WINDOWS NT

Cisco Internetworking with Windows NT & 2000

TOBY J. **VELTE** AND AMY **HANSON**,
WITH ANTHONY T. **VELTE**

Osborne/**McGraw-Hill**

Berkeley New York St. Louis San Francisco
Auckland Bogotá Hamburg London Madrid
Mexico City Milan Montreal New Delhi Panama City
Paris São Paulo Singapore Sydney
Tokyo Toronto

Osborne/**McGraw-Hill**
2600 Tenth Street
Berkeley, California 94710
U.S.A.

For information on translations or book distributors outside the U.S.A., or to arrange bulk purchase discounts for sales promotions, premiums, or fund-raisers, please contact Osborne/**McGraw-Hill** at the above address.

Cisco Internetworking with Windows NT & 2000

1234567890 DOC DOC 019876543210

ISBN 0-07-212083-5

Publisher
  Brandon A. Nordin
**Associate Publisher and
Editor-in-Chief**
  Scott Rogers
Executive Acquisitions Editor
  Wendy Rinaldi
Project Editor
  Emily Rader
Acquisitions Coordinator
  Monika Faltiss
Technical Editor
  Rex Hale
Copy Editor
  Carol Henry

Proofreader
  Linda Medoff
Indexer
  Jack Lewis
Computer Designers
  Jani Beckwith
  Roberta Steele
Illustrators
  Beth Young
  Brian Wells
  Bob Hansen
Series Design
  Peter F. Hancik

This book was composed with Corel VENTURA ™ Publisher.

About the Authors . . .

Toby J. Velte, Ph.D., MCSE+I, CCNA, CCDA, is cofounder of Velte Systems, Inc. (www.velte.com), a voice/data network and information systems security consulting firm. He is also a cofounder of Intelligent Networks, Inc. (www.intelligent-networks.com), a network software development company. Dr. Velte is an experienced network consultant who enables organizations to best use technology to meet their business needs. He has published numerous networking articles in *Windows NT Magazine, NT Systems*, and *Windows Pro Magazine*; and has coauthored the following books: *Windows NT Enterprise Networking* (Osborne/McGraw-Hill, 1998) and *Cisco: A Beginner's Guide* (Osborne/McGraw-Hill, 1999). Dr. Velte is available for consulting and public speaking. He can be reached at tjv@velte.com.

Amy Hanson, CCNA, is a senior network engineer for Velte Systems, Inc. She specializes in Cisco network security, including security network assessments and recommendations, firewall implementations, and security policy development; as well as authentication solutions such as Biometric technologies. Amy has also worked on LAN/WAN architecture design, implementation, and support for government, healthcare, and manufacturing organizations. She can be reached at akh@velte.com.

Anthony T. Velte, MCSE+I, CCNA, CCDA, is president and cofounder of Velte Systems, Inc. He is also a cofounder of Intelligent Networks, Inc. Mr. Velte is the coauthor of *Windows NT Enterprise Networking* (Osborne/McGraw- Hill, 1998) and a contributor to *Cisco: A Beginner's Guide* (Osborne/McGraw-Hill, 1999). He also speaks to organizations and professional groups. Mr. Velte has over 15 years of experience designing and implementing network technologies, network services, and security systems on national and global networks. He can be reached at atv@velte.com.

To my wife, Sandra—
Your friendship sweetens every achievement.
—TJV

To the people I love most—
My parents, my brothers and sister, and my best friend, Corey.
—AKH

To Anne Marie and Luke—
You are the answer to my question.
—ATV

CONTENTS

Part I
Windows Meets the Network

Part II

Building a Cisco Network with Windows 2000

Part III

Managing a Cisco/Windows Network

Part IV

Intranet/Extranet Strategies

ACKNOWLEDGMENTS

Books are enormous projects that encompass many individuals and their skills. This book is no exception, and we are indebted to those who helped turn this project into paper. First off, Wendy Rinaldi provided the inspiration and motivation to take on this challenge. Others at Osborne/McGraw-Hill were crucial, including the editor, Emily Rader; the general coordinator, Monika Faltiss; the computer designers, Jani Beckwith and Roberta Steele; and the illustrators, Beth Young, Brian Wells, and Bob Hansen. We'd like to thank John McManus, for his excellent contribution of Appendixes A and C, as well as countless additions throughout the book; and Tom Shaughnessy, for providing his prose expertise on a couple of chapters. Certainly, we are indebted to Rex Hale, CCIE, for his careful read of the entire book and for the inclusion of some of his expert tips. The book is definitely improved because of Rex. Of course, if it weren't for my co-authors, Amy and Tony, this volume would never have taken shape. To all of you—thank you very much!

—TJV

First and foremost, I want to thank Toby and Tony for giving me the opportunity to not only assist with the development of this book, but also for the good fortune of working for a company that provides endless opportunities; for my position, which is equally challenging and rewarding; and for the ability to work with the most talented people in the industry. I would also like to thank Osborne/McGraw-Hill for reviewing the material and bringing it to press. In addition, I would like to thank my family: my parents, Roger and Kathleen Hanson, for their infinite wisdom and direction; my bothers and sister, Troy, Kim, and Brent, for their sincerity and humor at the right times; and all of them for their love and support. Last, but most certainly not least, I want to thank Corey Benedict for being the most caring, patient, and understanding person—not only during the writing of this book—but every day of our lives.

—AKH

I want to thank Amy, Toby, and the rest of the Velte Systems crew, as well as our team at Osborne/McGraw-Hill, for doing such an amazing job on this project, especially with so many other projects going on at the same time. As always, I am very lucky to be working with such wonderfully talented people. I also want to thank my wife, Anne Marie, for supporting me in this effort while also carrying our first child, Luke Anthony, who is due any day now . . . we can't wait to meet you, little guy!

—ATV

INTRODUCTION

This book covers a variety of topics that are important to those designing, building, and maintaining networks with Cisco and Microsoft products. It makes sense to take a holistic approach to internetworking; most books tend to focus too much on one side of the technology fence or the other. This book recognizes that networking hardware and server software need to be designed, integrated, and managed in concert with each other.

Networks are complex beasts that require advanced skill and planning to tame. With over 70% of the Internet backbone comprised of Cisco gear, it comes as no surprise to learn that Cisco's networking hardware makes up a large percentage of the installed base in corporate networks around the world. Once thought of as a problem for Internet service providers or telecommunications experts to figure out, Cisco routers, switches, and firewalls are increasingly falling under the dominion of the corporate LAN/WAN administrator. And if projections about Cisco come true, more and more Cisco hardware and software will start to appear on administrators' desks. Users and administrators will need to get better acquainted with Cisco hardware and software.

Administrators and users alike are much more familiar with the Windows operating system than with Cisco's. Its installed base is also growing, and is, of course, the most used desktop operating system in the world. While many of these are Windows 95 or 98 systems instead of NT systems, this trend will soon shift. As Windows 9x systems slowly die off, they will be replaced with Windows 2000 systems. The current NT systems will also be converted to Windows 2000. The convergence is apparent: Windows NT and 2000 are getting ever closer to the Cisco networking gear; and for many users, administrators, and IT decision makers, this is evident already.

From convergence in the IT community springs new challenges. Users and administrators will have to become more familiar with both Cisco and Microsoft systems—particularly with the areas in which they work together. This book examines Microsoft and Cisco technologies, and describes the space in which they intersect. Look inside to find the tools you need to tame that beast you call your network.

WHAT THIS BOOK COVERS

This book contains 16 chapters and 4 appendixes. The chapters are broken down into four major sections. The first discusses Cisco and Windows convergence; the second explains the nuts and bolts of building networks; the third focuses on managing a network once you've built it; and the fourth outlines strategies you can use to connect others to your network.

Part I: Windows Meets the Network

The first section of this book introduces the background information you need in order to grasp how Cisco and Microsoft are shaping your future network today. This section also gets technical, covering the technologies that form the foundation of modern networking.

Chapter 1, "Cisco and Windows Converge"—This chapter discusses the recent news on Microsoft's Windows 2000 and on Cisco's latest strategies. It also introduces concepts necessary to properly understand and get the best use of the material found in this book.

Chapter 2, "Directory-Enabled Networking (DEN)"—This chapter describes the history behind the Directory-Enabled Network initiative. It also introduces the fundamental concepts of DEN and policy-based networking.

Chapter 3, "Networking Fundamentals"—This chapter introduces essential networking subjects, such as the OSI model, as well as various protocols (Ethernet, Token Ring, and Fast Ethernet), including routing protocols. These and other subjects are discussed as they relate to Cisco hardware and software, and as they relate to Microsoft Windows 2000.

Part II: Building a Cisco Network with Windows 2000

This section covers the hands-on aspects of configuring network components using simple and advanced software interfaces. It features a wide variety of Cisco and Microsoft tools that help make the job easier, and includes expert tips and shortcuts.

Chapter 4, "Cisco Hardware and Internetworking Tools"—This chapter covers the wide variety of available hardware options, including routers, switches, hubs, access servers, and firewalls, and highlights many of their unique features and functions. It also covers the Cisco Internetwork Operating System (IOS) in detail; and finally, it examines cables, connectors, and various management and troubleshooting tools.

Chapter 5, "Configuring Routers and RRAS"—This chapter covers router configuration and installation. It stresses the process of testing new equipment and testing IOS version upgrades in a lab environment, provides a simple preconfiguration checklist that you can use, and takes you step-by-step through the router boot process. It also covers Cisco ConfigMaker and NetSys Baseliner in detail, as well as setting up TCP/IP on Windows machines, the Windows route table, and Microsoft's Routing and Remote Access Service (RRAS).

Chapter 6, "Setting Up Switches and VLANs"—This chapter covers Cisco switches, including those supporting high-performance desktop connectivity, enterprise workgroup aggregation, and dispersed building aggregation. It carefully describes Cisco's Web-based Visual Switch Management (VSM) software, as well as the Spanning Tree Protocol (STP) and the Switched Port Analyzer (SPAN). It also covers VLAN configuration issues, trunking, and VLAN management.

Chapter 7, "Configuring Cisco Hubs"—This chapter covers the fundamentals of repeater technology, Ethernet standards, and IEEE 802.3 10BaseT and 100BaseT specifications. It reviews Cisco's FastHub Series of Class II repeaters and provides cabling specifications. This chapter also includes scenarios in which hubs can be installed cost-effectively in the network.

Part III: Managing a Cisco/Windows Network

This section focuses on the products and methods used to manage a Cisco/Windows network. This includes advanced Active Directory design and management strategies, Cisco device management, and naming services for Windows NT and Windows 2000, such as DNS, WINS, and DHCP.

Chapter 8, "Managing Devices"—This chapter covers a wide variety of applications used to manage and configure Cisco/Windows networks. This includes HP OpenView and CiscoWorks2000, and their add-on components. It also covers tools that help manage switches, networks (including ATM networks), and specific Cisco devices such as

CiscoWorks Switched Internetwork (CWSI), CiscoView, VLANDirector, TrafficDirector, and ATMDirector.

Chapter 9, "Managing Directory Services"—This chapter carefully delves into Windows 2000 Directory Services management. It covers the Microsoft Management Console and the various tools that enable smoother, faster, and less-expensive management of a Windows 2000 domain. This includes Windows 2000 multi-master replication techniques, IP Security (IPSec) configuration in Windows 2000, Systems Management Server (SMS), IntelliMirror technology, and the Distributed File System (Dfs).

Chapter 10, "Network Traffic Testing"—This chapter covers both the preventive and troubleshooting aspects of network traffic monitoring, as well as tools used to manage the process. This includes the use of network analyzers, such as the Windows 2000 Network Monitor Tool and Cisco's TrafficDirector. It covers advanced simulation methods and tools such as COMNET Predictor, and carefully outlines several different types of tests that you can conduct, including single- and dual-analyzer captures. In addition, it demonstrates application testing and "what if?" network simulations. The chapter also walks through the process of creating a topological map of your network.

Chapter 11, "IP Address and Naming Services"—This chapter covers naming services, including DNS and DDNS, NetBIOS NBT name services, WINS, and DHCP. It addresses integration of these services to help provide a comprehensive solution, and discusses other essential solutions such as forwarding broadcasts on Cisco routers and fault tolerance strategies. It also covers design options for naming services and overviews of the latest Windows 2000 and Cisco Network Registrar (CNR) DNS/DHCP tools.

Chapter 12, "Designing Windows 2000 Domains"—This chapter covers the latest information on Windows 2000 domain design. It presents the subject in a way that helps you make the most of your Cisco/Windows network. It carefully examines the technical steps required to build new networks or migrate existing networks to the new Windows 2000 domain model, and addresses real-world issues such as client migration and namespace design. It also provides several examples of network designs appropriate for small-, medium-, and enterprise-sized organizations. Finally, it covers tools such as DirectManage, DirectAdmin, DirectScript, and FastLane's Domain Management Suite (DM/Suite).

Part IV: Intranet/Extranet Strategies

Now that you have the foundation of building Cisco/Microsoft networks, you can explore specific, more advanced, connectivity solutions.

Chapter 13, "Web Services"—This chapter covers Web-based technologies offered by Cisco. Cisco's DistributedDirector, LocalDirector, and Web Cache Engine are all reviewed in detail. The chapter also discusses Cisco's Web browser interface, which allows the execution of Cisco IOS commands through a Web browser.

Chapter 14, "Secure Connections"—This chapter covers security hardware and software solutions from Cisco and Microsoft. It details Cisco IOS access control lists, Cisco Firewall IOS, and Cisco PIX Firewall, including treatment of the Network Address Translation (NAT) on the router IOS, on the router Firewall IOS, and on PIX Firewall. In addition, Cisco's real-time intrusion detection system, NetRanger (recently renamed CiscoSecure Intrusion Detection System), is fully covered.

Chapter 15, "Ensuring Quality of Service"—This chapter covers the implementations of Quality of Service (QoS) past, present, and future. It also covers Microsoft's implementation of LDAP with Active Directory (included with Windows 2000), Directory-Enabled Networking (DEN), IP QoS, and QoS commands in Cisco's IOS operating system.

Chapter 16, "Authentication, Authorization, and Accounting"—This chapter covers mechanisms you can use to protect against unauthorized access, control legitimate access, and track detailed information about the who, what, where, and when of access to your network. It defines the concepts behind Authentication, Authorization, and Accounting (AAA), and discusses CiscoSecure Access Control Server, NetSonar (recently renamed CiscoSecure Scanner), TACACS+, RADIUS, and CryptoCards.

Part V: Appendixes

The appendixes contain handy references to help you with router configuration, understanding the TCP/IP protocol suite, and getting Cisco and Microsoft Certifications. They also provide you resources for getting all the help and information you need.

Appendix A, "Basic Cisco Router Configuration"—This appendix contains information and tips on configuring a Cisco router. It contains a step-by-step walkthrough of a simple router configuration.

Appendix B, "Map of the TCP/IP Protocol Suite"—This appendix contains an excellent summarization of the TCP/IP protocol suite. It uses helpful descriptions and diagrams to describe TCP/IP and how it fits into the network.

Appendix C, "The Road to Certification"—This appendix covers all the little details about available Microsoft and Cisco certifications and how to get them. Some of the certifications covered are CCNA, CCDA, CCDP, CCIE, MCP, MCSE, and MCSE+I.

Appendix D, "Getting Help: Cisco and Windows Resources"—This appendix includes tips on where to find and how to use Microsoft's Online Help, Command Line Help, TechNet, online support packages, consulting services, Internet site, newsgroups, and Windows NT Resource Kits. It also covers Cisco resources such as Cisco Connection Online (CCO), CCO Software Center, Technical Assistance Tools, and the Cisco Documentation CD-ROM.

PART I

Windows Meets the Network

CHAPTER 1

Cisco and Windows Converge

Both Cisco Systems and the Microsoft Corporation are much in the public eye of late. Among other developments, Microsoft has announced the next generation of Windows, called Windows 2000, and Cisco is experiencing rapid growth through acquisition. Both companies have been pioneers of their respective industries and consistently stand above their competition. Yet there is another set of events that arguably will have a much greater impact on users and businesses than will recent product releases and corporate purchases.

A significant relationship has been developing between Cisco and Microsoft for the past several years. They have jointly agreed to undertake the challenge of making Cisco's products and Internetworking Operating System (IOS) run more cooperatively with Microsoft's new directory service, Active Directory (AD). Concurrently, Microsoft will cooperate with Cisco to make Windows 2000 more aware of Cisco network devices and of the general conditions that exist on an organization's network.

Every user who is on a network will feel the impact of these advancements. Features will be added to applications and Windows itself that would not be possible without this network OS/desktop OS alliance. Third-party applications will be redesigned to use information gathered from the network devices, and to subsequently interact directly with these devices to change service. A new breed of "intelligent" applications will be built upon the interaction between the network itself and the Windows system. Already, new standards such as Directory-Enabled Networking (DEN) have benefited from the Cisco/Microsoft association. Great things will undoubtedly come of this relationship—but to make the most of them, you'll need to understand how Cisco IOS and Windows 2000 will interact.

This book covers the areas where Cisco and Windows overlap. Here in this first chapter, we'll look at the current state of these areas of overlap, and where they will be in the coming years. We'll introduce Windows 2000 and the Active Directory, and then move on to DEN concepts and Cisco networking fundamentals.

WHY CISCO AND WINDOWS?

In Las Vegas, May 1997, Microsoft made an announcement. The press release was titled "Microsoft and Cisco Collaborate to Establish Directory Services Standard." The opening paragraph sums it up best:

> Microsoft Corp. and Cisco Systems Inc. today announced a letter of intent in which Cisco will license Active Directory from Microsoft for use in managing network infrastructure and to provide richer network services. As part of this agreement, Cisco and Microsoft will jointly develop extensions to Active Directory to integrate advanced management of network elements and services. Products developed as a result of this agreement will make it possible for network managers to unify their network infrastructures and to accelerate the development of richer network services via Cisco IOS software. It will also allow

service providers to simplify service delivery and provide new sets of services for their customers.

Merging the network with the desktop operating system is a natural direction to take as user communities get more connected. Increasingly, the real benefit of using computers is sharing information, reaching well beyond local PCs to information stores on corporate networks and on the Internet. Technologies that facilitate this direction will be well received but will need the support of the network and the desktop OS—enter Cisco and Microsoft.

Cisco is the world's most popular networking hardware vendor, owning approximately 80% of the market share on the Internet. Cisco systems may not have the fastest throughput of the day or the latest gigabit technology, but they are rock-solid in terms of functionality. Big businesses and mission-critical environments (such as the Internet) use Cisco gear because it is reliable, consistent, and supported by a skilled pool of individuals who know how to configure and maintain it. With its steady growth and frequent acquisitions, Cisco is gaining a stronger foothold and increasing its long-term viability. Cisco is being built to last—and basing a technology on Cisco IOS is a pretty good bet.

For desktop operating systems, Microsoft has been the leading supplier since its inception. It comes as no surprise that they were recently declared a monopoly by the U.S. Department of Justice. Though flawed, Windows technology is ubiquitous; and it is improving (especially by dropping the 9x versions). There is no question of its pervasive presence and momentum. Windows, too, will be around for some time. A pairing of Windows and Cisco is clearly logical. The result will be not only great financial reward for the two companies, but for many smaller ones as well, if they are nimble enough to take advantage of related opportunities. Everyone involved, from the single Internet day trader to the enterprise of thousands, will benefit.

Features arising from the Cisco/Windows relationship promise to ease administration, increase security, and provide unprecedented access to information. In this light, the value of a standards-based infrastructure becomes paramount.

Cisco Becomes Windows Aware

In addition to integrating its devices and IOS into Windows 2000, Cisco has already taken steps to become more Windows friendly. In the past, nearly all Cisco applications were written to run on UNIX systems exclusively. Lately, the trend has been to port these applications (such as CiscoSecure, NetSonar, and so on) to Windows NT. Cisco has even started writing (or acquiring) applications that run primarily on Windows NT (such as CiscoWorks2000). Cisco often releases versions for UNIX systems, as well, supporting the many network administrators who are loyal to UNIX reliability.

Cisco is wise to not alienate other vendors. They often release a product for Windows NT and coincidentally create the application as a Web-based tool, so that users of other systems can still administer the application from any system that can run a browser. They are working toward similar goals of interoperability with Novell, too, and will likely form business relationships with other vendors.

With the introduction of Windows 2000, Windows awareness extends far beyond the creation of 32-bit Windows applications. Windows 2000 brings robust directory services to a huge base of users and opens up a whole new category of opportunity for Cisco. Active Directory will be available to user workstations and e-mail servers, and to Cisco network devices such as routers, switches, and firewalls. These devices will be able to read and write information to and from the directory. The number of potential applications for this capability are enormous.

Windows Understands the Network

Just as Cisco has worked to make its applications Windows compatible, Microsoft must hold up its end of the deal and make some room in Active Directory for Cisco. This is only the first step in what Microsoft will have to do to make the Windows OS network aware. Since the Cisco routers, switches, and other devices will need to talk to the AD, Microsoft must build the intelligence of the AD so it can understand what the devices are telling it. New entries in the AD will be necessary, and a design created to use that information to provide better service and greater features to users. In addition, Microsoft must provide an environment that is scalable, secure, and will communicate with non-Microsoft enabled devices using open standards. Should Microsoft fail to make these accommodations, they are likely to find limited adoption (of network devices communicating with AD). Organizational users are no longer willing to accept a non-scalable OS, poor security, and applications that only work with their own components. If these needs are not met, users may look elsewhere for their network solutions.

The remaining portion of this chapter examines Microsoft's actions of late to ensure that their OS is chosen in the future.

Windows 2000: Which One?

In retrospect, the original name of Windows 2000—Windows NT 5.0—was probably inappropriate given the extensive features included in this release. The jump from NT 4.0 to 5.0 is far greater than for any previous upgrade. This is without a doubt Microsoft's biggest project to date; indeed, much of the NT code is completely rewritten. So much work has been done across the entire OS that it will take quite some time for most users to realize the full potential of the release. In this book, we'll focus on the new features as they relate to the network in general and to Cisco products in particular. Note that all the Cisco applications discussed in this book will run on Windows NT 4.0 as well. Not until we begin to manipulate the Active Directory directly from Cisco hardware and software will we see some of the more "futuristic" elements of the Microsoft/Cisco initiative.

Microsoft announced on October 27, 1998, that its next version of Windows NT (called NT 5.0) would be named Windows 2000. The renaming of NT is an obvious marketing move—since Windows 9x will be retired after Windows 98, Microsoft cannot abandon these users and expect them to move to NT. Many users associate NT with high-end, complicated, expensive workstations that have no business on their desk or in their homes. On the other hand, the 9x line of product, though less expensive, was abysmal compared with NT. It was unreliable and largely constrained due to its DOS heritage. Clearly, the future for Windows was not with Windows 9x.

To make NT 5.0 more palatable for 9x users, its name was adjusted to seem more familiar to Windows users in general. Corporate and individual users alike will all be using essentially the same operating system. Because of this consolidation, Microsoft plans to release four versions of Windows 2000, allowing some flexibility of choice to both home and corporate users. Nevertheless, even if they are sold in different market segments, these subspecies are nearly identical except for perhaps a service or two difference between them.

Let's take a look at the four versions of Windows 2000.

Windows 2000 Professional

Windows 2000 Professional is NT Workstation in disguise. This version will be the most popular with home and business users. The Professional version is the client to the server version and operates on standard, single-processor Pentium systems. Although very much like a server, the number of network users that can connect to it at any given time will be limited. Nor will Professional be able to run many of the network enabling services such as DNS, Active Directory, and DHCP Server.

Windows 2000 Server Standard Edition

This version is the workhorse of the network. Windows 2000 Server Standard Edition is a file and print server that can run as a domain controller (DC) with Active Directory. It also supports all of the BackOffice line of applications, including Transaction Server, IIS, Exchange, SQL Server, and so on. Server Standard Edition can run DNS, DHCP, and WINS services. This version is, of course, what NT Server was in the NT 4.0 world. It supports up to four-way symmetric multiprocessing (SMP) and 4GB of physical memory.

Windows 2000 Advanced Server

The Advanced Server version is, in general, an evolution of Windows NT 4.0 Server, Enterprise Edition. Enterprise Edition came about with the development of the Microsoft clustering service. This allowed two NT 4.0 servers to operate in tandem, so that if one failed, the other picked up the extra work without a hiccup. Windows 2000 Advanced Server extends this clustering service even further and can support up to 8GB of physical memory, and eight-way SMP.

Windows 2000 Datacenter

Windows 2000 Datacenter is really the same as the Advanced Server version with some additional scalability enhancements. It can support up to 64GB of physical memory and up to 32-way SMP. A few years ago, it would have been almost impossible to imagine that such CPU horsepower would be harnessed by a Windows operating system. It won't be long, however, before groups of these servers are commonly used for extremely intensive applications (scientific modeling, financial transactions, and Web hosting for a large site, for example), displacing mainframes, minis, and UNIX-based systems.

WINDOWS 2000 COMPONENTS

Windows 2000 is far more than a name. As stated earlier, it is the most significant project to date for Microsoft and involves the most new lines of code ever. Microsoft has loaded up the new OS with brand-new administration interfaces and features, from Active Directory to enhanced security. There is something for everybody. This section starts by describing some of the pitfalls of Windows 4.0 that were addressed in Windows 2000. Then we'll introduce some key concepts you'll need to know about Windows 2000 and its new features.

Why NT 4.0 Falls Short

To better appreciate Windows 2000 and all its advancements, it is worth a moment to reflect on some of the shortcomings organizations have encountered with Windows NT 4.0. These deficiencies all center around the lack of scalability.

Many of the improvements in Windows 2000 address the user limitations and administrative problems associated with NT 4.0. In NT 4.0, user information is stored in a flat file located within the Registry. This restricts the total number of users in a domain to about 40,000. Long before you add this many users, however, you'll begin to see other scalability issues with NT 4.0.

One of the most notable issues is felt by administrators of midsize to large NT networks on which several people are responsible for domain administration. First of all, in large, dispersed network environments, administrators get poor response time when viewing and manipulating the user accounts over a busy network, or on one on which the primary domain controller (PDC) is located on the other end of a WAN link. Many of the management tools bog down and become cumbersome to use in such conditions or when the domain comprises a large number of user accounts or groups. Also, in larger networks, the administrators must delegate some rote tasks to others. But NT 4.0 uses an all-or-none security policy. Administrators have all rights over the domain, or they have none. It is thus necessary to delegate total authority to others, which may not be in the best interest of the organization.

Since NT 4.0 and earlier versions do not have a centralized directory, any application or OS that requires a directory service must create its own. The result is a collection of usually incompatible directories in the domain. Users suffer because they must have multiple sign-ons and must learn to work the different directories. Administrators have extra upkeep on these disparate directories. Management sees the total cost of ownership soar and security degrade, as users fall into negligent behavior with their passwords.

NT 4.0's lack of scalability has generated other problematic issues, as well. The limitations imposed by NT 4.0 and earlier incarnations resulted in some convoluted enterprise designs. Large companies were forced to create more domains than they really needed just to support the number of users (often in different sites) and to overcome the all-or-none security delegation problem. Disparate domains remained connected to each other with one-way trusts, just so a user in one domain could see resources in another domain. These trust relationships had to be maintained for all domains a user might want to connect to. Such an arrangment is very difficult to maintain once the number of domains grows to more than five domains.

Key Concepts

Obviously, there is a great need to solve these scalability issues, and Microsoft has addressed it head on. They did not patch existing software or methods to improve scalability. Rather, they developed new strategies to attack the resulting problems. These new concepts, described in the following paragraphs, are the building blocks for Windows domains in the future.

Active Directory (AD)

AD is the database of all objects contained within a domain or collection of domains. Objects include users, directories, printers, computers, and so on. Unlike flat-file directories, such as the Registry, the AD is hierarchical and stored in a database. Because the database is free of the space restrictions imposed on Security Account Manager (SAM), up to about 10 million objects can be stored in AD, as opposed to the roughly 40,000 maximum users you can use with the SAM.

The AD is kept consistent through frequent replication among domain controllers and is always readily available to users because each DC can contain a copy. This is important because Microsoft, as well as third-party applications, will frequently refer to the contents of and write entries to the AD.

The power of a single, centralized database will be enormous. For example, instead of having to remember multiple passwords for separate databases, users need only log in once; their credentials are stored in the AD for access by other applications as needed. Also, looking for resources means checking only one database. In the AD, a user (for instance) can be searched or based on any attribute that has been collected, such as a phone number.

LIGHTWEIGHT DIRECTORY ACCESS PROTOCOL (LDAP) Applications, users, and devices will want to communicate to the AD from across the network. They will need to do lookups on the AD database and also place or change values in the AD database. This will be done using an open networking protocol designed to interact with directories: Lightweight Directory Access Protocol (LDAP).

LDAP is an Internet Engineering Task Force (IETF) initiative and is on track to become an Internet standard. By using an open standard, Microsoft encourages other vendors to write applications that communicate with the AD. Currently, Windows 2000 supports LDAP versions 2 and 3 as described in RFCs 1777 and 2251, respectively.

Schema

The *schema* is the part of the AD that defines objects and their attributes. Although the concept is initially a little difficult to grasp, a schema is really just a definition and rule set for the container objects within the AD. It defines where the objects will be present in the AD and where in the tree they can be found. A schema is very specific but can be customized to fit your needs. Just remember that disparate domains must share the same schema in order to understand each other's ADs.

If you are familiar with SNMP and MIBs, think of the schema as the MIB framework for which SNMP devices fill in the blanks. Otherwise, you might compare the schema to a directory tree that contains no files of actual data but provides a tree to which real data is attached. For example, a schema might have the container User with a subcontainer called userName. The schema doesn't really give you any new information, but whatever is entered into the userName container might. (Incidentally, the schema itself is contained within AD.)

Directory-enabled networking (DEN) extends the standard Microsoft schema to include containers for network devices and their current settings and status. For example, Cisco might extend the schema to include a container to which a Cisco 6000 series switch can enter the current throughput rate through one of its ports. (Chapter 2 discusses DEN in greater detail.)

Global Catalog

A user or application searches for an object in the AD from the top down. If all the attributes of an object are not known, you can start searching at the root of the tree and proceed down through all domains until you find a match.

Since many enterprise networks have sites separated by links of small bandwidth, it is impractical to have all partial queries start at the root of the tree, consuming a huge amount of bandwidth. To reduce Wide Area Network (WAN) utilization, some Windows 2000 servers can be configured to contain a *global catalog*. It contains only some of the attributes for all the objects in the AD. It might, for example, hold only users' last names and business units. You would configure these attributes to be the ones used most often in searches. The global catalog allows users to examine a local source that may provide the location of the object they are looking for. If the global catalog doesn't contain the needed information, searches can then be performed at the root of the tree.

Global catalogs are required for user login; therefore, each site must have at least one global catalog. (Sites are defined just below.)

Organizational Units (OUs)

Domains can be subdivided into separate administrative divisions called *organizational units* (OUs). This arrangement addresses a limitation in the distribution of administrative rights in previous versions of NT. Basically, administrators had total control over the domain and were unable to dole out administrative rights to others so that regional administrators could manage their users and resources without having administrative rights in the entire domain.

There is no limit to the number of OUs within a domain. Since each OU can contain a very specific delegation over administrative functions, you can finely tune all of your assignments.

Site

In AD parlance, a *site* in the enterprise network comprises one or more subnets (that is, independent network segments) connected via a high-speed link (~10 Mbps or better). Typically, a site is a geographic location, either a building or a cluster of buildings. If multiple buildings are connected via a high-speed link (to form a MAN), then the building may all be considered the same site.

Sites are used primarily for replication boundaries. Replication of the AD occurs more often within a site. A site may consist of only part of a domain or more than one domain.

Windows 2000 Namespace

The Windows 2000 namespace is the DNS namespace used to describe the relationships of computers on IP-based systems such as the Internet. For example, the namespace of a tree (domains share the same namespace within a tree, as described just below) might be velte.com for the parent, with two child domains called marketing.velte.com and research.velte.com. A child domain of marketing.velte.com might be us.marketing.velte.com. And so on.

DDNS

Windows 2000 domain names follow the DNS naming scheme conventions. In fact, DNS is intimately connected with Active Directory and Windows 2000. In Windows 2000, DNS serves to resolve the location of the LDAP-based AD objects. Dynamic DNS (DDNS) is so crucial to Windows 2000 and AD that there must be at least one DDNS server installed in order for AD to function properly. The reverse is not true; DNS can run just fine by itself.

Active Directory contacts the local DDNS server and publishes its record as a Service Location (SRV) resource record. This way, other computers can find an AD just by knowing the domain name and querying DNS. If a client uses AD and wants to see what's in the AD of another domain, the client need only point to the domain name and an AD will be contacted automatically.

TIP: WINS is used as a name locator in NT 4.0 networks. In Windows 2000 networks, WINS is not required unless NT 4.0 or other down-level clients are still active.

Although Microsoft recommends using its own DNS server, you can use any DNS server that meets the following criteria:

▼ Supports SRV Records (RFC 2052)

■ Supports dynamic DNS (RFC 2136) for full functionality

▲ Uses BIND version 8.1.1 or higher

You are not required to use the same DNS zone name as the name of the domain, although it will make administration much simpler. For example, the naming convention might be as follows:

Windows 2000 domain	research.velte.com
DNS zone	research.velte.com
Client	my-pc.research.velte.com

Tree

A *tree* is a group of domains linked via trust relationships and sharing the same namespace, global catalog, and schema. The tree has an uppermost domain (parent), and may have domains under it (children domains) in the tree hierarchy, linked via Kerberos trusts.

Forest

Trees or domains that do not share a common namespace can be linked together via one-way trusts to form a *forest*. For example, if velte.com and microsoft.com were linked by a trust relationship but shared a common schema and global catalog, the pair would be considered a forest. By default, trust relationships are formed by the tops of the trees; however, the trusts can be created to form alternate pathways for security measures.

Multimaster Replication

Windows 2000 uses *multimaster replication* within domains to keep the AD current. Instead of having one central computer (PDC) for the domain, which is replicated to subordinate servers (BDCs) (as is done in NT 4.0), Windows 2000 treats all DCs as peers. If you can update a record on any DC, it will update all Domain Controllers after a time. This way, all DCs have the same database, and users can update the AD on any DC.

An Example

Figure 1-1 illustrates many of the Windows 2000 concepts explained in this section. In this example, velte.com is the root domain for a tree that contains two other child domains (marketing.velte.com and research.velte.com) and two OUs (Sales and PR). This tree has a consistent schema that is contained within the AD. Updates from the three domains are carried out via multimaster replication.

Tree A could be connected to another tree, provided that tree adopts the same schema. Here, Tree B is connected at the two root domains by an explicit trust relationship between velte.com and microsoft.com. Within each tree there are implicit trusts enabling users in children domains to use resources throughout the tree (provided they have permission); thus, users in one tree can use resources in another tree (again, if they are granted permission).

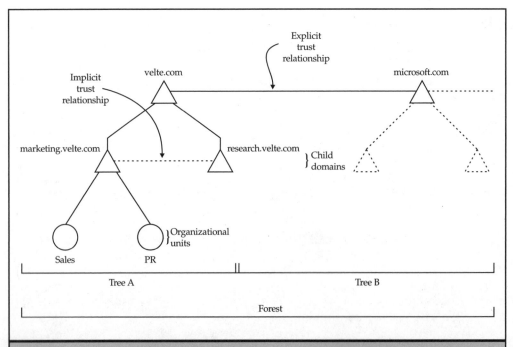

Figure 1-1.   Domain architecture in Windows 2000

The Enterprise Under Windows 2000

As you can imagine, you'll have substantial flexibility in how you organize your enterprise under Windows 2000. The building blocks have been augmented. Primary domain controllers (PDCs) and backup domain controllers (BDCs) are gone. Instead, groups of domain controllers (DCs) are in charge of authenticating users and keeping track of resources. All DCs are considered equivalent peers, and an update to your nearest DC will eventually propagate to the other DCs. OUs are primarily used to separate authority over a subset of the domain, because you can create users for a particular OU. For example, your domain might be ny.company.com, with OUs called Finance and Marketing. The Finance people get full control over their resources, as do the Marketing folks.

Interdomain trusts are no longer one-way. Instead, *transitive* trusts are used. Thus, if company.com has a child domain called us.company.com, which has two child domains called ca.us.company.com and ny.us.company.com, then users of either lower domain can view objects throughout the entire collection of domains. When more domains are added, the benefit of this trust arrangement becomes prominent: it can save a lot of time in administration, with fewer of the access problems common to trusting domains.

IMPORTANT NEW FEATURES

In addition to the internetworking concepts described in the preceding sections, Windows 2000 offers a host of other new features to tempt you toward migration. Let's take a look at new management features that focus on managing a Windows 2000 tree or forest, and at added tools for heightening network security.

Management

Windows 2000 promises to simplify management tasks while reducing management costs. Chapter 9 examines some of the new tools available to administrators and shows you the configuration basics for your new Windows 2000 domain. Some of the most exciting additions to the toolbox include the Microsoft Management Console (MMC) and IntelliMirror.

MICROSOFT MANAGEMENT CONSOLE   By using a single framework for all its management applications, Microsoft expects to make system management easier and less costly. This is the concept behind the Microsoft Management Console (MMC). The MMC is absolutely useless by itself. When you load it (type **mmc** at a command prompt), the interface is empty and has no function (see Figure 1-2). Only when "snap-ins" are loaded into the MMC does it become a useful management tool.

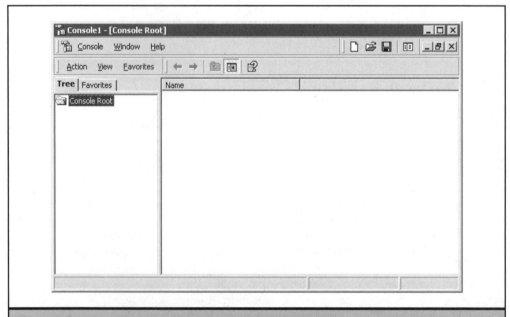

Figure 1-2.   The MMC is only a framework for administrative tools

A consistent framework for all management tools will reduce time spent learning how to use a variety of tools. In addition, you can customize your own tools by loading more than one administrative feature into the MMC and then saving it as a specific console. Later, you can call up just those tools by selecting that particular console. For example, if you typically work with a specific set of utilities for, say, troubleshooting a server, you can build a console with those utilities. Figure 1-3 shows an MMC loaded with five security management tools.

INTELLIMIRROR   Microsoft's set of new technologies, called IntelliMirror, allow many of the system management functions to be automated. We're not talking scripts here; this is something a bit more advanced. With IntelliMirror, administrators can automatically distribute software, control users' policies, and install Windows remotely. What's more, applications can be set up to detect corrupt files and then repair themselves by downloading the appropriate file from a central server.

For the most part, IntelliMirror's technologies focus on the tasks associated with providing data to users. By spreading the data over many servers, users are ensured quick and reliable access, even in the event of a server failure.

PERFORMANCE ENHANCEMENTS   One of the most common and valid complaints against Windows NT made by UNIX administrators is the frequency of administrative reboots.

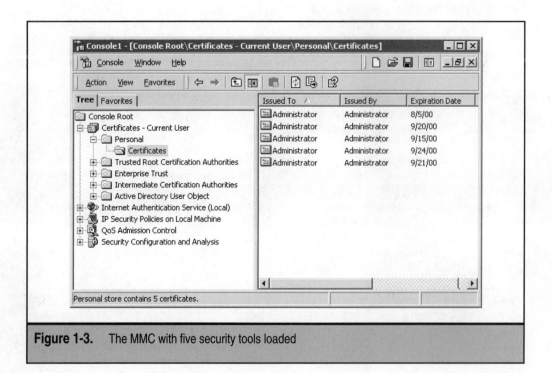

Figure 1-3.   The MMC with five security tools loaded

This consumes the administrator's time, severs open connections, and temporarily denies access to resources. No wonder this sort of maintenance must be carried out after hours (causing additional annoyance to the administrator, of course).

During typical NT maintenance, the administrator must frequently reboot the system for new settings to take effect. Reduced frequency of reboots is one of the promised performance enhancements with Windows 2000. While this is the case, there are still more required reboots with Windows 2000 than for a comparable UNIX system. Nonetheless, NT administrators will be very pleased by this reduced frequency in which they must watch Windows boot up. While this is a benefit, in our experience Windows 2000 takes a bit longer (especially the Domain Controllers) to boot up than NT.

Built-in load balancing is another enhancement that promises to give Windows 2000 a better running record. Up to 32 servers running Advanced Server can be set up to evenly distribute incoming server requests. These systems appear to be a single server to the end user. If you need to take one of the servers down for maintenance, the others simply take over the downed server's load. The end result is increased reliability and scalability.

Security

It's safe to say that in Windows 2000, security gets an overhaul. Many aspects of Windows NT security are scrapped and replaced with better controls, and more open policies and procedures.

KERBEROS LOGIN   All users are affected by the changes to login security. A user will still be prompted for a username and password, but authentication of this information in the domain is done quite differently from NT 4.0's standard check against the Security Account Manager (SAM). In Windows 2000, Kerberos (developed at MIT) is used to communicate from the DC to the user's computer.

NOTE: Kerberos borrows its name from Greek mythology. The three-headed dog, Kerberos (or Cerberus), protected the entrance to the underworld, Hades.

By using an open standard, other operating systems can log into a Windows 2000 domain. In theory, Apple, Novell, UNIX, and anyone using Kerberos version 5 can authenticate to a Windows 2000 domain (see Figure 1-4).

Other clients, too, can log in using various protocols. For Windows NT 4.0 clients, the Windows DC still accepts NT LAN Manager security until the domain is completely switched over to all–Windows 2000 systems (a state called *native* mode). Web users can still use the Secure Socket Layer (SSL) protocol, and AS/400 users can go through a Windows SNA Server.

PUBLIC KEY INFRASTRUCTURE (PKI)   In public key cryptography, a user's public key is used to encrypt certain data that is to be deciphered only by that user. Once this is done, that user deploys his or her own private key to decrypt the message that was encrypted

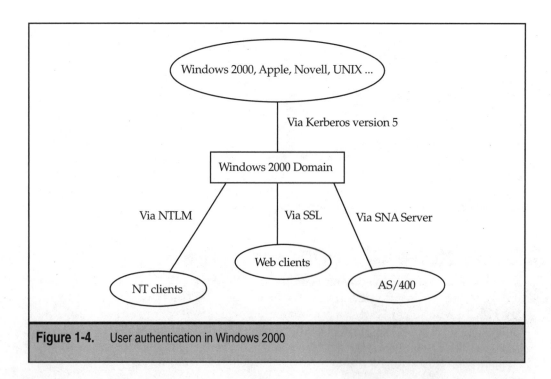

Figure 1-4.   User authentication in Windows 2000

using his or her public key. Keys are transported in digital certificates, which are maintained by a trusted Certificate Authority (CA) such as VeriSign.

Windows 2000 provides a public key infrastructure (PKI) that allows Windows 2000 servers to act as CAs within a Windows 2000 domain. Moreover, the PKI keeps track of certificates, generates new ones, and lets users know when one is out of date. This infrastructure allows an organization to use public key cryptography completely internally. Although standard Windows security can take care of the same functions as a PKI, the certificate method allows interoperability among non-Windows systems within an organization, or with users (even if they are corporate users) outside of a Windows domain. This could be useful for companies doing business with other organizations over the Internet, or even for the employees of an organization when they connect via the Internet.

IPSEC   IP Security (IPSec) integration is one of the outstanding additions to the Windows OS platforms. It allows full-blown, standards-based encryption to be easily implemented. With advanced authentication techniques to positively identify a user, you may want to encrypt the data transmitted across the network so it cannot be intercepted, viewed, or copied in route. To perform this function, Microsoft has (thankfully) adopted the IPSec standard. What follows is a brief overview of this technology; the subject is covered in more detail in Chapter 9.

IPSec negotiates between a sender and a receiver about how exactly to encrypt the data portion of IP packets as they traverse the network. This negotiation is normally completely transparent to the end user because it occurs between the application and the server. This is because IPSec is implemented below the application in the TCP/IP stack. Therefore, the user and the application probably don't even know the data is being encrypted.

With Windows 2000, you can create security policies on servers that designate levels of security users. You might, for example, dictate that all users must use IPSec to access certain directories on a server because they contain private information. In another directory you might set the policy to use IPSec if the client *can* use it, and otherwise not to use any security at all. Rather than simply encrypting everything, inducing a large processor overhead on your servers and clients, you can fine-tune your encryption methods and standards as desired.

WINDOWS 2000 MIGRATION

You are almost certainly in an organization using Windows NT 4.0 and planning a move to Windows 2000 at some point in time. It will not be a wholesale swap-out to a new Windows 2000 environment. Rather, a careful migration plan will have to be created and then implemented, so that disruption of the network is minimal. Chapter 12 studies those issues in depth; but, for now, let's get a taste of how a migration might take place. You'll be surprised at how much you have already learned about Windows 2000.

Domain Migration Example

Since you're probably not going to build your enterprise from scratch, we'll look at how Windows 2000 and AD will help you grow your existing network. For this example, we already have a domain with OUs. We have just acquired another company that has an overstuffed NT 4.0 domain with all the associated problems. Our job is to join the two organizations and allow users on both sides to access all resources in both domains (normal permissions—that is, Access Control Lists—presiding, of course).

With NT 4.0, we'd pretty much be stuck with joining the two units via a pair of one-way trusts. Users would be able to see some resources on the other domain, but we wouldn't gain the management and security benefits of AD. Additionally, the problems associated with managing each of those domains would now be compounded because they are separate but joined. This solution may work in the short term, but things will head downhill from here.

Another, easier choice is to assimilate another domain into the AD of the target domain. In this example, we convert the new domain to Windows 2000 and assign it as a child domain to the first domain, or as a child domain to the parent of the first domain. We next add OUs to parcel out the domain and make management easier. Now users from all over either domain can search the AD for resources, all with a single sign-on. We've cut management time, increased security, and made more resources available. This setup is illustrated in Figure 1-5.

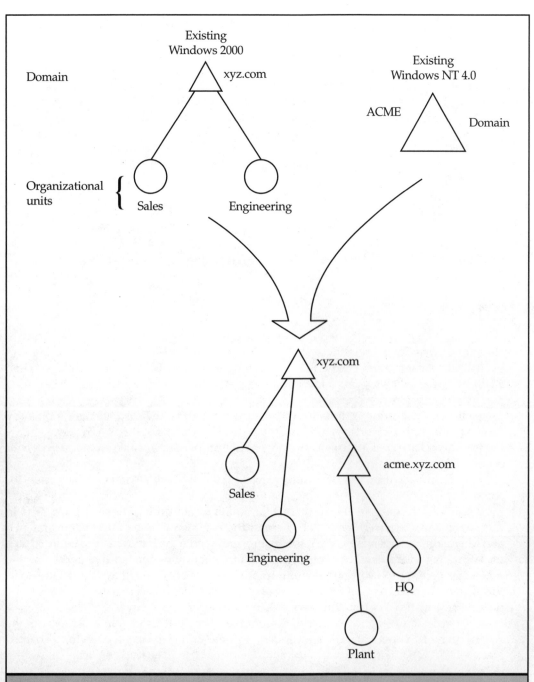

Figure 1-5.   Merging an NT domain into a Windows 2000 domain

"Omigod," you say, "I just got NT 4.0 up and running. Why do I have to migrate to a new OS already?" To begin with, you may *not* have to do it right away. The advantages of moving to Windows 2000 may not weigh heavily for your organization. Not everybody should feel compelled to move to Windows 2000 right away. If your network and server environment is meeting your business requirements, you are in a position to take the time necessary to map out a strategy for migrating when the time is right for your organization.

On the other hand, good candidates for an early move would include organizations that already have NT running, are large (more than 5,000 users), and are not located in a single facility. These environments have the most to gain by migrating to Windows 2000. The return on investment may not be significant to small- and medium-sized companies until application developers have had a chance to develop programs that fully leverage what Windows 2000 has to offer.

Note, too, that there are benefits to Windows 2000 other than improved security, lower-cost management, and increased network design flexibility. These benefits include the Distributed File System (Dfs), a new encrypted version of NTFS, enhanced support for newer hardware, and Dynamic DNS, all of which are covered in subsequent chapters.

SUMMARY

When Cisco and Microsoft announced they would work together to bring the network closer to the Windows operating system, a whole new realm of comput+ing became possible. This type of integration between the machines *using* the network and the machines that *are* the network will allow for a level of network reliability, security, and true integration that has never before been possible.

By centrally locating information about the network's devices and their status (by means of the Active Directory), opportunity opens up for applications to read this information and make decisions based not only on user properties, but also on the current condition of the network.

The full impact of the Cisco/Windows technological pairing won't be felt by users for some time. To get the most out of this relationship, users, administrators, and developers must study the technology ahead of time, and plan for it by adopting Windows 2000. In this chapter we reviewed the history behind the heightened integration between Cisco and Microsoft, the reasons for the relationship, and where the initiatives are likely to take us. We reviewed the new concepts necessary for properly understanding and using the new version of Windows, and how to migrate to it. We also looked at Active Directory, the new naming convention for Windows workstation and server, and some of the more notable new features of the Windows 2000 operating system.

In Chapter 2, we'll move ahead to discuss the Microsoft/Cisco relationship from the perspective of the network device vendor, and we'll introduce the Directory-Enabled Network (DEN) initiative.

CHAPTER 2

Directory-Enabled
Networking (DEN)

It's true that Active Directory's single view of users and network-based applications solves the scaling and administrative problems that plagued NT 4.0. By providing a common store of data across internetworks of any size, Active Directory takes a big step toward organizing user and application information in a central location. But what about the network itself? Users and applications are only two parts of a three-part equation. The third part—the network infrastructure—is the roadway over which everything travels. To realize ideal data communication, directory services must integrate the network infrastructure as the final element in attaining an environment that can adapt intelligently to changing conditions in order to always provide the best service to users.

POLICY-BASED NETWORKING: SUPPORT FOR QoS

Since the dawn of client/server computing, the Holy Grail has been to build the "intelligent network," simplifying the operation of distributed systems. The goal is to achieve policy-based controls that can be applied dynamically to network resources. This notion of *policy-based networking* promises as its major payoff the ability to provide selected, guaranteed levels of service needed to run ever-more-powerful network applications. This requires close control over parameter settings inside devices, something not yet possible under today's standard practice of telnetting into individual devices and implementing changes one by one. Under policy-based networking, however, settings will be made all at once from a central management console, and the devices will thereafter adjust their own behavior as needed, based on current operating conditions.

The sheer size and complexity of today's internetworks has created an urgent need for policy-based networking. But beyond magnitude, a new breed of applications is also driving the computer industry to provide better real-time control over network operations. These applications—videoconferencing, Voice over IP (VoIP), and others—require committed levels of service in order to work. It may be acceptable for a DNS lookup or an e-mail to be a little tardy, but video and voice packets are sensitive to the transmission timing and sequence. Without guaranteed network service levels, these high-powered applications don't work well. Robust directory services that put all network devices on the same informational page are necessary to guarantee these committed service levels.

Policy-based networking is most often associated with Quality of Service (QoS)—a robust technology despite its hype-sounding name. QoS is a suite of protocols, algorithms, and applications that work in concert to exert fine-grained control over real-time network operations and guarantee users or applications the network throughput levels they need. At least, that's the idea. Still a nascent technology, QoS should start realizing its promise during the first few years of the twenty-first century. Cisco has built a number of QoS commands into its IOS operating system, and has even rolled out a product named Cisco QoS Policy Manager to provide an operations console for QoS-enabled networks. QoS is covered in Chapter 15 of this book.

The mission of QoS is to allocate bandwidth and other network resources dynamically, based on interrelated factors such as user, application, location, time of day, and the like.

Once QoS technology is achieved, network behaviors can be adjusted automatically, on-the-fly, to respond to events as they occur. Such events include reprioritizing network traffic demand, according to a mix of factors such as available routes or a new service demand. For example, a major videoconference being set up by an R&D group might get priority status. Once attained, such pervasive network automation and control will enable designers to scale up to ever-larger networks running an increasingly broad mix of applications (most of the new ones are bandwidth hungry by nature). The new breed of applications includes real-time videocasting, VoIP, public key infrastructure (PKI) security, various audio services, and so on.

Video	VoIP	Audio	PKI
QoS			
DEN			
Existing directory services			

To make this dynamic bandwidth management scenario work, QoS needs an integrated directory service that talks *about* the network. In other words, a common set of data must exist for all three parts of the intelligent network equation: users, applications, and network infrastructure. Traditional network management tools such as Simple Network Management Protocol (SNMP) and Remote Monitor (RMON) talk *to* individual network devices, which is fine for per-device management. But they do nothing to control overall network behavior.

A new industry standard called Directory-Enabled Networking (DEN) has evolved to meet the urgent need for integrated directory services. Under the DEN initiative, existing directories remain in place but are able to share critical information freely, giving a comprehensive real-time view of users, applications, and the network infrastructure. DEN makes this possible by giving the directories a common language to speak.

A BRIEF HISTORY OF DEN

DEN was jointly proposed by Microsoft and Cisco Systems in 1997. For its original specification, the two companies drew heavily on existing directory standards and protocols. The motives behind the DEN initiative are understandable enough: Microsoft needs leverage to establish Windows as a true enterprise-class server operating system, especially to compete with UNIX. For Cisco's part, it wants to fulfill the vision of Internet convergence, where all communications media travel over the Internet—using Cisco hardware, of course.

DEN as a De Jure Standard

In 1998, the first draft of the DEN specification was submitted to the Desktop Management Task Force (DMTF), an industry group formed to develop standards for management of client/server systems. The specification wasn't handed over to the Internet Engineering Task Force (IETF) because the biggest part of the DEN is derived from the Common Information Model (CIM), a standard developed by the DMTF. In addition, most of the entities that will reside in DEN-compliant directories will come from applications and systems, not from network devices and media.

One point of confusion surrounding DEN is that it will be a "superdirectory," handling all network service applications. In fact, the opposite is true. DEN isn't intended to replace directory products at all. It's meant to foster their interoperability, thereby creating the common directory data store needed to take computing to the next level.

DEN common namespace						
DHCP	DNS	RADIUS	Kerberos	ERP	White pages	Others

Not a directory at all, DEN is a specification of generalized data structures organized into a comprehensive schema. (A schema is an outline that is universally applicable to a general purpose.) DEN designates the object classes needed to create a truly common *namespace* across the entire network, from ERP to DNS, to security, QoS, and beyond. A namespace is a set of names that are all unique and significant. The DEN mission is to foster a rigorously defined set of unique names and data formats for all network objects—hardware components, QoS policies, protocols, network media, applications, security policies, and more—to be shared by all directories.

With a common namespace, the various types of directories will be able to interoperate. Given such a broad scope, the only way to make the DEN initiative feasible is to leverage existing technology wherever possible. DEN does this by incorporating three existing directory standards:

▼ **CIM** Most DEN objects describing hardware and software are derived from the DMTF's Common Information Model.

■ **X.500** Much of the DEN specification describing persons and organizations is derived from X.500, the global directory standard from the International Standards Organization (ISO).

▲ **LDAP** DEN designates the Lightweight Directory Access Protocol (LDAP) to be the vehicle for directory intercommunication. Originally developed by the University of Michigan, LDAP is now under the auspices of the IETF.

Industry Acceptance of DEN

The DEN initiative has gathered considerable momentum, with nearly 200 major vendors now signed on. DEN version 3 was issued in the summer of 1999. Although the DEN specification is approaching completion, it will always remain for vendors to make their products compliant. Microsoft claims that the initial release of Windows 2000 is DEN compliant—specifically, that Active Directory complies with DEN.

Cisco has announced a DEN-compliant product called Cisco Directory Services (CDS). In addition, a new management software product will be distributed, called Cisco Networking Services for Active Directory (CNS/AD), which combines CDS with Active Directory to manage Cisco devices. CDS will integrate support for Novell's NDS in a later release.

Other major DEN development joint efforts are underway. Novell has built DEN support into NetWare 5.0 NDS with three key components: DHCP, DNS, and RADIUS. Netscape, Nortel/Bay Networks, Lucent, 3Com, and others are also now releasing DEN-compliant products.

THE DEN SPECIFICATION

Enterprises can no longer justify trying to coordinate a dozen or so disparate directories across their internetworks. Doing so is not only time consuming, but greatly increases the chance for error. This isn't exactly breaking news; for some time now it's been widely accepted that having individual directory services for such things as white pages, e-mail, ERP, security, and the like is ineffective and inefficient. The easiest example of how integrated directories will help is that not every device will be affected when something must be updated, such as creating a new user on the network. But the benefits of a common DEN namespace go beyond mere labor saving in routine administrative tasks. DEN will for the first time make it possible to apply fine-grained policies, at runtime, against complex multifactor rules drawing on information from many directories having to do with security, ERP application, white pages, and so on.

Clearly, there is strong motivation to improve on directory services. Yet substantial time, money, and training have been invested in legacy directory systems, so completely replacing them isn't the answer. And, given that the directories use various data formats and protocols, integrating and synchronizing them seems an impossible task. So how can the industry deliver truly integrated directory services in time for the new class of bandwidth-intensive network applications the world is counting on?

The answer is DEN. In practical terms, DEN offers the various directory services a common namespace can use, regardless of the services' respective protocols or data formats. The central features of DEN's design are as follows:

▼ **Least effort compliance**   DEN does not start from scratch, but rather leverages existing technology and know-how by building upon the best of existing directory technologies.

■ **Integration of network infrastructure**   DEN extends existing directory technology to include network devices, protocols, and media.

▲ **Extensibility**   DEN is an abstract standard that lets individual vendors implement their particular products as they see fit, as long as upper-level compliance is maintained.

Although DEN has received a fair amount of publicity over the past year, many are confused about what DEN is, exactly—because of what it's not. DEN is not a technology, not a protocol, and not an API or a product—it's not even a directory. It's a *specification* that defines how directories should store and exchange information about networks and their users.

DEN Defined

Technically, DEN is an open specification that defines an object-oriented information model for network entities. It defines these entities as classes, which together form the data model for all possible network information (in theory, at least). Not limited to network infrastructure devices and software, these classes include the breadth of client/server systems and applications. Additional classes profile users and policies to control the use of network resources.

Each DEN class describes a set of objects that share the same attributes, operations, methods, relationships, and semantics. A DEN object is a network element that exists within a class, with a well-defined boundary: an identity that encapsulates state and behavior. In other words, DEN is a very detailed specification that describes anything a human or machine using a network is likely to need to know. Each such element description is a class.

DEN class descriptions are as neutral as possible in order to maximize the scope of its usage. For example, the DEN class for network security protocols must be usable just as easily by a Kerberos product as by a CHAP product. Therefore, security protocols are contained within DEN's Security Service class, a subclass of the AAA class. (If you're new to networking lingo, AAA stands for Authentication, Authorization, and Accounting—a loosely defined standard for managing network security.) The AAA class is, in turn, a subclass of the Network Service class, and so forth on up the line, as depicted in Figure 2-1.

Thus, the AAA class is a container of various service classes, including the Security Service class. In the parlance of data models, a *container* is a class whose instances are collections of other objects, and not an object that itself represents something concrete.

The important focus in Figure 2-1 is the DEN terminology.

▼ A *class* is a prototype of a unique data structure designed to serve as a template for a particular entity.

■ The *data structure* arranges the class's attributes (also called *variables*) in a record that best represents the relationships of the attributes. A class inherits some of its properties from a parent class higher up the food chain, and classes below it derive some of their properties from the higher class—thus the terms *superclass* and *subclass*. (Veterans of object-oriented programming will recognize here that DEN uses a single-inheritance model.)

▲ An *object* is a unique instance of a class's data structure—in other words, a unique list of attributes. The idea is for a unique property to be stored in only

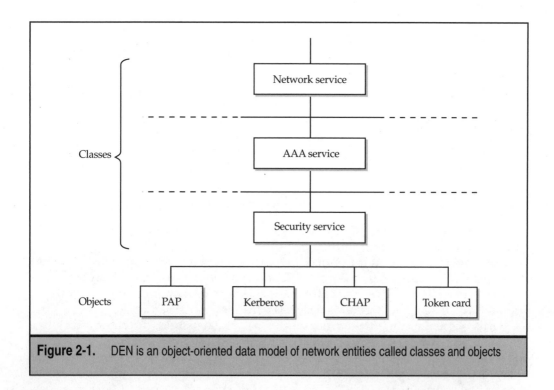

Figure 2-1.   DEN is an object-oriented data model of network entities called classes and objects

one place. When a DEN-compliant directory passes a message, the receiving directory knows where to find specific objects and how to map them into its particular data structure format.

NOTE: In *multiple inheritance*, a class inherits properties from more than one parent—for example, a Layer2Protocol DEN object inheriting from both the NetworkProtocol and Service objects. DEN specifies single inheritance for simplicity. Directories are, in essence, "name-search engines," and by using single inheritance, any name can be resolved by simply accessing the first property signature match encountered. In a multiple inheritance scheme, several matches might be found pointing to different parents, requiring a choice.

DEN Takes an Open Approach to Networked Directories

It's best to think of the DEN specification as a taxonomy of network objects to which directory services map their particular data. In other words, DEN attempts to classify network objects systematically, in a way that makes the most sense to all the directories that support it. DEN does this by detailing implementation-neutral schema for describing objects. As mentioned, DEN only provides the organization and the higher-level objects. It's up to the vendor to fill in the blanks to make its product interoperable using DEN.

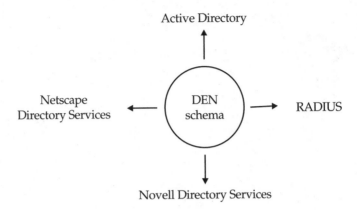

Directory services are physically distributed but logically centralized. In other words, directories sit on machines in various areas of the network topology, but the directories contain a common set of information. The network thus gains the intelligence on where resources are located, how they can be used, and who may use them. If directory services were held in a physically centralized store, they would be harder to find and slower to use, and would generate unacceptable levels of network overhead traffic.

Further distinguishing them from other types of data stores, directories work best with data that changes infrequently. For example, network management systems using the SNMP protocol like to take updates every five minutes or so, on such metrics as "packets per second" and the like. By contrast, directories work best with data elements that are updated every day or so. An example of this would be Cisco's CDS taking in new QoS policies from a network manager on a weekly basis.

Even a hierarchical directory is relatively flat and, therefore, no substitute for a database. Directories don't have relational data structures, don't support transaction semantics or stored procedures, can't do two-phased commits, don't support a sophisticated query language such as SQL, and don't have integral reporting capability. Without the room to store large objects such as BLOBs (binary large objects), directories aren't a good substitute even for a robust file system. Last, directories lack the support for connectionless transport that DNS has, and are not seen as a potential replacement for DNS—the world's largest distributed database.

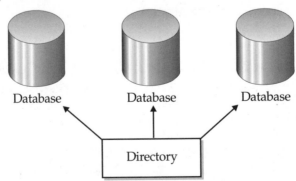

What DEN *does* do is define a base schema of classes for the types of things that appear in network directories. This alone is evidence that, while not itself a technology, DEN is nonetheless an undertaking of great scope. Not only must it provide a taxonomic structure that captures all data stored in the various directories—security data for RADIUS, domain-to-IP address mappings for DNS, and so on—but DEN must do so in a way that accommodates the subtle differences in each vendor's implementation of services in its own products. In other words, DEN must provide a directory namespace sufficiently broad and accurate to handle the stable of network directory services as they now exist.

LDAP: the Mechanical Superstructure for DEN

There is some confusion about how DEN and LDAP fit together, probably because LDAP looks so much like DEN. The DEN metadata model is interested only in defining a scheme to bring network infrastructure into a common directory data store, *not* in creating yet another new directory technology. Thus, DEN uses LDAP for a big part of DEN's superstructure (see Table 2-1).

LDAP was created to fix X.500's infamous problems with bloated overhead and difficulty of use. X.500 is such a glutton that only UNIX servers for the most part can run it, but the vast majority of users are on PCs. LDAP was designed to simplify and streamline X.500 in order to resuscitate the integrated directory service movement. LDAP has apparently succeeded: the IETF released LDAP v3 in 1997, and there are now dozens of LDAP applications in the marketplace.

LDAP is said to be "the way to implement DEN in the real world." It should be noted, however, that LDAP (much like DEN) is not presented as a stand-in for relational databases, file systems, or DNS. LDAP is an integrated directory service, pure and simple. Table 2-1 lists LDAP version 3's eight major features, and how DEN incorporates them to make itself desirable and feasible.

Both LDAP and DEN are abstract specifications. LDAP isn't a "product" any more than DEN is: rather, it's a spec on how vendors can design directory products that will interoperate within IP networks. The point to remember is that DEN incorporates LDAP for its mechanical infrastructure, and in so doing also subsumes a big part of X.500. But DEN goes a step farther to incorporate CIM classes, as well, to handle general computer-platform objects. Last, DEN redefines a number of classes on its own to handle network objects that are addressed by neither X.500 (via LDAP) nor CIM addresses.

LDAP is being implemented in a broad array of Web browsers, e-mail programs, and other types of network applications. It has also been adopted by the powerhouse directory services products. Perhaps most significantly (from a market share standpoint), LDAP is the primary access protocol for Active Directory.

LDAP Specification	LDAP Functionality/Relationship to DEN
Information model	LDAP defines attributes and values, inherited from X.500, almost without alteration. DEN incorporates "person-organization" elements for use in many types of network device transactions.
Schema	LDAP defines how "person-organization" elements are organized into objects. DEN incorporates LDAP's schema, but also borrows schema from CIM.
Naming model	In order to be easily implemented by any LDAP-compliant directory product, DEN incorporates the LDAP naming convention.
Security model	In order to be easily implemented by any LDAP-compliant directory product, DEN incorporates LDAP's specification for security. DEN has no particular spin on network security.
Functional model	The specifics of client access to and updating of directory information are left up to the LDAP specification. The DEN model deals only with data, not with runtime logistics such as add, delete, search, and compare operations.
Protocol	DEN relies totally on LDAP to map onto TCP/IP for transport.
API	DEN relies on product-specific APIs for implementation. In that regard, LDAP's API—or, rather, its implementation within an LDAP-compliant product—must be used to extend or tap into a DEN-compliant directory.
LDIF	The LDAP Data Interchange Format (LDIF) provides a simple text format for representing directory entries. LDIF is used to map to and perform data exchange operations with X.500 directories and proprietary directories. DEN has no equivalent tool, relying instead on LDIF.

Table 2-1. The DEN Model's Incorporation of LDAP

THE DEN INFORMATION MODEL

DEN builds an information model that holds "meta-information" in its schema. That is, the DEN information model is made up of "information about information" instead of the actual information itself. For example, DEN specifies data to be stored on routing protocols, but leaves it to individual DEN-compliant directory products to determine how and where to store that data.

As a highly abstracted object model, DEN seeks to standardize the data formats and relationships for objects down to the level at which individual vendors diverge according to market niche, technology of choice, and design style. A vendor of fiber-optic transmission technology, for instance, has data needs different from those of a vendor making infrared wireless media. But as layer-1 physical media, the products of these vendors share certain characteristics (such as maximum transmission distance). The DEN model has a common placeholder for that property shared by the two media types. This is said to be *inheritance*, where common properties are shared by the parent's subclasses.

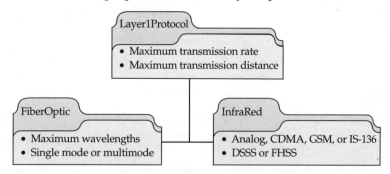

In our example of fiber-optic and infrared media objects, not only do the two media types share common objects by inheritance, but they use their own to store data-specific information. This data schema technique is called *generalization*. In relational databases it has the positive effect of having to store a particular type of data only in a single place. For DEN, generalization through inheritance also has the advantage of making it easier to link disparate directory formats within the data schema.

In essence, DEN works by setting up a hierarchy of classes that contain related objects. The higher you are in the DEN information model, the more removed you are from the actual things (routers, servers, users) being stored—in other words, things are more abstract at the higher levels. The farther down the model you go, the closer you are to real objects. But everything remains, nevertheless, abstract, because the DEN specification leaves off where vendor and user implementation begin.

To take another example, DEN has a class for microchips, but it does not have classes for particular kinds of chips. This is what's meant by *base* schema. Network device makers that are incorporating the specific Motorola or IBM chips are responsible for deciding what data about those devices to store, which they do by creating subclasses to hold information specific to particular product lines. This is what's meant by *extended* schema—the schema is extended from a superclass to a subclass. As a DEN-compliant technology, Active Directory features this type of extensibility.

The Heritage of DEN Classes

By way of their respective backgrounds, CIM and X.500 are complementary. CIM's roots are in desktop management. While the DMTF (CIM's sponsoring organization) is preoccupied with computer platform hardware and software, CIM has been developed to handle such things as PCs, disks, files, NICs, databases, operating systems, and the like. In contrast, X.500's focus has been primarily on people, organizations, and places. Neither technology, however, has focused on network infrastructure. That was left to SNMP, which is a closed management protocol and not a directory service. This heritage can be seen in the depiction of DEN v3.0 schema in Figure 2-2.

The lineage of DEN's classes isn't quite so orderly as illustrated in Figure 2-2. Specifically, DEN extends several CIM classes to realize the physical characteristics particular to network devices. One case of this is the NetworkASIC class, an enhanced DEN base class that extends the Chip class from the CIM schema. NetworkASIC has attributes to accommodate the special data needs of network devices, such as handling fast switching rather than just modem communication. This enhancement of CIM classes makes more sense than creating a separate class for network device hardware apart from computer platform hardware. After all, whether it's a PC or a router, hardware is by and large still hardware.

Inside a DEN Class

All DEN classes share a common format. The classes might behave differently or contain different types of information, but schematically they're laid out the same way, under

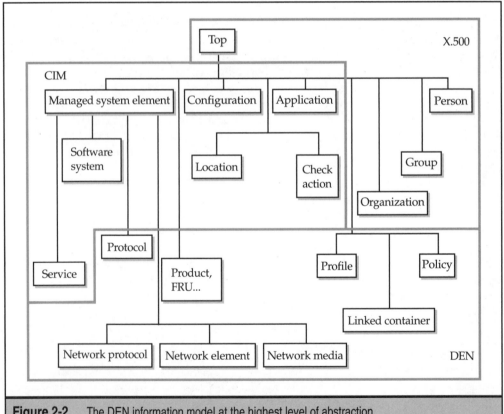

Figure 2-2. The DEN information model at the highest level of abstraction

one set of taxonomic rules. To be DEN compliant, a base class must define the elements in Table 2-2.

The four types of DEN classes—abstract, structural, container, and auxiliary—define what the classes can do. The most important distinction is that an abstract class cannot be directly instantiated (used); it exists only to serve as a parent of other classes. An abstract class holds no useful information itself. A container class exists only as a collection of other objects. In other words, its definitions can be referenced only by those classes it contains, not by outside classes. Auxiliary classes are used to include their attributes with the attributes of another class. An auxiliary class can be created once and referred to by separate classes. The vast majority of DEN classes are structural classes; they're the ones that do the actual work.

OIDs are widely used as unique identifiers in computing architectures. Perhaps the best known example is the use of OIDs to identify SNMP Management Information Bases (MIBs), software agents that sit on managed devices to collect information. By convention, all MIB OID numbers begin with the root notation 1.3.6.1.2.1. The ISO administers a regimented OID numbering scheme whereby computer systems should never be confused by duplicated numbers. It's a way to keep messages straight. At this writing, the OID root for DEN directories has yet to be assigned, but it's likely they'll begin with the notation 1.3.6.1.1—the ISO generic root number for directories. The fifth digit (the second 1) denotes that the numbered entity is a directory. For example, The OID for a Cisco direc-

DEN Class Element	Definition
Description	A text statement defining the purpose of this class.
Type	Type of class: abstract, structural, container, or auxiliary.
OID	Object Identifier, a unique number identifying this object.
Derived From	The superclass for this class.
Possible Superiors	A list of classes that may serve as a parent of instances of this class.
Auxiliary Class	A class used to bind one class of objects to another—for example, to bind hostConditionAuxClass and routeConditionAuxClass, together, to the policyCondition structural class.
Must Contain	List of attributes this class *must* contain.
May Contain	List of attributes this class *may* contain.
Relationships	List of associations and/or aggregations defined for this class.

Table 2-2.   Generic Layout of a DEN Class

tory might be 1.3.6.1.1.3. (In case you're wondering, the 2 in the root notation for MIBs stands for management, as in "systems management.")

The DEN specification provides a long list of attributes for use with objects. Where DEN *classes* are placeholders of information, the DEN *attributes* are used to express actual informational values. For example, a DEN attribute called NumberOfUsers defines the number of user sessions an operating system is actually handling at any given moment. Table 2-3 shows the layout of DEN attributes.

In addition to the usual list of syntax definitions (integer, Boolean, OID, and so on), DEN provides special syntax elements in order to fulfill its particular mission. Notable among these are DirectoryString and Object. DirectoryString is the syntax used to refer to a name taken from a known set of mutually agreed terms, such as the NameFormat set defined for the SystemName property. These are base DEN attributes that can be extended by vendors, in much the same way that base DEN classes can be extended.

How DEN Represents Object Relationships

Information models comprise both data and relationship models, and DEN is no exception. As you've seen, the DEN data model's schema is a collection of classes and attributes that directories can use to represent the data characteristics of their content. By contrast, DEN's relationship model specifies the relationships among various objects in the schema. There are three types of relationships in the DEN information model:

▼ **Link**   A relationship between two object instances.

■ **Association**   A group of links with a common structure and semantics.

▲ **Aggregation**   A special type of association in which some objects are "part of" others

Let's study some examples to bring this high-concept stuff down to earth. *Object instances* are actual pieces of directory data using a particular object. For example, the DEN

DEN Attribute	Definition
Description	A text statement defining the purpose of this attribute.
OID	Object Identifier, a unique number identifying this attribute.
Syntax	The structure of the grammar used to handle this attribute string.
Single Valued	Whether this class has one or several values.

Table 2-3.   Layout for DEN Attribute Definitions

class UserProfile is used to define what individuals are described to do. Persons stored with profiles in a directory each have their own object instance of the UserProfile class. These persons might be linked together as part of a domain; that's a *link*.

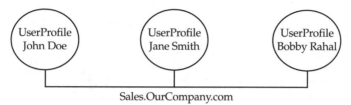

It may happen that the directory needs to group a number of DEN links together in order to apply a Kerberos security to them as a unity. This is an *association,* and it definitely beats having to describe security domain by domain.

Sometimes, however, it makes sense to *aggregate* things. For example, an Active Directory might want to publish a global catalog to avoid the inefficiency of publishing complete associations throughout the internetwork. The AD could do this by representing the entire associated group as one directory entry. That's *aggregation*.

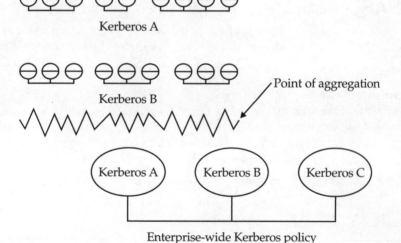

DEN Relationship Element	Definition
Purpose	A statement of the purpose of this relationship
Type	The type of this relationship: link, association, or aggregation
Cardinality	The relative order of each role within this relationship

Table 2-4. Layout of DEN Relationships

Relationships, then, are formed within DEN-compliant directories by linking, associating, or aggregating. In the mechanical sense, relationships are formed by listing the object to which "this" object relates in the Relationship property field of the base class for the object. Table 2-4 shows the format used to represent a DEN relationship.

Relationships are, of course, what brings any directory system to life. Directories (even hierarchical ones) may be flat and dumb compared to relational databases, but they put useful network information together by forming relationships between object entities on a massive scale. That, after all, is the very purpose of making directories in the first place: to construct a place where a user, resource, or policy resides. Because client/server directories are distributed, they must form and store relationships in order to work. At the DEN metadata level, the DEN classes strive to tie all various types of distributed directories together into a single content exchange that uses the above formats as their common currency.

DEN HIERARCHIES

A directory service mapping its data and relationships to the DEN information is of little use in and of itself. Profiles and policies are necessary to put this information to work. For example, if you wanted to exchange VLAN security policies between a Cisco CDS directory and a directory sitting on a Nortel carrier-class backbone switch, the DEN information infrastructure would make this possible (Nortel is implementing DEN, too).

Remember that more advanced network services, QoS in particular, require that policies be applied according to the real-time context of the application. Advanced applications such as videocasting and VoIP are all about speed, so there's no time for human intervention. This requires that the various directories feed the policy the information it needs to be in synch.

Policy-Based Networking

Policy-based networking requires profiles against which policies can be applied. Don't make the mistake of thinking that only users are profiled, however. Organizations, devices, and services are, as well. Let's look at an example of how a policy needs a profile: if a Cisco QoS Policy Manager server is trying to decide which of two services—video conferencing or distance learning—should get the most bandwidth, that server would refer to the profiles of the two services. Therefore, DEN defines profile schema for the gamut of network element types.

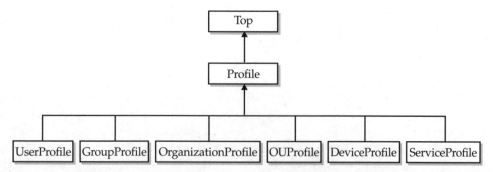

The Possible Superiors for UserProfile are Organization, OrganizationalUnit, and Group, which exist in the User Class Hierarchy portion of the DEN schema (the portion largely derived from X.500). Note that these possible parent classes should not be confused with their profile equivalents. For example, there is an Organization class as well as an OrganizationProfile class.

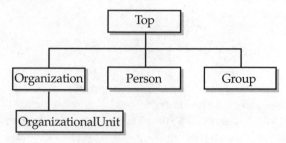

To support a policy, a DEN-compliant directory must either contain a policy, or must map to one in a cooperative directory via a relationship of some type. To do this, the DEN information model specifies schema for the variety of policy types.

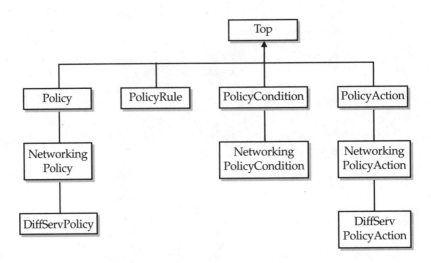

Here again, the Policy class is an abstract class put there only to let the NetworkingPolicy and DiffServPolicy classes exist. A networking policy might be one that determines how to condition traffic according to per-hop behaviors. DiffServ policies are used in QoS to differentiate service levels—for example, to provide better end-to-end bandwidth levels for one application over another.

Naturally, policy-based networking is largely concerned with operating conditions as they exist from moment to moment, and the actions to take in the event such conditions arise. A QoS policy might specify, for instance, that some action be taken if bandwidth utilization rises above a certain percentage—perhaps to detour a certain class of user sessions to another route, or to shut them down altogether in order to maintain higher-priority sessions at guaranteed-throughput levels.

Policy Class Hierarchies

The Policy class hierarchy illustrates interobject relationships. A policy might have several rules on file, each for a particular predefined condition. When the condition is sensed by the server, the associated action is triggered. The server could be a QoS server, a RADIUS security server, and so on. The point is that the relationships exist "side-to-side" so that policies can be applied to meet desired operating parameters. To accomplish this, disparate directory services must be somehow integrated, and that is what DEN does.

Dozens of other DEN class hierarchies are specified, and we won't enumerate them here. The hierarchies span the breadth of networking activity, including devices, components, network links, operating systems, routing protocols, applications, services, and more, down to the last nut and bolt. For example, there's a class called Chassis that must contain such attributes as ChassisSlotLayout, MaxChassisSlotSpacing, NumberOfCardSlots, HeatGeneration, and other objects. When the DEN spec writers aimed for fine-grained control, they really meant it!

To view the hierarchies in detail, visit the DMTF Web site at http://www.dmtf.org.

DEN IMPLEMENTED

Active Directory is envisioned as a critical network resource that developers will want to tie into applications that would benefit from knowing the information it holds. For example, a programmer writing an HR application might want to connect it to an Active Directory domain controller machine, for the purpose of tapping into the most up-to-date information on file for, say, employee cell-phone numbers. Thus, a programming environment would be needed for exchanges with Active Directory.

With that in mind, Microsoft provides a number of tools for working with Active Directory. Notable among them is Active Directory Services Interface (ADSI), an API that defines a directory service model and a set of interfaces to communicate with the AD. ADSI, used in place of the network-specific API calls, provides a single set of interfaces to communicate with any namespace that provides an ADSI implementation. As a Microsoft product, ADSI naturally supports standard Component Object Model (COM) features. ADSI has bindings to Visual Basic, Java, C, and C++. In addition, it enables administrators to automate such tasks as adding users and setting permissions on network resources. And ADSI gives developers access to other directory services, such as LDAP and NDS.

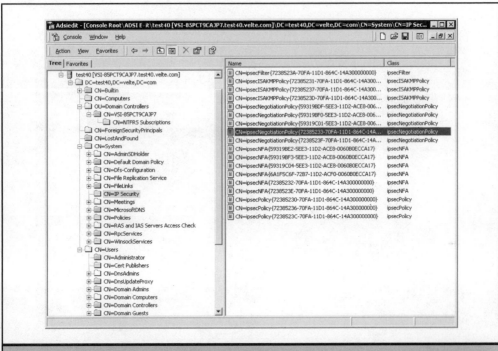

Figure 2-3.   The ADSI Editor snap-in gives developers an API for writing Active Directory hooks

ADSI installs with the Windows 2000 Resource Kit. Figure 2-3 illustrates the ADSI Editor, a Microsoft Management Console (MMC) snap-in application. Here you can see LDAP's heritage in the form of X.500 mnemonics (CN for common name, OU for OrganizationalUnit, and so on). The right pane in Figure 2-3 happens to be open to the IPSec (IP Security) class hierarchy, with a number of IPSec object instances identified in the Name column. Notice that there are multiple instances of the various IPSec objects.

This chapter does not offer a DEN-specific example because (at this writing) DEN has yet to be implemented in Widows 2000. A future release of Windows 2000 will ship DEN classes in Active Directory. Microsoft can't deliver these until the DEN spec is finalized, however, and until the vendors (especially Cisco) clarify what their extensions will look like. We do know that there will be, for example, a class tree called Device spanning from the abstract ManagedSystemNetwork class. How the Device structural class will be extended by the various network device makers, however, remains to be seen.

In Figure 2-4 you see the Active Directory Schema Manager, another MMC snap-in. The example in Figure 2-4 is open to the Classes folder, with applicationProcess classes listed. Looking at the tree on the right, notice the general look and feel of what we've been

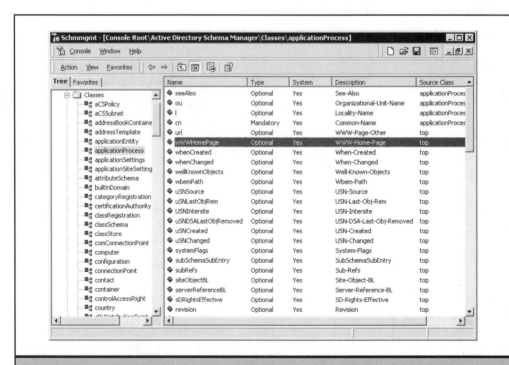

Figure 2-4.   Active Directory will eventually ship with a full set of DEN classes

talking about in DEN. The tree in the left-hand window lists the classes, and the right-hand pane lists its subclasses.

As DEN classes are delivered, the Active Directory Schema Manager is where developers will write programs to access Active Directory data on network infrastructure. Doing so will become routine, as network resource management under policy-based networking evolves.

SUMMARY

DEN is often mistaken for a directory technology. Rather, DEN is an architectural template intended for use by software engineers in designing directory products. For example, the folks designing forthcoming versions of Active Directory are referring to the DEN specification. Another misconception is that DEN is a superset of Active Directory, LDAP, or other directory technologies. DEN isn't a superset of any existent specification. As shown in this chapter, however, DEN incorporates LDAP for its communications infrastructure, and in so doing subsumes many X.500 class hierarchies. In addition, DEN separately incorporates CIM class hierarchies and extends several of them to work better with the particulars of network media and devices. That's what DEN is: an extension of the LDAP and CIM architectures to encompass network infrastructure. DEN's role is to bring infrastructure in as the third segment of the three-part equation to be solved by integrated directory services of the future.

It will be interesting to see how the DEN initiative plays out. The initial crowd of 200 vendors signed on so far is certainly impressive, and the list is likely to grow. But the big question is whether the level of implementation is deep enough to support true interoperability. Industry vets remain skeptical, in view of vendors' manipulation of SNMP implementations on their respective devices in order to protect turf—leaving customers in the lurch, stuck using network management systems with significant blind spots. Yet there is much optimism for DEN. Sponsors such as Cisco and Microsoft are sure to effect sufficient motivation to toe the architectural line. DEN's payoff could be huge for vendors and users alike. If disparate directories can exchange information at the level DEN has specified, users will see increased functionality and administrators will enjoy cheaper and more intelligent tools.

CHAPTER 3

Networking Fundamentals

A t this point, we have learned about the features and capabilities of Windows NT/2000 and about Cisco hardware. In Part 2, "Building a Cisco Network with Windows 2000," we will begin to put the pieces together that are necessary in constructing a fast, efficient network. Before we begin that process, however, in this chapter we'll take a look at some of the essential networking technologies that make up a network environment.

The language of networking is filled with acronyms and confusing terminology. However, learning a few key concepts will take you far toward understanding networking as a whole. This chapter begins by outlining the *Open Systems Interconnection (OSI) reference model* that most networking devices use in one way or another when sending and receiving data. After that we will examine the difference between rout*ed* and rout*ing* protocols. Finally, we will cover networking addressing—a necessary component to any internetwork that comprises other networks.

THE OPEN SYSTEMS INTERCONNECTION (OSI) SEVEN-LAYER MODEL

Standards organizations serve a very useful purpose. They work hard to ensure a fair and compatible networking environment that allows us to own and manage functional networks using products from many different vendors. When the networking community adopts a standard, the end user benefits most. It is almost always the only way to get competing vendors to implement solutions that work seamlessly across multiple platforms. One model that has been adopted by virtually all networking vendors is the *OSI seven-layer model* of networking. This section outlines the OSI reference model and its benefits.

The International Organization for Standardization, founded in 1946, published the Open Systems Interconnection (OSI) reference model in 1978 to meet the demand of networking vendors and users. This seven-layer model has become the standard for designing communication methods among network devices. It serves more as a template than a technical standard, but you will see that it permeates all things related to networking.

The OSI reference model has seven functional layers. Each defines a function performed when data is transferred between applications across a network, as illustrated in Figure 3-1. Each layer of the stack defines a set of functions that may be performed by any number of protocols. Although a given layer really only communicates with the layers immediately above and below it, there is a virtual communication stream between layers and peers, which is an equivalent implementation of the same protocol on a remote system. For example, a network-layer protocol will communicate through the protocol stack to the network protocol at the other computer. Each protocol layer is only concerned with communication to a peer at the other end of a link and thus creates a virtual link to the other system at the level of the OSI reference model. For example, the Transmission Control Protocol (TCP) is a transport-layer protocol that communicates with the transport layer on remote systems to ensure proper delivery of packets from one system to the other.

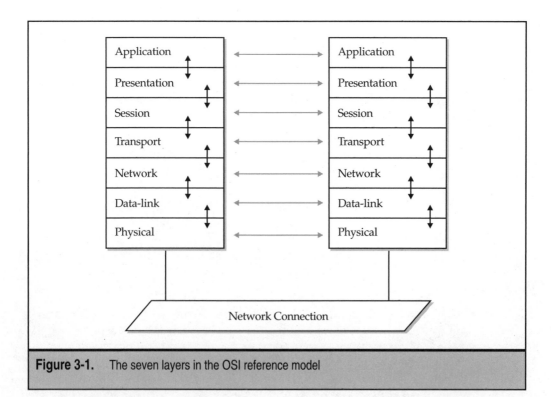

Figure 3-1. The seven layers in the OSI reference model

As mentioned, each layer is concerned with a certain set of functions. The layers communicate up and down the stack to remote systems until a virtual connection is established with the equivalent layer in the remote computer. Following are descriptions of the primary functions of each layer:

▼ **Layer 1**   The *physical layer* deals with the actual transport media that are being used. This layer defines the electrical and mechanical characteristics of the medium carrying the data signal. Some examples of physical media include coaxial cable, fiber-optics, twisted-pair cabling, and serial lines.

■ **Layer 2**   The *data-link layer* controls access onto the network and partially ensures the reliable transfer of packets across the network. This layer controls the synchronization of packets transmitted, as well as the error checking and flow control of transmissions. Some examples of data-link controls include token-passing protocols (such as Token Ring) and collision-based protocols (such as Ethernet's CSMA/CD).

■ **Layer 2**   The *network layer* is concerned with moving data between different networks or subnetworks. This layer is responsible for determining the network address of the destination device for which the data is intended. Internet Protocol (IP) and IP routing are functions of layer 3 of the OSI model.

■ **Layer 4**   The *transport layer* takes care of data transfer, ensuring that the data reaches its destination intact and in the proper order. The Transmission Control Protocol (TCP) and User Datagram Protocol (UDP) operate at this layer.

■ **Layer 5**   The *session layer* establishes and terminates connections and arranges sessions to logical parts. The Lightweight Directory Access Protocol (LDAP) and Remote Procedure Call (RPC) provide some functions at this layer.

■ **Layer 6**   The *presentation layer* is involved in formatting data for the application layer. Data encryption, and character-set translation such as ASCII <--> EBCDIC, are performed by protocols at this layer. Telnet is an example of a presentation-layer protocol.

▲ **Layer 7**   You are probably most familiar with *application-layer* protocols. These protocols are used by applications to communicate with the applications on the remote system. For example, protocols for electronic mail (Simple Mail Transfer Protocol) and file transfers (File Transfer Protocol) work at layer 7.

LOWER-LEVEL PROTOCOLS

The lower-level protocols (layers 1 and 2) define much of the physical network. At the lowest layer (physical), the type of cabling must be chosen (such as twisted-pair Category 5). Next, you have to decide what layer 2 Local Area Network (LAN) topology you will use. For example, Token Ring, Ethernet, and Fast Ethernet will all run over category (cat) 5 cabling. However, an Ethernet Network Interface Card (NIC) is quite different from a Token Ring NIC. To help you decide what technology is best for you, this section discusses the most popular LAN topologies, their advantages, and expected throughputs.

LAN Topologies

You will encounter three common types of LAN topologies most frequently today: Ethernet, Token Ring, and the Fiber Distributed Data Interface (FDDI). Each of these protocols is distinctly different from the others. Each has its own advantages and has a different role to play in your networking environment. You will probably have a mix of these topologies in your enterprise. Therefore, it's useful to understand the basic functioning of each so you can better choose which one to deploy when designing and building your own network.

Ethernet

Ethernet is undoubtedly the most popular LAN topology in use today. It is a simple and low-cost protocol that was developed jointly in the late 1970s by Xerox, DEC, and Intel Corporations. In its first incarnation, Ethernet was designed to move data at speeds up to 10 Mbps (megabits per second).

ACCESS CONTROL   Ethernet is a *contention-based protocol*. That is, all devices sharing a network segment are unaware of the other devices' intentions to use the media, so it is possible that more than one device may start sending bits along the wire at the same time.

The *Carrier Sense Multiple Access with Collision Detection (CSMA/CD) protocol* acts as a traffic cop to control access to the wire and to ensure the integrity of transmission.

Before attempting to transmit a message, a device determines whether or not another device is transmitting a message on the media. It does this by listening to see if there is a carrier on the wire. If it doesn't hear a carrier for 9.6 microseconds, the device will attempt to transmit the message. It must continue to listen while it's transmitting. In the event that two devices try to transmit at the same time, a *collision* occurs. Both devices must then back off from their transmission and retry after a random waiting period.

Because the media are shared by all devices, when a device transmits data, every device on the LAN receives the data. Each device checks each data unit to see whether the destination address matches its own address. If the addresses match, the device accepts and processes the packet. Otherwise, the packet is disregarded.

THE PHYSICAL CONNECTIONS   The physical connections for Ethernet have evolved from a backbone configuration to a star topology. The first Ethernet networks were built using a thick, semi-rigid, 0.4 inch-diameter coaxial cable as a backbone. Each cable could support 100 devices and could be no more that 500 meters long because of signal attenuation. Although segments could be connected by repeaters to amplify the signal, no more than two repeaters could be used. This limited the distance between any two stations on the Ethernet network to no more than 1,500 meters. This type of network is called Thicknet, or 10Base5 (which stands for 10 Mbps, baseband, 500 meters per segment).

Thin Ethernet was developed to reduce the cost of installation. Thin Ethernet uses a flexible RG58 coaxial cable for connecting to devices. It still uses a backbone topology, where a single cable runs from machine to machine. The cable connects to the NIC using a British Naval Connector (BNC) connection. These BNC *T connectors* are installed on the cable by cutting the cable, fitting each end of the cut with a female connector, and inserting the T-connector between the two new female connectors. Thin Ethernet is called 10Base2 (10 Mbps, baseband, 185 meters per segment). Both 10Base2 and 10Base5 use 50-ohm terminators on each end of the cable that act as signal "drains." This prevents the electrical signal from being reflected at the end of the cable and bouncing back and forth along the cable.

An obvious disadvantage of both Ethernet and Thin Ethernet is reliability. All it takes is a single cut in the wire, and all devices fall off the network. Also, a bad T-connector, a failed NIC, or a clumsy user can bring down the network.

To circumvent this issue, most Ethernet networks today are constructed using unshielded twisted-pair (UTP) wiring in a star topology. At the center of the network is a hub or switch. A separate run is made from the hub or switch to each device, as illustrated in Figure 3-2. This allows networks to be installed using horizontal cabling plants that terminate in a wiring closet, thus locating all wiring termination points centrally. This makes it much easier to implement moves, adds, and changes and prevents a single user or cable failure from taking down the network.

Ethernet built on twisted-pair cabling is known as 10BaseT (10 Mbps, baseband, twisted-pair cabling).

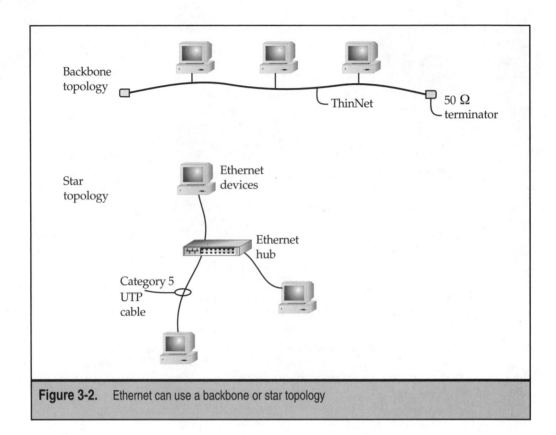

Figure 3-2.   Ethernet can use a backbone or star topology

Fast Ethernet

Fast Ethernet, or 100BaseT, is very similar to standard Ethernet. It uses the same contention-based protocol and is usually run over Category 5 UTP cabling. Interconnections are made using hubs, switches, and repeaters, just like 10BaseT.

The most obvious difference is that 100BaseT transmits data at 10 times the speed of 10BaseT. The required amount of time for a workstation to detect no carrier on the wire before transmitting is reduced by a factor of 10, from 9.6 to 0.96 microseconds. 100BaseT also uses a different coding scheme to represent bits on the network, making this protocol incompatible with 10BaseT.

Fast Ethernet (100BaseTX) typically runs over Category 5 UTP wiring, but it is possible to run it over Category 3 cabling using four pairs of wires. This is called 100BaseT4. Three pairs are used for transmission of data, and one is dedicated to handle collision detection. 100BaseFX is Fast Ethernet for Fiber Optic Cabling. Using fiber-optic allows for greatly increased transmission distances. Often, 100 Mbps switches or hubs are connected vertically from floor to floor in a building using 100BaseFX.

Token Ring

Token Ring is a LAN standard that avoids the Ethernet topology's contention of shared media. Instead, Token Ring uses a token-passing protocol to regulate data flow. All devices (called ring stations) are logically configured in a ring (the physical topology is still a star), and a frame called the token is passed around the ring. Only the device with the token may place data on the shared media. This token-passing protocol eliminates collisions and increases the utilization of the network. Token Ring runs at either 4 Mbps or 16 Mbps.

A basic Token Ring network consists of ring stations connected into a concentrator using Category 5 UTP or STP cabling located centrally in a wiring closet. Larger rings can be built by connecting multiple Token Ring hubs using special ports called Ring In (RI) and Ring Out (RO), or by using bridges or routers to connect multiple token rings.

TOKEN RING FRAME TYPES   Frames are the fundamental unit of transmission when referring to the lower two layers of the OSI model. Three important types of frames are transmitted on a token ring: tokens, MAC frames, and LLC frames.

▼   *Tokens* are used to control the transmission of data onto the ring. There is only one token on a ring at a time. Ring stations with something to say must claim the free token in order to transmit. This means only one station can transmit at any one time, eliminating collisions.

■   Media Access Control (MAC) frames are used by the ring stations to communicate with other ring stations. These frames are used to control the operation of the ring and to report errors. Token Ring has a very robust set of built-in controls to ensure proper operation.

▲   Logical Link Control (LLC) frames are the frames with user data. These frames use higher-level protocols such as TCP/IP, IPX/SPX, and others to transmit user data.

SPECIAL RING STATIONS   The first ring station on a Token Ring is called the Active Monitor. All subsequent ring stations become Standby Monitors. The Active Monitor ensures the ring is operating properly. It provides master clocking to the ring, removes any frames not claimed by other stations on the ring, compensates for frequency jitter, and ensures there is always only one token on the ring.

In the event that the Active Monitor doesn't detect a token or a frame on the ring within 10 milliseconds (ms), it will create a new token. Before it sends the new token onto the ring, the Active Monitor transmits a Ring Purge frame. The Ring Purge frame serves to reset the timers on all the ring stations. Once Active Monitor receives the returned Ring Purge frame, it transmits a new token onto the ring. If the Ring Purge frame isn't back within 4 ms, Active Monitor transmits another Ring Purge. This can continue for up to 1 second, at which time a new Active Monitor is elected.

BEACONING   Token Ring also has a troubleshooting method called *beaconing* to identify and attempt to correct hardware errors. This can be a fairly complex process, but basically, when a ring station sees a loss of signal on the ring, it sends a Beacon Frame containing the ring station's own address and the address of its Nearest Addressable Upstream Neighbor (NAUN). If the Beacon Frame travels all around the ring and reaches the NAUN, that NAUN station will pull off the ring and try to re-insert. The idea is that if the Beacon Frame gets all the way to the NAUN, the problem must reside in the NUAN. The re-insertion process includes a self-test that should cause the faulty station to remain off the ring. It doesn't always work, though.

FDDI

For high-speed, fault-tolerant networks, the *Fiber Distributed Data Interface (FDDI)* protocol is often used. Like Token Ring, FDDI is a token-passing protocol that uses fiber cabling to transmit data at 100 Mbps. It has several differences from Token Ring, however, that make FDDI an ideal media for network backbones or server network segments.

FDDI GOES THE DISTANCE   FDDI is faster than Token Ring—100 Mbps as compared to 16 Mbps. As you'll read about in the next section, token-passing protocols allow more use of the throughput than collision-based protocols. The second distinction from Token Ring is the distance you can obtain with fiber. Category 5 UTP cabling allows stations to be about 100 meters from the hub or switch; fiber runs, on the other hand, can go many kilometers before repeaters are required.

Distance capabilities and fault tolerance make FDDI an ideal media for network backbones. It is often used within a data center as a part of the network backbone, as a high-capacity medium for connecting high-volume servers, and for interconnecting multiple buildings in a "campus" environment.

REDUNDANCY IS BUILT IN   FDDI is composed of two parallel rings that connect each station to its neighbors with two links, as shown in Figure 3-3a. Each ring transmits data in the opposite direction, although only one ring is operational at a time. These rings are called the primary and secondary rings. Under normal operation, the secondary ring sits idle and is only used in the case of failure on the primary ring.

When a failure occurs on the primary ring, such as a break in the fiber or a faulty NIC, the ring isolates the damaged station by wrapping around to the secondary ring, as shown in Figure 3-3b. Data can then reach all remaining stations. However, when this occurs, the ring is no longer fault tolerant, and measures must be taken to fix the primary ring.

Throughput Expectations

LAN protocols operate at speeds in excess of 100 Mbps, but many people are surprised to learn that the achievable data rate is never as high as the specification for the LAN protocol. This section outlines some rudimentary methods you can use to gauge the *actual* throughput you can expect for collision- and token-based networks. Based on these calculations, you can better plan your network.

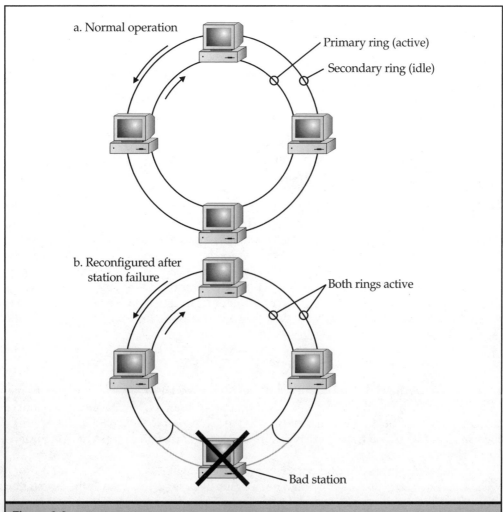

Figure 3-3. Dual-attached stations connect to two FDDI rings

NOTE: Since these calculations represent theoretical or ideal throughput values, they should not be used when designing a network around specific traffic requirements. Even though the numbers can serve as a first approximation and an upper bound on performance, actual throughput based on typical traffic and loading patterns on your network should be used in the design process.

Physical Properties

For us to examine the limitations of networks, we must first look at the physical properties of bits on the transmission medium. This will help us understand how packets and, ultimately, our data are transferred across the physical media. Remember the following values used in these descriptions of a network's physical characteristics:

▼ R = data rate (for example, 10 Mbps)

■ d = distance of network in meters (for example, 10 m, 100 m, 100 km)

■ V = propagation velocity of signal; about 2×10^8 m (for copper wire)

▲ L = length of frame in bits (for instance, 1000 b, 5000 b)

The number of bits that can be on the wire at any time is defined by Rd / V. This is the length of the medium in bits, given a certain data rate and length of the network. So, for a 10 Mbps Ethernet segment that is 500 m long, the bit length is 25. Think of this value as the number of bits that can be placed on the wire before they start spilling out the other end. As the data rate and the length of the wire increases, more bits can fit onto the wire at one time.

Since a sending device will want to put its entire frame on the wire, a useful way to think about the length of the network in bits is to put it in relation to the size of the frame that is being transmitted on the wire. We use the variable a to represent the length of the medium in relation to the frame size:

a = length of wire (b) / length of frame (b) = Rd / VL

If a = 1, then the length of the physical medium is equal to the length of one frame. Usually, a is much less than 1 for LANs, however. This means the frame is much longer than the length of the medium in bits. In the Ethernet example used above, the length of the wire was 25 bits, but frames are typically much larger than this on LANs—thousands of bits, thus a = 0.01 to 0.1.

Figure 3-4 illustrates an Ethernet segment that has a value of a that is less than 1 for a given frame size. Because this segment has a value of a that is less than 1, the last station will start to receive the frame before it is finished being transmitted. This is just fine; in fact, the short physical length is preferred so that a frame can get on and off the wire as quickly as possible.

The Theoretical Maximum Utilization

The *theoretical maximum utilization* (percentage of capacity used) of a segment goes down as the value of a (the length of the medium in relation to the frame size) goes up. How does this work? The media must be clear before another frame can be transmitted. If a is large, then the stations must wait for the frame to be sent the length of the medium before it is clear. It is important to remember that when data is on the wire, utilization is 100%. When no data is on the wire, utilization is 0% and cuts into the overall utilization of the medium.

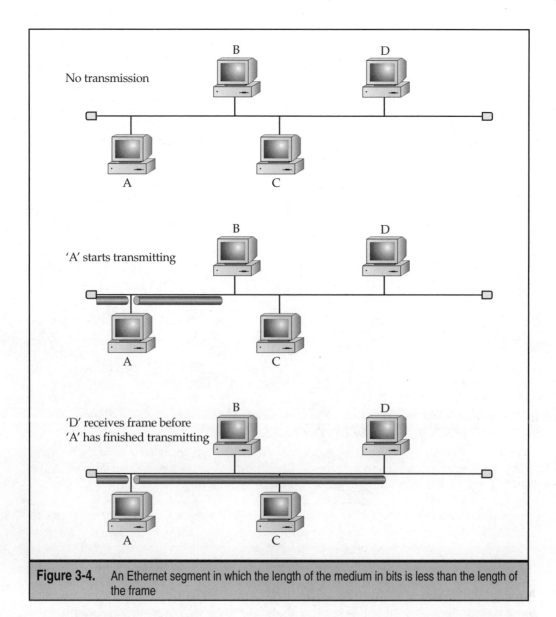

Figure 3-4.   An Ethernet segment in which the length of the medium in bits is less than the length of the frame

If, for example $a = 1$, then the maximum utilization of the medium can be at best only 50%. As soon as the start of the frame hits the end of the wire, the end of the frame is being transmitted. All devices must wait for the end of the frame to leave the wire. Since the length of the wire in bits is the length of the frame, the same amount of time used to transmit the frame is now spent waiting for the frame to propagate all the way down the wire. Thus the wire is only used to transmit data half of the time, so utilization is at best only 50%.

This is the best-case scenario; there is no overhead, no collisions, no errors, no lost data, and another frame is there to be sent at the exact point the first frame leaves the wire. The following table illustrates several cases of a 10 Mbps segment that uses 5000-bit frames. As the length of the cable increases, *a* goes up and the theoretical maximum utilization starts to go down dramatically. You can see why it is important to keep *a* as low as possible.

Length (m)	a	Maximum Utilization
10	0.0001	0.999
100	0.001	0.999
500	0.005	0.995
1,000	0.01	0.990
5,000	0.05	0.952
10,000	0.1	0.909
100,000	1	0.500

Since the maximum length for many media is about 100 meters, it is impossible for some LAN protocols (including Ethernet) to even approach the length required to get a large value for *a*.

Keep in mind that this calculation is theoretical and should be used to understand how networks work. In the real world, network performance can be influenced by a variety of factors.

Relative Throughput for Token-Based Protocols

When considering network technologies, it's useful to define the *relative throughput* value. Relative throughput is the ratio of the achieved data rate over the theoretical limit of the throughput. For example, if you measure only 20 Mbps of data transfer on your 100 Mbps segment, your relative throughput is 0.2.

The token-passing and collision-based protocols each have their own calculations to determine the relative throughput of a given type of LAN. These equations are different because the two LAN protocols have different methods of carrying data.

Let's start with token-based arrangements. You'll remember that in token-based protocols, a frame is transmitted from the token-holding station to the medium. The frame travels from station to station until it comes full circle and is received by the sending station. This station passes the token along to the station's neighbor, so that it can place a frame on the network if it needs to. If this station doesn't have any frames to send, it passes the token farther along.

Token Rings that carry minimal amounts of network traffic have low utilization values because the station wishing to send a frame must wait for the token. The time spent waiting for the token is time when data is not being sent. This reduces the utilization time. Token passing works better on a busy segment than do collision-based protocols, however, because the token is passed in sequence; every station has an equal chance to place a frame on the network. Since there is little time spent waiting for the token (between two stations that have data to send), the realized throughput goes up.

Relative Throughput for Collision-Based Protocols

Collision-based LANs function entirely differently than Token Ring LANs. Instead of passing a token that allows a station to send a frame, the collision-based protocol places a frame on the medium when the protocol senses that the medium is not being used. When two stations get the idea to send a frame at the same time, their frames collide, and both stations back off for a random amount of time before resending their frames.

To get at the relative utilization in this arrangement, we have to look at the probability that the wire is being used. First, if each station has the same probability of successfully capturing the wire for transmission, then the probability that a single station has captured the wire decreases as the number of active stations increases. Also, the interval between contentions decreases. That is, the station is less likely to grab command over the wire; and once it does, it is more likely to be interrupted by another station. Therefore, the maximum throughput for collision-based protocols occurs when there are only two stations on a subnet. This cuts down on contention for the medium and reduces the contention interval.

Figure 3-5 illustrates the theoretical throughput for token-passing LANs vs. collision-based LANs, for two different values of a.

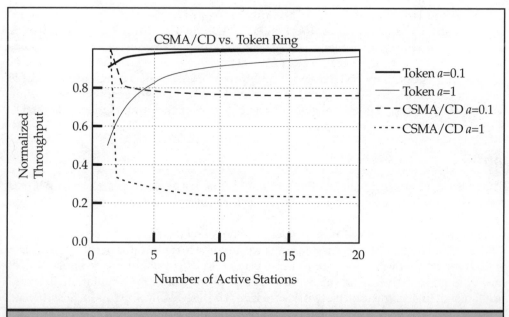

Figure 3-5. Normalized throughput for collision- and token-based protocols as the number of active stations increases to 20

Collision vs. Token Passing Protocols

You can see that token-passing protocols increase their utilization of the transmission media as more active stations are added. These protocols are, nonetheless, still susceptible to the problems associated with an increasing value of a as the physical size of the ring grows. Notice that the use of the available capacity is very poor when there are only a couple of stations. This is the result of the stations' waiting until they can transmit again (waiting for the token to come around).

The efficiency of collision-based protocols obviously suffers as more stations attempt to transmit frames. Increasing the speed of the protocol is one way to put off contention. Upgrading to 100 Mbps Ethernet from 10 Mbps Ethernet would shorten the amount of time the frame is on the wire and decrease the likelihood of a collision. Another strategy is to reduce the length of the segment. By breaking up large Ethernet segments, you reduce the bit length of the segment as well as the number of active stations. To get the most out of an Ethernet segment, you should break up the segment until you have only two stations on a segment. When one transmits, the other is receiving, and vice versa. This is essentially what happens when you connect a single device through a switch port—the device and the switch can carry on conversations without having to contend with other devices.

UPPER-LEVEL PROTOCOLS

In the previous section, we discussed the lower-level protocols, which form the foundation on which the upper-level protocols run. As with the lower-level protocols, there is usually more than one upper-level protocol at work in any large network. Network administration is easier if there is only one protocol to manage, but the requirements of businesses and applications have made multiprotocol networks commonplace. It is important to familiarize yourself with the various beasts you might encounter in working with these networks. This section gives you an overview of the primary protocols used in a typical Microsoft/Cisco networking environment.

TCP/IP

One of the definitions of *protocol* in a dictionary is that it's a set of rules governing how a process or function works. Upper-level networking protocols fit this definition. In the case of TCP/IP, a whole group of protocols work closely together to form the most widely used set of protocols in network communications today, called the *TCP/IP protocol suite.*

The utility of the OSI reference model starts to come to light at this point. As you have read, a variety of lower-level protocols are used to transfer data. If each combination of lower- and upper-layer protocols were a specific proprietary implementation, it would result in a rigid, incompatible network structure. The task to develop products that could interact while retaining their unique operating principles would be extremely costly and complex, if not impossible. Fortunately, since each layer is concerned with only the layer above and below it, it is possible to mix and match upper- and lower-level protocols. That is, you can have IP running over Ethernet, Token Ring, and FDDI.

You can see that the communications requirements for allowing layers to talk to each other requires a modular design. TCP/IP was developed with this very principle in mind by the Defense Advanced Research Projects Agency (DARPA), and was implemented on the Advanced Research Projects Agency Network (ARPANET). The TCP/IP suite of protocols have been deemed Internet standards by the Internet Architecture Board.

TCP/IP operates on the upper five layers of the OSI model. The lowest layer on which it operates is layer 3, the network layer. Layers 1 and 2 are able to understand a single LAN but are incapable of dealing with multiple LANs. Enter the network layer; it allows lower-layer protocols to transport data to other networks. This provides a solution for the entire internetwork, whether you have Ethernet, Token Ring, FDDI, wide area networks (WANs), or all of these.

One of TCP/IP's strengths is its ability to work with very large networks. This explains its widespread acceptance on the Internet and in enterprise computing.

A few of the many protocols included in the TCP/IP protocol suite are listed in the following table. We'll concentrate on the ones at the network and transport layers.

ARP	Address Resolution Protocol
FTP	File Transfer Protocol
HTTP	HyperText Transfer Protocol
ICMP	Internet Control Message Protocol
IP	Internet Protocol
NFS	Network File System
RIP	Routing Information Protocol
RPC	Remote Procedure Call
SMTP	Simple Mail Transfer Protocol
SNMP	Simple Network Management Protocol
TCP	Transport Control Protocol
Telnet	Character-oriented terminal emulation
TFTP	Trivial File Transfer Protocol
UDP	User Datagram Protocol

It's been estimated that Cisco products make up 80% of the Internet's backbone, so it's not surprising that almost all Cisco products include highly robust support for the TCP/IP protocol suite. Windows NT/2000 also includes built-in support for TCP/IP. When Windows and Cisco meet at the network, it's almost always via TCP/IP or IPX/SPX.

IPX/SPX

The *Internetwork Packet Exchange/Sequenced Packet Exchange (IPX/SPX)* was developed by Novell, Inc., for use with their networking product, NetWare. IPX/SPX is a derivative of the XNS network protocol developed by the Xerox Corporation.

The IPX portion of IPX/SPX operates at the OSI network layer, handling the addressing of the network devices (including IP) and keeping track of the routes within the IPX network.

NOTE: Lower-layer hardware devices used in networking, such as hubs, are specific to a single protocol (Ethernet, for instance). Upper-layer devices such as routers might support more than one protocol (TCP/IP and IPX/SPX, for instance). A router with this capability is called a *multiprotocol router.*

SPX operates on the OSI transport layer (like TCP). It provides for the reliability of the end-to-end communication link. SPX provides guaranteed packet delivery and packet sequencing. Its role in internetworking is to attempt to guarantee delivery of all routed packets.

IPX/SPX shares information about its services to network servers and routers by way of the Service Advertising Protocol (SAP). Services in an IPX network use SAP to advertise themselves and their network addresses. Workstations use the information made available through SAP to obtain the network addresses of servers that offer needed services. By default, SAP broadcasts the information onto the network every 60 seconds. This can become a problem as the network grows and, along with it, the information in the SAP table being broadcasted.

NOTE: Microsoft NT Workstation comes with the IPX/SPX protocol, and services that allow NT Workstation to act as a client to a Novell Server. Windows NT Server has built-in support for the client, as well as gateway services for NetWare.

NetBEUI

NetBIOS was developed by IBM in the mid 1980s. It was intended as a common application programming interface (API) for application programmers to use as a mechanism to deliver their applications to the network. An API is a set of functions or procedures for a programming language that enable the application to use services provided by other software. Microsoft later developed *NetBIOS Extended User Interface*, or *NetBEUI*, to provide communication within a local area network.

NetBEUI locates other devices on the LAN by using NetBIOS machine names—those familiar computer names consisting of, at most, 15 characters. When a computer has data it needs to send to another device on the LAN, it broadcasts onto the LAN looking for a specific NetBIOS name. Every device on the LAN looks at the broadcast packet to see if it's intended for them. The device with the broadcast name responds to the source device, and the sending device can then send the data onto the LAN with a specific address. This process is called *NetBIOS name resolution.* The simplicity of the NetBEUI protocol makes it very quick on a small network. However, as the network grows, this broadcast methodology can quickly begin to consume more and more of the available bandwidth because of the growing number of broadcasts. This is especially troubling when networks are connected over slower WAN links.

NetBEUI, by nature of its role resolving names by use of broadcasting, is not aware of other networks and by itself is not routable. NetBIOS can encapsulate itself inside network and transport protocols such as TCP/IP or IPX, however, to enable routing in a routed network environment. Windows NT uses NetBIOS over TCP/IP (called NBT) to run on a routed TCP/IP network.

Systems Network Architecture (SNA)

It seems that almost every large, well-established network has some need for *Systems Network Architecture (SNA)* support. This is because the IBM mainframes are prevalent and still in use. SNA was developed to provide networking to the terminals of older mainframes.

In the early days of large mainframe computing, terminals were used for specific applications. Users who needed to access more than one application had to have multiple terminals in their workspace. In 1974, IBM announced SNA, which defined the framework around which IBM built its data communications functions and protocols. IBM took the communications out of the applications themselves and provided for shared communication functions for all applications, similar to the modularity of the OSI model. The benefits are the same, achieved by putting the network definitions into a common networking application with common interfaces that all applications can use. Any changes or additions can be made in one place, instead of requiring changes to every application.

SNMP and MIBs

The *Simple Network Management Protocol (SNMP)* is a member of the TCP/IP protocol suite and is mentioned here because you will see it at work throughout this book. It runs at the application layer of the OSI model and is used to help manage TCP/IP-based networks.

The intelligence for an SNMP-managed network lies in the Network Management Station (NMS). The NMS polls the network devices, or SNMP agents. These agents keep information about themselves in the form of a Management Information Base (MIB). The MIB provides a standard representation of what information is available for the SNMP agents and where it is stored. From the MIBs, the NMS extracts and keeps a database of all the information about all the SNMP agents it is managing. This method allows for low overhead on the SNMP agents themselves, reducing the complexity and, therefore, the cost of implementation.

Hewlett-Packard's *Openview* is an example of an SNMP management station. Windows systems are capable of acting as SNMP agents—that is, they can share information about themselves in a MIB format that can be polled from an SNMP management station. Most Cisco devices, as well, can share information about their configuration and utilization via SNMP. You will learn more about SNMP and network management in Chapter 8.

ROUTING PROTOCOLS

As you recall from earlier in this chapter, it is important to limit the number of devices sharing the same subnet. This reduces collisions and increases utilization. However, once a destination is beyond the local subnet or broadcast zone, a device acting as a *router* must be used to forward the packets to the correct network. If internetworks consisted of only a handful of networks, this would not be an issue. But when many dozens of networks are being fed from many routers, the routers must be able to communicate among themselves about all possible destinations. Moreover, the routers must be able to update their route tables dynamically, as networks and/or routers become available or unavailable.

Routing protocols keep a recent view of the network and all the available routes within that network. These protocols enable the routers they serve to keep track of all the other devices in the network, the state of those devices, and the best routes available for passing data along the network.

Distance-Vector Routing

There are two primary types of routing protocol: *distance-vector* and *link-state*. The first routing protocols used the distance-vector method. A network device using distance-vector routing periodically broadcasts data packets to its immediate neighbors, typically every 60 to 90 seconds. These packets contain all the information the device currently has about the network's topology. To determine the best path, distance-vector routing protocols typically use information about *link speeds* and *hop counts* to make their routing decisions. The hop count is increased by 1 for each router that must be traversed. The number of hops to the destination is considered the router's *metric* or *cost* to get to the destination.

After receiving this information, routers incorporate it in their routing tables before passing the information along to their neighbors. Through this periodic checking and broadcasting, which is performed at regular intervals regardless of whether the network has changed, all routers are kept updated with the correct network addresses for all devices on the network, as well as with the best route for transferring data between any two devices. If a device several hops away from a sending router fails, it can take time for the sending router to discover the fact. In larger networks, this slow convergence of route tables can lead to misdirected network traffic and cause further erroneous entries in the route information propagated throughout the network.

Routing protocols that use the distance-vector method are simple to configure and deploy. As networks grow larger in size, however, the periodic announcements used by them may cause excessive traffic on the network. Typically, distance-vector protocols are used on networks with fewer than 50 routers; most larger networks employ other routing protocols. The advantages and disadvantages of distance-vector protocols are summarized here:

Advantages	Disadvantages
Easy to configure	Slow to converge
Widely accepted	15-hop count limit
Lower resource requirements on the router	No variable-length subnetting

The *Routing Information Protocol (RIP)* is probably the most common distance-vector routing protocol. Cisco developed its own protocol called the *Interior Gateway Routing Protocol (IGRP)*, which was later improved and called *Enhanced IGRP* or *EIGRP*.

Link-State Routing

Link-state protocols were developed to address many of the limitations of the distance-vector protocols. Link-state protocols can adapt more quickly to changes in network topology and are thus better for managing large, complex networks.

Link-state protocols communicate changes in network topology to other devices in an incremental manner. When a network link changes state (up to down, or down to up), a notification called a *link state advertisement (LSA)* is flooded throughout the network. All routers note the change and recompute their routes accordingly using their link-state algorithm. This method is more reliable, easier to debug, and consumes less bandwidth than the distance-vector method. On the other hand, it is more complex and more demanding of CPU resources and memory. As the size of the network increases, the memory and CPU utilization required to run link-state routing protocols becomes a primary consideration in network design.

The advantages and disadvantages of link-state protocols are summarized here:

Advantages	Disadvantages
Fast convergence of route tables	Higher requirements for CPU and memory
No hop-count limit	Difficult to configure
Variable-length subnet masking (defined in the section "VLSM" under the main heading "TCP/IP," later in this chapter)	
Reduced bandwidth consumption (fewer updates)	

Examples of link-state protocols include the *Open Shortest Path First (OSPF)* protocol, which is part of the TCP/IP protocol suite; the *Intermediate System-to-Intermediate System (IS-IS)* protocol, a router-to-router protocol that is part of the OSI suite; and the *NetWare Link Services Protocol (NLSP)*, Novell's link-state protocol for IPX networks.

RIP

The *Routing Information Protocol (RIP)* is a distance-vector protocol that uses the Bellman-Ford algorithm. RIP routers usually broadcast a routing update message containing known routes every 30 seconds. A timer is started when a route is learned from a routing update message. A route that hasn't been learned again within 180 seconds is removed from the router's table. This leads to a "chatty" protocol. Try to imagine a dozen routers sending their entire route table to neighboring routers every 30 seconds.

RIP's Limitations

Because RIP cannot detect or correct routing loops (explained in the following section), routes learned with RIP that exceed 15 hops are treated as invalid and unreachable. This means any given source and destination on your network cannot be separated by more than 15 hops. This hop-count limit can make RIP impractical for large networks.

Another limitation is a long convergence time. This is the time it takes for a network to stabilize after a change in one of the networks. For example, if a router in a 10-hop network goes down, it could take five minutes (30 seconds times 10 hops) for the most distant router to learn of it. All the while, that distant router has been sending packets as if the downed router were still up.

Removing Routing Loops

Routing loops occur when routers send packets from router to router and never actually deliver the packets to the destination LAN. Routing loops can be frustrating and difficult to troubleshoot and can wreak havoc on a network. To eliminate routing loops and decreasing convergence times, RIP can use the *split-horizon method* with *poison-reverse updating*. These are schemes for controlling the way a router advertises a route to the neighbor from which it learned the route.

In split-horizon updating, routes are not sent back to the router that advertised the routes initially. For example, if router A announces its available routes to router B, router B does not send this information back to router A in an update. It is never useful to send information about a route back to the router that generated the information in the first place. Split-horizon updating eliminates routing loops that occur between two adjacent routers.

Split-horizon with poison-reverse updating eliminates routing loops that can occur when you have many routers. It works by temporarily inactivating routes that have increased in hop count by more than 1. An increasing hop count for the same route indicates a routing loop, and temporarily removing or inactivating the route will stop the looping. If the route continues to loop, then the route is declared invalid and is not used.

RIP Support in Microsoft NT/2000

Windows NT/2000 servers can participate in a RIP environment. RIP is installed as a service and requires very little configuration.

To install RIP for Windows NT 4, load the software from the Network Properties applet. To open the applet, right-click the Network Neighborhood icon, or get to the applet from the Control Panel. Click the Services tab and then Add. This brings up a list of network services that haven't been installed on the system, as illustrated in Figure 3-6.

Starting RIP under Windows 2000 is done via the Management Console for RRAS, as described for OSPF in the upcoming section.

This implementation of RIP has the following features:

▼   Uses the split-horizon and poison-reverse methods of updates

■   Allows for route filters, so you can choose which networks to announce or to accept announcements from

■   Can filter packets based on IP ports

■   Works with IP and IPX for NetWare

■   Uses a GUI and command-line interface with scripting capabilities

■   Can be managed remotely

▲   Works with virtual private networking (VPNs) using the Point-to-Point Tunneling Protocol

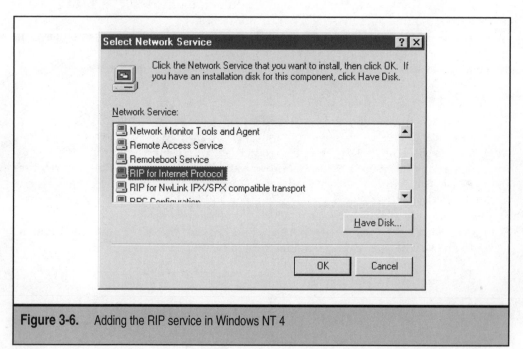

Figure 3-6.   Adding the RIP service in Windows NT 4

As networks grow, the limitations of RIP become the driving force to adopt a link-state routing protocol. Once a network has exceeded 10 hops or approximately 50 routers, upgrading to a link-state protocol should be considered. OSPF is a primary candidate for IP networks because of its universal acceptance and scalability.

> *TIP:* If you have a single NIC on your Windows server and a single router on your local network, do not enable routing. Simply define a default gateway in your server, pointing to the IP address of the router. Even if you have multiple Cisco routers, you may employ HSRP (Hot Standby Routing Protocol) between the routers. The server will continue to use a simple default gateway.

OSPF

The most common link-state protocol is the Open Shortest Path First (OSPF) protocol. OSPF was developed by the Internet Engineering Task Force (IETF) and designed expressly for large IP environments such as the Internet.

OSPF directly addresses many of the limitations of RIP. For example, OSPF is not limited to a hop count, can use other metrics besides hop count to determine best path, and sends changes to the routing tables only—not the whole routing table. This can greatly reduce the consumption of expensive bandwidth .

Another advantage of OSPF is that it passes *subnet mask* information (see "TCP/IP," later in the chapter) in its routing updates. This allows routers to handle variable-length subnet masks within an IP network. It also lets them accommodate IP networks that are noncontiguous. This gives the IP address administrators much greater flexibility and efficiency in the assignment of those precious IP addresses.

All of this sounds great, but there is a catch to OSPF. The cost of all this intelligence is greater consumption of router CPU cycles and memory, and an increased complexity in design and management.

OSPF Areas

OSPF allows sets of networks to be grouped together. Such a grouping is called an *area*. The routers in each area know only about the other routers in the area and build their topological maps based on those routers. The routers in an area share their route tables only with other routers in their area. Area border routers (ABRs) pass routing information among areas. This reduces the overhead requirements for each router and creates a modular network design that is very scalable. This concept is illustrated in Figure 3-7.

OSPF networks all have an Area 0, which is considered the backbone area. All other OSPF areas must connect to the backbone area—if not directly, then through a virtual direct link. The backbone area manages all inter-area traffic.

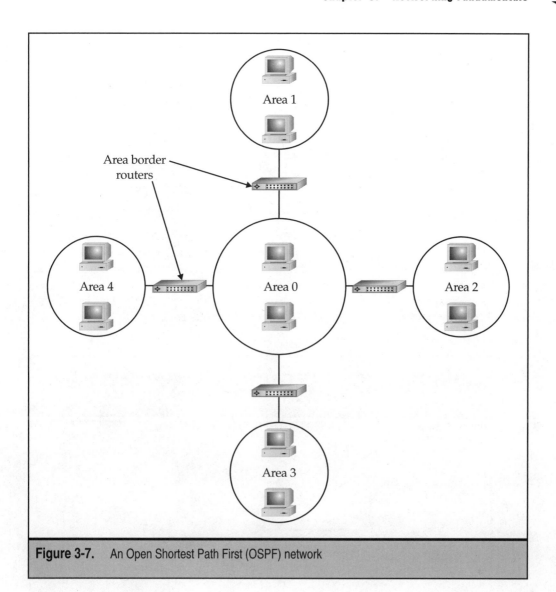

Figure 3-7.   An Open Shortest Path First (OSPF) network

OSPF Support in NT

Realizing the limitations of RIP in larger networks, Microsoft has implemented OSPF as part of the *Routing and Remote Access Server (RRAS)* solution. OSPF can be run on NT 4 after downloading an RRAS update, or natively on Windows 2000. The Windows NT 4

RRAS update pack can be found at http://www.microsoft.com/ntserver/nts/downloads/winfeatures/rras/rasdown.asp. Installing OSPF is easy to do:

1. In Windows 2000, open the Routing and Remote Access Management Console located in the Administrative Tools menu.

2. If RRAS has not been installed, install it now. Once this process is complete, you can add a routing protocol by right-clicking the server and selecting Install Routing and Remote Access Service.

3. From here you will need to add the OSPF protocol. This is accomplished by right-clicking the General heading under the IP Routing icon.

4. Then select New | Routing Protocol, as illustrated in Figure 3-8.

OSPF might be used to convert an NT or Windows 2000 system into a router. The Windows machine must have at least two NICs, and statically defined addresses. A scenario similar to that in Figure 3-9 would be ideal for turning a Windows system into a backup router. In this example, most traffic would be routed through the router. In the case of router failure, traffic would flow through the Windows systems. This provides a level of redundancy at a fraction of the cost of an additional router.

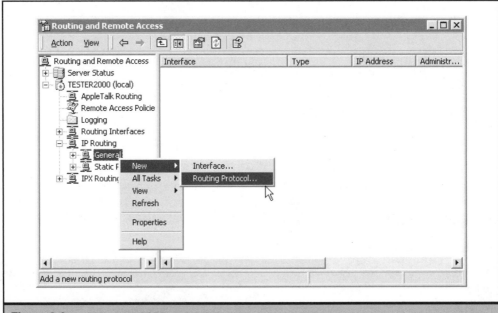

Figure 3-8.   Adding the OSPF routing protocol

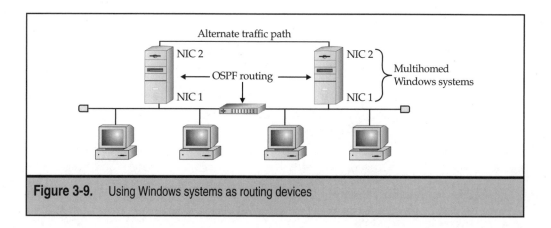

Figure 3-9.   Using Windows systems as routing devices

The surviving redundant system must be able to handle the additional traffic that was being handled by the failed system. Therefore, Microsoft's router solution does not compete with larger, dedicated hardware routers that can process many more packets per second compared to a PC running RRAS (40,000 as compared to millions). Dedicated routers also have other features that may be needed in a large or complex network environment. Nonetheless, RRAS and OSPF may be ideal for smaller to mid-sized sites and locations where larger routers are not required, or for redundancy.

Cisco's IGRP/EIGRP

The Interior Gateway Routing Protocol (IGRP) is a distance-vector routing protocol developed by Cisco Systems to overcome some of the shortcomings of RIP. RIP uses a single metric for basing its routing decisions: the hop count. Therefore, a 10 Mbps segment gets the same priority as a 56 Kbps link. IGRP has incorporated several additional metrics into the routing decision, including internetwork delay, bandwidth, reliability, and load. Each of these can be adjusted by the network administrator. Another enhancement IGRP made over RIP was the ability to load-share traffic over multiple, equal cost links.

Cisco later developed an enhanced version of IGRP that combined the advantages of both link-state and distance-vector routing protocols. The new routing algorithm is called Diffusing Update Algorithm (DUAL) and was incorporated into Enhanced IGRP (EIGRP). EIGRP has a fast convergence time because it propagates only the updates required to advertise topology changes in the network—as opposed to IGRP, which, as a distance-vector protocol, broadcasts its entire routing table every 90 seconds. EIGRP also can send these updated route changes to only the routers that need them. This feature is known as *bounded updates*.

Another enhancement within EIGRP that puts it ahead of all other distance-vector protocols is support for variable-length subnet masks, which was discussed earlier as an advantage of link-state protocols. Unfortunately, IGRP and EIGRP are proprietary protocols and only work with Cisco routers; they will not work with Microsoft's RRAS product. If you have an all-Cisco router environment, you are probably using IGRP or EIGRP and may not want to switch over to OSPF just to incorporate NT servers with your other routers.

WAN TRANSPORT SUMMARY

Cisco routers are designed to support a variety of wide-area connectivity options over serial and ISDN interfaces. This section briefly describes some of the most common transports.

ISDN

Integrated Services Digital Network (ISDN) was originally designed for enhanced voice communication and to support additional services that extend beyond standard POTS (plain old telephone service).

Cisco routers can be configured to use *basic rate interface* ISDN (BRI) and *primary rate interface* ISDN (PRI). BRI incorporates two 64 Kbps digital channels for data, and one 16 Kbps digital channel for management signaling. PRI incorporates 23 digital channels of 64 Kbps, and a single 64-bit digital channel for management signaling.

BRI is used in most smaller network installations. In larger networks, ISDN might be used for dial backup services, for backing up a point-to-point or Frame Relay WAN. In this scenario, the remote locations would use a BRI connection, while a data center would use a PRI connection.

ISDN has become quite common in most areas of the United States as well as in other parts of the world. In some cases, it may be your only option when attempting to establish a network connection to a remote site.

Frame Relay

The most commonly implemented WAN protocol in use today is *Frame Relay*. This packet-switching protocol is most often configured using PVCs (permanent virtual circuits) but may also be implemented using SVCs (switched virtual circuits). The use of the permanent virtual circuit is analogous to a point-to-point connection between two routers, as illustrated in Figure 3-10.

The difference in a PVC configuration is that after the data leaves the router, it may be switched through several devices within a Frame Relay cloud. However, the upper-layer protocols see the connection as a direct point-to-point connection. One advantage of using Frame Relay is that the interfaces can be configured to support multiple PVCs over a single serial interface. This is accomplished using subinterface commands and is covered in more detail in Chapter 5.

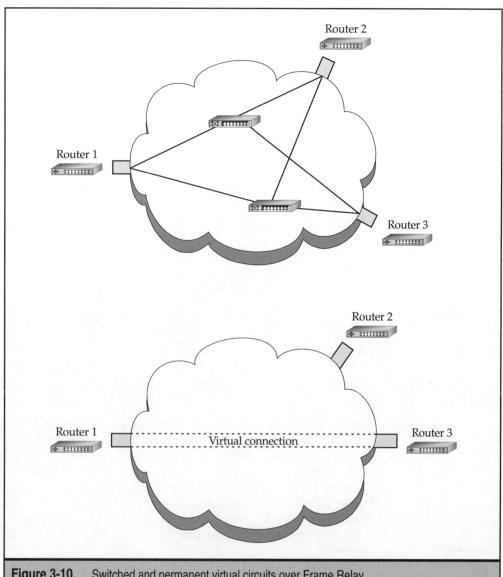

Figure 3-10. Switched and permanent virtual circuits over Frame Relay

ATM

Asynchronous Transfer Mode (ATM) is a cell-relay–based technology that uses fixed 53-byte cells. Although the industry had been slow to adopt ATM, its popularity has been increasing. ATM can be found in the backbone of larger networks and is being used to build high-capacity WANs. ATM is optimized to handle services on the network that extend beyond standard data services into voice and video applications. Similar to Frame Relay, ATM passes cells instead of frames across the network.

ATM Features

Cisco has shown a considerable interest in ATM and in 1991 co-founded the ATM Forum with Sprint, Net/Adaptive, and Northern Telecom. The ATM forum has been working to ensure that ATM remains and evolves with interoperability in mind. Because of this, ATM has slowly gained wide acceptance and has been implemented by a large number of vendors.

Cisco ATM switches support voice, data, video, LAN Emulation (LANE), compression, and Quality of Service (QoS) mechanisms, including dynamic bandwidth allocation. Like Frame Relay, ATM must set up a circuit to the remote end before communicating. The sending and receiving stations remain unaware of the intermediate switches in between.

ATM also incorporates advanced QoS mechanisms into the specifications. ATM is built from the ground up to support managed data flows through virtual channels. When applications require higher bandwidth, ATM can throttle other forms of data, allowing data with the higher bandwidth requirements to pass through the network unobstructed.

LAN Emulation

Besides increased bandwidth, one of the most immediate benefits of ATM is the integration of voice- and LAN-based traffic on a single platform. ATM utilizes LAN Emulation (LANE) to allow Ethernet and Token Ring network devices to use ATM transport by employing layer 2 MAC encapsulation; in effect, this is *bridging*. These bridged segments are called ELANs. An ATM network can have several ELANs; however, since the ATM network is really just tunneling the traffic, you must still rely on routers outside the ATM network to route traffic between ELANs. For full routing and switching, you must install ATM interface cards on your network devices. In this way, you can begin to realize the full potential of ATM in the traditional network environment.

HDLC

The *High Level Data Link Control (HDLC)* protocol allows Cisco routers talk to each other over serial interfaces. This protocol is typically used on point-to-point WAN connections. This is the default encapsulation on a Cisco serial interface, and it supports all of the most common network protocols.

PPP

The *Point-To-Point Protocol (PPP)* supports TCP/IP, IPX, and AppleTalk. PPP uses the lower-level Link Control Protocol to establish, set up, and maintain the link or line connections. PPP also uses the Network Control protocol to support IP and IPX and AppleTalk. This is used mostly in dial-up connections between routers and other devices. Microsoft clients dialing into a Cisco access server should typically use PPP.

NETWORK ADDRESSING SCHEMES

Every networking protocol that is routable must have a scheme for identifying the specific host machine and the network it resides on. It is the router's job to read the network address and route the packets to the correct network. Then the packets are directed to the device on that network, using the host portion of the address. Each of the most popular networking protocols has its own addressing scheme. When you're building and designing networks, it is imperative to understand each major networking scheme. In this section, we will discuss how TCP/IP and IPX/SPX use network addressing.

TCP/IP

TCP/IP assigns every connection point on the network a unique 32-bit address (for example, 10.1.100.56). Each address consists of two parts, a network portion and a host portion. The network and node designations in an address are required for the routing of packets through a network. Determining which part of the IP address is the network and the host can be tricky.

IP Numbers and Addresses

The 32-bit IP address is represented as four 8-bit octets. In binary it looks like this:

11111111.11111111.11111111.11111111

where each 1 could be a one or a zero. The value for each of the eight positions equals 128, 64, 32, 16, 8, 4, 2, 1. If a 1 occupies a position within the eight bits, it is considered "on," and the value for that bit is added to the value of other "on" bits for that octet. For example, 01000011 equals the sum of $64 + 4 + 2 = 70$. In this way, you can create any number from 0 (00000000) to 255 (11111111) for each octet.

This important concept is worth another example. Let's say we want to create an octet with a value of 201. We need to turn on only those bits that will add up to 201.

Bit On/Off	Bit Value
1	128
1	64

Bit On/Off	Bit Value
0	32
0	16
1	8
0	4
0	2
1	1

The sum of all 1 bits = 128 + 64 + 8 + 1 = 201 or, in binary, 11001001.

You can make it easy on yourself by using the Windows Calculator application in scientific mode to figure out binary IP addresses. Type in a number and then click the Calculator's Bin radio button to see see the binary representation. For a complete cop-out, you can use a subnet calculator to figure out all your crucial subnet numbers. Cisco provides an IP subnet calculator in some of the network management tools such as ConfigMaker (see Chapter 5). Or you can go online and use a Web-based version at

http://www.cisco.com/techtools/ip_addr.html

IP Classes

IP addressing is divided into five "classes" of addresses. The address range of the network portion of the address determines the class, and the remainder of the address is for hosts. Therefore, when you have few networks, you can have many hosts, and vice versa. IP classes are identified by the values of the first five bits of the first octet, as demonstrated in Table 3-1.

Address Class	1st Octet	Range of Numbers	Number of Hosts	Number of Networks
A	0xxxxxxx	0–127	16,777,214	126
B	10xxxxxx	128–191	65,534	16,384
C	110xxxxx	192–223	254	2,097,152

Table 3-1. Number of Hosts and Networks for the IP Address Classes

Class A addresses contain a 0 in their first bit and a smaller number of bits for networks and, therefore, accommodate a smaller number of possible networks but a very large number of possible hosts in each network. These addresses are reserved for very large sites with a huge number of hosts.

Class B addresses contain a 1 in their first bit, and a larger number of network numbers are available, with a fewer number of hosts in each network as compared to Class A addresses. Class B addresses are used in networks with a large number of sites that have a large number of hosts at each site.

Class C addresses have a 1 in the first two bits of their addresses. They offer a very large number of network numbers, but fewer hosts in each network. These addresses are used in smaller sites that have fewer hosts on each network.

All these address classes are analyzed in Table 3-1.

IP Addressing by the Numbers

The address ranges are represented by the value of the first octet, although the numbers of networks and hosts are determined by the entire number of bits included in the network and host portion of that address, for each particular address class. By default, Class A addresses, for example, use only the first octet for network numbers. Class B addresses include the first two octets as part of the network address. Class C addresses include the first three octets as part of the network address, leaving only the fourth and last octet for host addresses.

Subnetting

The dividing line between networks and hosts is really determined by the *subnet mask*. *Subnetting* is used as a way to divide the hosts' portion of an IP address into separate "subnetworks," with a smaller number of hosts assigned to each subnet. This gives the IP address administrator more flexibility in determining the distribution of network assignments and host assignments within the IP address assigned from the InterNetwork Information Center (InterNIC). The InterNIC controls the assignment of all IP addresses available. This ensures a unique address for everyone using IP addresses for communicating with other TCP/IP entities. The Internet is a perfect example of this, although intercorporate communication via alternate pathways is becoming more prevalent.

IP address subnetting is accomplished through the use of the subnet mask. A subnet mask is a 32-bit binary number that is compared with the IP address using the logical AND function to determine which bits of the IP address are part of the IP subnet. A subnet mask essentially answers the simple question the computer or router wants to know: "What part of the address is the network?" A subnet mask places a 1 in the bits that are for the network. That is, if the computer sees a subnet mask of

11111111.11111111.00000000.00000000

then the computer knows that the first two octets determine the network and the last two are for the host. This bit mask is equivalent to 255.255.0.0.

Here are the default subnet masks for each major class:

Class A	255.0.0.0
Class B	255.255.0.0
Class C	255.255.255.0

By increasing the subnet mask, an administrator can increase the addressing space for networks (thus increasing the number of networks available for use), while decreasing the numbers available for hosts. The example in Table 3-2 shows a Class B IP address that is using a subnet mask to increase the number of available subnetworks.

Because the address in Table 3-2 is a Class B address, the first two octets represent the actual address as assigned by InterNIC (minus the first two bits, which identify this as a Class B address). The third octet now becomes useful in describing the subnet, because the network administrator has extended the subnet mask to include the third octet as part

Subnet Mask (Dotted Decimal)	Binary Representation of Third and Fourth Octets	Number of Subnets	Number of Hosts
255.255.192.0	11000000.00000000	2	16,382
255.255.224.0	11100000.00000000	6	8,190
255.255.240.0	11110000.00000000	14	4,094
255.255.248.0	11111000.00000000	30	2,046
255.255.252.0	11111100.00000000	62	1,022
255.255.254.0	11111110.00000000	126	510
255.255.255.0	11111111.00000000	254	254
255.255.255.128	11111111.10000000	510	126
255.255.255.192	11111111.11000000	1,022	62
255.255.255.224	11111111.11100000	2,046	30
255.255.255.240	11111111.11110000	4,094	14
255.255.255.248	11111111.11111000	8,190	6
255.255.255.252	11111111.11111100	16,382	2

Table 3-2.   Subnet Masks Increase the Number of Available Hosts

of the network portion. The dotted decimal representation of this subnet mask would be 255.255.255.0. Now, instead of having a Class B address with one network and 65,534 hosts available, you have 254 subnetworks available with 254 hosts available in each subnet. Table 3-2 shows the possible subnet masks available for a Class B address, and the number of networks and hosts provided by each mask.

DISALLOWED AND RESERVED SUBNET ADDRESSES You'll notice that some possible subnet addresses are missing from Table 3-2. IP addressing specifications mandate that a minimum of two bits are required for subnet and host addresses. It's also important to note that the presence of all 1's in the host portion of an address indicates a broadcast address for that subnet, and therefore it can't be assigned to a host. Also, the presence of all 0's in the host address represents "this subnet," and it can't be assigned to a host, either. These two conditions represent the upper and lower limits of a block of host addresses and are unusable by hosts. Although a network address could use all 1's or all 0's (making 10.255.0.0 with a subnet mask of 255.255.0.0 possible), it is not considered good practice to do so.

A number of addresses are reserved by InterNIC, as identified in RFC 960:

▼ 0.*x.x.x*

■ 127.*x.x.x* (loopback address)

■ 128.0.*x.x*

■ 191.255.*x.x*

■ 192.0.0.*x*

■ 223.255.255.*x*

▲ 224.0.0.0 through 255.255.255.255 (multicast and experimental addresses)

Certain addresses in each class are not routed on the Internet, as detailed in RFC 1597. These are commonly used within organizations because obtaining large blocks of addresses from the InterNIC can be impossible. This provides a measure of security against outside intruders and against the organization's data accidentally being placed on the Internet. These reserved addresses are as follows:

Class A	10.0.0.0 through 10.255.255.255
Class B	172.16.0.0 through 172.31.255.255
Class C	192.168.0.0 through 192.168.255.255

SUBNETTING ON CISCO DEVICES When configuring Cisco devices, you will encounter several different schemes for displaying the IP address and subnet mask. It is possible to enter the subnet mask in the decimal format, as in 255.255.0.0. Often you will be asked for the number of bits in the subnet field. This query might look like this:

```
Number of bits in subnet field [0]
```

For the most part, Cisco devices know the class of the IP address for which you are entering the subnet mask, and you'll be asked for how many additional bits should be included along with the default for that class of IP addresses. For example, 10.1.10.1 is a Class A address, and thus Cisco assumes a mask of 255.0.0.0. If you want a subnet mask of 255.255.255.0, then you need to add 16 bits to the default for a total of 24 bits in the subnet mask. So the answer to the number-of-bits query would be 16.

NOTE: You will frequently see the IP address displayed with the subnet mask bits indicated by the "slash" notation. For example, the address 10.1.10.1 with a subnet mask of 255.255.0.0 could be displayed as 10.1.10.1/16, where the 16 represents the total number of bits in the subnet mask.

VLSM   You have seen how subnetting can greatly increase the number of available networks by reducing the number of hosts. Let's say that we are given a Class B network address 130.1.0.0. The default subnet mask is 255.255.0.0. This is a single network address with over 65,000 host addresses. We want to use additional subnet bits to increase the number of networks and decrease the number of hosts per network to something more reasonable. If we change the subnet address to 255.255.255.0, we can look at Table 3-2 to calculate how many networks we can capture and how many hosts will be available for each network.

In this example, the 255.255.255.0 mask allows for 255 networks and 254 devices per network. This is probably appropriate for most LANs—but what about serial point-to-point connections between routers? This type of network only requires two addresses. It seems like a waste to dedicate a whole network to only two addresses.

The solution is to change the subnet mask to allow for more networks and fewer hosts just for those addresses. For example, we could use a subnet mask 255.255.255.252 and get only two hosts per network, but it would greatly increase our use of those addresses. Networks with more than one subnet mask in use are considered to be using *variable-length subnet masking (VLSM)*. As discussed previously under "Routing Protocols," some routing protocols cannot propagate the subnet mask with the route. This obviously leads to problems and misrouting when VLSM is being used.

Supernetting

Supernetting is, in concept, the opposite of subnetting. In subnetting we add bits to the default mask to increase the number of networks. However, in some instances, it makes sense to decrease the number of networks. For example, let's say an organization has been given a contiguous block of Class C address such as these:

209.98.224
209.98.225
209.98.226
209.98.227

A Class C address has the default mask of 255.255.255.0. This means that the above addresses are all separate networks. However, the company may want to treat all the addresses as part of the same network for routing purposes. In that event, a subnet mask of 255.255.224.0 would be used so that all the above addresses are in the same network.

IPX/SPX

Novell's IPX/SPX protocol suite is similar to TCP/IP, in that it is a popular protocol and can be routed over many networks. Like TCP/IP, IPX/SPX must have a representation of devices on each LAN and an addressing scheme that can segregate among LANs. This section explains how IPX/SPX accomplishes this.

The Node Number

Each device on any given Novell LAN has a unique *node* number—a 48-bit number typically taken from the MAC address of that device's LAN interface. Since these MAC addresses are unique, you are almost guaranteed to generate a unique number. Usually these numbers are expressed as 12 hexadecimal values, each comprising 4 bits per node. An example is

00-00-A0-00-38-00

which is displayed on Cisco routers as

0000-a0000-3800

A device's node number does not have to be assigned to the MAC address of its NIC. You can manually change it to any 48-bit number you wish, as long as it is unique for that given LAN. There may be circumstances that dictate using a manually chosen and entered node number. One such case is on routers. If a LAN segment has more than one LAN interface, the node address of the first LAN interface will, by default, be the node address of the others. You will probably want to change one of these addresses to some other, unique value.

The Network Number

For moving traffic to devices located on other LANs, there must be a way to identify and route to those machines based on something more than their unique node number.

IPX/SPX uses the two-tiered approach, like TCP/IP. Where the node number defines a device on a LAN, the *network* number describes which LAN is the destination for the packets. Unlike the node number, the network number is not automatically generated; it must be chosen in advance and manually configured on each interface of all the routers. This number is a 32-bit number that is typically represented, together with the node number, as the *network.node*. This completely describes the address of each device on a network.

All devices on a given LAN segment share the same network number. However, NetWare servers have a different internal network number than the local network number. This is because the NetWare server acts as source address for many NetWare services. NetWare Servers need the internal IPX network number to perform functions related to the server and give the server a unique identity. If, for example, a node with an address of 00.00.A0.00.38.00 is on the network 500, the node's complete IPX network address would be 500.00.00.A0.00.38.00. Note that the network number for the LAN segment and the internal network numbers must all be unique, throughout the enterprise.

TIP: Lay out your IPX network numbering scheme in advance, and maintain accurate records of which numbers are used. Duplicate addresses will cause substantial problems on your network. In addition, you may choose to use network numbers of different length for the Internal network number and the LAN segment number. This makes the server addresses easy to identify for troubleshooting or filtering, if needed.

Of course, there is nothing to preclude the simultaneous existence of TCP/IP and IPX/SPX on the same client. The client will need to have the proper drivers and protocol stack to run each protocol suite. Since each can use Ethernet and Token Ring, this scenario is common. Multiprotocol routers must be used, and configured to route and share routing information with other routers for each protocol. Although this configuration adds to the complexity of the network and cost of management, it is often deployed to provide the most compatibility with legacy systems or during an interim cut-over period.

SUMMARY

This chapter has introduced many essential topics for Cisco internetworking. You have learned about the OSI seven-layer model and its importance, as evident by its permeation into networking hardware and software. We discussed some of the most popular lower-level technologies used to transport bits across the wire from device to device.

The upper-level protocols were covered here as well. This information will be useful when it comes time for you to actually configure and manage your network devices.

Routing protocols also play a crucial role in the efficiency of any large network. The most common routing protocols were discussed in this chapter, and in Chapter 5 you will have the opportunity to see how to configure routing protocols to work in a laboratory environment.

WAN transports and the most common addressing schemes are the common foundation of a network. Having a good understanding of these core components will assist in building and managing a high-quality network. Knowledge of these essentials will support your understanding of the information in Chapter 5, Chapter 6, and all the chapters in Part 3.

PART II

Building a Cisco Network with Windows 2000

CHAPTER 4

Cisco Hardware and Internetworking Tools

Networks comprise a wide variety of network devices, computer platforms, cables, and connectors. For example, network devices include routers, hubs, switches, firewalls, and access servers. And if this isn't complex enough, you also need to consider the connectivity between these devices, including the appropriate interfaces and their corresponding cables. Such complexity makes it a challenge, indeed, to design the optimal network infrastructure.

With dozens of technologies to understand and hundreds of devices to consider, it can be an intimidating task to purchase and design successful internetworking solutions. Fortunately, Cisco Systems has created a hierarchical structure for their product lines. This simplifies the challenge of choosing the right device.

This chapter describes the differences among Cisco's various models, highlighting the most important features and providing advice about when and where to use each device. The software that runs the devices (Cisco IOS) will be explained, along with some useful troubleshooting tips. We'll also show you some of the most effective commands for configuring your devices. Also, we'll give you an overview of management tools and protocols.

CISCO HARDWARE

In order to have an optimally effective network, you have to use the best hardware for the environment. Cisco offers a wide range of internetworking devices. Many of these devices can satisfy multiple situations. However, by analyzing features, functionality, scalability, and price, you'll be able to choose the components that are best suited for your environment.

All Cisco devices are similar in terms of the protocols they support, the way they are configured and managed, and even the way they look. However, each device also has unique features and functionality to offer and was developed for a specific purpose. This section defines the types and models of network devices offered by Cisco.

Routers

Routers provide the following:

- ▼ Communication across WANs
- ■ Communication using different protocols
- ■ Partitioning of broadcast domains
- ▲ Limited security

Cisco offers several series of router models, described in the following sections. Each series provides unique functionality and purpose, including the support of particular WAN circuits and serving companies of certain size and capacity. For more information on how to configure routers, see Chapter 5.

Cisco 700 Series

The Cisco 700 Series is a family of ISDN routers suitable for home offices or small remote offices that require Internet access or access to corporate headquarters. The 700 Series offers two plain old telephone service (POTS) RJ-11 interfaces to connect a telephone, fax, or modem on the same ISDN line as your computer. There are no module slots available on the 700 Series. This means you don't have the option of adding modules or cards that would provide scalability for growth. (A device with module slots is called *modular,* and a device with module slots only is called *fully modular.*)

The Cisco 700 Series supports Port Address Translation (PAT), Multilink PPP (MP), and Dynamic Host Configuration Protocol (DHCP) relay agent and server for dynamic addressing. Although the 700 Series does not support the standard Cisco IOS, it is fully operable with Cisco IOS–based routers.

All routers in the Cisco 700 family feature a Microsoft Windows 95 or Windows NT 4.0 graphical software package that allows you to set up and monitor your router quickly and easily. The following are suitable uses for the 700 Series.

▼ Internet Ready

■ Small Office/Home Office (SOHO)

▲ Remote Office

Figure 4-1 illustrates an environment using the Cisco 700 Series.

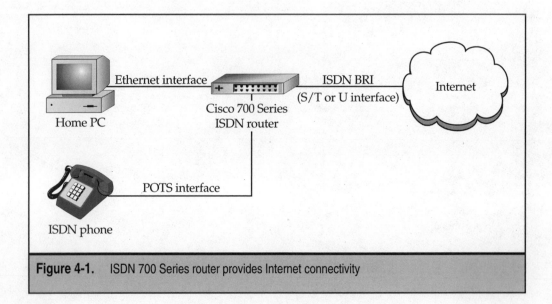

Figure 4-1.   ISDN 700 Series router provides Internet connectivity

Cisco 800 Series

The Cisco 800 Series of ISDN routers is similar to the 700 Series. The 800s provide additional enhanced security and are targeted for users requiring ISDN connectivity to the Internet and a corporate LAN. Unlike the 700 Series, the 800 Series does support standard Cisco IOS.

The 800 Series offers two POTS RJ-11 interfaces to connect a telephone, fax, or modem on the same ISDN line as your computer. The 803 and 804 also provide a built-in four-port hub to connect perimeter devices such as printers or additional workstations. Figure 4-2 illustrates an environment using the Cisco 800 Series.

Cisco 1600 Series

The Cisco 1600 Series is a family of routers for small branch offices or small businesses needing a connection to the Internet or to a company's intranet or corporate LAN through various supported WAN connections. The 1600 Series supports one Ethernet and one serial or ISDN interface, and an extra WAN interface module for flexibility and scalability. The 1600s also offer integrated CSU/DSUs supporting speeds up to a T1. Figure 4-3 illustrates an environment using the Cisco 1600 Series.

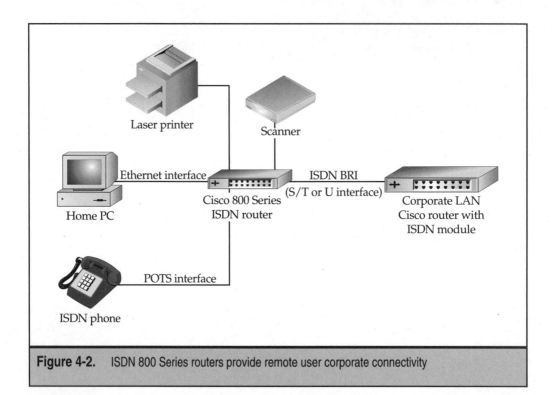

Figure 4-2.   ISDN 800 Series routers provide remote user corporate connectivity

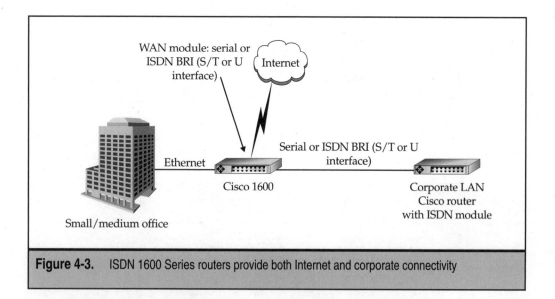

Figure 4-3.   ISDN 1600 Series routers provide both Internet and corporate connectivity

Cisco 1720 Virtual Private Network (VPN) Access Router

The Cisco 1720 virtual private network (VPN) access router provides a secure solution for small to medium businesses, and remote users who want to deploy secure Internet/intranet access and VPNs. Using the VPN router, you can take advantage of Internet bandwidth instead of shouldering the expense of private circuits. The 1720 provides one 10/100 auto-sensing Ethernet port and two WAN interface slots for serial or ISDN connections, with optional built-in CSU/DSU. Figure 4-4 illustrates an environment using the Cisco 1720 VPN access router.

Cisco 2500 Series

The Cisco 2500 Series provides router functionality to networks that only require data transport (voice is not supported). There are several types of routers in this series, including LAN routers, router/hub combinations, access servers, high-density serial routers, dual LAN routers, and single LAN routers. This series is the most commonly used to connect branch offices to corporate headquarters. It supports Ethernet, Token Ring, and ISDN. Figure 4-5 illustrates an environment using several models of the 2500 Series.

Cisco 2600 Series

The Cisco 2600 Series gives remote branch offices a solution for data/voice/video integration, departmental dial services, and VPN access. These routers provide some versatility with their capability of sharing modular interfaces with the Cisco 1600 and 3600 Series. Figure 4-6 illustrates an environment using the 2600 Series.

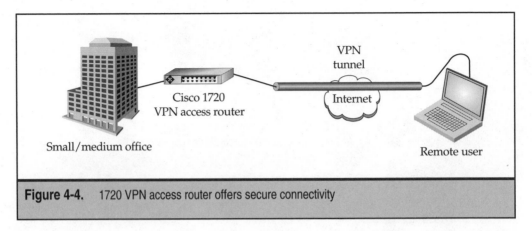

Figure 4-4.   1720 VPN access router offers secure connectivity

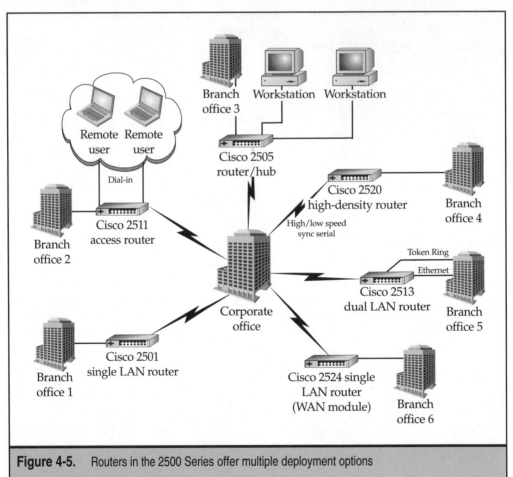

Figure 4-5.   Routers in the 2500 Series offer multiple deployment options

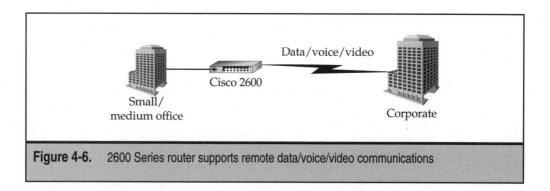

Figure 4-6. 2600 Series router supports remote data/voice/video communications

Cisco 3600 Series

Routers in the Cisco 3600 Series provide the same functionality as the 2600 Series, plus ISDN and asynchronous dial-up connectivity. Figure 4-7 illustrates an environment using the 3600 Series. This is a very versatile and modular route; some consider it to be a much better value, providing more flexibility than the aging Cisco 4000 line.

Cisco 4000 Series

The Cisco 4000 Series routers are completely modular routers, supporting the full suite of Cisco IOS's feature set. This series is diminishing, however. Unlike the 3640, which offers six slots and supports mixed media interfaces, the 4000 Series has only 3 slots with limited interfaces. Only the 4500 and 4700 router series are still being produced. This causes

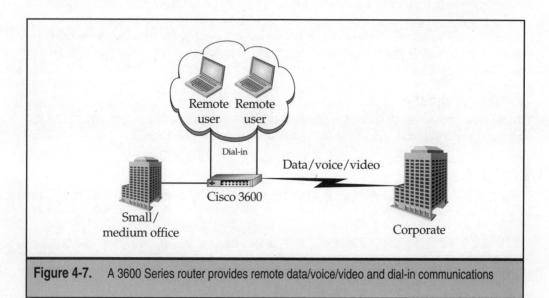

Figure 4-7. A 3600 Series router provides remote data/voice/video and dial-in communications

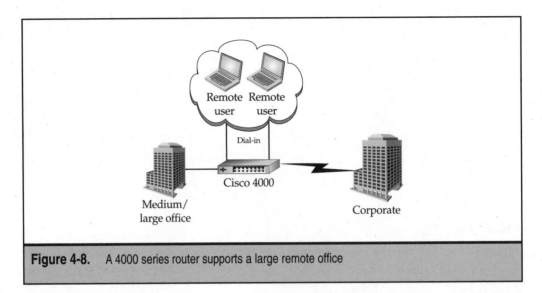

Figure 4-8. A 4000 series router supports a large remote office

some concern that Cisco may be planning to discontinue the entire 4000 Series and use the 3600 Series as its replacement. (Similarly, the 2500 Series is being replaced with the 2600 Series.) Figure 4-8 illustrates an environment using the Cisco 4000 Series.

Cisco 7000 Series

The Cisco 7000 Series is implemented in corporate offices where dual power supplies, full support of Cisco IOS, and high-performance switching is required. This family of routers is designed for today's most mission-critical internetworks; it combines proven software technology with reliability, availability, serviceability, and exceptional performance features. The 7500s use the processing capabilities of Versatile Interface Processing (VIP) and Cisco Express Forwarding, providing performance exceeding a million packets per second. Figure 4-9 illustrates an environment using the Cisco 7000 Series.

Router Summary

Table 4-1 summarizes the target market of each series; the table lists supported technologies and gives Web addresses for obtaining additional information.

Switches

Switches are an alternative to hubs and bridges. Switches alleviate bandwidth congestion by providing the following:

- ▼ Reduction of collisions
- ■ Control of broadcast and flooding
- ▲ Segmentation of traffic by using Virtual LANs (VLANs)

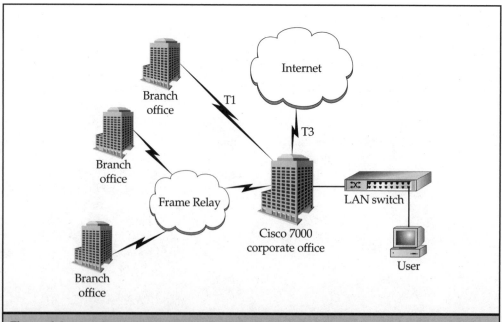

Figure 4-9.   A 7000 Series router supports a campus backbone

Series	Market	Fixed Ports	Modules	Comments	http://
700	Home office or small remote office	1 ISDN/BRI; 1 Ethernet	None	Optional 2 analog telephone ports	www.cisco. com/go/700
800	Home office or small remote office	1 ISDN/BRI; up to 4 Ethernet	None	Optional 2 analog telephone ports; advanced security features	www.cisco. com/go/800
1600	Small remote office or small business	Ethernet; 1 serial or ISDN/BRI	1 WAN interface slot	Modular for scalability	www.cisco. com/go/1600

Table 4-1.   Cisco Router Comparison

Series	Market	Fixed Ports	Modules	Comments	http://
1720	Small to medium business, or mobile or remote user	1 10/100 Ethernet	2 WAN interface slots	Virtual private network (VPN) solution	www.cisco. com/go/1720
2500	Branch offices	Depends on model	Depends on model	Single LAN router; router/hub; access server; high-density router; dual LAN router; single LAN router (modular)	www.cisco. com/go/2500
2600	Small to medium business or remote office	1–2 port Ethernet; Port Token Ring (optional)	2 WAN interface slots; 1 network module slot; 1–2 voice slots	Supports voice/fax over IP	www.cisco. com/go/2600
3600	Medium to large business of remote office	None	2–4 LAN/ WAN slots	Supports voice/fax over IP; wide variety of media support	www.cisco. com/go/3600

Table 4-1. Cisco Router Comparison *(continued)*

Series	Market	Fixed Ports	Modules	Comments	http://
4000	Medium to large business	None	3 LAN/ WAN slots	Modular; high density; wide variety of media support	www.cisco. com/go/4000
7000	Campus backbone	None	2–13 LAN/ WAN slots	High performance; high density; wide variety of media support	www.cisco. com/go/7000

Table 4-1.   Cisco Router Comparison *(continued)*

Like routers, each series of Cisco switches offers unique functionality and targets a certain market. For more information on switches and their configuration, see Chapter 6.

Cisco 1548 Micro Switch

The Cisco 1548 Micro Switch offers eight auto-sensing 10/100 ports—perfect for a small office or home office (SOHO). The switch is now manageable with simple configurations. Its simplicity contributes to an easy installation and deployment process. If you have the IP address assigned to the switch, you can display the Cisco 1548 Switch Manager from your intranet, to configure and monitor the switch.

Catalyst 1900 Series

The Catalyst 1900 Series of switches offers ten or twenty-four 10BaseT ports; and two 10BaseTX (Fast Ethernet) uplink ports, or one 10BaseTX and one 10BaseFX (Fiber) uplink port. The uplink ports are for the backbone connection to connect the switch to other switches or servers. Switches from the 1900 Series should be implemented to provide 100BaseT connections to backbones or servers, and 10BaseT connections to hubs and workstations.

Catalyst 2900 Series

The Catalyst 2900 Series is similar to the 1900 Series, but the 2900s offer 10/100 auto-sensing ports instead of 10BaseT. The 2900 Series switches should be used when your network has a combination of 10BaseT and 100BaseT workstations and servers, and printers.

Catalyst 4000 Series

The modular Catalyst 4000 Series provides 24 Gbps of switching bandwidth and offers expansion to 96 ports of 10/100 Ethernet or 36 ports of Gigabit Ethernet. These switches deliver superior performance, value, and optimized total cost of ownership for 10/100/1000 Ethernet switching. The 4000 Series is typically implemented in wiring closets requiring advanced network services.

Catalyst 5000 Series

The Catalyst 5000 Series is fully modular and offers Ethernet, Fast Ethernet, Fast EtherChannel, Gigabit Ethernet, FDDI/CDDI, Token Ring, and ATM modules. A route switch module and NetFlow switching card are also available for the 5000 Series, to provide layer-3 functionality (routing). The 5000 Series is the most powerful solution for switching between different media types and supporting all the advanced features of the Cisco IOS.

Catalyst 6000 Series

The Catalyst 6000 Series provides gigabit scalability, high availability, and multilayer switching solutions for campus networks. This series delivers application intelligence, Quality of Service mechanisms, and security. Up to 384 Fast Ethernet and 130 Gigabit Ethernet ports can be supported, to offer high-performance switching and services for large wiring closets.

Catalyst 8000 Series

The Catalyst 8000 Series was developed for multiservice core backbones requiring a mix of high-capacity routed interface types, especially for Gigabit Ethernet, ATM, and SONET (Synchronous Optical Network). This series is ideal for aggregating multiprotocol traffic from multiple wiring closets or from workgroup switches. By providing both layer-2 and layer-3 switching, throughput of more than 6 million packets per second (pps) can be obtained. There is one fixed Ethernet port for out-of-band management, two serial ports, and up to 13 modular slots.

Switch Summary

Table 4-2 summarizes the features associated with each series of switches and gives the Web site where additional information can be found.

Series	Market	Fixed Ports	Modules	Comments	http://
1548	Small office/home office (SOHO)	Eight 10/100 auto-sensing ports	None	Not manageable	www.cisco.com/go/1548
1900	Medium-sized offices requiring high-speed connections to servers and/or workstations	10- or 24-port 10BaseT; 2-port 100BaseTX; or 1-port 100BaseFX and 1-port 100BaseTX	None	Manageable; supports VLANs; security features	www.cisco.com/go/1900
2900	Medium to large offices	8-, 12-, or 24-port 10/100 auto-sensing; 2-port 100BaseTX, or 2-port 100BaseFX	2 (2916M XL and 2924M XL only)	Advanced security; high density; supports VLANs	www.cisco.com/go/2900
4000	Medium to large offices requiring advanced network services in wiring closets	None	3-slot chassis (one slot for supervisor engine and two slots for switched port modules); one chassis can support up to 96 10/100 Fast Ethernet or up to 36 Gigabit Ethernet	Provides range of port densities from 10/100 to 1000 Mbps; layer-2 switching only	www.cisco.com/go/4000

Table 4-2.   Cisco Switch Comparison

Series	Market	Fixed Ports	Modules	Comments	http://
5000	Large offices	None	2, 5, 9, or 13 (depending on model)	Supports up to 384 user ports; high performance; high density; full system redundancy	www.cisco.com/go/5000
6000	Large offices with Ethernet backbones and server aggregation environments requiring very high densities of Fast or Gigabit Ethernet	None	6- and 9-slot versions; support for up to 384 10/100 Ethernet, 192 100FX Fast Ethernet, and up to 130 Gigabit Ethernet ports	Layer-3 services such as QoS, security, and traffic management	www.cisco.com/go/6000
8000	Large offices with requirements to aggregate multiprotocol traffic from multiple wiring closets or from workgroup switches	1-port Ethernet; 2-port serial	5–13 modular slots	Aggregates throughput of 6 million pps; layer-2 and layer-3 switching	www.cisco.com/go/8000

Table 4-2. Cisco Switch Comparison *(continued)*

Hubs

Cisco makes several models of hubs that offer economical and scalable solutions to creating LANs. A hub consolidates connections from nodes such as workstations, servers, and printers, and forwards the traffic to routers or switches. For high-traffic bandwidth requirements, a hub often is replaced with a switch. For more information on hubs, see Chapter 7.

Cisco 1500 Series Micro Hub

The Cisco 1500 Series Micro Hub provides 10 Mbps Ethernet hubs you can use to create LANs. Each hub has eight ports; you can also stack up to five hubs and create a single manageable stack with 40 possible connections.

Cisco HP 10BaseT Hub-16M

The Cisco HP 10BaseT Hub-16M offers sixteen 10BaseT Ethernet ports. Rather than stacking the HP 10BaseT-16M hub, an MDI/MDI-X switch port is used to cascade up to four switches together to create a single collision domain. This hub provides additional security, including intruder prevention, eavesdrop prevention, network management alarm, automatic port disabling, and password protection.

Cisco 1528 Micro Hub 10/100

The Cisco 1528 Micro Hub 10/100 is an eight-port hub similar to the 1500 series hub, but the 1528 also provides 10/100 auto-sensing Fast Ethernet. This hub cannot be managed remotely—it only has LED indicators for visual monitoring and troubleshooting. Unlike the 1500 Series, the 1528 hub is not stackable; but up to two 1528 hubs can be cascaded together.

Cisco FastHub

Cisco also has a line of fast hubs. These hubs provide 10/100 auto-sensing and 100 Mbps ports for server farms and for enterprise power workgroups and users.

▼ The 200 and 300 series provide integrated management, including SNMP, RMON, Telnet, and out-of-band console.

▲ The 400 series is a new line of products with features similar to Cisco's other FastHub series. In addition, the 400 series has a slot for an optional switched uplink module, providing long-distance connectivity to the network core.

Hub Summary

Table 4-3 summarizes the characteristics of Cisco's series of hubs and provides a Web address for obtaining additional information.

Series	Market	Fixed Ports	Modules	Comments	http://
1500 Micro Hub	Small remote office	Eight 10/100 auto-sensing	None	Manageable; up to 5 hubs can be stacked	www.cisco.com/go/1500
HP 10BaseT Hub-16M	Small to medium office	16-port 10BaseT; 1 AUI	None	Cascaded up to 58 users; manageable via SNMP, Telnet, or terminal-based	www.cisco.com/go/hp16m
1528 Micro Hub	Small remote office	Eight 10/100 auto-sensing	None	Not manageable (other then LED lights)	www.cisco.com/go/1528
FastHub	Medium or large office	12-, 15-, 16-, or 24-port Ethernet 10/100-BaseTX (depending on model)	2 (316T and 316C); 1 switched uplink module (400)	Manageable and unmanaged (depending on model); stackable and unstackable (depending on model)	www.cisco.com/go/fh100 www.cisco.com/go/fh200 www.cisco.com/go/fh300

Table 4-3.   Cisco Hub Comparison

Voice

Cisco IOS provides a means of leveraging voice transmission over in-place data networks. Compared with traditional phone lines, leased lines, and other dedicated alternatives, using data networks to transfer voice costs less. Voice-over-data networks provide options such as standard telephone calling, fax transmissions, videoconferencing, whiteboard discussions, and voice calls from World Wide Web pages. However, Voice over IP (VoIP) will only work when deployed on supported network devices. Currently, the 2600, 3600, and 7200XVR router series support VoIP.

VoIP is the most flexible choice for voice transport because it can run over any layer-1 or layer-2 infrastructures. An integral part of providing multiservice connectivity to remote sites is the capability to switch voice among the sites. This flexibility is particularly important in heterogeneous environments in which remote sites may be interconnected with Frame Relay links. Voice over Frame Relay (VoFR) is configured on supported Cisco routers to carry voice traffic such as telephone calls and faxes over a Frame Relay network. VoFR protocol is different from the VoIP protocol; therefore, when the media changes to Frame Relay, the VoIP protocol has to be switched to the VoFR protocol. On Frame Relay links, high-quality levels of service for voice and video are provided by the FRF.11 and FRF.12 standards. FRF.11 provides compliant VoFR trunking; FRF.12 provides compliant end-to-end fragmentation. Cisco's MC3810 Multiservice Concentrator enables organizations to integrate voice, fax, video, data, and LAN traffic over a single network backbone. In addition to the MC3810, the 2600 and 3600 routers also support VoFR.

Asynchronous Transfer Mode (ATM)

Asynchronous Transfer Mode (ATM) can be used in both WAN and LAN environments. Because ATM is somewhat complicated and ATM equipment is more expensive, certain companies have stayed away from this technology. Despite this fact, ATM does offer important benefits, such as support for better Quality of Service (QoS) than other LAN protocols.

ATM uses fixed cell lengths. Switching of these cells can be done by hardware, which is much faster than software because there is no fragmentation and reassembly of packets, as in Ethernet. ATM is also a connection-oriented technology that usually offers better QoS. This QoS makes ATM a good choice for videoconferencing, imaging, telephony, and other applications that require excessive bandwidth. Unfortunately, ATM only offers QoS guarantees if the whole network is based on ATM and workstations are using an ATM protocol stack. Since the majority of networks aren't centered on one technology, however, it's hard to maximize ATM's capabilities without replacing an entire network. The Cisco Lightstream (described shortly) is a network device developed by Cisco to support networks based on ATM.

ATM is gaining popularity as a WAN transport. It delivers better support for various levels of service than traditional Frame Relay. Most of the midsize routers support ATM interfaces. The 3810 is often used for interfacing to a T1 ATM network for multiservices, voice, and data.

Cisco Lightstream 1010

The Lightstream 1010 is a five-slot modular chassis featuring the option of dual, fault tolerant, load-sharing power supplies. It offers the functionality required for a true ATM production environment. For more information on the Lightstream 1010, see Cisco's Web site at http://www.cisco.com/go/ls1010.

SECURITY AND INTERNET PRODUCTS

With more and more users on the Internet, and growing instances of security breaches, companies are concerned more than ever about the safety of data. Many companies are considering or have installed a *firewall* to protect internal networks. A firewall can be a dedicated hardware box or a software application running on a PC or server. It is used to separate two networks or subnets by deploying security policies that decide which traffic to permit and which to deny. Typically, a firewall is developed around the support of authentication and authorization, data confidentiality, data audits, and policy management and control.

A Cisco router can act as a firewall by enabling *access lists* on its interface(s). The security provided by access lists is limited, but installing Cisco's Firewall IOS software on a router will increase the security and security-related configuration options. Offering even better security than the Cisco Firewall IOS is the Cisco PIX Firewall. In addition to the Firewall IOS and the PIX Firewall, Cisco offers NetSonar for assessment of network device security, and NetRanger for security intrusion detection. These utilities will be covered in more detail in Chapter 14.

Firewall IOS

Cisco Firewall IOS security is a solution for securing Internet access in small- to medium-sized businesses, and in branches and remote offices. This Firewall IOS solution is supported on Cisco's 1600, 2500, 3600, 4000, and 7000 Series routers at this time. The Firewall IOS is based on Cisco's IOS, using similar commands but with enhanced security features. These enhancements include event logging, authentication schemes, network address translation (NAT), and Context-Based Access Control (CBAC).

CBAC is a form of packet filtering available as part of the Cisco IOS Firewall feature set. CBAC examines not only network- and transport-layer information, but also application-layer protocol information. CBAC is defined further in Chapter 14.

PIX Firewall

Cisco PIX Firewall is a dedicated firewall solution. Unlike other firewall solutions, the PIX Firewall offers dedicated security without deteriorating performance. This is largely due to the PIX's adaptive security algorithm (ASA) and cut-through proxy.

ASA tracks the source and destination addresses, TCP sequence numbers, port numbers, and additional TCP flags of each packet. This information is stored in a table, and all inbound and outbound traffic is compared against this table. Traditional firewalls, on the other hand, check every packet at the application layer of the OSI model (the highest layer), which is process intensive. A Cisco PIX can query an authentication database server (such as TACACS+ or RADIUS). When a user is approved, the PIX Firewall no longer checks at the application level for that particular session. Session state information is maintained, and all packets applicable to that session are allowed to pass through ("cut through").

NetSonar

NetSonar (recently renamed CiscoSecure Scanner) is a vulnerability assessment tool that gathers detailed information about all devices on your network, including servers (HTTP, e-mail, FTP, and so on) and network devices (including routers and switches). Services and protocols running on these devices are checked to determine security vulnerabilities. The data collected can be generated into reports and graphs for monitoring and improving network security and security policies.

NetRanger

NetRanger (recently renamed CiscoSecure Intrusion Detection System) is an intrusion detection security system used to detect, report, and terminate unauthorized activity in your network. The content of packets is analyzed to verify traffic authorization. Traffic such as SATAN attacks and ping sweeps can be detected (assuming they are configured in the policy) in real time. NetRanger Director management console will then remove the offender from the network.

REMOTE ACCESS SERVERS

Cisco's remote access security includes authentication, authorization, and accounting. Access security offers remote users a secure means to dial into corporate resources. These services are supported with TACACS+, RADIUS, and Kerberos V authentication methods, which are explored in a later chapter.

Cisco AS5200/AS5300 Series

The AS5200/AS5300 Series offers asynchronous serial and ISDN line service to accommodate both mobile users and high-bandwidth dedicated telecommuters. This series supports all protocols and services on all asynchronous ports.

Cisco AS5800

The Cisco AS5800 is a high-density and high-performance access server that offers multiple areas of redundancy. It can answer both ISDN and 56K modems and has up to 48 channelized T1/E1/PRI or 2 channelized T3 interfaces—providing extensive bandwidth capacity.

AccessPath

The AccessPath server is also a large-scale integrated solution, having the capability to terminate over 2,500 concurrent calls. It can terminate up to 84 channelized T1/E1/PRI or 3 channelized T3 interfaces, offering even more bandwidth capacity than an AS5800.

Access Server Summary

Table 4-4 summarizes the features of each access server and gives a Web address for additional information.

Series	Market	Fixed Ports	Modules	Comments	http://
AS5200/ AS5300	Hybrid async and ISDN remote users	1–2 port Ethernet; 2-port sync and 2-port PRI or 4-port PRI	3	Supports 48 to 128 integrated modems	www.cisco. com/go/ AS5200 and www.cisco. com/go/ AS5300
AS5800	Hybrid async and ISDN remote users. Accommodates both mobile and high-bandwidth users	None	Fully modular	Supports up to 48 channelized T1/E1/PRI or 2 channelized T3 interfaces; multiple areas of redundancy	www.cisco. com/go/ AS5800
AccessPath	Complete solution for dial and IP telephony POPs	2520 async connections (TS3) or 480 async connections (LS3)	None	Terminates up to 2530 concurrent calls; up to 84 channelized T1/E1/PRI or 3 channelized T3 interfaces	www.cisco. com/go/ apath

Table 4-4.   Cisco Access Server Comparison

CISCO IOS

The Cisco IOS technology leads the industry in developing and offering standards and plays a major role in standards organizations such as IETF and IEEE. Standards have provided a means for Cisco's hardware solutions to be compatible and to perform internetworking. Although Cisco IOS varies somewhat from platform to platform, there is consistency in the overall structure. This makes it easy to navigate and support multiple devices and platforms.

IOS Releases

This section describes the four types of releases of the Cisco IOS: major, maintenance, general deployment, and early deployment. The release you choose to implement on an individual device or network of Cisco devices will depend on your requirements for features and stability.

Major Releases

A major release supports a fixed set of features and platforms through the life of the release. This introduction of significant features, functionality, and/or platforms is released to support customers needs. The goal of a major release is to deliver stable, high-quality software for general deployment in a customer's production networks. In a release number, the number(s) before the decimal point indicate the major release: **11.**0(1), **12.**0(1), etc.

Maintenance Releases

After a major release, there are several periodic revisions. These revisions are regression tested and incorporate the most recent bug fixes. No new platforms or features are introduced in maintenance releases. Their focus is to improve product stability and/or add platform or feature support. The maintenance release number follows the decimal point in the release number: 11.0**(2)**, 12.0**(3)**, etc.

General Deployment Releases

General deployment releases are major releases that are appropriate for general, unconstrained use in customers' networks. The software's stability has been proven internally by Cisco and externally by customers. By assigning the status of general deployment release, Cisco is designating the associated major release suitable for unconstrained use in customers' networks. General deployment releases include all the subsequent maintenance updates of a release. So, if release number 11.0(8) was the general deployment release, it would also include 11.0(9), (10), etc.

Early Deployment Releases

Early deployment releases introduce significant new features, functionality, and/or platforms. They are based on a major release and will not achieve general deployment status. Early deployment releases should be used to provide support for newly emerging technologies. They are fully regression tested and incorporate the most recent bug fixes (including those from major releases). Their numbering is followed by a T, as in 12.0(3)T.

Table 4-5 lists key attributes and examples of each type of Cisco IOS release.

IOS Connectivity

Cisco IOS software provides a wide range of connectivity services by supporting major protocols and media types.

Link Types

Cisco supports link types for both LAN and WAN environments. Common LAN link types include

▼ Asynchronous Transfer Mode (ATM)

■ Ethernet

■ Fast Ethernet

■ Fiber Distributed Data Interface (FDDI)

■ Gigabit Ethernet

▲ Token Ring

Type of Release	Key Attributes	Example of Numbering
Major	Focuses on stability	11.0(0)
Maintenance	Improves stability and/or adds platform or feature support	11.0(3)
General deployment	Designates associated major release suitable for unconstrained use in customers' networks	11.0(4) and every maintenance release after this major release
Early deployment	Early delivery of new platforms and features	12.0(2)T

Table 4-5. Characteristics of IOS Releases

LAN link types are supported on routers, access servers, and switches.
Common WAN link types include

▼ Asynchronous and synchronous serial

■ ATM

■ Digital subscriber line (DSL)

■ Frame Relay

■ Integrated Services Digital Network (ISDN)

■ Point-to-Point Protocol (PPP)

■ Switched Multimegabit Data Services (SMDS)

▲ X.25

These WAN link types are supported with Cisco IOS running on routers and access servers.

Protocols

Cisco IOS software supports most major protocols and the possible translation among them, including

▼ TCP/IP

■ IPX

■ AppleTalk

■ Banyan Vines

■ DECnet

■ Systems Network Architect (SNA)

■ Advance Peer-to-Peer Networking (APPN)

■ Data-Link Switching Plus (DLSw+)

■ Novell NetWare

■ Open Systems Interconnection (OSI)

▲ Xerox XNS

IOS Advanced Features

In addition to the standard protocols and link types, Cisco IOS provides the advanced features described in the following paragraphs.

Tag Switching

Tag Switching is the technology of layer-3 routing scalability and flexibility combined with layer-2 high-performance switching. The first packet of a session is tagged, and all subsequent packets are expedited to the final destination. This reduces time needed for router processing and packet transfer.

NetFlow Services

NetFlow technology meters traffic to provide utilization reports, usage-based billing, network planning, network monitoring, and measurements for Quality of Service (QoS). This information can be particularly useful for companies that share bandwidth with customers, providers, and other business partnerships.

Cisco Express Forwarding (CEF)

Cisco Express Forwarding (CEF) works with Tag Switching and NetFlow services to increase performance across network backbones. CEF relies on a Forwarding Information Base (FIB) for information on packet forwarding for all routes in the routing table. This eliminates the need for route caches and incorrect cached information. The Express Forwarding algorithm reduces the process overhead on network hardware by not being sensitive to traffic patterns and certain cache behaviors.

Network Address Translation

Network Address Translation (NAT) accomplishes two things: securing the IP address structure of your internal network, and eliminating the need to purchase or lease blocks of IP addresses. NAT translates internal addresses (possibly illegal) to legal addresses for transport over a public network infrastructure such as the Internet. All external recipients of data see the NAT address rather than the real internal IP address assigned to your machine.

Software-Based Compression

Cisco IOS data compression is used to compress packets at one end of the WAN segment and decompress at the other end. This technology supports efficient use of expensive WAN bandwidth. Cisco supports several compression technologies including Hi/fn Stac LZS, Predictor, and Microsoft Point-to-Point Compression (MPPC).

Both ends of the compression transaction must support the same algorithms. In addition, compression requires valuable processor cycles in the router that can slow down performance and cause network latency. It is important to make sure compression is appropriate and to provide optimization.

IOS Management Features

Cisco IOS management features give network administrators an easy way to set up and configure devices, monitor network activity, optimize performance, and troubleshoot problems quickly. Network management is typically done by using a centralized tool that is compatible with the majority of the network devices deployed. Management tools may offer discrepancy reports, configuration tips, or possibly even the capability for you to simulate your network prior to implementation.

Management Information Bases (MIBs)

Management Information Bases (MIBs) are databases of information that are accessed using the Simple Network Management Protocol (SNMP). The database provides a standard representation of what information is available for the SNMP agent, and where it is stored.

Browser Interfaces

The majority of Cisco network devices offer a user-friendly browser application interface that can be used instead of the command line interface (CLI). Using a Web browser, you can easily perform configuration modifications without having to know the command syntax of Cisco's CLI.

IOS Reliability

Network redundancy is accomplished through Hot Standby Router Protocol (HSRP) and Simple Server Redundancy Protocol (SSRP). HSRP provides seamless failover between routers; and SSRP provides automatic routing among routers and ATM switch groups following the detection of device failures.

In addition, Cisco IOS provides the following reliability features:

▼   Deterministic Load Distribution (DLD), for load balancing among multiple links

■   Fast Ether Channel (FEC), which uses multiple ports to provide additional bandwidth and redundancy between switches, routers, and servers

■   Enhanced Interior Gateway Routing Protocol (EIGRP), which supports convergence for load balancing, as well as backup across redundant links and Cisco IOS devices, to minimize congestion

▲   Cisco Express Forwarding (CEF), to maintain full-forwarding state and performance even during network topology and routing changes

CABLES, CONNECTORS, AND INTERFACES

As discussed just above, the majority of Cisco network devices are compatible with several types of links for both LAN and WAN connections. Depending on the link type, different cabling and connectors are required to support traffic flow. The following sections describe some of these link types and the connections and cables they use.

WAN Interfaces

WAN connections are required when companies need to communicate among buildings or across distances. Several types of WAN connections are available for various bandwidth and availability requirements. Most WAN connections are made through serial interfaces. This section gives a brief overview of ISDN technology, followed by details on the various types of serial connectors and their cable requirements.

Integrated Services Digital Network (ISDN)

ISDN is a digital data-transport service offered by local telephone carriers. Similar to a Frame Relay or direct connection, ISDN supports the transmission of text, graphics, video, music, voice, and other types of data over telephone lines. ISDN is usually more economical than Frame Relay or direct connections because it uses existing infrastructure. Therefore, ISDN is an alternative solution to remote-access users who require more bandwidth than an analog dial-up line. ISDN availability is limited, so it's not an option for everyone.

An ISDN circuit consists of 64 Kbps bearer (B) channels that carry user transmissions, and one delta (D) channel that is a signaling channel. The D channel carries control information, such as call setup and disconnect signals.

There are two types of ISDN interfaces: Basic Rate Interface (BRI) and Primary Rate Interface (PRI). The BRI is used in situations in which the ISDN circuit is terminated in a network device supporting limited bandwidth, such as a remote user or a remote office. BRI consists of two B channels and one 16 Kbps D channel. This provides 128 Kbps of bandwidth for the end user. The ISDN circuit is terminated at the remote user's office, or at the remote site in an ISDN BRI router.

The PRI is used in situations in which multiple ISDN circuits are consolidated and terminated. The ISDN circuits of remote users and remote sites would terminate at corporate headquarters into a PRI network device. A PRI consists of 23 B channels and one D channel. This provides a 1.544 Mbps pipe into the PRI termination network device.

Serial

Serial connections are most appropriate when traffic is constant and service is required on demand. A dedicated circuit and Frame Relay connection are two types of serial connections that would use a serial interface on a router. Prior to establishing communication between two serial interfaces, you need to know three things: the device type, the signal type, and the connector type.

1. Determine whether the device is of type Data Terminal Equipment (DTE) or Data Circuit-Terminating Equipment (DCE).

   Serial connections usually need to be terminated in a DCE. Typically, however, a router is of type DTE, and so you need to have additional hardware to support this circuit termination. An example of a DCE is a CSU/DSU. The DCE will provide a clocking signal to synchronize the data prior to passing it on to the DTE. Figure 4-10 illustrates a typical serial connection.

   Channel Service Unit (CSU) is a device used in digital transmission; it connects network devices to the local digital telephone loop. Data Service Unit (DSU) is a device used in digital transmission that connects the physical interface on the network device to the transmission circuit (for instance, T1). The DSU is also responsible for signal timing. These two devices are often referenced together as a CSU/DSU.

TIP: Cisco does offer serial interfaces with a built-in CSU/DSU on some routers. The router can function as both a DTE and DCE. An internal CSU/DSU eliminates extra external perimeter devices and cables.

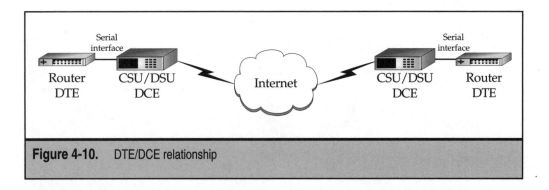

Figure 4-10.   DTE/DCE relationship

2. Determine the type of signal being used.

   A standard serial interface is used to connect communication devices such as a CSU/DSU. The CSU/DSU then connects to a network device such as a router. Some type of signal is needed to allow communication between the CSU/DSU and the router. The most common serial-interface signal is the EIA-232 standard (formally known as RS-232). There are other signals, as well, depending on your equipment, distance, and speed requirements. The different signals and their corresponding properties are listed in Table 4-6.

   Each type of signal has its own speed and distance limitations. The data rate of a signal generally determines the distance it is able to travel. The slower the data rate, the longer the distance. The rate of a signal is typically measured in *baud*, representing the number of times per second that the state of a communication line (signal) changes. The higher the baud, the faster the data rate. Table 4-7 lists the maximum distances achievable, assuming the corresponding data rate (baud) for an EIA/TIA-232 signal. Table 4-8 lists the maximum distances achievable for EIA/TIA-449, V.35, X.21, and EIA-530 signals.

3. Determine the type and gender of the connector.

   You must specify DTE or DCE; generally, it is DTE. By counting the number of pins or pinholes on a connector, you can tell what size the connector is. For instance, a DB25 has either 25 pins or 25 pinholes. If there are pins, then the connector is a DB25 male connector. If the connector has 25 pinholes, then the connection is a DB25 female connector. Keep in mind that just because externally the connector fits, it does not mean the wires are terminated to the pins and pinholes internally.

LAN Interfaces

Ethernet and Token Ring are the most common of several LAN interface connections supported by Cisco network devices, and this section focuses on those two.

Type of Signal	Circuits	Signal Speeds	Network Device End Connector	Network End Connector	DCE Available	DTE Available
EIA/ TIA-232	Unbalanced	Up to 64 Kbps	DB-60	DB-25	✓	✓
EIA/ TIA-449	Balanced and unbalanced	Up to 2 Mbps	DB-60	DB-37	✓	✓
V.35		Up to 56 Kbps	DB-60	DB-15	✓	✓
X.21	Balanced	Up to 64 Kbps	DB-60	DB-15	✓	✓
EIA-530	Balanced	Up to 4 Mbps	DB-60	DB-25		✓

Table 4-6.   Serial Signal Properties

Data Rate (Baud)	Distance Measured in Meters
2,400	61
4,800	30
9,600	15
19,200	15
38,400	15
64,000	8

Table 4-7.   Speed and Distance Limits for EIA/TIA-232 Signals

Data Rate (Baud)	Distance Measured in Meters
2,400	1,220
4,800	625
9,600	312
19,200	156
38,400	78
56,000	31

Table 4-8.   Speed and Distance Limits for EIA/TIA-449, V.35, X.21, and EIA-530 Signals

Ethernet

Ethernet is a cost-effective technology used to transport data from point A to point B on a network. Ethernet has become so popular that most computer companies have chosen it for the NICs of their own computers.

Ethernet is a physical and data-link layer protocol that defines the standards of frames transmission across a LAN. Depending on cabling, NICs, and network device modules and ports, Ethernet can support 10, 100, and 1000 Mbps speeds.

ETHERNET CABLE AND CABLE PINOUTS   When establishing Ethernet connections in a network, you have to determine what type of Ethernet cabling and connectors are in use. Cisco network devices use 10BaseT, Fast Ethernet, and AUI ports. Following are descriptions of the four cable types and pinouts on which Ethernet is supported.

▼ **10Base5 (AUI)**   Ethernet 10Base5 is run on thick coaxial cable, also called thick Ethernet or Thicknet. This cable has a distance limitation of 1640 feet. AUI interfaces are also commonly used to connect to a transceiver. Transceivers can be purchased to support many media types, including 10Base2, 10BaseT, and 10BaseFL.

■ **10Base2**   Ethernet 10Base2 (Thinnet) is the coaxial cable version of Ethernet that was widely installed in the 1980s. Its popularity was comparable to 10Base5, but 10Base2 was easier to handle and cheaper.

■ **10BaseT**   Ethernet 10BaseT is run on unshielded twisted pair (UTP) cable. This is the most common type of Ethernet protocol. It looks like telephone cable but meets additional electrical standards that telephone cables do not. It has a distance limitation of 100 meters from a hub to a workstation. Two pairs of wires are used, one for receiving data and one for transmitting data. RJ-45 jacks are at the end of cables. Table 4-9 shows the pinouts for 10BaseT Ethernet.

Pin	Description
1	TX+
2	TX–
3	RX+
4	-
5	-
6	RX
7	-
8	-

Table 4-9. Ethernet 10BaseT RJ-45 Pinouts

Higher grades of cable, such as Category 5, can be used for Ethernet as well. Category 5 cable provides for future growth into faster transmission technologies such as 100BaseT.

▲ **100BaseT (Fast Ethernet)**   Fast Ethernet is run on UTP cable with the same pinout as 10BaseT. This makes it easy to upgrade NICs to Fast Ethernet and still use existing network cabling. Fast Ethernet has the same distance limitation of 10BaseT (up to 100 meters).

Token Ring

Token Ring is a physical and data-link layer technology similar to Ethernet. However, unlike Ethernet, Token Ring connects devices in a LAN based on a logical ring and a token-passing environment. In this environment, a small token is passed from node to node. The node having the token in its position has the rights to transmit data. If it has no information to send, it passes the token on to the next node.

TOKEN RING CABLE PINOUTS   A Token Ring environment uses two types of cabling: Shielded Twisted Pair (STP) and Unshielded Twisted Pair (UTP).

▼ **Shielded Twisted Pair (STP)**   Table 4-10 shows the pinout for Token Ring STP ports. DB-X stands for a data bus connector. This is a type of connector that is used to connect serial and parallel cables to a data bus. DB connector names are in the format DB-x, where x represents the number of wires within the connector. Each line is connected to a pin on the connector; but in many cases, not all pins are assigned a function. DB connectors are defined by various EIA/TIA standards.

Pin	Signal
1	RX–
2	Ground
3	+5 Volt, fused
4	Ground
5	TX–
6	+RX
7	Ground
8	Ground
9	+TX

Table 4-10.   Token Ring DB-9 Pinout for STP Port

▲ **Unshielded Twisted Pair (UTP)**   Table 4-11 shows the pinouts for Token Ring UTP ports.

SPEED AND DISTANCE LIMITATIONS   STP and UTP cables have different distance limitations. UTP cabling has a maximum distance limitation of 100 meters. STP cabling has a

Pin	Signal
1	Ground
2	Ground
3	TX
4	RX
5	TX
6	RX
7	Ground
8	-
9	-

Table 4-11.   Token Ring DB-9 Pinout for UTP Port

maximum distance limitation of 500 meters. The Token Ring protocol can operate at 4 Mbps and 16 Mbps ring speeds, but all devices on the ring must agree on the speed.

Console and Auxiliary Ports

Cisco network devices come standard with a console port and an auxiliary port. This section explains the difference between the two ports and describes their typical roles.

The asynchronous and auxiliary ports on Cisco network devices provide access to device configurations. Access can be achieved remotely using a console terminal or terminal-emulation application, or by using a modem.

The main difference between the auxiliary port and the console port is that the auxiliary port supports hardware flow control and the console port does not. Hardware flow control paces the transmission of data between the sending and receiving devices. It ensures that the receiving device has room in its buffer to receive the data before the sending device will send it. If the receiving device's buffer is full, the device sends a message to the sending device to suspend transmissions until it receives a message that the buffer has room for additional data.

Since the auxiliary port supports hardware flow control, it is ideal for use with modem transmissions. Console terminals and terminal-application software transmit at a slower speed than modems; therefore, the console port is suitable for these environments.

Network devices such as routers include a console and auxiliary cable kit. This kit contains the cable and adapters you need to connect a console terminal or modem to your router. The following items are included in the kit:

▼ RJ-45–to–RJ-45 rollover cable

■ RJ-45-to-DB-9 female DTE adapter

■ RJ-45-to-DB-25 female DTE adapter

▲ RJ-45-to-DB-25 DCE adapter

The RJ-45-to-RJ-45 rollover cable consists of eight wires. A rollover cable reverses the order in which the wires are terminated, unlike a straight-through cable where no swapping of wires takes place. Figure 4-11 illustrates the difference between a rollover cable and a straight-through cable; the wires are labeled 1 through 8.

You can tell the difference between a rollover cable and a straight-through cable by comparing the two plugs on the ends of the cable. If you hold the two plugs side by side and the first wire on the first plug is the same color (typically white) as the last wire on the second plug, that cable is probably a rollover cable. A rollover cable connects pins 1 and 8, 2 and 7, 3 and 6, and 4 and 5.

Each wire is responsible for carrying a particular signal, based on the type of adapter used (this is discussed in the upcoming sections). There are two groups of signals: signals that are sent and signals that are received, as defined in Table 4-12.

Console Port Overview and Pinout

The combination of a rollover cable with either the RJ-45–to–DB-9 female DTE adapter or the RJ-45-to-DB-25 female DTE adapter generates a specific signal. This signal allows

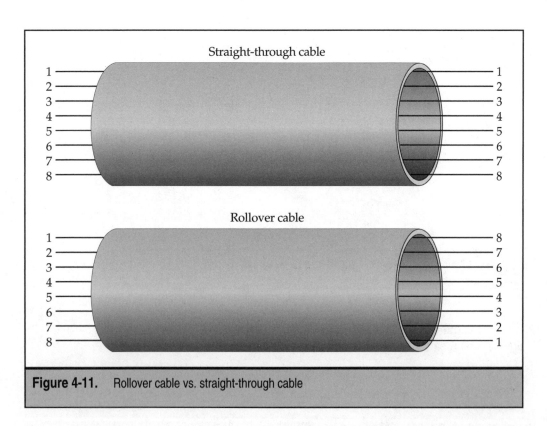

Figure 4-11.   Rollover cable vs. straight-through cable

Signal Sent	Function	Signal Received	Function
RTS	Request to Send	CTS	Clear to Send
DTR	Data Terminal Ready	DSR	Data Set Ready
TxD	Transmit Data	RxD	Receive Data
GND	Ground	GND	Ground
GND	Ground	GND	Ground
RxD	Receive Data	TxD	Transmit Data
DSR	Data Set Ready	DTR	Data Terminal Ready
CTS	Clear to Send	RTS	Request to Send

Table 4-12.   Signals and Functions

Console Port Signal	RJ-45–to–DB-25 Adapter Pin Used	ASCII Terminal Signal
RTS	5	CTS
DTR	6	DSR
TxD	3	RxD
GND	7	GND
GND	7	GND
RxD	2	TxD
DSR	20	DTR
CTS	4	RTS

Table 4-13.   Console Port-to-ASCII Terminal Signal Translations

communication to occur either through an ASCII terminal (using the RJ-45–to–DB-25 adapter) or through terminal-emulation software (using RJ-45–to–DB-9 adapter).

ASCII TERMINAL   The RJ-45–to–DB-25 adapter should be used with the rollover cable when connecting the console port to an ASCII terminal. This adapter uses seven of its 25 pins (pin 7 combines two wires) to provide translation of each signal sent from the console port to each signal received by the terminal. Table 4-13 lists the pins used, and the signals sent and received.

PC-TERMINAL EMULATION SOFTWARE   The RJ-45–to–DB-9 adapter should be used with the rollover cable when connecting to a PC running the terminal-emulation software. This adapter uses seven of its nine pins (pin 5 combines two wires) to provide translation of each signal sent from the console port to each signal received by the PC running the terminal-emulation software. Table 4-14 lists the pins used, and the signals sent and received.

AUXILIARY PORT OVERVIEW AND PINOUT   To connect a modem to the auxiliary port, use the RJ-45–to–RJ-45 rollover cable with the male RJ-45–to–DB-25 adapter. This adapter uses seven of its 25 pins (pin 7 combines two wires) to provide translation of each signal sent from the auxiliary port to each signal received by the modem. Table 4-15 lists the pins used, and the signals sent and received.

ACCESSING EQUIPMENT

The internal configurations of Cisco network devices can be accessed in three ways: through the console port, through a browser interface, or through a Telnet session. Before

Console Port Signal	RJ-45–to–DB-9 Adapter Pin Used	Terminal Emulation PC Signal
RTS	8	CTS
DTR	6	DSR
TxD	2	RxD
GND	5	GND
GND	5	GND
RxD	3	TxD
DSR	4	DTR
CTS	7	RTS

Table 4-14. Console Port-to-Terminal Emulation PC Signal Translations

using Telnet or Web access, an IP address must be assigned to the network device and Telnet must be enabled. This means initial configuration is done by using console port access.

Console Access

The majority of Cisco hardware comes with a console connection kit. This kit and its contents are described in the earlier section, "Console and Auxiliary Ports." Once you have

Auxiliary Port Signal	RJ-45–to–DB-25 Modem Adapter Pin Used	Modem Signal
RTS	4	CTS
DTR	20	DSR
TxD	4	RxD
GND	7	GND
GND	7	GND
RxD	2	TxD
DSR	8	DTR
CTS	5	RTS

Table 4-15. Auxiliary Port-to-Modem Signal Translations

the cables connected in the right place, this section tells you what to do next to connect a PC running terminal-emulation software.

PC Terminal-Emulation Software

Hyperterminal is the free terminal-emulation software that comes with Windows NT and Windows 9x. To launch it, follow these steps:

1. Select Start | Program | Accessories | Hyperterminal.

2. When prompted, enter a connection name and select the icon you would like associated with that name. (For convenience, you can copy the icon to the desktop as a shortcut.)

3. Next, you'll be prompted for connection information, including country code, area code, phone number, and communication port. The country code and area code will default to your machine's configuration values. Phone number is irrelevant for connecting to a console on a network device. For the port, use the default COM 1, unless another peripheral device on your computer is using it.

4. The next screen contains the communication port properties. Configure these as shown in Figure 4-12.

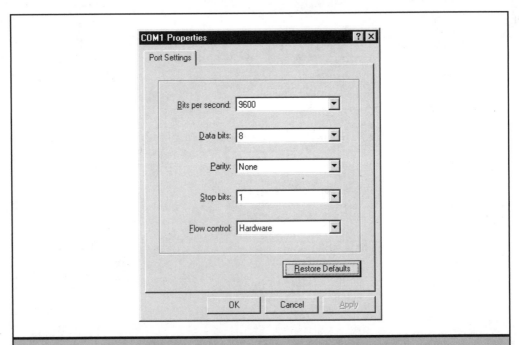

Figure 4-12.   Communication port properties for connecting a terminal-emulation PC

5. Click OK, and the terminal-emulation software will connect to the console port and provide you with the network device user prompt. (You might have to press ENTER a couple of times before you see a prompt.) From this prompt, you can enter the privileged EXEC mode and begin the necessary configurations.

Browser Interface Access

Most Cisco network devices provide a browser interface application that can be used to modify and view configurations. This type of access is probably the easiest—especially if you aren't familiar with Cisco's command line interface (CLI). Before accessing a network device, verify that your browser supports the Web application. Then you'll need to set certain parameters based on what type of browser you are using. These parameters may be dependent on the type of network device, and are covered in the chapters for the individual network devices (Chapters 4–7).

Once you have all the parameters set, launch the browser by double-clicking its icon. Type in the IP address of the device you want to access. You will then be prompted for the enable password. Once you have been authenticated, you have access to the Browser interface home page for that particular network device. Menu options at the top of the home page will help you navigate around the device to perform configurations and obtain network device information.

Telnet Access

The network device identifies each Telnet session as a virtual terminal. If configured, many simultaneous virtual terminal accesses can be supported—meaning you can have multiple Telnet sessions to the same device at the same time. The maximum number of Telnet sessions for most network devices is five.

In order to have Telnet privileges, you need to define Telnet permissions on the network device. The following is an example of commands for permitting five simultaneous Telnet sessions (0–4) to a router:

```
VelteRouter(config)#line vty 0 4
VelteRouter(config=line)#login
VelteRouter(config=line)#password password
```

Windows NT and Windows 9x offer the basic Telnet client application. Launch Telnet by typing **Telnet** at a DOS prompt, or by selecting Start | Run and typing **Telnet**, followed by the IP address of the network device you are trying to access.

When using the Telnet application included with Windows NT and Windows 9x, it may be useful to modify the buffer size of the screen output so you can scroll up and down your configuration display. In the Telnet window, go to menu option Terminal Preferences. Change the buffer size to 200. Figure 4-13 illustrates this option.

The majority of Cisco network devices offer a common CLI following a Telnet session into the device. This CLI is described next.

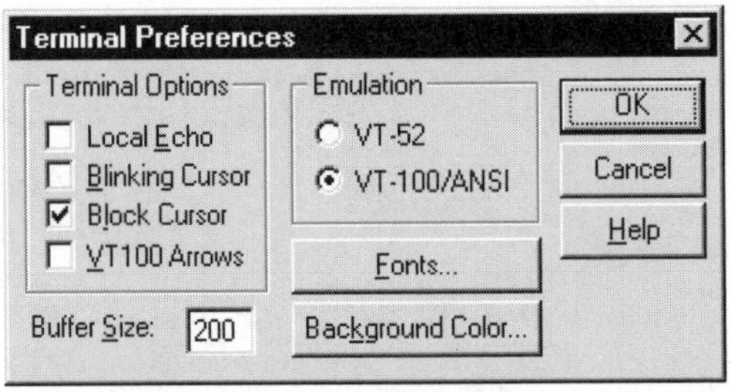

Figure 4-13.   Changing Telnet buffer size

COMMAND LINE INTERFACE

The command line interface (CLI) is used to perform network configurations through the console port or through a Telnet session from any node in the network. The commands issued on the CLI are applied only to the network device where you're currently logged in. This means you're limited to obtaining statistics of other network devices when using the CLI.

From the CLI, you can Telnet to any network device and perform network operations (assuming Telnet capabilities are enabled). To issue a CLI command, type the command at the prompt and press ENTER. If there is an output associated with your command, it will be displayed on your screen. If the output is continuous (for example, if you've turned on debugging to capture all of a certain traffic), the output on the screen will be interweaved with any additional commands you generate. Cisco CLI allows you to send your output to a file for viewing at a later time. This is handy when your output is extensive or you would like to maintain historical information.

Cisco's switches, routers, and even the PIX Firewall, to some extent, all support the traditional Cisco CLI. Managed devices maintain configurations and collect statistics that are useful for troubleshooting. Hubs, as well, provide some limited information. The remainder of this section discusses the capabilities of higher-layer devices such as the switches and routers.

Levels of Access

In the Cisco user interface, there are two levels of access: user EXEC level and privileged EXEC level.

User EXEC Level

The user EXEC level is the lowest level of access defined by the Cisco IOS. This level is represented by the > sign in CLI prompts.

```
Router>
```

Permissions at the user EXEC level are limited to viewing the status of network devices. No configuration changes are permitted.

Privileged EXEC Level

Access at the privileged EXEC level, also referred to as *enable mode,* is required in order to perform configuration changes, use debugging utilities, and view network device configurations. You enter the privileged EXEC level by typing the **enable** command at the user EXEC level CLI:

```
VelteNetworkDevice>enable
Password: enablepassword
VelteNetworkDevice#
```

The prompt changes to # to indicate enable mode.

Once in the privileged EXEC access level, you can view the configuration file and the status of the network device. However, in order to make configuration modifications, you need to go one step higher, into *configuration mode.* You can only go to configuration mode from privileged EXEC mode. Following is the command for entering configuration mode, which causes the prompt to change again, reflecting the mode change:

```
VelteNetworkDevice#config terminal
VelteNetworkDevice(config)#
```

All configuration commands entered at this prompt will be applied to the entire network device. An example of a configuration command would be defining the default gateway.

There is one additional access level that allows configurations to be applied to individual interfaces versus the entire network device. This is called the *interface mode.* An example of an interface mode command would be configuring the interface's IP address. Following is the necessary command for the interface configuration mode:

```
VelteNetworkDevice(config)#interface ethernet0
VelteNetworkDevice(config-int)#
```

Again, the prompt changes to reflect the level or mode you've entered. This prompt helps you remember what level you're in and what privileges you have.

Useful CLI Commands

The Cisco IOS CLI is a hierarchical structure that offers several useful keystrokes and commands to simplify the management and configuration of Cisco network devices.

Editing Keys

By default, your ten most recent commands are maintained in the CLI history. You can increase or decrease this number by typing **terminal history** x in the configuration mode, where x is the number of historical commands you'd like maintained. On an ANSI/VT100 terminal or emulation software, the UP ARROW key goes backward in command history and the DOWN ARROW key goes forward. On a machine other an ANSI/VT100 terminal or emulation, you press CTRL-N for the next command in the command history, and CTRL-P for the previous command. Once you have the command you are looking for displayed at the prompt, you can use the LEFT ARROW key to modify that command.

Several commands, specifically in configuration mode, tend to be very long. You may notice a misspelled word just as you are finishing the last characters in one of these long commands. To bring your cursor quickly back to the prompt, press CTRL-A. Pressing CTRL-E does the reverse and returns the cursor back to the end of the command.

To finish entering a command automatically, you can press TAB. For instance, if you type **conf** and then press TAB, the remainder of the command (**config**) would automatically be typed. Keep in mind when using the TAB shortcut that you do need to type in enough characters to uniquely identify the command from others that begin the same way.

The ? (Help) Command

When you press the **?** key (context-sensitive help), the network device will display all commands available at that particular level and a brief definition of each. The following shows an example of some of the help commands that are similar between Cisco's network platforms and their corresponding functions:

```
vsigate#?
Exec commands:
<1-99>           Session number to resume
access-enable    Create a temporary Access-List entry
access-template  Create a temporary Access-List entry
clear            Reset functions
clock            Manage the system clock
clock            Manage the system clock
configure        Enter configuration mode
connect          Open a terminal connection
copy             Copy configuration or image data
debug            Debugging functions (see also 'undebug')
disable          Turn off privileged commands
disconnect       Disconnect an existing network connection
enable memory    Turn on privileged commands
exit             Exit from the EXEC
help             Description of the interactive help system
lock             Lock the terminal
login            Log in as a particular user
logout           Exit from the EXEC
name-connection  Name an existing network connection
no               Disable debugging functions
ping             Send echo messages
reload           Halt and perform a cold restart
resume           Resume an active network connection
```

```
rsh              Execute a remote command
send             Send a message to other tty lines
setup            Run the SETUP command facility
show             Show running system information
systat           Display information about terminal lines
telnet           Open a telnet connection
terminal         Set terminal line parameters
test             Test subsystems, memory, and interfaces
traceroute       Trace route to destination
tunnel           Open a tunnel connection
undebug          Disable debugging functions (see also 'debug')
where            List active connections
write            Write running configuration to memory,
                 network, or terminal
```

To determine the next required parameters and arguments for any of these commands, type one of the commands followed by a **?**. Type in one of these parameters followed by another **?**. Continue to do this until you see the <CR> option. This means you have entered all the parameters, and by pressing ENTER you will activate the command. In the following example, the **?** command is used to set the clock on the network device:

```
vsigate#clock ?
read-calendar  Read the hardware calendar into the clock
set        Set the time and date
update-calendar Update the hardware calendar from the clock
vsigate#clock set ?
hh:mm:ss Current Time
vsigate#clock set 15:40:10 ?
<1-31> Day of the month
MONTH  Month of the year
vsigate#clock set 15:40:10 Apr ?
<1-31> Day of the month
vsigate#clock set 15:40:10 Apr 23 ?
<1993-2035> Year
vsigate#clock set 15:40:10 Apr 23 1999
```

You can also enter the **?** command directly after a partial command, to determine all commands that start with that character sequence. For example:

```
vsigate#te?
telnet terminal test
```

The show Command

Cisco IOS CLI also offers a **show** command that provides a quick reference for interface information, access lists, debugging status, and many other statistics. This information helps you confirm specific configurations without having to go through the whole configuration file. Routers and switches have similar **show** commands. Following are some of the more useful **show** commands that can be executed on a router or on a switch:

```
Switch or Router#show ?
  access-lists     List access lists
  accounting       Accounting data for active sessions
  aliases          Display alias commands
  arp              ARP table
  cdp              CDP information
  clock            Display the system clock
  configuration    Contents of Non-Volatile memory
  controllers      Interface controller status
  debugging        State of each debugging option
  history          Display the session command history
  hosts            IP domain-name, lookup style,
nameservers, and host table
  interfaces       Interface status and configuration
  ip               IP information
  line             TTY line information
  location         Display the system location
  logging          Show the contents of logging buffers
  memory           Memory statistics
  privilege        Show current privilege level
  processes        Active process statistics
  queue            Show queue contents
  queueing         Show queueing configuration
  registry         Function registry information
  reload           Scheduled reload information
  rhosts           Remote-host+user equivalences
  rmon             rmon statistics
  running-config   Current operating configuration
  sessions         Information about Telnet connections
  snmp             snmp statistics
  spanning-tree    Spanning tree topology
  stacks           Process stack utilization
  startup-config   Contents of startup configuration
  subsys           Show subsystem information
  tcp              Status of TCP connections
  tech-support     Show system information for Tech-Support
  terminal         Display terminal configuration parameters
  users            Display information about terminal lines
  version          System hardware and software status
  vlan             VTP VLAN status
```

Debugging Commands

The debugging commands are very useful when you're troubleshooting network communication problems. Debugging lets you actually see the traffic that is being sent through the network device.

NOTE: Although debugging commands are very useful, it's very important to be careful of what type of debugging is turned on. By debugging common, universal traffic, you may overload the network device's processor and cause it to lock up. One debugging command that should be especially avoided is **debug all**, which turns on all debugging options.

SENDING DEBUGGING COMMANDS TO THE SCREEN   To view logging results, you can have them displayed to the terminal screen. If you're attached directly to the console port, the messages will appear immediately on the screen following the debug command. If you attached through a Telnet session, you'll need to enable the network device to copy the messages to your Telnet session. This is achieved by using the following command in the configuration mode of the network device:

```
velte(config)#logging monitor debugging
```

USEFUL DEBUGGING COMMANDS   Here's a list of the common debugging commands used by both Cisco routers and switches:

```
Switch or Router#debug ?
aaa                 AAA Authentication, Authorization and Accounting
all                 Enable all debugging
arp                 IP ARP and HP Probe transactions
cdp                 CDP information
custom-queue        Custom output queueing
domain              Domain Name System
ethernet-interface  Ethernet network interface events
ip                  IP information
list                Set interface or/and access list for the
                    next debug command
modem               Modem control/process activation
packet              Log unknown packets
priority            Priority output queueing
snmp                SNMP information
telnet              Incoming telnet connections
tftp                TFTP packets
```

Typically, the debugging tool is used when you're trying to determine whether or not traffic is traversing the router. You turn on debugging for specific protocol(s) you want to watch for. Then start the traffic. If the traffic you have generated is hitting the router (assuming it uses the same protocols you are debugging), you can actually see the packets on the router through your console or Telnet session. The router will display information such as traffic source and destination. Common protocols you can capture are IP, SNMP, Telnet, and TFTP.

Several of the debugging commands have additional parameters that can make the command more specific. For example, you don't have to turn on debugging for all of IP or all of TCP in order to verify that traffic is able to reach a network device. With the **ICMP** debugging parameter, you can turn on ICMP debugging for the remote network device, and then ping from your workstation to the device. If the network device generates log statements, verifying your ICMP traffic, then you know the routes from your workstation to that device are correct. Here is the command to enable ICMP debugging on either a router or a switch:

```
Router or Switch#debug IP ICMP
ICMP packet debugging is on
```

SENDING DEBUGGING COMMANDS TO AN INTERNAL BUFFER   The most efficient way to have the router report debug information is to use the **logging buffered** command in the config mode. The debugging information within the log file can then be viewed using the **show log** command (you must first exit config mode before doing the **show** command). These commands are illustrated as follows:

```
Switch(config)#logging buffered
Switch(config)#exit
Switch#show log
Syslog logging: enabled (0 messages dropped, 35 flushes, 0 overruns)
Console logging: disabled
Monitor logging: level debugging, 0 messages logged
Trap logging: level informational, 5571 message lines logged
File logging: disabled
Buffer logging: level debugging, 5567 messages logged
Log Buffer (4096 bytes):
```

> **NOTE:**   As of IOS version 11.2, you can issue a **clear log** command to clear the log buffer. It can be helpful to get rid of old unneeded messages while you are debugging a problem.

Network Device Configurations

The various network devices require specific configurations. Hubs and switches will work if they are simply plugged in to the network and powered up. This doesn't use all their potential features, however—especially in the case of the many features of a switch. Other network devices, as well, including firewalls, routers, and access servers, require configuration in order to work.

There are two types of configurations: first-time, and then recurring configurations for modifications.

First-Time Network Device Configurations

When you connect a network device to a terminal and power it up for the first time, there will be no configuration in memory and the network device will go into the initial configuration dialog box. You'll be prompted for specific information regarding the device's configuration. Depending on the device being configured, this information may include any of the following:

▼ Host name
■ Enable secret
■ Enable password
■ Virtual terminal password
■ SNMP configurations
■ Routing protocols
▲ Interface IP addresses

You can also return a network device to this initial unconfigured state by typing **write erase** in privileged EXEC mode. This command erases the current configuration in memory and allows you to start fresh.

Modifying Network Device Configurations

Modifications can be made using the console port or through a Telnet session.

TIP: Keep in mind that if the network device is currently being used, any configurations done through Telnet or the console port are valid as soon as you press ENTER. Make sure, if you are configuring an interface from a Telnet session, you are not modifying the interface that you're connected to. This could result in disconnection of your Telnet session. If this happens, establish a connection through the console port and perform the necessary modifications. Or have someone power the router off and then back on, which will eliminate the new config parameters that were not yet written to NVRAM.

An alternative method of modifying configurations is to use a TFTP server. The network device configuration files are plain ASCII text. The devices read their text files during boot-up and generate their running configuration files. These text files can be saved as plain text on a TFTP server. Using a screen editor, you can modify the files and reload them into the network device through TFTP. Even if you decide to make configuration changes on-the-fly, without using a TFTP server, it's a good idea to TFTP your most recent configurations to a TFTP server as backup.

To TFTP a file to a TFTP server, you must first create the file in the directory the TFTP server is using, and verify that you have write privileges for that file. The following commands illustrate the process of copying the configuration file of VelteNetwork Device (which is a router) to the TFTP server at 10.4.5.6:

```
VelteNetworkDevice#write network
Remote host [ ]?10.4.5.6
Name of configuration file to write [router-confg] velte.conf
Write file to velte.conf on host 10.4.5.6 [confirm]? <ENTER>
Writing velte.conf:!!!!! [OK]
```

After the file is modified, following are the commands used to copy it back into VelteNetworkDevice:

```
VelteNetworkDevice#configure network
Host or network configuration file [host]?<ENTER>
Address of remote host [255.255.255.255]?10.4.5.6
Name of configuration file [router-confg]velte.conf
Configure using velte.conf from 10.4.5.6 [confirm]?<ENTER>
Loading velte.conf from 10.4.5.6 (via Ethernet 0) !!!!!!!
```

Rebooting Network Devices

When you reboot a network device, the device can pull its system image from three places. If you configure all three options, the network device will try to boot from the first option. If that fails, it will try to boot from the second option and then from the third option, if necessary. The three options are ROM, flash memory, and the network server.

READ-ONLY MEMORY (ROM)   ROM is nonvolatile memory that can be read from but not written to by the microprocessor. ROM contains a copy of the IOS that the network device is using. When it boots up from ROM, the device is referring to the ROM chips. The location of the ROM chips varies among network devices. In high-end devices, the ROM chips can be upgraded to contain newer versions of the IOS. These chips are read only and therefore do not contain any configurations you may have applied.

In most cases, you would boot from ROM as your last alternative. This is because ROM typically is a subset of the Cisco IOS software, possibly lacking in protocols, features, and configurations of full IOS software. Also, the software could be an older version if you have upgraded your router since it was purchased.

NOTE: The Cisco 7200 Series and Cisco 7500 Series cannot boot from ROM.

FLASH MEMORY   Flash memory is nonvolatile storage that can be electrically erased and programmed so that software images can be stored, rebooted, and written as necessary. Flash memory contains the current version of the IOS running on the network device. The **show flash** command reveals the image file currently supported in flash memory—in addition to total memory and memory available on your network device. Following is an example of output generated by the **show flash** command:

```
vsigate#show flash
System flash directory:
File Length  Name/status
 1  3218108 c4500-is-mz_112-17.bin
[3218172 bytes used, 13559044 available, 16777216 total]
16384K bytes of processor board System flash (Read/Write)
```

NETWORK SERVER   A system image can also be loaded from a network server such as a TFTP server. Network devices use the filename and TFTP server's IP address to determine the IOS file from which to boot. To copy the current system image file from the network device to the TFTP Server, use the **copy flash** command in privileged EXEC mode:

```
Router#copy flash tftp
```

Make sure you have the TFTP file created and write privileges enabled.

To manually copy the file from the TFTP server to the network device, use the **copy tftp** command in privileged EXEC mode. Flash will be erased to make room for the new image.

NOTE: You can put comments in the file on the TFTP server by starting the line with an exclamation mark (!). When the file is copied to the network device, all lines beginning with the exclamation mark will be removed.

Here are the commands to configure the automatic sequential booting of the three options:

```
VelteNetworkDevice(config)#boot system flash
VelteNetworkDevice(config)#boot system rom
VelteNetworkDevice(config)#boot system backupfile 10.1.2.3
```

The order in which the commands are entered is the order they will be placed in the configuration file upon failure of the previous command.

Following these or any other configuration changes, do a **write memory** to write the updated configurations to NVRAM. NVRAM is nonvolatile RAM that retains its content when the network device is powered off. It can be read and written to by a microprocessor and therefore is used to store the devices configurations.

TROUBLESHOOTING TOOLS

There are several troubleshooting tools available for determining problem information, such as links or devices that are down, loops in your network, and/or poor routing statements. A few of these tools are discussed in the following sections.

Ping

The Internet Control Message Protocol (ICMP) was defined by the Department of Defense as part of the Internet layer protocols. ICMP serves four functions: flow control, unreachable destination alerts, redirecting routes, and checking remote hosts.

The ICMP echo message, also known as **ping**, sends a packet to a specific destination and requests a response. Using the MAC and IP address, and the ping-defined destination IP address, the request is sent. If the destination is connected to the network and receives the request, it will respond. This send-and-respond process will occur five times. Successful responses are represented by am exclamation mark (!), and unsuccessful responses by a period (.). The **ping** command also provides statistics on the success rate, as well as the minimum, average, and maximum milliseconds it took for the ping packet to travel from source to destination and back to source.

Here is an example of a successful ping:

```
vsigate#ping 10.1.1.13
Type escape sequence to abort.
Sending 5, 100-byte ICMP Echos to 10.1.1.13, timeout is 2 seconds:
!!!!!
Success rate is 100 percent (5/5), round-trip min/avg/max = 1/1/1 ms
```

Here is an unsuccessful ping:

```
vsigate#ping 10.1.1.253
Type escape sequence to abort.
Sending 5, 100-byte ICMP Echos to 10.1.1.253, timeout is 2 seconds:
.....
Success rate is 0 percent (0/5)
```

If your **ping** command is not successful, check the following factors:

▼   Is the destination physically plugged into the network?

■   Is there a link light on the destination's NIC?

■   Does the destination have the correct default gateway?

■   Does the destination default gateway have the correct routes?

■   Does the source have the correct default gateway?

■   Does the source default gateway have the correct routes?

■   Is there some type of router access list or firewall intercepting the traffic that may be blocking ICMP?

■   Are the interfaces up on all applicable network devices (no port failure has occurred)?

▲   Are the subnet masks correct?

If fixing any of the above possible problems does not fix your inability to ping, the **traceroute** or extended **ping** commands may be useful. Extended ping allows you to set some additional parameters, including the source of the **ping** command. An example of extended ping is shown here:

```
vsigate#ping
Protocol [ip]:<Enter>
Target IP address: 209.98.98.98
Repeat count [5]:<Enter>
Datagram size [100]:<Enter>
Timeout in seconds [2]:<Enter>
Extended commands [n]: y
Source address or interface: 10.1.1.1
Type of service [0]:<Enter>
Set DF bit in IP header? [no]:<Enter>
Validate reply data? [no]:<Enter>
Data pattern [0xABCD]:<Enter>
Loose, Strict, Record, Timestamp, Verbose[none]:<Enter>
Sweep range of sizes [n]:<Enter>
Type escape sequence to abort.
Sending 5, 100-byte ICMP Echos to 209.98.98.98, timeout is 2 seconds:
!!!!!
Success rate is 100 percent (5/5), round-trip
min/avg/max = 16/16/16 ms
```

Traceroute

The **traceroute** command is similar to **ping**, except it defines the hops included in its path to the destination. When the **ping** command is unsuccessful, entering the **traceroute** command shows you the hops defined by the network routing statements that choose the route the packets will take. If the packets are being blocked or not being routed correctly, the trail of hops will help you determine which network device is blocking packets or has incorrect routing information.

In addition to the hops, traceroute also discloses the latency between hops. This is particularly useful in determining possible bottlenecks in your network.

Telnet

Telnet is the login and terminal-emulation protocol that operates over TCP/IP networks. Its primary function is to facilitate users' login to remote host systems. By having this capability, you can establish a Telnet session at multiple hosts along a path and perform testing at each step. For instance, if you are unsuccessful getting from point A to point B, verifying connectivity at each hop from point A to B may help identify a possible point of failure.

Other Tools

In addition to **ping** and **traceroute**, several other commands are useful as troubleshooting tools. **Show** commands display existing configurations, interface status, access-list counters, and other beneficial information. Debugging commands are particularly helpful in monitoring traffic as it passes through a device. Debugging can also be used to verify source and destination IP addresses, protocols, port numbers, and so on. Common debugging commands are described in the "Command Line Interface" section of this chapter.

EQUIPMENT MANAGEMENT

It's a good idea to restrict remote access to your network devices, making it available only from a limited number of network management stations. Certain devices can then be defined to allow configurations, monitoring, and management to take place within the management stations. This reduces the possibility of security breaches and malicious activity.

This section examines several management tools on the market that provide centralized network device management. Most of these tools rely on standard management protocols, such as Simple Network Management Protocol (SNMP). Chapter 8 offers thorough information on these management tools.

SNMP

Simple Network Management Protocol (SNMP) is an application-layer protocol running on top of the user datagram protocol (UDP). SNMP is used to gather statistics, obtain configuration information, and change the configuration of SNMP-enabled devices.

The network management tool runs on a network management server, which makes configuration requests to a network device or agent using SNMP. SNMP relies on *community string(s)* to provide verification of authority prior to passing configuration and statistical information. The same community string(s) must be configured on both the server and the agent. Unfortunately, prior to SNMP version 2, the community string is passed in cleartext across the network.

The community string consists of two parts: the read community string (public) and the read/write community string (private). (As discussed in the following section, "SNMP Security Issues," it's not good business practice to use the default strings, public and private.) Management tools that only read the statistics and configuration information of network devices require the read community string. Management tools that read the network device's statistical and configuration information, as well as provide configuration changes, require both the read and the read/write community string.

Access lists on certain network devices can be configured to permit read or read/write privileges limited by the management device's IP address.

SNMP Security Issues

It is important to disable the SNMP process and/or modify the SNMP community strings on the network devices if you are not using SNMP for network management. By default, the majority of Cisco devices assign the read community string to **public**, and the write community string to **private**. It would be the best guess of any hacker to try the default community strings first, anticipating that the majority of network engineers probably don't change them.

When the SNMP server is enabled and the SNMP community strings are configured, the configuration and statistical information of the network device is being passed across the network. Thus, a network analysis tool could be configured to pick up SNMP packets. These packets could then be deciphered to obtain network configurations, resulting in possible security breaches and network attacks. Chapter 10 has more information on the capabilities of network analysis tools and examples of how to use them.

MIBs

After the network management server or workstation is authenticated to issue SNMP commands, the network device's Management Information Base (MIB) can be queried. The MIB stores all the device's statistical and configuration information. SNMP can issue **get** commands to obtain information from the MIB, or **set** commands to apply configuration changes to the MIB.

Remote Monitoring (RMON)

The standard MIB, discussed just above, lacks the ability to provide statistics on data-link and physical layer parameters (layers 1 and 2 of the OSI model). This means Ethernet traffic and Token Ring statistics are not accessible. In the 1990s, RMON MIB was developed to address these shortcomings. RMON MIB provides for network managers the important statistics about the links on which the network devices reside. The RMON agent must be present on the network device in order to provide information about its links.

Types of Management Tools

There are two ways a management tool can obtain network device information: through a *trap* or via a *polling device*.

Traps

A trap is sent to the network management server whenever a monitored event happens on a network device (for instance, when a serial interface goes down). Traps aren't particularly reliable because they depend on not only the device's recognizing these defined events, but also that every link and intermediate device within the network path be up and running.

Polling

Polling is somewhat more reliable than traps, but it generates additional traffic. The network manager server initiates polling and proactively requests information from all managed devices. The larger the network, the more network devices to be monitored, and the more traffic is generated by polling. Therefore, network management servers that rely totally on polling work better in smaller networks.

Other Management Protocols

Although SNMP is the most common management protocol, Cisco does support other management protocols. Some of these protocols operate independently, and some were developed to work directly with SNMP.

Cisco Discovery Protocol (CDP)

Cisco Discovery Protocol (CDP) is a management protocol that runs on Cisco routers, access servers, and switches. When CDP is enabled, each device sends periodic messages to a multicast address and listens to the periodic messages sent by other devices. These messages hold information about neighboring devices and when their interfaces go up or down. With CDP, network management applications can learn the device type and the SNMP agent address of neighboring devices. This enables network management tools to send SNMP queries to neighboring devices. Here is the command generated on a network device to display its CDP neighbors:

```
vsigate#show cdp neighbors
Capability Codes:
R - Router, T - Trans Bridge, B -Source Route Bridge
S - Switch, H - Host, I - IGMP, r - Repeater
Device ID          Local Intrfce    Holdtme    Capability    Platform    Port ID
Switch.velte.com   Eth 1            150        S             WS-C2924M-Fas 0/8
vsitest7           Tok 1            147        R             RSP2        Tok 6/0
Lab-Router-04      Tok 0            146        R             4500        Tok 0
```

Common Management Information Protocol (CMIP)

The Common Management Information Protocol (CMIP) defines network standards based on the OSI model—similar to SNMP. However, even though CMIP is richer in functionality, its slow acceptance has resulted in few CMIP products.

ping and traceroute

The **ping** and **traceroute** commands (as defined in an earlier section) can be used as network management protocols. Many network management tools work with the ping and traceroute protocols to verify connectivity in combination with one of the above protocols (particular SNMP).

SUMMARY

Cisco offers a wide variety of hardware options, including routers, switches, hubs, access servers, and firewalls. Each network device targets a select market and offers unique features and functions. These characteristics must be considered when determining a solution for your network.

The majority of Cisco's network devices are based on Cisco IOS. Cisco IOS provides support for a variety of link types and protocols. It also offers advanced features such as Tag Switching, NetFlow services, Cisco Express Forwarding (CEF), Network Address Translation (NAT), and software-based compression. Cisco's IOS has a command line interface (CLI) that is, for the most part, standard across the platforms that support it. This CLI offers several common and useful commands, including the debugging commands. The debugging commands are useful for troubleshooting and problem resolution. Other troubleshooting tools include ping, traceroute, and Telnet. The Cisco IOS release you should deploy will depend on your own requirements for features, stability, and reliability.

Cisco supports several types of links and protocols. The necessary cable and connectors for an interface are based on the link type and protocol. The two basic interfaces are LAN and WAN. LAN supports protocols such as Ethernet and Token Ring, and WAN supports protocols such as ISDN and serial connections.

Regardless of the types of network devices being used, or the link types and protocols being supported, it is important to provide proper management and maintenance over the devices. SNMP, among other management protocols, is supported on the majority of Cisco's hardware. These management protocols, along with Cisco's management software or that of another third party, will assist you in maintaining an optimal network solution.

Next, Chapter 5 will provide more specific information on the features and functions of routers, where they should be deployed, and how they are configured. Chapter 5 will also describe configuration tools that simplify the router configuration process.

CHAPTER 5

Configuring Routers and RRAS

The Cisco IOS (Internetwork Operating System) offers a wide array of configuration options—so many that, initially, router configuration can seem daunting. However, all the commands and capabilities offered by the latest IOS will simplify the task of getting your network up and running and help you keep it optimized. It's best to take the time to do a little planning and get to know the basics before starting. From there, you'll be able to customize the IOS to suit the exact needs of almost any network.

Since there are many sources of information about configuring specific routers, and since changing IOS versions impact how a router is configured, we'll take a quick look at the router boot process and router setup and configuration, and then focus on tools like ConfigMaker that are used to build and manage a variety of router configurations. Then we'll cover Netsys Baseliner, a tool used to model and analyze the configuration of routed networks. Finally, we'll focus on Windows NT and Windows 2000 TCP/IP setup, Windows route tables, and Microsoft's Routing and Remote Access (RRAS).

ROUTER FUNDAMENTALS AND SETUP

In the following sections, we will discuss the various hardware and software components of a working router. Also, we will step through basic installation procedures and try out various TCP/IP router configurations that illustrate several common configuration options.

Test Before You Implement

Whether you are adding new segments to your LAN or new sites to your WAN; installing an Internet connection; upgrading router software; or adding support for video or voice, or even TN3270 mainframe support, you will at some point have to make changes to a production network. Make it a rule to always test new equipment (including model changes) and IOS software in a lab environment first, where it won't interfere with the production network.

You don't have to have a million-dollar lab to perform testing. Just make sure the test environment has enough equipment to mimic a subset of your production network.

NOTE: Complex configurations may require more equipment and resources than you can reasonably keep on hand for testing. In these cases, look to your local or regional Cisco office or a Cisco Certified Partner. They may have lab environments to suit your requirements. If not, they will certainly be able to assist you in finding the equipment, information, and resources necessary to accomplish the task.

Although testing is usually not required when you're installing additional components of the same model, nor for many IOS configuration changes, testing should be conducted when performing IOS upgrades, enabling new feature sets, or installing new equipment models. When you make changes to a production network, always be prepared to back them out should they cause problems on the network. Also, it never hurts to be the first one on site the morning after a major network change, no matter how late you might have been there the night before to install the change. In Chapter 10, you'll find suggestions and advice about network analysis, testing, and simulation techniques that will help you plan and implement network alterations while keeping the risks to a minimum.

Getting Ready to Test

Whether you are setting up a new router or modifying the configuration of an existing one, the first place you should look for configuration information is in the documentation for your existing routers and in the latest network documentation. You will need to understand your network addressing scheme, the routing protocols in use, and the configuration of your LAN and WAN topologies, and you will need the addresses of any servers on the network that will be used by the router. These include Domain Name System (DNS), Trivial File Transfer Protocol (TFTP), Remote Access Dial-In User Service (RADIUS), and Terminal Access Controller Access Control System (TACACS) servers. Part of the initial discovery process should include preparation of a checklist of information necessary to properly configure your new routers or reconfigure existing routers.

In addition, don't forget that you will need to follow any change control processes that your organization has established. Remember to allow plenty of time to document, test, and execute the changes you plan to make, especially when the changes are major.

Preconfiguration Checklist

To make life a little easier, have ready all the information necessary to properly configure your routers, before you start the process. With very simple network configurations, this information may be nothing more than a name for the router, some passwords, a couple of TCP/IP addresses, and a subnet mask. For networks that are more elaborate, you will need information specific to the routing protocols on the network, as well as a host of other items.

The following preconfiguration checklist covers a basic TCP/IP installation:

- ▼ Router host name
- ■ Physical configuration (slots, cards/modules, ports)
- ■ Ports currently active (serial 0, Ethernet 2, Token Ring 3, etc.)
- ■ Ports currently shut down
- ■ Ports to activate
- ■ Port IP addresses with subnet masks
- ■ Routing protocols
- ■ Autonomous system number
- ■ Serial encapsulation (Frame Relay, etc.)
- ▲ Passwords

For complex configurations you will also need:

- ▼ Parameters unique to the network
- ■ Parameters for each network segment

▲   Information specific to the router's functions

Although you may not need all this information for a particular setup, this checklist is a good reference to make sure you have what is required before getting started. If you don't already have a configuration checklist template, it's a good idea to build one and include it with your network documentation. That keeps it handy for the next update and for anyone conducting that update.

NOTE: When installing new routers, one way to get a quick look at key configuration parameters is to Telnet to either a production router similar to the ones you plan to install, or to a neighboring router, and execute the **show running-config** command.

Installing Routers

Before installing a router, you will need to make sure you have a licensed copy of Cisco's Internetwork Operating System (IOS) appropriate for your particular requirements. The IOS is essentially the configurable brains of the router—an operating system, just as NT or UNIX is an operating system, but highly specialized for data communications. As network technology advances, Cisco continues to add new features and upgrade existing features by modifying the IOS. Each new version fixes problems and adds support for new technologies. The IOS provides functions as basic as sending network packets from one interface to another, and functions as advanced as data encryption, mainframe connectivity, access control, and prioritized network traffic management using QoS (Quality of Service) mechanisms. More information about the most current version of IOS available for your router hardware can be found on the Cisco Web site. The procedure for copying the IOS over to the router's memory is outlined later in this section. For now, let's focus on getting the router hardware installed.

As is true for all network equipment, location is everything for a router. Routers can generate a fair amount of heat. If they have little ventilation and inadequate cooling, a rack full of routers can drive up the heat of a small network closet anywhere from 5° to more than 15° (C). This can cause intermittent problems leading to complete failures of routers and other equipment. Even in areas with sufficient cooling, make sure there is adequate clearance around the fan and vent areas of the router.

Like hubs, switches, and other devices, routers should be installed with the following in mind:

▼   Install in a cool, clean, and dry operating environment

■   Keep the chassis free of obstructions

■   Keep the router and its cables away from equipment that would cause interference

■   Provide adequate and reliable power

▲   Provide proper strain relief for all power and data cables and their connectors

It's also very important to control physical access to the routers. Only authorized persons should have access, to prevent the network from being compromised.

Administrative Access

Gaining access to the router to upgrade software or modify the configuration can be done in several ways. Table 5-1 summarizes these methods.

The most common access method when setting up one or a small number of new routers is via a console port connection. This direct connection allows configuration of the basic parameters necessary to connect to the network. Usually this first set of parameters is completed, then the router is connected to the network, and then administrative access is gained via a network connection.

Console Port

The console port is on the rear of the router. On the Cisco 4700 (Figure 5-1), the console port is a male DB-25 serial connector to which an RJ-45–to–DB-25 female terminal adapter can be connected. An RJ-45–to–RJ-45 rollover cable is then used to connect to a DB-9 serial or other type of terminal adapter that is compatible with the terminal, host, or PC used to connect to the router console.

When using a Windows system to connect to the router console, you connect the serial connector to one of the PC serial ports. Make sure you know which serial port (COM 1,

Connection Type	Description
Console port	"Dumb" terminal (VT100) using a serial line connection
Auxiliary port	"Dumb" terminal (VT100) using a modem connection
Telnet	Virtual terminal (VT100) or scripted access using a TCP/IP-based network connection
HTTP	Web browser using a TCP/IP-based network connection
TFTP	Direct connection via Ethernet or Token Ring cable, or using a TCP/IP-based network connection
SNMP	Simple Network Management Protocol connection over a TCP/IP-based network connection

Table 5-1.   Methods of Administrative Access

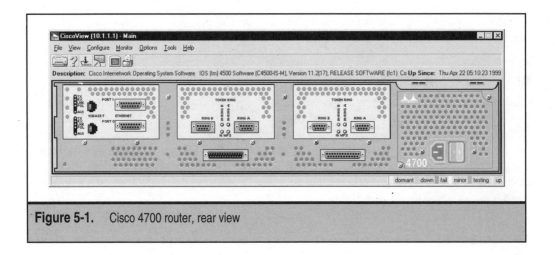

Figure 5-1. Cisco 4700 router, rear view

COM 2, etc.) is going to be used, and configure the terminal software serial port with the following parameters:

Baud rate	9600
Data bits	8
Stop bits	1
Parity	None
Flow control	None
Terminal type	VT100

Once connected, the router should be accessible with a few presses of the ENTER key. If it isn't, make sure you have configured your terminal software to use the correct serial port (usually one of COM ports 1–4). Then, if the router is still not responding, verify that you are using the serial adapters and rollover cable provided with the router and that the connectors are securely attached. (Also, having missed this obvious detail a time or two ourselves, make sure the router is powered on.)

Base Configuration

The minimum configuration that allows administrative access on a TCP/IP network includes assigning a password, an "up" network interface (using the **no shutdown** command), an IP address, a subnet mask, and the routing protocol used in your network. Note that you also need to have a password set on the vty ports to allow administrative access via the LAN. On a lab router, our initial configuration included the following:

```
interface Ethernet0
ip address 10.1.10.2 255.255.255.0
media-type 10BaseT
```

```
!
router ospf 1
network 10.0.0.0 0.0.0.255 area 0
!
```

The routing protocol specification—in this example, OSPF—allows the router to ac-quire the information necessary for dispatching network traffic through the router from local subnets to those on other routers. From this basic configuration, the router can be connected to the network, and a Telnet or HTTP session can be established for further configuration. This also allows for configuration via Cisco's ConfigMaker, scripts, or other tools, as well as provides a path for online upgrades to the IOS via TFTP.

Telnet Access

Once a router is connected to the network, access via a Telnet client is straightforward. You can use the Telnet application included with Windows, or any of a large number of third-party and shareware Telnet applications.

NOTE: One very helpful application that offers several enhanced features is CRT from Van Dyke Technologies, Inc. It supports Telnet, VT100 terminal emulation, Telnet proxy firewall support, auto-mated login capabilities, and modem-dialing support using Windows TAPI. You can download an eval-uation of CRT from http://www.vandyke.com/products/crt/index.html.

To connect to a router on the network using Telnet, configure the application to use VT100 terminal emulation and enter the router's host name or IP address. If the router is on the network and configured properly, you will be prompted for a password just as you would in a console connection.

HTTP Access

IOS version 11.*x* introduced an integrated HTTP server that allows administrative access to the command line interface (CLI) via a standard Web browser.

For HTTP access to a router, you will need to configure the router with the following command:

```
Lab-Router-04 #conf t
Enter configuration commands, one per line.  End with CNTL/Z.
Lab-Router-04 (config)#ip http server
Lab-Router-04 (config)#
```

To "hide" HTTP access from users browsing the network and from applications look-ing for HTTP servers on the standard HTTP port 80, you can enter the following com-mand, using an arbitrarily assigned port number (in this case, 6969):

```
Lab-Router-04 #conf t
Enter configuration commands, one per line.  End with CNTL/Z.
Lab-Router-04 (config)#ip http port 6969
Lab-Router-04 (config)#
```

This will require that any user attempting to access the router's HTTP server enter the IP address or host name followed a colon and then by the port number the server is listening on, as shown in the following example:

```
http://router.anyoldnetwork.com:6969
http://10.200.30.40:6969
```

For additional control of access to the router's HTTP server, you can use the following command to specify an access list:

```
Lab-Router-04#conf t
Enter configuration commands, one per line.   End with CNTL/Z.
Lab-Router-04(config)#ip http access-class?
<1-99>  Access list number
Lab-Router-04(config)#
```

At this point you will notice that you need to specify which access list (number 1–99) you would like to use when controlling access via HTTP. The following example illustrates the command for creating an access list and then applying it to the HTTP server:

```
Lab-Router-04#conf t
Enter configuration commands, one per line.   End with CNTL/Z.
Lab-Router-04(config)#access-list 99 permit tcp host
 10.1.1.10 eq http
Lab-Router-04(config)#ip http access-class 99
Lab-Router-04(config)#
```

Note that access to the HTTP server requires the enable-level password.

For more information on access lists, refer to Chapter 14.

TFTP

When booting a router, the Trivial File Transfer Protocol (TFTP) can be used as a primary or secondary IOS image store. TFTP can also be used to copy IOS image files into the router's flash memory. It is often used to copy a new IOS version to routers when upgrading, and as a backup image location that routers can use during bootup (should the image in flash memory get corrupted).

If you don't already have a TFTP server, you can download Cisco's free TFTP Server for Windows 95/Windows 98/NT 4.0 at http://www.cisco.com/public/sw-center/sw-other.shtml.

Booting the IOS from TFTP

By default, the router will try to boot the IOS from flash memory by checking the configuration register 0x2102, which tells the router where in memory to boot from. The following configuration command explicitly tells the router to look for and boot the IOS from flash memory.

```
Lab-Router-04(config)#boot system flash
```

Cisco IOS software can also be booted across a TCP/IP network using the TFTP protocol. A common scenario is to configure the router to boot from flash memory first. If, for some reason, the IOS image in flash memory is corrupted or erased, the router can be booted from an image residing on a TFTP server. Additional boot system commands, entered in the same order you would like the router to use, will tell the router where to look should it not find the IOS image in flash.

The following configuration commands are used to specify the TFTP boot servers:

```
Lab-Router-04(config)#boot system tftp 10.200.30.41
Lab-Router-04(config)#boot system tftp 10.100.7.233
```

You can also boot a mini-version of the IOS from ROM should you need to get the router up and running under adverse circumstances. This will come in handy if the IOS in flash memory has been erased or corrupted and there is no TFTP server available. Make sure this configuration command is the last boot system statement entered:

```
Lab-Router-04(config)#boot system rom
```

NOTE: Entering the flash, TFTP, and ROM boot system commands into the configuration increases fault tolerance and is critical when supporting a number of routers remotely.

Storing and Transferring Router Configurations and Images

A TFTP server can also be used as a configuration storage and management tool, allowing you to keep several versions of the router configuration and IOS images. This is handy for backing out changes should there be a problem, or for keeping a copy of the current configuration in case the router fails completely and must be quickly replaced.

The **copy** command options are listed here:

Command	Description
copy bootflash	Copy from boot flash
copy flash	Copy from system flash
copy rcp	Copy from an RCP server

Command	Description
copy running-config	Copy from current system configuration
copy startup-config	Copy from startup configuration
copy tftp	Copy from a TFTP server

The following example is the command and resulting dialog for copying the current configuration to a TFTP server:

```
Lab-Router-04#copy running-config tftp
Remote host []? 10.1.1.99
Name of configuration file to write [Lab-Router-04-confg]? y
Write file y on host 10.1.1.99? [confirm]y
Building configuration...
Writing ....
```

By changing the name of the configuration file to write to the TFTP server, you can maintain multiple versions of the configuration for the router. This is advisable when making major configuration changes.

TFTP is not very forgiving when it comes to copying an IOS image or configuration file to a router. If you enter the filename incorrectly, it may wipe out the current IOS image or configuration file, leaving you with a blank space in the router memory. Always verify the filename and make sure you have entered it exactly as it appears on the TFTP server.

The following illustrates the process of copying an IOS image from a router's flash memory to a TFTP server:

```
Lab-Router-04#copy flash tftp rsp-jsv-mz.120-2.XE1.bin.bku
IP address of remote host [255.255.255.255]? 10.1.1.99
Name of file to copy []? rsp-jsv-mz.120-2.XE1.bin.bku
writing rsp-jsv-mz.120-2.XE1.bin.bku!!!!!
Lab-Router-04#
```

NOTE: The file for the IOS image must already exist on the TFTP server. You can use the **touch** command in UNIX, or create an empty file in the TFTP server file directory using Windows Notepad. Once the file exists there, you can then successfully copy the file from the router using TFTP.

The next example illustrates the process of copying an IOS image from a TFTP server to the router's flash memory:

```
Lab-Router-04(config)#copy tftp flash
System flash directory:
File  Length   Name/status
```

```
   1    3218108   c4500-is-mz_112-17.bin
[3218172 bytes used, 13559044 available, 16777216 total]
IP address or name of remote host [255.255.255.255]? 10.1.1.99
Name of file to copy ? rsp-jsv-mz.120-2.XE1.bin
Copy rsp-jsv-mz.120-2.XE1.bin from 10.1.1.99 into
 Flash address space ? [confirm]y
112573bytes available for writing without erasure.
Erase Flash address space before writing? [confirm]y
bank 0...
bank 1...
Loading from 10.1.1.99
!!!!!!!!!!!!!!!!!!!!!!!!!! [OK - 3218108/2112573 bytes]
Verify checksum...Verification successful:
Length = 3218108, checksum = 0x4C1B
```

Although the TFTP process may seem complicated, it is very useful. If you are unfamiliar with TFTP, it's a good idea to run through all of the TFTP procedures a few times on a test router before doing any production work.

Cisco Router Software Loader

If you don't want to run a TFTP server, you can load selected software images via a direct cable connection by using the Cisco Router Software Loader (RSL) application. RSL version 7.0 allows image, configuration, and modem file downloads for the following routers and access servers:

▼ 1000

■ 1600

■ 2500/2600

■ 3600

■ 4500/4700

■ 7200

▲ AS5200/5300

To directly connect to a router, you will need an Ethernet crossover cable, or a straight-through twisted-pair cable for Token Ring. Also, RSL requires Windows 9x to run. The application is available on CD-ROM or online. As of this writing, the URL for downloading RSL is http://www.cisco.com/univercd/cc/td/doc/product/software/ios113ed/fp113rn/cdril2.htm.

Note, however, that since the URL is located under the Cisco IOS version 11.3 documentation, an updated document may become available under the IOS 12.x area at a later date.

CONFIGMAKER 2.4

Configuring devices via the CLI can be challenging, particularly for an occasional user or someone new to router configuration. GUI interfaces have made configuration tasks easier across several platforms. Cisco's contribution to this group is ConfigMaker, an easy-to-use software tool based on Windows 9*x* and NT 4.0 with SP3 (or greater) installed.

ConfigMaker is designed to simplify the most common functions of the existing Cisco IOS CLI. It is intended for resellers and network administrators of small- to medium-sized networks of roughly 20 routers (although ConfigMaker itself does not restrict the number of network devices). Administrators of ConfigMaker should be proficient in LAN fundamentals and basic network design.

NOTE: The ConfigMaker software is free and included in the feature pack CD typically included with your new Cisco hardware. You can also download the latest version of ConfigMaker from the Cisco Web site. As always, URLs are subject to change; but at the time of this writing, ConfigMaker was available at http://www.cisco.com/warp/public/734/configmkr/.

ConfigMaker Functions

Cisco ConfigMaker assists you in configuring a small- to medium-sized network of Cisco routers, switches, hubs, and other devices from a single PC, and at the same time creating an interactive network drawing. The user-friendly interface helps you set up your network without necessarily having in-depth knowledge of Cisco IOS. Figure 5-2 shows Cisco ConfigMaker's main interface.

Before using ConfigMaker, you will need to understand your current network infrastructure and topology, and be able to verify that ConfigMaker supports all of your devices and connections. Check out the section on ConfigMaker's supported devices and protocols to determine whether or not your devices and connections are supported.

ConfigMaker Wizards

Cisco ConfigMaker consists of several wizards. Each wizard simplifies tasks such as identifying devices, configuring devices, connecting devices, and other actions necessary for you to create a network diagram.

When you draw your network, you must first add your devices, using the AutoDetect Wizard or the Device Wizard, and then add connections between the devices, using the Connection Wizard. The AutoDetect Wizard, Device Wizard, and Connection Wizard all assist you in developing a network diagram within ConfigMaker. The Firewall Wizard then assists you in applying a security policy to supported devices. Finally, once you have confirmed the configurations are complete, you can use the Deliver Configuration Wizard to actually deliver the configurations to the appropriate device(s).

AUTODETECT DEVICE WIZARD   There are two ways you can draw your network in ConfigMaker. One way is to add devices and connections manually to the Network Diagram window by using the Device Wizard, which is defined in the next section. The

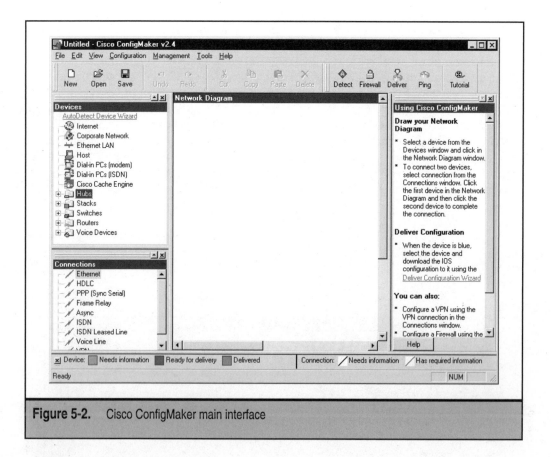

Figure 5-2.   Cisco ConfigMaker main interface

second way is to use the AutoDetect Device Wizard. This wizard automatically identifies a device in two ways:

▼   Over your network based on the IP address or host name

▲   When directly connected to the COM port on your computer

If the device has already been configured, ConfigMaker will prompt for the user and
privilege passwords. After it has been authenticated against these passwords, ConfigMaker
then collects the device's configuration, including the type of NICs, the IOS version, and so
on. Once the information is gathered by the AutoDetect Device Wizard, the icon related to
the model of the device is automatically drawn in the Network Diagram window.

DEVICE WIZARD   The AutoDetect Device Wizard automatically detects a device and
adds it to your Network Diagram window. The Device Wizard allows you to do the reverse. It allows you to set up a device in ConfigMaker and then have the option to down-

load the configurations to a device on your network or attached to your computer's COM port. In order to do this, you must first click a device in the Devices list box on the left-hand side of the main interface. Drag the device to the Network Diagram window. After you release your mouse, the Device Wizard is displayed. With a series of dialog boxes, the Device Wizard steps you through the configuration of the device you selected. Each dialog box asks you to provide configuration parameters, including the definition of passwords, IP addresses, and even the hardware installed on your device (assuming it is modular). Although ConfigMaker collects the data necessary for the basic configuration, many times you may not be prompted for specific parameters you want to have configured. In this scenario, you have the option to append configuration parameters to the actual configuration file. To add additional configuration parameters to the device, right-click the device in the Network Diagram window and select Device Properties. Click the IOS Configuration tab and then select Add/Modify IOS commands. An Add/Modify IOS commands window appears. Type any additional commands in this window and click OK. Figure 5-3 illustrates the Add/Modify IOS commands window.

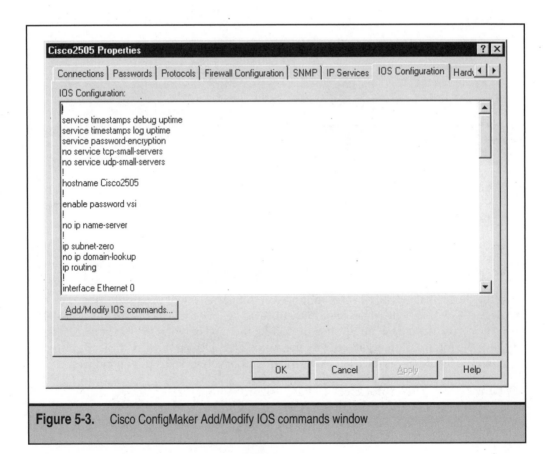

Figure 5-3.   Cisco ConfigMaker Add/Modify IOS commands window

CONNECTION WIZARDS   The next step after you have two or more devices defined in your Network Diagram window is to connect the devices with the proper connection type. Click a connection type from the Connections list box on the left side of the screen. Then click a device in the Network Diagram window (the device selected must support the selected network type on at least one of its interfaces). Click the second device. The Connection Wizard is then displayed. The connection wizard asks you to enter information such as protocols, passwords, and addresses for the connection being made.

FIREWALL WIZARD   The Firewall Wizard helps you define a policy for the router connected to the Internet or corporate network. Click the Firewall button on the Cisco ConfigMaker toolbar or select Configuration | Firewall from the menu bar. The Firewall Wizard is then displayed. A wizard page is displayed for each network or device that can have a security policy. A red checkmark appears next to the name of each network or device when the security policy has been completed. The Firewall Wizard Summary dialog box then reports the security settings you selected. Figure 5-4 is a network diagram illustrating an Internet connection, and Figure 5-5 is an example of the Firewall Wizard Summary dialog box for the security policy applied to this Internet connection.

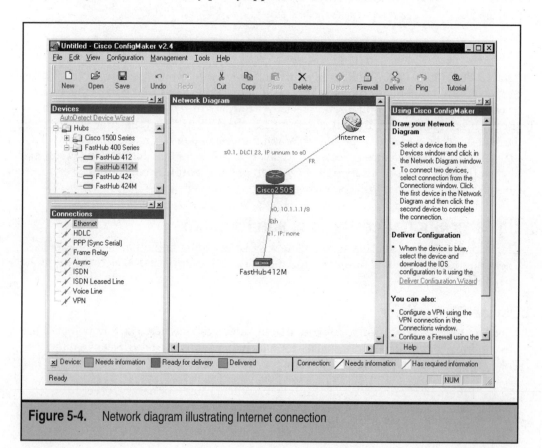

Figure 5-4.   Network diagram illustrating Internet connection

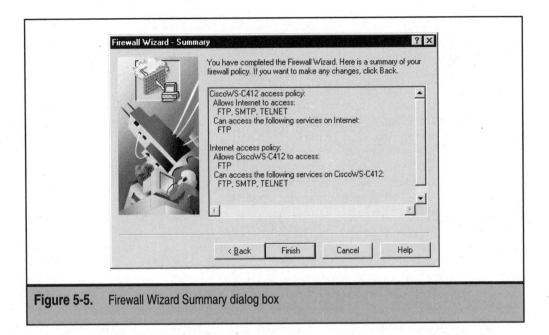

Figure 5-5. Firewall Wizard Summary dialog box

DELIVER CONFIGURATION WIZARD Using the Deliver Configuration Wizard, ConfigMaker can send configuration files through a connection from the PC's COM port to the device's console port or send the configuration files over the network, provided the locations have already been configured with an IP address. Click the device or device(s) to which the configuration will be delivered. The Deliver Configuration dialog box is then displayed. This dialog box lists all the devices selected for delivery in the order that delivery will occur and by their delivery method (through the COM port of your computer or across the network). Click OK, and the wizard will complete the delivery process.

ConfigMaker-Supported Devices and Protocols

Cisco ConfigMaker supports various routers, switches, hubs, and other network devices. The series numbers, model numbers, and modules of the supported devices are outlined in Table 5-2.

Device Connectivity

There are several connection topologies that link devices together. The following is a list of supported connections and scenarios for which they would be used. Keep in mind that Token Ring is not a supported connection type at this time.

▼ **Ethernet** Connects a hub, hub stack, switch, router, or access server to an Ethernet LAN segment. Several access servers or routers can be connected to a single Ethernet LAN segment.

- **HDLC**   Connects an internal router to the Internet or a corporate network router. All routers must be Cisco supported.

- **Async**   Connects two routers; or an asynchronous modem, dial-in line, or POTS (Plain Old Telephone Service) connection can be made between a router and a dial-in PC with a modem. Asynchronous connections can also be used in

Device and Series	Model Numbers	Modules
800 router	801, 802, 803, 804, 805	
1000 router	1003, 1004, 1005	
1600 router	1601, 1602, 1603, 1604, 1605-R	WAN interface cards (WICs): 1 Serial, 1 56/64 Kbps CSU/DSU, 1 ISDN BRI (U, S/T), 1 T1 CSU/DSU, 1 ISDN BRI (S/T) LL
1720 router	1720, 1750	WAN interface cards (WICs): 1 Serial, 2 Serial, 2 async/sync, 1 ISDN BRI (U, S/T), 1 56/64 Kbps 4-wire CSU/DSU, 1 T1/FT1 CSU/DSU Voice interface cards (VICs): 2 Voice FXS, 2 Voice FXO, 2 Voice E/M
2500 router/ access server	2501, 2503, 2505, 2507, 2509, 2509-RJ, 2511, 2511-RJ, 2514, 2516, 2520, 2522, 2524	WAN interface cards (WICs): 5-in-1 serial, 1 ISDN BRI (U, S/T), 1 T1 CSU/DSU, 2-wire 56/64 Kbps CSU/DSU, 4-wire 56/64 Kbps CSU/DSU
2600 router	2610, 2611, 2620, 2621	Network modules: 1 10BT Ethernet, 4 10BT Ethernet, 4 async/sync, 8 async/sync, 16 async, 32 async, 4 ISDN BRI (U, S/T), 8 ISDN BRI (U, S/T), 1 T1 ISDN PRI, 2 T1 ISDN PRI,1 E1 ISDN PRI, 2 E1 ISDN PRI, 1-slot VIC, 2-slot VIC WAN interface cards (WICs): 1 Serial, 2 Serial, 1 ISDN BI (U, S/T), 1 56/64 Kbps CSU/DSU, 1 T1 CSU/DSU, 2 async/sync Voice interface cards (VICs): 2 Voice FXS, 2 Voice FXO, 2 Voice E/M

Table 5-2.   Supported Devices for ConfigMaker

Device and Series	Model Numbers	Modules
3600 router	3620, 3640	Network modules: 1 Ethernet, 4 Ethernet, 1 Ethernet 2 WAN slot, 2 Ethernet 2 WAN slot, 1 Fast Ethernet, Compression module, 4 ISDN BRI (U, S/T), 8 ISDN BRI (U, S/T), 1 10/100 Ethernet 1 T1/ISDN PRI, 1 10/100 Ethernet 2 T1/ISDN PRI, 1 10/100 Ethernet 1 E1/ISDN PRI, 1 10/100 Ethernet 2 E1/ISDN PRI, 1 T1 ISDN PRI, 2 T1 ISDN PRI, 1 E1 ISDN PRI, 2 E1 ISDN PRI, 4 Serial, 4 Async/sync, 8 Async/sync, 16 Async, 32 Async, 1-slot VIC, 2-slot VIC
		WAN interface cards (WICs): 1 Serial, 1 56/64 Kbps CSU/DSU, 1 ISDN BRI (U, S/T) {WIC-1B}, 1 ISDN BRI (U, S/T) {WIC36-1B}, 1 T1 CSU/DSU
		Voice interface cards (VICs): 2 Voice FXS, 2 Voice FXO, 2 Voice E/M
4000 router	4500, 4500M, 4700, 4700M	Network modules: 1 Fast Ethernet, 2 Ethernet, 6 Ethernet, 2 serial, 4 serial, 2 serial 16 async/sync, 4 ISDN BRI (U, S/T), 8 ISDN BRI (U, S/T), 1 T1 ISDN PRI, 1 E1 IDSN PRI
Hubs	Cisco 1500 Series: 1538, 1538M Cisco MicroHub 10/100 stack Cisco FastHub 400 Series: 412, 412M, 424, 424M Cisco FastHub stack	
Switches	Cisco 1548, 1548M, Micro Switch 10/100	
Internet/intranet devices	Cisco Cache Engine	

Table 5-2. Supported Devices for ConfigMaker (continued)

backup configurations. Cisco ConfigMaker automatically sets the modem lines to answer incoming calls when you make an asynchronous connection. It does not support the PAP password authentication method, outgoing calls to PCs and Macintosh computers, or asynchronous connections to the Internet or a corporate network.

- **Frame Relay**   Connects two routers with Frame Relay interfaces. (Remember, a single port on a router can have more than one virtual circuit.) When you order a Frame Relay line from the service provider, you need to specify the destinations for the data. The service provider configures the virtual circuits for each location and assigns a Data-Link Connection Identifier (DLCI) for each end of the virtual connections (the DLCIs are used to configure your Frame Relay connections).

- **PPP Synchronous Connections**   Connects a synchronous serial port on a router or access server to a serial port on an external router or access server. The external router can be a non-Cisco device.

- **ISDN**   Connects a group of PCs with ISDN BRI lines to a router, or connects a router or access server to another router or access server using ISDN BRI. ISDN connections between routers can share a group of BRI or PRI interfaces. That is, a router may call more than one router and receive calls from more than one router. However, ISDN connections to the Internet, a corporate network, or ISDN dial-in PCs cannot share a group of interfaces. Cisco ConfigMaker defaults to using one B channel (of each ISDN BRI line) for a single call. You can change this to use all available B channels in the ISDN BRI line for a single connection. However, your ISDN BRI service provider might bill each B channel as a separate call.

- **Voice Line**   Connects a voice device (such as a phone, fax, or PBX) to a router that has a voice interface card (VIC) installed. Cisco modular routers support FXS, FXO, and E&M VICs interfaces. You must first add a voice slot before adding a VIC to a router in the NIC selection window.

- ▲ **VPN**   Connects a private tunnel between point-to-point sites by allowing you to configure IPSec and Internet Key Exchange (IKE). Using preshared key methods for authentication attempts, you can configure hashing methods, encryption methods, and security association (SA) timeout values.

Connectivity Protocols

Device connections are listed in the bottom-left window of the ConfigMaker main interface. After selecting a connection type there, click in the Network Diagram on the two devices to be connected. Cisco ConfigMaker then prompts you for specific information when a connection type is chosen. Table 5-3 outlines the information required to configure each particular connection type.

Cisco ConfigMaker supports Information Protocol Version 2 (RIPv2) and Enhanced IGRP. All devices in the network must use the same routing protocol. Since EIGRP does not work over ISDN and Asynchronous connections—they will use snapshot routing. In

Type	Ethernet	HDLC	Frame Relay	ISDN	Voice
Port interface/number	✓		✓	✓	✓
IP address	✓	✓	✓	✓	
Network bits/subnet mask	✓	✓	✓	✓	
IPX number	✓				
IPX frame type	✓				
Ethernet port for IP unnumbered		✓	✓	✓	
NAT		✓	✓	✓	
WAN internal IP address		✓	✓	✓	
Global address pool		✓	✓	✓	
Static address of local host, global address, IP service		✓	✓	✓	
Easy IP				✓	
LMI type			✓		
DLCI (source and destination)			✓		
Option to back up			✓		
Group name					
Either ISDN PRI interfaces (x23)				✓	
T1 frame type				✓	
Dial-in PC pool address				✓	
Usernames and passwords of each user				✓	
or ISDN BRI interfaces (x2)				✓	
Services provider identifiers (SPID)				✓	
Corporate network phone number				✓	
Chap password				✓	
Remote router name				✓	

Table 5-3.   Information to Configure for Various Connections

Type	Ethernet	HDLC	Frame Relay	ISDN	Voice
Phone number (all digits)					✓
External mapping to telephone numbers					✓

Table 5-3.   Information to Configure for Various Connections *(continued)*

addition, EIGRP does not work over LAN connections when using native IPX and AppleTalk protocols in ConfigMaker. Instead, LAN connections will use RIP for IPX and AppleTalk protocols even though the rest of the network will use EIGRP.

IP, IPX, and AppleTalk are the routed protocols supported by ConfigMaker—assuming all your network devices support these protocols. The IP protocol is set by default.

Set your routed protocols in the initial ConfigMaker Device or AutoDetect Device Wizards. If you want to change the routed protocol parameters of existing devices, right-click the device and select Device Properties. Then click the Protocols tab (Figure 5-6). By Selecting different routed protocols here and clicking Apply, you apply those parameters only to the devices selected in the Network Diagram window of the main ConfigMaker interface.

When you add routed protocols to network devices, you may need to run the connection wizards again to establish the connections. To start the wizard, double-click the connection between the devices in which protocols were added in the Network Diagram window. After completing the connection wizard, deliver the altered configurations to the devices, using the Deliver Configuration Wizard. ConfigMaker cross-checks the common protocol between locations when connections are enabled, thereby preventing incompatible configurations.

Installing and Configuring ConfigMaker

Installation of ConfigMaker is straightforward and should be uneventful. The application takes up just under 16MB when installed on a clean machine and even less when installed on a machine that already has the necessary shared DLLs and controls. You don't have to reboot after installation.

Machine/Implementation Requirements

Following are the minimum requirements for installing and using Cisco ConfigMaker 2.4:

▼   Pentium-class or 80486-based computer with 16MB of RAM

■   20MB hard disk space

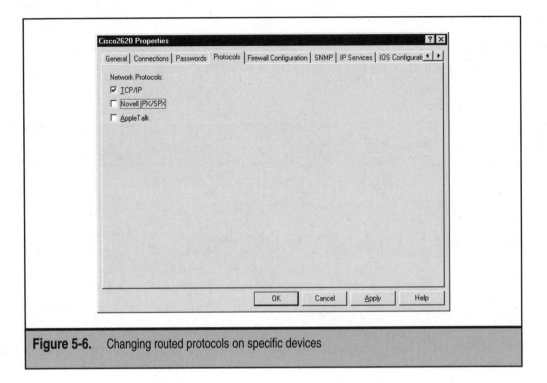

Figure 5-6.   Changing routed protocols on specific devices

- SVGA monitor at 800 × 600 pixel display with at least 256 colors
- CD-ROM drive
- Windows 9x or Windows NT 4.0 SP3
- ▲ Cisco IOS 11.2 or later on your routers

In addition, the following capabilities are recommended:

- ▼ Internet connection on the PC running ConfigMaker
- ▲ Netscape Navigator 3.0 or later *or* Microsoft Internet Explorer 3.0 or later

USING CONFIGMAKER

The ConfigMaker interface has a task list in the right-hand side of the main window, which defines the steps you need to take to configure and draw your network. This task list is helpful when using ConfigMaker for the first time.

Drawing the Network Devices

You can draw your network by adding devices and connections manually to the Network Diagram window, from the Devices and Connection lists on the left side of the main interface. Or you can use the AutoDetect Device Wizard.

To add a device manually, click a device in the Devices list and drag it to the Network Diagram window. The Device Wizard will lead you through a series of dialog boxes, asking you for the configuration parameters. The configuration parameters are dependent on the type of device selected, but they may include things such as user and privilege passwords, routed protocols, and the cards installed (assuming the device is modular). Specific information related to the interface configurations (including IP addresses) is defined when you establish a connection between two devices.

The AutoDetect Device Wizard can identify supported devices by a connection to a device through a console port or through a direct network connection. During device detection, if a Cisco modular router is found, the wizard also identifies the network modules, WAN Interface Cards (WICs), and Voice Interface Cards (VICs). This wizard helps you detect devices on your network and reports important information about them, such as the type of installed NIC and the IOS software version number.

Connecting Devices

Once you've added all supported devices to the Network Diagram, the next step is to establish connections between those devices. To make a connection between two devices on the Network Diagram window, click the connection type in the Connections list at the bottom left of the interface. Then click the two devices you want to connect. The Device Wizard will prompt you with a series of dialog boxes to collect configuration parameters, dependent on the type of connection selected. Included in these parameters is the information necessary to properly configure the interfaces being connected, such as IP addresses. Continue these steps until all supported routers, switches, hubs, and other devices are accurately represented on the Network Diagram window.

The following sections define the different IP addressing options supported by ConfigMaker.

Network Address Translation

ConfigMaker supports Network Address Translation (NAT) on the router with the connection to the Internet or to a corporate network. However, the router must use the Cisco IOS software image 11.2P, or greater than 11.3. By using private IP addresses on your internal network, NAT allows your network to have fewer public IP addresses.

In *simple static* NAT, an internal private IP address is statically mapped to an external public IP address. In *extended static* NAT, an external public IP address is statically mapped to an internal IP address with a specified destination port number. The gateway router translates addresses and routes the traffic appropriately.

Figure 5-7 illustrates simple and extended static NAT.

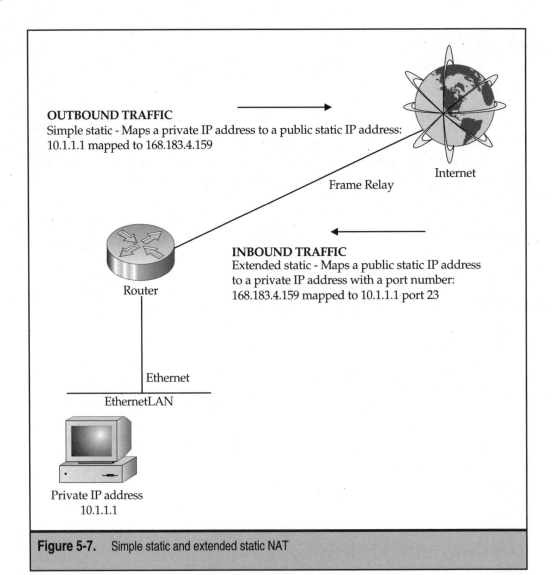

OUTBOUND TRAFFIC
Simple static - Maps a private IP address to a public static IP address:
10.1.1.1 mapped to 168.183.4.159

Internet

Frame Relay

Router

INBOUND TRAFFIC
Extended static - Maps a public static IP address
to a private IP address with a port number:
168.183.4.159 mapped to 10.1.1.1 port 23

Ethernet

EthernetLAN

Private IP address
10.1.1.1

Figure 5-7. Simple static and extended static NAT

If you have an internal device such as a Web server to which an external user may need access, first add the host device and then define a static address translation for it. Double-click the external connection link in the Network Diagram window on the main interface and then click the Network Address Translation tab.

Easy IP

ConfigMaker also supports EasyIP on the gateway router. Easy IP is a feature that allows a router to automatically receive its WAN interface–registered IP address. The ability to negotiate a WAN IP address works only for PPP, ISDN, or ISDN leased-line connections. The WAN interface–registered IP address is then used to translate many IP addresses to one IP address. Figure 5-8 illustrates Easy IP.

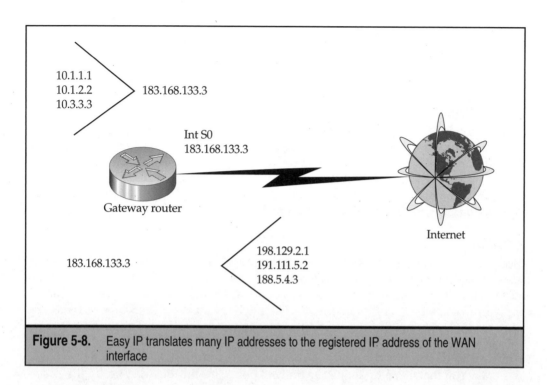

10.1.1.1
10.1.2.2   183.168.133.3
10.3.3.3

Int S0
183.168.133.3

Gateway router

Internet

183.168.133.3

198.129.2.1
191.111.5.2
188.5.4.3

Figure 5-8.   Easy IP translates many IP addresses to the registered IP address of the WAN interface

Easy IP (Phase I) is supported in IOS software release 11.3. Routers running this IOS image essentially have Port Address Translation (PAT) and the ability to configure a single WAN IP address. PAT dynamically maps hosts to private addresses by keeping track of the port number used in the session.

Easy IP (Phase II) is supported in IOS software release 12.01. Routers running this IOS image have all the features of Easy IP Phase I, plus full support for DHCP. Full support of DHCP extends the ability to dynamically assign private addresses to PCs and other hosts connected to the network. It also provides DHCP server functionality that allows a configured router to act as the DHCP server for the network.

The use of Easy IP on your network does not prohibit the use of NAT; however, Easy IP and NAT can be configured on only the gateway router and on only one router in the network. (NAT and PAT are covered in more detail in Chapter 14.)

IP Unnumbered

When configuring the interface for a PPP, HDLC, Frame Rely, ISDN BRI, or asynchronous modem connection, ConfigMaker provides the option of choosing IP Unnumbered. By selecting IP unnumbered, you are choosing that the specified Ethernet IP address be applied to additional interfaces on the router. IP unnumbered allows you to save a registered IP address.

Security

After defining your devices and connections, you can configure a VPN using the VPN connection in the Connections window, or configure a firewall using the Firewall Wizard.

VPN Connections

In order to create a VPN connection, you must have created two devices with connections to the Internet. Once you have done that, click VPN from the Connections window, click the first router, and then click the second router (you do not have to click the Internet connection). The VPN Wizard will then lead you through a series of dialog boxes, requesting configuration parameters that are dependent on the type of devices and also providing information, such as the definition of the Pre-Shared key.

Firewall

Cisco ConfigMaker also provides you with the option of applying different levels of firewall security to the router connected to the Internet or corporate network, or any *one* router if there is no Internet or corporate network. Click the router in which you want to apply firewall security and then double-click the Firewall Wizard, located in the Using Cisco ConfigMaker window on the right side of the main interface. The Firewall Wizard will then prompt you to verify whether or not the Cisco IOS Firewall Feature Set is installed on the device. If it is not installed on the device, ConfigMaker will configure access lists only. You then need to define the firewall policy for this device. Specify the IP services permitted or denied for the client on the internal side of the router accessing the Internet. Similarly, you then define the IP services permitted or denied for the Internet on the external side of the router accessing an internal device. The Firewall Wizard will then provide a summary of the policy you have defined for both directions. A lock will appear on the router in the Network Diagram window to illustrate that security has been applied to that device.

There are obvious benefits to using the Cisco IOS Firewall feature set versus access lists. The Cisco IOS Firewall feature set provides integrated enhanced security capabilities such as Context-Based Access Control (CBAC), Java applet filtering, denial-of-service detection and prevention, and audit trail and real-time alert logging.

Delivering Configurations from ConfigMaker

Configurations can be delivered through the console port, or through a LAN (but only if your network is running IP and the device you are delivering the configurations to has previously been configured and has an IP address). During the configuration of an established network, Cisco ConfigMaker creates an automatic backup of existing configurations and then downloads the new configuration files.

Click the device or devices to receive new configuration files upon delivery (for multiple configuration files, hold down the CTRL key while clicking the devices). Click Deliver Configuration Wizard in the Using Cisco ConfigMaker window on the right side of the main interface. When you're delivering more than one configuration, ConfigMaker displays the Deliver Configuration - Preview dialog box. This dialog box lists all the devices selected for delivery in the order that delivery will occur. It also lets you determine whether to deliver the configuration to the device via the COM port of the computer (the default) or over your LAN.

Configuring SNMP Parameters

ConfigMaker performs network management by utilizing basic SNMP parameters, including community strings, trap managers, and general device information. You can set SNMP configuration specifically for a selected device, or you can apply default configurations to all devices in the network. To access the configuration parameters, right-click the selected device and choose Device Properties. Then click the SNMP tab, as shown in Figure 5-9.

ConfigMaker supports SNMP trap managers. This feature allows configuration of the destination IP address's trap information, and a community string used to authenticate messages sent between a management station and a router containing an SNMP agent.

NETSYS BASELINER

Cisco's NetSys Baseliner is a modeling tool that allows network administrators to design and analyze network configurations prior to implementation. This application assists the

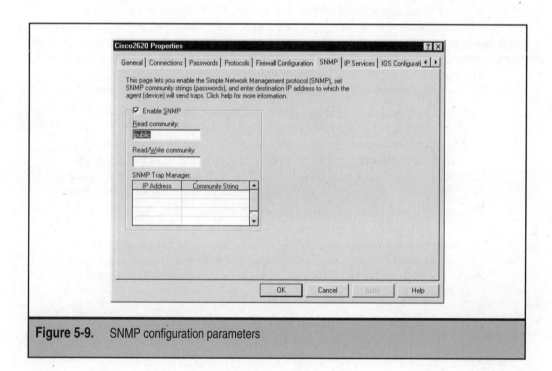

Figure 5-9. SNMP configuration parameters

network administrator by proactively monitoring configuration changes and providing graphical views based on selected topologies.

Product Overview

NetSys Baseliner audits the actual configuration files of all included routers, identifying configuration conflicts and reporting on their nature and location. According to Cisco, there are more than 100 common yet hard-to-locate configuration problems that NetSys Baseliner can identify.

NOTE: Keep in mind that not all identified "problems" necessarily need to be corrected. Use NetSys Baseliner to generate a list of potential problems, evaluate them, and then make *proper* configuration adjustments.

Features of NetSys Baseliner

NetSys Baseliner offers a full view of your network configuration, along with many powerful analysis and reporting features.

▼   **Maintenance of Router Integrity**   NetSys Baseliner compares the configuration files of all submitted routers. It validates their consistency as a whole, and evaluates individual configuration files to identify problems. Misconfigurations are explained, including identification of the device and/or interface where they occur. This helps to reduce time-consuming fault isolation and repair. Not all misconfiguration reports merit reconfiguration of the devices. For example, NetSys Baseliner has a tendency to bark at static routes. Static routes are required, however, when you aren't extending your routing protocol to a certain subnet (possibly your Internet connection).

■   **Offline Configuration Testing**   NetSys Baseliner helps you modify configuration files and run them through the evaluation process prior to committing them to the live network. This helps reduce costly downtime. Configurations that may work smoothly in the model won't necessarily run without incident in a live network. You'll want to consider hubs, switches, printers, and workstations in your configuration modifications and testing.

■   **Graphs**   NetSys Baseliner will graphically display customized router configurations and multiple protocols for each supported device (the various topology views are discussed in the section "Using NetSys Baseliner"). The graphs display both physical and logical connections between routers and protocols. Network administrators can view both physical and logical connections in either a flat or separated view.

▲   **Reports**   NetSys Baseliner generates reports containing detailed configuration problems, configuration changes, and historical router configuration files. You can customize and filter this information as needed.

Supported Devices

Today's network designs are becoming extremely complicated. Companies are deploying many types of network devices above and beyond routers and basic hubs. In addition, switch technology is becoming very aggressive. Even basic network devices have unique configurations that may add to network management complications. Unfortunately, NetSys Baseliner only supports Cisco router configurations. (It also recognizes Bay routers.)

Supported Protocols and Topologies

The NetSys Baseliner software supports the following protocols and topologies:

▼   **LAN topologies**   ATM (Asynchronous Transfer Mode), Ethernet, Fast Ethernet, FDDI (Fiber Distributed Data Interface), and Token Ring

■   **WAN connectivity**   BRI (Basic Rate Interface), Channelized T1, Frame Relay, HSSI (High-Speed Serial Interface), IP Unnumbered, Serial, SMDS (Switched Multimegabit Data Service), X.25, Asynchronous, Dialer, ATM, and POTS (Plain Old Telephone Service)

■   **Network protocols**   (IP) Internet Protocol, IPX (Internet Packet Exchange), SAP (IPX Service Advertisement Protocol), and SNA (Systems Network Architecture)

▲   **Routing protocols**   RIP (Routing Information Protocol), IGRP (Interior Gateway Routing Protocol, EIGRP (Extended Interior Gateway Routing Protocol), OSPF (Open Shortest Path First), BGP (Border Gateway Protocol), IS-IS (Intermediate System to Intermediate System), IPX-RIP (Internet Package Exchange-Routing Information Protocol), RSRB (Remote Source-Route Bridging), STUN (Serial Tunneling), and DLSw+ (Data Link Switching Plus)—Cisco's representation of DLSw standard for SNA and NETBIOS traffic forwarding

Target Market and Price Structure

NetSys Baseliner is a tool used for network administrators and/or engineers who are responsible for router configurations.

The list price of the Windows NT NetSys Baseliner 4.0 with unlimited router configurations (BASE-4.0-UNL-NT) is $6,995. The URL for NetSys Baseliner is www.cisco.com/warp/public/734/baseliner.

Installation of NetSys Baseliner

NetSys Baseliner is easy to install (assuming you have the correct licensing), and it uses moderate machine resources.

Following are the minimum system requirements:

▼ Windows NT Workstation (or Server)

■ 64MB RAM

■ 200MB free disk space

■ CD-ROM drive

■ Video display set to show at least 32,768 colors

■ Netscape Navigator 3.0 or later/Explorer 4.0 or later

▲ Web server software (if reports will be published on the internet via HTTP)

Prior to installation, have the following information at hand:

▼ **Host ID**   If the hard drive of the host machine is partitioned, make sure you use the host ID of the C drive—regardless of the drive on which you install NetSys Baseliner.

■ **Product serial number**   Use the product serial number that is provided during setup.

▲ **License key**   A 24-digit hexadecimal number. You can obtain the license key by calling Cisco Tech Support at 1-800-553-2447. Otherwise, you can fill out the registration form during the installation process (this will take longer, however, because you have to wait for them to get your request and respond).

Setup will prompt you to create your *baseline*, which is the term used to define the network model based on the configuration files that have been pulled and evaluated. Prior to installation, you should have copied all applicable router configuration files into a single directory to which the NetSys Baseliner workstation has access. During installation, you can use all the configuration files or only specific files. The router configuration files are then copied to the NetSys Baseliner subdirectory identified by your baseline name. Additional configuration files can be evaluated through the Collect Cisco Router Configuration option, discussed later in the section "Using NetSys Baseliner."

When you first launch NetSys Baseliner by clicking its icon, the main window will be empty except for the menu bar and status line. If your license is invalid (for example, if you mistyped your application key), you'll be notified when the application starts, and you'll have the opportunity to reenter the licensing values without having to re-install the application.

USING NETSYS BASELINER

NetSys Baseliner does not require extensive configuration prior to use. The majority of its options involve the generation of view-related topology graphs and reports.

> **WARNING:**   Access to the NetSys Baseliner application provides the key to access a network's configurations and security controls. Therefore, NetSys Baseliner access should be monitored, controlled, and limited.

Configuring NetSys Baseliner

You need to complete the following three tasks to configure NetSys Baseliner. These tasks are further defined in the sections that follow.

1. Create the baseline that your network model will represent.
2. Define the routers on which configuration files will be updated/replaced, and the parameters for those routers.
3. Following modifications to your router configuration, collect the configurations and update your baseline.

Creating a Baseline

The first task after launching NetSys Baseliner is to create a baseline. This model is developed based on the router configuration files.

When you create a new baseline, NetSys Baseliner copies the router configuration files to a subdirectory in the NetSys Baseliner data directory. *Do not edit this file.* Instead, use NetSys Baseliner to make needed changes to the configuration files. This allows you to experiment on your model network without affecting production.

To create a new baseline, select File | New Baseline to open the Create a Baseline Wizard. Identify the location of your configuration files, as illustrated in Figure 5-10. You have the option to use all the configuration files or only the ones you select. Click the Next button, and a progress window will be displayed while the baseline is being created.

Setting Up Router Access

The NetSys Baseliner network model is based on the routers and their configurations in your baseline. These elements are updated by the Collect Cisco Configuration Wizard, which pulls configurations from the list of routers in the database. You use the Setup Router Access Wizard to add, edit, or deletes router configurations from the database. Select Tools | Set Up Router Access to launch this wizard. You then select existing routers or modify/add additional routers for which to collect configurations. Parameters must then be defined for all routers whose configurations are being collected. See Figure 5-11.

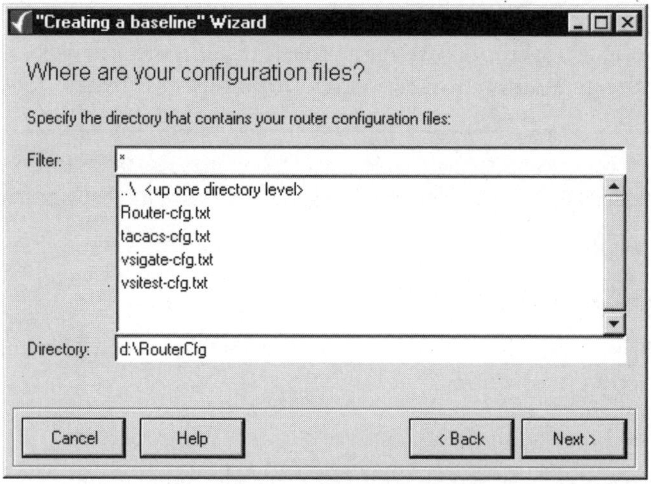

Figure 5-10. Specifying the location of configuration files in the Creating a Baseline Wizard

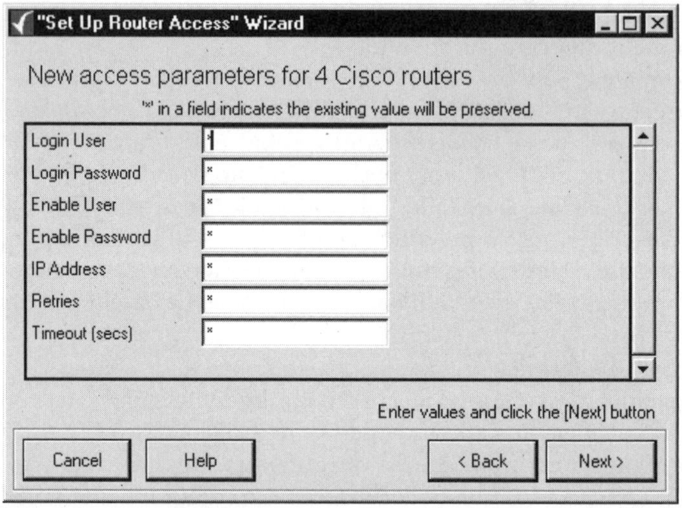

Figure 5-11. Use the Set Up Router Access Wizard to establish router parameters

The IP Address parameter enables you to define an IP address to obtain a configuration file through the router's IP address (just in case the domain name fails). The configuration files are obtained through a TCP/IP Telnet session using the **write term** command. It will initially find the router based on the domain name. If the domain name cannot be resolved, it will then find the router based on the IP address.

The Set Up Router Access Wizard states that parameters can be generic for all routers or unique to each router. If you want to use the IP address as a backup for domain name failure, this statement is not true. You have to enter the unique IP addresses for each router. When modifying the parameters of an existing router, use * to maintain existing parameters.

NetSys Baseliner lacks application security; it displays cleartext when you type in the passwords (Login and Enable) for router access. Whenever the Set Up Router Access Wizard is launched, these parameters can be viewed, which ultimately could allow access to your router configuration files. It is therefore important to secure and limit access to the NetSys Baseliner application.

Collecting Cisco Configuration

The Collect Cisco Configuration Wizard does a Telnet **write term** to the selected routers to collect actual configuration files. This wizard uses domain names and the passwords defined in the router access parameters. If the domain names fail, the routers' IP addresses (also defined in the parameters) are used. Configuration files can either be written directly to your baseline or saved to a specified directory for later use (depending on your intentions).

After execution of the Collect Cisco Configuration Wizard, you can verify that no errors occurred during the collection. If any errors occurred, they would be identified by selecting View | Collection Logs, as shown in Figure 5-12. If there was a problem with the collection, you can double-click the entry in the Status column to obtain a more detailed report.

NetSys Baseliner Views

After a baseline has been created, the main window of NetSys Baseliner looks like Figure 5-13, with a navigation panel on the left and a data display panel on the right.

The navigation panel allows you to select various views of the network and its data. You can select a view by clicking one of the three tabs (Reports, Topology, and Elements) at the top of the navigation panel, or by clicking View in the menu bar and selecting a view.

Topology View

The topology view is a graphical display of how all of the network's devices are linked together. You can limit the topology display to only those parts of your network that are of interest (for example, all devices supporting a particular protocol). To open a topology view, choose View | Topology View and double-click the view under the data tree.

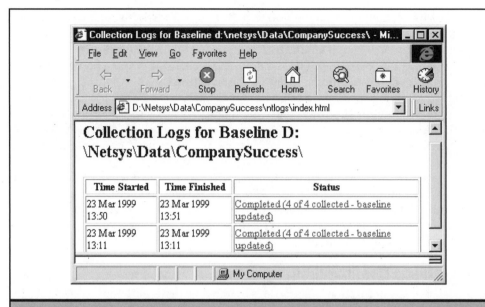

Figure 5-12. Use the View | Collection Logs display to check the status of collected configurations

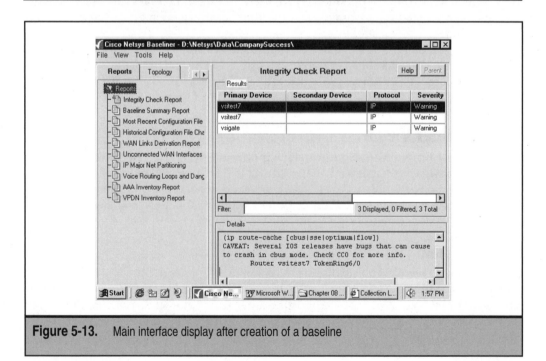

Figure 5-13. Main interface display after creation of a baseline

NetSys Baseliner provides the following topology views:

Topology View	Description
Campus	Displays any of the network's devices grouped into areas as identified by WAN connections in the configuration files.
Flat	Displays any of the network's devices without regard to location. Caution: This view takes a long time to generate—especially for large networks.
RSRB	Shows only those network element rings based on SRB, RSRB, Token Ring, or DLSW protocols.
OSPF	Shows all routers that support OSPF or IGP, or are grouped into campuses.
OSPF-Areas	Similar to OSPF view, but without regard to autonomous system number.
AppleTalk	Shows routers supporting the AppleTalk protocol, grouped into campuses according to their primary zones.
DECnet	Shows all DECnet devices.
BGP	Displays devices that support BGP.
IS-IS	Displays devices that support the IS-IS protocol.
By-Name	Groups routers into campuses by assigning a campus name to a group of routers.
Voice Routing Loops and Dangling Routes	Provides a list of routing loops and dangling routes that carry voice data.
VPND	Displays all devices that support the VPDN protocol.

Figure 5-14 shows a campus topology view.

Reports View

Reports can be viewed in the NetSys Baseliner main window, or you can view HTML versions in a Web browser. Reports are generated based on the current contents of the configuration files in your baseline. (Remember—if you modify those configuration files, you need to reopen your baseline in order to refresh the baseline configuration and update the data displayed by the reports.)

Reports can be saved in three different formats:

▼ CSV format can be imported into a spreadsheet.

■ ASCII format can be imported into a text editor or word processor, or sent as e-mail.

▲ HTML format can be transported to a remote location in an easily printed format.

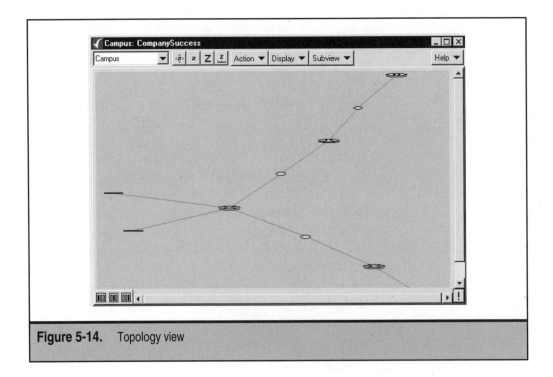

Figure 5-14. Topology view

NetSys Baseliner offers the following reports:

Report Format	Description
Integrity Checks	Identifies syntactical and semantic errors found in router configuration files.
Baseline Summary	Lists eight subsidiary reports that summarize your baseline.
Most Recent Configuration File Changes	Displays the results of a comparison of the most current and most recent previous versions of the baseline configuration files.
Historical Configuration File Changes	Displays changes in the configuration files since the baseline was created.
WAN Links Derivation	Provides information about how the NetSys Baseliner software identified the WAN connections.
Unconnected WAN Interfaces	Provides a list of all dangling interfaces (an interface is left dangling if there is no matching IP address associated with any other router on the network).

Report Format	Description
IP Major Net Partitioning	Provides a list of the network's major IP networks and their IP addresses.
Voice Routing Loops and Dangling Routes	Identifies routing loops and dangling routes in networks that transport voice traffic.
AAA Inventory	Identifies all Authentication, Authorization, and Accounting servers connected to the routers and the protocols used.
VPDN Inventory	Provides information about the source router, domain name, home gateway, and tunnel used to transmit data over a VPDN.

Elements View

This view provides access to the baseline copy of the configuration files for the network devices. You can then access a configuration file by right-clicking the device you wish to view. Figure 5-15 shows a device configuration file displayed in Notepad.

By modifying this element version file, you can experiment and observe the effects of your changes without risk to your production network. If you then want to incorporate

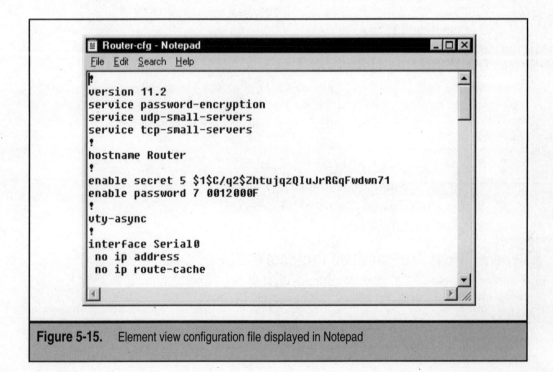

Figure 5-15.   Element view configuration file displayed in Notepad

your changes into the network, you'll need to copy the baseline version of the configuration file onto your network, or log in to the router itself and perform the configuration changes.

> **TIP:**   The typically continual evolution of configuration files is a good reason to automate the process of collecting and reporting on configurations. By using a batch processing program, you can create batch files that will automatically update the baseline and generate new reports. Two examples of such batch processors are Wilson Window Ware's WinBatch (http://www.windoware.com) and Unisyn Software's AutoMate (http://www.unisyn.com).

IP INTERNETWORKING ON WINDOWS NETWORKS

A crucial component in building networks with Windows is to have the Windows workstations and servers properly configured to use the network infrastructure. This includes the basic TCP/IP setup and extends to having servers and workstations perform functions typically left to dedicated routers. Although it is preferable to have dedicated routers perform the routing in most networks, sometimes a Windows NT or Windows 2000 workstation or server may need to route traffic. Common situations include those in which a server is acting as a remote access point of entry into the network, or in which a server is acting as a termination point for PPTP or IPSec tunnels. This section describes how to configure Windows NT or Windows 2000 systems to use TCP/IP, and covers NT and 2000 internal routing and RRAS.

IP Setup for Windows Networks

When you first install Windows, you are asked to provide specific information about the Network Interface Card (NIC) and the workstation if you select to install networking and the TCP/IP protocol. You might have to re-install TCP/IP networking for the following reasons:

▼   You are adding TCP/IP to the workstation.

■   You need to re-install Windows.

■   Your machine has moved to a new location.

▲   You have added a new NIC.

Dynamic Host Configuration Protocol (DHCP)

If you do re-install TCP/IP networking, you first need to determine if you use the Dynamic Host Configuration Protocol (DHCP) on your local network, or if each system has a statically defined IP address. DHCP is a service that listens to workstations as they boot up. If a NIC requires an IP address, the DHCP responds and keeps track of the numbers it doles out. More information about DHCP is included in Chapter 11.

If you find that you do use DHCP, then you're in luck. All you need to do is check the appropriate button in the TCP/IP configuration window, depending on your version of Windows:

▼ For Windows NT, select "Obtain an IP address from a DHCP server."

▲ For Windows 2000, select "Obtain an IP address automatically."

If you don't use DHCP, you'll have to obtain several pieces of information before continuing:

▼ The IP address of the workstation (for example, 10.1.1.15)

■ The subnet mask for your network (for example, 255.255.255.0)

▲ The IP address of the default gateway (for example, 10.1.1.1)

For additional functionality, you should also have the following:

▼ The IP address of at least one DNS server so DNS name resolution is possible

■ The IP address of at least one WINS server so WINS name resolution is possible

▲ The default IP host name and domain name (for example, www and microsoft.com) to simplify name lookup when accessing hosts in the same domain

Armed with this data, you can configure any Windows system. How and where you enter this information will depend on the type of Windows system you are configuring.

TCP/IP for Windows NT

Access the TCP/IP Protocol configuration window by selecting the Network icon in the Control Panel. Open the Protocols tab and make sure TCP/IP is listed. If it isn't, add it using the Add button. Also, you'll want to be sure you installed a NIC before configuring TCP/IP.

When all is in order, click TCP/IP in the Protocols tab and select the Configure button. Figure 5-16 illustrates the main TCP/IP configuration window.

Add your IP information in the appropriate boxes. Click the DNS and WINS Address tabs and set those up, as well, if you have that information. The Routing tab is used only for systems with more than one NIC. The Advanced button lets you restrict what sort of IP traffic is allowed to pass in or out of this NIC. This is mostly used for systems on the Internet. When you have entered all your TCP/IP properties, click OK. Some changes will be made to Windows networking, and you'll be prompted to reboot for the changes to take effect.

After rebooting, your NIC should be functional. If it isn't, first check the Event Log (choose Settings | Control Panel | Event Viewer) to see if there were services or drivers that failed to load properly.

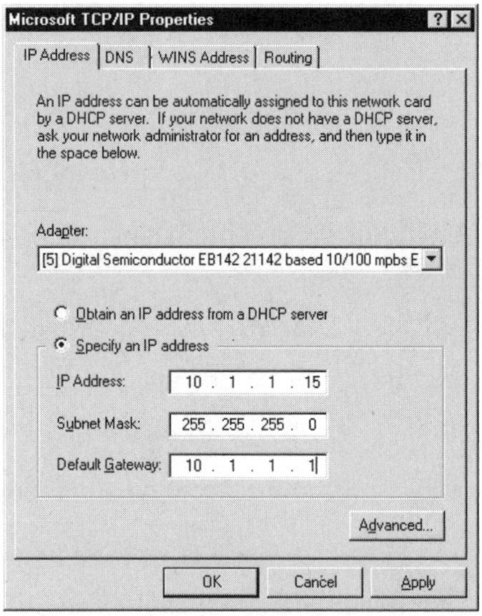

Figure 5-16.   Windows NT TCP/IP configuration window

TCP/IP for Windows 2000

Configuring TCP/IP in Windows 2000 is straightforward, although the location of the main TCP/IP configuration window is slightly hidden. To find it, choose Start | Settings | Network, and select Dial-up Connections. You can also click the Network and Dial-up Connections icon in the Control Panel, or even right-click My Network Places on the desktop and select Properties. All three paths lead you to the Network and Dial-up Connections window, the main networking configuration window.

From the Network and Dial-up Connections window, click the Local Area Connections icon. This displays a small window that displays the current statistics about your NIC. You'll see numbers on how long it has been operational, how many packets have been transferred, and the speed at which it is operating.

To actually configure the NIC, click the Properties button. This calls up the General Networking Properties window, where Internet Protocol (TCP/IP) should be listed. If it isn't, add it by clicking the Install button. To configure TCP/IP, click to highlight Internet Protocol (TCP/IP), and then click the Properties button. This brings up the actual configuration window, shown in Figure 5-17.

If you aren't using DHCP, enter your IP address here. Check the "Obtain DNS server address automatically" option only if your DHCP server also provides this information to its clients (most do). To access the WINS, advanced DNS, and security settings, click

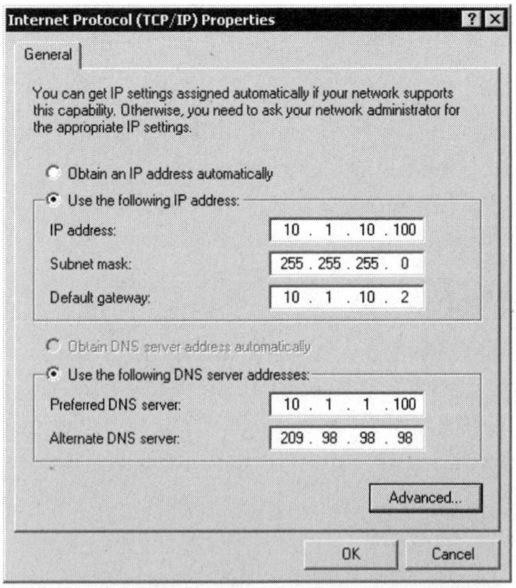

Figure 5-17. Windows 2000 TCP/IP configuration window

the Advanced button. When you have finished with these options, click OK until you've closed the General Networking Properties menu.

Managing the Routing Tables

Routing tables are at the heart of a router's ability to efficiently transfer packets from one point in the network to the packets' destinations. Routers need these tables to be on hand and accurate, for use in quickly identifying destination networks and making routing decisions.

Here is how routers use route tables: When a router receives a packet, the router looks in its routing table for the destination subnet for that packet. Then the router passes the packet to the interface with the lowest cost route to reach the next router in the path. When the next router receives the packet, it repeats this process and forwards the packet on to the next hop. This process continues until the packet reaches its final destination.

Because even single-homed machines (with one network address) need to make routing decisions, all NT systems with at least one NIC have a simple routing table created by default (provided the TCP/IP protocol stack has been installed). Information in a routing table includes the following:

▼ All the reachable subnets in the network

■ The routing cost to reach each subnet

■ The address of the next router in the destination path

▲ The router interface to which packets are forwarded to reach that next destination.

The route table also lists any *static routes* that have been entered manually. Note that although static routes will work for smaller networks, it would become an organizational nightmare to maintain static routes for a larger network, as you will see. This is why routing protocols such as RIP and IGRP are so important.

Viewing the Routing Table

All static routing functions are accomplished using the **route.exe** command-line utility. For a full list of **route** command arguments, type **route /?** at the command prompt.

To print a listing of a route table, type **route print** at the command prompt. You'll get a listing similar to the one in Figure 5-18. Here are descriptions of the information in this report:

▼ **Network Destination** Destination address for routed packets.

■ **Netmask** The portion of the network address that must match the destination address in order to use that route. For instance, a mask of 255 (all 1's) means that the octet in the destination address (that is to be routed) must match exactly that of the network address.

■ **Gateway** Location where the packets need to be sent so they are routed. This is usually the address of the default gateway.

■ **Interface** Points to the IP address of the NIC that will be used to get to the gateway. It may be the same as the gateway location, or a NIC address, or 127.0.0.1, which is the software loopback address.

▲ **Metric** The number of hops to reach the destination address. All local destinations are one hop away. If you statically define a route, a larger metric may apply if the destination subnet is more than one hop away.

Adding Static Routes

The network destination 0.0.0.0 is the *default route,* which applies for all destinations not included in the route table. So that your computer knows how to reach subnets (and the computers on those subnets) that are not directly connected or not reached via the default route, you include static routes in the routing table.

Static routes solve the problem illustrated in Figure 5-19. In this network, there are three subnets: 10.1.1.0, 10.1.10.0, and 10.1.11.0. Your computer is sitting on the 10.1.1.0 network and has the IP address of 10.1.1.15. The default route is defined as the local address for your firewall (10.1.1.100, in this example). This means all requests for computers other than those in 10.1.1.0 will be sent out the firewall.

You want to reach the computer that is sitting on the 10.1.11.0 network and has the IP address of 10.1.11.15. However, your computer is only aware of the subnet that is directly

```
 ■ Prompt                                                        _ □ ✕
<C> Copyright 1985-1996 Microsoft Corp.

C:\>route print
==================================================================
Interface List
0x1 ......................... MS TCP Loopback interface
0x2 ...00 00 a0 00 38 00 ...... DEC DC21143 PCI Fast Ethernet Adapter
0x3 ...00 00 00 00 00 00 ...... NdisWan Adapter
==================================================================
==================================================================
Active Routes:
Network Destination        Netmask          Gateway       Interface  Metric
          0.0.0.0          0.0.0.0          10.1.1.1      10.1.1.15    1
         10.1.1.0    255.255.255.0         10.1.1.15      10.1.1.15    1
        10.1.1.15  255.255.255.255        127.0.0.1       127.0.0.1    1
        10.1.10.0    255.255.255.0          10.1.1.1      10.1.1.15    1
        10.1.11.0    255.255.255.0          10.1.1.1      10.1.1.15    1
        10.1.12.0    255.255.255.0          10.1.1.1      10.1.1.15    1
   10.255.255.255  255.255.255.255         10.1.1.15      10.1.1.15    1
        127.0.0.0        255.0.0.0        127.0.0.1       127.0.0.1    1
        224.0.0.0        224.0.0.0         10.1.1.15      10.1.1.15    1
  255.255.255.255  255.255.255.255         10.1.1.15      10.1.1.15    1
==================================================================

C:\>
```

Figure 5-18.   A route table in a Windows network

connected (10.1.1.0) unless you are running a routing protocol (see Chapter 3). So if you try to reach 10.1.11.15, the request will be sent out the firewall and die shortly thereafter. Adding a static route solves this problem.

Adding a static route to the routing table is accomplished using the **route** command with the **add** argument. First you list the destination, and then the netmask (optional), followed by the gateway and the metric (also optional). To add a route for the example above, we would type the following command at the command prompt:

```
route add 10.1.13.0 Mask 255.255.255.0 10.1.1.1 Metric 3
```

This tells the table to route all traffic destined for the 10.1.13.0 subnetwork through 10.1.1.1 rather than the default route.

You can see from this "simple" example that static routes can become prohibitively complex in larger networks. In those environments, you will certainly use dynamic routing protocols such as EIGRP, RIP, and OSPF. Nonetheless, static routes are useful for exceptional situations, such as a small site where you don't want to dedicate a router or to involve the NT server with dynamic routing protocols.

In most cases, there is a single default route and static routes usually don't enter the picture. However, in the preceding example, users of the 10.1.1.0 network have two potential paths to leave the local network. This is where RRAS enters the picture.

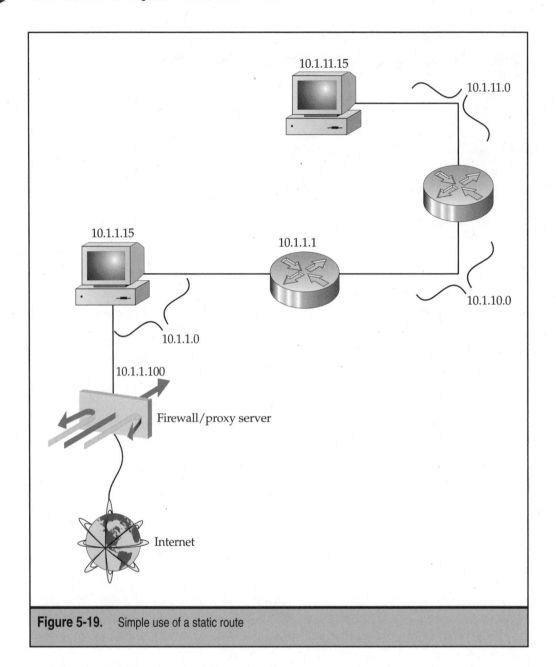

Figure 5-19. Simple use of a static route

Microsoft's RRAS

When a Windows NT system has more than one network connection as a router, you must install and run Microsoft's Routing and Remote Access Service (RRAS). The RRAS software (formerly code-named "Steelhead") provides an extensible platform for multiprotocol routing and internetworking. Businesses can use RRAS for LAN-to-LAN routing, and for remote site connectivity over WANs or over the Internet via VPN connections. Although you should seriously consider using dedicated routers for all of your network routing requirements, RRAS may help you in a pinch or where budgetary constraints apply (although the savings will not be great). Nonetheless, RRAS offers some useful features, such as Point-to-Point Tunneling for virtual private networks, demand-dial routing, Microsoft Point-to-Point Compression (MPPC), IP and IPX packet filtering, and PPP Multilink Channel Aggregation.

RRAS runs only on Windows Server; it replaces the older RAS and Multi Protocol Router (MPR) add-on. RRAS is available now from Microsoft as a free download, at http://www.microsoft.com/ntserver/nts/downloads/winfeatures/rras/rrasdown.asp. You will also find excellent documentation there about the use and configuration of RRAS.

RRAS Features

RRAS has the following advantages:

▼ Integrated with the operating system

■ Provides a unified routing/remote access service solution

■ Not as difficult to use and configure as traditional routers

■ Works with most standard PCs and NICs

▲ Has APIs so that developers can create custom routing solutions

RRAS features include the following:

▼ Network protocols, including IP and IPX

■ Routing protocols, including RIP (Routing Information Protocol), SAP (Service Advertising Protocol), and Open Shortest Path First (OSPF)

■ Remote administration using graphical user interface

■ Command line interface with scripting

■ Demand-dial routing to connect remote LANs

■ PPTP server-to-server for secure virtual private networks

■ Remote Authentication Dial-In User Service (RADIUS) client support

▲ Packet filtering for security and performance

NOTE: RRAS works with Microsoft's Proxy Server 2.0 if you have applied Service Pack 4 or higher.

Perhaps the greatest attraction of RRAS is that it is integrated within NT and intimately tied to other Windows components, such as the user database and Proxy Server. Additionally, RRAS is much easier to configure and implement compared with standalone routers.

ROUTING PROTOCOLS   RRAS includes a robust set of routing protocols. It supports RIP versions 1 and 2 for IP, OSPF for IP, IPX RIP, IPX SAP, and DHCP. In addition, RRAS contains APIs to enable third-party vendors to make other routing protocols work with the new service. For example, Border Gateway Protocol (BGP), Interior Gateway Routing Protocol (IGRP), and NetWare Link Services Protocol (NLSP) can be plugged in. This added functionality moves NT's routing capabilities to a level where they can play a role in the internetwork, but the stability and scalability of RRAS in the enterprise network has yet to be proven.

PACKET FILTERING   Packet filtering is another feature that has been added to RRAS. For IP routing, RRAS supports packet filtering based on TCP port, UDP port, IP protocol ID, ICMP type, ICMP code, source address, and destination address. For IPX packet filtering, RRAS supports source address, source node, source socket, destination address, destination node, destination socket, and packet type. This greatly enhances the network administrator's ability to control network traffic, for security reasons as well as increased network performance.

RADIUS   One of the latest features added to RRAS is a security enhancement: support of Remote Authentication Dial-In User Service (RADIUS). RADIUS is a distributed security solution for use in enterprise and public-carrier networks. RRAS also has added authentication and encryption support.

Installing RRAS on Windows NT 4.0

When you install RRAS in NT 4.0, it replaces any existing RAS software. Before installation of RRAS, you should have already incorporated the NT Service Pack 4 or later. Next, you must delete any of the following services that are installed on your NT Server, because RRAS replaces them:

▼   RAS

■   RRAS (beta 1)

■   RIP for Internet Protocol

■   RIP for NwLink IPX/SPX

■   SAP Agent

▲   BOOTP/DHCP Relay Agent

NOTE: Before removing RAS, back up your existing RAS configuration files, including the Switch.inf and Modem.inf files.

Next, you should install any of the appropriate protocols or services listed in the following table *before* installing the RRAS upgrade, if you want them to be available within RRAS.

If You Use:	Install This Service or Protocol:
IP routing	TCP/IP protocol
IPX routing	NwLink IPX/SPX–compatible transport
SNMP management	SNMP Service

The last step before beginning the RRAS installation is to ensure that all your network hardware adapter cards are correctly installed and functioning. RRAS works with any LAN or WAN cards that are supported by NT.

To start the installation, double-click the executable file you have downloaded from the Web. You will be asked where you want to install RRAS. There are three related components available for installation:

▼   **Remote Access Service** is the replacement for RAS. (You must have at least one RAS-capable device installed.)

■   **LAN Routing** supports LAN-to-LAN routing and LAN-to-WAN routing.

▲   **Demand Dial Routing** enables NT to connect to nonpersistent links such as modems, when users request access to remote resources.

After selecting the components of RRAS you wish to install, you are prompted with a few routing configuration options. Then you must restart the server. After your system reboots, you can complete the configuration of the routing services or monitor the routing using the new RRAS Administration tool.

RRAS Administration

With the RRAS Administration tool, administrators can manage routers and RAS servers in their networks. This utility is found under Programs | Administrative Tools in NT Server. It has a tree view on the left displaying the installed network and routing components of RRAS. The list in the right-hand window displays the interfaces for a selected protocol, as illustrated in Figure 5-20.

You can use RRAS Admin to configure components such as protocols or interfaces, by right-clicking the desired object in the tree view. This tool is also useful to view routing tables, whether they are static or generated by networking protocols. By way of this GUI, you can complete other administrative routing duties, as well, including

▼   Adding routing protocols and interfaces

■   Adding a demand-dial interface

■   Deleting or disabling interfaces

■   Administering RAS servers

■   Viewing RAS servers in a domain

■   Granting dial-in permissions to RAS clients

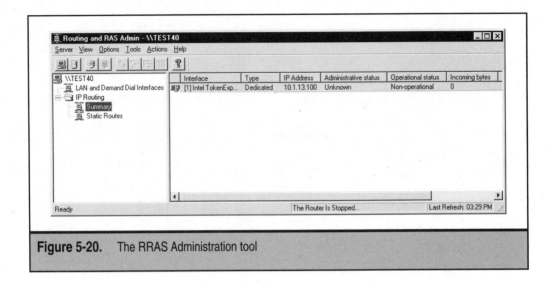

Figure 5-20.   The RRAS Administration tool

- Adding and deleting static routes
- Adding and deleting packet filters
- Adding local host filters
▲ Adding PPTP filters

RRAS can be used in place of a traditional router in many situations. It might be used as a low-cost dial-up solution, or as a router/proxy server for a small remote site. Note that RRAS is not nearly as capable a routing device as a real Cisco router, however. For example, RRAS can process about 40,000 packets per second, while average stand-alone routers can process millions of packets per second.

Installing RRAS Under Windows 2000

RRAS is not installed by default for Windows 2000 servers, although a management plug-in for the Microsoft Management Console is provided under Programs | Administrative Tools. You must open this menu item to install RRAS. Figure 5-21 illustrates the RRAS Management Console when RRAS is not installed. To initiate installation, right-click the name of the local server and select Install Routing and Remote Access.

Installation of RRAS is wizard based, like most installations within Windows 2000. One of the first decisions you make is about what components you want to install. The two choices are

▼ Using the server to route on LANs and WANs
▲ Enabling remote access

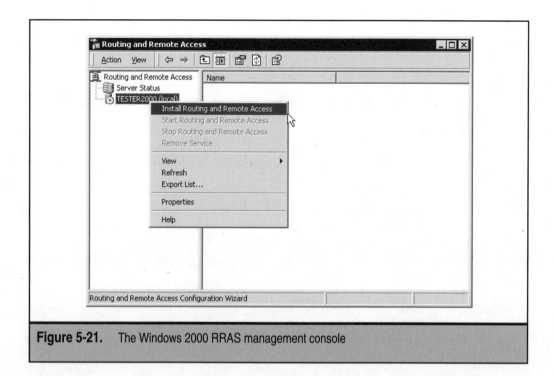

Figure 5-21.   The Windows 2000 RRAS management console

After you have made this choice, the installation copies files and finishes by asking if you'd like to start the RRAS service. Unlike previous versions of Windows, a reboot is not required to start RRAS. When you use the management window, additional information about the interfaces RRAS uses will be available, as illustrated in Figure 5-22.

From the RRAS management console, you can configure the LAN and WAN interfaces you want to use in RRAS, routing protocols, and remote access policies. You can also view various statistical tables on the protocols you are using, and specific information about any given interface. Chapter 3 contains more information about setting up routing protocols such as RIP and OSPF in Windows 2000.

SUMMARY

In this chapter, we studied router configuration and installation. We learned the importance of testing new equipment and upgrades of IOS versions in a lab environment before deploying them on a production network. We examined several important areas and key items necessary to ensure a clean router deployment on a network, including a simple preconfiguration checklist. This chapter described the Cisco IOS versions and images, how they are booted by the router hardware, and how they are accessed and configured

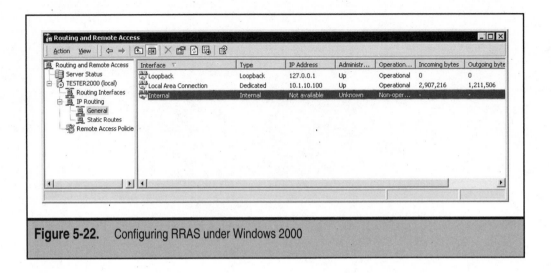

Figure 5-22.   Configuring RRAS under Windows 2000

by network personnel. Additionally, the chapter discussed the IOS feature sets and reviewed the specific categories Cisco uses to identify the IOS releases.

As for other network equipment, you should always remember to install routers in a secure, cool, and dry location, making sure that cables are properly supported to prevent cable strain. We also discussed the various ways a router can be accessed administratively: the console port, auxiliary port, Telnet, HTTP, TFTP, and SNMP. We also covered two valuable tools that can be used in building, testing, and managing router configurations. Cisco ConfigMaker allows you to build a configuration and distribute it to routers on your network. It runs on Windows 9x and Windows NT 4.0. The interface helps you draw your network graphically for manual device identification, and offers an automatic detection wizard to capture information about network devices. ConfigMaker also supports Network Address Translation, as well as Easy IP and the Cisco IOS Firewall feature set configurations. NetSys Baseliner is a modeling tool that allows administrators to design and analyze network configurations before rolling them out on a production network. This product is particularly valuable when you have multiple configurations and multiple locations.

Finally, we looked at IP internetworking topics for Windows environments. We covered the basic setup of TCP/IP on a Windows machine and examined the information available in the Windows route table. We covered Windows static routes, and looked at Microsoft's Routing and Remote Access (RRAS) and the routing protocols it supports.

In the next chapter, we'll dive into switches and VLANs.

CHAPTER 6

Setting Up Switches and VLANs

The centralization of servers and services, plus bandwidth-hungry applications like audio and video, all contribute to the growing congestion on LANs. *Switches* provide a solution to alleviate bandwidth congestion, by reducing collisions and by controlling broadcasts and flooding. They can also segment traffic by using *virtual LANs (VLANs)*. Users can be grouped together by department or by functional team and assigned to a VLAN. The communication within these groups becomes isolated on their VLAN, eliminating their specific traffic from the rest of the network and thus reducing bandwidth congestion. Communication among VLANs is enabled with a routing or switching device operating at the IP level, layer 3 of the OSI model.

This chapter provides an overview of switches and VLANs and the tools used to configure them.

SWITCHES

Switching is a technology that reduces congestion. You can purchase switches that support Ethernet, Token Ring, and other media types. When upgrading from 10 Mbps Ethernet to 100 Mbps Ethernet, acquiring the compatible hubs, network interface cards (NICs), and cabling may be costly. Switches provide an alternative solution to improve network performance by eliminating contention for the same bandwidth.

Prior to the introduction of switches, connections from each workstation were run to the network closet and then typically terminated in a hub or bridge. Switches became popular in the mid-1990s as a way to create smaller collision domains on LANs. These smaller collision domains reduce contention for bandwidth on a LAN and thus improve performance. A switch behaves similarly to a bridge but offers higher performance.

Hubs, Bridges, and Switches

When a *hub* receives packets, it regenerates the signals out each port. A hub does not have the capability to send the packet only out the destination port. All the connected stations appear to be on the same wire. Therefore, to make sure the traffic reaches its destination, the hub sends the traffic out on every port. Figure 6-1 illustrates the flow of traffic without a switch.

A *bridge* is a device that connects two or more LAN segments. A table of known destinations is created on a bridge by using the MAC addresses of the datagrams that flow through the bridge. When a datagram passes through, it will be dropped if the destination is on the same interface as the source; or transmitted to the destination interface; or flooded to all interfaces if the destination is not contained in the table.

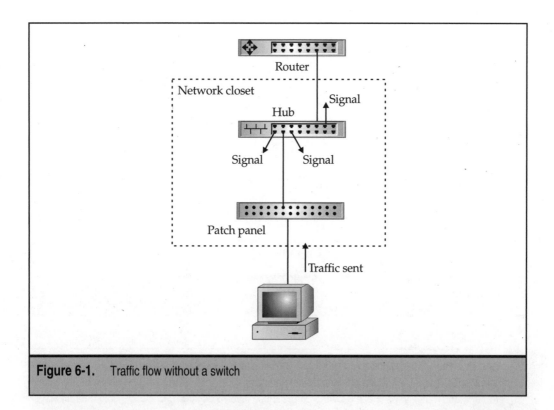

Figure 6-1.   Traffic flow without a switch

The most common LAN medium is Ethernet. Prior to a host's transmitting on an Ethernet segment, the host checks to see if data is currently being transmitted. If the network is in use, transmission is deferred. Often two hosts check at the same time, see that the network is clear, and simultaneously send data. This results in a collision, and each host enters a back-off phase and retransmits later. Figure 6-2 demonstrates Ethernet collisions.

Unlike a hub, each port on a switch or bridge is its own collision domain. A bridge is a *store-and-forward* device. This means it will collect the complete frame, determine the destination port, prepare the frame, calculate a cyclic redundancy check (CRC) error-detection scheme, and then transmit the frame.

Switches are similar to bridges, except they usually have a higher port density and operate at much faster speeds than a bridge. A switch, like the bridge, can act as a store-and-forward device—and has the added bonus of opting to use *cut-through processing*. In cut-through processing, the switch first looks at the destination address of the frame, determines the outgoing port, and then immediately starts sending bits to the outgoing port. This is a much faster method, resulting in lower latency than with a bridge.

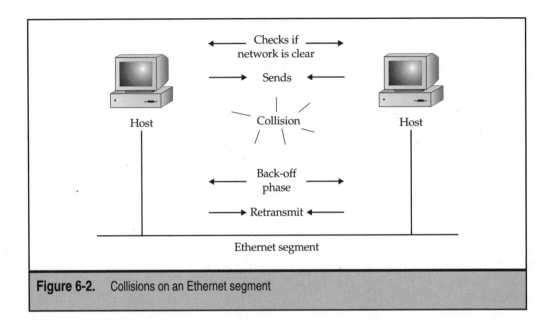

Figure 6-2. Collisions on an Ethernet segment

NOTE: The term *switch* refers to a layer-2 (data-link layer) device. Some vendors use the term *switch* more generically, using product names such as layer-3 switching, routing switches, switching routers, and multilayer switching (forwarding). These layer-3 devices can handle both data-link layer and network layer switching.

Catalyst 2900 Series XL

The Cisco Catalyst 2900 Series XL switch offers many features attractive to the SOHO (small office/home office) market. Let's take a closer look at the 2900 Series XL.

Most of the features and functions of this series are similar to all the other switches offered by Cisco. The Catalyst 2900 Series XL is a full line of 10/100 auto-sensing Fast Ethernet switches supporting a maximum of 64 port-based VLANs. There are five different models within the 2900 Series XL. Each model offers different port densities, configuration options, and pricing, to meet a broad range of network design requirements. All models support the grouping of multiple ports to provide redundant, high-bandwidth connections between switches, servers, and other key network stations. Table 6-1 outlines the features of each model in the 2900 Series XL.

In addition to the 2900 Series XL, Cisco offers switches in the 1900 series for small offices; the 3000 series when modular stacking is required; the 3900 Token Ring series; the 5000 series for full modular and high-performance requirements (typically for larger companies); and the 8500 series for campus backbones. Chapter 4 includes an overview on the Cisco switch product line and the appropriate scenario for each series.

Features	Model 2912 XL	Model 2912 MF XL	Model 2924 XL	Model 2924C XL	Model 2924M XL
10/100 auto-sensing ports	✓	✓	✓	✓	✓
Full- or half-duplex auto-sensing	✓	✓	✓	✓	✓
4-port switched 10BaseT/100BaseTX auto-sensing module uplink		✓			✓
2-port switched 100BaseFX				✓	
12-port switched 100BaseFX		✓			

Table 6-1.   The 2900 Series XL Hardware Features

Example Network Designs for 2900 Series XL Routers

Routers and switches play major roles in VLAN design. Switches are the core devices that control the grouping of ports into VLANs. Routers provide the mechanism for communication among the VLANs. The Catalyst 2900 series offers a variety of switches that, when selected and installed correctly, will optimize network performance.

The 2912 XL, 2924 XL, and 2924M XL are ideal to provide high-performance desktop connectivity. This is accomplished by connecting 10/100 bandwidth directly to each workstation and then connecting back to an Enterprise switch or router. The 2924M XL contains two 100BaseFX (FX are fiber) ports for networks that offer connectivity over longer distances (more than two kilometers).

EtherChannel, or port grouping, is an additional feature supported by the 2900 series. Port grouping allows you to combine multiple ports using Fast EtherChannel and provide redundancy and increased bandwidth back to an enterprise switch or router. Figure 6-3 is a network diagram of high-performance desktop connectivity.

The Catalyst 2924M XL is also suitable to be deployed in network closets with connections from Ethernet hubs, switches, and local servers; or as a backbone switch for a small to mid-sized company. Each server can be allocated its own port, or can take advantage of EtherChannel and use multiple ports for redundancy and greater bandwidth. Workstations can be connected to hubs, smaller switches, or directly into the switch backbone. Figure 6-4 is a network diagram for workgroup aggregation.

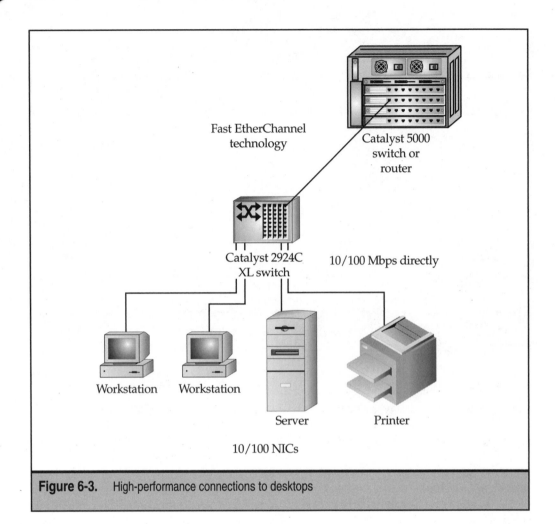

Figure 6-3. High-performance connections to desktops

The 12-port Catalyst 2912MF XL is ideal for aggregating geographically dispersed Fast Ethernet workgroups, over 100BaseFX fiber connections on a small or mid-sized campus environment connected with fiber. Figure 6-5 is a network diagram for dispersed building aggregation.

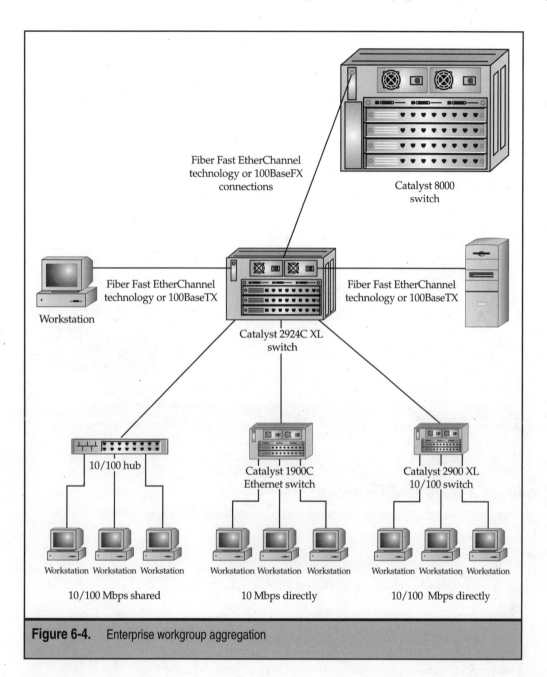

Figure 6-4.   Enterprise workgroup aggregation

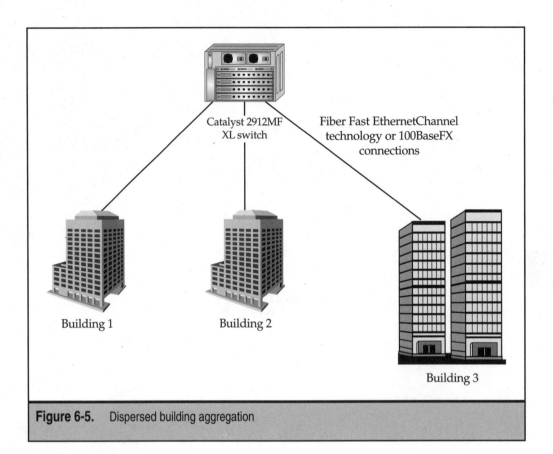

Figure 6-5.   Dispersed building aggregation

Profile of a Switched Network

A properly switched network is composed of three basic components:

▼ The physical switching platform

■ A common software infrastructure

▲ Network management tools and applications

Switching Platforms

There are three types of platforms available to provide the switching technology: LAN switches, ATM (Asynchronous Transfer Mode) switches, and routers. ATM switches and routers provide limited switching technology and are described here only briefly. This discussion focuses on LAN switches.

LAN SWITCHES   A LAN switch consists of many ports that connect to LAN segments. A switch may have all Token Ring LAN ports, or it may have Ethernet LAN ports in addition to a high-speed port (such as 100 Mbps Ethernet, FDDI, or 155 Mbps ATM) that connects to other network devices. Depending on your network architecture, the high-speed ports could be connected to a network device such as a backbone switch or router. This connection allows the switch to have connectivity to other LANs and WANs.

The LAN interfaces can either be dedicated to one workstation or server, or be attached to a hub that connects several workstations or servers together. Performance can be improved by connecting existing hubs, populated with lower-end users, to a switch port. The collision domain will then be reduced to the number of users on the hub. The other ports in the switch can be used to connect servers or high-end users that require substantial bandwidth.

Figure 6-6 shows the difference between shared and dedicated interfaces.

NOTE: Use a crossover cable, or the crossover port, when connecting a hub to a switch.

ATM SWITCHES   To maximize the unique capabilities of Asynchronous Transfer Mode, an ATM switch will typically be deployed with ATM technology. There are several types of ATM switches:

▼   Workgroup ATM switches

■   Campus ATM switches

■   Enterprise ATM switches

▲   Multiserver access switches

ROUTER SWITCHING   Switch technology on routers is used for communication between unique LANs and WANs. Since a router is not a true switch, but rather just offers switching technology, router switching is not discussed in great detail in this chapter. Following are some key differences between a switch and a router used for switching:

▼   The LAN switch is based on layer 2. A router is based on layer 3 of the OSI model.

■   Switches forward packets based on the MAC address. Routers forward packets based on the IP address.

■   A router understands IP subnets and unique IP networks. A switch only understands subnets.

■   A switch's security is limited to creating filters based on layer-2 options such as the destination and source MAC addresses, protocol type, and packet length. A router can provide additional security based on layer-3 TCP/IP ports and network IP addresses.

▲ A router doesn't care what type of media are being switched, because it forwards traffic based on the IP address and not the machine address. Therefore, it does not require the translation overhead.

Common Software Infrastructure

During the design of a switched network, it's important to have a common software infrastructure that will create a compatible platform between a variety of switching platforms (LAN, ATM, and routers). Choosing one network manufacturer for all the network hardware will make it easier to manage the logical topology. In addition, you'll be able to monitor and control sensitive or private traffic by using a standardized mechanism for traffic security.

Cisco IOS switching software uses standard protocols to create a common infrastructure that provides switching across a switched network, in addition to advanced capabilities such as virtual LANs.

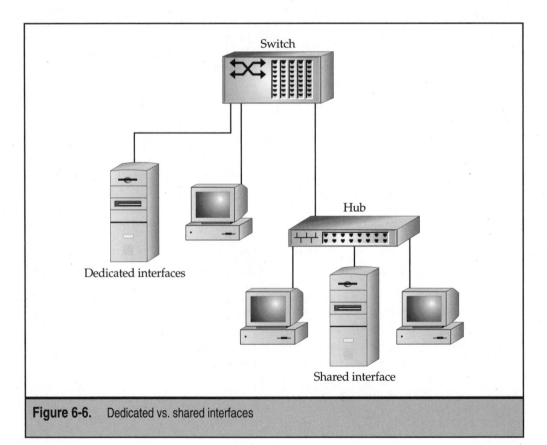

Figure 6-6. Dedicated vs. shared interfaces

Network Management Tools and Applications

In order to maintain a switched network, the network engineer needs to be able to monitor, configure, plan, and analyze the network's devices and services. There are several management tools that offer these capabilities, including

▼ Cisco Visual Switch Manager Software

■ Cisco IOS Command-Line Interface

■ CiscoWorks for Switched Internetworks (CWSI)

▲ SNMP Network Management Platforms (including HP OpenView and SunNet Manager)

Cisco Visual Switch Manager and the Cisco IOS Command-Line Interface are used primarily for day-to-day configuration of your switches. These tools do offer limited management and monitoring capabilities; but for those of you with large networks that are harder to manage one switch at a time, we recommend you use a more dedicated tool such as CiscoWorks for Switched Internetworks (CWSI) or some other type of SNMP Network Management Platform.

CISCOWORKS SWITCHED INTERNETWORKS (CWSI)   CiscoWorks Switched Internetworks (CWSI) is a network management platform based on the Simple Network Management Protocol (SNMP) and Remote Monitoring (RMON). CWSI also leverages the information-sharing capabilities of Cisco Discovery Protocol (CDP), Virtual Trunk Protocol (VTP), and Inter-Switch Link (ISL), which are technologies used by switches. CWSI is a configuration and analysis tool for optimizing LAN and WAN performance, reducing the complexity of managing switched internetworks and providing a graphical display.

CWSI contains VlanDirector, a virtual LAN management application for Cisco Catalyst switches. VlanDirector helps you to centrally create, modify, and manage VLANs. VlanDirector is defined further later in this chapter.

Preconfiguration of Switches

Unlike some other network devices, you don't *have* to configure a switch; it will function straight out of the box. It may not do exactly what you intended it to do, but it will work. As soon as you plug in a switch attached to your network segments, the switch will start forwarding packets to the compatible devices.

The settings you may need to modify on the switch are as follows:

Settings to change the configuration of the port:

▼ Set the speed.

■ Change to full-duplex or half-duplex.

■ Make the port a trunk port (trunk ports will be defined in a later section).

▲ Allocate the port to a VLAN other than the default.

Management settings:

▼ Set the IP address, mask, and default gateway.

■ Designate SNMP community names.

■ Set SNMP trap receivers.

▲ Record administrative information such as the switch name, location, contacts.

To secure access to the switch:

▼ Set authentication items; TACACS+ or local usernames and password.

▲ Designate EXEC password.

Default Settings for Switches

Table 6-2 lists default settings for more switches.

Switch Information Checklist

It's important to designate at least a subset of the default switch settings (specifically the security settings), and more than likely you'll want to modify other defaults to take advantage of the switch's functions. Use the following checklist to gather needed information beforehand, so you can easily and properly configure your switch.

▼ Switch host name

■ Switch IP address

■ Switch IP mask

■ Switch default gateway

■ Domain

■ Switch DNS server

■ Identified active ports

■ Identified VLANs and port members

■ SNMP community strings

■ Passwords

■ Port speeds

■ Port duplex mode

▲ Ports requiring security

Although every setup won't need every item in this checklist, it helps to have a starting point for collecting the information you'll need for configuration. More complex configurations will require additional information, including parameters for Spanning Tree

Feature	Setting	Default
Management	IP address, subnet mask, and default gateway	0.0.0.0
	Cisco Discovery Protocol (CDP)	Enabled
	Address Resolution Protocol (ARP)	Enabled
	Static address assignment	None assigned
	Network view	Always enabled
	VLAN membership	All ports are members of VLAN1
Performance	Auto-negotiation of duplex mode	Enabled
	Auto-negotiation of port speeds	Enabled
Flooding control	Broadcast storm control	Disabled
	Flooding unknown unicast and multicast packets	Enabled
	Network port	Disabled
	Cisco Group Management Protocol (CGMP)	Enabled
Network Redundancy	Spanning Tree Protocol	Enabled
	Port grouping	None assigned
Diagnostic	SPAN port monitoring	Disabled
	Console, buffer, and file logging	Disabled
Security	Password	None assigned
	Addressing security	Disabled
	Trap manager	0.0.0.0
	Community strings	public
	Port security	Disabled

Table 6-2.   Switch Default Settings

Protocol (STP), Cisco Group Multicast Protocol (CGMP), and Cisco Discovery Protocol (CDP). Each of these protocols and their options are discussed later in this chapter.

SWITCH SETUP AND INSTALLATION

The setup and installation of a switch is relatively painless. You can pretty much just plug the nodes into a switch, power it up, and walk away, and the switch will work. You'll have to do a little more work, however, in order to maximize the switch's capabilities.

Cisco IOS Versions

Switches use a special release of the Cisco IOS software. Because the software needs to be modified to support switches, the software is not released on the same eight-week maintenance cycle that is used for routers.

A switch can be ordered with Standard Edition or Enterprise Edition software. The following are key features of Standard Edition software for release 11.2(8)SA6, which supports a subset of the Catalyst series including the 2900 Series XL:

▼   Automatic discovery and creation of *clusters* of up to 16 switches that can be managed through a single IP address. Cluster support includes

    ■   Unified management and authentication of clustered switches

    ■   HTML, the Cisco IOS command-line interface (CLI), and SNMP management interfaces for cluster, switch, and port management

    ■   Browser-based tools to upgrade all the cluster switches

■   Support for between 64 and 250 virtual LANs (VLANs), depending on the model (for 2900 Series XLs, it's 64)

■   IEEE 802.1D Spanning Tree Protocol (STP) support on a per-VLAN basis

■   Network Time Protocol (NTP) to provide an external source for time-of-day information

■   Fast and Gigabit EtherChannel support for high-speed connections between switches and servers

■   Auto-negotiation of speed, and half- or full-duplex operation on 10/100 ports

▲   Cisco Group Management Protocol (CGMP) to limit the flooding of IP multicast traffic

The Enterprise Edition software for Cisco IOS includes all the features of the Standard Edition software, as well as the advanced VLAN functionality. The following additional features are included in the Enterprise Edition software:

▼   VLAN Trunk Protocol (VTP) version 2

■   Inter-Switch Link (ISL) and IEEE 802.1Q Trunking

■   Dynamic-access VLANs

▲   Load sharing and redundancy over parallel trunks

During the writing of this book, the Cisco IOS Enterprise Edition software was at Release 11.2(8) SA6. The majority of switches can be upgraded to the Enterprise Edition, and some of the high-end switches can only run the Enterprise software. You can upgrade to the Enterprise Edition by purchasing the Enterprise Edition Software Upgrade Kit and downloading the file to your PC or workstation; then do a TFTP transfer of the files to the switch.

NOTE: If you previously configured your system to support Cisco's Web-based management software, it might be a good idea to delete existing HTML files and disable access to the HTML pages before you do the upgrade. This will eliminate disruption of the upgrade by users accessing the manager software pages during the transfer of the new software.

Maintenance releases and future versions of Cisco IOS are posted to Cisco Connection Online (CCO) in the Cisco IOS Software area.

The Setup Program/Process

As with other Cisco network devices, your initial means of connecting to a switch is through the console port. After this initial connection and configuration, you have three options for connecting to a switch: via the console port, via Telnet, and via the browser-style Visual Switch Manager software. The initial connection, and configuration through the console port and with Telnet, are discussed in the following paragraphs. Configuration using Visual Switch Manager software is discussed in more detail in a later section.

Connecting via the Console

Included with the purchase of a switch is a rollover cable. Connect one side of this RJ45 cable into the console port. The other side goes into an adapter, either an RJ-45–to–DB-9 female DTE adapter, or an RJ-45–to–DB-25 adapter.

Your terminal emulation software needs to communicate with the switch using hardware flow control. The terminal type should be set to VT100. Several terminal software applications are available, including the Hyperterminal program that is included with Windows 9x and NT 4.0. Hyperterminal and most of the other terminal programs provide an easy path to the console port. The following configuration supports a serial connection to the switch's console port:

Baud rate	9600
Data bits	8
Stop bits	1
Parity	None
Flow control	None
Terminal type	VT100

Configure the terminal emulator using these parameters and then, if you haven't already done so, power up the switch. Press ENTER a couple of times until you see a prompt.

The first time you boot up the switch, you'll be prompted for IP information. Although this information is not required for the switch to work, it is necessary to allow connectivity through a Telnet session or Visual Switch Manager software. The initial IP information can only be configured using the console port. This is also a good time to set your passwords for the switch, and change the default SNMP community strings (even though these configurations can be done through a Telnet session or Visual Switch Manager).

If you decide against using the software prompts during the initial powering of the switch or if you want to change these configurations, you can use the CLI. The following procedure describes how to change the IP information for the 2900 Series switches using the CLI (this process is similar across the majority of switches):

1. Enter privileged EXEC mode:

   ```
   Switch>enable
   ```

2. Enter global configuration mode:

   ```
   Switch#configuration terminal
   ```

3. Enter the interface configuration mode and specify the interface to which the IP information is being assigned:

   ```
   Switch(config)#interface VLAN1
   ```

   VLAN1 is by default the switch's interface.

4. Assign the IP address and subnet mask:

   ```
   Switch(config-if)#ip address ip_address subnet_mask
   ```

5. Define the IP address of the default router:

   ```
   Switch(config-if)#ip default-gateway ip_address
   ```

In addition to providing IP information, you'll need to enable Telnet on the switch in order to connect to the switch through a Telnet session. Here is one way to enable Telnet connectivity and a password for Telnet authorization:

1. Enter privileged EXEC mode:

   ```
   Switch>enable
   ```

2. Enter global configuration mode:

   ```
   Switch#configuration terminal
   ```

3. Enter the interface configuration mode for the Telnet session:

   ```
   Interface switch(config)#line vty 0 4
   ```

   where 0 and 4 indicate a range of 0–4 (total of five) Telnet sessions allowed at one time.

4. Enter a password.

```
Switch(config)#password password
```

Telnet

A connection through Telnet is useful for remote administration of network devices. Once you have the IP address assigned and the password configured, launch the Telnet application. Windows NT, Windows 9x, and Windows 2000 include a Telnet application that will do the trick. Enter the IP address of the switch you would like to connect to. You will then be prompted for a password. Once it's authenticated, you'll be at the switch's command line interface.

Cisco's IOS command line interface (CLI) is generally referred to as an EXEC session. There are two levels in an EXEC session: user mode (denoted by the > prompt) and privileged mode (denoted by the # prompt). The user level is obviously very limited, and privileged mode gives you the keys to the kingdom. Luckily, both levels can be password protected. Changing the default password should be one of your first configuration changes.

TELNET CONNECTION ISSUES   Once you have connected to a switch using Telnet and entered the user-level password, the CLI is similar to that for a Cisco router. One thing that might be a little confusing, though: For a router, configurations can be assigned to a router's interface. For a switch, configurations can be assigned to a VLAN or to a switch's interface, depending on what type of configuration is being applied.

For example, here is the **int** command to configure a particular interface for a router:

```
Router(config)#int Ethernet0
Router(config-if)#
```

However, in a switch, the configurations can be assigned to VLANs or interfaces, so you'd type one of these **int** commands:

```
Switch(config)#int VLAN1
Switch(config-if)#
```

or

```
Switch(config)#int Fast Ethernet 1
Switch(config-if)#
```

Notice that Cisco returns the prompt

```
Switch(config-if)#
```

instead of

```
Switch(config-VLAN)#
```

which it should have returned in the case of assigning configurations to a VLAN. The **if** prompt in a router refers to an interface, but here it refers to a VLAN—thus there can be confusion about whether your configurations are being assigned to the switch interface or a VLAN of the switch. Make sure you know whether the configurations should be applied to the interface or to the VLAN before using sthe **int** command.

When connecting to a switch via Telnet, another consideration concerns the login. When you log into a switch, you are in the user mode. To access the privileged mode, type **enable** at the > prompt. The CLI will then prompt you for the enable password. Even though the switch does not echo either the user or privileged password, Telnet will send the password in clear text across your network, which is a security concern.

Cisco Visual Switch Manager Software

Using Cisco's browser-style Web-based management software is the easiest way to configure a switch. Cisco offers Cisco Visual Switch Manager and the Switch Network View for configuring and monitoring switch activity. These applications use your Web browser's GUI and are both discussed in detail later in this chapter.

When You Can't Access the Switch

If the switch is not responding, check for the following possible causes:

▼ Look for an incorrect or bad cable. If there is no link light at one end or the other of the cable, try using a crossover cable instead of a straight-through cable (or vice versa).

■ It may be that Spanning Tree Protocol (STP) is checking for possible loops. Wait 30 seconds or so for the LED to turn green and then try the switch again.

▲ Verify that you configured the correct IP address and mask for the switch, and that the default gateways for both your PC and the switch are correct.

SPECIAL SWITCH PROTOCOLS

Switches provide the option of configuring additional protocols to help maximize their efficiencies. Two common protocols—Spanning Tree Protocol and Cisco Group Multicast Protocol—create a more effective switching process. Also, the Cisco Discovery Protocol is helpful for viewing the devices attached to a switch. By default, all of these protocols are enabled. They are included on the Device menu of the Visual Switch Manager utility.

Spanning Tree Protocol (STP)

Spanning Tree is a protocol designed to eliminate loops in a network. When a machine has two potential paths to another machine, looping can occur.

Figure 6-7 demonstrates a potential loop. If Workstation A sends a frame to Workstation B, Switches 1 and 2 update their tables to indicate that Workstation A is located on Interfaces 1/0 and 2/0, respectively, and they pass the frame out the opposite interface.

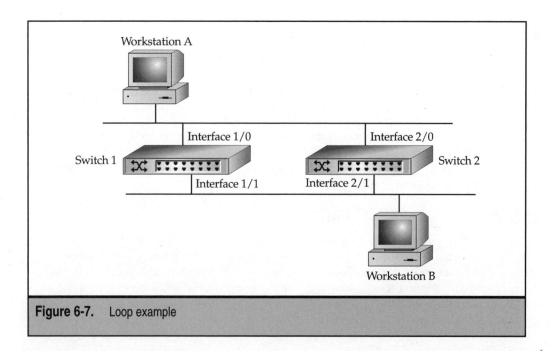

Figure 6-7.   Loop example

However, each switch will see the frame sent by the other switch. Both will update their tables again to indicate that Workstation A is located on Interfaces 1/1 and 2/1, and will pass the frame out the opposite interface. This is the beginning of a loop.

The Spanning Tree Protocol (STP) solves the problem of loops by exchanging routing information through Bridge Protocol Data Unit (BPDU) frames. Switches use the routing information to disable multiple interfaces that could create a loop. (Technically, the interface isn't disabled but rather placed in a mode in which it can't forward packets.) The switches still maintain awareness of the two interfaces, so the alternative route can be used if necessary.

Switches can be configured to use *load sharing*. Load sharing allows both interfaces to be enabled, and then the traffic is divided between the two paths. Load sharing is configured by assigning *STP port priorities* or *STP port costs*. Assign STP port priorities and port costs by selecting **Devices | Spanning-Tree Protocol** from the menu bar in the Web-Based Management application. Then select the VLAN ID, and click Modify STP Parameters.

Load sharing divides the bandwidth supplied by parallel trunks connecting switches. To avoid loops, STP normally blocks all but one parallel link between switches. With load sharing, you divide the traffic between the links according to which VLAN the traffic belongs to. In order to assign STP port priorities, both load-sharing paths must be connected to the same switch. STP port costs, on the other hand, can be assigned to load-sharing paths connected to the same switch or two different switches.

Cisco Group Multicast Protocol (CGMP)

Cisco Group Management Protocol (CGMP) forwards IP multicast packets to *only* IP multicast clients that have been defined based on groups. A CGMP group contains a member list of multicast clients. When a multicast client sends a *leave* message, that client is dropped from its group. The switch checks to see if there are other multicast clients on that port. If so, the group is maintained; if not, the group is deleted.

CGMP-enabled switches also communicate with the routers to determine whether any of their attached users are part of a multicast group. To accomplish this, CGMP works with Internet Protocol Group Management (IGMP); therefore, the switch requires a connection to a router running both CGMP and IGMP.

Cisco Discovery Protocol (CDP)

Cisco Discovery Protocol (CDP) runs on all Cisco-manufactured equipment, including routers, bridges, access and communication servers, and switches. CDP enables you to collect and view information about all the Cisco devices directly attached to the switch. This protocol runs on the data-link layer and is independent of all other protocols.

To enable CDP and show information about CDP neighbors, type the following commands at the command line interface (CLI):

```
Switch(config)#cdp enable
Switch#show cdp neighbors
```

Following is an example of the data displayed by this command:

```
Capability Codes: R - Router, T - Trans Bridge, B - Source Route
                  Bridge, S - Switch, H - Host, I - IGMP,
                  r - Repeater
Device ID       Local Intrfce   Holdtme  Capability  Platform    Port ID
tacacsrouter    Tok 0           167         R        4500        Tok 0
Switch.velte.com Eth 1          128         S        WS-C2924M-Fas 0/8
vsitest7        Tok 1           154         R        RSP2        Tok 6/0
```

CDP is configured for each interface (or, in the case of switches, for VLANs). Besides enable/disable, the only other option for CDP is configuring how often the information is received. The allowed range is from 5 to 900 seconds, with the default being appropriately placed at 60 seconds. Cisco hardware enables CDP by default.

MANAGING WITH CISCO VISUAL SWITCH MANAGER

A centralized tool for performing configuration modifications and reviews makes switch management easier. It's inconvenient to have to connect a PC to the console port and do configuration through a frequently changing command line interface.

Web-based management software simplifies the complexity of using the CLI by enabling network managers to make centralized configuration changes using a GUI. Cisco Visual Switch Manager is Cisco's Web-based management tool embedded in the Flash memory of Cisco switches. This is an appreciated alternative means of access.

Cisco Visual Switch Manager software uses your Web browser to provide a GUI for configuring and monitoring switch activity. By using a supported browser with a few modified parameters, you can access this GUI by just typing the switch's IP address. The GUI then provides a standard menu-selection interface that simplifies the configuration process.

Getting Started with Cisco Visual Switch Manager

In order to use Cisco Visual Switch Manager, you need to have a browser that will support it. Certain versions of Netscape Communicator and the Microsoft Internet Explorer will support Cisco Visual Switch Management, as described in Table 6-3.

Both browsers require configuration modifications prior to accessing a switch. Use the following procedures.

Setting Up Netscape Communicator

1. Select Edit | Preferences from the menu bar and click Advanced.

2. Select the Enable Java, Enable JavaScript, and Enable Style Sheets options.

3. Click OK.

4. Select Edit | Preferences from the menu bar.

5. Click Advanced Cache and select Every Time.

6. Click OK.

Operating System Running Visual Switch Manager	Netscape Communicator	Microsoft Internet Explorer
Windows 95 Service Pack 1	4.03+	4.01 Service Pack 1
Windows 98	4.03+	4.01 Service Pack 1
Windows NT Service Pack 3	4.03+	4.01 Service Pack 1
Solaris 2.51+ (with patch cluster and Motif library patch 103461-24)	4.03+	

Table 6-3. Browser Requirements for Cisco Visual Switch Manager

Setting Up Microsoft Internet Explorer

1. Select View | Internet Options from the menu bar and click the Advanced tab.

2. Under Java VM, select Java JIT Compiler Enabled and Java Logging Enabled, and then click Apply.

3. Go to the General tab. In the Temporary Internet Files section, click Settings.

4. Select Every Visit to the Page; then click OK.

5. Go to the Security tab. In the Zone drop-down list, choose Trusted Sites Zone.

6. In the Trusted Sites Zone area, click the Custom option.

7. Click the Settings button, and scroll down to the Java options. Under Java Permissions, choose Custom.

8. Click the Java Custom Settings button.

9. In the Trusted Sites Zone area, click Edit Permissions.

10. Under Run Unsigned Content, select Enable and click OK.

11. Click OK in the Security Settings Window.

12. Click Security in the Internet Options window; and in the Trusted Sites Zone section, click Add Sites.

13. In the same section, deselect the Require Server Verification option.

14. Enter the switch IP address in the Add This Web Site to the Zone field using the https:// format.

15. Click Add and then OK.

16. In the Internet Options window, click Apply and OK.

Using the Cisco Visual Switch Manager

After you have made the changes to your browser, you can access the switch using Cisco Visual Switch Manager. Launch your browser and, in place of an http address, type the domain name or the IP address of the switch you'd like to access. You will be prompted for a username and password. Unless you are using an external authentication method (such as TACACS+), you only have to enter the enable password (no username). Following authentication, the page shown in Figure 6-8 is the first one you'll see.

The commands on the access page simulate typed-in commands at the CLI, by going behind the scenes and performing the keystrokes.

▼ If you are familiar and comfortable with Cisco's IOS, you can select the Web Console link to do configurations on the switch.

■ Although you can use the Telnet link on this access page, this link to the switch will prompt you again for passwords. If your goal is to Telnet to the switch, you're better off to use your Telnet emulation program so you aren't prompted twice for passwords.

▲   If you want to use the helpful Web-based interface, click the Visual Switch Manager link, and the Switch Manager's home page (Figure 6-9) will pop up. This interface is especially useful for someone who isn't familiar with Cisco's IOS.

NOTE: Unfortunately, if you want to go back to the initial access page (Figure 6-8), you will have to launch another browser session. The Visual Switch Manager home page doesn't provide a link back to the access page.

A graphic of the switch is located at the bottom of the home page, providing you with a status of its ports. There are three status types: Link Up, No Link Status, and Link Faulty/Port Disabled. Port configurations can be done by double-clicking one of the ports in the switch or by selecting Port Configuration from the Manager software's Port menu. Unlike accessing the port configurations from the switch, the Port | Port Configu-

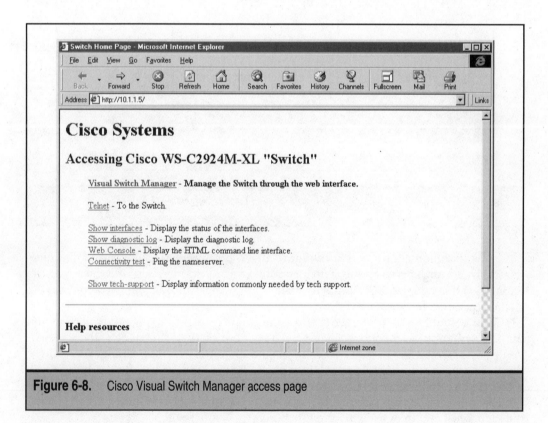

Figure 6-8.   Cisco Visual Switch Manager access page

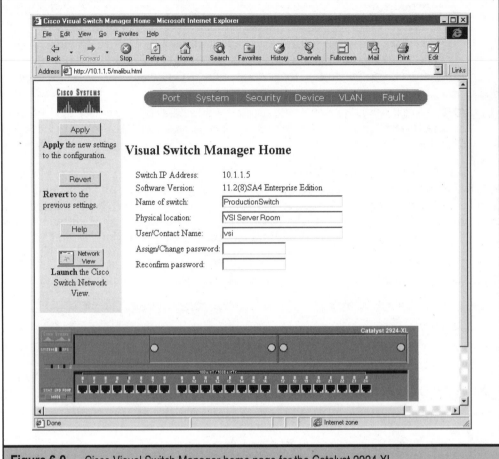

Figure 6-9. Cisco Visual Switch Manager home page for the Catalyst 2924 XL

ration menu option allows you to configure all the ports at once. Since the communication back and forth between the switch and the Web-based interface isn't the speediest, we suggest that you use the Port menu when configuring multiple ports, to avoid having to click each port individually.

Cisco Visual Switch Manager is simple and fairly easy to navigate. Any time you make a configuration change, you click the Apply button on the left side of the screen. If you enter a change and decide you want to go back to the previous setting, you can use the Revert button as long as you haven't yet clicked Apply. The Revert button will redisplay the previous settings.

The following section describes several menu options within Visual Switch Manager that will assist you in optimizing the functionality of your switch.

SWITCH CONFIGURATION GUIDELINES

In this section, we will examine the elements of switch configuration, using the menus in the Cisco Web-based management software (see Figure 6-9). This user-friendly interface is beneficial for configuring the following settings of the switch:

▼ System elements

■ Port parameters

■ Security optimization

▲ VLANs

NOTE: Starting with this section, you'll be reading about configuring an installed switch. The best thing you can do before you start this process is to have your switch's parameters all predetermined and documented. Identify the items in the Switch Information Checklist provided earlier in the chapter, as well as the physical location of the switch and its connections to the network.

System Configurations

The elements of a switch's core system configuration are similar to those of other network devices. These include IP management, SNMP management, and switch software management. The following sections define these elements as they pertain to switch configuration. In Visual Switch Manager, they are managed with commands on the System menu.

IP Management

IP addresses, masks, broadcast addresses, default gateways, the DNS server, and domain names are configured on a switch to optimize its capabilities. Although none of these fields is required, their configuration is required for managing connections via Telnet and the Web-based management software. Configuring this information also makes it easier to manage and troubleshoot the switch device.

SNMP Management

The switch supports Simple Network Management Protocol (SNMP). SNMP consists of three parts: SNMP manager, SNMP agent, and Remote Monitoring (RMON) Management Information Base (MIB). The RMON MIB provides statistics only as high as data-link and physical-layer platforms such as the switch, and therefore no statistics are provided on IP or application-layer information.

For example, the Catalyst 2900 supports four RMON groups:

▼ **Statistics**   Provides traffic and error statistics for a specified interface.

■ **History**   Periodically samples statistics; can be used to establish baselines.

■ **Alarms**   Generates alarms defined by the network administrator.

▲ **Events**   Sends traps or notifications from the alarm group to the SNMP manager.

The switch acts as an SNMP agent, and the network management software (Cisco-Works, for instance) acts as the SNMP manager. The SNMP manager gathers data from the MIB and uses it to generate statistics about the SNMP agent. The SNMP agent can also be configured to send traps or notifications of certain events, such as password failures, to the SNMP manager.

SNMP community strings (used to authenticate) and a trap server must be configured to order for a network management tool (such as CiscoWorks) to function. SNMP is enabled and configured in the manager software, using the System | SNMP Configuration menu option. Figure 6-10 shows the SNMP page from the Web-based management interface.

Switch Hardware/Software Management

Using Cisco's Web-based management system, you can easily view the current version and status of the Cisco Switch IOS, hardware platform, and memory. If additional features are required in connection with a later Cisco IOS release, the manager software also

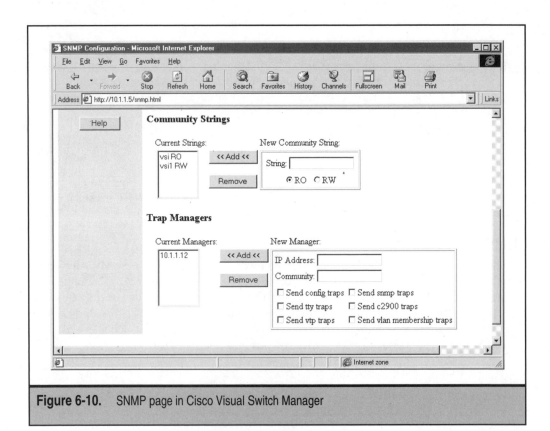

Figure 6-10.   SNMP page in Cisco Visual Switch Manager

simplifies the task of upgrading the Cisco IOS image. This new image is downloaded onto the TFTP server. Using the Visual Switch Manager, select System | System Configuration. Enter the IP address of the TFTP server, a filename to copy from, and a filename to copy to. The Cisco IOS image will then be upgraded (assuming enough memory is available and the IOS version is supported).

Port Configurations

There are several configuration options for the ports of a switch, including enable/disable, port speed, duplex mode, port name, and so on. In Visual Switch Manager, they are configured with commands on the Port menu. Using pull-down menus and selecting check boxes, you can enable or disable the switch, assign 10 or 10/100 auto-sensing to Ethernet ports, choose half or full duplex, and assign a port name. After you have selected the desired configuration for each port, click the Apply button. Figure 6-11 shows the Port Configuration options in Visual Switch Manager.

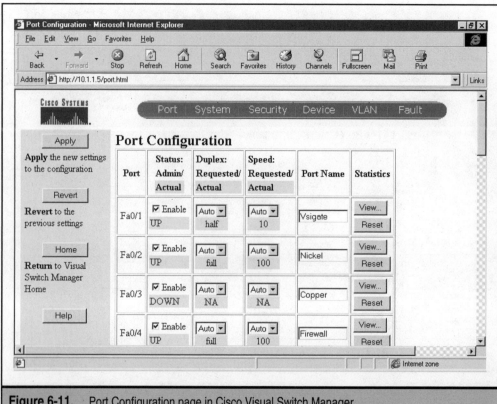

Figure 6-11.   Port Configuration page in Cisco Visual Switch Manager

TIP: If you explicitly define the port speed on the switch, rather than let the switch set it, it's good practice to configure the attached device to use that speed, as well. This can help you avoid problems with auto-speed negotiation that may impair connectivity.

Port Groupings (EtherChannel)

EtherChannel port groups are logical high-speed connections between switches. You can group up to eight 100BaseT ports or Gigabit Ethernet ports, and create up to 12 groups. When these ports are grouped, a switch considers the group to be a single logical port. Thus, a configuration change made to one port is applied to all other ports in that specific group. All ports in a group are in the same VLAN and have the same VLAN port mode, as explained in "VLAN Port Membership Modes," later in the chapter. To assign ports to port groups, select Port | Port Grouping from the menu bar in Cisco Visual Switch Manager. Figure 6-12 shows the layout of the Port Group page.

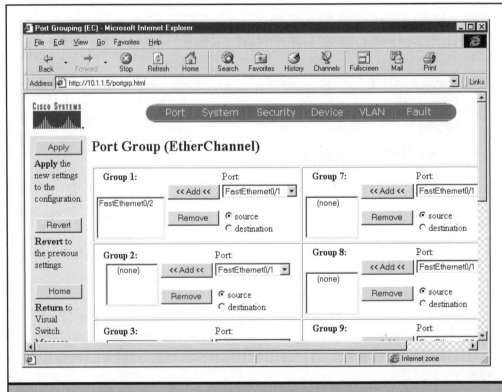

Figure 6-12.   Cisco Visual Switch Manager Port Group page

TIP: Here's a useful deployment of EtherChannel: Instead of keeping a redundant link for fault tolerance, use port groups to provide redundant links. If one port fails, one or more of the others automatically takes over. In the meantime, the traffic is spread out evenly among all ports in the group.

Trunks can be included in port groups, but all trunks must have the same configuration. When you first create a group, all subsequent ports added to the group automatically take on the first ports' configurations. As is the case for the LAN ports, if you change
the configuration parameters related to trunk configuration, the switch propagates the
settings to the rest of the ports. Not all switches and ports support EtherChannel, so you
need to verify what is supported on the particular platform or card when selecting a
switch. Later in this chapter we'll take a closer look at VLAN trunks.

TIP: If you are not using the EtherChannel function, turn it off—especially if you are not connecting
the port to another EtherChannel-capable switch.

ETHERCHANNEL FORWARDING METHODS   The Catalyst 2900 Series XL supports two kinds
of port groups: source-based forwarding and destination-based forwarding. In source-
based forwarding, packets received from ports outside the group are distributed based on
the packet's source address. Port groups that forward based on source address can have as
many as eight ports. Source-based forwarding is enabled by default.

In destination-based forwarding, packets received from ports outside the group are
distributed based on the packets' destination addresses. Port groups that forward based
on destination address can have any number of ports.

Switched Port Analyzer (SPAN)

Switched Port Analyzer (SPAN) is a diagnostic feature that lets you assign a port as a
monitor port where you can receive a copy of traffic flowing through a different port or
multiple ports. This is useful if you want to place a sniffer on the monitor port, to analyze
traffic without the possibility of disrupting it.

If the ports to be monitored have been assigned to a VLAN, a monitor port can only
monitor ports in the same VLAN. You can't change the VLAN of the ports being monitored unless you first disable monitoring. By default, all ports are assigned to the
static-access VLAN port membership mode; but if you create VLANs, you have the option to change this mode. If VLANs are assigned to the monitor port, however, it must remain a static-access port. (VLAN port membership modes are described later in this
chapter.)

To select the ports you want to have monitored, select Port | Port Monitoring from
the Cisco Visual Switch Manager. You can select up to 15 ports to have monitored at a
time (before clicking the Apply button). Then continue to select ports, if necessary, making sure you only select 15 at a time and always click Apply when finished.

Flooding Controls

When a node needs to communicate with the entire network, it sends a datagram to MAC address 0xFFFFFFFF—also known as a *broadcast*. Any NIC that receives a broadcast message responds by interrupting the CPU. When a host needs to communicate with part of the network, it sends a datagram to MAC address 0xFFFFFFFF with the leading bit of the vendor ID set to 1—also known as a *multicast*. NICs with that vendor ID respond to a multicast by adding to its group addresses. The switch uses Cisco Group Management Protocol (CGMP, described previously in the section "Special Switch Protocols") to forward IP multicast packets to only IP multicast clients. *Unicast* is similar to a broadcast, except that unicast sends a copy of each packet to each destination. Figure 6-13 illustrates the difference between the three types of traffic to three different hosts (A, B, C).

By *flooding* broadcast and multicast traffic out every port, the switch ensures that packets will arrive at their destinations, and this is appropriate in some situations. However, unicast and multicast packets generate substantial traffic, and in a switch the traffic is flooded across that switch's VLAN. When a port belongs to more than one VLAN, it also floods the other VLANs. This trickling effect means all VLANs could be flooded.

You can control flooding in a switch using three methods. (To achieve the best results, use a combination of the three.)

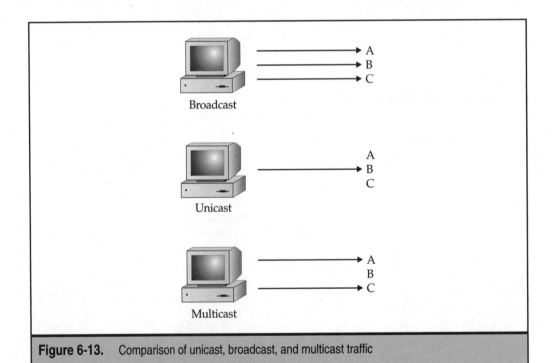

Figure 6-13. Comparison of unicast, broadcast, and multicast traffic

▼   Enable what is called a *network port*, which will then receive all traffic with unknown destination addresses instead of flooding it out all interfaces. (To define a port as the network port, select Port | Flooding Controls in Cisco Visual Switch Manager.)

■   Disable unicast and multicast traffic on ports that you know would never need to receive unicast and multicast traffic (for example, a port that has all known destinations). To also disable unicast and multicast traffic on the ports you have defined, use the same Flooding Controls page as defined in the previous bullet.

▲   The third method is the most common and recommended in most situations: controlling of broadcast storms by enabling *filtering* and setting *thresholds*. The higher the threshold, the less effective the filtering. This threshold can be monitored by enabling the trap state and configuring a trap manager to send a trap if the threshold is crossed. (These settings are accessed by selecting System | SNMP Configuration in the Visual Switch Manager software.)

Security

A switch provides layer-2 security options. MAC addresses can be filtered and bandwidth can be reserved. MAC address filtering, and filtering at layer 2 in general, are very cumbersome and administratively intensive operations. If you have a need for filtering, it's more effective to do it using IP addresses at layer 3 with a router.

In Visual Switch Manager, switch security options are managed with commands on the Security menu.

Port Security

Configuring secure ports allows you to allocate the bandwidth of a port to one workstation or to a group of workstations. By enabling a secure port, you can define a number of nodes (1–132) to have access outbound through that port. Configuring a number from 1–132 only limits how many different MAC addresses can connect at one time—not necessarily who has the privilege to connect. However, you can configure a specific MAC address using the Secure Address Table (explained in the next section, "Address Management").

Secure ports can also send SNMP traps and/or shut the interface down when it receives an address not defined in the Secure Address Table. A trunk cannot be a secure port.

Address Management

The switch uses the Address Management Table as a reference of MAC addresses and associated port numbers. Using the MAC Address Table, the switch knows the location of the destination and forwards traffic out one port, instead of having to flood the traffic out all interfaces. There are three types of addresses, and thus three tables that need to be maintained.

▼   **Dynamic Address Table**   As datagrams pass through a switch, the switch captures the source and destination MAC addresses and dynamically updates the

Dynamic Address Table. As nodes are removed and added to the network, the switch is smart enough to update its Dynamic Address Table. MAC addresses that haven't been used for a defined time period (known as the *aging time*) will be removed from the table. Resetting the switch does not reset the aging time.

■ **Secure Address Table**   A secure address is a manually defined unicast address with only one destination port. Multiple secure addresses can have the same destination port. The destination port may or may not be a secure port. Secure ports can send traps or shut the interface down when there is an address violation. If the secure port is defined to have, say, 130 MAC addresses, and you only define five MAC addresses in the Secure Address Table for the same interface, the switch will learn the source addresses of incoming packets. It will then automatically assign them a secure address until it reaches 130 total secure MAC addresses. The five defined MAC addresses have reserved spots.

▲ **Static Address Table**   A static address is manually entered into the Static Address Table and must be manually removed. It can be either a unicast or a multicast address. When you add a static address, you define the MAC address, the port the address will come in on, and the port(s) the address should be forwarded to.

You can also define a port group as the destination of a single static address. However, if your port group is a source-based port group, you should configure the static address to forward to all ports (in order to eliminate lost packets). For a destination-based port group, configure the static address to forward to only one port to eliminate redundancy. See the section "Port Grouping," later in the chapter, for more information.

MANAGING WITH THE CISCO SWITCH NETWORK VIEW

You access the Cisco Switch Network View software by clicking the Network View button near the bottom-left of the Visual Switch Manager home page. The Switch Network View gives you a picture of your network and allows you to manage multiple switches at one time. Like the Visual Switch Manager, the Network View uses your Web browser's GUI. Network View also requires the same type of browser and configuration modifications as for the Visual Switch Manager.

Before Launching Cisco Switch Network View

The Cisco Discovery Protocol (CDP) is used to exchange information with other CDP-capable devices to create a graphical display. This means you need to verify that all devices have CDP enabled (it is enabled by default). When CDP messages are exchanged, Cisco Switch Network View creates a network topology. The device in which the software is executed is the primary device.

If you have multiple switches stacked together, only the three connected to the lowest port numbers of the primary server will be displayed. All other switches within the stack are considered edge devices and will be displayed with less detail. SNMP must be enabled and the community string set to **public** on all stack members.

Using Cisco Switch Network View

When you click the Network View button, the application will take a while to collect the information necessary to display a map of your devices. A new window opens, containing all devices running CDP and the links between them.

This Network View application is primarily a display tool, offering you options for device and link reports. These reports provide limited configuration information that cannot be modified. You have to use the Switch Manager application to perform modifications. Figure 6-14 illustrates a simple map of two devices running CDP.

VIRTUAL LANs (VLANs)

A virtual LAN (VLAN) is configured to group related users together regardless of their physical connection to the network. A "group" of users typically includes those who share common resources—a department, for example, or a functional group. The VLAN acts as a group's own little network.

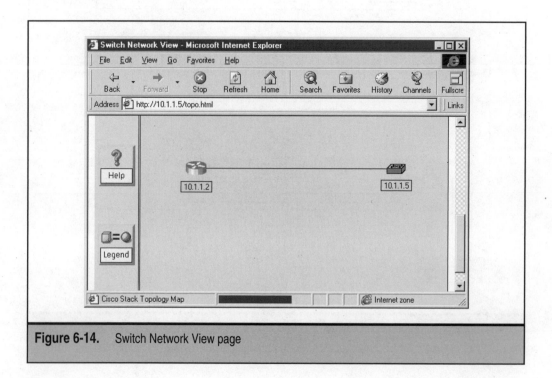

Figure 6-14.   Switch Network View page

The users in various VLANs are logically separated and function just as if they were on separated physical hubs. The virtual network allows its users to communicate without having to travel across several network devices. Assignment of users no longer involves moving a physical cable in the network closet—in the virtual environment, user adds, moves, and changes are all achieved using network management tools. These tools allow you to reconfigure the users in a VLAN logically, in seconds. Figure 6-15 illustrates a VLAN switched network.

A VLAN adds several benefits to a switched network, including broadcast control, security, performance, and network management. The switch isolates collision domains for attached hosts and only forwards appropriate traffic out of a particular port. The virtual

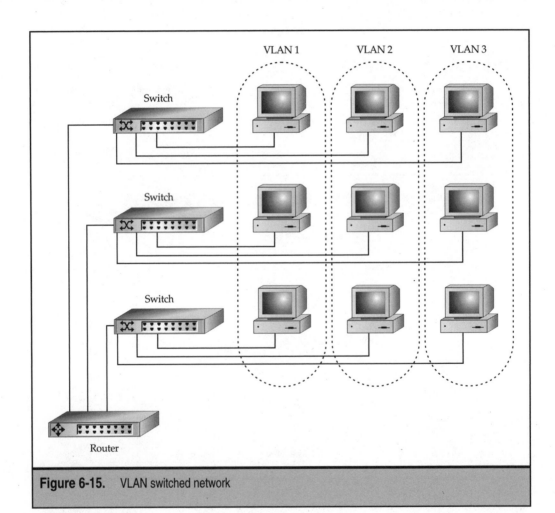

Figure 6-15.　VLAN switched network

network environment, however, takes this concept one step further and provides isolation between VLANs. A VLAN is a bridging domain that contains all broadcasts and multicast traffic. By grouping related users into VLANs, their related traffic stays within the VLAN.

A switch needs to know how to forward traffic between VLANs—traffic within the switch, and traffic among other switches. This is done by maintaining ARP tables that include MAC addresses and their corresponding ports. ARP tables are used internally by the switch and are continually broadcast to other switches. The following ARP table contains the MAC address and VLAN ID that correspond to a host IP address.

```
Switch#show arp
Protocol   Address          Age (min)   Hardware Addr   Type   Interface
Internet   10.1.1.15                4   0000.a000.3800  ARPA   VLAN1
Internet   10.11.3.13               4   0000.a002.36ad  ARPA   VLAN2
Internet   10.11.3.1               70   0060.2fa3.fabd  ARPA   VLAN2
Internet   10.1.1.5                 -   0050.8055.6f00  ARPA   VLAN1
Internet   10.10.2.100              4   0010.5a9b.b5e6  ARPA   VLAN3
```

Cisco has proposed VLAN standards, including IEEE 802.1Q and ISL (Inter-Switch Link). Both of these protocols are discussed in more detail later in this chapter.

VLAN Implementations

There are four types of VLAN solutions: port grouping, MAC-layer grouping, network-layer grouping, and IP multicast grouping. Port grouping is the most common and is supported by the Catalyst 2900 series.

Port Grouping

Typically, VLAN implementations define VLAN membership by assigning a VLAN to port numbers. For example, ports 1, 3, 4, 5, and 6 are VLAN1, and ports 2 and 7 through 24 are VLAN2. Network administrators may mimic the ports associated with VLAN1 and VLAN2 (in this example) on separate switches throughout their network. Such port grouping is the most common method of configuring VLANs, and the configuration is fairly straightforward. There is a downside: if a workstation moves but needs to remain in the same VLAN, the network engineer needs to reconfigure the user's new port number.

MAC Addresses

MAC-layer addresses are hardwired into the workstation's NIC. In VLANs based on MAC addresses, network engineers can move a workstation to a different physical location and the workstation will automatically retain its VLAN membership without any reconfiguration on the switch. When MAC-layer addresses are used, all users must be configured initially to be in at least one VLAN. Administration of this arrangement can become extremely tedious and complicated in large networks.

Network Layer Grouping

Layer-3 VLANs can support a virtual network based on network layer addresses (or subnet addresses for TCP/IP networks). Unlike a router, however, in this arrangement the traffic is still switched, using the Spanning Tree Protocol (STP)—not routed. Network layer grouping can be a disadvantage to performance, because inspecting a layer-3 address will take longer than for a layer-2 address (each packet has to go one step higher in the OSI model).

IP Multicast Grouping

When an IP packet is sent via multicast, it goes to an address that is a proxy for a defined group of dynamically assigned IP addresses. Workstations join a particular multicast group by responding to a broadcast notification. All workstations that join an IP multicast group can be seen as members of the same VLAN. VLANs defined by IP multicast groups would inherently be able to span routers and thus WAN connections. The Cisco Group Multicast Protocol (CGMP) is used to forward IP multicast packets to only IP multicast clients. These are layer-2 multicasts—not to be confused with the layer-3 multicasts that routers support.

VLAN Configuration Limitations

There can be up to 68 defined VLANs. Since four are reserved for Token Ring and FDDI, the Catalyst 2900 Series XL supports only 64. VLANs can be configured using the CLI or the Visual Switch Manager interface. Prior to assigning a VLAN to a port, you need to verify that the switch is in VTP server or VTP transparent mode. If VTP is not enabled on the switch, it will not be able to automatically send updates of its configuration changes to other devices. In the Switch Manager, use the VLAN | VLAN-VTP Management option to enable and configure VTP on a switch.

The port on which the VLAN is being configured can have either the static-access or multi-VLAN membership mode, assigned via the VLAN Membership page of the Switch Manager interface. See the next section, "VLAN Port Membership Modes."

Because a VLAN is considered a separate logical network, it contains its own MIB with the switch's parameters and network data. The VLAN is accessible by SNMP; SNMP configuration applies to the entire switch.

The VLAN switch also supports its own implementation of the Spanning Tree Protocol. Each VLAN has its own instance of STP, and when you enable STP for one switch, you enable it for all other VLANs.

VLAN Port Membership Modes

As discussed in the preceding section, the most common method of defining a VLAN (and the method supported by Cisco) is by assigning VLANs to ports, or port grouping. (VLAN port grouping is not to be confused with EtherChannel port grouping.) Ports as-

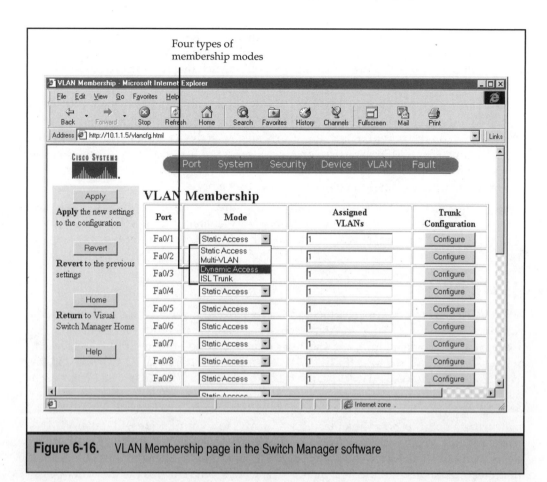

Four types of
membership modes

Figure 6-16. VLAN Membership page in the Switch Manager software

signed to VLANs are assigned a membership mode that determines the type of traffic carried by each port, and the number of VLANs the port can belong to.

There are four membership modes for a VLAN or multiple VLANs: static-access mode, multi-VLAN mode, dynamic-access mode, and trunk mode. Figure 6-16 shows the VLAN Membership page of the Switch Manager software (select VLAN | VLAN Membership in the menu bar). This page helps you assign a membership mode to a port, as well as the VLANs it will support.

▼   A *static-access* membership mode is the default. A port assigned this type of mode can only belong to one VLAN. In order to perform port monitoring of traffic where the traffic from one port is duplicated over to another monitoring port, the monitoring port must be assigned static-access membership.

■ A *multi-VLAN* membership mode is manually configured on the port. A port with this type of membership can belong to as many as 64 different VLANs. A multi-VLAN port cannot be configured on a switch that has a trunk configured. A multi-VLAN port will not allow traffic encapsulation.

■ *Dynamic-access* membership mode is configured dynamically using the VLAN Membership Policy Server (VMPS). VMPS assigns a MAC address to a VLAN based on the port on which the VLAN sits. Each device can belong to only one VLAN. The VMPS database containing the entire list of MAC addresses and their associated VLANs must use the switch's naming convention for naming ports; you can't assign your own names to the ports.

▲ *Trunk* membership mode is exactly as it sounds: The port is connected to a trunk. In this mode, the port (or trunk) is a member of all VLANs in the VLAN database. You can, however, limit membership by configuring the allowed VLAN list.

VLAN TRUNKS

When VLANs were developed, a method was needed to make sure traffic destined to a particular VLAN went to that VLAN. Cisco developed two methods for this monitoring: one is ISL (Inter-Switch Link), and the other is an adaptation to the IEEE 802.10 security protocol usually referred to as IEEE 802.1W. Cisco ISL and IEEE 802.1Q, discussed in this section, are the protocols used to carry traffic of multiple VLANs over a 100BaseT or Gigabit Ethernet trunk.

A VLAN trunk is configured either between two switches or between a router and a switch. It is a point-to-point link that allows VLANs to communicate with other VLANs. When a switch receives a frame from an administratively defined VLAN, the switch attaches a unique identifier to the frame prior to forwarding it. Each device examines this identifier and passes it to the next device. The last switch removes the identifier before passing the frame on to its destination.

By default, a trunk port sends and receives traffic from all VLANs in the VLAN database. You can, however, delete VLANs from the VLAN database and eliminate their traffic from the trunk. This configuration is useful for a VLAN of machines containing highly proprietary information, when these machines do not need access to any other VLAN devices.

Inter-VLAN Routing Protocols

This section describes the three protocols based on layer 2 of the OSI model, available for creating a trunk to allow communications between VLANs:

▼ ISL

■ IEEE 802.1Q

▲ ATM LAN Emulation

These protocols do not provide a mechanism for inter-VLAN communications; rather, they provide a means to transport multiple VLANs across the same physical link. A router, or MPOA in the case of ATM, would provide inter-VLAN connectivity.

Table 6-4 summarizes the network communications protocols supported by each VLAN routing protocol (assuming Cisco IOS version 11.1 or greater).

Inter-Switch Link (ISL)

ISL is a Cisco protocol defined to maintain VLAN information as it is transferred between switches and/or routers. ISL operates in a point-to-point environment maintaining full bandwidth performance and supporting up to 1000 VLANs.

In order to extend VLAN information among switches, you need to define a communication link, an *ISL link (trunk)*. To use ISL, you need to configure the ports on both sides of the link as trunk ports. By default, no VLAN traffic will be forwarded across this ISL link unless you specify identical VLANs on the trunk ports.

ISL encapsulates an Ethernet frame with a header containing the VLAN ID (this ID is only attached when the frame is destined to nonlocal networks). ISL enables the protocol on the router or switch, enables the protocol on the interface, defines the encapsulation format as ISL, and then customizes the protocol according to the topology of your network.

ISL links/trunks are used to connect VLAN-capable Fast Ethernet devices (such as the Catalyst 5000 switch and 7500 router). Figure 6-17 illustrates switches in an ISL environment.

IEEE 802.1Q Protocol

The IEEE 802.1Q protocol is Cisco's adaptation of IEEE 802.10. It can run over any LAN or HDLC serial interface to provide connectivity between VLANs. VLAN identification is

Network Communications Protocol	ISL	ATM LANE	IEEE 802.10 (Cisco's IEEE 802.1Q)
IP	✓	✓	✓
Novell IPX	✓	✓	✓
AppleTalk Phase II	✓	✓	
DECnet	✓	✓	
Banyan Vines	✓	✓	
XNS	✓	✓	

Table 6-4. Protocols Supported by Inter-VLAN

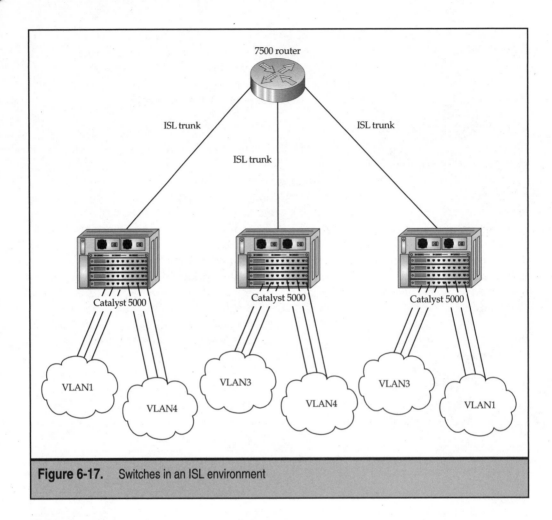

Figure 6-17. Switches in an ISL environment

placed in a frame between the MAC and LLC headers of the frame (layer 2). This VLAN ID allows switches and routers to selectively forward packets to ports with the same VLAN ID. The IEEE 802.1Q protocol ensures data integrity and confidentiality by using authentication and encryption methods.

ATM LAN Emulation Protocol

The ATM LAN Emulation (LANE) protocol enables routing of all major protocols among VLANs, so that networks can take advantage of ATM.

VLAN Trunk Protocol (VTP)

VLAN Trunk Protocol (VTP) has similar functionality to the inter-VLAN routing protocols (IEEE 802.1Q, ISL, and ATM LANE), but VTP provides additional management capabilities. VTP is an optional but highly recommended protocol to have enabled on a switch prior to setting up VLANs.

The majority of networks have a combination of different media types, including FDDI, 10 Mbps Ethernet, 100 Mbps Ethernet, and ATM. Instead of having to create separate VLANs for each of these links, Cisco developed the VLAN Trunk Protocol. VTP is a layer-2 messaging protocol included in the switch IOS that automatically manages the addition, deletion, and renaming of VLANs. This protocol is required in order to have those changes automatically forwarded to all the other switches in the network.

VTP Versions

Whether you choose VTP version 1 or 2, all switches in the same VTP domain must run the same version. By default, version 2 is disabled. If you enable version 2 on one switch, every other switch that is version 2–capable will automatically enable version 2. This is a really handy feature because it saves you the time of logging into each switch and manually updating it. Make sure to verify, however, that every switch within each VTP domain does indeed support version 2.

NOTE: If your network environment has Token Ring, you must use VTP version 2.

VTP Domains

When VTP is used, each switch must be configured to be a member of a VTP domain. A switch can be a member of one VTP domain only. Domains can be grouped according to campus, site, or other categorization. VTP domains are used to forward VTP advertisements.

The following sequence of commands configure a VTP domain name and password for a switch:

```
Switch#vlan database
Switch(vlan)#vtp domain floor1
Switch(vlan)#vtp password password
```

VTP Modes

VTP switches can be configured as a server, as a client, or to be transparent.

▼ If the switch is configured to be a VTP server, it can manage configuration parameters for the entire group of servers.

■ As a VTP client, the switch would advertise and synchronize its VLAN configurations to other switches in the VTP domain. Unlike a VTP server, however, the switch cannot create, modify, or delete VLANs.

▲ In VTP transparent mode, VTP is disabled on a switch. In this mode, a switch does not advertise or synchronize its configurations, but only forwards the advertisements of other switches (which, obviously, aren't VTP transparent).

In the privileged EXEC mode, the following commands allow you to configure the VTP in client, server, or transparent mode:

```
Switch#vlan database
Switch#vtp vtpmode
```

VTP Advertisements

VTP servers and VTP clients advertise their configurations to other VTP servers and clients using the VTP protocol. Transparent VTP switches only pass on the advertisements received from VTP client and VTP server switches. These advertisements consist of the following:

▼ VTP domain name

■ VTP configuration revision number

■ Update identity and update timestamp

■ MD5 digest

■ VLAN ID

■ VLAN name

■ VLAN type

■ VLAN state

▲ Additional VLAN configuration information specific to the VLAN type

VTP Pruning

VTP also has a feature known as *pruning*. Pruning blocks flooded traffic to VLANs that are included in a list. Pruning will automatically stop the forwarding of a VLAN's traffic across a trunk if there are no members of VLAN active on the switch at the receiving end of the trunk. Pruning is turned off by default on the Catalyst 5000.

Unfortunately, pruning is currently not available on all switches, including the popular Catalyst 2900 Series XL. According to Cisco, this feature will be supported in a future release.

Summary of VTP Settings

Table 6-5 summarizes the default VTP configuration settings of a 2900 switch, as discussed in the preceding sections. Figure 6-18 illustrates VTP support for VLANs on a switched network.

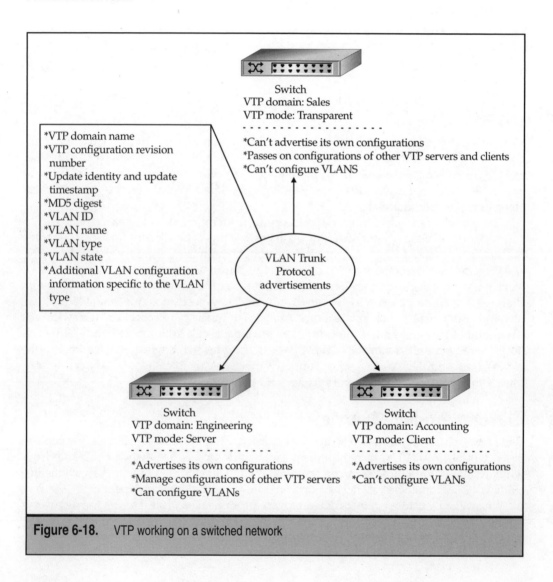

Switch
VTP domain: Sales
VTP mode: Transparent
- - - - - - - - - - - - - - - - -
*Can't advertise its own configurations
*Passes on configurations of other VTP servers and clients
*Can't configure VLANS

*VTP domain name
*VTP configuration revision number
*Update identity and update timestamp
*MD5 digest
*VLAN ID
*VLAN name
*VLAN type
*VLAN state
*Additional VLAN configuration information specific to the VLAN type

VLAN Trunk Protocol advertisements

Switch
VTP domain: Engineering
VTP mode: Server
- - - - - - - - - - - - - - - - -
*Advertises its own configurations
*Manage configurations of other VTP servers
*Can configure VLANs

Switch
VTP domain: Accounting
VTP mode: Client
- - - - - - - - - - - - - - - - -
*Advertises its own configurations
*Can't configure VLANs

Figure 6-18. VTP working on a switched network

Setting	Default State
VTP domain name	Null
VTP mode	Server
VTP version 2 enable state	Version 2 disabled
VTP password	None
VTP pruning	Not available

Table 6-5.   Default VTP Configurations

VLANDIRECTOR

VlanDirector is a virtual LAN-management application for Cisco Catalyst switches. It allows you to create, modify, and manage VLANs, reducing the complexity and time needed for switch configuration. Multiple windows within the application display various configuration statuses and provide both physical and logical views of the switches being managed and maintained.

The growth of switched internetworks results from the need for increased bandwidth and network efficiency. Switches allow business systems to better contain broadcast traffic, and to optimize LAN segment traffic through the use of logically defined VLAN workgroups. The deployment of such powerful solutions requires equally capable network management products. Network managers need to quickly configure and assess changes to their switched network environment. They need tools for visualizing their physical and logical switch connections. Analysis of traffic patterns across the switched environment takes on added importance as managers seek to optimize bandwidth and improve resource efficiency. On a daily basis, managers face the need for tracking individual users and devices to resolve connectivity issues, or to change VLAN configurations as required for evolving workgroups and personnel shifts.

VlanDirector Product Overview

VlanDirector is an SNMP-based switch management application that provides graphically based virtual LAN (VLAN) management capabilities for Cisco switches. Drag-and-drop windows allow for simple port configurations. VlanDirector also monitors functions including VLAN topologies, switches, port configurations, and workgroups.

When VlanDirector is launched, a discovery process takes place. During the discovery process, VlanDirector determines all the devices in which the Cisco Discovery Protocol (CDP) is enabled, collecting information such as VLAN device names, topologies, and ports.

Supported Switches

VlanDirector supports the creation and modification of VLANs on the following Catalyst series switches: 5000, 3900, 3000, 2900, 2830, and 1900.

Supported VLANs

VlanDirector supports three types of VLANs:

▼ **Ethernet VLANs**   This is the most common VLAN design, consisting of logical users independent of their position on the network. All users connecting to the same VLAN are assigned to the same Ethernet VLAN, as well.

■ **ATM VLANs**   This design spans an ATM network bridging two or more Ethernet VLANs using LAN Emulation (LANE).

▲ **Token Ring VLANs**   In this arrangement, a set of rings are interconnected through a bridging function. There are two Token Ring VLAN types defined in VTP version 2: Token Ring Concentrator Relay Function (trCRF) comprises logical ring domains formed by defining groups of ports that have the same ring number. Token Ring Bridge Relay Function (trBRF) is a domain of interconnected rings formed using an internal multiport bridge function.

Installation of VlanDirector

VlanDirector is included in the CiscoWorks Switched Internetwork (CWSI) application as part of CiscoWorks 2000, and can be installed as a stand-alone application or can be fully integrated with CiscoView.

Since CWSI installs on a system with the Essentials applications already installed, there are no more additional hardware or software requirements for VlanDirector. CWSI requires Essentials because the two share some back-end processing and databases. You can install CWSI with other network management stations such as HP OpenView. Refer to Chapter 8 for more details on the minimum requirements for CWSI.

Installation Requirements

Prior to the installation of the VlanDirector software, certain required configurations must be in place on the network.

ENABLE CDP   Switches use Cisco Discovery Protocol (CDP) to maintain information about neighboring devices that also support CDP. This information includes device type, links between devices, and the number of ports on each device. CDP must be enabled on all the switches in the network being monitored and managed.

To enable CDP on a switch using the command line interface, enter this command:

```
Rouer(config)#set cdp enable all
```

To enable CDP from the Visual Switch Manager software, select Device | Cisco Discovery Protocol and click the button to run CDP.

NOTE: CDP can be disabled for specific ports on a switch. This is a useful feature when you do not want to exchange information with a certain device.

ISL REQUIREMENTS   Cisco's Inter-Switch Link (ISL) protocol, described earlier in this chapter, is defined only on Fast Ethernet. If there are switches on the network that are connected with Fast Ethernet and have more than one VLAN running, ISL needs to be enabled on both devices. Use the following steps to define a port as an ISL trunk port, which by default will send and receive traffic from all VLANs in the VLAN database.

1. Enter global configuration mode:

    `Router#`**`configure terminal`**

2. Specify the interface port to be defined:

    `Router(config)#`**`interface Fa0/1`**

3. Configure the port to be in trunk mode:

    `Router(config-if)#`**`switchport mode trunk`**

4. Configure the port to support ISL:

    `Router(config-if)#`**`switchport trunk encapsulation isl`**

All switches being managed and maintained must be running a minimum of switch software version 1.2.

COMMUNITY STRINGS   VlanDirector uses the default community strings (public and private) when it is launched, unless directed otherwise. It's wise to change from these default names to prevent unauthorized access. To specify a new or different set of community strings, use the following command in VlanDirector:

`Vldirector#`**`csf`** **`switch_name`** **`read_community_string write_community_string`**

By leaving the switch name value blank, you tell VlanDirector to assume all switches use the same read and write community string. To allow the assignment of unique community strings to each switch, repeat this command as many times as needed.

STARTING DEVICE FOR DISCOVERY   During installation of VlanDirector, the system will prompt you for a host name or IP address of a switch. This is the switch that will act as the starting device for the discovery process used to determine other devices. This switch is typically the core switch from which other switches branch.

Chapter 8 includes more information regarding the installation of CWSI, which contains VlanDirector.

Using VlanDirector

Before using the VlanDirector application, you need to have documented your network design, including the design of your VTP domains. As discussed earlier in the chapter, a VTP domain can be a server, client, or transparent. VlanDirector requires at least one VTP server for each VTP domain. In most situations, the other switches should be configured as clients.

When you start the VlanDirector application, the VlanDirector window opens as shown in Figure 6-19. This main window consists of the following elements:

▼ **Menu bar** Contains all the commands used to create, modify, and delete VLANs.

■ **Toolbar** Provides icons for common tasks such as creating, deleting, and showing VLANs. In Figure 6-19, the toolbar is directly under the menu bar.

■ **Names window** Displays names of existing VLANs and contains a toolbar for performing tasks such as organizing and managing VLANs.

■ **Membership window** Contains link status, port number, and IP address of devices. If there is information to be displayed, the Membership window will appear on the right side of the VlanDirector window.

▲ **Status bar** Displays system messages, including number of domains, fabrics, and VLANs discovered. The status bar is in the bottom-left corner of the VlanDirector window.

Finding VLANs

There are two ways to find the VLANs on your network. From within the VlanDirector Names window, you can either click the plus sign next to the folder in which the VLAN resides and scroll down to the VLAN you are looking for, or you can use the Find button in the toolbar (the binoculars icon). The Find button lets you enter the VLAN name or scroll through a list of all VLAN names. When the VLAN is found, it is automatically highlighted in the Names window.

Creating and Modifying VLANs

VlanDirector can be used to configure Ethernet, ATM, and Token Ring VLANs.

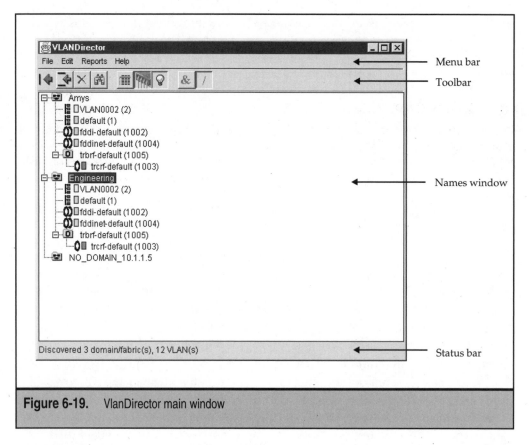

Figure 6-19.   VlanDirector main window

ETHERNET VLANS   To configure Ethernet VLANs, in the Names window click the folder of the domain in which you are creating the VLAN. Select Edit | Create from the menu bar, and enter the appropriate settings, shown here:

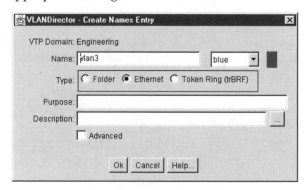

ATM VLANS   For ATM VLANs, you have to configure a server and LAN Emulation (LANE) server for the default ATM VLAN in your ATM network. You can use Configure | Config Server (from the Edit menu) to add and change the priority of backup configuration servers, and to delete configuration servers.

To create an ATM VLAN, select Edit | Create from VlanDirector's menu bar and enter the following information in the Create Names Entry dialog box:

▼   Name for the VLAN

■   Color to identify the VLAN

■   Type of VLAN

■   Purpose of the VLAN

▲   Description of the VLAN contents

Advanced options include the following:

▼   VLAN index (automatically assigned)

■   802.10 SAID (automatically assigned)

■   LANE Services to bridge the VLAN across ATM network

■   Config (represents an LE server on the device)

■   Device (the host name and module/port numbers)

▲   Order (the priority number of the server; automatically increments)

TOKEN RING VLANS   To create Token Ring VLANs, you must first configure the trBRF parent VLAN, and then the trCRFs that you want associated with the trBRF. A trBRF is a logical grouping of trCRFs; therefore, you need to create the trBRF before creating the trCRFs. Both trBRFs and trCRFs are created by selecting Edit | Create in the Names window menu bar, and entering the appropriate settings as follows:

▼   A name for the VLAN

■   A color to identify the VLAN in the Names window

■   The type, which is either trBRF or trCRF

■   The purpose of the VLAN

▲   A description of the contents of the VLAN

There's only one Advanced option: a VLAN index, which is automatically assigned.

You can only modify VLAN characteristics that are not default or automatic, such as the index. To modify, select the VLAN in the Names window (or locate the VLAN using the Find button) and select Edit | Modify from the menu bar.

Deleting VLANs

Deleting a VLAN removes it from the Names window, VTP servers, VTP-enabled transparent devices, and other devices not running VTP. A Token Ring trBRF can only be deleted if the BRF does not contain any trBRFs, or by deleting both the trCRFs and the trBRF.

Configuring Links and Ports

After using VlanDirector to create a VLAN, you can add links and ports to it. Links on switches running VTP are automatically configured to forward packets for VLANs. If you add a link to a VLAN, the link is enabled to carry packets for that VLAN.

To add, move, or delete VLAN ports, go to the CWSI campus map and select the device you want to modify. Click the right mouse button and select Device Ports.

▼ To add ports, select on the CWSI campus map the ports you want to add and drag them to the desired VLAN in the Names window.

■ To move ports, highlight the VLAN in the Names window. Then, in the Membership window, select the ports you want to move. Drag the ports from the Membership window into the destination VLAN in the Names window.

▲ To delete a port, in the Names window select the VLAN from which you want to delete ports. In the Membership window, select the ports you want to delete. Click the Reset button in the Names window toolbar. Note: You cannot delete a link port.

VlanDirector's Reporting

VlanDirector provides reporting functionality that includes discrepancies or inconsistencies in your network's VLANs. These reports are useful to help identify and troubleshoot problems. To produce reports, select Reports in the VlanDirector menu bar and choose Discrepancies.

The discrepancies reported by VlanDirector's can include any or all of the following:

▼ **VLAN Name Conflict**   ISL numbers have the same name in different VTP domains.

■ **VLAN Index Conflict**   VLAN names have the same ISL number in different VTP domains.

■ **VLAN SAID Conflict**   Different SAID numbers are on the same VLAN in different domains.

■ **VTP Disconnect Domain**   A link in the VTP domain is not set to trunk.

▲ **No VTP Server**   No VTP server exists in the VTP domain.

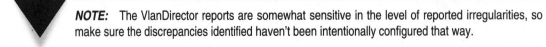

NOTE: The VlanDirector reports are somewhat sensitive in the level of reported irregularities, so make sure the discrepancies identified haven't been intentionally configured that way.

SUMMARY

Switches offer features and functionality in addition to that provided by hubs and bridges. For some network managers, replacing hubs with switches is an appropriate decision. A switch will reduce Ethernet collisions and provide cut-through processing to help reduce network latencies. Cisco Group Multicast Protocol (CGMP) is used to forward multicast packets to only multicast clients, reducing broadcast traffic.

An efficient switched internetwork consists of a switch platform, a common infrastructure, and effective management tools. Three types of devices provide switching technology: LAN switches, ATM switches, and routers. The selection of platform depends on the current network infrastructure and the requirements of the switch. The switch offers solutions to various network arrangements, including high-performance desktop connectivity, enterprise workgroup aggregation, and dispersed building aggregation. Like other network devices, switches can be accessed and configured through the console port, via a Telnet session, or using Cisco's Web-based Visual Switch Management software. Once the switch is installed, powered up with network connectivity, and working, several options can be set (in addition to the common IP address assignment and passwords) that will increase efficiency. Spanning Tree Protocol (STP) can be enabled to eliminate possible loops in the switched network. Switched Port Analyzer (SPAN) can be configured on a port to receive traffic from other port(s) to be diagnosed. Ports can be grouped together into an EtherChannel to increase bandwidth and provide redundancy.

A VLAN is configured to group related users together regardless of their physical connection to a switch or switches. When a VLAN is assigned to each group of ports, this is considered to be a Port Grouping type of VLAN. This is the most common and easiest type of VLAN to configure.

VlanDirector provides an accurate campus view of Cisco switches in addition to simplifying configuration and monitoring functions. VlanDirector assists in maintaining configuration consistency and providing useful discrepancy reporting.

The demand for bandwidth is increasing with the growing usage of applications such as voice and audio. For bandwidth-intensive applications, workstations should be directly connected to switches in order to provide high-performance desktop connectivity. Workstations that may not require as much bandwidth can connect to a hub that is connected to a switch. In Chapter 7, we'll take a closer look at hubs.

CHAPTER 7

Configuring Cisco Hubs

The increased usage of high-bandwidth applications is driving the need for faster networks. There is a per-user increase in bandwidth requirement that is compounded by the addition of more users on the network. Although many argue that hubs are going the way of the dinosaur, many cost-conscious network designers and administrators use hubs to keep costs down, add users, and deploy network connectivity to areas of the network that do not yet require dedicated switch ports. Let's face it—although everybody says they need the speed of 100 Mbps Ethernet or Gigabit Ethernet, most really don't. In fact, a large majority of single-user PCs in use today can't put enough data on the wire to fully utilize a 10 Mbps connection.

In several areas of the network, hubs can be cost effective and can meet all the necessary bandwidth requirements. These areas are workgroups found in small offices; branch offices; segments within a larger office network; and, increasingly, networks in the home. The other primary area for hubs is in the server room or data center, where ports must be available for additional low-volume servers, network monitors, administrative PCs, printers, and other equipment. Instead of spending additional money to provide dedicated switch ports when they're really not necessary, the savvy network professional is deploying the new breed of low-cost, manageable hubs.

Where bandwidth is or may become an issue, 100BaseT hubs can be a wise investment that affords users more bandwidth at minimal expense. As we saw in Chapter 4, hubs have come a long way from their black-box repeater days; they are faster, manageable, modular, and more reliable. With the integration of management- and port-level control and visibility, hubs have evolved to suit the needs of the modern network.

In this chapter, we will walk through the installation and configuration process for several of Cisco's most popular hubs, to see how hubs can be a cost-effective part of your switched network. We'll take a close look at the management features built into the latest hubs from Cisco, as well as how to take advantage of the SNMP and RMON capabilities of these newer devices. Finally, we'll examine several network-design scenarios (workgroup LANs, and server room/data center connectivity) that will illustrate how you can use hubs effectively.

HUBS EXPLAINED

To better understand where you should use hubs, it doesn't hurt to know a little more about what they do and how they do it. After a look at the basic features common to all hubs, we'll discuss the important issues of data cabling. Then we'll examine the current 10BaseT and 100BaseT standards, and delve into 100BaseTX and 100BaseFX.

Ethernet Hubs

A *hub* is a network device that allows multiple stations to be cabled together in a star topology. When the hub supports Ethernet, it is generally referred to as a hub, a *concentrator*, or a *repeater*. If the network is Token Ring, the hub is typically referred to as an MSAU

(Multi-Station Access Unit). Because most new installations are Ethernet, we will focus here on the various types of Ethernet hubs.

Ethernet hubs allow the network to be configured in a star topology, in which the PCs are located at one end of the segment and terminated into the centrally located hub. This keeps cable and network adapter failures from affecting every user. If a station cable is damaged by a piece of office furniture, only one PC (the one the cable is connected to) will get disconnected from the network. In network configurations using a bus topology, in which all of the PCs are connected to a single run of cable, any damage to the cable will either take the entire network down or, in effect, split it into two segments at the break. This is one reason why star topology networks are the most commonly deployed configurations.

NOTE: From a technical point of view, Ethernet and IEEE 802.3 are different specifications. Ethernet was originally developed by Xerox and further enhanced by a consortium of Digital, Intel, and Xerox. This early implementation of Ethernet did not allow for the variety of network topologies that we use today. The IEEE-defined international standards for all LAN technology, including 802.3 and 802.3u, are referred to in this chapter as Ethernet.

As you learned in Chapter 3, Ethernet is a *shared media protocol*. Each participating station on a particular segment has to share the wire with the other stations. Every station can send data onto the wire at any time, and every station on the segment can "hear" what the other stations are sending. The trouble is, the wire is capable of carrying only one "conversation" at a time. If there were no rules to follow, the segment would be saturated with fragments of all the attempted conversations. When two stations talk at the same time, they cause a *collision*. In other words, when more than one station sends data to the wire, each listens to determine if the data was sent during a time in which no other stations were sending. If it detects that another station was trying to send at the same time, the listening station knows that the data is corrupt as a result of the collision. Both stations then back off and wait a random amount of time before trying to send data again.

Keeping the number of collisions down means limiting the number of stations on the segment. As the collisions increase, the network's performance drops. Because hubs simply retransmit frames to all attached cable segments, what might have been fast with 12 users can become unbearably slow with 30 users because of the increased number of collisions. Of course, it all depends on the type and amount of traffic each station typically sends, so don't assume anything without analyzing your network traffic patterns.

Class I and II Repeaters

Each station sees the network as a single cable; but in a network based on the star topology, there are many runs of cable. A hub in this environment is sometimes called a repeater because it simply repeats the signal internally to the other ports, as opposed to routing the signal the way a router would. Individual repeaters can also be used to resend the signal to another repeater, to allow for longer distances. Multiple hubs can form a single logical repeater. Since a repeater functions at the physical layer, it cannot route traffic.

It simply carries and amplifies electrical signals across a single segment. There are two types of repeaters commonly used today, *Class I* and *Class II repeaters.*

A Class I repeater uses an analog-to-digital conversion of electrical signals coming into the repeater. This allows the repeater to pass traffic between different Ethernet implementations (100BaseTX and 100BaseFX, for example). Because the conversion process introduces a time delay, there is a limit of one Class I repeater in any individual network segment.

A Class II repeater doesn't perform any signal conversion, it simply retransmits the electrical signal to the other ports in the repeater. Since there isn't much delay, additional repeaters are possible on a single segment.

NOTE: The Cisco FastHub 100, 200, 300, and 400 Series are all Class II repeaters.

Cable Distances

One rule of thumb to use when cascading Class II repeaters to create a single segment is to ensure that maximum station-to-station cable lengths are not exceeded. With a single Class II repeater (hub) using 100-meter station-to-hub cable runs, the 200-meter station-to-station cable length is maintained. When cascading Class II repeaters, you will need to consider the length of the cable used to connect the repeaters and reduce the length of the station-to-hub cables accordingly. For example, consider station runs terminating in two separate network closets with one hub in each of the closets, and say the length of cable between the two hubs is 20 meters. To get the maximum station-to-hub length allowable, you would need to factor in the 20 meters used to connect the two hubs. You would also need to factor the hub-to-station runs on both hubs. In this example, the maximum station-to-hub cable length would be 90 meters instead of 100 meters. We arrived at this length by subtracting 20 meters from the 200-meter maximum length. We then split the remaining 180-meter allowable length between the two hub locations giving us the 90-meter limitation per hub location.

This calculation can be visualized in the following scenario: An Ethernet frame is sent between a client PC and a Server. Traffic between the client station (PC) connected to Hub 1 and the host station (Server) connected to Hub 2 needs to traverse the 90-meter length of cable to get to Hub 1. Then the traffic crosses the 20-meter uplink cable to Hub 2. Finally, the traffic crosses the 90-meter length of cable between Hub 2 and the host station (Server). By adding the three lengths together (90+90+20), we arrive at the 200-meter, station-to-station cable distance.

Additionally, EIA/TIA standards recommend that you reserve 10 meters of that distance for patch cabling. This limits the "in-the-wall" cable distances even more.

Table 7-1 lists the maximum allowed distances between a hub and station.

Ethernet Type	Maximum Hub-to-Station Cable Distance
Standard 10BaseT (Category 5)	100 meters
Standard 10BaseFL (Multimode Fiber)	400 meters
Standard 100BaseTX	100 meters
Standard 100BaseFX	400 meters

Table 7-1.   Hub-to-Station Cable Distances

When you add up the two 100-meter station-to-hub distances, you arrive at the 200-meter maximum distance between any two stations for Category 5 UTP. As mentioned earlier, if you cascade hubs you'll need to account for the length of cable used between them. When designing the FastHub series, Cisco recognized that many cable installations would be at the 100-meter station-to-hub length. To accommodate existing cable plants, Cisco engineered the FastHub to exceed the IEEE 802.3u specifications and allow for up to a 23-meter uplink between FastHubs that already have the maximum 100-meter station cabling. This extends the overall segment length to 223 meters when using two FastHubs (see Table 7-2).

Although some hubs, including the Cisco FastHub Series, allow you to extend the cable distances somewhat, it's a good idea to stick to the limits defined in the standards. Ethernet is especially sensitive to the delay introduced by longer cable distances, and performance can degrade quickly when a cabling standard is exceeded.

Number of Hubs (Class II Repeater) Category 5 UTP	Maximum Overall Cable Distance (Station A to Hub, to Station B)
1 (standard 100BaseT hub)	200 meters
2 (standard 100BaseT hubs)	200 meters
1 (Cisco 100BaseT FastHub)	200 meters
2 (Cisco 100BaseT FastHubs)	223 meters

Table 7-2.   Overall Category 5 Cable Distances for a Single-Collision Domain

Cable Specifications

An important part of every network is the network cabling. The most common cable is unshielded twisted pair (UTP). There are several categories of UTP, with each category offering higher speeds. Category 5 cable can support 10BaseT at 10 Mbps, all the way up to 100BaseTX at 100 Mbps. Categories 4 and 3 support speeds up to 20 Mbps and 16 Mbps, respectively. The following list summarizes the Category 3, 4, and 5 specifications:

▼ *Category 3* cable is rated up to 16 MHz and supports 10BaseT.

■ *Category 4* cable is rated up to 20 MHz and supports Token Ring and 10BaseT.

▲ *Category 5* cable is rated up to 100 MHz and supports 100BaseT, 10BaseT, and Token Ring.

Although 10 Mbps network devices can use Category 3, 4, or 5 cable, 100 Mbps network devices must use at least Category 5 cable. When you start incorporating 100 Mbps equipment into your network, you'll need to make sure that all the cable segments (including patch cables) are Category 5 certified. You may be able to get the network up and running if you try to run 100 Mbps equipment on the Category 3 cable typical in older, 10 Mbps networks. It won't be reliable, however, and will be prone to errors (if it works at all). If you don't know whether your cabling can support 100 MHz traffic, have it tested and certified by a reputable cabling company. You can save yourself a lot of headaches and cost by removing cable issues from the equation *before* you get started configuring a network with hubs.

An alternative to copper cabling is fiber-optic cabling. It can support 10BaseFL and 100BaseFX segments. Because fiber-optic will run over distances of 2 kilometers (2,000 meters), it's typically used when distances are longer than 100 meters (although repeater-to-station lengths are limited to 400 meters). Popular uses include connecting buildings in a campus environment, connecting devices on a network backbone within a data center, and connecting remote hubs and switches from a central router or switch within a large building.

10BaseT Hubs

We've had 10BaseT hubs for a long time. The most common implementation of the 10BaseT standard in use today is based on the IEEE 802.3i specification. It was designed to run over two pairs of Category 3 unshielded twisted pair (UTP) cables. Each station is connected in a star topology to the hub. Token Ring has been the primary competition, but 10BaseT's low cost and ability to support most of the common network protocols has made it a network industry standard. Equipment that supports it is commonplace and much less expensive than Token Ring. Finding network adapter cards for 10BaseT is easy, and the cards themselves are inexpensive. Aside from being fairly fast and easy to work with, its adoption as a standard has been driven by a huge range of network and software vendors giving network designers many options.

100BaseT Hubs

With the onslaught of new applications today, including those providing voice and video, high transmission speeds are required. One of the most popular methods of increasing network speed is to incorporate 100BaseT switches into the network. Because 100BaseT can auto-negotiate the speed from 10 to 200 Mbps (full duplex), transition from 10 Mbps Ethernet to 100 Mbps Ethernet can be accomplished with relative ease. The network equipment, including switches and hubs, can be upgraded to 10/100 components; and then the workstations can be upgraded with 10/100 cards gradually, at a convenient pace.

The 100BaseT network is based on specifications defined in the IEEE 802.3u standard. It requires two pairs of Category 5 unshielded twisted-pair (UTP), or four pairs of Category 3 or 4 UTP. It also can run over single and multimode fiber-optic cabling. The primary competition for 100BaseT includes Fiber Distributed Data Interface (FDDI), Asynchronous Transfer Mode (ATM), and Gigabit Ethernet.

Fast Ethernet 100BaseT has many of the same features as 10BaseT. It uses the same frame formats and frame lengths as 10BaseT. It uses CSMA/CD and runs over Categories 3, 4, and 5 UTP cabling. Interconnections are made using hubs, switches, and repeaters, just like 10BaseT. However, 100BaseT does have some important differences from 10BaseT. First, data is transmitted at ten times the speed of 10BaseT. For example, the required amount of time for a workstation to detect no carrier on the wire before transmitting is only 0.96 microseconds, as opposed to 9.6 microseconds with 10BaseT. The second important difference is that 100BaseT uses a different coding scheme to represent bits on the network.

Fast Ethernet has been defined by three different physical layer specifications: 100BaseTX, 100BaseT4, and 100BaseFX.

▼ 100BaseTX is fast Ethernet over Category 5 UTP and uses RJ-45 connectors, as 10BaseT does. 100BaseTX requires two pairs of wires for transmission of data.

■ 100BaseT4 is simply Fast Ethernet over Category 3 or 4 UTP cabling, except that it requires four pairs of wires. Three are used for data transmission, while the fourth is used to manage collision detection. Implementation of 100BaseT4 is fairly uncommon, and the standard is not compatible with the hubs discussed in this chapter. It was designed because there are some cases in which the existing voice-grade Category 3 cabling cannot be replaced economically by Category 5 cabling. The 100BaseT4 standard allows those installations to realize the benefits of 100 Mbps transport without having to upgrade cable plants.

▲ 100BaseFX is fast Ethernet for fiber-optic cabling. Fiber-optic allows greatly increased transmission distances. 100BaseFX uses the same MIC, ST, and SC connectors for the fiber-optic cabling as FDDI. It also uses both single-mode or multimode fiber, just like FDDI.

BASIC HUB SETUP

Although the latest hubs incorporate more features, they are only slightly more difficult to set up. Cisco has several different hub offerings (Chapter 4) that incorporate various features to meet a wide variety of network requirements.

The Cisco FastHubs (100, 200, 300, 400 Series) can all run at 100 Mbps (200 Mbps in full-duplex mode), making them suitable for almost any configuration in which a hub is desirable. Most are available with or without integrated management, and they come in a variety of form factors. The 100 and 400 Series also have hubs that can run at 10 Mbps and 100 Mbps; the 200 and 300 Series are able to run at 100 Mbps only. If you are looking for a 100 Mbps hub and don't need to provide any 10 Mbps connectivity, you can save a few dollars by buying a 100 Mbps hub.

Cisco also has the 1528 and 1538 Series of Micro Hubs. They are all 10/100 Mbps auto-sensing and are available with integrated management. These 8-port hubs can be stacked and connected using a special cable. By stacking four of them, you can create a 32-port repeater segment.

Setting up Cisco hubs is a very simple process, and there is very little difference in setting up the different models (where there is, the Cisco documentation does a fine job describing the process). So here we'll just run through one quick hardware setup example, using the Cisco FastHub 216T with integrated management.

FastHub 216T

The FastHub 216T is a 100BaseT Class II repeater (hub) that is designed to be used in a variety of situations. It is rack and wall mountable and can be connected to another Class II repeater, creating a 30-port segment. It also supports and can be managed using the Simple Network Management Protocol (SNMP), Remote Monitoring (RMON), and Telnet, as well as the familiar Cisco console port to allow for additional ports on the network segment. For detailed specifications on this and other Cisco hubs, refer to Chapter 4.

The FastHub 216T model has 16 100BaseTX ports, and an additional 100BaseTX uplink port that allows you to use a straight-through cable when connecting to another hub, switch, or router.

NOTE: You can only use one of the two ports (16x or 16). The straight-through port is provided as a convenient way to uplink the hub to a switch, router, or another hub. Attempting to connect devices to both ports will cause both ports to shut down.

Figure 7-1 illustrates the proper wiring scheme for the standard crossover cable used with ports 1 through 16x.

Category 5 UTP cable consists of four pairs of 22-26 AWG (American Wire Gauge) wire. Only two pairs (four wire strands) are required for 10BaseT and 100BaseT. Figure 7-2 illustrates the proper wiring scheme for a straight-through cable.

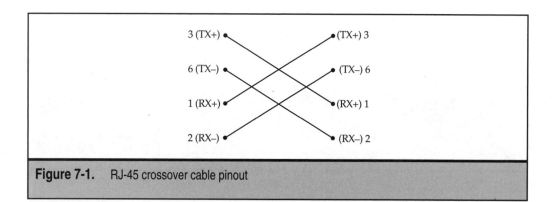

Figure 7-1. RJ-45 crossover cable pinout

CiscoView (covered in Chapter 8) provides a physical representation of the front panel of the hub, shown in Figure 7-3. Here you can see the 16 available ports, as well as the uplink port described earlier.

The front of the 216T hub also provides information about hub and link status via a series of LEDs. By default, the LED above each port indicates the port state, as follows:

Solid green	Active connection; no Ethernet traffic.
Flashing green	Active connection; Ethernet traffic.
Green/amber alternating	Port is resetting or experiencing hardware problem.
Amber	Port has been deactivated via hub management interface.
Off	No active connection (PC may be turned off, incorrect cabling may be in use, or there may be a loose connector).

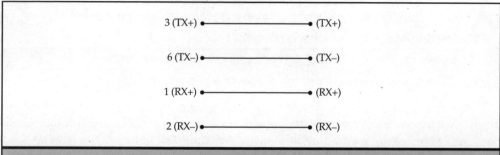

Figure 7-2. RJ-45 straight-through cable pinout

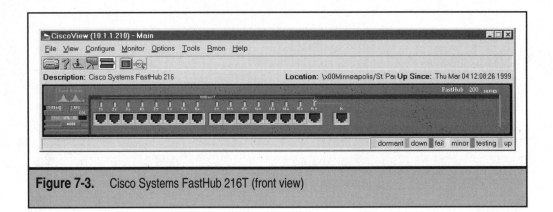

Figure 7-3. Cisco Systems FastHub 216T (front view)

Installation and Configuration

It is very important that you carefully select a good location for installing the hub if you want it to be reliable and give you many years of service. If you don't treat your network hardware right, someday it will return the favor, probably at about 11:45 P.M. the night before the month-end financials are due, or early on the Monday morning you're stuck in traffic, while everybody is arriving and logging in.

Following is a list of items to keep in mind before installing the FastHub (or any network hardware, for that matter). Also, make sure that you are not exceeding the cable distances defined earlier in Tables 7-1 and 7-2.

▼ Install the hub in a cool, clean, dry operating environment.

■ Keep the hub free of obstructions.

■ Keep the hub and cabling away from equipment that might cause interference. It is generally recommended that you keep network devices and cabling at least 48 inches away from large motors and transformers, and at least 12 inches away from fluorescent lighting, small transformers, and lighting ballasts.

■ Provide adequate and reliable power.

■ Make sure that you are not exceeding the cable distance limits.

▲ Provide proper strain relief for all power and patch cables.

The tips in the list above may seem obvious, but we've seen hubs mounted in some pretty creative places. In one case, the hubs were stacked on a table under hundreds of patch cables; when we reached into the mess, we could feel quite a bit of heat trapped around the hubs. It was only a matter of time before they'd start failing. In the very same network, all of the copper cable was run along and inside an elevator shaft. For months, network administrators tried to identify what was causing sporadic outages on the network. Finally, an elevator went past while the cable was being tested with an analyzer, and the mystery was solved. The elevator was generating strong interference as it went past the bundle of copper cable. Each time, it would knock a few users off the network; sometimes it would cause the entire network to fail briefly, but enough to disrupt hundreds of users. The moral of the story: it pays to take great care in the placement of your network equipment and cable runs.

The Cisco hubs can be powered from a 90 to 127 or 200 to 250 VAC power source and should be on a UPS if possible. You can also power the FastHubs via a Cisco Redundant Power Supply (RPS) by connecting the RPS to the RPS receptacle on the back of the unit. Note that you cannot connect both AC and RPS to the hub.

Once you have selected the location for the hub, you may want to supply it with the initial configuration before installing it into the final location. The most common method for supplying the initial configuration to a hub is to use the console port. The rear of the hub (Figure 7-4) has an AC input, RJ-45 console port, and a DC input for the optional Redundant Power Supply (RPS). As with other Cisco products, the console port is a serial connection from the PC's serial port to an RJ-45 rollover cable.

Use the provided RJ-45–to–RJ-45 rollover cable, and either the RJ-45–to–DB-9 female terminal adapter or the RJ-45–to–DB-25 female terminal adapter. Connect the appropriate adapter to a serial port on your PC, and insert the RJ-45 head directly into the console port on the back of the hub.

When connecting, configure the terminal software's serial port with the parameters listed on the following page and illustrated in Figure 7-5. Also, don't forget to set your terminal type to VT100. Hyperterminal, shown in Figure 7-5, is included with Win9x and NT4. Once it's configured for the correct serial port and terminal settings, HyperTerminal (like many other terminal applications) provides an easy method of accessing the console interface.

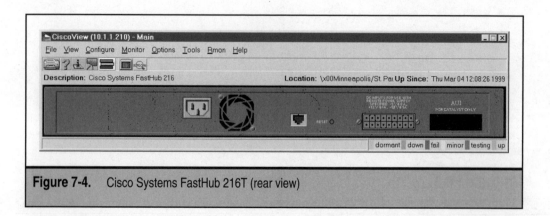

Figure 7-4. Cisco Systems FastHub 216T (rear view)

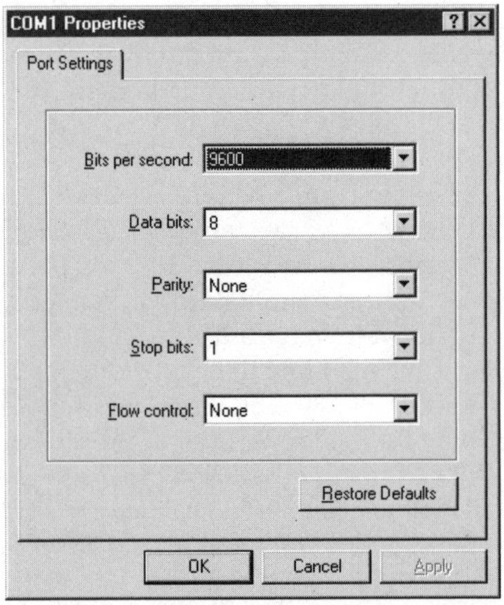

Figure 7-5. Terminal software COM port settings

As shown in Figure 7-5, terminal software can be configured to support a serial connection to the Cisco console port using the following parameters:

```
Baud rate: 9600
Data bits: 8
Stop bits: 1
Parity: none
Flow control: none
Terminal type: VT100
```

Once the parameters are set, power up the hub if you haven't done so already. At the terminal window, press ENTER. You should see the initial Console Login screen. The first time you access the console, no password is required; so press ENTER to proceed to the main menu.

Console Main Menu

The main menu lists all of the available selections used in configuring and managing the hub, as shown in Figure 7-6. The keys for navigating the management console are listed in Table 7-3.

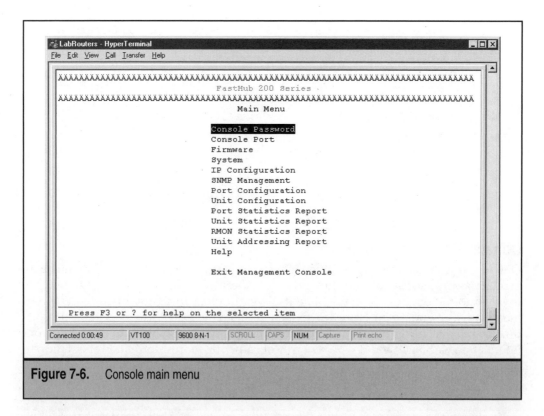

Figure 7-6.   Console main menu

Out of the box, the hub has several default settings that you will want to change first. Keep in mind that you may need to set your configuration in accordance with your particular requirements.

Key	Action
ARROW (UP, DOWN, LEFT, RIGHT)	Move cursor within text entry fields
ENTER	Select
TAB	Jump to OK and Cancel
HOME and END	Jump to beginning and end of text entry fields
F3 or ?	Access help topics

Table 7-3.   Management Console Navigation Keys

Here is a quick checklist you can use as a guide to your initial configuration. Each menu item is described in detail in the sections that follow.

▼ Set password, intrusion threshold, and silent time (Console Password menu).

■ Adjust terminal settings as necessary (Console Port menu).

■ Assign system name, contact, and location (System menu).

■ Set IP Address, mask, gateway, DNS servers, and Domain name (IP Configuration menu).

■ Disable Routing Information Protocol (RIP).

■ Set SNMP read and write strings (SNMP Management menu).

▲ Disable authentication trap generation (SNMP Management menu) .

Console Password Menu

Unless you want unsolicited help managing your network equipment, setting management passwords should be your first priority. Otherwise, somebody may eventually try to telnet to the device and manipulate its configuration. In tightly managed environments in which unused ports are deactivated, the telnetter's goal will most likely be to activate additional ports. However, an unscrupulous person may want to access network information via SNMP and RMON as a way of gathering more information about the network and its users. So it's a good idea to have a password management scheme in place. Also, have an established password to enter when you first configure the hub, so the task is not accidentally forgotten.

In the Console Password menu, you'll configure the Password Intrusion Threshold. Setting this to a relatively low number (3–5) will help thwart attempts at password guessing, by locking the console for the specified time should somebody try a few password guesses. Set the threshold in accordance with your security policy, if available.

The Silent Time Upon Intrusion Detection item is the number of minutes the console will remain locked after somebody has tried to log in with bad password attempts. This interval is typically referred to as Intruder Lockout and may be defined in your formal security policy.

Console Port Menu

The Console Port submenu (Figure 7-7) allows you to adjust the baud rate, data bits, stop bits, and parity settings in the event your terminal or modem requires a setting other than the default.

Configuration items include the following:

Match Remote Baud Rate   You can leave this enabled unless you're having
(Auto Baud)   trouble with your modem or terminal.

Auto Answer	If enabled, tells an attached modem to answer an incoming call automatically.
Time Delay Between Dial Attempts	The number of seconds the hub will wait before initiating a dial-out call.
Number for Dial-Out Connection	The phone number you want the hub to use when dialing out.
Initialization String for Modem	The AT command set that you want the console to send to the attached modem. Typically, you would enter **AT&F** to reset the modem to its factory configuration, followed by additional AT commands to set the baud rate and other parameters.

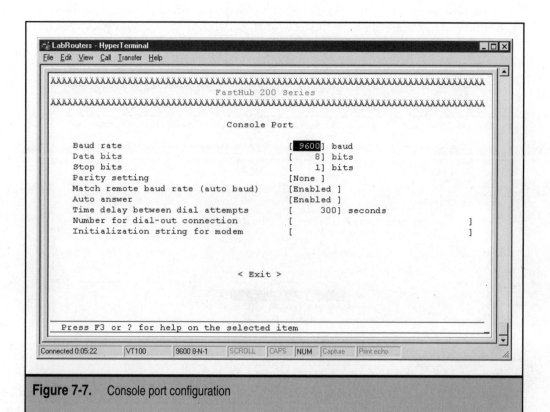

Figure 7-7.   Console port configuration

NOTE: Be careful when adjusting the Console Port settings. You may accidentally lock yourself out of the console, especially if you're accessing the console remotely via modem. Doing so will require that you access the hub via the console port after performing a reset. If you forget the password, you'll have to perform a reset while connected to the console port, and then enter the Diagnostic Console Systems Debug Interface and select the View Management Console Password menu.

Firmware Menu

The Firmware submenu (Figure 7-8) lists the bootstrap firmware version, as well as the management firmware version. This information is helpful in determining the need for an upgrade.

    The Firmware submenu also provides a field to set whether or not the hub will accept a TFTP upgrade. If you use a TFTP server to manage and load router IOS and configuration, you can benefit by enabling this setting. Note that upgrading firmware is not a frequent event and should only be done when necessary.

    Fields are also provided for specifying the name or IP address of the TFTP server, and the filename of the firmware to be loaded. An alternative to TFTP is to use XMODEM to

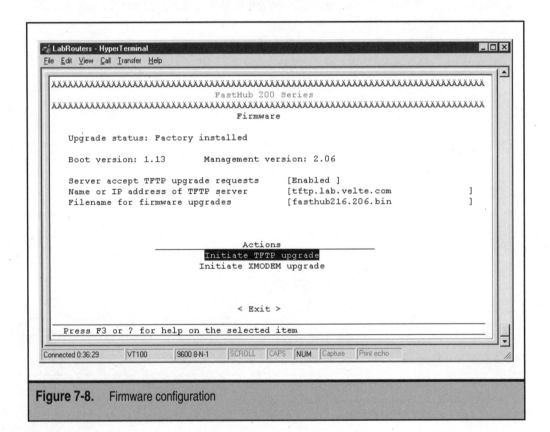

Figure 7-8.   Firmware configuration

"transfer" the upgrade to the hub from your terminal application. In this case, make sure the firmware upgrade file is accessible from your terminal. Then start the process by selecting Initiate XMODEM Upgrade, and begin the file transfer at the terminal application.

NOTE: As of this writing, the firmware for the FastHub 216T is located on the Cisco CCO Software Center at http://www.cisco.com/kobayashi/sw-center/sw-switching.shtml, under the Cisco FastHub 200 Series link. Also, you can download the Cisco TFTP server for Windows NT/98 at http://www.cisco.com/kobayashi/sw-center/sw-other.shtml, under the Cisco TFTP Server for Windows 95/Windows 98/NT 4.0 link.

System Menu

The System submenu (Figure 7-9) allows for the definition of the system name, contact name, and location. All are handy fields when you have to manage more than a few devices. The system name should follow a logical naming convention. This submenu also displays system Up Time, which can be useful in determining if a power outage has occurred, or if the hub has been tampered with.

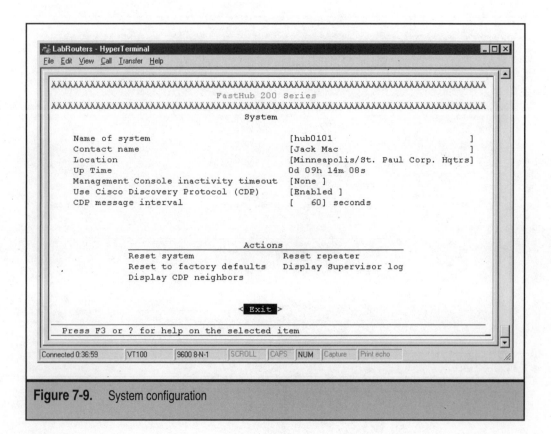

Figure 7-9. System configuration

This menu provides a Management Console inactivity timeout interval, which drops a console session after the designated period of inactivity. You can also specify whether or not the Cisco Discovery Protocol (CDP) is running. If it is, the default CDP Message Interval is set to 60 seconds. The Cisco Discovery Protocol (CDP) is used by the hub to identify other devices on the network. It also allows the hub to advertise its presence on the network. If CDP is enabled, selecting the Display CDP Neighbors action will let you see other CDP-enabled neighboring devices.

Additionally, the System configuration menu provides access to the Supervisor Log, as well as a setting to invoke a reset of the hub via the Reset Repeater submenu.

IP Configuration Menu

To manage the hub using SNMP and to connect to it using Telnet, the hub must be configured with an IP address, subnet mask, and default gateway at a minimum. If for some reason you don't need to manage the hub from the network, it's not necessary to provide any addressing information. The IP Configuration submenu (Figure 7-10) also displays the MAC (Ethernet) address of the hub.

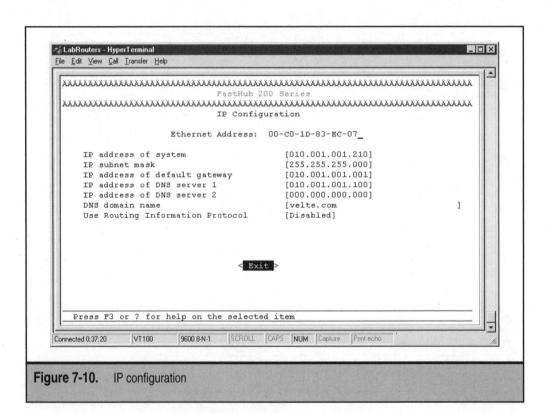

Figure 7-10.   IP configuration

The following fields allow for manual entry of the TCP/IP configuration:

▼   IP Address of System

■   IP Subnet Mask

■   IP Address of Default Gateway

■   Addresses of primary and secondary DNS servers

▲   The default domain name

In this menu, you can also enable the hub to receive Routing Information Protocol (RIP) updates so that it can automatically discover gateway information.

SNMP Management Menu

Before we examine the SNMP configuration options, let's quickly run through an overview of the SNMP protocol. See Chapter 8 for more detail on SNMP.

SNMP includes the Agent residing on the hub, and the Network Management Station (NMS). The NMS and the Agent communicate specific information as defined in SNMP MIBs (management information bases) that they both share. *MIBs* are basically text databases of information that can be collected from a device so that both the NMS and the Agent are able to exchange specific pieces of information defined in the MIB. The NMS uses the MIB to formulate get requests and get-next requests that it sends to the Agent on the hub. The Agent responds to the requests with a get response packet containing MIB information, as specified by the NMS. If configured with Authentication Trap Generation, the Agent can also send a trap (an event message) to the NMS without having received a get request or a get-next request from the NMS.

The FastHub supports SNMP MIBs and MIB-II, but does not yet support SNMPv2. The FastHub 216T supports the following MIBs:

▼   RFC 1213 (MIB-II)

■   RFC 1643 (EtherLike)

■   RFC 1317 (MIB)

■   RFC 1516 (SNMP-REPEATER)

■   RFC 1757 (RMON groups 1–4)

■   Cisco Structure of Management Information (SMI)

■   Cisco Stackmaker

■   Cisco CDP (Cisco Discovery Protocol)

▲   Cisco FastHub

The NMS can gather quite a bit of device-specific information, as long as the Agent and NMS support the same MIBs. Figure 7-11 shows some of the information the NMS

SNMP Table - hub0101

🔘 Read-only variable.

Cisco Systems FastHub 216

Variable	Value
sysDescr	Cisco Systems FastHub 216
sysObjectID	1.3.6.1.4.1.9.1.169
sysUpTime	1 days 3 hours 29 mins 31.14 secs.
sysContact	Jack Mac
sysName	hub0101
sysLocation	Minneapolis/St. Paul Corp. Hqtrs
sysServices	9
ifNumber	2

Close · Start · Set · Copy · Log... · Options... · Help

Figure 7-11. HP OpenView SNMP table view

(HP OpenView, in this case) has received from the agent. Notice that this is the same information accessible via several of the Console menus.

With the RMON MIB loaded, the NMS can gather even more information. RMON groups 1–4 provide the NMS with access to real-time hub statistics, including frame counts, error statistics, frame sizes, and more.

The SNMP Management submenu (Figure 7-12) helps you configure SNMP parameters for network management. The READ and WRITE Community String fields should be configured with the same strings defined in your network management tool.

TIP: Default names for community strings are often "public" for Read Only and "private" for Read/Write. It is highly recommended to remove these default community names and use other names unique to your enterprise. Otherwise, unscrupulous people can gain access using the commonly known defaults.

When you enable Authentication Trap Generation, the hub will send an authentication trap to the SNMP management tool if the hub receives SNMP requests without a valid Read or Write string. For additional security, you should configure the Write Manager and Trap Manager fields to point to your SNMP management host(s). When configured with an IP address or host name, the hub will not accept or send SNMP data to any other addresses.

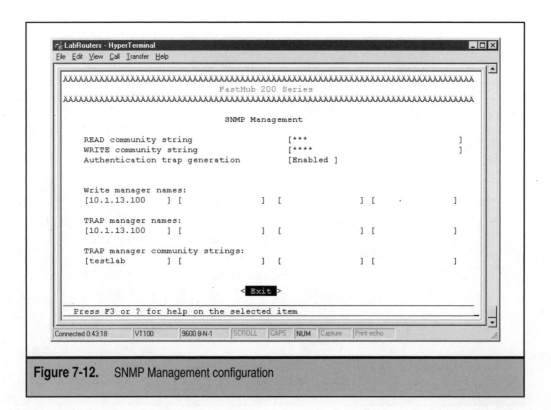

Figure 7-12.   SNMP Management configuration

The final item on the SNMP Management menu is the definition of Trap Manager community strings that act as the authentication for traps sent by the hub to an SNMP management host.

Port Configuration Menu

The Port Configuration submenu allows you to view port-specific parameters and assign a name to each port. In addition, each port can be activated and deactivated individually. Here are descriptions of each menu option:

Port Linkbeat Status	Reports whether or not the port is receiving an active linkbeat from the adapter connected to it. This can also be determined by a steady green LED above each port.

Port Autopartition Status	Reflects a fault in either the station adapter or wiring when the port is auto-partitioned. In this state, the offending station is removed from the network until the condition is corrected, to protect the other stations on the hub. The LED above the port will alternately flash green and amber. If the station is active and functioning normally, this field will indicate that it is not auto-partitioned.
Port Connector Type	Reflects the hub port connector type (in this case, RJ-45).
Last Source Address	Reports the last MAC address received on the port.
Source Address Changes	Shows the number of MAC addresses in use on a particular port. This is particularly handy in discovering hubs "daisy-chained" off the main hub.
Port Name	An assigned name for a particular port; may be a location ID, a cube number, a user name, or left unassigned.
Port Status	Allows the port to be toggled on or off; can be used to prevent unauthorized access to the network.

Unit Configuration Menu

The Unit Configuration submenu displays basic information about the hub hardware, as follows:

RPS Status	Indicates the status of an externally attached redundant power supply.
Power Source	Indicates where the unit is drawing its power (Internal vs. RPS).
Boot Version	Displays the bootstrap software version.
Management Version	Displays the management firmware version.
Main Board	Displays the main board version number.

You should always check this unit configuration information before performing any upgrade to the system. Nothing is a bigger waste of time than upgrading something to the same version it already is.

Port Statistics Report Menu

The Port Statistics Report submenu (Figure 7-13) allows you to examine a variety of network statistics on a port-by-port basis. This information, explained in the following table, can be very helpful in troubleshooting a problem. It can also be periodically checked

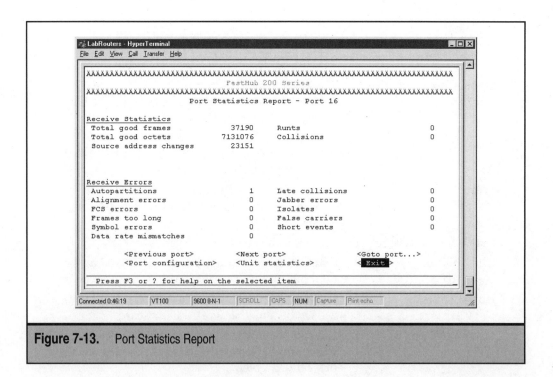

Figure 7-13. Port Statistics Report

via the console or an SNMP management station to verify the condition of the network segment.

Total Good Frames	A cumulative count of good frames.
Total Good Octets	The octets, or bytes, received in good frames.
Source Address Changes	Total number of different MAC addresses used on the port.
Runts	Frame fragments usually caused by collisions. A count higher than the Collisions count (next field) could reflect a faulty network adapter card.
Collisions	These occur routinely in Ethernet networks, but a high number indicates excessive network traffic.
Auto-partitions	These occur if the hub detects a problem with the device connected to the port. Disconnecting and reconnecting a device can cause a small number of auto-partitions, but a higher number suggests a problem.

Alignment Errors	Usually a result of a cable problem but can sometimes be caused by a bad network adapter card. When troubleshooting, check the cable plant first.
Frame Check Sequence Errors	These, like alignment errors, are a result of a cable problem but can sometimes be caused by a bad network adapter card.
Frames Too Long	Can be caused by hardware or cable errors, but most likely are the result of protocols other than TCP/IP running on the attached station.
Symbol Errors	Errors within a frame; if these occur, they are usually associated with another error that can indicate the source of the problem.
Data Rate Mismatches	Can indicate a bad network adapter card.
Late Collisions	Usually caused by the segment being too large; check total cable distances between stations and repeaters.
Jabber Errors	Usually the result of a cable problem, but can also be caused by a bad network adapter card.
Isolates	Indicate the number of times a port is isolated (disconnected) from the network, usually the result of a cable problem.
False Carriers	These occur if the hub detects a problem, with the device connected to the port. Disconnecting and reconnecting a device can cause a small number of false carriers, but a higher number suggests a problem.
Short Events	Indicative of interference being introduced onto the network. Cable or network equipment could be too close to a source of interference.

Unit Statistics Report Menu

The Unit Statistics Report illustrated in Figure 7-14 is the same as the Port Statistics Report, except that it is the aggregate of all the port data. A quick check of the Unit Statistics Report can alert you to problems on the network without having to check each port individually.

RMON Statistics Report Menu

The RMON Statistics Report (Figure 7-15) presents information collected by the RMON groups supported on this hub. These statistics were described previously in the "Port Statistics Report Menu" section.

▼ Total frames (received)

■ Total octets

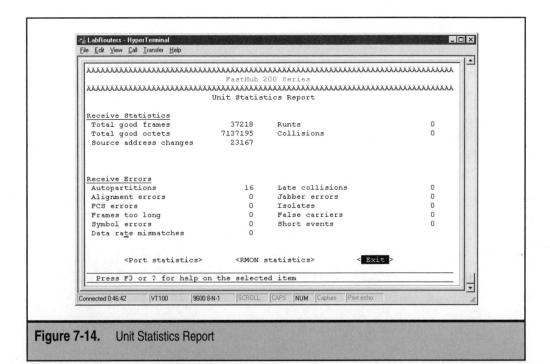

Figure 7-14. Unit Statistics Report

- Runts
- Good broadcast frames
- Good multicast frames
- Total collisions
- FCS (Frame Check Sequence) errors
- Alignment errors
- Jabber errors
- Oversize frames
- ▲ Undersize frames

The benefit of RMON support is that you can gather the information in a network management tool and display the data in a variety of views. Figure 7-16 shows a bar graph representation of the data available.

Unit Addressing Report Menu

The Unit Addressing Report shows the source address (MAC) of the station currently accessing the specified port. This report is helpful for troubleshooting when you know the MAC address of a device and are trying to find the port it's connected to.

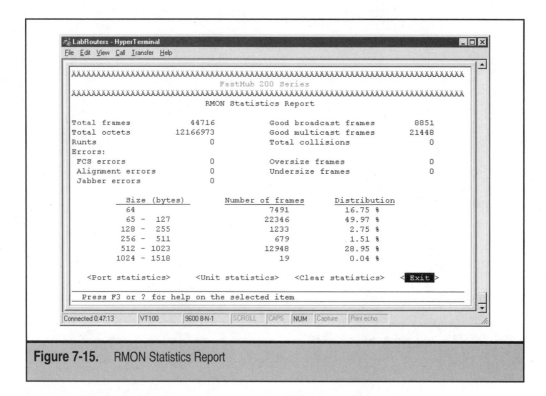

Figure 7-15.   RMON Statistics Report

INTEGRATING HUBS INTO THE NETWORK

Hubs still have their place in the Ethernet network. True, it's only a matter of time before they are eclipsed by a new breed of low-cost switches. However, until the cost per port is equal, hubs will always be of use on the network.

The two primary areas in which hubs hold their own are the workgroup environment and the server room. At the workgroup level, 10/100 hubs provide a low-cost way to get desktops on the network. The setting may be a remote office with 10 users, two servers, and a small-office/home-office (SOHO) router, where 100 Mbps shared is more than adequate bandwidth. It may be in a server room, where the high-volume servers all have dedicated 100 Mbps switch ports and a handful of low-volume servers; and miscellaneous administrative workstations share a single 100 Mbps switch port through, say, a FastHub 424M 10/100. It's always nice to have a few extra ports available, anyway, and a hub is the least expensive option. The other bonus offered by a hub is that it can quickly be swapped out for a switch without much pain and suffering. That said, let's take a look at the role of a hub in a workgroup and in a server room.

The Workgroup

This workgroup scenario consists of a small 10-user segment with two file/print servers, one printer, and a small wide-area router connected back to headquarters. This same

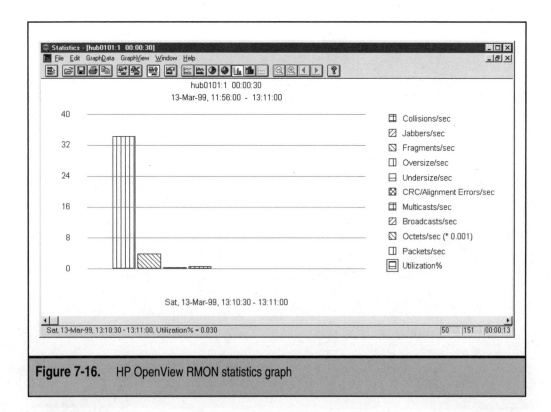

Figure 7-16.   HP OpenView RMON statistics graph

setup could just as well be a small segment in a campus network, where the router is connected to the network backbone instead of a WAN.

We'll use two Cisco 1538 hubs. The first one is a 1538M (with Management) and the
second an unmanageable 1538. These two 1538 Series hubs will be stacked using the integrated stacking connectors and the stacking cable. Our small office will have 16
ports—enough to attach all our devices with a few open ports left over. Since the 1538 is
auto-sensing, we'll be able to connect the 10 Mbps workstations and printers, as well as
the 100 Mbps servers, to the same stack. A router serves as a connecting point from our
network to a WAN link that connects to headquarters.

This network scenario is illustrated in Figure 7-17. It's a very compact configuration
and can be installed into the smaller areas typical of small/remote offices available for
network equipment.

The Server Room

The server room scenario comprises a collection of high- and low-volume servers, three
administrative PCs, and two printers. The switch is connected directly to the network
backbone via a router.

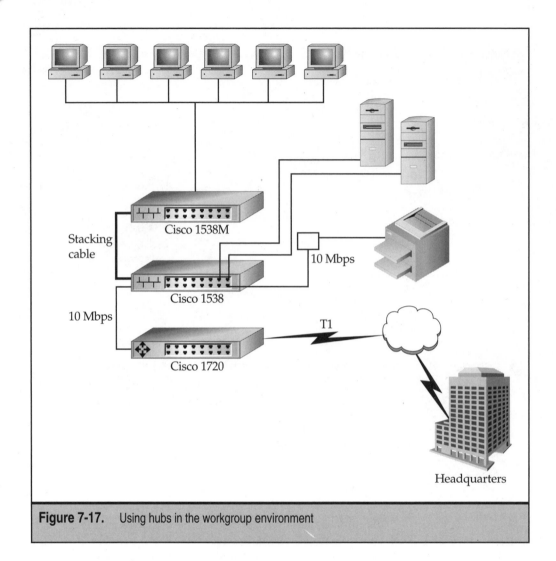

Figure 7-17. Using hubs in the workgroup environment

It has been determined that three of the servers, both printers, and two of the administrative PCs have fairly low bandwidth requirements and could be on the FastHub 424M 10/100. The remaining two servers and one administrative PC all have high requirements for bandwidth and will have to be on the 100 Mbps switch. This places the low-bandwidth devices strategically on a shared media, while high-throughput devices reside on their own collision domain (off the switch). This scenario is illustrated in Figure 7-18.

One major benefit to this arrangement is the availability of additional network ports without much additional expense. In dynamic environments, there is often need for additional ports; having some available lets you deploy additional servers quickly while additional dedicated switch ports are being acquired.

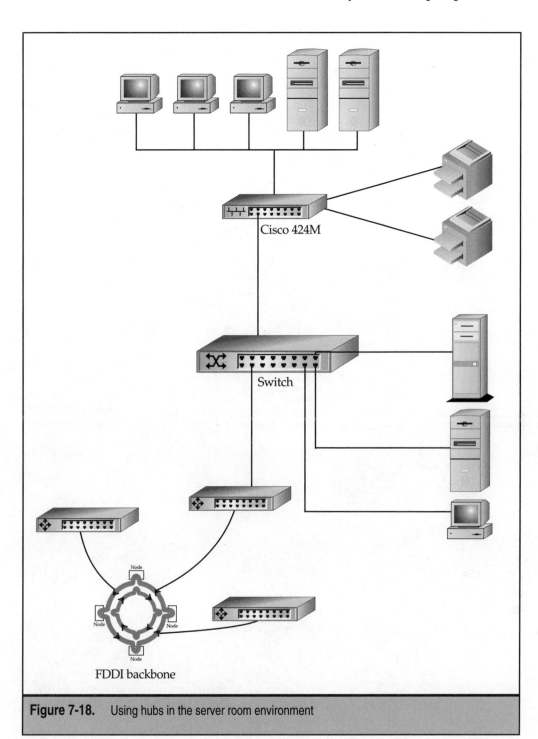

Figure 7-18.   Using hubs in the server room environment

SUMMARY

In this chapter, we reviewed the fundamentals of repeater technology, Ethernet standards, and IEEE 802.3 10BaseT and 100BaseT specifications. In doing so, we highlighted the differences between Class I and Class II repeaters. We learned about Cisco's FastHub Series of Class II repeaters, and covered the cabling specifications used when connecting to and cascading repeaters. We took a closer look at cable specifications commonly used in today's networks, as well as other cabling options such as fiber-optic cabling and its support for 10BaseFL and 100BaseFX.

This chapter's walkthrough of the installation and configuration of a Cisco FastHub 216 gives us a good representation of the entire Cisco FastHub Series. We discussed the importance of ensuring that the equipment be installed in a clean, cool, and dry environment, and that the network equipment and cabling be kept free of obstructions and away from sources of electrical interference.

We also took a look at the SNMP configuration options and identified the key statistics generated by the SNMP and RMON management interface.

Finally, we looked at two scenarios in which hubs can be installed cost-effectively in the network.

This chapter concludes Part II. The next section focuses on managing these networks we have learned how to build.

PART III

Managing a Cisco/Windows Network

CHAPTER 8

Managing Devices

Networks grow unruly over time: devices proliferate, applications bloat, and network administrators struggle to keep up. To get a grasp on today's problems and proactively prevent future fires, network administrators can choose from a variety of Cisco and third-party *network management packages.* These applications were once found only in large companies on UNIX systems—a healthy budget and detailed training were required to make good use of them. Today, for the first time, Cisco internetworking management tools have arrived for Windows NT. This chapter discusses some of the most useful ones. So roll up your sleeves, clear some space on your hard drive, and jump in.

NOTE: Additional management tools, other than those discussed here, are available from Cisco and third-party vendors. We discuss many of those applications throughout this book in the most appropriate location, even though almost every one of them performs some management functions. For example, Cisco's ConfigMaker is used to manage Cisco routers, although its main function is to help create configurations for routers; therefore, it is located in Chapter 5. The applications examined here in this chapter, on the other hand, are used to manage a myriad of devices and have many management functions.

THE NEW MANAGEMENT SUITES: FROM CHARACTERS TO GUIs

It's no secret that management of Cisco devices has typically involved using the cryptic command line interface (CLI). The CLI is serial; only one command can be entered in at a time, and only one set of results of an informational query can be displayed to the administrator at a time. This text-only interface does not have an in-depth help system; nor does it tolerate any commands that do not exactly match a Cisco IOS command. The result is an interface that is slow to use, hard to learn, and unfriendly.

Although the CLI is still the favorite of senior, more experienced Cisco engineers, it was only a matter of time before a colorful GUI was added to the Cisco family. The CLI will remain the best way to perform some simple tasks on individual devices, but the new GUI-based applications are highly useful. They allow the uninitiated to get familiar with Cisco devices, and the experts to make changes to many configuration parameters across many devices, in relatively little time.

Understanding Management Suites

Because many of the management applications are altogether new (or new to Windows), they can be a little thin on features or not quite as stable as the mature, proven UNIX products.

Surprisingly, one of the biggest drawbacks is their confusing naming convention. It seems that, for some reason, the names of these products are actually not names of applications at all. Instead, they are names of application families or suites. For example, you may already know of the Microsoft Management Console, CiscoWorks, and Hewlett-Packard's HP OpenView. None of these are applications, but rather names of product suites that contain one or more applications. But the applications in a management suite also have names that usually sound much like the suite name, or the applications themselves sometimes appear in more than one product suite (as in the case of CiscoView). To further confuse matters, many of these applications overlap in functionality with other applications by the same vendor!

Another important element to understand before you get enamored of these powerful tools is that they are resource intensive. It may be their UNIX roots, their enterprise scale, or their makers' Fortune 500 budgets that foster such brazen consumption of enormous quantities of RAM and hard-drive space. Whatever the reason, these applications are not for laptops, and not for servers running other mission-critical applications. For example, to run CiscoWorks2000 you need a minimum of 256MB RAM and at least 4GB of hard-drive space.

SNMP and MIBs

Almost all application suites rely on the Simple Network Management Protocol (SNMP). It is used as a TCP/IP-based communication channel from the management application and the network device. There are essentially two components to SNMP: the Network Management System (NMS), and the SNMP agent that resides on the network component to be managed. SNMP agents can run on a variety of devices, including

▼ Routers

■ Hubs

■ Switches

■ UPS battery backup systems

■ Servers (hardware and software levels)

■ Workstations

▲ Printers

The NMS polls network devices for specific pieces of information at a specified interval. The agents, in turn, respond to the requests. The agents keep a set of data about themselves as specified in the Management Information Bases (MIBs) that they are configured to support. A MIB provides a standard representation of what information is available for the SNMP agent and where it is stored. Typical MIBs in use on a Cisco network include the following:

▼ Basic MIB (RFC 1317)

■ Basic MIB-II (RFC 1213)

■ Ethernet-like interface types (RFC 1643)

- SNMP-REPEATER (RFC 1516)
- RMON (RFC 1757)
- CISCO SMI Management Information
- ▲ CISCO CDP (Cisco Discovery Protocol)

NOTE: There are a host of other MIBs that contain information specific to various devices. If you have an SNMP manageable server, router, or switch with advanced/enhanced functionality, it very likely supports several MIBs.

The NMS keeps a database of the information extracted from the MIBs for all of the SNMP agents managed by that NMS. This allows the SNMP agents to provide information specific to a particular device, reducing complexity as well as CPU and network overhead.

To send and receive SNMP data, the NMS and agents exchange information over TCP/IP. UDP ports 161 and 162 are used to send and receive messages called Protocol Data Units (PDU) between the NMS and the agents.

SNMP Messages

The following five packet types are used for SNMP messages:

Packet Type	Sender/Receiver	Purpose
Get Request	NMS to SNMP agent	Retrieves the values of specific MIB variables from an SNMP agent
Get-Next Request	NMS to SNMP agent	Retrieves the next instance of information for a particular variable or device
Set Request	NMS to SNMP agent	Alters the value of objects that can be written to the MIB
Get Response	SNMP agent to NMS	Contains the values of the requested variables
Trap	SNMP agent to NMS	Contains information about an event that caused an unsolicited message from an SNMP agent

Proxy SNMP Agents

In some cases, you may have a network device that cannot support the SNMP-required protocols. An *SNMP proxy agent* can be used to manage these devices. This allows the NMS to send an SNMP query to the proxy agent, which converts the request into the managed device's native management protocol and delivers it. The device can reply in its native protocol to the proxy agent, which then forwards the reply back to the NMS.

Polling

As a managed network grows in size, so will the SNMP traffic. There are two simple methods to reducing the SNMP traffic overhead on the network:

▼ Adjust the *polling interval.* This reduces the amount of time the NMS waits between requests for information from each device on the network.

▲ Configure the agents to send trap packets. The agent sends information to the NMS only when a specific event has occurred.

SNMP with Windows NT and Windows 2000

Like management-enabled Cisco devices, Windows has an SNMP agent. The Windows SNMP agent runs as a service and accesses the Registry. It is able to reply with information because the Registry data is converted into a MIB format that can be queried by standard SNMP managers.

Windows NT and Windows 2000 support multiple MIBs via an agent API. This allows third-party vendors to create MIBs specific to their NT application. Following are several Windows-based MIBs:

▼ **Internet MIB-II**   Defines objects used for fault analysis as defined in RFC 1213.

■ **LAN Manager MIB-II**   Defines objects used for user and login information.

■ **Microsoft DHCP Service MIB**   Contains information about the use of the DHCP service.

■ **Microsoft Internet Information Services MIB**   Defines statistics describing the use of the HTTP, Gopher, and FTP servers.

▲ **Microsoft WINS Service MIB**   Defines statistics and database information about the use of the WINS Service.

SNMP Standards

Although there are other RFCs that touch on the subject, most SNMP and MIB information is defined in the following RFCs:

RFC 1155	Structure and Identification of MIBs for TCP/IP
RFC 1157	Original SNMPv1 RFC defining architecture, protocol, MIB, etc.
RFC 1213	Structure and Identification of MIB-II for TCP/IP
RFC 1902	MIB Structure for SNMPv2
RFC 1903	Textual conventions available to all SNMPv2 MIB modules
RFC 1904	Conformance Statements for SNMPv2
RFC 1905	Protocol Operations for SNMPv2
RFC 1906	Transport Mappings for SNMPv2
RFC 1907	MIB definition for SNMPv2

For most applications, you won't need to refer to the RFCs. Should you need a more thorough understanding of the SNMP protocol, the RFCs listed here will be helpful.

HP OPENVIEW

HP OpenView is the de facto application suite for managing integrated networks, systems, applications, and databases. With HP OpenView, the products in the HP OpenView professional suite, HP OpenView Network Node Manager for Windows NT, and HP OpenView Network Node Manager for UNIX can share information and network status with other network management applications. The compatible interface, coupled with the industry's high demand for simplified network management, have together guaranteed success for Hewlett-Packard. HP OpenView is installed at over 100,000 locations worldwide!

Introduction to HP OpenView

HP OpenView is the Hewlett-Packard network management architecture that simplifies management and reduces the cost of supporting multivendor networks. Advancing technologies, multiple protocols, and diverse network components are among the several elements that create network-management nightmares for IT professionals. The majority of a network engineer's time is divided between end users' needs and network problems—there isn't much time left over to devote to proactive network monitoring. Each additional network device constitutes an additional management cost. HP OpenView focuses on simplifying network management, which ultimately reduces management costs.

Features of HP OpenView

HP OpenView offers an array of features that enable managers to regain control over the IT environment.

MAPPING Most people are visual learners, and for this reason maps have become very well suited for communicating information to personnel at various levels of technology. The map uses icons to represents the managed network devices. When an event on a device occurs (such as a reboot or a crash), the icon changes color to represent a different status. HP OpenView maps are represented with hierarchy views. These views allow you to display the managed network devices and their topology at a high level, or you can double-click on various icons and step through the network based on subnets.

EVENT MANAGEMENT An event is an occurrence that changes the status of a managed network device. When an event occurs, an alarm is sent to the HP OpenView management console. HP OpenView uses Event Management to handle common events as well as specially configured events.

DISCOVERY Before it can add a device to its map, HP OpenView must be aware of the device. By using routes, ARP cache tables, and other diagnostic services such as ping, HP OpenView determines all managed network devices, assigns each one an appropriate icon, and adds them to the map. IP and IPX devices use separate discovery tools.

MANAGEMENT DATABASE Historical data can be very beneficial in resolving problems, determining trends, and forecasting. Access to historical and real-time data, and having the capability to graph and generate reports, play major roles in effective management. HP OpenView has many partners who offer snap-in solutions to satisfy the requirement for a management database.

COMMUNICATION INFRASTRUCTURE HP OpenView uses SNMP and Desktop Management Interface (DMI) in providing a communication channel between the management console and the devices being managed. This communication infrastructure allows HP OpenView to support multiple protocols and therefore a wide range of network devices.

INTEGRATION SERVICES HP OpenView was developed so it could seamlessly integrate with partners whose products added functionality within the HP OpenView framework. Application Programming Interfaces (APIs) provide access to underlying communications, event management, and database services. Later in this chapter, you'll see how Cisco's management tools can integrate with HP OpenView.

NODE MANAGEMENT HP OpenView allows you to customize the management of devices. Devices can be separated based on type, location, and so forth, and then grouped accordingly. This allows network managers to monitor a subset of all the discovered devices on a network or the network as a whole.

HP OpenView provides monitoring and management of networking devices such as routers, hubs, switches, servers, desktops, and printers, as well as other network software-based applications. A more extensive list of these supported devices along with specific uses is defined later in the "Supported Devices" section.

HP OpenView's Platforms

HP offers three primary HP OpenView platforms:

- ▼ HP OpenView professional suite
- ■ HP Node Manager for Windows NT
- ▲ HP Network Node Manager for UNIX

Each individual platform can be used on its own or combined with other management applications to further enhance the capabilities. The three variations have been developed to satisfy the diversity in network infrastructures. Table 8-1 summarizes the key differences between the three HP OpenView network management solutions. The remainder of this section focuses on the HP OpenView professional suite platform.

Features	Professional Suite	NT Network Node Management	UNIX Network Node Management
Company size	Small to medium	Medium to large	Large to global
IT staff size	1–10 basic knowledge	5–30 IT experts	20–100+ IT experts
Network type	LAN	LAN/WAN	LAN/WAN
Average managed nodes	10–500	100–1,000	1,000–10,000
Operating systems	Win 95, NT 3.51, 4.0	NT 3.51, 4.0	HP-UX, Sun Solaris
Management consoles	1 master console/remote access via PCAnywhere	Up to 15 concurrent management consoles	Up to 25 concurrent management consoles
Task customization	3 operator categories	Unlimited operator categories	Unlimited operator categories
Solution style	Integrated applications in same box for network and system management	Network management solution	Network management solution
Partner solution	100+ "snap-in" applications	170+ partners committed to integrating their applications	300+ "snap-in" applications
Price (U.S. list)	$1,495	N/A	N/A

Table 8-1.   Differences in HP OpenView's Primary Platforms

Supported Devices

The OpenView professional suite supports management of the devices listed in the following table:

Devices	Management Services Provided by OpenView
PCs/desktops	Automates the identification of the names and versions of software running on networked PCs. Monitors software license usage to plan for future software purchases, and provides audit information. Provides remote power On/Off and Reboot PC functions, allowing PC management tasks to be done after office hours.
Servers	Provides failure prediction alerts (such as temperature monitoring) and other preconfigured alerts. Monitors and reports security breaches by unauthorized user access to servers. Displays usage rates via graphs. Provides utilities to view information on one or multiple servers.
Network devices	Provides the ability to proactively monitor, configure, and manage devices.
Printers/plotters	Installs, configures, troubleshoots, and manages printers remotely. (The printers and plotters must be HP machines and, obviously, connected to the network.)
Uninterruptible power supply (UPS)	Performs real-time diagnostics; monitors voltage, current, and battery runtime. Receives immediate notification of power failures or other power alerts (for APC-brand UPS).

In addition to management of these devices , the OpenView professional suite allows you to monitor network traffic among the devices. You have the capability to monitor individual packets or packet samples. Top talkers can be identified, and traffic loads can be balanced to optimize traffic flow. Preventive actions can be taken by using traffic and network health-monitoring tools that are based on real-time situation analysis.

Supported Protocols

HP OpenView professional suite is an open network- and systems-management platform based on SNMP and DMI industry standards. SNMP was covered earlier in this chapter. DMI is an industry standard defined to provide management applications with a set of rules to query desktop device hardware and software, and to provide configuration of multiple PCs on the network. (Desktop devices must be DMI-compliant.)

Assuming the proper products are installed and configured, HP OpenView can support IP and IPX routed protocols.

HP OpenView Target Market and Cost

The target market for HP OpenView professional suite comprises small- to medium-sized companies with a staff of up to ten IT professionals responsible for the general overall network support. The professional suite is supported on Windows 95, and on Windows NT 3.51 and 4.0. HP OpenView professional suite has several interconnected management workgroups over LANs and WANs; these workgroups forward events to one master management console. PCAnywhere, which works over IP, IPX, and high-speed modems, provides remote access to the master management console.

The list price of HP OpenView professional suite is $1,495. A free evaluation CD-ROM is available if you are located in the U.S. For more information, contact Hewlett-Packard at www.openview.hp.com.

Installation and Configuration

Installation of HP OpenView requires a suitable system and at least some expertise and familiarity with the network architecture.

Machine Implementation Requirements

The HP OpenView professional suite for Windows NT and Windows 95 has the following system requirements:

- ▼ Installed TCP/IP and SNMP services
- ■ Windows 95, Windows NT 3.51, or Windows NT 4.0
- ■ 166 MHz or faster Pentium processor
- ■ VGA monitor
- ■ 64MB of RAM
- ▲ 600MB of disk space

The foregoing requirements should support all the products offered by the professional suite (see the following section, "HP OpenView Installation"). Keep in mind that these products have their own individual requirements, and the amount of memory needed depends on the number of products you have running simultaneously. As always, the more memory, the better. We have never encountered an application that has a problem with too much memory.

If you plan to discover and manage IPX devices on Windows NT, the following network software must be added when configuring the network settings:

▼ Novell's Client 2.5 *or* Client Services for NetWare

▲ NWLink IPX/SPX-compatible transport

HP OpenView Installation

During the installation process, you can select which of the suite's products you want to install. For some products, you must enter information about your network, or choose a client or server for installing the various components of the product. The sections that follow list all the products included in the HP OpenView suite and a summary of their functions. Each product has been categorized as to Management Platform, Device Management Applications, Desktop Management Applications, Traffic and Network Health Management, Software Bridges, and Miscellaneous.

MANAGEMENT PLATFORM: HP WORKGROUP NODE MANAGER   Assists in the administration of PCs, hubs, routers, and servers. The following features are also included: network maps, AutoDiscovery and Layout, status polling, alarm log, trap management, SNMP Manager, DMI Manager, console security, alarm forwarding, automatic paging, automatic e-mail, and Visual Basic custom controls.

DEVICE MANAGEMENT APPLICATIONS: HP TOPTOOLS FOR SERVERS   Remotely collects and monitors component inventory, security, and diagnostic data through a Web-based interface providing powerful monitoring and proactive alerting.

▼ **HP OpenView Exposé**   Provides management for NetWare and Microsoft Windows NT servers.

■ **HP Jet Admin**   Manages the configuration and status of printers.

▲ **Win APC PowerNet Manager**   Collects and displays graphics related to UPS status from PowerNet SNMP Agents and Adapters. Win APC PowerNet Manager also shuts down connected devices when a power shortage occurs.

DESKTOP MANAGEMENT APPLICATIONS

▼ **Remote DMI Management (built into Workgroup Node Manager)**   Creates inventory tables by retrieving current inventory information.

■ **HP NightDIRECTOR (built into Workgroup Node Manager)**   Performs PC administration during off-hours so productivity isn't disrupted.

■ **HP TopTools for Desktops**   Remotely collects and monitors HP Vectra PCs, Kayak PC workstations, and OmniBook notebook PC information. Statistics include component inventory, security, and diagnostic data.

▲ **Network Associates Zero Administration Client (ZAC) Suite**   Provides software distribution and license metering in addition to monitoring of remote PCs' software/hardware inventory.

TRAFFIC AND NETWORK HEALTH MONITORING

▼ **HP Advance Stack Assistant (ASA)**   Uses HP EASE technology to monitor network traffic and overall utilization, broadcasts, errors, and top talkers. (HP EASE utilizes statistical packet sampling.) In addition, by analyzing network trends, ASA learns more about what is affecting network performance.

▲ **HP NetMetrix**   Monitors network traffic (similar to HP Advance Stack Assistant) but utilizes RMON packet-capture mechanism instead. HP NetMetrix requires at least one RMON-capable network device.

SOFTWARE BRIDGES   These products increase management capabilities.

▼ **Microsoft SMS Integration**   Provides an interface to alternate between HP OpenView and Microsoft System Management Server.

▲ **CA Unicenter Bridge**   Enables additional HP device-management applications such as NetServer Assistant, Advance Stack Assistant, and TopTools to be launched from CA's Unicenter TNG Framework and Unicenter TNG.

MISCELLANEOUS

▼ **PCAnywhere**   Provides remote access to management console via a modem or network.

■ **Action Manager (built into Workgroup Node Manager)**   Performs configured functions (sounds, forward alarms, pages, e-mails) whenever a device sends an alarm to the HP OpenView management console.

▲ **HP OpenView Network Node Manager Bridge**   Enables enterprise-level users to access suite applications by allowing the professional suite to be run from HP Network Node Manager for NT.

Installations of Workgroups Network Node Manager, JetAdmin, Exposé, and PCAnywhere are performed on the management console. PCAnywhere must be installed on remote PCs, requiring remote management capabilities. DMI Clients need be installed on your PCs that are to be managed. Exposé needs to be installed on network servers.

SNMP ROUTER CONFIGURATION   SNMP community strings need to be configured on all network devices being monitored. HP OpenView uses the RO community string. The following lines are from a router configuration file. You will need to log into the router in Privileged Exec mode and execute the following commands:

```
snmp-server community stringname RO
snmp-server host 198.189.2.1 stringname
```

The value **stringname** is your community string name, and **198.189.2.1** is the IP address of your management console.

Following the installation of HP OpenView and your selected products, and assuming all the SNMP community strings have been enabled, you can begin configuring HP OpenView to satisfy your network management requirements.

Using HP OpenView

HP OpenView offers several options in tailoring the application to your desired level of management. This section focuses on the basic configurations using only the HP Workgroup Node Management product. Increased granular network management can be accomplished by installing additional products included in the professional suite.

As discussed in the HP OpenView Installation section, all monitored network devices must have an SNMP community string defined. All monitored network workstations must be DMI compliant.

Configuring Discovery Networks

In order for HP OpenView to detect the devices you want managed on your network, you need to enter the IP settings of the management console, and the IP addresses of the network/subnets you want managed. Figure 8-1 illustrates the IP setting configurations entered under AutoDiscovery | Configure Discovery Networks. As shown in this figure, you can also define maximum IP and IPX hops (a *hop* is a jump from one router to the next router). This hop limit is useful if you want to gather management information for only a specific subnet of your network.

Customizing SNMP Traps

Traps are SNMP messages sent by managed devices on the network as a result of preconfigured abnormal statuses. HP OpenView has a default set of values/actions associated with each generic trap that a network device can generate. These defaults are listed under Options | Customize Traps and shown in Figure 8-2.

By default, the trap configurations will be applied to all managed devices on the network. However, you can also configure a unique set of traps, values, and actions for each

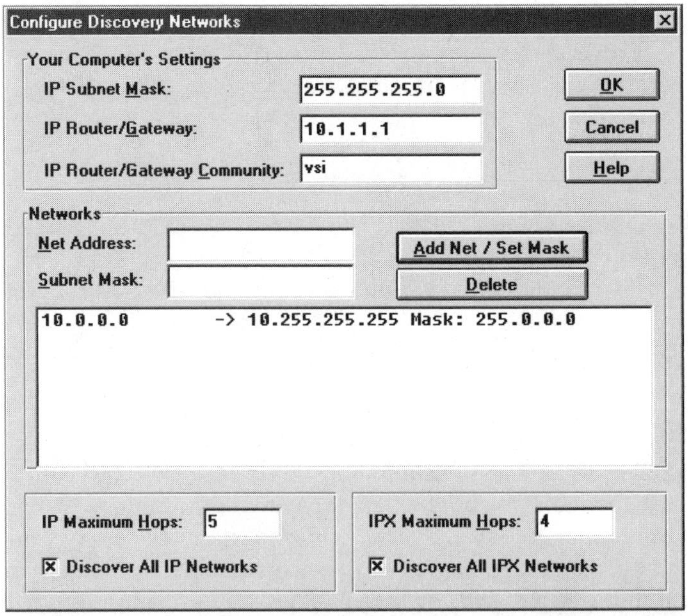

Configure Discovery Networks		☒
Your Computer's Settings		
IP Subnet <u>M</u>ask:	`255.255.255.0`	<u>O</u>K
IP Router/<u>G</u>ateway:	`10.1.1.1`	Cancel
IP Router/Gateway <u>C</u>ommunity:	`vsi`	<u>H</u>elp

Networks

<u>N</u>et Address:		Add Net / Set Mask
<u>S</u>ubnet Mask:		<u>D</u>elete

```
10.0.0.0          -> 10.255.255.255 Mask: 255.0.0.0
```

IP Maximum <u>H</u>ops:	`5`	IPX Maximum <u>H</u>ops:	`4`
☒ Discover All IP Networks		☒ Discover All IPX Networks	

Figure 8-1. Preparing to discover networks

---

device being managed on the network. (Keep in mind that certain traps will have to be specially configured/enabled on your devices.)

To add a new device to the list, click Add in the Device Class Name list box. This will display a list of device types and their Enterprise numbers. Select the Enterprise number of the device you want to customize. (If the device is not on the list, you'll need to add it to the OpenView/Ovfiles/Devices file.) After defining your device, use the bottom section of the Customize Trap Alarms window to configure the trap values and actions you want associated with that device.

NOTE: Although Customize Trap Alarms can create a very detailed network management tool, it can also become confusing if you have several traps resulting in different actions for each network device being monitored. Traps from selected devices can also be ignored; click the Ignore button on the right to designate this.

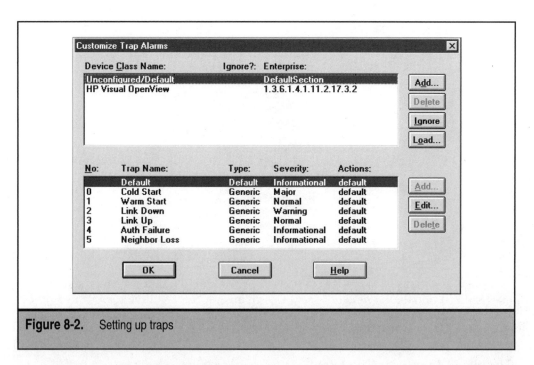

Figure 8-2.   Setting up traps

Following are descriptions of the trap characteristics you can manage for either a unique device or for all the managed devices:

Trap Characteristic	Description
Type of trap	Generic: Equal to HP OpenView's default setting or a generic trap value. Custom: The default settings have been altered. Specific: Trap applies to unique device(s) and not all the network devices.
Severity of trap	Trap Severity is HP OpenView's method of categorizing traps, defined just below in the Status Legend illustration.
Trap actions	You can configure specific actions to take place when a trap occurs, including playing a sound, launching a program, sending a page, sending an e-mail, forwarding the event (trap) to another management system, updating map status, and/or logging a trap. Actions can be customized for each trap; or you can tie actions to the Severity categories using Options | Customize Alert Alarms.

SNMP TRAP CATEGORIES The various Severity levels for traps are categorized as shown in the following Status Legend illustration. Each category has a corresponding color.

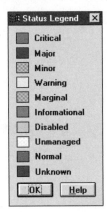

When the actions of a trap from a network device are defined to change the severity category and update the network map, this change of color will be represented on the map. This feature makes it easy for a network manager to determine which devices need attention just by viewing the map.

Running Discovery Manager

After HP OpenView is configured, you are ready to run Discovery Manager. Figure 8-3 shows you the Discovery Manager window, available through the AutoDiscovery | Discovery Manager command.

Discovery Manager generates queries to each router and ultimately to each network device being managed, and creates a list of devices it will continue to poll at a defined rate.

Managing the Polling List

After running Discovery Manager, you can view a list of the devices being polled (Monitor | Polling | View Polling List). You can poll any managed device that has an IP or IPX address.

At any time, you can change the list of devices you want to poll. While in the View Polling List table, select the device you no longer want to poll and click Remove. You can also change the current polling parameters for a specific device, by selecting the device you want to modify and then clicking Configure. For changes in the polling list to take effect, you must stop and restart polling.

Polling is active when the icon at the far-right on the main interface is rotating and shows color. You can also access the Polling menu by clicking the Polling icon.

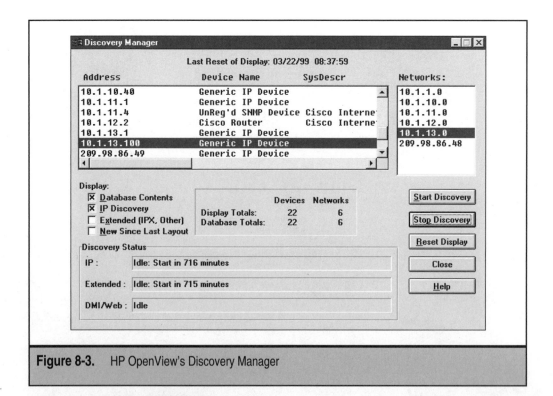

Figure 8-3.   HP OpenView's Discovery Manager

Creating the Network Map

Discovery Manager can be configured to automatically create/update a *network map* every time it runs, or you can create a map with the AutoDiscovery | Layout | Do Basic Layout command. Figure 8-4 illustrates a simple network map.

By double-clicking on a gateway device (router) in the network map, you can access the next layer of the map. When a trap alert changes the Severity (and the color) of a device, the network gateway device changes color also. This feature allows the network manager to see problems at all levels/views of the network map.

To access the Alarm Log, right-click an icon/device on the map and click Alarms. The alarm log will show you current alerts or historical alerts for that particular device. By choosing Acknowledge All in the Alarm Log, the Severity type of the network icon will turn back to normal. A sample view of the Alarm Log is shown in Figure 8-5.

NOTE: In addition to the basic configurations and features described in this chapter, HP OpenView has several details you can tailor to create a more granular network-management architecture. When determining how explicit you want your configurations, be sure to maintain consistency within device types, subnets, timeframes, and so on. HP OpenView is a product aimed at simplifying network management and reducing your management costs. Too much detail could defeat this purpose.

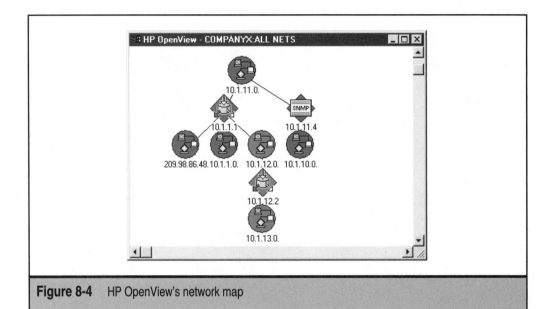

Figure 8-4   HP OpenView's network map

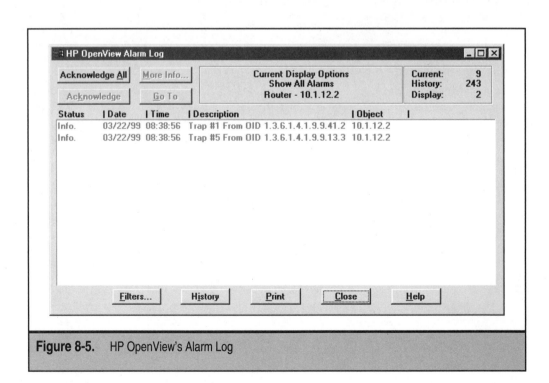

Figure 8-5.   HP OpenView's Alarm Log

THE CISCO MANAGEMENT TREE

Let's step back and get a big-picture view of the two Cisco management suites we will be discussing in this chapter. Table 8-2 schematically outlines two very different application suites: CiscoWorks for Windows and CiscoWorks2000.

CISCOWORKS

CiscoWorks for Windows is a GUI-based suite of applications that runs on Windows 9x, or Windows NT. It is designed for small- to medium-sized businesses that want to take command over troubleshooting and management of their Cisco networks. The applications use SNMP exclusively to communicate with sundry Cisco routers, switches, or hubs. You can get amazingly detailed information about a device or even change its settings—bringing a router's interface up or down, for example.

Cisco Suite Name	Application Group Name	Application Name
CiscoWorks for Windows	N/A	CiscoView Configuration Builder
CiscoWorks2000	Resource Manager	Availability Manger Device Configuration Manager Software Image Manager Inventory Manager Change Audit Service Syslog Analyzer CCO Service Tools Cisco Management Connection
	CWSI (CiscoWorks for Switched Internetworks)	Network Topology Discovery and Display VLAN Management Traffic Monitoring and Performance User Tracking ATM and LANE Service Configuration and Status Monitoring CiscoView Graphical Device Management

Table 8-2.   The CiscoWorks Application Tree

Getting Started with CiscoWorks

The first thing you must do, of course, is obtain a copy of the software. You can purchase a copy for about $500 from a Cisco reseller or directly from Cisco's Web site. (You'll be offered better deals from a reseller, however.) If you *are* a reseller, you might be able to get an evaluation copy from a friendly competitor or channel partner.

The CiscoWorks CD-ROM takes up about 220MB of space, but much of this is left untouched by most users, as explained later in the "Supported Devices" section.

The second thing you must take care of is securing some additional documentation prior to attempting the installation. Although the installation and configuration are not difficult, every installation is as different as the network it runs on, and supplementary information will undoubtedly prove essential to a successful evaluation or implementation. If you purchase the CiscoWorks software, you will receive a few documents; but these are quite thin. Also, there isn't much information on the CiscoWorks for Windows CD-ROM. Go to Cisco's Web site for downloadable Adobe .PDF files, at http://www.cisco.com/univercd/cc/td/doc/product/rtrmgmt/cwfw/index.htm.

Application Suite Overview

Our discussion of CiscoWorks for Windows will cover the two major applications: CiscoView and Configuration Builder. Additional functionality for CiscoWorks for Windows is also available for purchase, in the form of these supported applications offered by Cisco:

▼ **Threshold Manager**   Sets threshold on RMON-enabled devices.

■ **StackMaker**   Manages switches and hubs when they are configured to be a member of a stack.

▲ **Flash File System**   Used to edit and display functionality for high-end router configuration files.

In addition to adding the above supporting applications, CiscoWorks for Windows can be integrated with the following network management applications:

▼ Castle Rock Computing SNMP

■ HP OpenView Network Node Manager for Windows NT

▲ HP OpenView Professional Suite for Windows

CiscoWorks for Windows can share data with these other management tools and access their database of information—thereby increasing CiscoWorks's own ability to manage Cisco devices. For the discussions in this section, however, we will use CiscoWorks as a stand-alone product to highlight its inherent abilities.

System Requirements for CiscoWorks

Before you can install the application suite, make sure the computer you choose has access to the network and sufficient resources to run CiscoWorks for Windows. You don't need a supercomputer (to the extent you do for CiscoWorks2000), but beware of cast-off or secondhand machines that might not meet the following requirements:

▼ **Operating system**   Windows 95 or NT 4.0

■ **Processor**   486 (Pentium @ 90MHz recommended)

■ **Graphics**   At least 1024 × 768 to see device images

■ **RAM**   32MB

■ **Hard drive space**   327MB to install (50–80MB after that)

▲ **Network interface card**   Required unless connecting to devices via the serial port

CiscoWorks for Windows is designed to interact with its environment. The environment itself, then, must meet certain requirements as well, in order to gain full functionality from the tool.

Supported Cisco IOS Versions

The version of Cisco IOS running on the devices may or may not support CiscoView. For the most part, CiscoView supports all routers with IOS release 10.2 through 11.3. This qualifies nearly all routers that are in production today, except the very oldest and some cutting-edge devices using Cisco IOS 12.0 or higher.

The Configuration Builder application also works on routers with code from IOS 10.2 to 11.3. Access servers require 10.3 or higher, and Cisco 3600 devices and 4000 series devices require 11.1 or 10.3, respectively. This wide range of eligible release code is quite generous; yet you will find that not all devices, especially newer models, are supported. Adding support for these devices is easy and will be covered later under "Adding New Packages."

Supported Devices

CiscoWorks for Windows ships with support for over 50 devices or series of devices (all the 4000 routers, for instance). These are called *packages* or .PKG files. (This device support is what accounts for 212MB out of the 220MB on the CiscoWorks for Windows CD-ROM.) New or revised packages are available for download from Cisco's Web site. The most common devices are supported out of the box and include the following:

▼ 700 series routers (most)

■ 2500 series routers (most)

■ 1200–5000 series switches (many)

■ 4000–7000 series routers (all)

- 216 and 300 series FastHubs
▲ AS5200–AS5800 access servers

Installing CiscoWorks for Windows

Let's walk through the download and installation of a new CiscoWorks package. If your environment meets the system requirements listed earlier, you are ready to install CiscoWorks for Windows. If you are using CiscoWorks with another management application, such as HP OpenView, you will need to have that application installed first. CiscoWorks detects it during installation and asks whether you'd like to work with it. Also, be sure you have backed up any data files from any previous version of CiscoWorks, including Configuration Builder. It is also recommended that you do not attempt to install CiscoWorks for Windows on a system that is also running CiscoWorks2000 (which includes CWSI, CiscoWorks for Switched Internetworks). If you do, CiscoWorks for Windows gets confused and mayhem follows.

1. Initiate the installation process by placing the CD in your machine and running the SETUP.EXE file.

2. After viewing the obligatory licensing agreement, you'll be asked whether you'll be installing the product stand-alone or in conjunction with another management application. Only specify another application if you already have it installed on the system and you want to integrate with it.

3. Select the directory in which you want to place all the files (approximately 50 to 80MB).

4. Next, you'll be asked which packages you want to install. There is no description of the packages, only the filename—you'll have to guess what the package includes. For example, the package called "4000.pkg" includes support for all 4000-series routers. Some choices are not as obvious, however, so choose carefully—because the installation takes quite some time depending on how many packages you select.

When the package installation process is finished, you can view the readme file or jump right in. Let's just jump right in.

CiscoView

When CiscoView is first started, it has a rather unassuming, diminutive window. It certainly doesn't look like it can do much, but that's because no devices have been loaded. CiscoView is waiting to show off, but first you need to connect to a device.

Connecting to a Remote Device

As you recall, CiscoWorks uses SNMP for all connections to remote devices. Therefore, you need to have at least the read-only SNMP community string for each device you want to view. If you intend to alter the device's configuration, you'll need the read/write community string. The other crucial piece of information you'll need is the IP number or host name (if the devices are registered with a name service). If you don't have any of this information or it is incorrect, you won't get connected to the device and will see an annoying error message instead. To connect to a device, follow these steps:

1. Click on File | Open Device.
2. Enter the IP number or host name of the device, and at least one of the SNMP community strings. Click OK, and CiscoView will attempt to make a connection with the device.

If all goes well, you'll see a graphical representation of the device, as illustrated in Figure 8-6 for a Cisco 4500 router. In this example, we are viewing the rear panel of the router. Three modules are currently installed in it: a 4-port ISDN module, a 2-port Token Ring module, and a single-port Ethernet module. When CiscoWorks calls up a device in this fashion, it color-codes each physical port so that you can instantly see which ports are active.

This initial image of the device is obviously quite useful, but CiscoView's features go beyond this.

Configuring Devices with CiscoView

In terms of basic configuration, what you can specifically manipulate depends on the device. To configure global features of the device, double-click on a port; or click a port to highlight it and select Configure | Port. This brings up a window like the one in Figure 8-7.

In this window, you can bring an interface up or down, or rename it in the Local Description field. Also, you can view some basic information about that port, including its

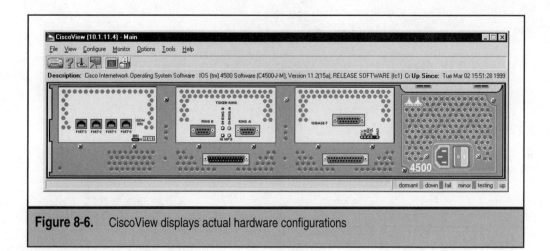

Figure 8-6. CiscoView displays actual hardware configurations

▼ MAC address

■ Last update time

■ Current status

▲ Current speed

Configuring the whole device (that is, its chassis) in this fashion allows you to view many of the device's current settings. Obtaining these values by hand would require sifting through the results of numerous **show** commands. The results describe information about the current Cisco IOS release, IP routing tables, history of changes made to the router, and a summary of the device's memory configuration. Not all aspects of a device are revealed here or are available for configuration, but you can save a lot of time by using these functions for the most common queries.

Monitoring the Network Devices

For real-time monitoring of almost any aspect of a device, CiscoView is the tool to use. You can watch the current utilization of any port on your network using CiscoView. Not only can you see basic utilization, but you can watch graphs of packet flow in and out of the ports and error frames, or a plethora of statistics specific for a given protocol such as Ethernet collisions.

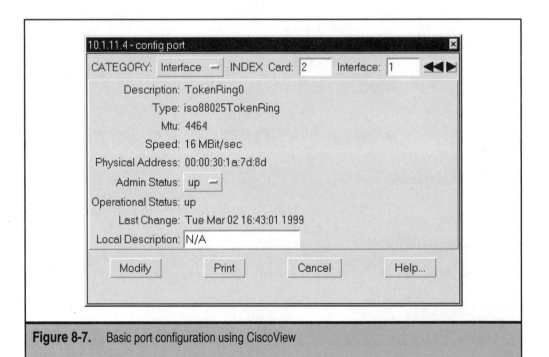

Figure 8-7. Basic port configuration using CiscoView

To start monitoring, select a chassis or port and click the Monitor menu item. This will call up a new window containing one or more graphs that are updated as frequently as you indicate. In most instances, you can select which aspect of monitoring you want to watch. For example, if you were curious about the temperature of the inside of your Cisco 7000 router; you could click the chassis, select Monitor, and then Environment in the next window that pops up. The result is shown in Figure 8-8. You can see the current voltage inside the device, and that the air flowing out of the router is 5° C warmer. (If you have ever turned on a 7000 and seen the house lights dim at the same time, you now know why—these babies burn some power.)

The Monitoring aspect of CiscoView is most valuable for troubleshooting. Even if the problem is with a device on the network and not necessarily the device you are monitoring, the monitoring might pick up errant frames and point you toward a solution. The fact that you can scan quickly through all the routers on your network greatly reduces the legwork associated with this level of troubleshooting.

Using Threshold Manager

Sometimes you want to be warned about pending problems so you don't have to enter the troubleshooting mode. CiscoView's menu of tools contains the Threshold Manager,

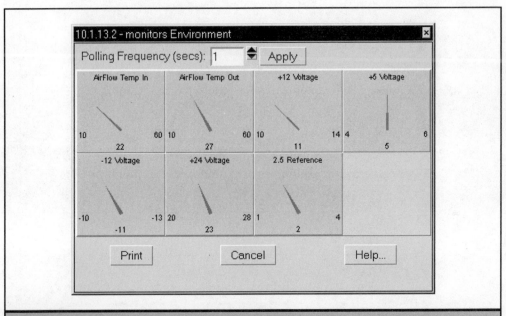

Figure 8-8. Checking the temperature inside a router

which you can use to watch specific counters and take action if the counter reaches a pre-determined level.

Select Tools | Threshold Manager to start the Threshold Manager. Initially, this calls up a blank window that lists all the active threshold policies. These policies describe the items or counters you have told the Manager to watch; and since you haven't specified any yet, the initial screen is blank. To add a watch, click the Config | Threshold menu item. Then select from a variety of preconfigured policies, or you can choose to create your own from scratch. Either way, you'll next see a screen like Figure 8-9.

In this example, we are setting a policy to watch the utilization of the CPU. There are fields to give the policy a description and designate the thresholds for the policy, as well as how frequently to poll the device. You'll want to set this last value at a reasonable level for catching the event, but not so often that you cause another event. Another key component is the action the policy takes when a threshold has been achieved. You can set the policy to simply log the event and/or send an SNMP trap to a network manger application such as HP OpenView. Fortunately, policies can be grouped together, saved, and applied to other devices or groups of devices.

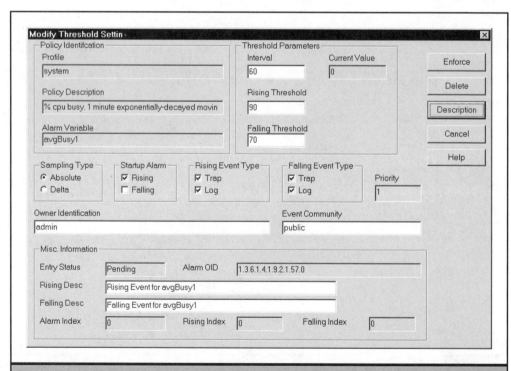

Figure 8-9. Threshold Manager will warn you about impending problems

Adding New Packages

It's just a matter of time before you'll come across a device with which you want to use CiscoView, but that won't be supported from the basic installation. In all likelihood, you can find a package for this device on Cisco's Web site. You'll probably need a CCO (Cisco Connection Online) account to retrieve it, though. The process of getting this account is covered in more detail in Appendix D.

To look for a CiscoWorks package that you want, point your browser to http://www.cisco.com/kobayashi/library/netmanage/cview/. From there, navigate the series of Web pages, selecting the device family and then eventually the device for which you need a package. Downloading the file is simple enough. Make sure you save it in a place where the CiscoWorks application can reach it.

To install the new package, select Programs | CiscoWorks Windows | Install New Device. You'll be prompted for the .PKG file. Once selected, the file is simply loaded and incorporated into CiscoWorks. Next time you start CiscoView, you'll be able to select the new device.

NOTE: You'll notice on the Web site that some of the newer packages for the latest devices have increased functionality. You might have to check back later to see if a package has been created for some of the most recent devices.

Configuration Builder

We've seen how CiscoView can be used to quickly view and troubleshoot network devices. Network administrators also need to be able to manipulate the configuration files that are loaded when the router or switch is started. The traditional option is to telnet or log into the device via the management port, and use the CLI to slowly build the configuration file by hand using individual commands. This method is obviously very time consuming and also prone to human error. Mistyping a single command can render the device useless. Configuration Builder offers a better way.

Configuration Builder is a GUI-based tool you can use to build configuration files and quickly distribute them to your Cisco devices. You start Configuration Builder by selecting Programs | CiscoWorks Windows | Configuration Builder. The first window that pops up is the New Configuration File window shown in Figure 8-10.

From here you can manually describe some essential device characteristics, or use the Learn feature to automatically query the device for the needed information. To use Learn, you'll need to know the device's IP number (unless you are using the console port), and the line and enable passwords. Using the Learn function is recommended, if possible, to reduce the possibility of human error. Either way, Configuration Builder needs to determine the following:

▼   IOS release level

■   Number and type of interfaces

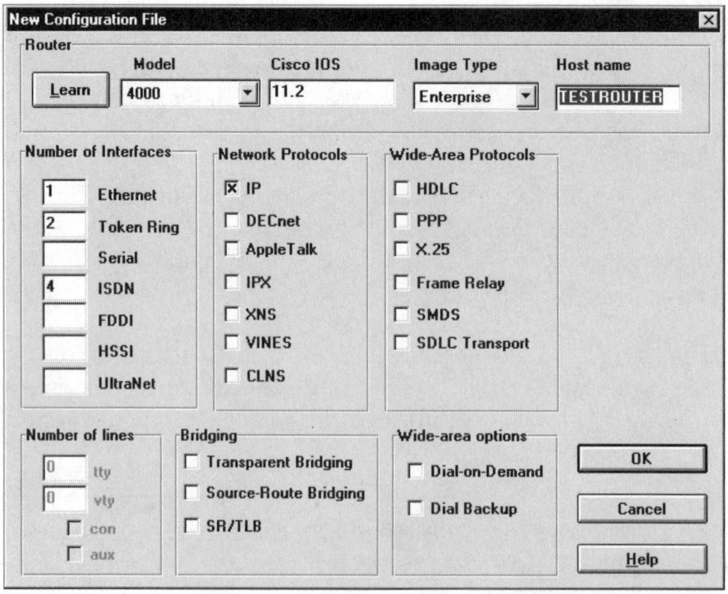

Figure 8-10.   Creating a new configuration file starts with the basic items

- LAN and WAN protocols in use
- Bridging options
- WAN options
- ▲ Device host name

When all this information is entered, click OK to return to the main screen. A window there will show a schematic for your device. The interfaces will be listed but crossed out because they have not yet been configured. You have two options to continue to build your configuration file: you can use the menu items to configure the interfaces, routing, bridging, WAN links, and so forth; or you can select the Global | Guided Configuration option and be led sequentially through the various settings. We'll follow the Guided Configuration process here so that we get a feel for all the options available. When we're finished, we'll have a configuration file we can roll out to our device or to many devices.

Using the Guided Configuration

Using the Guided Configuration option is a handy way to make sure you haven't left anything out of a new configuration file. After selecting Guided Configuration, a series of windows will ask you for information. Sometimes you must provide answers (such as the IP addresses for IP-configured interfaces), or the information might be optional (as in the case of SNMP management). In this example, we'll be creating a configuration file for a 4500 series router.

Basic Configuration

The first screen, Basic Configuration (Figure 8-11) asks for some essential information about the device. You can change the host name, enter the passwords required to log into the device, and add an optional banner for displaying to users when they log into the router. Make sure there's no checkmark in the Shutdown column for interfaces that you want to use. When you've finished, click OK.

TIP: You can change the value in the Bandwidth column so that routing protocols will increase or decrease the attractiveness of using that path.

SNMP Configuration

Configuration Builder will now present the main view; to continue, you need to return to the Global menu and select Guided Configuration. This approach seems unintuitive

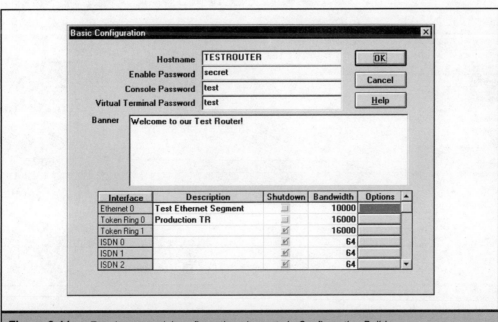

Figure 8-11.   Entering essential configuration elements in Configuration Builder

because it doesn't follow the "back and next" formula used in many configuration tools or wizards.

The next window is the SNMP Configuration window. Here you configure the basic SNMP parameters, including the community strings, what events to send SNMP traps on, and where to send those traps. Remember, to take advantage of the management functions of the tools described in this book, SNMP must be configured correctly and running on the device. Click OK when you have finished.

IP Routing Configuration

Depending on what protocols you selected on the initial configuration screen (Figure 8-10), you'll be presented next with a more detailed configuration window for those protocols. In Figure 8-12, you see information required for a basic IP configuration. You'll need to provide an IP address and subnet mask for each active interface. Also, you might want to include descriptions of the interfaces for troubleshooting purposes.

An excellent feature provided by Configuration Builder is the ability to import or create access lists and incorporate them into your configuration file. For each interface, you can import a previously saved access list or use the GUI access list creator to make new lists. Then you can save these lists for later use. When you click OK to close this window, you have finished creating the most essential elements of your configuration file.

Interface	Description	Enabled	IP Address	Subnet Mask	Access List	Second.
Ethernet 0	Test Ethernet Se	✓	10.1.10.2	255.255.255.0	▼	
Token Ring 0	Production TR	✓	10.1.11.4		▼	
Token Ring 1					▼	
ISDN 0					▼	
ISDN 1					▼	
ISDN 2					▼	
ISDN 3					▼	

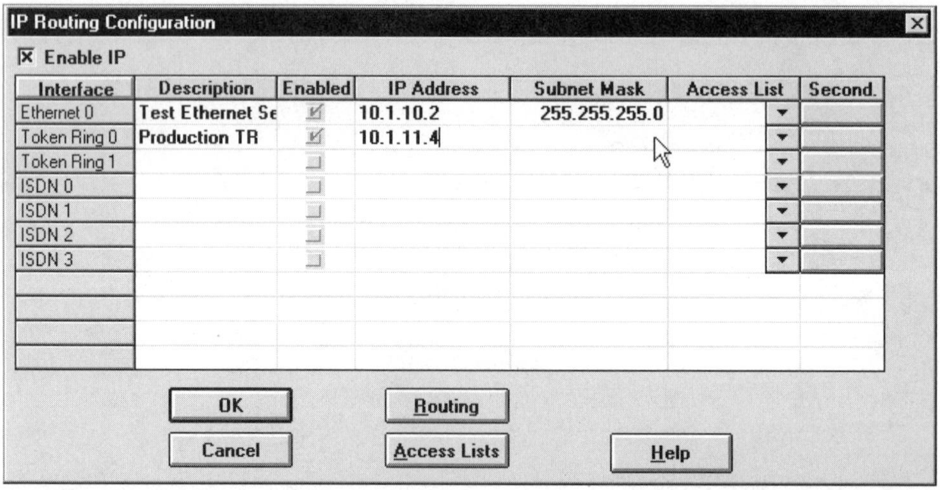

Figure 8-12.   Adding essential IP information

Adding IP Routing

For the router to function, you need to add information about IP routing protocols so routes will be shared with and learned from other routers. To do this, you select Routing | IP | Routing Protocols to get the IP Routing Protocols window, shown in Figure 8-13.

In this example, we want to include this 4500 router in the local OSPF autonomous system on the backbone area (area 0). First, select OSPF and the correct autonomous system number. Then include the area number for all interfaces with which you want to share routes. It really is just that simple. Click OK, and you'll return again to the main window.

Figure 8-14 illustrates the main Configuration Builder window with our sample router configured in the new configuration file. Notice that the two interfaces we configured (Ethernet 0 and Token Ring 0) are now valid and have IP addresses assigned to them, while the other interfaces are still crossed out.

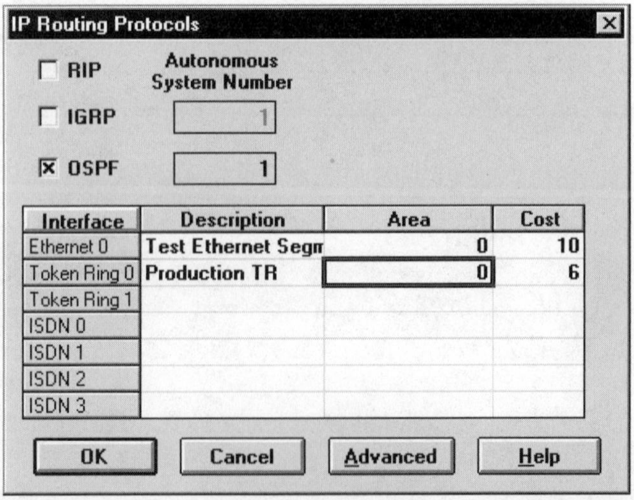

Figure 8-13. Setting up OSPF

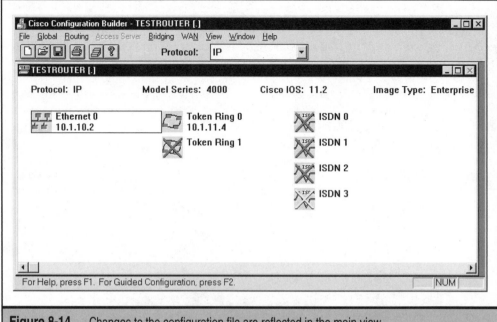

Figure 8-14.   Changes to the configuration file are reflected in the main view

Sending the Configuration File

Now that the configuration file exists, you can save it to disk so you can view it and then send it to the actual router. The configuration file created in this example is listed here:

```
!*********************************************************************
!
!                    Cisco Router Configuration File
!
!
!
!                 Generated by the Cisco Configuration Builder
!
!                      Wed Dec 15, 1999 - 16:11:34
!
!*********************************************************************
!
!
!
hostname TESTROUTER
```

```
banner motd #
Welcome to Test Router 4 !!!
#
enable password secret
line console 0
login
password test
line vty 0 4
login
password test
isdn switch-type basic-5ess
!
ip routing
no decnet routing
no appletalk routing
no ipx routing
no xns routing
no vines routing
no clns routing
!
snmp-server community public RO
snmp-server community private RW
!
router ospf 1
network 10.1.10.2 0.0.0.0 area 0
network 10.1.11.4 0.0.0.0 area 0
!
interface ethernet 0
description Test Ethernet Segment
no shutdown
bandwidth 10000
no priority-group
ip address 10.1.10.2 255.255.255.0
ip ospf cost 10
no ip access-group
!
interface token 0
description Production TR
no shutdown
bandwidth 16000
ring-speed 16
no priority-group
ip address 10.1.11.4 255.255.255.0
ip ospf cost 6
```

```
no ip access-group
!
interface token 1
no description
shutdown
bandwidth 16000
ring-speed 16
no priority-group
!
interface bri 0
no description
shutdown
bandwidth 64
no priority-group
.
.
.
```

Once you have verified that the statements in the configuration file are the ones you intended, you can send the file to the router. The router will start using the new configuration immediately, so make sure your settings are exactly correct. Select File | Send and enter the IP address for your device, as well as the line and enable password. You also have the option of writing the configuration to NVRAM. Do this only if you know the configuration will work; otherwise, you might be in for a load of work getting the device up and running again. Click OK, and if the communication parameters are correct, the router should receive its new file without skipping a beat.

CISCOWORKS2000

CiscoWorks for Windows will be a workhorse for some time, but Cisco is nevertheless planning to replace it with CiscoWorks2000. Therefore, you shouldn't attempt to use both products simultaneously on the same machine (or the same network, for that matter). Like CiscoWorks for Windows, CiscoWorks2000 is really a name for a family of applications. However, CiscoWorks2000 is further divided into two major groups: Resource Manager Essentials and CiscoWorks for Switched Internetworks (CWSI). These two groups of applications form an integrated foundation for management of Cisco routers, switches, hubs, and access servers. Each group comes on its own CD-ROM.

The sheer complexity of this management suite prevents us from covering all the details of every application. This section outlines the most basic features found within each of CiscoWorks2000's two basic groupings.

Getting Started

CiscoWorks2000 is rather finicky about its platform, is somewhat of a resource pig, and requires careful planning before installation. Not only do you have to set aside a powerful workstation, you must also configure the server with stringent software requirements.

System Requirements for CiscoWorks2000

First, you must decide whether you'll be installing just one group of applications or both. The Resource Manager Essentials is required for CWSI, so you'll probably install both. The requirements are a little less demanding if you plan to use only the Essentials server. Following are the minimum requirements for a CiscoWorks2000 system:

▼ **Processor**   Pentium 300 MHz or faster

■ **RAM**   256MB

▲ **Hard drive space**   4GB (NTFS recommended)

Of course, these are the minimum requirements for the server. If you'll be deploying it in a large enterprise, then you should get an even faster machine with even more RAM and hard drive space. Once a CiscoWorks2000 server consumes all its available resources, it starts using the swap file and slows to a crawl.

Software Requirements for CiscoWorks2000

The software requirements are quite specific, and if you don't meet any one of the conditions, CiscoWorks2000 will not load or run properly.

To start, you'll need Windows NT 4.0 Server or Workstation, with Service Pack 3 or higher (currently SP 3 is the recommended and tested environment; do not use anything higher for CiscoWorks2000 release 2.0). You cannot run CiscoWorks2000 on a Primary or Backup Domain Controller. Also, CiscoWorks2000 is not supported on Windows 2000 yet.

Certain Web-based applications, as well, must be installed before installing CiscoWorks2000. You'll need to have Microsoft Internet Explorer 4.01 with Explorer Service Pack 1 (no Active Desktop). You must also have Option Pack installed with the following components: Data Access Components 1.5; Microsoft Management Console; Internet Information Services 4.0 (or Personal Web Service if you are installing it on NT Workstation); and Windows Scripting Host (not selected by default).

Resource Manager Essentials

Because CWSI depends on Resource Manager Essentials (hereafter called just "Essentials"), you must always install Essentials first after you have verified that your system meets the software and hardware requirements.

Installing Essentials

The Essentials installation is straightforward. Run the SETUP.EXE program on the product CD-ROM. You'll be asked where you want to install the files and which applications to install. Unless you know specifically about each application, it's best to include them all (select the Typical installation); they don't take up much space. Most of the 4GB of required space is for the swap file and for future log and configuration files. After a reboot, you can start using Essentials or install CWSI. Either way, you'll need to configure Essentials before you can start using it.

Configuring Essentials

Essentials is completely Web based, so any access to it is through a Web browser on the server or, more likely, on a remote client machine. To access the Essential's Web interface, you need to point your browser at the name of the server and port number 1741. For example, the address http://ciscoworks.test.com:1741 would work if the server's name was ciscoworks in the domain test.com.

CiscoWorks2000 uses Java throughout the Web page, so you'll need to run Microsoft's Internet Explorer 4.01 (with Service Pack 1) or Netscape's Navigator 4.04 or 4.05. Performance will be slow unless you have a fast Pentium (350 MHz or faster). Also, it seems no monitor on earth is big enough to hold all the information that these pages display; so the larger, the better. To get the most out of the GUI interface, you'll need to change a few settings in your browser:

▼ Enable Java and JavaScript.

■ Configure the browser to accept cookies.

■ Set the browser to compare each page against its cache.

▲ Allow the use of Style Sheets.

THE MANAGEMENT CONSOLE   Once you've specified the name of the server and port 1741 in the address field of your browser, you should see the management console illustrated in Figure 8-15. The left-hand pane presents the login window, the navigational tree, and a message pane at the bottom. The message pane displays periodic messages that provide tips and other useful information. The center pane is where tables and graphs are presented. These correspond to the item selected in the navigational pane on the left. (Before you log in, however, only the CiscoWorks2000 splash screen is displayed.)

You can log in at first as either the administrator or as a guest. Once you've logged in as the administrator, you can add users, change the default passwords, and customize the rights of any user.

▼ The default administrator login is

   Username: **admin**
   Password: **admin**

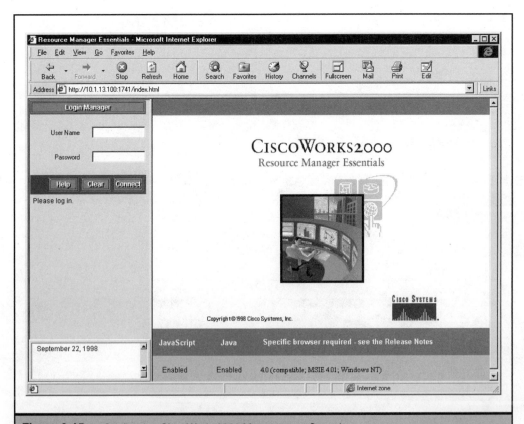

Figure 8-15. Configuring CiscoWorks2000 Management Console

NOTE: It is recommended that you change the default administrator password on your first login.

▲ The guest account is named **guest** and has no default password.

ADDING DEVICES Even though all the menu items are activated, you will not be able to monitor, manage, or manipulate a single device until you have populated CiscoWorks2000 with those devices. There are a couple of ways of doing this: you can enter them in one at a time; select them from the Select Devices menu, as shown in Figure 8-16; or import them from the following sources:

▼ Local or remote network management system: CWSI 2.2 or 2.1; HP OpenView; CiscoWorks

▲ A Comma Separated Value (.CSV) file

More information about the syntax of the .CSV file is provided in the on-line help. The preferred method is to pull devices from the locally installed CWSI or from a local copy of HP OpenView. Either way, this "importing" is a quick process and, once completed, will get you on your way to reaping the benefits of CiscoWorks2000.

NOTE: Even though you import devices, many of the Essentials management views will be empty for some time until each device has been polled. Be patient—soon you'll have plenty of data collected from your devices.

The Resource Manager Essentials Applications

Essentials is full of tools that will streamline the management of your Cisco network. Although there is not enough space here to walk you through all of the available ways to display data about your network, we will take a look at some of the most useful applica-

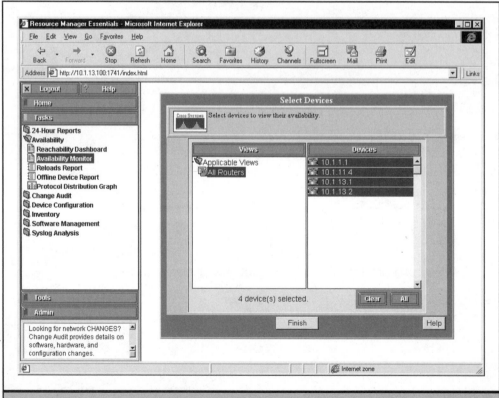

Figure 8-16. Selecting multiple devices for analysis

tions. "Applications" in this context means separate menu items that perform functions independently from other items. This is different from the usual meaning of application as a program that is run separately from all others. Nonetheless, all applications use the underlying Resource Manager Essentials as a foundation and are contained within one of the four major menus: Home, Tasks, Tools, and Admin.

Availability Manager

The Availability Manager is useful in getting a bird's-eye view of the network's overall status. Basically, you can gauge the ability of each device to respond to CiscoWorks2000. To view the Availability Manager, select Tasks | Availability. Click the Availability Monitor and you'll be presented with a list of devices. Select only the devices whose availability you want to check. You can select multiple devices or all of them, as shown in Figure 8-16.

From here, click Finish, and another browser window will pop up. The graph in this window lists the overall availability statistics for each device you selected. These stats include up time, time of last update, and overall reachability represented as a percentage of time. Clicking any single device allows you to view over 15 other information pages on the device, such as

▼ Reachability over time

■ Response time

■ Interface status

■ Configuration reports

▲ Traffic distribution by protocol

Device Configuration Manager

The Device Configuration manager is found under the Tasks | Device Configuration menu. It is the one-stop shop for all your configuration file questions. This feature will automatically download the configuration files from all sorts of devices and store them in a database. You can even compare a current version with a previously stored copy and learn who changed it, what was changed, and when it was last changed.

One of the Device Configuration Manager's greatest contributions is its ability to search through hundreds of configuration files and pull out only the ones that match a criterion. If you don't feel like wading through a long configuration file, you can click the name of a certain aspect of the file (such as an interface) and display only that part of the configuration file. See Figure 8-17.

Software Manager

What used to take days can now be accomplished in minutes with the Essentials' Software Manager. This tool is also located in the Tasks tab and controls the inventory and distribution of Cisco IOS software.

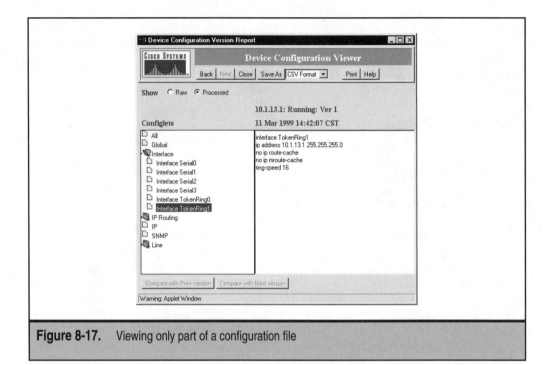

Figure 8-17.   Viewing only part of a configuration file

Before you can distribute any IOS software, you must first build a library of IOS releases. This can be done via a Web connection to CCO, from files on your network, or from the devices themselves. Software Manager can actually pull all versions of Cisco IOS currently on your network and centralize their storage.

When you want to upgrade a Cisco IOS, for example, you can select only those devices that meet a certain criteria, such as "all 4000 series routers with an IOS release value of 10.3." Then you select an IOS from your library to push down to those devices. This constitutes a job that can be scheduled for off-hours in order not to disrupt normal network traffic. CiscoWorks2000 is smart enough to let you know if you're trying to load an incompatible Cisco IOS, or an IOS onto a device that does not have the required system resources.

Inventory Manager

Related to the Software Manager is the Inventory Manager, which keeps track of virtually every aspect of what physically exists in your network. For example, you can view all your devices based on class of device, such as routers, hubs, and switches. Then you can drill down to a more detailed level showing individual devices and even specifics within one device.

Figure 8-18 illustrates a basic summary of all network devices located in a particular test environment. This graph shows each device type as a percentage of all devices. You can see that half of the devices in this network are routers. These data are especially useful in capacity planning, or to quickly count devices of a certain type for the purpose of planning upgrades.

Change Audit Service

The Change Audit Service is located under the Tasks tab. From here you can view all the changes that have taken place for the software, hardware, and configuration on any device in the CiscoWorks2000 database. This central reporting tool lets you know, for example, that a particular router's configuration file was changed by CiscoWorks2000 at 2:00 P.M. last Wednesday. Of course, you can sort the changes based on type and time.

Syslog Analyzer

Most Cisco devices have the ability to generate a system log (syslog) when a deleterious event has taken place. CiscoWorks2000 can capture these log files from the devices, and the Syslog Analyzer (in the Tasks tab) helps you sort and prioritize the log entries.

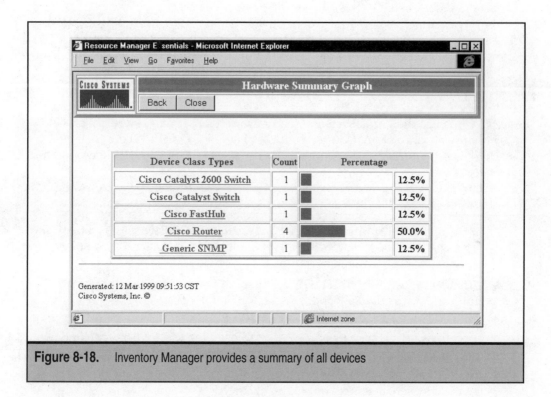

Figure 8-18. Inventory Manager provides a summary of all devices

Syslog Analyzer's ability to sort and prioritize the events cuts down on troubleshooting time. You can customize the reports and create filters so only the most important events are displayed.

Cisco Connection Online (CCO) Service Tools

The CCO menu item is located under the Home tab as well as through the Tools | CCO Tools command. It is your link to the most relevant Web pages on Cisco's Web site. You'll find information about using CiscoWorks2000, Cisco IOS upgrades, technical information, technical tips, and specific information about Resource Manager Essentials.

NOTE: You will need a CCO account to get into some parts of the Web site. Obtaining an account is explained in Appendix D.

CiscoWorks Switched Internetwork Campus

The second component of CiscoWorks2000 is CiscoWorks Switched Internetwork (CWSI, often pronounced "swizzee"), which can certainly do more than just manage switches. CWSI can form the foundation of your network topology map using a systematic discovery operation much like HP OpenView's.

Also, you launch other applications from within CWSI, including CiscoView, VLANDirector, TrafficDirector, and ATMDrector. These and other applications offer performance management capabilities by collecting RMON data from devices and distilling it down into simple graphs and charts.

Installing CWSI

Since CWSI is installed on a system already running Essentials, there are no CWSI-specific hardware or software requirements. CWSI requires Essentials because they share some back-end processing and databases. You can install CWSI with HP OpenView and other network management systems.

Start the installation process by running SETUP.EXE from the application CD-ROM. You'll need to address the following during installation:

▼ **Location for the application files**   Be sure to select a drive with plenty of space, because the program will fill it up with topological maps and other device-specific information.

■ **Whether to integrate CWSI with another network management application**   In all likelihood, you'll select StandAlone.

■ **Choosing the device packages you want to include**   This is for the benefit of CiscoView, and is the same process as for installing CiscoWorks for Windows.

■ **Whether to include the TrafficDirector or ATMDirector applications**   Obviously, if you know you won't be using them, don't waste precious system resources by loading them.

- **Picking a seed device for network topology discovery** This is the IP address for the first device that CWSI will query to determine your network layout.

▲ **The AniServer** CWSI uses a background process called Asynchronous Network Interface (ANI) to run the discovery process, so you need to enter the name of the AniServer. If this is the same as the local machine, AniServer will work.

After a reboot, you'll be up and running with the complete CiscoWorks2000 suite of applications. Before discovery can take place, you'll need to enter correct SNMP community strings. Select Edit | SNMP Communities, which opens a text file in which you add the appropriate read-only and read/write community strings for your devices. Instructions are given in the top of the file. That is all you need to do to set CWSI up before making a discovery of your network.

Making a New Discovery

To initialize the CWSI discovery process, click the button with the circular arrow, on the left end of the CWSI Campus toolbar. Discovery will take a few minutes, depending on the size of your network. CWSI uses CDP (Cisco Discovery Protocol) as one of the mechanisms to find Cisco devices. CDP runs at layer 2 of the OSI model, and so can discover devices without IP or SNMP installed, such as Cisco switches.

Figure 8-19 shows an example of the discovery map; in this case, we discovered our local test network. All connections, devices, and even interface information are displayed on the map. Double-clicking any device will open CiscoView and load the device. You can also right-click a device and list its ports and other basic attributes. Once you have a topological map with devices, you can use the applications included with CWSI to manage and monitor them.

REMOVING DEVICES FROM THE MAP Once CWSI discovers a device and adds it to the map, it cannot be deleted. Currently, you have two other options for removing an object from the discovery map:

▼ Delete the lines attached to the object, and then hide the unwanted object in a part of the screen that is not viewed.

▲ Delete the CWSI database and rediscover the network without the unwanted object. The map will then need to be organized and saved.

NOTE: If you want to discover devices more than one router hop away, you must select the Jump Router Boundaries box under Options | Properties | Discovery.

CWSI Applications

The applications included with CWSI are listed in Table 8-3. Most of these are really separate applications and are simply launched from within CWSI and use the CiscoWorks2000 database of devices. In any event, it's easy to use them because they're all centrally located in this fashion.

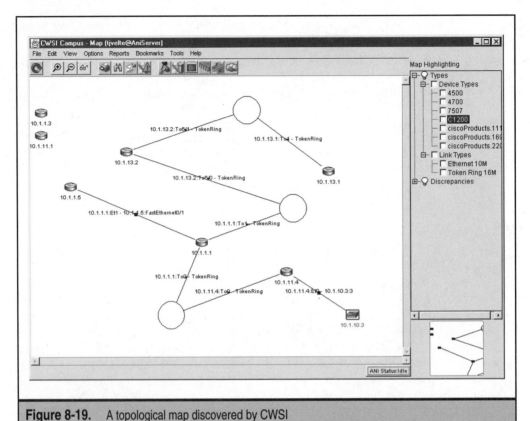

Figure 8-19. A topological map discovered by CWSI

NTMANAGE

NTManage by LANWARE (www.lanware.net) is a network management and trouble-shooting application that runs on Windows NT Workstation and Server. Like CWSI, NTManage has an auto-discovery feature that, given a seed router, searches your network and creates a topological map of it. NTManage has real-time reporting functions so that fault detection and device management are easy and quick.

Installing and Configuring NTManage

Installation of NTManage is simple and straightforward; just be sure you have the SNMP service already running. This is accomplished through the Control Panel. Open the Network icon, click the Services tab, and select SNMP Agent. The system must be rebooted for the SNMP agent to take effect. After that, your NT system is capable of sending SNMP

CWSI Application	Features/Functions
CWSI Discovery	The CWSI Campus map provides a logical view of devices and links in your network. You can also view the topology of your virtual LAN (VLAN) configuration in relation to the physical topology.
VLANDirector	VLANDirector is a configuration and management tool that enables you to display, modify, and manage VLANs. You can also generate reports on VLAN status and membership.
UserTracking	This tool tracks end-user information for VLAN updates. For example, if a user's workstation is moved and plugged into another port, UserTracking provides MAC information so that the device can remain on the original VLAN without manual reconfiguration.
CiscoView	CiscoView, covered in detail earlier in the chapter, displays a graphical representation of a device and allows you to configure and monitor device chassis, port, and interface information.
TrafficDirector	TrafficDirector, described in Chapter 10, provides RMON and application-usage monitoring for quicker troubleshooting of network performance problems.
ATMDirector	ATMDirector is essential for Cisco networks with ATM switches. This application discovers ATM switches, physical links, and permanent and switched virtual circuits. It provides performance monitoring and traffic analysis of RMON-enabled ATM links.

Table 8-3.   CWSI Applications

alerts to an SNMP Manager (such as HP OpenView) or can be queried by an SNMP Manager to divulge information about the condition of the computer.

Once the program has started, you'll be asked to create a new network topology map. Again, this is a logical view of the devices on your network. Unless you have a very small network (fewer than ten devices), you'll probably elect to use the auto-discovery feature: You provide a range of IP numbers that matches the range in use by your devices, and NTManage sequentially cycles through the numbers, querying each for information. Figure 8-20 shows the resulting topological map for a test network created for NTManage to discover. All devices on this test network were successfully discovered, including the printer server and non-NT devices such as the UNIX system and the router.

The left pane of NTManage's window shows a list of devices and an icon indicating the device's current state (up or down). You can see by the direction of the arrow on the icon for the UNIX server (10.255.4.99) that it is down. Also, in the right-hand pane, all devices that need attention have a large red box as a background. And, as you'll see, NTManage can go far beyond this map in its ability to tell an administrator that a problem has developed.

Although the auto-discovery function works well for learning the fundamental information about network devices, none of the devices that are initially discovered are automatically connected to one another. The user has to manually select two devices at a time and join them via the menu. Another related drawback: although the auto-discovery will learn of all the network devices, to make NTManage useful you may have to select each device and provide more information about it. In the example in Figure 8-20, we wanted

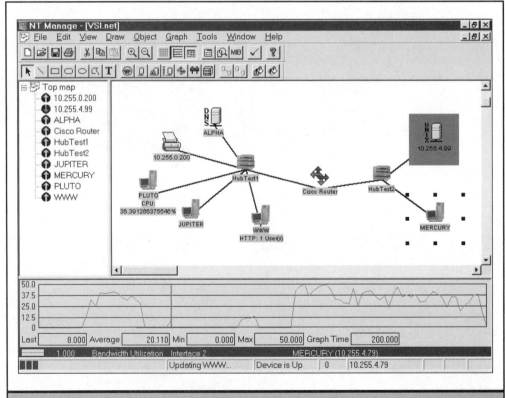

Figure 8-20. NTManage automatically discovers network devices

to indicate which computer was the DNS server, which was the Web server, and so on. In a large network, keeping the topological map current can consume a good measure of time and resources.

Monitoring Objects

In Figure 8-20, NTManage is telling you if a device is up or down but not much else. For full functionality, you'll need to configure NTManage to monitor specific counters or ports on one or more devices. The variety of objects to report on is staggering. Plus, you can use VBScripts to customize monitoring properties. Some of the canned monitoring options include CPU utilization; any TCP/IP port; performance counters (on NT systems only); and NT services.

The options for reporting an event are also diverse. You can set up NTManage to send an e-mail message, use paging services, sound alarms, write to log files, run a VBScript, or plot the results in a window below the map (Figure 8-20, bottom). For example, it's possible to monitor the number of users attached to your Web server (via a built-in VBScript) and play a .WAV file the first time the count exceeds an arbitrary number of concurrent users. Obviously, setting up and maintaining counters and alarms requires time, but if an administrator focuses on key systems and key counters, this is time well spent.

Perhaps the best feature of NTManage is its ability to automatically report the current status of your network to a Web server, via a tool called WEBVIEW. This tool allows you to set the location of the Web server and the frequency of updates to the files stored there. You can also customize the appearance of the pages, and whether or not IP numbers are displayed for the devices (for security's sake). With this setup in place, you can be anywhere in the world where you can reach that Web server, and presto—up pops the current status for all your network devices.

The amount of detail on the Web page is not as great as what you get from the console. In Figure 8-21, you can see that two devices are unreachable. From here you can see how long they have been down (by checking the last update), and which of the other devices are up and running.

One drawback of traditional management applications is that they rely on software agents running on each system to be monitored, or network probes dutifully reporting statistics back to the NMS (such as HP's OpenView). NTManage has only a single console that queries a seemingly unlimited number of network devices, without the need to install agents on each device. (And so you only pay for one console license; approximately $2,500 U.S.) This arrangement is made possible in part by NT's performance counters that can report a wealth of statistics—from CPU utilization to percent of free space on the page file. For non-NT systems, NTManage uses SNMP to query those devices.

What makes NTManage different from the other management tools discussed in this chapter is its ability to glean more information from NT systems than what you can get from SNMP queries. Of course, NTManage's ability to monitor Cisco equipment is not as great as a Cisco product's ability. However, if your primary interest is in how your servers are doing, and you want to track only some basic characteristics of the Cisco devices, it makes sense to use a tool like NTManage.

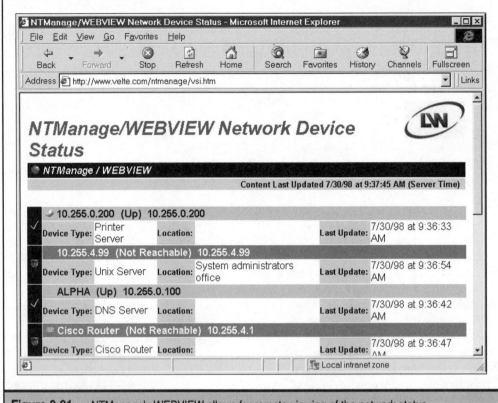

Figure 8-21.   NTManage's WEBVIEW allows for remote viewing of the network status

SUMMARY

There are a plethora of applications available to help manage and configure your Cisco/Windows network. We covered some of the most powerful and widely used management applications in this chapter. At the heart of most arrangements is a network management system such as HP OpenView or CiscoWorks2000. They use the SNMP protocol to communicate with network devices, learning everything about the devices' configuration and usage statistics. The data is often centrally stored, simplified, and displayed in an easy-to-grasp topological map. From here, the network administrator has the option to drill down into any device and see details about the device.

A fair number of ancillary applications are contained within the CiscoWorks product suite. Some help manage switched networks, ATM networks, or particular Cisco devices. This flexibility allows the administrator the ability to customize the management suite to fit the needs of their network, because no two networks are exactly the same. In the next chapter we will turn our attention to managing Windows systems, exploring some new tools that are available for today's network administrators.

9

Managing Directory
Services

A long with a dizzying array of network devices that must be configured and managed, a network administrator must also contend with setting up and managing the Windows domain controllers, stand-alone servers, and clients. Windows 2000 aims to make this a simpler and less costly task. Preceding this likely improvement, however, the period of transition from Windows NT 4.0 to Windows 2000 will be especially taxing financially and will place a burden on the technological resources of any company. During the transition period, both operating systems will be running simultaneously, and administrators will need skills in both OSs and must be able to deal with the incompatibilities that will surely arise.

This chapter highlights many of the administration tools for configuring and managing Windows 2000 networks. We will concentrate on the tools most likely to be unfamiliar to administrators of NT systems, with an emphasis on programs for managing Windows/Cisco networks. We'll start with the common framework in which all management tools reside: the Microsoft Management Console. Then we'll study examples for some of the most important administrative functions, including user/group properties, security delegation, and site replication. Then we'll explore some of the tools required to manage many of the new features included with Windows 2000.

THE MICROSOFT MANAGEMENT CONSOLE

A recurrent theme in Windows 2000 is *centralization*. This concept is best illustrated in the Active Directory (AD). The AD is located at the heart of the domain and provides all the information needed by applications and network operating systems to function properly in the Windows 2000 environment. It only makes sense to have one database for users, rather than a separate database for each of perhaps hundreds or thousands of applications. (Imagine trying to keep all those databases current!) Active Directory centralizes this function by providing a core database of information that can be used extensively by all applications.

The Microsoft Management Console (MMC) carries the centralization theme a step further by creating a framework in which management tools serving a variety of specific functions can be accessed from within a single user interface. The management tools must comply with the MMC specifications so that they can run inside this framework. The end result is that all management tools will have the same look and feel. If you can use one, you can become familiar with them all. The ultimate result is less time taken for learning the tools, and thus reduced costs.

The goal for MMC is easier management through an extensible, consistent, and intuitive interface for all administrative applications. The Management Console is a Windows-based multiple document interface (MDI) that resembles Internet Explorer. Because it's just a framework, MMC has no functionality by itself. To give it a purpose, you have to apply individual *snap-ins*—management components—into the MMC as the common host. For example, snap-ins exist for most of the current Windows Administrative Tools, such as the Disk Administrator.

Your collection of snap-ins is entirely customizable and can be created from scratch; it can even include browser-based interfaces. Once you define the MMC with the snap-ins you want, you save that group of snap-ins as a *tool*. You can include in a single MMC tool only those snap-ins needed to perform all elements of a set of complicated administrative tasks. There's no need to switch around among several applications.

Running MMC on Windows NT

Although MMC has been designed with Windows 2000 in mind, it is possible and sometimes beneficial to run the MMC on Windows NT and 9x machines. This arrangement has nearly all the functionality of the version for Windows 2000. The snap-ins available for Windows NT and Win 9x are limited, however. Currently, most are from Microsoft, for Microsoft applications. Often Microsoft bundles the MMC framework with other, more advanced software such as Routing and Remote Access (RRAS) for NT, and the NT Option Pack 4.0. You can expect that any subsequent new version of Microsoft software will come with an MMC-friendly snap-in. When you install these administration services on NT, you also install the MMC and will use it to administer the services.

NOTE: You can download the MMC for Windows NT directly from the Web site http://www.microsoft.com/MANAGEMENT/MMC/download.htm.

Whether you explicitly install the MMC or it's installed with another package, you start it by typing **mmc** at the command prompt. Figure 9-1 shows the MMC framework without any tools or snap-ins loaded.

You will need to load at least one snap-in to be able to manage anything. From the Console menu, select Add/Remove snap-in. The selection of available snap-ins displayed will depend on what software has been installed on your computer. Simply select one and it will be loaded. You can then go back and select others to create a completely customizable application.

As stated earlier, you can load more than one snap-in to create customized management tools. Each configuration is saved in an MMC-saved console file, .MSC, usually located in the My Documents folder). Next time you need a specific collection of tools, you just open that particular MMC configuration.

Running MMC on Windows 2000

If you are running Windows 2000, you don't have a choice about whether or not to use the MMC. All Microsoft administrative tools use it by default. From the Start menu, select Programs | Administrative Tools, and you'll get a list of tools that all use the MMC as their framework. The list will vary depending on what software is installed on that computer.

Under Windows 2000, you'll have more snap-ins available to you. And, just as in the Windows NT/9x version, you can add snap-ins and create your own specialized set of tools by combining just the snap-ins you need.

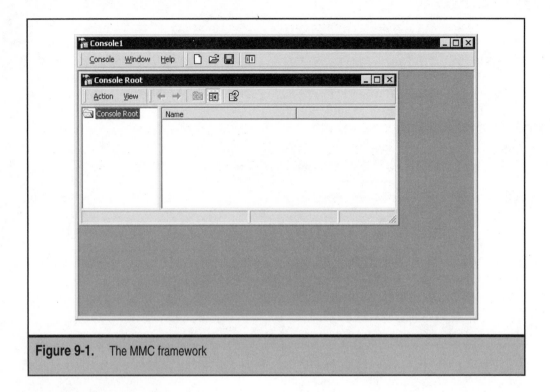

Figure 9-1. The MMC framework

The Snap-In Design

Under Windows 2000, the MMC is pervasive and the only gateway to many, if not all, administrative functions. These include the functions to manage an individual machine, as well as those to manage network-wide services such as DNS. To get familiar with the basic layout, let's take a look at the MMC with the Computer Management snap-in loaded (Figure 9-2). This particular MMC tool is started by right-clicking on the desktop's My Computer icon and selecting Manage from the shortcut menu. This snap-in is not available under Windows NT.

The basic window layout is the same for almost all snap-ins inside the MMC. At the top of the parent frame is the master menu and toolbar. Here you will find familiar items that control file and window management tasks, such as setting properties, changing the view, and Help. The tools in the toolbar will vary but generally offer navigational assistance and commands such as Create New and Delete.

The frames within the parent frame are called child frames; and though they may vary significantly in content, generally there are only two frames. The left frame contains the hierarchical organization specific to the snap-in, and the right frame presents data specific to the item that is highlighted in the left frame. In Figure 9-2, the Device Manage-

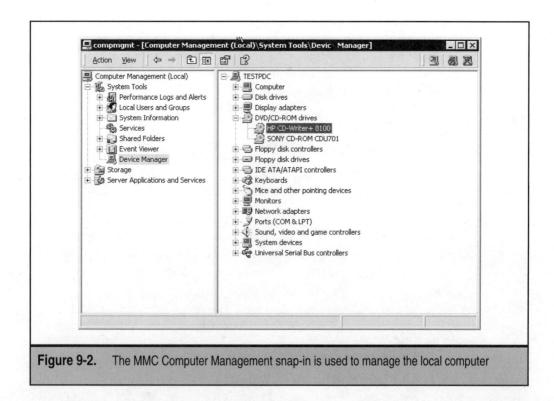

Figure 9-2.   The MMC Computer Management snap-in is used to manage the local computer

ment object is highlighted on the left, and a subset of its properties are listed on the right. To manage a specific device, simply double-click that particular device.

Now that you've seen the framework, let's dig in and start using the tools.

NETWORK ADMINISTRATION WITH MMC

Windows 2000 and the MMC fundamentally change the way administrators manage Windows/Cisco networks. At first use, when making the transition from Windows NT, these changes may cause even a seasoned network administrator some confusion. Nearly all of the familiar management tools from Windows NT have been renamed, moved, or merged with other tools in Windows 2000. Initially, it may be a little hard to remember that Microsoft is trying to centralize network management and *reduce* the complexity of its management tools.

This section illustrates MMC method through examples of the basic tasks expected from network managers in Windows 2000.

Active Directory Tasks

Active Directory has had plenty of press as the most significant change in Windows 2000. Here is where the rubber meets the road. Even the most fundamental administrative tasks are accomplished differently in Windows 2000.

Computer Properties

Let's return to the MMC with the Computer Management snap-in loaded, shown in Figure 9-2. You will notice that many tools that used to have their own application in NT are now included in this centralized snap-in. There are three major groups listed on the tree in the left frame: System Tools, Storage, and Server Applications and Services.

▼ **System Tools**   This group contains many of the individual tools from NT systems, including the Performance Monitor, Event Viewer, and Services.

■ **Storage**   The Storage items comprise all things related to the local storage media: the Disk Manager, Removable Storage, and a new Disk Defragmenter tool.

▲ **Server Applications and Services**   The items listed under this object will depend on what software is loaded on the local computer. You will be able to manage applications such as Internet Information Services, Domain Name System, and Telephony services here.

Users, Groups, and Organizational Units

To manage users, groups, and Organizational Units (OUs), select the Active Directory | Manage option from the Windows 2000 Configure Your Server window that opens automatically when you boot into Windows 2000. (When it's appropriate, you can discontinue display of this screen by unchecking the Show This Screen at Startup check box.) Next you'll see the MMC with the Active Directory Users and Computers snap-in, as illustrated in Figure 9-3.

Creating users, groups, and Organizational Units is a straightforward process, and nearly the same for each element. Right-click the object you want to create and select New, and then the type of new object you want to make. This will invoke another window in which you enter more specific information. For example, if you right-click the domain company.com and select New | Organizational Unit, you call up another window for entering the new OU's name and other specifications.

NOTE: Don't be confused by the title bars at the top of the MMC window. The somewhat cryptic string starts with the name of the snap-in. The words contained within brackets is the full path to the application.

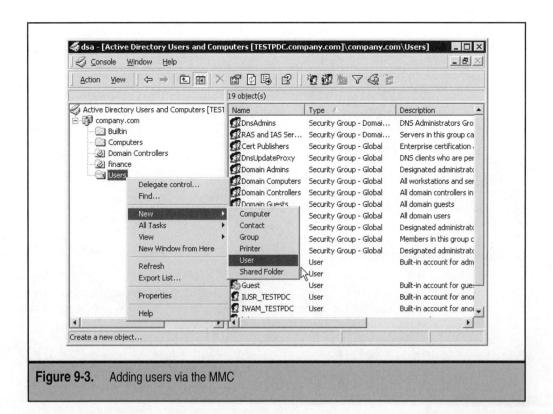

Figure 9-3. Adding users via the MMC

You'll want to be careful when using MMC to manage the AD. It's important to pay attention to where you are creating new objects, because you can add new objects just about anywhere in the hierarchy. It's possible (and encouraged) to create OUs within other OUs. If this is what you intend to do and you actually create the new OU under the domain, the results are completely different from creating an OU under a domain controller directly and will affect all members of that OU. The same can be said for users and groups—the placement of these objects in the AD hierarchy has dramatic impact on the objects' properties. For example, creating a new user under the domain will give the new user rights over all objects beneath it in the hierarchy, including all member OUs. This is quite different from creating a new user in an OU that has very restricted rights (as for guest users) and is possibly contained wholly within another OU.

WARNING: The Computer Management snap-in lets you easily move users, groups, and OUs around the domain tree. Be aware that a simple move might have impact on many users.

Here is the information you should have on hand when creating new users, groups, and OUs:

▼ **Users** Domain placement, name, login name, downlevel name (for Windows NT networks), password, and password policy

■ **Groups** Domain placement, name, downlevel name (for Windows NT networks), scope of group, and type of group (see Table 9-1)

▲ **Organizational units** Domain placement and name

To further configure and manage these objects, simply right-click them in the MMC and select Properties. This lets you add significantly more information. For example, you can enter information about users such as their home page, contact information, and dial-in rights.

Authority Delegations

One of the first things you will want to do once you have created groups, OUs, and other domain objects is to set up users to manage these objects. Right-click an object and select Delegate Control to invoke the Delegation of Control Wizard that will step you through the delegation process.

One of the first steps is to verify that you want to add a delegation or change the current delegation of the selected object. In this example, we'll add control over the Sales OU by a group called SalesAdmins that is local to the Sales OU. We will assume for this example that the OU and group have already been created and that the SalesAdmins group has been populated with at least one user or group.

The next step involves selecting a group or user to have control over this OU. In Figure 9-4, we have selected the SalesAdmins group.

Next, we can select predefined groups of rights that are common to administrative roles, or create our own custom control by choosing only the rights we want. In Figure 9-5, a predefined role for a user account manager has been selected. You will be shown a summary of your selections before committing them. Once you click the wizard's Finish button, the delegation policy will be enforced.

Group Scope	Visibility	Contains
Domain Local	Local domain	Users, Global, or Universal groups
Global	Throughout forest	Users or Global groups
Universal	Throughout forest	Users, Global, or Universal groups

Table 9-1.   Relationships of Group Types and Scopes

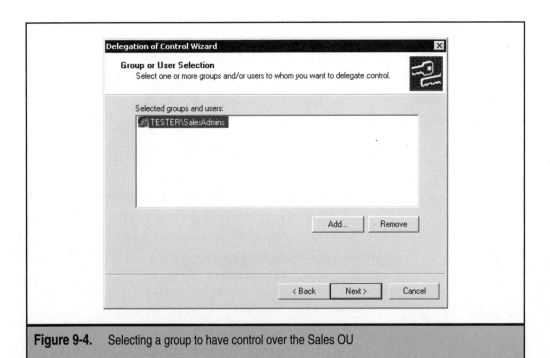

Figure 9-4.   Selecting a group to have control over the Sales OU

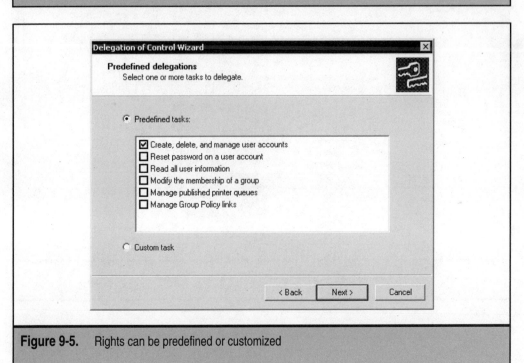

Figure 9-5.   Rights can be predefined or customized

Here's how to verify the delegation settings:

1. In the MMC main window, click View | Advanced Features.
2. Right-click the Sales OU and select Properties.
3. Open the Security tab and click the Advanced button.
4. Select the SalesAdmins item and click the View/Edit button.

This displays a window like that shown in Figure 9-6. Here you can not only review the object's rights, but add to or delete them as well. Once you are familiar with the process of delegating permissions, you might forego the wizard and proceed right to this dialog box, using the MMC to directly configure the delegation of rights.

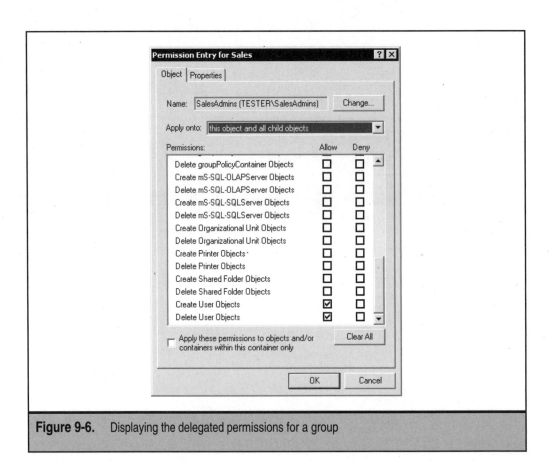

Figure 9-6.   Displaying the delegated permissions for a group

NOTE: Permissions flow through the domain tree by default. Objects with permissions at the root of the tree will have permissions through all member objects unless those rights are specifically denied. For example, if an OU permits access to a file, but the domain specifies that the users in that OU do not have access to that file, the user will not have access to the file.

Group Policies

One of the most powerful administrative controls in Windows NT is the combination of the System Policy Editor and User Profiles. With these tools, and administrator can enforce how systems on the network are configured and what functions are available to users. Judicious use of these tools can reduce the total cost of ownership (TCO) by allowing lock-down of users' systems and, thus, control of user errors and problems.

The System Policy Editor and User Profiles have a new look and are joined in the same snap-in for Windows 2000. They are now called the Group Policy snap-in for the MMC and can be applied to almost any object. You might, for example, create and apply a group policy to a domain, to an OU, and to a group within the OU. The policies follow the hierarchy of the domain tree; if a policy higher up the tree is in conflict with a lower-level policy, the higher-level policy takes precedence by default.

To start the Group Policy snap-in, right-click an object such as the domain. Select Properties, and click the Group Policy tab. Select Default Domain Policy and click the Edit button. This invokes the Group Policy snap-in as shown in Figure 9-7.

There are two major configuration groups in the domain group policy: Computer Configuration and User Configuration. These correspond to the System Policy Editor and User Policies, respectively. Each group contains three major containers for policies:

▼ **Software Settings** Policies for installing software on specific computers or on users' systems

■ **Windows Settings** Policies for setting security parameters and running scripts at startup or shutdown of Windows

▲ **Administrative Templates** Policies for controlling the appearance and behavior of Windows

Once you have selected a particular policy you want to alter, right-click it and select Properties. You have the choice of disabling or enabling the policies listed in the right-hand frame. In this example, we have enabled the Remove Documents Menu item in the Start Menu policy. Now the Documents item will not be displayed in the Start menus of all users in the domain.

Now that we have covered some of the basic administrative tasks associated with users, we'll turn our attention to administration of the domain servers under Windows 2000.

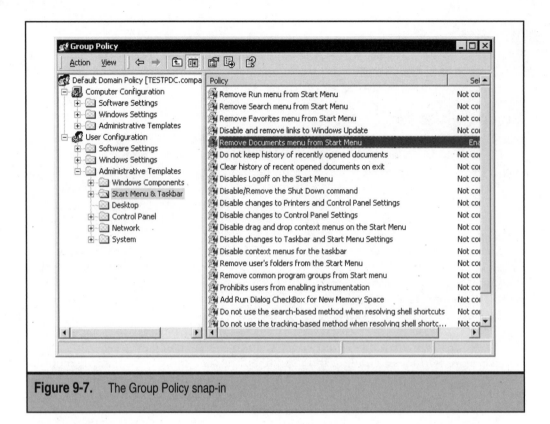

Figure 9-7.   The Group Policy snap-in

Domain Replication

For a Windows 2000 domain tree to function properly, the contents of the Active Directory must be updated to all domain controllers (DCs) in a timely fashion. Windows 2000 employs *multi-master replication techniques* using Site Links to achieve consistent information among the peer DCs. Note that all the connections discussed in this section run on top of an existing network infrastructure. This infrastructure dictates which links are formed, who is a member of a given site, and how frequently you should schedule updates.

Multi-Master Replication

Instead of having one central database for the domain that is replicated to subordinate domain controllers, as is done in NT 4.0, Windows 2000 treats all domain controllers as peers. You can update a record on any domain controller and expect that it will, after some time, update all domain controllers. Replication is passed from one DC to another only when they have new information, and only the information that has changed is sent to the replication partner.

To tackle the issue of having information changed on one DC while it is being changed on another, domain controllers use timestamps and *update sequence numbers* (USNs) to track DC updates. A USN is a 64-bit number that is advanced when a change is made to the Active Directory. Each DC keeps track of the USNs of its replication partners. When a replication is called, the DC requests all changes since the last time it received an update and then resets its USN for each of its replication partners.

If a DC attempts to update another DC with conflicting information, they both first check their USNs; the DC with the largest (most recent) USN will win and be replicated. If the USNs are the same, then timestamps are used to determine which change was most recent. (This is why it's important to keep all computers, especially DCs, synchronized to a standard clock.)

By default, replications are called every five minutes within the same site. To ensure a smooth replication, the Knowledge Consistency Checker (KCC) creates a logical ring topology of all DCs within a site and automatically creates connections to achieve this topology. The KCC is a software component that runs on DCs. The replication proceeds around the ring until it reaches the starting DC.

Determining Subnets and Sites

A *site* in Active Directory parlance is a part of the network that comprises one or more subnets (an independent network segment made up of a set of IP addresses on TCP/IP networks). These subnets are typically connected to each other with high-speed links (10 Mbps throughput or better). A site may contain only part of a domain or more than one domain. Typically, a site is a geographic location—perhaps a group of users in a single building, or multiple buildings that are connected via high-speed links.

AD needs to know about the assignment of DCs to sites, because this information is used to

▼ Help users find the closest DC upon login.

▲ Determine replication. Replication *within* sites is uncompressed to reduce CPU utilization, whereas replication *across* sites is compressed to reduce bandwidth utilization. Replication *within* a site is triggered by the arrival of updates, whereas replication *across* sites is based on a defined schedule to reduce use of bandwidth.

Configuring Connections and Site Links

The KCC creates connection objects to connect DCs within the same site. These are logical constructs the KCC uses to organize connectivity. They are automatically created by the KCC when the DC is introduced to the site. Normally, the administrator would not need to add connections unless they're needed to reduce update latency. Think of these connections as routes in a routing table. That is, although protocols are in place to automatically build and update the routes for routers, you can also add your own static routes to ensure a certain path is taken.

Site Link objects are unidirectional connections between two or more sites. Although links within sites are automatically created by the KCC, a network manager might still want to create additional links to create a specific group of sites that replicate on a specific schedule.

To build a Site Link, open the MMC with the Active Directory Sites and Services tool. If this tool is not available under Administrative Tools on the Startup menu, you can always start it by typing **mmc** at the command prompt to invoke the MMC, and then adding the Sites and Services snap-in. (Adding snap-ins is described earlier in this chapter.) Figure 9-8 shows the Sites and Services snap-in open in the MMC.

To create a Site Link, you will need to

▼ Have at least two sites set up.

■ Determine the replication schedule.

▲ Calculate the link cost (higher cost means a less-desirable link).

The link cost, like that for routes, gauges the benefit of sending replication information down that link. The links you create will probably follow physical connections along

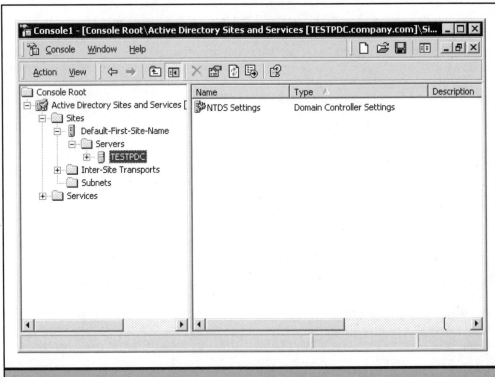

Figure 9-8.   Using the Sites and Services snap-in to build Site Links

WAN links. For example, if you have a point-to-point connection between Boston and New York, you might make a Site Link between those two sites. If you have a Frame Relay connection connecting Los Angeles, San Francisco, and Minneapolis, you could create a single Site Link for each link between the three sites. Both arrangements are illustrated in Figure 9-9.

> **NOTE:** Although a site can contain more than one Site Link, routing among these links is not automatic. A Site Link Bridge, described next, is used to accomplish this.

Configuring Site Link Bridges

Site Link Bridges, like bridges within a router, connect multiple Site Links so that replication can pass among Site Links. For example, if Boston and Los Angeles are a Site Link with a cost of 5, and San Francisco, Los Angeles, and Minneapolis are a Site Link with a cost of 4, a Site Link Bridge can be established with a cost of $4 + 5 = 9$. The Site Link Bridge enables replication to occur across each Site Link, allowing Boston to replicate to Minneapolis via Los Angeles and vice versa. One stipulation for a Site Link Bridge is that each Site Link in the Bridge must have at least one site in common; otherwise, a route cannot be calculated.

Setting the cost for links is very important. To continue our example, an additional Site Link might be created with Minneapolis and Boston as the only members. If the ad-

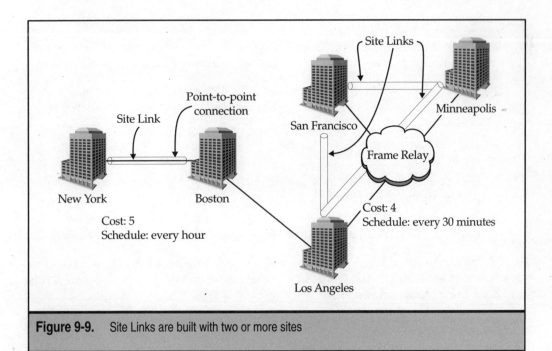

Figure 9-9. Site Links are built with two or more sites

ministrator then assigns this Site Link a cost lower than 9, then replication will follow this link as opposed to the Site Link Bridge just described.

Site Link Bridges can help reduce the number of Site Links that must be created in larger networks. It's best for administrators to keep these as simple as possible, however, and try to follow the physical topology of the network. This will keep the demands on precious WAN bandwidth to a minimum.

IP Security (IPSec) Configuration

Windows 2000 includes many new security features that not only help lock down the information on the network and its servers but also simplify that job and better organize your security policies.

Security functions over TCP/IP networks are greatly enhanced with Windows 2000 adoption of IP Security (IPSec). Microsoft's version of IPSec is based on the emerging technology developed by the Internet Engineering Task Force (IETF) IPSec working group.

IPSec can be used to create an end-to-end security solution that results in encrypted transmission of data. An IPSec solution can offer

▼ **Confidentiality**   Individuals cannot intercept a message and read it.

■ **Authentication**   Receivers of messages are sure of the sender's identity.

▲ **Integrity**   The message is guaranteed not to be tampered with along the way.

How IPSec Works

Figure 9-10 illustrates schematically how IPSec works. A host with an active security policy wants to attempt to communicate with another computer running a security policy.

1. Host computer A attempts to send data. The IPSec driver communicates with the IPSec driver on Host B to set up a *security association* (SA, covered in the next section).

2. The two computers conduct a secret key exchange, establishing shared and secret keys.

3. Using the methods of security negotiated in the SA, Host A signs and encrypts packets destined for Host B.

4. Host B receives the packets, and the IPSec driver checks the signature and key on the packets. If authenticated, the data is passed up the stack to Host B.

Of course, the entire IPSec process occurs rapidly and without the knowledge of either user at Hosts A and B. Additional CPU cycles are consumed, however, in encrypting and decrypting these packets.

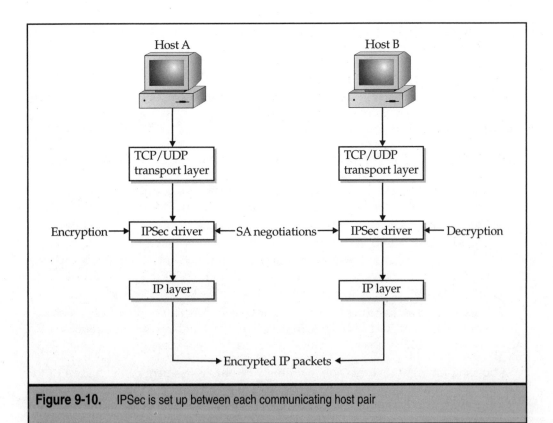

Figure 9-10.   IPSec is set up between each communicating host pair

IPSec Negotiation

An IPSec *policy agent* resides on each computer in a Windows 2000 network. Whether it is active or not is up to the administrative policies in place. If the agent is active, it will retrieve the IPSec policy and enforce it on the local computer. The policy will describe the local *security association* (SA) that should be enforced on the computer.

An SA is a contract between two communicating computers that is set up before any data is transferred. This negotiation determines specifics about how the two computers will communicate data, including the following:

▼ **The IPSec protocol**   Uses an authentication header and an encapsulating security payload.

■ **An integrity algorithm**   This is either Message Digest function 5 (MD5) or Secure Hash Algorithm (SHA).

▲ **An encryption algorithm** This is Data Encryption Standard (DES), or Triple DES, or 40-bit DES, or none.

Establishing IPSec Policies

By default, Windows 2000 provides three predefined security policies that will satisfy most cases. You can also start with one of these predefined policies and customize it to fit your needs.

▼ **Client (Respond Only)** This policy instructs the computer to use IPSec when requested to do so by another computer. The computer with this policy does not request IPSec when it initiates communications and will normally not use it. Therefore, this policy is for computers that contain little or no sensitive data.

■ **Server (Requests Security)** This policy is for servers that should use IPSec if possible but should not deny communication if the client does not support IPSec. This policy is useful in environments in which not all the clients can use IPSec—for example, during a migration to Windows 2000. If total security is required, the Secure Server policy (described next) should be used.

▲ **Secure Server (Requires Security)** For your servers that contain sensitive data, this policy requires use of IPSec for all clients. All outgoing communications are secured, and all unsecured requests from clients are rejected.

Choosing the right security policy requires careful assessment of the nature of the data. Indiscriminately assigning the highest level of security for all users and servers will put unnecessary strain on the servers and clients' workstations because of the overhead for encrypting and decrypting all network traffic. On the other hand, allowing any type of client to connect to a secure server would endanger secure information.

NOTE: Setting up a security policy between users and domain controllers is not necessary, because their communication is already encrypted when required using Kerberos v5.

Creating and Applying IPSec Policies

The MMC is used to create and configure IPSec policies. The IPSec snap-in must be added to the MMC as shown in Figure 9-11. When the IPSec snap-in is first opened, the three default policies are present for you to use and alter as needed, or you can create your own using the IP Security Policy Wizard.

If you choose to make your own security policies, you will be prompted to do the following:

▼ Set the default reply to request for secure connections.

■ Set the method of security to be used.

■ Select the authentication method.

▲ Decide which connection types will apply this policy (LAN, remote, or all).

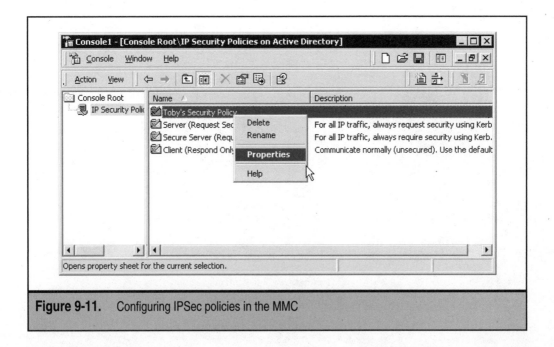

Figure 9-11.   Configuring IPSec policies in the MMC

You can also establish settings pertaining to handling of keys, and the timeout values of shared information. It is also possible to import new and improved security methods as they become available. When you have finished making your changes, the policy is added to the default selections so you can alter or view its properties at a later time.

An IPSec policy can be assigned to a group policy, in which it will be applied to all member computers and users of the policy. Unlike many other security policies, in IPSec the local policies take precedence over policies higher up the hierarchy. For example, the local OU IPSec policy will override a policy included with the domain.

Security Templates

Security templates are a way to organize all the security features (except IPSec and public keys) for desktop computers into a single file. These files or templates can later be loaded into a group policy that may apply to hundreds or thousands of computers. Importing security templates saves administration time because nearly all the security features can be configured from one tool and then set for many computers.

To configure a security template, open the MMC and load the Security Configuration and Analysis snap-in. The first time you create a template, you'll need to right-click Security and Configuration Analysis and select Open Database. Rather than selecting an existing database, type in the name of the new security database (.SDB) file. This file will hold all your security settings. Next, select a template to load. The template choices pertain to certain aspects of security, such as local computer settings and domain controller settings.

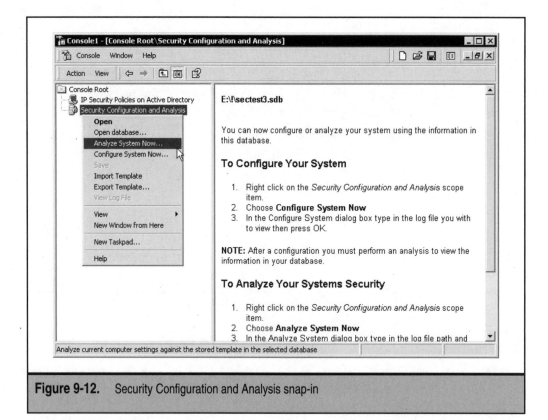

Figure 9-12.   Security Configuration and Analysis snap-in

In Figure 9-12, you can see the Security Configuration and Analysis snap-in at work. When you first open a new security database file, you must either configure it immediately or choose to have your system analyzed for potential security problems before configuring the policy. It's usually a good idea to analyze your system from time to time to validate that your security policies are in effect. To do this, select the Analyze System Now menu item and specify where to store the results.

ANALYZING SECURITY SYSTEM   When you select Analyze System Now on the Security Configuration and Analysis menu, the results are stored in a text file. Using this report, you can be better prepared to set policies for other computers in the domain. Here's a portion of a sample analysis:

```
-------------------------------------------
05/30/1999 10:42:53
----Analysis engine is initialized successfully.----

----Analyze Group Membership...
```

```
         Analyze Replicator.
         Analyze Backup Operators.
         Analyze Print Operators.
         Analyze Server Operators.
         Analyze Account Operators.
         Analyze Guests.
         Analyze Users.
         Analyze Administrators.

         Group Membership analysis completed successfully.

----Reading Configuration info...

----Analyze Registry Keys...
0 mismatches found under machine.

         Registry keys analysis completed successfully.

----Reading Configuration info...


----Analyze File Security...
4 mismatches found under e:\.

         File security analysis completed successfully.


----Analyze General Service Settings...

         General Service analysis completed successfully.


----Analyze available attachment engines...

         Attachment engines analysis completed successfully.
----Reading Configuration info...


----Analyze Security Policy...
         Analyze password information.
         Analyze account lockout information.
         Analyze account force logoff information.
         Analyze other policy settings.
```

CONFIGURING SECURITY POLICIES To configure the policy, select Configure System Now from the Security Configuration and Analysis menu. You can configure the following:

▼ **Account policies** Passwords, account lockouts

■ **Local policies** User rights, logging of security events

■ **Group restrictions** Local group security administration

■ **Registry settings** Security for local registry keys

■ **File system** Security for local file system

▲ **Services** Configuration of startup and security for local services

NEW WINDOWS 2000 FEATURES

In this chapter, we have described basic administrative functions in the Windows 2000 environment. Previously, these jobs have been carried out using other NT tools, running programs from the command prompt, or by a combination of third-party tools and methods.

New in Windows 2000 comes a collection of features added to existing tools such as SMS 2.0; completely new applications such as IntelliMirror; and new technologies that can be implemented in NT environments now. These new tools promise to simplify administration and provide users with additional functionality. For example, an administrator will be able to easily install Windows 2000 over the network to remote computers without having to be in front of the machines. And users' desktop settings, applications, and data can follow them to any machine in the domain.

Systems Management Server (SMS) 2.0

Although Systems Management Server (SMS) has been around for years, SMS 2.0 has some significant new features. One of the most important for Windows 2000 deployment is the capability of SMS to install Windows 2000 to remote machines.

Remote OS Installation

Here is how remote installation works:

1. You first create a system that has everything installed on it that you want to copy over to new systems. We'll call this the *gold image*.

2. Next you run the Sysprep tool to clone the system and copy the necessary files to a local server running the Remote Installation Services (RIS).

3. Then you configure the client to begin installation from the gold image on the RIS server. If the client computer supports the Pre-Boot eXecution Environment (PXE), then the client can load the gold image without any human intervention. If not, a special floppy disk will direct the client where to find the gold image.

Once the process of remote installation is initiated, the installation wizard prompts the user to log in. Depending on the user's rights, certain installation customization options may be available.

SMS Computer Inventory

Another feature of SMS 2.0 that will prove quite useful is its ability to take an inventory of all the systems in the network. Before deploying Windows 2000, you will certainly want to know which systems will be able to support the upgrade. You will also want to generate reports about installed software. These functions will help you identify the programs you want to include in the upgrade and which ones, if any, are not supported by Windows 2000.

IntelliMirror

Like CiscoWorks (discussed in Chapter 8), IntelliMirror does not describe a single product or application, but rather is a set of features provided by indigenous tools found within Windows 2000. We have already discussed some of these tools earlier in this chapter (such as the Group Policy snap-in). The IntelliMirror features promise ease of use and administration by allowing users to have their settings, documents, and applications available to them no matter where in the domain they log in. The following three sections describe benefits that can be achieved by adopting IntelliMirror.

NOTE: You probably won't want to enable all of IntelliMirror's features for all users. The impact of such a universal deployment on the network has not been determined at this time.

Applications Follow Users

In this arrangement, when a user logs into a system and the system detects that it does not have software required for that user, the system begins installation of that software. To determine what software to install for each user, the computer-based software installation Group Policy is checked when the user logs in. (Remember that a policy can be applied to domains, OUs, groups, and individual users.) If the policy requires an application that is not present, the computer is directed to load it.

Applications can be *published* to users, or *assigned* to them. Users have the option of installing published software packages, but they must install assigned software.

Settings Follow Users

This arrangement is not new. It is provided in Windows NT by what is called a *roaming* profile. Under Windows 2000 the job is taken over by the Group Policy, as described earlier in the chapter. This policy dictates how the desktop, menu items, and other application properties are presented to the user at login. This promises a comfortable familiarity to the user. For the administrator, it means the ability to lock down restricted parts of the OS.

Data Follows Users

Special folders can be set up to replicate to a network drive. For example, while you are working with a document in the My Documents folder, it can be replicated to a secure network location. When you log out and then in on another machine, the system checks with the special folder, identifies the most recent files, and retrieves your documents in that folder. The Offline Folders, Synchronization, and Group Policy tools all play a role in providing this feature.

Distributed File System (Dfs)

Another feature available now for NT 4.0 users and one that will be standard in Windows 2000 enhances the scalability of Windows networks. The Distributed File System (Dfs) allows you to collect network shares and reshare them as a single share on any Windows server. This enables consolidation of many disparate shares into a single namespace. Users no longer have to mount each share on a different machine with a new drive letter, because all the shares they need will be under a single share on a Dfs server. The Dfs server doesn't actually house the shares; they remain on the computers where they were stored before consolidation.

Dfs is built into Windows 2000, so there are no additional components to install. Currently, Dfs can be installed as a service on NT 4.0 machines. An NT 4.0 workstation can act as a client to a Dfs server, but the workstation cannot itself host a Dfs share. NT 4.0 servers can host a single Dfs share and can also act as a Dfs client. You can download the Dfs software from the following Microsoft address:

http://www.microsoft.com/ntserver/nts/downloads/winfeatures/NTSDistrFile/default.asp

Creating a Dfs Root

There is an upgrade path for Win 9*x* machines to be able to act as a Dfs client. First, you create a share on a Windows server; you might call this "corp-share" or "s-drive." Next, you use the Distributed File System tool (in the Programs | Administration Tools menu) to create the root for the Dfs share. From the Dfs main window (Figure 9-13), you can configure and manage any Dfs on your network if you have administrative rights.

To get started, select New Dfs Root Volume to start the wizard that walks you through creating a new root. It is located in the Action menu item or can be invoked by right-clicking Distributed File System in the left pane and selecting New Dfs Root. The root share can be an existing share or a new one. You must also designate whether you want the share to be tracked within Active Directory. This allows more general accessibility and a degree of fault tolerance. As an example, consider a new root called Acct. Once this is created, we can add other volumes (called child nodes) to this root, as shown in Figure 9-13. Or we can create another root.

With the root set up, we can begin to add more shares to it. Right-click the new root object and click New Dfs Child Node on the shortcut menu. This displays a window re-

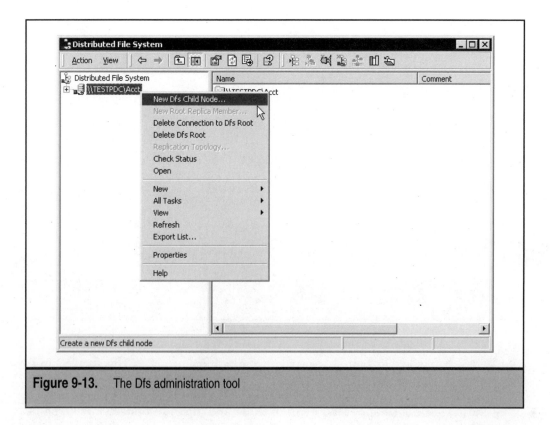

Figure 9-13.   The Dfs administration tool

sembling Figure 9-14. From here, you can map a directory from the root Dfs to a share located on another computer. The remote shares may be on any NT, Win 9*x*, or even Windows 3.11 computers. They can be of either the FAT or NTFS type.

NOTE: Some shares have restrictions on the number of connected users honored within the Dfs. For example, NT Workstation shares allow up to ten concurrent connections. This restriction holds true while the share is part of a Dfs root, as well.

Advantages of Dfs

Because Dfs maps the physical location of the shares into a single namespace, the location of the data stored on shared drives becomes transparent to users and applications. In addition to being much easier to organize and search, this arrangement has several ramifications.

It is possible to create redundant drives. Let's say, for example, that you have two shares that are identical in content and read-only for normal users, both located on sepa-

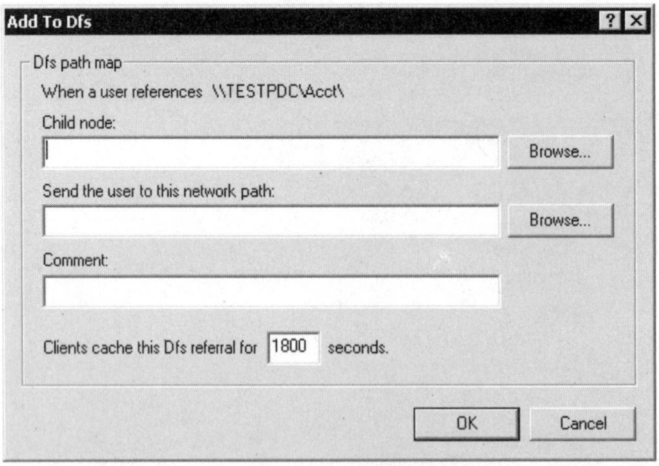

Figure 9-14. Adding shares to a Dfs volume

rate servers. We could map both shares to the same location in the Dfs. This is called an *alternate volume.*

Alternate volumes can be used for redundancy. If a user is accessing one of the volumes and it crashes, the application will time out and, upon reconnection, will be restored to the identical, alternate volume. In the best of cases, the switch over to the alternate is transparent to the user or application.

Alternate volumes can also be used for load balancing. When users request data from a particular namespace on the Dfs, they will be given access to one of the two alternate volumes, thus distributing the traffic between the two. If Dfs is used with Active Directory, users will be given the logically closest share, because the AD is aware of sites and will forward the request to the share at the same site as the user's.

Here are a couple of examples of practical use of Dfs: You might, for instance, create a Dfs share consisting of only file systems that you want to have backed up. Then you can tell your backup software to connect to a single Dfs share and back up the entire collection of systems, and thus avoid having to hunt down and connect with multiple server shares. You'll have to ensure that the shares are in their original position if you need to restore data from the backup media.

Another beneficial use of Dfs is on a Web server. Let's say you have a central home page that links to a page or set of pages for each department. Instead of all departments having to access your server and update it when they have new material, you could create a Dfs share on the Web server. This share's elements are shares located in each department. So you have your root home page, and all departments located in the next directory. The departments don't have to relinquish their security rights to you nor you relinquish your security rights to them.

Connecting to Dfs Shares

Connecting to a Dfs share is as easy as connecting to any other share. You simply provide the Universal Naming Convention (UNC) name of the Dfs server, followed by the Dfs share name of the root, and then any subsequent paths. For example:

    \\ServerName\Dfs_ShareNameRoot\Path\FileName

Security is managed by the usual methods in NT, via Access Control Lists maintained at the source of the share (not at the Dfs share). Dfs requires no other security mechanism to be set up or configured.

SUMMARY

Windows Network Operating System management is undergoing a revolution. In Windows 2000, the Microsoft Management Console will hold all management tools. Many tools used in Windows NT 4.0 and earlier will be moved, merged, or deleted in Windows 2000. Although this move to centralize management functions will ultimately enable smoother, faster, and cheaper management, the transition will be challenging for many administrators. This chapter focused on many of the changes resulting from centralization, and highlighted some of the tools required to manage a Windows 2000 domain. We also examined some new features that will add functionality for your network users.

The next chapter digs a bit deeper into management, exploring techniques for monitoring and predicting network traffic.

CHAPTER 10

Network Traffic Testing

In any organization, the data network is the digital nervous system that connects all users with the information resources they need. When any part of this nervous system fails, users are without service or cut off from the rest of the organization. Although many organizations wait for expensive failures before jumping into action, it is far more prudent for network administrators to take prophylactic action against such costly outages. Both troubleshooting and network planning can be accomplished more effectively by using some form of *network traffic testing*.

This chapter discusses both preventive and troubleshooting aspects of network traffic monitoring. For those who find themselves having to quickly respond to network outages, application problems, and other "fire fighting" issues, we'll introduce some powerful tools you can use to quickly pinpoint the cause of the failure. For the network administrator who is trying to get a leg up on outages by using proactive testing, we'll show you how to use network analyzers and simulation tools to properly quantify the impact an application has on your network. There is no doubt—when armed with this information, you can better predict how your network will behave in the future and reduce unexpected outages.

TESTING YOUR NETWORK

Chapter 8 covered many aspects of network monitoring: the concept of using an application to watch the behavior of the network. Typically, this involves setting *thresholds* for various feeds of "interesting" information, so that an action occurs when the thresholds are reached or exceeded. Then the monitoring application sends an *alarm* or *trap* to a network manager. In this section, we'll discuss how to go about taking a more assertive approach to acquiring data about your network.

Benefits of Testing

Though the costs are greater up front, the benefits of testing will far outweigh the initial investment over a fairly short period of time. Because of the growing size and complexity of today's networks, administrators are finding that they cannot remain in a reactive mode—they want to start doing something to reduce the number of fires. Let's look at some of the benefits of testing.

Cost Savings

Proactive network testing can achieve tremendous savings. How does the saying go? "An ounce of prevention . . ." Here are some areas in which proactive testing can save an organization money.

▼ **Application rollout** Testing a new application before rolling it out to the production network will allow you to gauge how it will function and affect the other applications.

■ **Reduce network slowdowns**   Certainly, network outages are aggravating and extremely costly—but a more frustrating and potentially more costly problem found in many networks is the insidious network slowdown. Outages get attention right away and are usually resolved relatively quickly. On the other hand, a slowdown due to proliferating applications and growing traffic loads may go unnoticed and, over time, prove more costly than an outage.

▲ **Product awareness**   Another cost benefit from testing is the leverage it gives you when you are working with a vendor. By testing a product ahead of time, you become familiar with the product and how it works in your environment. Testing helps you define hardware requirements such as processor power and bandwidth. You don't want to pay for a point-to-point T1 circuit when a 256 Kbps Frame Relay connection will meet all the traffic requirements.

Accurate Capacity Planning

It's common knowledge in the industry that computer systems are becoming more distributed in nature. Servers are holding more and more of the data users are accessing, and these servers are located remotely, away from the user's LAN. Some enterprise applications are widely distributed (for example, e-mail, group organizers, and database applications such as Lotus Notes). This means more traffic is traversing the network, and users must depend on network efficiency for crucial and timely information.

Increased traffic load causes network slowdown and sometimes outages. Typically in the past, only a few people were affected by a network outage. These days, however, nearly every person in the corporation depends on the network to do their jobs. For some, an outage may be an annoying inconvenience; but, for others, loss of access may translate into a loss of revenue or customers.

Installing unlimited bandwidth for each user is not financially feasible, so administrators must use the existing bandwidth intelligently. Testing and planning can help you determine what throughput you need to meet the demands of the applications, so users can do their jobs without undue delays.

Testing Directives

Before you start to plan a test, you'll have an idea about what kind of test you want to run. One of the biggest threats to a successful test is a poor plan—a plan with no clear directives. Without a plan, you cannot efficiently test everything there is to test about any given application.

Testing directives are particular criteria that you need to test against. This will focus on the items most likely to affect rollout success or failure. It is imperative that you start by clearly defining your test objectives: What is it specifically that you want to know? What questions do you want answered? Here are some possible questions:

▼ Is a 256 Kbps line going to be enough for my network devices?

■ If this application fails, does it cause others to fail?

- How many users can run this application concurrently?
- Is this new version of software stable?
▲ Is this application time dependent?

Before setting out to test an application, you'll want to plan your testing scenario. Following are descriptions of five major types of tests that you can conduct. You will probably find that your testing directives entail a combination of these approaches. This is expected and will be useful—provided that you clearly define exactly what it is you are trying to test, and test only one aspect of an application at a time. Trying to answer too many questions simultaneously will confound your results and invalidate your work.

Throughput

Another name for *throughput testing* could be *bottleneck detection*. Here, you are looking for the component of the network that is preventing the application from running faster. This bottleneck could be in the CPU of the server, the user's NIC, or even the users themselves. The most common bottleneck is in WAN links because of their restrictive throughput.

Reliability

Reliability testing looks to see if a hardware or application element functions satisfactorily for an acceptable percentage of time. For hardware, this is usually measured in uptime or Mean Time Between Failures (MTBF). For software, you'll want to test after you artificially increase the load on servers or otherwise tax the application. Often, an application will eventually succumb to an increasing load.

Ideally, you should know the limitations of every piece of hardware and software in your network. In a Microsoft/Cisco network, the most likely piece to fail is an application or a data circuit. It's not usually the hardware—Cisco hardware is extraordinarily reliable (although nothing can achieve 100% reliability).

Functionality

Functionality testing verifies that all the features of an application perform as desired. A product vendor's claims are sometimes not supported in every network. You will want to run the application in a test environment that is as close to your production environment as possible, to emulate the same load and traffic the application will encounter once it is put into service.

Regression

Regression testing is similar to functionality testing, except that regression testing addresses the performance and functionality of a new software version or a hardware upgrade. New versions of software are supposed to fix old bugs, but they can also introduce new bugs that may be worse than the old ones. Here are some events that might warrant regression testing:

▼ A new Cisco IOS release

■ A new Microsoft NT Service Pack

■ A new Web-browser Client

▲ A new version of an in-house application

Acceptance

Acceptance testing checks to make sure everything is working as planned before a new application or hardware solution is rolled out into production. This is why acceptance testing is often the last type of testing performed. Outside contractors or consultants often provide a Service Level Agreement (SLA) that guarantees a certain level of throughput or other measure of quality. You will want to test your network to make sure these levels of quality are met.

NETWORK PROBES VS. ANALYZERS

To capture network traffic for troubleshooting or network planning purposes, you will need nothing more than a computer and a NIC that operates in promiscuous mode (many network adapter cards do), and some special software. These data-capturing tools can be classified in two main groups: network analyzers and network probes. There is some overlap in what these devices do toward your network analysis tasks, although both serve a specific purpose.

Network probes are dedicated devices that typically sit near routers and hubs and other such network devices. The probes tap into network segments and watch traffic 24 hours a day. The traffic patterns are summarized into a variety of statistics at the probe. A network management station queries many probes and receives a summary of the statistics.

Probes can be PCs with probe software installed on them, or they can be separate hardware devices that are smaller than PCs with no monitor or keyboard attached. Either way, they sit quietly attached to the network and gather predefined data.

Network analyzers can provide detailed network information much as a probe does, but they can also provide single-packet analysis. Because network analyzers capture all traffic and do less consolidation of statistics than probes do, they can collect an enormous amount of data in a short period. That is why analyzers are typically used in troubleshooting a LAN, or to test a single application in a controlled environment.

Analyzers are usually PCs with special software such as Network Monitor (described later in the chapter), Distributed Sniffer System, or Net X-Ray. These machines do not have permanent homes, unless it's in a testing lab or on a very disruptive network segment.

Network Analyzers

Network analyzers, sometimes called protocol analyzers, are designed for troubleshooting (although, as you'll see, they can be quite handy for other purposes as well). They excel at recording information at the lowest layers in the OSI model: the physical and data-link layers.

Troubleshooting

Analyzers can be used to troubleshoot many kinds of network problems, including faulty NICs, boot problems, broadcast storms, and errant applications. Here is an example of a network analyzer used for troubleshooting:

A network's users are reporting extremely slow response, although all users are able to access the network. The first thing a seasoned administrator will do is ask what has changed since the network was running fine. If there's no satisfactory answer, the administrator may place a network analyzer on the local segment where users are reporting slow response time.

All sorts of statistics will be immediately available, such as number of bad frames, number of broadcast messages, or even a particular conversation between two computers. In our example, it was revealed that there were an unusually high number of runt frames caused by a faulty NIC in one computer. This dysfunctional NIC was retransmitting a small frame over and over—filling the local network so other traffic could not flow properly.

Other Uses of Analyzers

Network analyzers have other uses than just troubleshooting. For example, most analyzers can record network traffic and play it back to the network at a later time. This is called *traffic playback* or *traffic generation* and can be quite useful when you want to test other systems' reactions to a specific request and you want control over the request. Additionally, you can generate traffic to stress-test your systems and determine their maximum load before they break down. Here is an example of that usage:

Cisco 2500 Series routers were intermittently crashing in a large network (no, they're not bulletproof after all!). The only error from the router indicated that the accounting process on the router was at fault. When these routers were placed in a lab, however, they did not crash. Since the amount of traffic in the lab is miniscule compared with the production network, the traffic load itself was suspected as being related to the crashes. Analyzers were used to flood traffic through the router. Sure enough, the routers started to crash. As it turned out, there was a bug in Cisco's IOS that caused crashes in certain cases when the accounting service was turned on. (The bug has since been fixed.) As mentioned earlier, analyzers can be used to gauge network traffic generated by a single application, because the analyzers can filter traffic based on host or destination addresses. This point will be explored later when we analyze a new application prior to deployment.

Some network analyzers are listed in Table 10-1.

Network Probes

Probes are workhorses, diligently collecting data about the network and summarizing the results in tables. This information is usually stored on the probe until a management

Company/ Product	Solution Type	LAN Protocols	WAN Protocols	Generate Traffic?	Cost in U.S. Dollars	Contact
Digitech Industries/ WAN900	Software and hardware	Ethernet, Token Ring, FDDI	RS-232, RS 449/442, V.35, T-1, FT-1, X-25, Frame Relay, ISDN, SMDS, ATM, DDS, E-1/FE-1, DS3	Yes	Starts at $5,000	http:// www. digitechinc. com
LANQuest/ Frame Thrower	Software and hardware	Ethernet, Token Ring	None	Yes	$1,595 to $2,795	http:// www. lanquest. com
Network Associate/ Sniffer Total Network Visibility	Software and hardware	Arcnet, Ethernet, Token Ring, FDDI, LocalTalk	RS-232, RS 449/442, V.35, T-1, FT-1, X-25, Frame Relay, ISDN, SMDS, ATM	Yes	Starts at $11,500	http:// www. nai.com
RadCom/ RC-155-c ATM Traffic Generator/ Analyzer	Software and hardware	Ethernet, Token Ring, LLC, SNAP, Token Ring Mac	ATM	Yes	$17,500	http:// www. radcom- inc.com
Xyratex/ Gigabit Ethernet Protocol Analyzer	Software and hardware	Ethernet, Fibre Channel	None	Yes	Starts at $25,000	http:// www. xyratex. com

Table 10-1.   Third-Party Network Analyzers

station requests certain pieces of the data. When the management station sends a request for information from the probe, it will only ask for specific responses from the probe. In this way, the analysis does not consume a tremendous amount of network bandwidth. Also, information gathered over a long period of time (days, months) can be retrieved and analyzed in a very directed and specific manner. This is the probe's biggest advantage over other management methods.

The primary disadvantage of a probe is that it must be installed and operational on each network segment you want to monitor. This can be quite expensive and very time consuming to set up and administer.

Using Probes for Baselining

In addition to monitoring all sorts of statistics about your network, probes are useful for *network baselining*. A baseline is a measurement of your overall traffic characteristics—for instance, usage for a particular time of day. With baseline statistics, you can gauge

▼ Network performance

■ Network efficiency

■ Network throughput

■ Traffic flow patterns

■ Traffic loads

▲ Application response time

This data can be quite important in understanding how your network works, and it's crucial that it is determined before major upgrades or redesigning of the network. Any good network architect will need baseline statistics before creating any design. Also, the numbers can be used to feed *simulators*, which attempt to predict the network's behavior when given a new condition. Simulators are discussed later in the chapter.

Placement of Probes

Larger networks often have many hundreds of network segments, and it will be impractical to place a probe on every segment. Therefore, determining the best possible locations for probes is very important.

To maximize traffic capture and minimize probe count, probes should be placed on network segments that are either *sources* or *sinks* of information flow. A sink of information is a segment with many servers on it. A sink is a target for client connections, whereas a source is a client initiating the communication. It's usually easier to target a LAN segment that's full of servers than it is a segment with all users, because users are scattered throughout an organization.

Although the probe market has been traditionally dominated by UNIX probes and UNIX management software, there are a large number of new offerings now ported to NT. Table 10-2 lists probes that work with various Windows NT management applications, including HP's newly ported OpenView product called Network Node Manager. Later in the chapter we'll show you how you can set up a Cisco switch to act as a probe—a very cost-effective way to increase the number of available probes on your network.

Product	Vendor	Solution	Cost in U.S. Dollars	Contact
NetClarity Remote Analyzer Probe	LANQuest	Software	$995 per probe	http://www.lanquest.com
StackProbe	Bay Networks	Software and hardware	$5,500 to $12,000	http://www.baynetworks.com
EcoScope	Compuware	Software	$3,000 to $12,000 per probe	http://www.compuware.com
Network Node Manager for NT	HP	Software	$4,995 for 250 nodes	http://www.hp.com/openview
NetScout Systems	NetScout	Software and hardware	$1,495 for software; $2,995 to $14,995 for probe hardware	http://www.netscout.com

Table 10-2.   Network Probe Vendors and Products

TIP: Oftentimes, vendors of network probes include additional capabilities in their products, over and above the standards-based capabilities. These enhancements are generally proprietary, and real benefits may not be realized unless the RMON NMS (remote monitoring, Network Management System) software supports those proprietary extensions. To get the most out of your monitoring system, be sure to evaluate the RMON NMS software in tandem with the hardware probes.

NETWORK TESTING STANDARDS

Before we discuss running specific tests, let's quickly review the various protocols, tools, and methods of analysis commonly used to test networks. This background will be useful when we use an analyzer and a probe to examine a particular application and monitor network traffic, respectively. Analyzers and probes predominantly use the Simple Network Management Protocol (SNMP) and Remote Monitoring (RMON) to gather data about your network traffic.

The only way one can collect data from a variety of network devices is to use some sort of network monitoring standards. Fortunately, standards organizations such as the

Internet Engineering Task Force (IETF) foster and maintain such standards. The details of these standards are typically published as Requests for Comments (RFCs) and subsequently adopted by vendors so that their products will comply with the standards and work smoothly with other vendors' products. This allows you to monitor all sorts of devices from a single application.

NOTE: An excellent source for downloading and learning about RFCs is at the InterNIC site, http://www.internic.net/ds/rfc-index.

SNMP and MIBs

As you read in Chapters 3 and 8, the Simple Network Management Protocol (SNMP) is the most popular method to monitor network nodes. SNMP is found on virtually any network device that can be managed. These include routers, switches, hubs, servers, UPSs, and WAN devices.

Although SNMP is the most common management protocol, its revisions are gaining in popularity. SNMP-2 is a major overhaul of the original SNMP and is covered in RFCs 1902 through 1908. SNMP-2 contains all the functionality of SNMP but addresses many of its performance and security concerns; for example, you can use encrypted management passwords in SNMP-2. Unfortunately, SNMP-2 is not widely used.

Recall from Chapter 8 that all the information that can be reported by a particular device can be found in its Management Information Base (MIB). The MIB is not the data itself; rather, it is a structured database of information pertaining to that node. The database contains the data you are requesting. The MIB is updated dynamically, so when you make a request, you get statistics for the immediate condition. Because managed devices are SNMP compliant, each one knows how to respond to standard queries issued by the network management protocols.

Some vendors (including Cisco) will create private MIBs as extensions to the standard ones. These extensions provide additional, proprietary information that can only be obtained using the vendor's management software (or another third-party management program that can read the extensions).

RMON

Remote network monitoring (RMON-1) is the first of a series of SNMP-based MIBs that defines device statistics for diagnosing LANs at the physical and data-link layers (layers 1 and 2 of the OSI model). The original RMON (RFC 1271) defines nine groups of Ethernet diagnostics:

▼ **Alarms**   Takes samples from the statistical group and compares the values against predefined thresholds. If a value exceeds a threshold, an alarm or trap is generated and sent to the management station.

■ **Events**   Controls the specifics about the generation and notification alerts.

■ **Filters**   Stores any filters you use. For example, you might add a filter to watch only the traffic going to a specific host.

■ **History**   Records periodic statistics for later retrieval from a management station.

■ **Host Top** *n*   Keeps a list of the top hosts in a given statistical group—for example, the top ten hosts based on generating network traffic.

■ **Hosts**   Maintains statistics for each host station on the network based on the host's MAC address.

■ **Packet Capture**   Essentially acts as a buffer for packets once they flow through a defined channel.

■ **Statistics**   Contains basic traffic data for each interface on the RMON agent.

▲ **Traffic Matrix**   Provides a table of the source and destination stations for conversations. If a new conversation is recorded for a pair of workstations, an entry is added to this matrix.

Many probes are called RMON probes because they contain this particular set of MIBs. Sometimes RMON can be part of another network device, such as a router or a switch. These devices are called *embedded RMON agents*.

RMON-2

RFC 2021 outlines the next generation of RMON, called RMON-2. RMON-2 gathers statistics at the network and application layers only, so it is not a replacement for RMON. The two generations are typically used together to get a more complete picture of the network traffic. RMON-2 uses the following eight groups to describe how traffic flows in packets (network and application layers):

▼ **Address Mapping**   Identifies hosts based on MAC addresses and Ethernet or Token Ring addresses.

■ **Application Layer Host Table**   Records packets, errors, and bytes based on the application, such as cc:Mail, ping, and HTTP.

■ **Application Layer Matrix Table**   Tracks conversations between two hosts based on the application.

■ **History**   Uses customized filters to track specific hosts or applications and store statistics based on the filter settings.

■ **Network Layer Host Table**   Records packets, errors, and bytes per network-layer protocol.

■ **Network Layer Matrix Table**   Tracks conversations between two hosts based on the network-layer protocol.

■ **Probe Configuration**   Enables remote configuration of probe settings, such as how and where error traps are sent and how to download new software.

▲ **Protocol Distribution**   Records percentage of traffic based on the network protocol, such as IP, IPX, and AppleTalk.

Although RMON-2 has many functional advantages over RMON alone, RMON-2 is CPU- and memory-intensive. It is estimated that RMON-2 can demand two to five times the resources used by RMON. Therefore, many current RMON devices will not be able to support RMON-2. You will need to upgrade these devices.

NOTE: If you are only using probes for troubleshooting physical and data-link layer problems, there is no reason to include RMON-2

RMON-3

RMON-3 is still in development and focuses on monitoring WAN links. For example, a new MIB will be created that deals exclusively with Frame Relay characteristics, including errors such as the Forward Explicit Congestion Notification (FECN) and Backward Explicit Congestion Notification (BECN).

MICROSOFT'S NETWORK MONITOR

As mentioned earlier, all you need to analyze the network traffic is a standard PC, a network adapter card, and some software. Fortunately, Windows NT and Windows 2000 ship with a network analyzer application called Network Monitor. Under Windows NT, the Network Monitor is installed from the Services tab in the Network configuration window. Under Windows 2000, it is installed from the Control Panel. Click Network and Dial-up Connections, then Local-Area Connections, and then Properties. Then click Install | Protocol and select Network Monitor Driver.

Network Monitor has two components. The first is called the Network Monitor Agent, available on all varieties of Windows NT and Windows 2000. The other component, the Network Monitor Tool, can only be installed on Windows NT Server or Windows 2000 Servers. If both components are installed on a Server, they are collectively called the Network Monitor Tools and Agent. Running Network Monitor Agents on other systems allows a server to collect data from the Agent's network segment as if it were physically connected to it. This means you don't need to physically bring an analyzer to every segment, as long as an Agent is already set up.

NOTE: The Network Monitor Tools and Agent that ships with NT Server allows you to capture only packets that are originating from or destined to the local machine. To capture packets headed for other machines, install the Network Monitor Tools and Agent included with the Systems Management Server. This will also allow you to install the full version of Network Monitor on Windows NT Workstation or Windows 2000 Professional.

Network Blueprints

Table of Contents

OSI Layers

7. Application Layer
- Provides interfaces to end users
- Provides standardized services to applications

6. Presentation Layer
- Specifies architecture-independent and data transfer format
- Encodes and decodes data; encrypts and decrypts data; compresses data

5. Session Layer
- Establishes and terminates connections
- Arranges sessions for upper and lower layers

4. Transport Layer
- Manages network-layer connections
- Provides reliable packet delivery mechanism

3. Network Layer
- Internet IP addressing
- Provides routing for internetworks

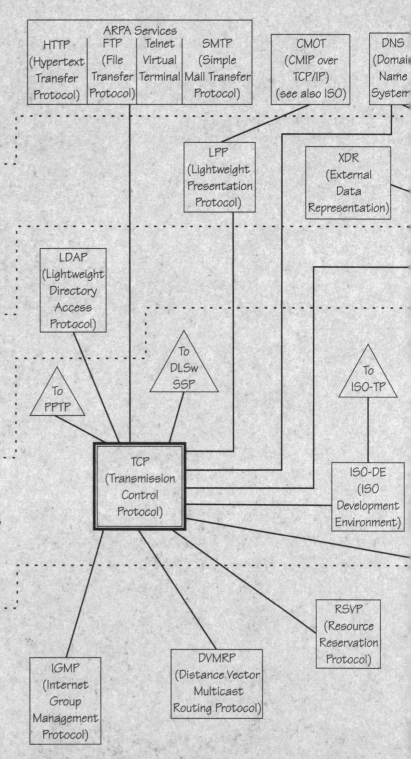

Suite

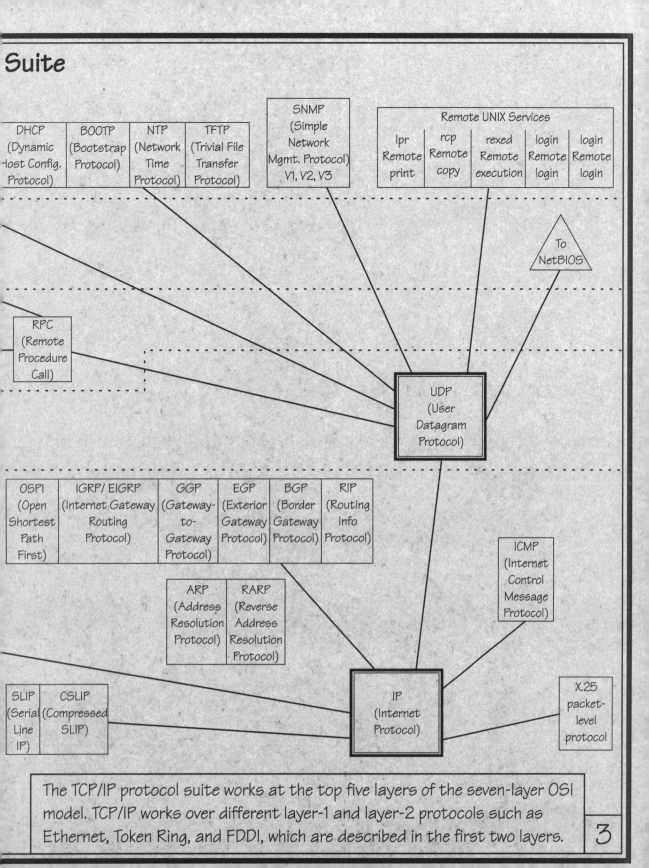

DHCP (Dynamic Host Config. Protocol)

BOOTP (Bootstrap Protocol)

NTP (Network Time Protocol)

TFTP (Trivial File Transfer Protocol)

SNMP (Simple Network Mgmt. Protocol) V1, V2, V3

Remote UNIX Services

| lpr Remote print | rcp Remote copy | rexed Remote execution | login Remote login | login Remote login |

To NetBIOS

RPC (Remote Procedure Call)

UDP (User Datagram Protocol)

OSPI (Open Shortest Path First)

IGRP/ EIGRP (Internet Gateway Routing Protocol)

GGP (Gateway-to-Gateway Protocol)

EGP (Exterior Gateway Protocol)

BGP (Border Gateway Protocol)

RIP (Routing Info Protocol)

ARP (Address Resolution Protocol)

RARP (Reverse Address Resolution Protocol)

ICMP (Internet Control Message Protocol)

SLIP (Serial Line IP)

CSLIP (Compressed SLIP)

IP (Internet Protocol)

X.25 packet-level protocol

The TCP/IP protocol suite works at the top five layers of the seven-layer OSI model. TCP/IP works over different layer-1 and layer-2 protocols such as Ethernet, Token Ring, and FDDI, which are described in the first two layers.

3

Complete Trust
Windows NT 4

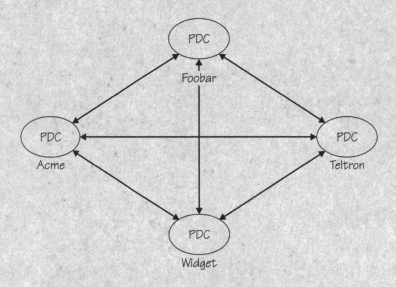

Twelve explicit one-way trusts must be maintained for these four companies to share resources.

Windows 2000

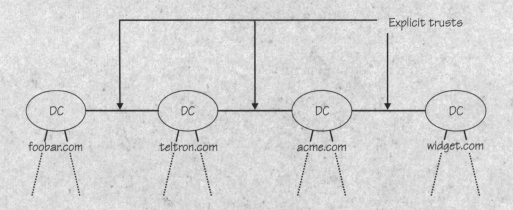

The four companies are joined by three trust relationships to form a forest. Each company maintains its own namespace, but they all share the same global catalog and schema for compatability.

Master Domain
Windows NT 4

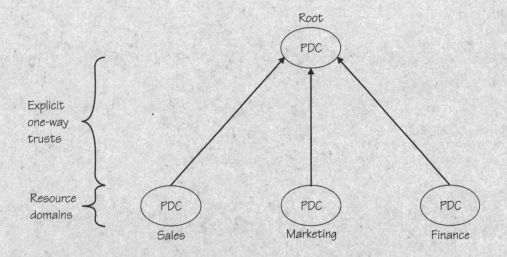

Root
PDC

Explicit
one-way
trusts

Resource
domains

PDC
Sales

PDC
Marketing

PDC
Finance

Four primary domain controllers and three trust relationships must be maintained to allow users access to the resource domains.

Windows 2000

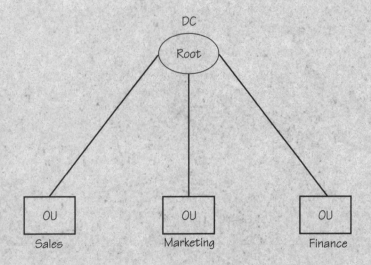

DC
Root

OU
Sales

OU
Marketing

OU
Finance

Trust is implied. Organizational units are used to delegate administrative authority to the three divisions.

Multiple Master Domain
Windows NT 4

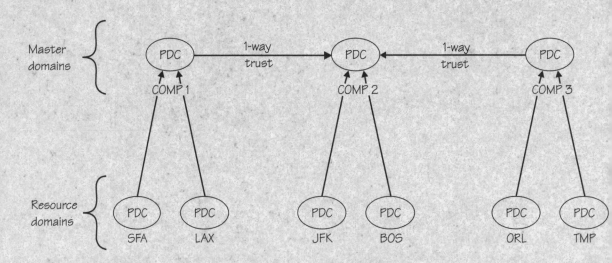

Master
domains

Resource
domains

COMP 1   1-way
trust   COMP 2   1-way
trust   COMP 3

PDC — PDC — PDC

PDC
SFA

PDC
LAX

PDC
JFK

PDC
BOS

PDC
ORL

PDC
TMP

Trust relationships must be set up and maintained to allow users access
to resources.

Windows 2000

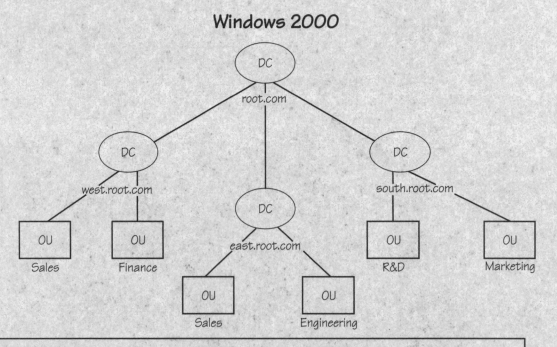

DC
root.com

DC
west.root.com

DC
east.root.com

DC
south.root.com

OU
Sales

OU
Finance

OU
Sales

OU
Engineering

OU
R&D

OU
Marketing

A single domain type needs no trust relationships to be maintained.
Trust is implied by membership in the tree.

6

Internet Connectivity w/Network Address Translation

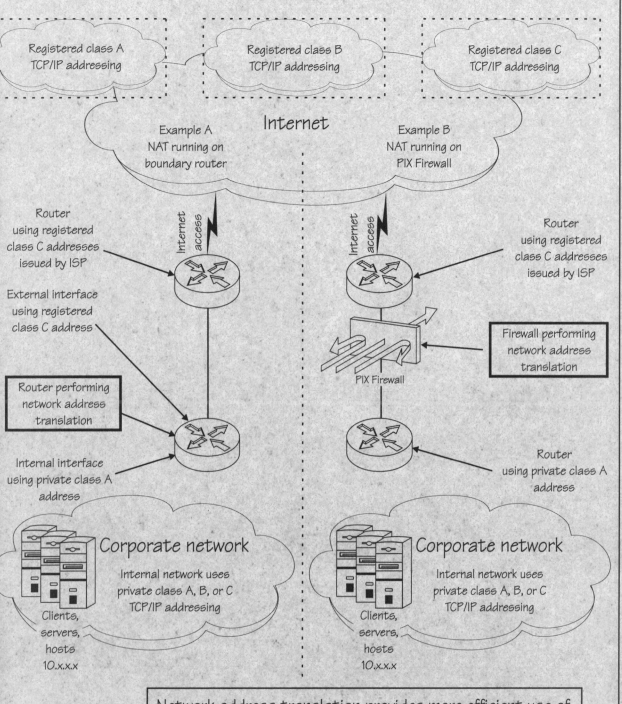

Registered class A
TCP/IP addressing

Registered class B
TCP/IP addressing

Registered class C
TCP/IP addressing

Internet

Example A
NAT running on
boundary router

Example B
NAT running on
PIX Firewall

Router
using registered
class C addresses
issued by ISP

Internet access

Internet access

Router
using registered
class C addresses
issued by ISP

External interface
using registered
class C address

Firewall performing
network address
translation

PIX Firewall

Router performing
network address
translation

Internal interface
using private class A
address

Router
using private class A
address

Corporate network

Internal network uses
private class A, B, or C
TCP/IP addressing

Corporate network

Internal network uses
private class A, B, or C
TCP/IP addressing

Clients,
servers,
hosts
10.x.x.x

Clients,
servers,
hosts
10.x.x.x

Network address translation provides more efficient use of
registered IP addresses, offers increased internal security,
and enables use of private addressing on internal networks.

7

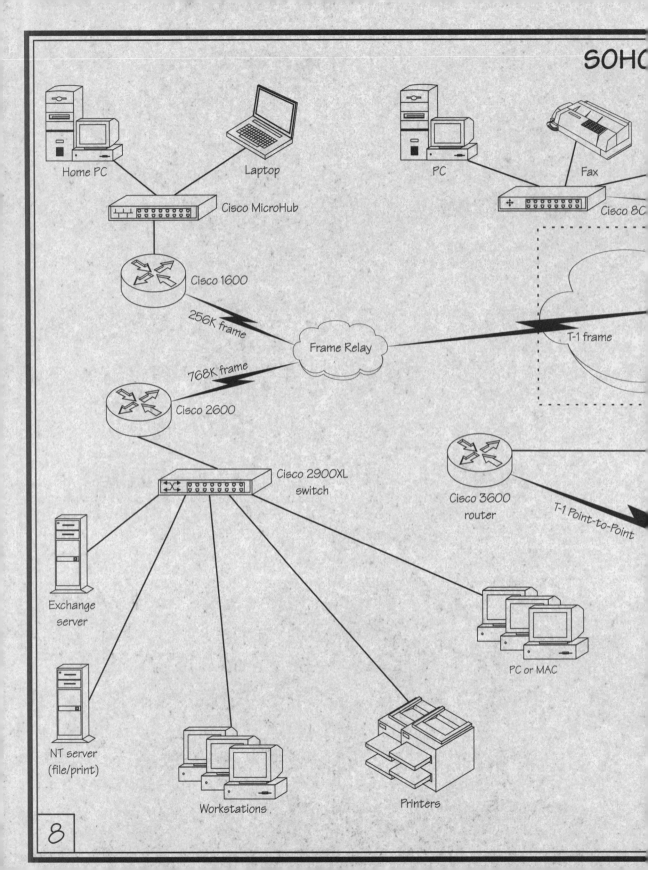

SOHO

Home PC

Laptop

Cisco MicroHub

PC

Fax

Cisco 8C

Cisco 1600

256K frame

Frame Relay

T-1 frame

768K frame

Cisco 2600

Cisco 2900XL
switch

Cisco 3600
router

T-1 Point-to-Point

Exchange
server

PC or MAC

NT server
(file/print)

Workstations

Printers

8

Solutions

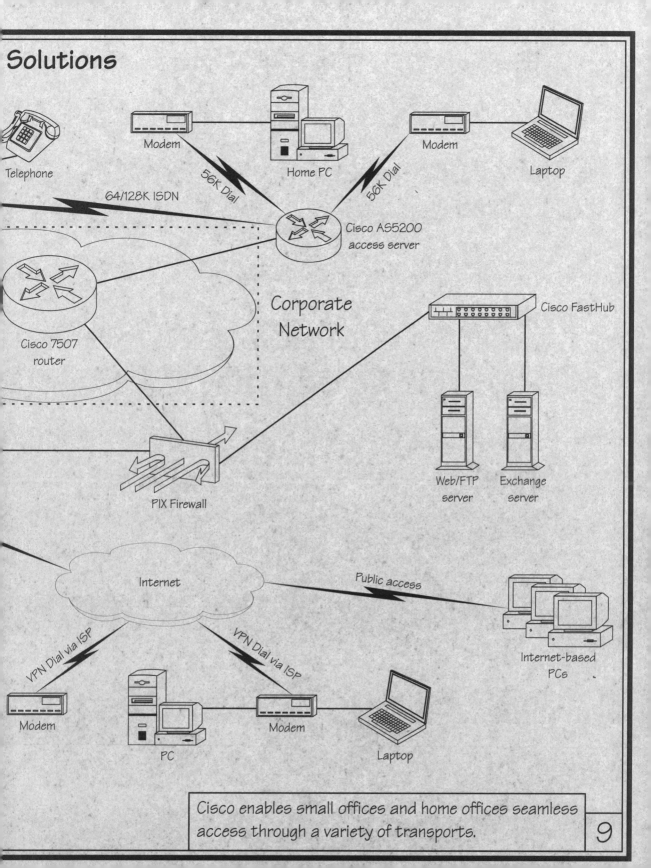

Telephone

Modem

Home PC

56K Dial

64/128K ISDN

56K Dial

Modem

Laptop

Cisco AS5200
access server

Cisco 7507
router

Corporate
Network

Cisco FastHub

Web/FTP
server

Exchange
server

PIX Firewall

Internet

Public access

Internet-based
PCs

VPN Dial via ISP

VPN Dial via ISP

Modem

PC

Modem

Laptop

Cisco enables small offices and home offices seamless
access through a variety of transports.

Traditional Fault-Tolerant Router Backbone

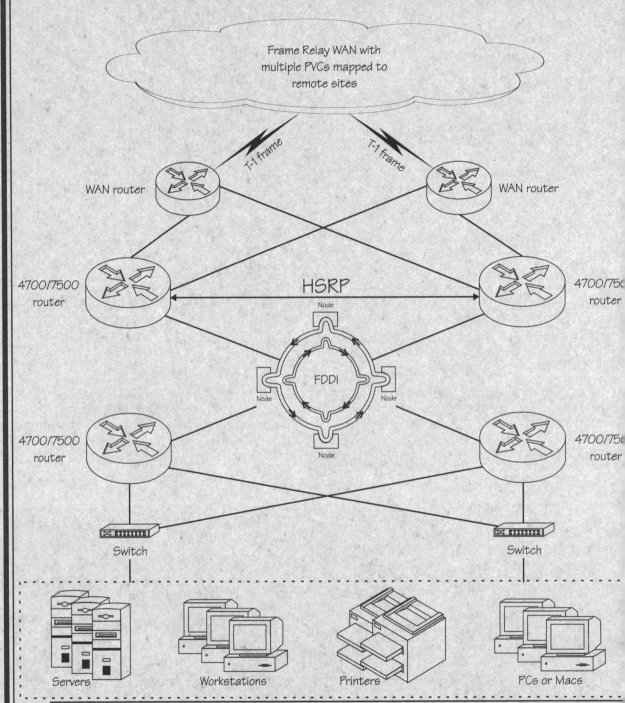

A typical fault-tolerant router backbone will include additional routers to insulat
against hardware failure and incorporate backup routers to other devices, or use
an extremely fault-tolerant technology such as a dual-attached FDDI ring.

Fault-Tolerant Switched LAN Backbone

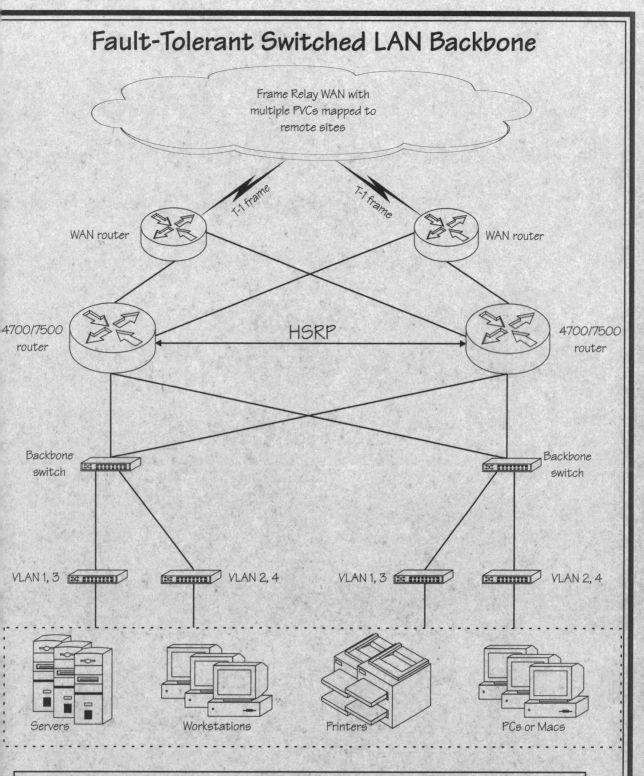

Frame Relay WAN with multiple PVCs mapped to remote sites

T-1 frame

T-1 frame

WAN router

WAN router

4700/7500 router

HSRP

4700/7500 router

Backbone switch

Backbone switch

VLAN 1, 3

VLAN 2, 4

VLAN 1, 3

VLAN 2, 4

Servers

Workstations

Printers

PCs or Macs

The switched backbone will include redundant routers for wide-area connectivity and VLANs supported by multiple switches for fault tolerance.

Business-to-Business Extranets

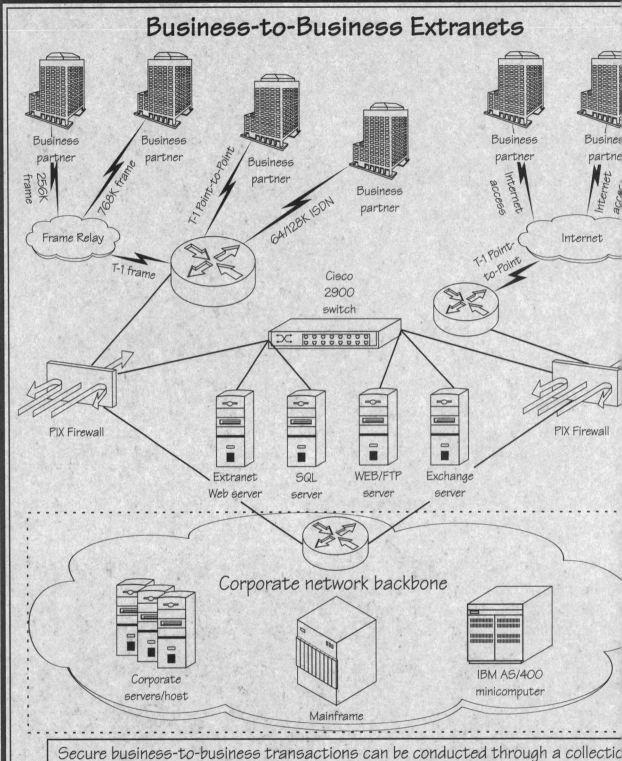

Business partner

256K frame

768K frame

Business partner

T-1 Point-to-Point

Business partner

64/128K ISDN

Business partner

Frame Relay

T-1 frame

Business partner

Internet access

Business partner

Internet access

Internet

T-1 Point-to-Point

Cisco 2900 switch

PIX Firewall

PIX Firewall

Extranet Web server

SQL server

WEB/FTP server

Exchange server

Corporate network backbone

Corporate servers/host

Mainframe

IBM AS/400 minicomputer

12

Secure business-to-business transactions can be conducted through a collectic of private business-to-business connections or via the Internet. In all cases, security is critical to protecting corporate information assets.

Firewall, Router, and PPTP-Based VPNs

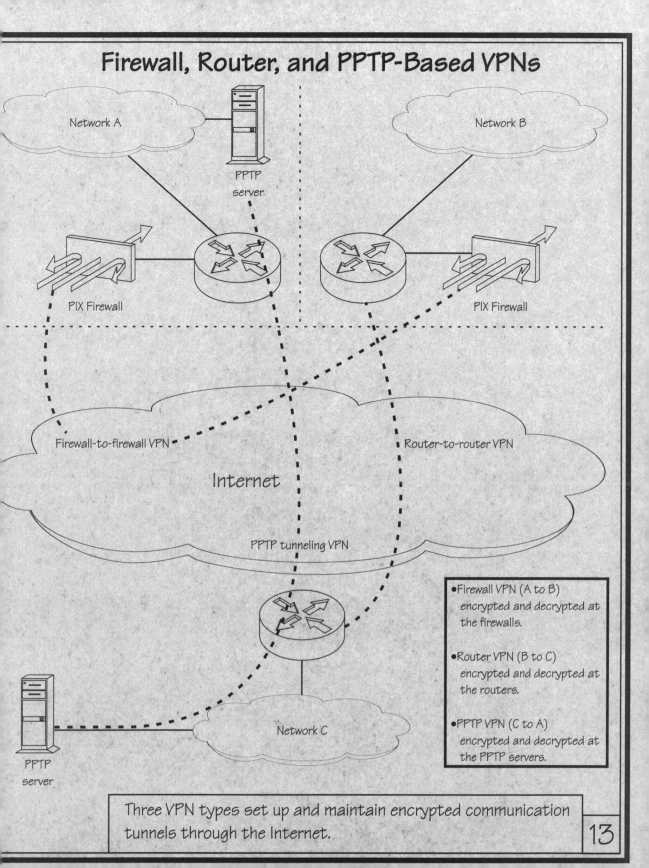

Three VPN types set up and maintain encrypted communication tunnels through the Internet.

13

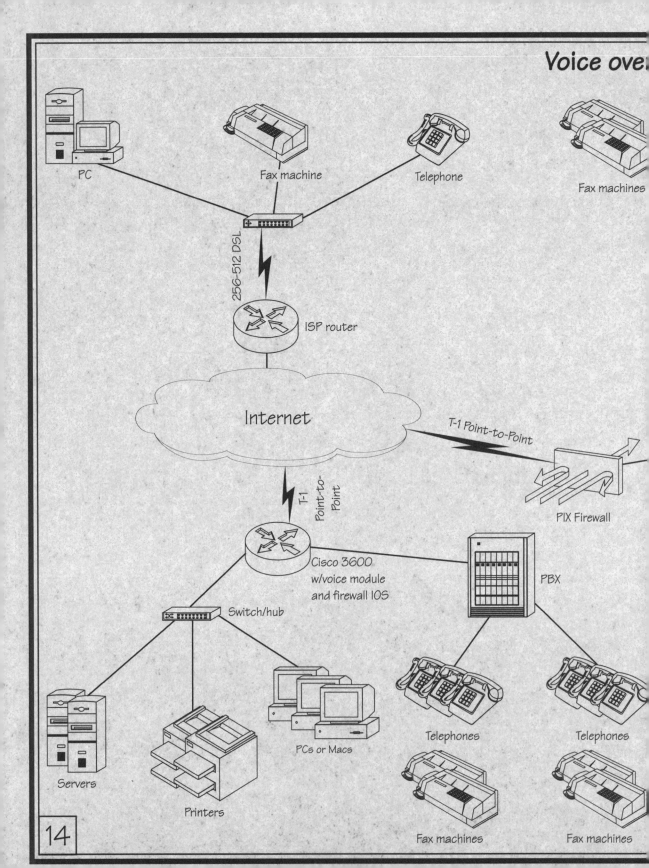

Voice over

PC

Fax machine

Telephone

Fax machines

256-512 DSL

ISP router

Internet

T-1 Point-to-Point

T-1 Point-to-Point

PIX Firewall

Cisco 3600
w/voice module
and firewall IOS

PBX

Switch/hub

Servers

Printers

PCs or Macs

Telephones

Telephones

Fax machines

Fax machines

IP (VoIP)

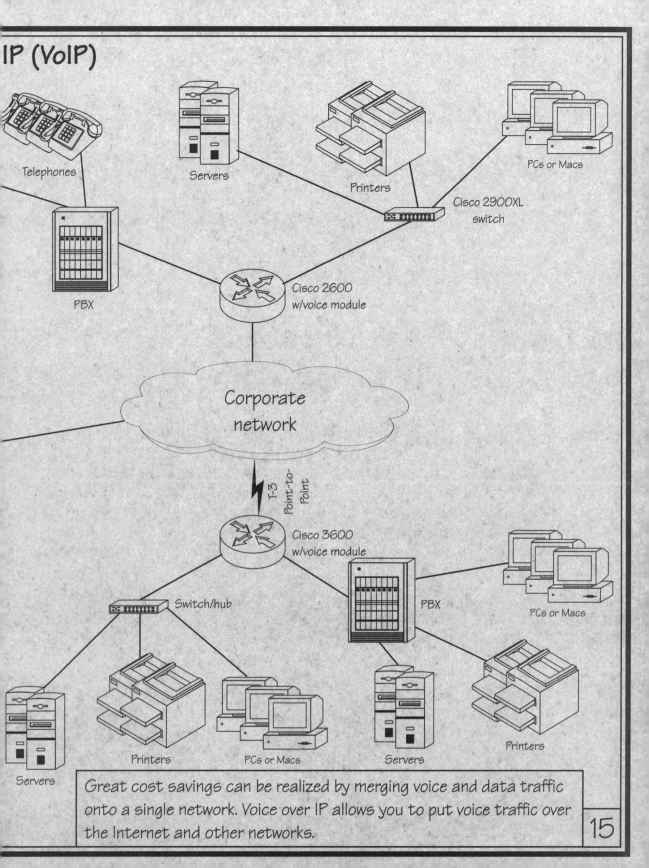

Telephones

Servers

Printers

PCs or Macs

Cisco 2900XL switch

PBX

Cisco 2600 w/voice module

Corporate network

T-3 Point-to-Point

Cisco 3600 w/voice module

Switch/hub

PBX

PCs or Macs

Servers

Printers

PCs or Macs

Servers

Printers

Great cost savings can be realized by merging voice and data traffic onto a single network. Voice over IP allows you to put voice traffic over the Internet and other networks.

15

Throughput

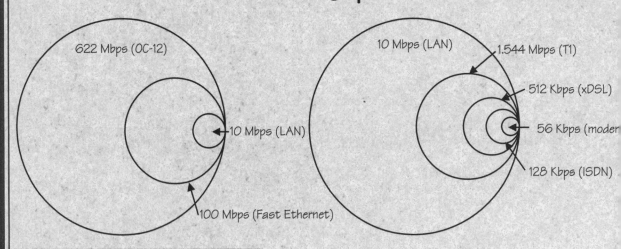

622 Mbps (OC-12)

10 Mbps (LAN)

1.544 Mbps (T1)

512 Kbps (xDSL)

56 Kbps (moder

128 Kbps (ISDN)

10 Mbps (LAN)

100 Mbps (Fast Ethernet)

The area of each circle represents
the amount of throughput each
technology provides.

Port Number Reference

Application	Port	TCP/UDP
echo	7	TCP/UDP
ftp-data	20	TCP
ftp	21	TCP
telnet	23	TCP
smtp	25	TCP
domain name system (DNS)	53	TCP/UDP
bootp	67	UDP
tftp	69	UDP
gopher	70	TCP
http	80	TCP
finger	79	TCP
pop3 (mail)	110	TCP
nntp (news)	119	TCP
ntp	123	UDP
NetBIOS name	137	UDP
NetBIOS datagram	138	UDP
NetBIOS session	139	TCP
snmp	161	UDP
snmp-trap	162	UDP
rexec	512	TCP
rlogin	513	TCP
shell	514	TCP
syslog	514	UDP
VPN	1723	TCP

Common predefined port numbers
and their applications.

Microsoft's Network Monitor is a powerful network analyzer. It can track information up to the network layer, perform filters on stations or protocols, and conduct packet analysis. Here's how to get started with Network Monitor:

1. Start the Network Monitor by clicking Network Monitor in the Administrative Tools menu, accessed from the Start | Programs menu.

2. Select an agent if your local agent is not running.

3. To connect to a Network Monitoring Agent running on another system, click Capture, and then select Networks from the menu. Then choose the name of the computer running the Monitoring Agent. (You need to have administrative rights on both machines when setting up this connection.)

4. Once the Network Monitor has connected to an active Agent, you'll see the main Capture window.

5. Click the Capture button (looks like a Play button) and watch the statistics start to accumulate, as shown in Figure 10-1.

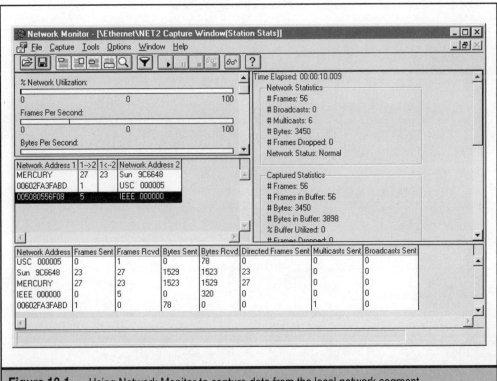

Figure 10-1.   Using Network Monitor to capture data from the local network segment

Network Monitor will continue to collect packets from the local network segment until you pause or terminate the capture. Don't worry, your hard drive won't fill up. This is because packets are sent continually to a buffer until the buffer fills up; then the newly arrived packets begin to overwrite older packets. You might want to set a small buffer if you are interested only in watching real-time network statistics, and not in capturing packets for analysis later. Once you have captured some network traffic, you'll need to stop the capture to view the captured data.

From the Capture menu, click the Stop and View item. This will end the capture and bring up the packet analysis window, as shown in Figure 10-2. In the first panel under the toolbar, double-click on a particular frame to open it and display its contents.

In this case, we have opened up a packet that was part of a Telnet session, and have highlighted a portion of the data (payload) portion of the packet. This is the part of the packet that carries the information the applications want to hear from each other. The other portions of the packet function only to properly deliver the payload; they contain addressing and other such information. In this case, the payload contains a portion of the password prompt that the Telnet user sees when first establishing a Telnet session with a host.

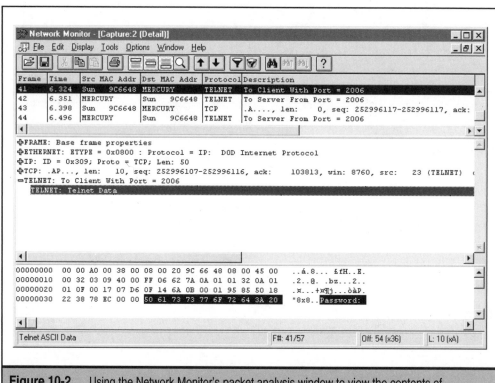

Figure 10-2. Using the Network Monitor's packet analysis window to view the contents of individual packets

NOTE: Telnet connects with a username and password that are sent as clear (unencrypted) text so that anyone with Network Monitor (and some time on their hands) could capture this information. It's something to keep in mind if you use Telnet to perform administrative functions.

CISCO'S TRAFFICDIRECTOR

If you recall from Chapter 8, CWSI contains an application called TrafficDirector (it's an option element when you install CWSI). TrafficDirector is a stand-alone application that acts as a management station and collects network traffic data from remote probes and switches. You can use TrafficDirector to monitor usage, troubleshoot problems, chart trends, and set alarms for severe network conditions.

TrafficDirector Agents

Like other probes, TrafficDirector sits centrally and queries remote probes to learn about traffic on the network. Once they're initiated, these probes are called *agents* and can be grouped together for easier administration. You can use three kinds of probes with TrafficDirector:

▼   **Dedicated SwitchProbe devices**   These devices are purchased from Cisco ($2,000–$12,000) and come in a variety of protocol types.

■   **A network analysis module**   This is a Cisco card you insert into a Catalyst 5000 to give it all the RMON and RMON-2 capabilities of a probe ($14,995).

▲   **Cisco switches**   Some Cisco switches can be configured to act as probes. If you have the switches, this is the most cost-effective way to create probes.

For switches configured to use RMON, Cisco uses what it calls mini-RMON. This only obtains a limited set of statistics. To get the full range of statistics in RMON and RMON-2, you will need to use a SwitchProbe or install a Network Analysis Module.

TIP: Some of Cisco's switches may not have the capability to support all the groups of RMON, but most support at least the first four groups. When you're looking at buying a switch that supports RMON, be smart and dig a little deeper and find out which specific groups the switch supports.

TrafficDirector's Interface

TrafficDirector is a very functional application with many features. Its interface (see Figure 10-3) is split into two sections.

The leftmost pane displays information about Agents of a particular AgentGroup. Here is where graphs and statistics are displayed. Most of the control over the program is managed via the icon buttons located in the right-hand pane.

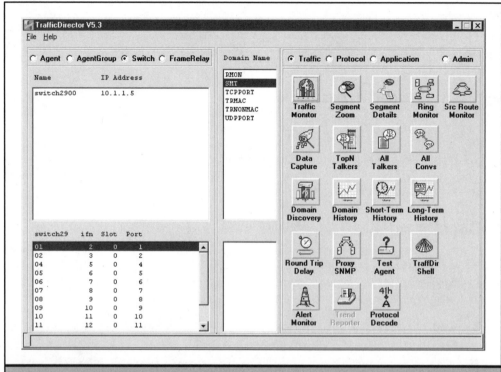

Figure 10-3.   TrafficDirector's user interface

The buttons at the top of the right-hand pane signify the four modes of TrafficDirector. Clicking one of these modes will change the array of icon buttons just below. These icons represent specific actions and functions available in the selected mode.

▼ **Traffic mode**   Used to display data-link layer (layer 2, RMON) information.

■ **Protocol mode**   Used to display network layer (layer 3, RMON-2) information.

■ **Application mode**   Used to display OSI layers 4–7 (RMON-2) information.

▲ The last button is for **Admin** mode. It is used to add agents, set up the SQL server database, and configure other aspects of the program.

Getting Started with TrafficDirector

In the following example, we'll start with nothing more than TrafficDirector and a switch on our test network. There are a few things we need to do before we can start receiving RMON updates, including adding at least one agent.

Enable SNMP on Switches

Before you can poll any device, it will have to be set up to use SNMP. Depending on your switch, this can be accomplished via the command-line interface or with the administrative browser-based interface. Although SNMP configuration can get somewhat complicated, all you really need to do to enable SNMP applications to use a switch is to enable SNMP on the device and create the read-only and read-write SNMP community strings. You'll need these passwords later when you add the device as a TrafficDirector agent. More information about setting up SNMP on switches is covered in Chapter 6.

Adding the Switch Agent

Open TrafficDirector; from the Start menu, select Programs | CWSI 2.2 | Start TrafficDirector. This will call up a window similar to Figure 10-3. At this point, TrafficDirector is fully functional, except there are no agents loaded. You won't be able to view any network statistics until you first add at least one agent.

To add an agent, click the Admin button at the top of the right pane, and then click the Config Manager icon in the array of buttons just below. This will open up another window in which all the agents are listed. Click Add, and in the next window enter the RMON agent's name, IP address, switch type, and SNMP community strings. As soon as you click OK, TrafficDirector attempts to communicate with the agent and scan its ports. If the scan is successful, you can close the window and return to the main TrafficDirector screen.

TrafficDirector Output

At this point, you should be able to gather at least the most basic RMON statistics from the switch or probe you've just added. In the left pane, click the Agent radio button at the top, and select the newly added agent in the main windows on the left (Name /IP Address box). Next, in the right-hand pane, click the button to enable Traffic mode, and then click the Segment Zoom icon. TrafficDirector's Segment Zoom window is illustrated in Figure 10-4. Here you can see the statistics about the local network segment, and that there appears to be some problems with collisions on this segment.

APPLICATION ANALYSIS

Whether you are troubleshooting an existing application on the production network or analyzing a new application before deployment, you will want to conduct an *application analysis*. The basic technique for this analysis is the same for all applications: You create an environment that emulates the production network—making it as realistic as possible in a laboratory. Then you reproduce the application that will be used, and at the same time you monitor the network traffic. For our examples here, we will assume we are assessing an application before deployment on the production network, so we can conduct our tests in a lab setting.

Outlined in this section are two examples of application testing. The first example uses a computer that runs software, called a *network analyzer*, which looks at each packet

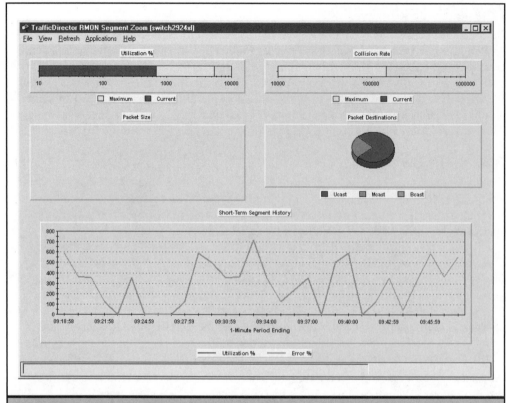

Figure 10-4. Statistics discovered by TrafficDirector

on the network to measure the amount of traffic generated for the various functions of the application. For the second application, we use two analyzers simultaneously, measuring latency as well as the overall speed of the application as it performs on the network.

Single-Analyzer Capture Example

As described in the section on Microsoft's Network Monitor, Telnet users send their usernames and passwords in cleartext over the network. If users are connecting to routers via Telnet, the line and enable passwords are easily captured by anyone with an analyzer. This is obviously a serious security risk, but it can be removed by using a Terminal Access Controller Access Control System (TACACS+) with Cisco routers. In this example, you'll see how one analyzer can be used to predict the effects of this added security application.

What Happens with TACACS+?

In a standard Telnet session, the user makes a connection with a router and the session is allowed to continue. With TACACS+, the user makes the same connection with the router, but the router then checks with a TACACS+ server. TACACS+ provides user authentication and checks on every command the user issues, to make sure the logged-in user has the correct level of permission. (See Chapter 16 for information on using TACACS+.) Although the user's password is still sent in the clear, you can force the user to log in using a security token whose password changes each time it is used. This way, even if the user knows the last password, it can't be used to Telnet to any device. A redundant TACACS+ server is always available in case the first one is unreachable.

Before deploying TACACS+, you'll want to know how much additional traffic will be placed on the network. This data is what the application analysis will provide. But before we can begin, we need to understand how the application will interact with the user and any other systems. Here is the basic outline of traffic flow with TACACS+ running (this traffic flow is illustrated in Figure 10-5):

1. A user initiates a Telnet session with a router.

2. The router prompts the user for a username and password (cleartext). Then the router sends this information (encrypted) to a TACACS+ server.

3. The TACACS+ server checks its database to see if the user is valid. If so, the server sends the OK (encrypted) to the router, along with a privilege level for the user.

4. Based on the TACACS+ information, the router allows the user access and the Telnet session continues (cleartext).

Analysis of Traffic Generated by TACACS+

Once you have identified the flow of traffic, you can start thinking about the different kinds of transactions that are possible within the application. For TACACS+ there are three categories:

▼ **Administrative**   These transactions include logging into the TACACS+ server to perform administrative duties.

■ **User**   These transactions include logging into routers and issuing commands there.

▲ **Replication**   This is traffic generated from one TACACS+ server to another to replicate their user database.

To conduct the tests, Microsoft's Network Monitor was placed on a test segment with a router, a test user, and the TACACS+ server, as shown in Figure 10-6.

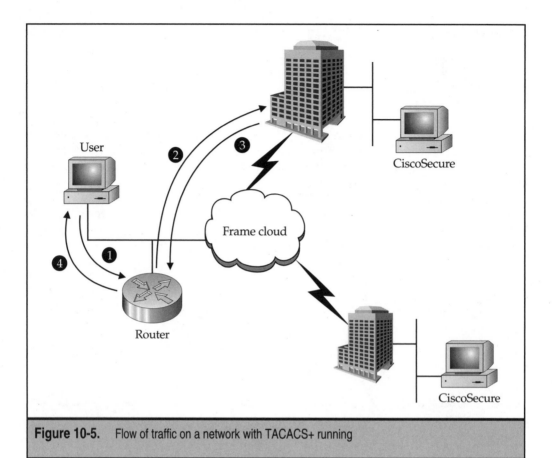

Figure 10-5.   Flow of traffic on a network with TACACS+ running

NOTE: Although this test scenario is unrealistic because there is no other traffic or slow WAN links in between any of the devices, we are only interested in testing how much traffic is generated—not how long it takes to get from device to device.

Network Monitor was started, and the filter function was set up to capture only traffic flowing between two devices. Then the user or server initiated a particular transaction, such as logging into a router or starting the replication process to another server. Each test was conducted sequentially, trying never to run more than one test per network capture. The results are shown in Table 10-3.

Our analysis determined that there were eight major transaction types to test. After a capture is complete, the last packet in the captured file is a summary log that Network Monitor places there for analysis. You can see how many packets were sent and received, as well as their cumulative size. The bytes total was divided by the time it would normally take for a user to issue the command to get a rate. The analysis shows that the high-

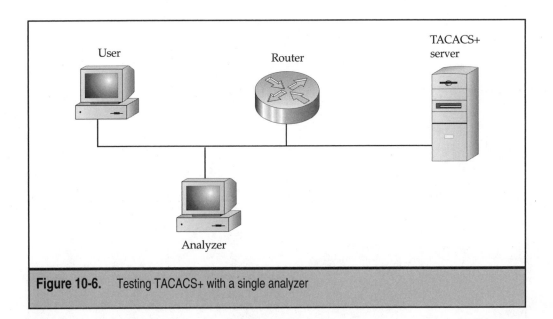

Figure 10-6. Testing TACACS+ with a single analyzer

est rate is only 16.5 Kbps. Therefore, no new links are going to be installed to run this application. To see how this new traffic will influence the rest of the network requires modeling (see the later section "Simulations and Capacity Planning").

TIP: The captured packets are in bytes and must be converted to bits, by multiplying them by eight.

Dual-Analyzer Capture

Single-analyzer captures work well when you want to determine the number of packets, the size of the transaction, or other characteristics about individual frames. But when you want to get detailed information about how long something takes, you'll need to run an application analysis using two protocol analyzers over a more complex test network.

Since information about the amount of traffic is almost useless without a comparative reference to time, you will often need to determine how much of the transaction time is taking place on the network. A single analyzer can know about when a packet passes by on the local segment, but the analyzer cannot know how long the packet takes to reach a remote server over a complicated network. Another analyzer must be located near the server to measure when the packet is received.

Network Setup for Dual-Analyzer Capture

Figure 10-7 is a schematic diagram of a test network. A user will be communicating with a remote server through a network. Analyzers are set up on the local segments for the user

Category	Traffic Description	Total Frames	Total Kilobytes	Rate (Kbps)
Administration	Login into TACACS+ Server to do admin	377	101.5	15.0
	Adding a user and modifying a group property	817	259.2	16.5
User	Login to router (host to router)	48	2.8	1.1
	Log into router (router to TACACS+ server)	43	2.9	1.2
	Issue command on router (router to TACACS+)	18	1.3	2.1
	Log into router and issue **show run** (All Traffic) command	148	11.6	3.7
Replication	Between two TACACS+ Servers (no new info)	184	107.5	9.5
	Between two TACACS+ Servers (update 10 users)	187	107.7	9.6

Table 10-3. Summary of Traffic Generated by Use of TACACS+

and the server. The cloud in this figure represents the rest of the network that separates the user from the server. This could be a single WAN link or a complete Frame Relay cloud with many routers and switches in between. It probably has a random delay associated with traffic passing through it.

Running the Dual-Analyzer Test

Here is how to run the test using two analyzers:

1. Configure the analyzers to only capture packets from the client and server computers. You can use Microsoft's Network Monitor or any third-party protocol analyzer.

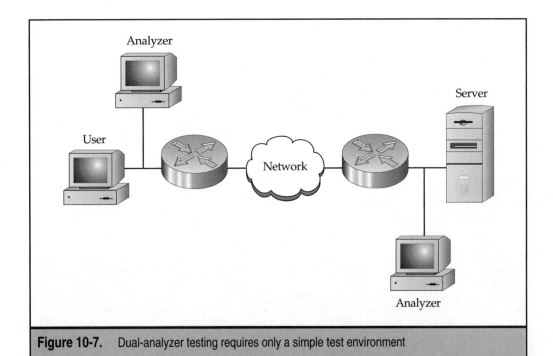

Figure 10-7.   Dual-analyzer testing requires only a simple test environment

2. Synchronize your analyzer with the person running the other analyzer so that both analyzers start capturing packets at the same time.

3. Use the client to request information from the server.

4. Stop capturing when the conversation is complete.

5. Repeat these steps for each kind of transaction (requesting a record, depositing a record, changing a record, and so on).

When you have finished, you will have two sets of analyzer trace files that hold the packets for each type of transaction. It is essential that you keep track of which files belong to what transaction and which analyzer. You will examine each trace file to determine the number of packets traveling in each direction, the number of bytes traveling in each direction, and delays at each computer and on the network. The traces from both analyzers should be almost identical, except for the times when packets were seen coming in.

To make sense of it all, you need a simple spreadsheet. Table 10-4 illustrates a spreadsheet with five conversations. Listed are the start and stop times, the application name, its protocol, the host and destination addresses, and packet and byte counts for traffic in both directions.

Start Time	Stop Time	Application	Protocol	Host A	Host B	#Pkts (A->B)	#Bytes (A->B)	#Pkts (B->A)	#Bytes (B->A)
"11/20/ 1999 13:30:54"	"11/20/ 1999 14:00:53"	"cc:Mail"	"IPX"	"Novell_ Client1"	"Novell_ Server34"	922	79,377	922	108,908
"11/20/ 1999 13:31:24"	"11/20/ 1999 14:00:33"	"WWW (Web)"	"IP"	"[132.207. 129.164]"	"[132.157. 182.24]"	95	38,130	70	7,245
"11/20/ 1999 13:32:50"	"11/20/ 1999 14:01:22"	"Novell Print Services"	"IPX"	"Novell_ Server41"	"Novell_ Server34"	88	6,394	88	24,417
"11/20/ 1999 13:30:11"	"11/20/ 1999 14:00:04"	"Telnet"	"IP"	"[132.189. 30.4]"	"[132.15. 244.152]"	29	9,354	44	4,562
"11/20/ 1999 13:32:26"	"11/20/ 1999 14:00:32"	"Oracle"	"IP"	"[132.143. 57.83]"	"[132.40. 215.61]"	675	337,690	831	54,314

Table 10-4. A Sample Spreadsheet Showing Five Conversations

Making Sense of the Results

Fortunately, all of the time delays can be measured because the analyzers record and time-stamp each packet as it moves by. However, the one-way network delay times cannot be measured unless the two analyzers were time-synchronized (with precision to the millisecond). Here is the problem: If the first analyzer is some seconds ahead of the other analyzer, you cannot determine exactly the length of the one-way network delay. This is because there are two unknowns: the offset time and the network delay.

You can determine the round-trip delay of the network by the following method:

▼ First, record the *total* round-trip delay from the client analyzer. This is how much time has passed since the request went out and until a reply is seen.

■ Then subtract the processing time of the server from the total round-trip delay, to determine the round-trip *network* delay.

▲ To calculate the server processing time, just record when the request was seen at the server (from the server analyzer) and subtract that value from the time the reply was seen leaving the server.

Conducting application analysis as outlined here helps pinpoint where in the system major delays are introduced. Very often, the delay is found in the network cloud. This variable is quite complicated, and clarifying the location of bottlenecks in complicated networks requires further analysis or network simulations.

> **NOTE:** Using the **ping** command also yields round-trip delays. These values, however, are often greater than what is normally found on a network because ping packets are given a low priority by networking devices.

SIMULATIONS AND CAPACITY PLANNING

The simple traffic analyses we conducted in the examples above can tell us a great deal about how a single application works by itself. However, no application runs alone in a Microsoft/Cisco environment. Determining how an application will interact in a complicated network alongside hundreds of other applications is a job for *network traffic simulations.*

Simulating Your Network

As a network evolves, the number and variety of devices and applications it supports will make it a real challenge to understand the system as a whole. It becomes next to impossible to predict with any accuracy how one traffic demand will affect another part of the network. There are simply too many devices, too many routes, and too many conversations going on simultaneously. Since you cannot use the production network as your laboratory, and it's impractical to build an exact replica, it makes sense to make a model of your network and run simulations on it. These simulations subject your "virtual" network to various designs and traffic loads to see how well it functions under those circumstances.

Building a model of your network is a very piecemeal process. To build a model that considers every aspect of the network and the traffic it carries is, essentially, to rebuild your network. Therefore, a model must include certain simplifications and assumptions. The trick is knowing what aspects can be altered without compromising the model. This section outlines the simulation process and helps you understand where to make those important simplifications.

Preparing to Simulate

In the preceding application analysis, we determined the network requirements of an application. We can use this information to ensure that users experience minimal delay when running that application. To really get a feel for how the application will behave in our production environment, we'll first build a model of the production environment. To that we add the information from the application analysis, and then we run a simulation to see how the network responds to the new load.

But before we can run a single simulation, we must create a representation of the production network. This consists of the network topology and the traffic that runs over it. This concept is illustrated in Figure 10-8. Once you have compiled a decent representation of the network topology and the network traffic, you can combine this information with a question you want answered about the network. This question may be a "What if?" question such as "What if we add 500 users to the New York site?" or "What is the impact on the network if we add a new application?" Once you have a question, you can run a simulation to help you answer that question.

Network Topology

The *topology* of the network includes the physical devices that constitute the network, as well as their logical settings. This is the framework for the model. Later, traffic will be laid down onto this framework. Some of the physical devices that must be included in the representation of the network are

▼ Computers

■ LANs

■ Point-to-point connections

■ Routers

■ Switches

▲ WAN links

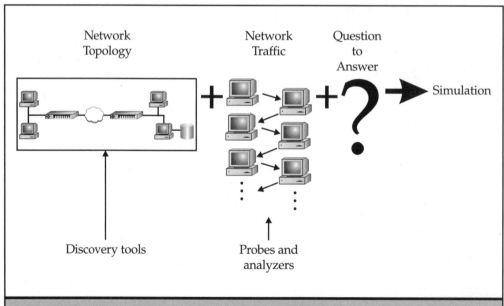

Figure 10-8. Simulations require a network topology, application traffic information, and a question to answer

Some logical parameters to be considered are

▼ Interface settings on routers

■ LAN speeds

■ Naming conventions

■ Router capabilities (such as backplane speed)

■ Routing protocols

▲ WAN speeds

Fortunately, there are programs available that can discover the physical and logical settings on your network; these tools include HP OpenView and CWSI (within CiscoWorks2000). You'll recall from Chapter 8 that most of these programs use SNMP to query the devices. Sometimes you need to provide a list of routers and their corresponding IP addresses. Other programs need only the address of a seed router. The discovery program learns what it can from the router's MIB, and then asks the router who its neighbors are. From there, the discovery steps through the entire network, learning about routers, interfaces, and devices on each network segment. Simulation programs often do not include a discovery tool; they import the topology from other network monitoring tools as described previously. In any event, you have just realized the first benefit of simulation: network documentation.

Building the topology of your network has the added benefit of creating an inventory of the most important devices on the network and their settings. The discovery programs take advantage of this by providing a Web browser–based interface to access this database. For example, CiscoWorks2000 allows you to search and sort the entire hardware database for specific devices or settings.

Application Traffic

If the network topology is the structure or skeleton of your network, the life-giving blood of any network is the application traffic that courses over links and through routers to its final destination. The importance of emulating the network traffic in as much detail as possible cannot be understated. Time and available computational power should be the only limiting factors. Application traffic can be modeled on two levels: the byte baseline, and based on application profiles.

BYTE BASELINE   Earlier in this chapter, we explained that *baselining* is the process by which you record the amount of traffic that is on the network over a period of time. This information can be obtained from RMON devices such as switches or dedicated devices. Since RMON deals only with the lowest layers of the OSI model, however, it cannot provide information about specific applications (this is reserved for RMON-2). All you learn is how many bytes per second have passed over your links or through your devices. This level of reporting does give you percentages of utilization for your links, and this information can be quite useful in its own right.

Without information about network protocols or applications, you cannot discern one program's traffic from another. Therefore, byte baselining has limited value for simulations, because you are interested in how individual applications behave on the network. Nonetheless, if a point-to-point link is nearing capacity, you don't need to know anything about applications to know that adding more traffic would not work well.

APPLICATION PROFILES An alternative to byte baselining is to use probes or analyzers that are capable of detecting information from passing packets about the network protocol and the application that generated the packets. These probes typically use RMON-2 or their own proprietary methods to gather this information. Although the probes are quite good at picking out what network protocol a packet is using (for example, IP, IPX, or AppleTalk), they need to be configured manually to identify Word, Telnet, NetMeeting, and other applications. Once this configuration is complete, however, you can identify every traffic conversation on the network. Here is some of the data that can be extracted:

▼ Application name

■ Destination computer

■ Duration of conversation

■ Latency for application

■ Network protocol

■ Number of bytes in each direction

■ Number of packets in each direction

▲ Source computer

These are the application profiles that can be imported into the modeling software. Other benefits can be realized, as well, from this data. The information can be used to

▼ Check latency for applications, for Quality of Service requirements

■ Identify the throughput requirements of particular applications

■ Check to see where your Web traffic is going

▲ Learn about which users are using which resources

Data Reduction

If you have multiple probes capturing conversations on your network, you will quickly have thousands of captured conversations. Since each conversation is entered into a simulation, this glut of conversations (over 30,000) will bog down even the most powerful machines. The best way to deal with the large number of conversations is to remove or consolidate them.

REMOVE DUPLICATE CONVERSATIONS Because you have multiple probes located on the network, there is a good possibility that two probes will capture and record the same conversation. When you collect the conversations from all the probes, some conversations will be represented twice if you don't eliminate duplicate traffic conversations.

Sometimes, the workstations that act as probe managers perform this consolidation for you, preventing traffic from being counted twice. If this task isn't being done by the probe manager, you'll have to create a utility that looks at each conversation and compares it against all others. When it finds two that have identical attributes, it can delete one of them.

REDUCE CONVERSATIONS   There are two other ways to reduce the number of conversations without significantly reducing the realism of the simulation: by eliminating insignificant conversations, and by consolidating like traffic.

You can safely eliminate conversations that are too small to have a significant impact on the network traffic. For example, you will find that about 40% of your conversations make up less than 1% of the total traffic. This is because these conversations have very few packets and very few bytes. Eliminating them will greatly increase the speed of the simulations, yet will reduce the realism of the simulation by only a small fraction.

In traffic consolidation, conversations that have the same source, destination, and application can be lumped into a single conversation. All packets and bytes are added in, so no traffic load is lost. Typically, you'll also have a time criterion, so you only consolidate conversations that are close together in time. Eliminating small conversations and consolidating the remaining ones can reduce your number of conversations by 40% to 70%. This allows you to make your simulations more realistic by running them for longer periods of time, or by including more of your network in the model.

Two Approaches to Simulation

Simulators usually take an analytical or a discrete-event approach to modeling the traffic. Discrete-event simulation takes the traffic data quite literally and analyzes each packet to determine its behavior. The analytical approach is usually much faster, because it reads in the application traffic and makes more assumptions about it before running a simulation. Indeed, many argue that the analytical method is just as accurate as the discrete event method. Because of the long simulation time involved in using the discrete-event method, it is recommended that, for larger networks (more than 50 routers), a simulation tool employing the analytical method be used.

NOTE: The complexity that goes into simulation tools baffles most of us. Just remember that the "garbage in, garbage out" rule applies to all simulators.

There are two major categories of questions that you should identify before running a simulation: *change analysis* and *fault tolerance*. It is imperative to have a specific question in mind before setting out on a simulation. The question will be concerned with changing something about the production network; or, for fault tolerance, it may question how failure of specific devices or groups of devices will negatively affect application demands. Here are some "what if?" questions you might ask for each category:

Change Analysis: What if we . . .

▼ Add or remove an application demand

■ Change or add routers

■ Change or add WAN links or LANs

■ Change routing protocols

■ Move servers

▲ Move users

Fault Tolerance: What if we . . .

▼ Fail a city

■ Fail a facility

■ Fail LANs

■ Fail network devices

▲ Fail WAN links

Answering these questions using the simulator will help your organization understand much more about its network. You will discover useful information relating to capacity planning, rollout validation, and disaster recovery. Simulators are obviously very powerful, so let's look at one now.

CACI Products

Simulators are software packages that have typically run on powerful UNIX workstations in the past. They usually cost $40,000 to $100,000 each and require detailed training to use. Because of the cost and complexity of simulation tools, many companies contract with a consultant (such as Velte Systems) that specializes in this type of work. The firm may provide the tools used in gathering the data and running the simulations.

CACI Products Company offers a simulation package, COMNET Predictor, that imports the topological map of the network and a collection of application conversations. This gives you a fairly realistic model of your network you can use to run simulations against.

COMNET Predictor and COMNET III

COMNET Predictor is an analytical modeling tool from CACI Products Company (www.caciasl.com). The company also sells a discrete-event modeling tool called COMNET III. COMNET Predictor runs on Windows NT; it is intuitive and quite easy to install. Alternatively, you can import your topology from third-party sources, such as

▼ Cabletron SPECTRUM

■ CACI SIMPROCESS

■ Castlerock SNMPc

- Digital POLYCENTER
- HP OpenView
- IBM Netview for AIX
- ▲ NAC MIND

Sample Simulation

Let's walk through a simple COMNET Predictor simulation on a lab network we will build from scratch. Figure 10-9 illustrates our test network. There are two LAN segments separated by a WAN link. There is an NT Server and Workstation on each LAN. The network building tools are located in the toolbar on the left side of the screen. Creating a network is as simple as clicking the tool for the network item (such as LAN or Server) and dropping the item into the main window. You connect devices with links and later define

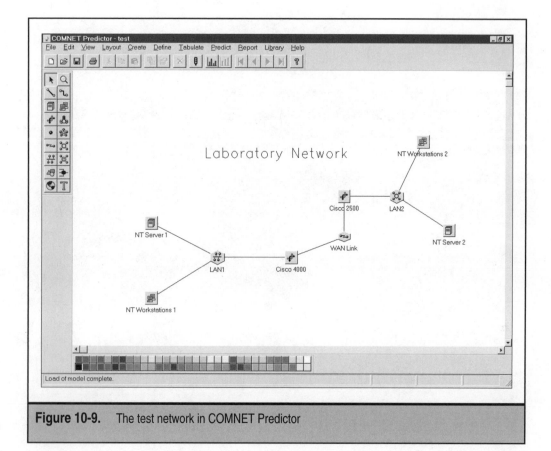

Figure 10-9. The test network in COMNET Predictor

their characteristics (such as a T1 or ISDN connection) by choosing from a predefined list or customizing your own specifications.

You can see we have two different models of Cisco routers in our test network. The simulation tool is familiar with the capabilities of most Cisco devices and will include those characteristics in the simulation.

Next we'll have to add traffic to the model. Again, in this case, we will keep it simple and create some fictitious traffic demands by hand. In Figure 10-10, you can see five traffic demands that were placed manually. They indicate the origin, destination, application, protocol, and rate for each traffic demand. You can pick applications from a predefined list, or create your own as we did in Figure 10-10 for cc:Mail. In a simulation of the production network, there may be thousands of conversations listed in this window. These, of course, are imported from the probes.

In this example, we have added traffic demands by hand because the network is so simple. In real life, though, you'll need to capture them with probes and import them into COMNET Predictor using one of the following sources:

▼ Axon Network LAN Servant

■ Compuware EcoScope

■ Frontier Software NETscout

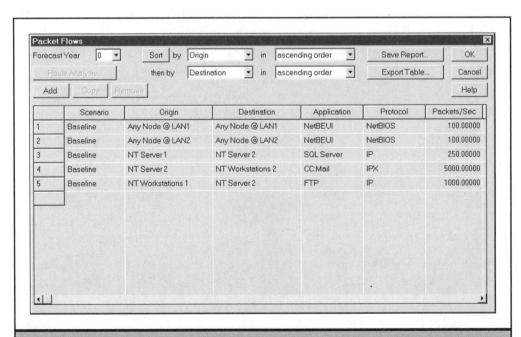

Figure 10-10.   Listing traffic conversations in the model

- HP Netmetrix
- Network General Distributed Sniffer System
- Network General Expert Sniffer
- ▲ Wandel & Golterman Domino Analyzer

With the topology and traffic demands in place, we are finally ready to run a simulation. We simply click the Run Simulation icon (the stoplight button near the center of the main toolbar), and the simulation is under way. Because this is a simple network with few demands, the simulation is over in a fraction of a second.

Numerous reports can be generated in the COMNET Predictor simulator, to examine utilization, forecasting, and network failures. Figure 10-11 is a report showing the percentage of utilization for each device or LAN in the network. Before we ran the simulation, we told Predictor that we expected a 10% growth in traffic each year. Predictor calculated the use of each device or LAN and projected its use for the next two years. From this report, we can see that we might want to keep an eye on our WAN link because it is approaching 40% utilization. For further analysis, we could easily change the throughput of the WAN link and run another simulation.

Network Resource Analysis

Resource type: Nodes and Links   Perf. measure: Util %   Help   Cancel

☐ Bottlenecks   ☐ Max 1-way if full-duplex   Save Report...

☐ Warnings and alarms   Rank method: descending order   Export Table...

in the rank year   Rank year: 2   Top N: 5   Top N Chart...

	Nodes and Links	Year 0 Util %	Year 1 Util %	Year 2 Util %
1	WAN Link	32.55	35.81	39.39
2	LAN2	31.75	34.92	38.42
3	Cisco 2500	15.63	17.19	18.91
4	LAN1	12.74	14.02	15.42
5	Cisco 4000	8.33	9.17	10.08
6	NT Server 2	0.63	0.69	0.76
7	NT Server 1	0.03	0.03	0.03
8	NT Workstations 1	0.00	0.00	0.00
9	NT Workstations 2	0.00	0.00	0.00

Figure 10-11. A COMNET Predictor report giving utilization percentages for each network device or link

SUMMARY

This chapter introduces many important concepts and applications to make sure your Microsoft/Cisco network stays up and running smoothly and efficiently. We examined the benefits of testing a network, along with several different types of tests that you can conduct. Network probes and analyzers were introduced, and application testing was demonstrated using one or two analyzers. By conducting traffic analysis, you can learn about the utilization on the LAN and WAN links as well as on network devices.

You learned about network simulations and the many benefits of proactive network testing. Conducting simulations is a very important part of lifecycle management for your network. Simulations should be carried out often, because today's network experiences many changes to its ever-evolving topological and traffic makeup.

We walked through the creation of a topological map of your network, using tools to take inventory of all the devices and their device-specific settings discovered using SNMP. We found that running the simulation allows you to answer many "what if?" questions to help validate the rollout of a new application or hardware. The model also helps you plan your capacity for future growth and determine your plan in case of network failures.

Remember that application testing and network simulation are neither the starting point nor the ending point for your network design questions. Because the digital landscape of your network changes constantly, you'll soon learn to appreciate the importance of staying one step ahead of the next big fire.

CHAPTER 11

IP Address and Naming Services

IP address and naming services—such as the Domain Name System (DNS), Windows Internet Naming Service (WINS), and Dynamic Host Configuration Protocol (DHCP)—play a very important role in TCP/IP-based networks.

At the simplest level, DNS is used by applications on client workstations, hosts/servers, routers, and other devices to resolve people-friendly host names—such as mailserver.abigcompany.com or router01.abigcompany.com—to the long string of numbers in IP addresses (and vice versa). Once an address is determined, the communicating device can send packets to the destination device using its IP address. An IP network can be functional without DNS, but its users would have to remember and use the IP addresses of destination devices. If the destination device were to be moved to another subnetwork, requiring an address change, all parties would have to be notified of and start using the new address. With DNS, devices can be moved and keep their same names. DNS also supports other network functions, such as reverse lookup, and provides support for resolving e-mail addresses, as discussed later in this chapter.

WINS, like DNS, is a naming service that maps names to network addresses. WINS, however, does its work to reduce or eliminate the need for broadcast traffic generated by NetBIOS-based networks, including those using Windows networking. The WINS service is available to all Microsoft-based network clients, and to WINS-compliant non-Microsoft clients. Later we will see how to set up and configure this necessary but somewhat cantankerous service on Windows NT/2000 servers.

DHCP provides a mechanism for automating the assignment of important IP information such as IP addresses and the default gateway. This protocol is commonly used to deliver address information to workstations and printers every time they boot up.

Although there are additional benefits to running DHCP and naming services (DNS, Dynamic DNS, or WINS) in a Windows NT/2000–only environment, most environments include non-Microsoft clients. It is important to understand the fundamentals of these services so a solution can be designed and installed that includes integrated support for IP-enabled Apple computers, printers, UNIX hosts, and other network devices.

Since running these services on a network can be quite complex, we'll look at some Microsoft and Cisco applications that ease those administration headaches. In the past, it was necessary to manually configure files containing the DNS records. Now, with Microsoft's DNS and Cisco's Network Registrar, the tasks of adding, modifying, and deleting records is done using various dialog boxes and forms. This greatly reduces the potential for error when manipulating record information. Cisco's Network Registrar and Microsoft's Integrated DNS, WINS, and DCHP management tools are reviewed in this chapter.

Finally, we'll walk through the steps necessary to configure Cisco devices to use DNS as a client. We'll also cover several router and switch configuration parameters used in facilitating the use of IP addressing services on the network, such as the **ip helper** and **dhcp server** configuration commands.

NAMING SERVICES: DNS

The most important function of a naming service is to translate an IP address to a people-friendly naming convention. Without this translation, we would have to remember the numerical IP addresses of every device we needed to communicate with. In the Windows world, our only other option for such translations would be to use WINS or a manually configured file (LMHOSTS or HOSTS) located on each client device. The LMHOSTS and HOSTS files, stored locally on a workstation, contain a list of hosts and their IP addresses. This allows the applications and the user to obtain a mapped name for the IP address of every host listed in the file. Unfortunately, these host files are manually updated and cannot, in any practical sense, contain all of the name-to-address mappings for every host on a large network or the Internet.

Under DNS, hosts can more easily be moved to different locations on the network. Moving a server to a new network subnet and assigning it a new address requires just one change to the DNS primary server. In contrast, using HOSTS or LMHOSTS files requires that every device be updated with the server's new IP address. Every client machine hoping to communicate with the server by name will need to have an updated HOSTS or LMHOSTS file. Consider a network having hundreds, thousands, or even millions of client machines, and you can easily see that DNS is a cornerstone service on almost every TCP/IP network. DNS bridges the gap between the IP address scheme and the Internet domain naming scheme. The following DNS primer section explains DNS functions and how it's able to accomplish such a Herculean task.

DNS Primer

Since the primary job of DNS is to translate Internet host and domain names into addresses and vice versa, let's look first at how Internet naming is organized. The *domain hierarchy* was established to organize domain naming into a meaningful and manageable structure. At the top of the hierarchy is the unnamed root, from which the top-level domains branch. The top-level domains are, for example, com, net, org, edu, and the two-letter codes assigned to each country. Underneath these are second-level domains such as .cisco, .microsoft, .amazon, and .barnesandnoble. Beneath these may be one or more subdomains; and finally, the whole structure ends with a host name.

You can see the entire convention by taking an Internet address and viewing it from back to front. Let's look at news.marketing.company.com, for example. Working from back to front, we would have com.company.marketing.news. Within this string, com is the top-level domain, company is the second-level domain, marketing is the subdomain, and news is the host name.

Zones

A *zone* is an area of one or many domains or subdomains for which a DNS host can resolve addresses. In most cases, one DNS host would be assigned primary responsibility over several domains and/or subdomains within a domain, while one or several other DNS hosts would be assigned secondary responsibility over the same domains and/or subdomains. Figure 11-1 illustrates this concept.

In the Figure 11-1 example, we have a large domain with several subdomains under it. DNS host A has primary responsibility for the two zones webfarm.velte.com and velte.com zones. DNS host B has primary responsibility for the notes.velte.com zone.

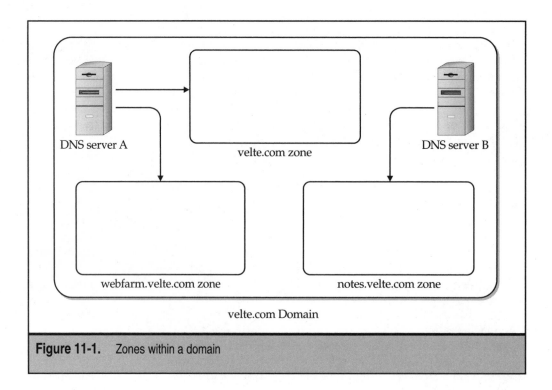

Figure 11-1. Zones within a domain

Using zone transfers (a method of sending and receiving DNS information from one DNS server to another), the two DNS hosts can cover their primary area(s) while acting as secondary DNS hosts for other zones.

Name Servers

To synchronize the DNS database on several hosts, only one host acts as the absolute authority over the zone information. This host is called a *primary name server.* For redundancy, additional hosts called *secondary name servers* can store a copy of the primary name server's zones. The primary name server is the final word on address-to-domain name mapping, but secondary name servers can be configured to receive a periodic zone transfers and can act as authoritative sources of name resolution for any DNS client.

Name Resolution

Name resolution is what DNS is all about. Any DNS client (workstation, router, server, or even another DNS host) can query a DNS host for the following three types information.

RECURSIVE QUERIES   The most common type of query is called a recursive query. This is sent from a DNS client to the DNS host lookup, requesting that the DNS host translate a host name (hostname.subdomain.domain) to an IP address. From the command line of a router, a recursive query is initiated when attempting to open up a Telnet connection to another host. Assuming that at least one DNS host has been entered into the router's configuration using the IP | name-server command, you can enter a valid host name at the prompt, or directly after a **connect** or **telnet** command, to execute a successful recursive query.

ITERATIVE QUERIES   Typically sent between DNS hosts, an *iterative* query is used when one DNS host is unable to service a DNS client request. The DNS host will send an iterative query to other DNS hosts in an attempt to find a host that can service the DNS client's request.

INVERSE QUERIES   An inverse query, or reverse lookup, occurs when a DNS client asks the DNS host to resolve an IP address to a host name. As the name implies, this query is the opposite of a recursive query.

DNS Record Types

Several DNS record types are used frequently by every DNS server. Together, they allow the DNS host to store and retrieve host and address information quickly and efficiently. See Table 11-1.

One common method of increasing server availability is to implement round-robin lookup using the CNAME record, allowing a single host name to be mapped to multiple IP addresses. This is accomplished by creating one CNAME record for each server's unique IP address, and then using the same host name as the Alias in each record. Round-robin is used when more than one server contains the same information, as you might find in a large Web site. Round-robin provides rudimentary load-balancing and fault tolerance by handing out sequential IP addresses as each DNS client request for the host name is processed. However, since the DNS host is not able to verify whether any server associated with an IP address is up and running, it is possible that DNS will send a bad address to the DNS client should one of the servers be down. When several servers are associated with the same host name, round-robin offers more fault tolerance than a single server name–to–IP address reference.

DNS Record Type	Description
A host record	A host record supports iterative queries. It contains a host name and corresponding IP address. A client requesting a name-to-IP address lookup receives the IP address associated with the host name in the host record. A record is established once for each new host entry.

Table 11-1.   DNS Record Types

DNS Record Type	Description
CNAME record	A CNAME record maps additional host names to an IP address. For example, say a single server provides Web pages, acts as an FTP server, and also is running a Telnet server. By adding CNAME records, a DNS client can look up a single server using any one of the following host names: www.superserver.skrumpy.com, ftp.superserver. skrumpy.com, or telnet.superserver.skrumpy.com.
MX record	The MX record contains a list of one or several e-mail servers configured to receive e-mail for a specific domain. Aside from helping to locate e-mail servers, this DNS feature allows for an increased measure of fault tolerance. Each e-mail server in the record has an associated number; the lower the number, the higher its preference. Should the server with the lowest number be unavailable, the server with the next lowest number would receive mail messages and hold onto them until the server with the lowest preference number is available.
PTR record	The Pointer record is essentially the opposite of a host record. It consists of an IP address and host name to support reverse lookups.
Name Server record	The name server record consists of an address and host name of a name server for a specific domain. There are usually many name-server records stored on an active DNS host. The records are used by the DNS host to quickly resolve a DNS client request, even if the host doesn't have information for the domain from which the client is requesting information.

Table 11-2.   DNS Record Types *(continued)*

NAMING SERVICES: NETBIOS

To support name-to-IP address resolution on networks running NetBIOS, it was necessary to establish a method of storing the broadcast NetBIOS names and their associated addresses. Since NetBIOS was originally designed to run on bridged networks, where every node is able to "hear" every other node on the network, there was no system in place to support its use on routed networks. In a routed environment, broadcasts are contained within their respective network segments (subnets) and are not usually allowed to traverse the router.

The Windows Internet Naming Service (WINS) was designed as the DNS of NetBIOS. WINS was designed to work around the broadcast limitation by serving as a central repository for the NetBIOS names and IP addresses. Using WINS, which we'll study later in this chapter, a client can look up a particular node by name and receive its IP address without a broadcast being transmitted across the network. In short, WINS provides dynamic registration and mapping of NetBIOS names to IP addresses. Let's take a closer look at the registration of NetBIOS names and how they are resolved.

Broadcast-Based Networking

In broadcast-based networks, each node is able to hear all the other nodes on the network. New nodes must first register themselves on the network by broadcasting the name they intend to use. The existing nodes listen to the broadcast and check to see if the new node's name is the same as theirs. If none of the existing nodes has the same name, the new node can start using the name.

When one node wants to communicate with another node (a client machine, printer, server, or other network device), it broadcasts a packet with the intended recipient's name. Every active network node will receive and examine the packet to verify whether or not the packet is intended for them. Once the packet has been examined, all nodes but the intended recipient ignore the packet. The intended recipient sends an acknowledgment that it's up and ready to communicate with the sender. When this acknowledgment is received, the two nodes begin communicating by establishing a session between each other.

Workgroups and Beyond

In workgroup environments, broadcast-based networking can simplify administration—as many have found when implementing a peer-peer network using NetBIOS over NetBEUI. (NetBEUI is Microsoft's NetBIOS Extended User Interface.) Broadcasting the node name and address, although typically limited to a single network segment, is an easy and low-cost method of providing name-and-address resolution. Larger networks, however, would see an unacceptable increase in the amount of broadcast traffic necessary to support browsing and name-and-address resolution. Aside from increasing the amount of traffic through each network node, routers must be configured to bridge the NetBIOS traffic, thereby requiring WAN links to carry additional traffic as well.

A step in the right direction is to use TCP/IP instead of NetBEUI to transport NetBIOS traffic. NetBIOS over TCP/IP (NBT) allows NetBIOS sessions to operate over routed TCP/IP-based networks commonly found in larger private and public systems (including the Internet). With standard TCP/IP, DNS can be used to resolve a host name to an IP address. Because of limitations with NetBIOS, however, this is not possible when NetBIOS sessions need name resolution. Without the ability to effectively broadcast to the entire network, NBT nodes cannot get the name resolution they require to set up NetBIOS sessions.

There are several solutions to this problem, the most common being WINS and WINS/DNS integration as described later in this section. Other methods include the use of a locally stored file called the LMHOSTS file to allow some broadcasts to propagate throughout the network using the **ip forward protocol spanning-tree** configuration in your Cisco routers. Let's take a look at these options, and then we'll move on to Windows 2000's Active Directory/DNS–based service.

LMHOSTS

The LMHOSTS (LAN Manager Hosts) file is located on each node. This file is most often updated manually, although methods do exist for managing it centrally. LMHOSTS is a standard text file that contains a list of remote resources (servers, printers, workstations, etc.), with their IP addresses and their domains.

NOTE: On Windows 2000 and NT 4.0 systems, the LMHOSTS file is located in %systemroot%\system32\drivers\etc.

Using this file, the client computer can look up the IP addresses of resources without having to rely on broadcasts or an outside naming service. The limitations are obvious: If any host moves to another subnet or otherwise changes its IP address, the LMHOST file on every node accessing the host must be updated. Also, if other host resources are added to the network, they must be added to every LMHOSTS file.

NOTE: Although extensions do exist to accommodate a pointer to a centrally located LMHOSTS file, there are other alternatives that offer greater functionality and integration with the network. For example, if you use or are planning to use DHCP, you might as well forget about using the LMHOSTS file for anything except special situations. With DHCP, IP addresses are dynamically assigned and therefore constantly subject to change. Keeping up with the registrations would be impossible. For that reason, Microsoft WINS and DHCP are engineered to work together.

Configuring a Router to Forward NetBIOS Name Server Broadcasts

If, for some reason, you don't want to use WINS to enable browsing and name services, or if you're not fully converted to a Windows 2000 environment, you can allow the router to forward the broadcasts. However, you'll want to carefully evaluate the impact (overhead, administration, etc.) of doing so.

NBT accomplishes broadcast name resolution using UDP port 137, and Server Message Block (SMB) datagram service on UDP port 138. Allowing these two ports to be open through the router will enable one subnet to browse another and resolve addresses. However, UDP broadcasts are not forwarded by the routers, thereby limiting you to the local subnet. To allow one subnet to broadcast to another, you'll need to take the following steps. First, at the router CLI, enter these commands:

```
Router(config)#ip forward-protocol udp 137
Router(config)#ip forward-protocol udp 138
```

Then enter the configuration mode of the interface from which you want the router to forward broadcasts (in this example, it is ethernet 0):

```
Router(config)#interface ethernet0
```

Then enter the **ip helper** statement along with the subnet to which you want the broadcasts forwarded:

```
Router(config-if)#ip helper 10.1.1.0
```

If you enter **ip forward-protocol** without specifying UDP and the port number, the forwarding of the following additional ports will be activated by default:

```
Time Service - port 37
TACACS - port 49
Domain Name System - port 53
BootP - port 67
Trivial File Transfer - port 69
```

NOTE: This configuration is uni-directional. If you wish both subnetworks to be able to browse each other, you'll need to configure both the local and remote routers.

MULTIPLE SUBNETS   If you want to give several subnets the capability to send and receive broadcasts, the ip forward-protocol should be implemented along with spanning tree on all routers with subnets requiring broadcasts, as shown here:

```
Router(config)#ip forward-protocol spanning tree
```

WARNING: The decision to implement spanning tree (or allowing broadcasts in the first place, for that matter) should not be a casual one. Before actually using spanning tree, be sure you analyze the effect it will have on the routers, network overhead, general network traffic patterns, and network administration. Using spanning tree as a quick fix or as a replacement for WINS or DNS is strongly discouraged.

If you decide against allowing broadcasts through your routers and don't plan on using the LMHOSTS file, you have other practical solutions: WINS, DNS, or Dynamic DNS (DDNS).

Resolving NetBIOS Names with DNS

When using Win 9x or NT, an alternative to using broadcasts or the LMHOSTS file is to use the option to Enable DNS for Windows Resolution available in recent implementations of Microsoft's TCP/IP client. In a Windows 2000–only environment, WINS is not necessary. In mixed Win NT/9x, Windows 2000 environments, however, WINS will be required. When Windows 2000 is operating in this environment, it is said to be operating in mixed mode. If all systems are Windows 2000, the network is in native mode.

The most common situation requiring WINS in a Windows 2000 environment will be supporting WINS name resolution for Windows 2000 clients accessing Windows NT 4.0 workstations and servers. The recommended arrangement for this situation is to implement Windows 2000 DNS, create a WINS referral zone, and configure the DNS server to refer to the WINS database. Windows 2000 DNS server can then handle name requests from Windows 2000 clients as standard DNS requests.

In Windows 2000, to reach the WINS configuration dialog box, go to Start | Settings | Network and Dial-up Connections | Local Area Connection | Internet Protocol(TCP/IP) | Properties | Advanced | DNS. Figure 11-2 illustrates the Windows 2000 client configuration when the WINS referral zone is named nt4domain.

Since clients configured to use the WINS referral zone feature don't automatically perform dynamic registration of their NetBIOS name when they come up on the network, the naming convention and process of assigning names to the nodes must be managed manually. To implement this, the NetBIOS name must match the name entered into DNS as the host name. To do so, assign participating nodes a unique machine name, and then enter a DNS host record using the machine name exactly as entered into the TCP/IP configuration. The NetBIOS name space is flat, so "matching" a WINS referral zone is limited to a single DNS domain. This is because name resolution requests are sent to the DNS under the assumption that the request is for the DNS domain "matched" with the WINS referral zone.

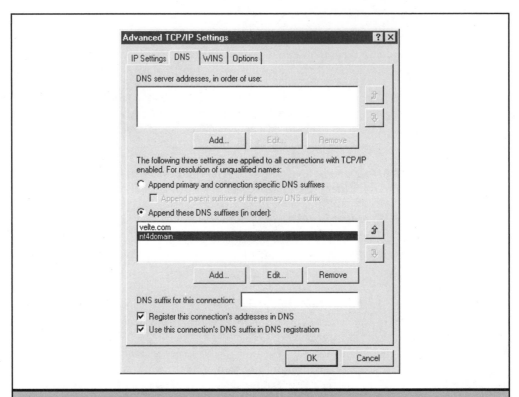

Figure 11-2.   Enabling WINS name resolution in Windows 2000

The reason for limitations has to do with the way NetBIOS name resolution works. Let's look at what happens when an application using NetBIOS attempts to locate a NetBIOS-based server. In this example, the application is looking for the server named database1. Since the TCP/IP client is configured to use DNS for Windows Resolution, the client constructs a DNS query using the NetBIOS name database1, and then adds the TCP/IP domain name before sending it to the DNS server. The query sent to the DNS server becomes a standard query, to which the DNS server can reply without knowing that the name originated from a NetBIOS-based request. The request would include the NetBIOS name database1, along with the DNS domain name domain.com as it was earlier entered into the TCP/IP client configuration. The standard DNS query sent to the DNS server would request the IP address of database1.domain.com. The DNS server would reply with an IP address, as it would for any other valid query. When the client receives the response from the DNS server, it can pass the IP address to the requesting NetBIOS-based application. The application then uses the address as though its request were processed by an LMHOSTS file, a broadcast, or a WINS server.

NOTE: Be aware that IP address assignments will have to be statically defined in DNS, and using DHCP will allow client addresses to change.

WINS is not without its limitations; but when properly implemented, it can help ease the administrative workload associated with NetBIOS name services. In the next section, we'll take a closer look at WINS.

NAMING SERVICES: WINS

Conceptually, WINS is very much like DNS. There are two sides to the service: the client and the server.

▼ The client has to register the client node with the WINS server and query the WINS server for IP-to-NetBIOS name resolution when necessary.

▲ The server has to receive and process WINS client registrations and queries. Part of providing this service also requires that the server communicate with other WINS servers on the network, to exchange the server's database of registrations using *replication*.

Name Registration, Renewal, and Release

When the WINS client's TCP/IP stack is initialized, one of its first tasks is to send a name registration request to the WINS server. The WINS server then checks its internal database to see if that name already exists. If there's no duplicate name, the client is allowed to use the requested name on the network. The WINS server also stores the requesting client's IP address and associates it with the newly assigned name. Not only is this used when other clients are requesting name-to-IP address mappings, but also to contact another client that may already own a requested name. Let's examine the registration, renewal, and release processes.

Registration

Once a client gets an IP address, requests a name registration, and is accepted and registered with the WINS server, the client will be able to successfully communicate with other machines on the network.

If, for some reason, the requested name is already being used on the network by another client, that client is asked to verify that it is still using the name. The server first sends a Wait for Acknowledgement (WACK) message to the client requesting the name. This is closely followed by a formal name query from the server to the client who originally registered the name. If the original owner responds with verification, the server informs the new client that the requested name is already registered to another IP address.

Once the check for duplicate names is completed and it is determined that the name can be registered on the network, the WINS server sends a positive name registration response to the requesting client. The process of name registration is complete.

Renewal

A WINS client may use its registered name only for a specific amount of time. This is called the *time to live* (TTL), or the *renewal interval*. The TTL prevents the database from filling up with old registration entries no longer in use. Clients can then register names that may have been in use previously. It is the WINS client's responsibility to keep track of the renewal interval and to reregister with the server when half of this interval has expired. If this doesn't happen, the registration is discarded and the name made available for future registrations.

Release

A release is processed when a WINS client gives up its WINS registration. When done as part of a normal shutdown, this is called an *explicit release*. During the shutdown process, the client sends a name release request to the WINS server. The WINS database entry for this registration is marked "released" by the server. If a workstation is improperly shutdown (due to a power failure, for instance) and the client cannot send an *explicit release*, the server will perform a *silent release*. This kind of release will occur only after the renewal interval has passed and the server has not received a request from the client to continue the name registration.

Node Types

One of the more confusing things about the WINS name resolution process is the method of a client's initial communication with the WINS server. On a NetBIOS over TCP/IP (NBT) network, WINS is not necessarily used when resolving name-to-IP address mapping, or it may not be used initially as part of name resolution. In fact, one node type, broadcast (b-node), doesn't use WINS at all. These facts are particularly important when WINS is down or not working well.

The node type in use on a workstation is often not considered, or it may be one of the last things checked. For example, a workstation configured to use b-node will check the NetBIOS name cache and do a local broadcast before giving up. Although the request may be checked against the LMHOSTS file and passed on to DNS, these steps will be performed only if the client is configured to do so. In any event, WINS is bypassed completely. Other node types will contact a WINS server to resolve name requests, but in various ways. Table 11-2 lists the node types along with a brief description of their name resolution behavior.

Node Type	Method of Name Resolution
Broadcast (b-node)	The *b-node* workstation uses local broadcasts to resolve names. Broadcasts are typically limited to LAN network segments and not routed across other portions of a network. This node doesn't attempt to contact a WINS server and has very limited functionality on any network larger than a small workgroup.
Point-to-point (p-node)	The *p-node* workstation attempts to resolve names using a point-to-point connection with a WINS server. This node doesn't attempt to broadcast, even if it cannot resolve a name using a WINS server. Therefore, if WINS servers are unavailable, p-node workstations will not be able to resolve addresses and subsequently communicate with other workstations.
Mixed (m-node)	The *m-node* workstation operates like a p-node, but includes the ability to first resolve by broadcasting (b-node). If the broadcast is unsuccessful, a point-to-point (p-node) connection with a WINS server is attempted.
Hybrid (h-node)	The *h-node* workstation uses a point-to-point connection (p-node) first and falls back to a broadcast (b-node) name resolution. This node type is recommended for most situations because it tries the WINS server(s) first but has the ability to broadcast, as well. The broadcast may allow the workstation to communicate with others workstations and servers, even if the process only resolves machines on the local network segment.

Table 11-3.   NBT Node Types

Windows NT/2000–based systems can use any of the node types, depending on how the client is configured. In both Windows 2000 and Windows NT/9*x*, WINS clients are configured as h-node by default. In Windows 2000, for the default LAN connection, you access the WINS Configuration dialog box with Start | Settings | Network and Dial-up Connections | Local Area Connection | Internet Protocol(TCP/IP) | Properties | Advanced | WINS. Figure 11-3 shows the Settings dialog box used to configure the system to use WINS.

To get information about your workstation's TCP/IP configuration, in Windows NT/2000 use **ipconfig /all** at the command line (see Figure 11-4). The node type will also be displayed. In Windows 9*x*, you can use the winipcfg.exe utility to display IP information, including the node type.

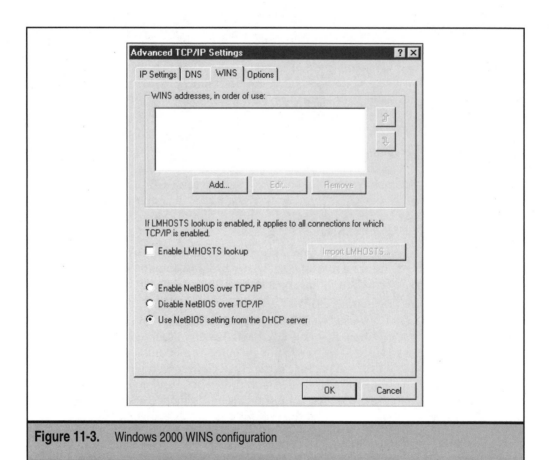

Figure 11-3. Windows 2000 WINS configuration

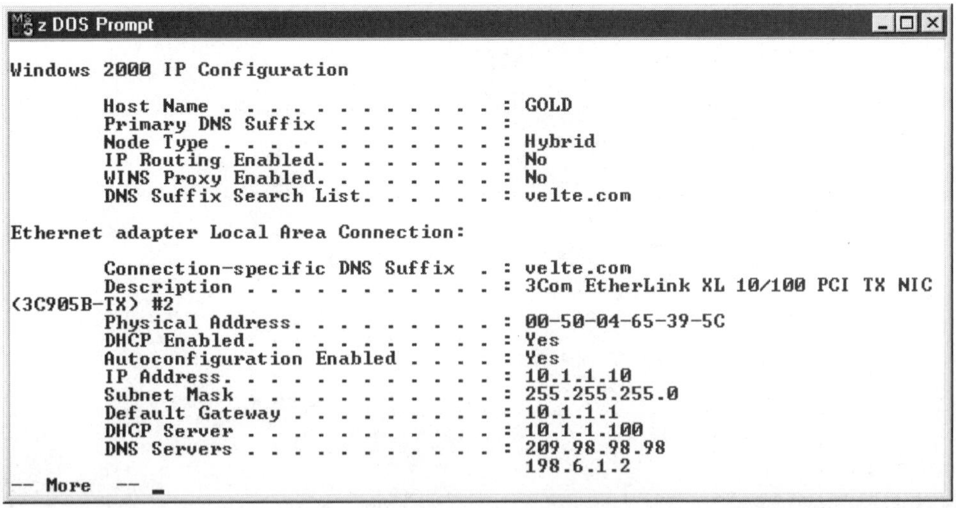

```
┌──────────────────────────────────────────────────────────────────────────┐
│ M§ z DOS Prompt                                                  _ □ ×     │
├──────────────────────────────────────────────────────────────────────────┤
│ Windows 2000 IP Configuration                                             │
│                                                                            │
│         Host Name . . . . . . . . . . . : GOLD                            │
│         Primary DNS Suffix  . . . . . . . :                               │
│         Node Type . . . . . . . . . . . : Hybrid                          │
│         IP Routing Enabled. . . . . . . . : No                            │
│         WINS Proxy Enabled. . . . . . . . : No                            │
│         DNS Suffix Search List. . . . . . : velte.com                     │
│                                                                            │
│ Ethernet adapter Local Area Connection:                                   │
│                                                                            │
│         Connection-specific DNS Suffix  . : velte.com                     │
│         Description . . . . . . . . . . . : 3Com EtherLink XL 10/100 PCI TX NIC │
│ <3C905B-TX> #2                                                             │
│         Physical Address. . . . . . . . . : 00-50-04-65-39-5C             │
│         DHCP Enabled. . . . . . . . . . . : Yes                           │
│         Autoconfiguration Enabled . . . . : Yes                           │
│         IP Address. . . . . . . . . . . . : 10.1.1.10                     │
│         Subnet Mask . . . . . . . . . . . : 255.255.255.0                 │
│         Default Gateway . . . . . . . . . : 10.1.1.1                      │
│         DHCP Server . . . . . . . . . . . : 10.1.1.100                    │
│         DNS Servers . . . . . . . . . . . : 209.98.98.98                  │
│                                             198.6.1.2                     │
│ -- More  --  _                                                            │
└──────────────────────────────────────────────────────────────────────────┘
```

Figure 11-4. IPCONFIG command-line utility

Name-to-Address Queries

A query is generated by the client in an effort to resolve a name to an address. On a broadcast network, this is done by simply broadcasting a name query out to all reachable nodes. Each node has to process the query to decide whether or not it needs to respond. Ultimately, the node with the name queried will respond with its address, and a conversation between the two machines can begin. With WINS, a name query is sent by the client directly to the WINS server. If the primary server is offline, the client will send the query to the secondary.

Even with a primary and secondary WINS server available, several other methods of name resolution are available. Figure 11-5 illustrates some of the other alternatives, including local cache, LMHOSTS file lookup, and DNS. Being prepared to use these options isn't a bad idea in view of the importance of name resolution services in network communication; and options are definitely good to have if you rely heavily on WINS.

Following is an example of the steps a workstation might take to resolve a name-to-IP address mapping:

1. The workstation begins the process by checking its local NetBIOS name cache. This offers the fastest name resolution, but only if the name has already been recently resolved. The name remains in memory (in the cache) so that the client can quickly look up recently resolved names from a list.

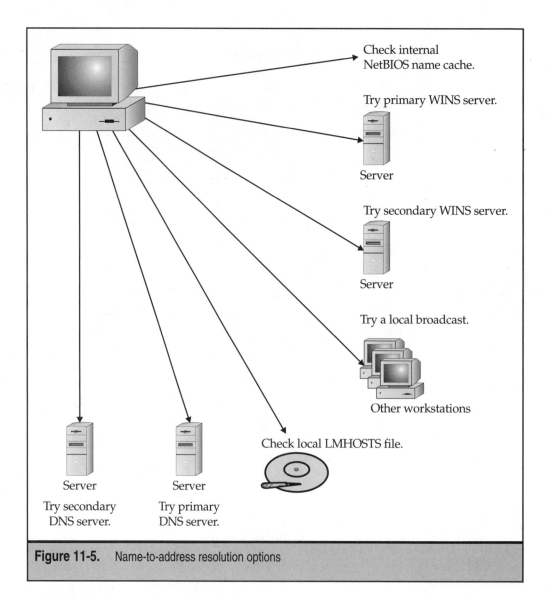

Figure 11-5. Name-to-address resolution options

2. If the name isn't found in the local cache, the client queries the primary WINS server.

3. If the primary WINS server cannot be reached or the client receives a negative name query response from the server, the client tries the secondary WINS server.

4. If the secondary WINS server cannot be reached or the client receives a negative name query response from the server, the client tries a broadcast.

5. If a broadcast yields no results, the client can, if configured to do so, check the LMHOSTS file found locally on the client's machine.

6. After all of the preceding options have been tried without successful resolution, the client may try to resolve the name using DNS. The client may perform the query on several DNS servers before failing the query completely.

These rather exhaustive measures may seem like overkill, but the process as a whole dramatically increases the odds that the query will be successful. And when it is, the client can communicate with other machines on the network, which is why the network is there in the first place.

Replication

WINS uses a *database replication process* to populate every WINS server with current name/address mappings. To keep things running smoothly, the information must be replicated in an organized manner. This starts with identifying servers to each other as *replication partners.*

The communication relationship between the partner servers is classified as push, pull, or both push and pull. A *pull* partner is one that receives updates from the other server by periodically requesting that server's WINS database entries. A *push* partner will send the other server update notifications as registrations occur and as the WINS database changes. The primary and secondary WINS servers, both of which should always exist for fault tolerance, must be push and pull partners with each other, as illustrated in Figure 11-6.

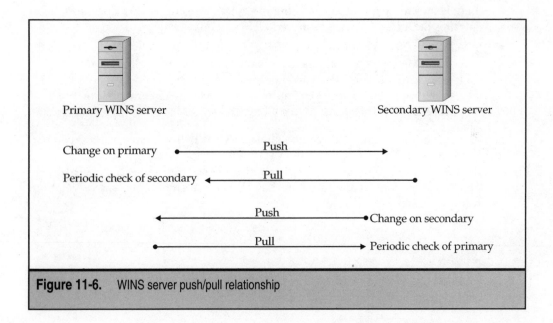

Primary WINS server   Secondary WINS server

Change on primary •————— Push —————▶

Periodic check of secondary ◀————— Pull —————•

◀————— Push —————• Change on secondary

•————— Pull —————▶ Periodic check of primary

Figure 11-6. WINS server push/pull relationship

In most cases, all WINS servers on the network will be push/pull partners so that the name space is kept as consistent as possible. Great care should be taken in designing and configuring a WINS server environment. One small oversight or error in the configuring can cause database inconsistencies and other problems that are difficult to identify and resolve.

INTEGRATING DNS WITH WINS/DHCP

The DNS servers for Windows NT and Windows 2000 can both be configured to use the WINS database to resolve NetBIOS name queries. This is done when DNS cannot resolve the name from its own host database. One of the primary reasons for this arrangement is to enable dynamic registration of DHCP clients, which was incorporated into WINS, for DNS services.

NOTE: In an environment where WINS is not required, as in a Windows 2000–only network, DHCP registration can now be accomplished by implementing the Dynamic DNS (DDNS) functionality integrated into Microsoft's Windows 2000 DNS server.

DHCP clients, which could automatically be registered in WINS, can now be resolved by using the "bridge" between DNS and WINS. Before this can happen, however, you must configure the DNS server to use WINS resolution.

▼ In Windows NT, this is accomplished via the DNS Manager; you right-click the zone you want to configure, and then choose Properties | WINS Lookup. From there it's a simple matter of checking the WINS Resolution check box and entering the address of one or more WINS servers.

▲ In Windows 2000, you click Start | Programs | Administrative Tools | DNS to launch the Microsoft Management Console (MMC) snap-in. In the MMC tool, click DNS | Hostname | Forward Lookup Zones | Zone and select the WINS tab of the Properties dialog box. Figure 11-7 shows the resulting dialog box. (For more on the MMC snap-in, see Chapter 9.)

Remember that there should always be at least two WINS servers for any given network that requires NBT name services. In addition, ensure that WINS is synchronizing the WINS database using push/pull replication between the replication partners. In more complex installations, make sure that the architecture and the replication relationship between servers is done carefully.

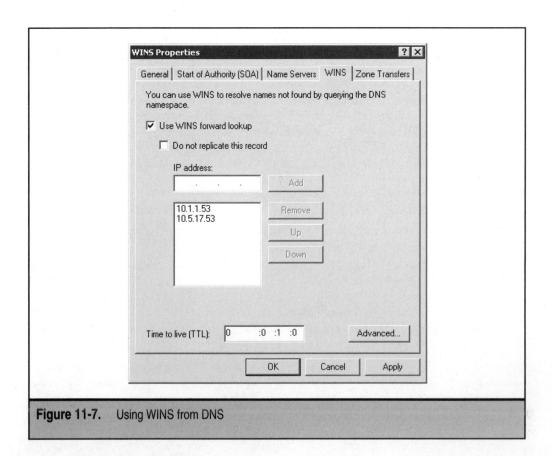

Figure 11-7.   Using WINS from DNS

WINS ARCHITECTURE

WINS will be a part of most Windows-based networks for some time to come and must be implemented properly. The first recommendation is to use only the default configuration parameters unless you have clearly identified reasons to change them.

One of the few parameters that should be "tuned" is the interval for replication between WINS servers. The interval should be based on where the WINS servers reside within your network. Generally, a replication interval of 15 minutes is suitable for WINS servers on the same LAN segment or connected by a 10/100 Mbps network. For higher-speed WAN connections, every 30 to 60 minutes is typical. For slower WAN connections, or those where bandwidth is scarce, you may want to use an interval of 60 to 90 minutes, or perhaps even 2 hours or more. Bandwidth constraints aside, you should also consider how often registrations occur, and how often you want updates to be available to nodes accessing this WINS database. If you need to ensure that WINS is synchronized across the network quickly, a shorter interval should be used.

Let's take a look at two common WINS deployment scenarios: WINS replication over a LAN, and WINS replication over a WAN. Since there are few reasons to alter most of the default settings, we'll leave the Renewal Interval, Extinction Interval, Extinction Timeout, and Verify Intervals parameters at their defaults. The only parameters affected to accomplish LAN/WAN tuning are Push Update Count and Pull Replication Interval.

LAN Implementation

Unless your network is very small, you should always set up two WINS servers. In addition, consider the physical and logical location of each server. At least one should be operational even if the other has been hit by a power failure or is attached to a network segment that isn't operating. Try to place the two servers in geographically separate areas, such as two different floors of a building. Figure 11-8 illustrates a LAN-based architecture. Since the servers are LAN connected, we'll assume there is plenty of available bandwidth.

In this example, the two WINS servers are configured as push/pull replication partners. The high-bandwidth network connection allows replication to occur often, so we'll configure the servers to replicate every 5 to 15 minutes and after every 5 to 15 record

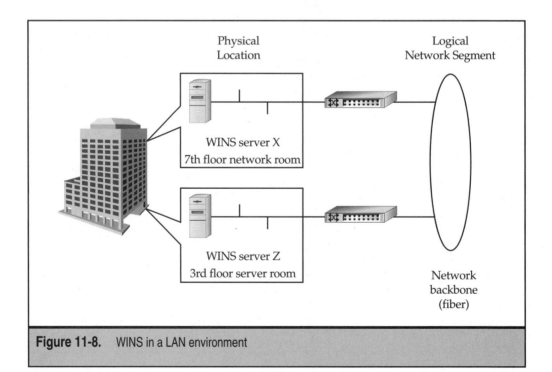

Figure 11-8.   WINS in a LAN environment

changes. This configuration ensures that the entire WINS environment is synchronized within 15 minutes or when 15 records have changed.

Wide Area Network Implementation

When replicating over a WAN, limited bandwidth and network reliability are at issue—more specifically, it's the balance between keeping the WINS environment synchronized and keeping the network utilization as low as possible.

A well-managed (cost vs. bandwidth vs. reliability) WAN environment, like the example in Figure 11-9, usually has just slightly more bandwidth available than is needed most of the time. Network administrators try to ensure that the delays associated with occasional overutilization are minimal. One way to keep unnecessary traffic off the wire is to keep your WINS environment from replicating frequently over the WAN. It becomes a balancing act of stretching out replication intervals as far as possible without influencing the working of the WINS environment.

In Figure 11-9, there are 500 users on both sides of the WAN. On each side, one WINS server is deployed. To keep most of the WINS server–querying traffic off the WAN, the clients on network X are configured to use WINS server X as their primary WINS server; clients on network Z are configured to use WINS server Z as their primary WINS server. For fault tolerance, the clients on network X are configured to use the WINS server on network Z as their secondary WINS server; the inverse is true for the clients on network Z. The same setup works nicely for DNS services as well.

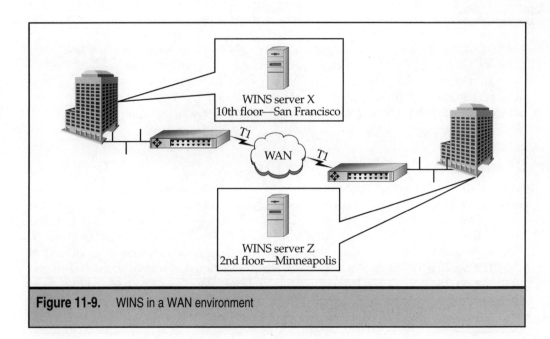

Figure 11-9.   WINS in a WAN environment

The goal is to balance the use of the WAN with the needs of the WINS server replication. The key to this balance is the frequency of name registrations. If network registrations are rare—that is, few network workstation and server moves/additions/removals occur, then replication doesn't need to happen as often. In the example, we'll assume this to be the case and that we want replication to occur every 60 minutes. So, we'll configure WINS X and WINS Z as replication partners with a replication interval of 60 minutes and 10 changes. The result is that the servers will synchronize every hour or every 10 changes, whichever comes first. Therefore, the maximum time needed for a record to be recorded on the other WINS server is 60 minutes.

DHCP PRIMER

The Dynamic Host Configuration Protocol (DHCP) is used to automate the assignment of TCP/IP addressing over the network. This protocol can also provide additional configuration parameters to workstations, printers, and other IP devices. This is initially done when the devices are booted up or initialized on the network.

The device sends out a DHCP request on the network, which is picked up by a DHCP server. The server contains one or several ranges of IP addresses grouped into DHCP *scopes*. A scope contains anything from a single TCP/IP address to all of the addresses in a subnet. When clients are configured to use DHCP, they request IP information from the DHCP as part of their boot process. The server replies with an IP address lease; the client has the right to use the address for the time specified in the lease, which can be a few minutes, hours, days or permanently. Halfway through the lease duration, the client will communicate with the server to renegotiate the lease renewal.

DHCP usually provides more than just the IP number, subnet mask, and default gateway. It can also provide WINS server addresses, DNS servers, and dozens of other variables. When using DHCP, it is advantageous to have clients get all or most of their IP configuration parameters from the server. When a DHCP environment is up and running, it requires very little, if any, manual configuration. Also, to create a high-performance and fault-tolerant environment, multiple servers should be available to respond to DHCP requests.

DHCP and BOOTP

DHCP is designed so that is doesn't interfere with current implementations of network protocols and the network devices that do not use DHCP; it even helps integrate support for those devices. Examples of these devices are servers and workstations whose IP addresses are statically configured by design, or that do not support DHCP. DHCP can support static address assignments and deliver them easily via the Bootstrap Protocol (BOOTP), because DHCP is based on BOOTP but adds functionality on top of it. The major difference between BOOTP and DHCP is that DHCP can lease an address to a client for a specified time period, whereas BOOTP cannot. An IP address delivered via BOOTP remains with the BOOTP client address indefinitely or until it is manually reassigned.

Another difference from BOOTP is that DHCP can provide additional IP configuration information such as DNS and WINS servers, and NBT parameters.

NOTE: DHCP uses UDP port 67 when the client is sending to the server, and UDP port 68 when the server is sending to the client.

INTEGRATING NAME SERVICES

Naming services are critical to achieving a reliable and usable network environment. Designing and implementing DNS, WINS, and DHCP services on any network requires careful planning. The first step in this process, when building a new network or enhancing an existing one, is to start with a detailed review and documentation of the existing network. Look for the following facts and statistics:

▼ Network node count
■ Remote location topology
■ Location of TCP/IP-based servers
■ Existing WAN capacity and reliability
■ Topology of network backbones
■ Internet connections (addressing, firewalls, points of entry, capacity, etc.)
■ Firewalls used to secure the network (NAT, PAT, etc.)
■ Geographical organization considerations
■ Organizational structure considerations (business units, multinational, etc.)
■ Private external connections to other organizations (capacity, topology, configuration)
■ Remote access points of entry
■ Existing NT domain architecture
■ Existing WINS architecture
■ Staffing to provide ongoing network support
■ TCP/IP addressing schemes in use and required
■ DNS servers outside the organization (usually at the ISP)
■ Network diagrams
▲ Workstation/printer/device configurations (assess ability to support naming services)

When you have all this information before designing a naming services solution, you'll be able to tackle many of the design issues quickly and efficiently.

Windows 2000 DNS

Windows 2000 was designed from the ground up to be fully integrated with Windows 2000 Active Directory service. The new AD service uses the Windows 2000 multimaster replication engine. Replication of DNS records from one DNS server to another (zone transfers) happens differently, and the concept of primary and secondary DNS servers changes. In a traditional DNS configuration, replication is based on a single master updating secondary DNS servers. In Active Directory replication, the DNS environment can be multimaster. Each DNS server in the network contains a complete copy of the DNS records. A change made on one DNS server will be quickly replicated to all other servers in the environment, thereby increasing the overall fault tolerance of the environment and the availability of current DNS record information.

Windows 2000 DNS Design

The usual basic design principles apply when designing a Windows 2000 DNS strategy for your network. You should have at least two DNS servers, located in physically and logically diverse locations on your network, and the DNS servers should be located in a secure environment with reliable power and network connectivity. DNS server distribution has one cardinal rule: Never put two mission-critical servers in the same location, using the same network segment, and plugged into the same electrical outlet. A Windows 2000–based network relies heavily on the availability of DNS, so much so that failure is not an option. If DNS doesn't work on a Windows 2000 network, you might as well go home and mow the lawn.

Figure 11-10 illustrates the deployment of primary and multiple secondary servers in common DNS scenarios found in NT-based networks. In Windows 2000, every server is a primary and a secondary, so the same topology can be used effectively. Note that the main servers are in well-protected data center environments.

Using DNS Caching Servers

In addition to distributing DNS servers, a caching server is deployed at the large site containing local TCP/IP-based servers.

NOTE: Windows 2000 also introduces the client-side caching resolver for DNS name resolution. This service can run on a Windows 2000 client and provide caching for the workstation. It won't cache all the lookups done by other workstations, as is done by a caching DNS server, but the caching resolver can improve lookup speed and keep some of the names-lookup traffic off the network.

You might also include a caching DNS server for resolving previously resolved name-to-address requests locally from the cache, rather than have all queries being transmitted over the WAN (like the other remote location in the example). Caching name servers work well in larger networks that have WANs. Since a caching server looks like a DNS server to the client, nothing special needs to be done when implementing them. All a caching DNS server does is receive a query from a client, check its cache for the informa-

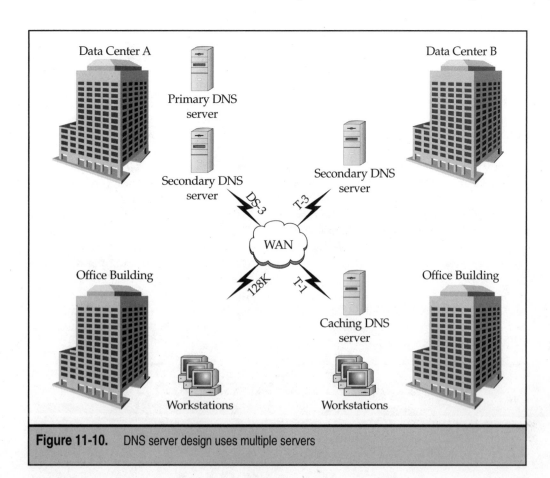

Figure 11-10.   DNS server design uses multiple servers

tion, and reply to the client. If it doesn't find what the client is looking for in the cache, the caching server will query a DNS server on the client's behalf. Once it receives the information from the DNS server, the caching server stores the information in its cache for later use and returns the information to the client.

The big deal with caching servers is that they can help reduce WAN traffic by keeping redundant queries on the local network instead of on the WAN. A caching server also provides a measure of protection against a WAN outage, because it will likely have cached name-to-IP address records for most if not all the hosts local to a site. This allows clients to resolve local host addresses even though the WAN is down.

Dynamic DNS (DDNS)

Dynamic DNS is one of the most exciting and long-awaited functions to be incorporated into the DNS standards. DDNS enables a client machine using DHCP to have its host name automatically registered in DNS, much like DHCP's ability to update WINS. This allows DNS to populate its host tables not only with static host entries, but also with host entries or workstations that have their IP addresses dynamically assigned at bootup using DHCP.

Windows 2000 DHCP server can be configured to update the DNS server host table when a client boots up as a DHCP client. In essence, this is why WINS can go away once a network has completely migrated to Windows 2000. In Windows NT environments, dynamically assigned workstations are disconnected from their common names. At the time a workstation gets an IP address from DHCP, DHCP can only tell WINS the workstation's name, so all systems much check with WINS for name-to-IP mappings. All systems must also be able to check with DNS for non-Windows-based systems or systems on the Internet. Now that the DHCP can register the names with DNS, a Windows 2000 user need only check with DNS for name-to-IP mappings. With the disappearance of WINS, you'll also see the elimination of NetBEUI-constrained names for workstations. Now, computer names will look much more like those used by DNS. So instead of SERVER1 in the FINANCE domain, a system might be known as server1.finance.company.com.

Enabling DDNS is done from the DHCP management interface. Figure 11-11 shows this arrangement. Click Start | Programs | Administrative Tools | DHCP to launch the DHCP MMC snap-in tool. Then click DHCP | Hostname | Properties, and select the WINS tab of the Properties dialog box.

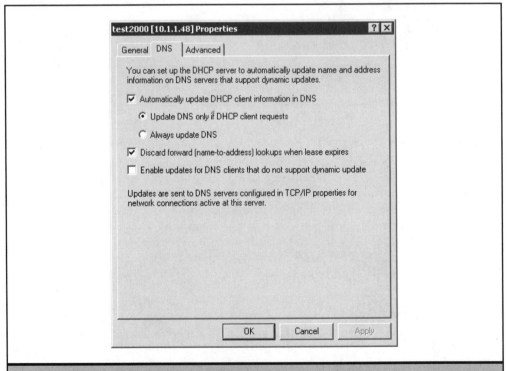

Figure 11-11. DDNS configuration in Windows 2000

NETWORK REGISTRAR

Cisco Network Registrar (CNR) provides an alternative to the Microsoft DNS and DHCP services. Like these services, CNR is a standards-based implementation that incorporates DNS and DHCP into an integrated package. Network Registrar incorporates a standards-compliant DNS and DHCP server. The DNS server supports incremental zone transfers and dynamic updates, and is compatible with other DNS servers. The DHCP server supports DHCP Safe Failover (for increased fault-tolerance), DDNS dynamic updates, and directory services integration via LDAPv3.

In Windows NT and Windows 2000, CNR's DNS and DHCP services are managed using the CNR Server Manager. After product installation, open the Registrar by selecting Start | Programs | Network Registrar | Network Registrar. Figure 11-12 shows the CNR Server Manager interface.

Upon examining the interface, which looks a lot like the MMC-based management tool, we can assume that Cisco will likely be offering an MMC-compatible snap-in interface sometime soon. In the meantime, the CNR 3.0 interface is similar to the Microsoft DNS/DCHP/WINS management interfaces. The interface is quite simple and easy to understand, and the configuration parameters are organized well within the two primary functions (DHCP and DNS).

Using CNR with DDNS

The CNR DNS server provides support for dynamic DNS whether it is used with CNR DHCP or another DHCP server supporting DDNS. The CNR DNS is configured from the

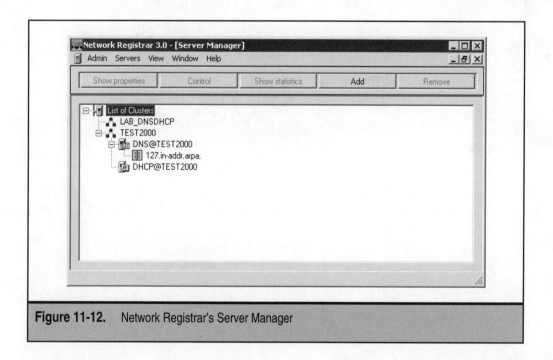

Figure 11-12.   Network Registrar's Server Manager

CNR Server Manager interface where the DNS server properties are accessed by selecting Server | DNS@hostname | Properties. The resulting tabbed dialog box, shown in Figure 11-13, gives you access to all the DNS configuration parameters.

The options under the General tab allow you to change the name of the server, and to show the Cluster Name and CNR DNS server version. The Forwarders tab contains settings for adding DNS server addresses to which you want forwarded unresolvable DNS requests (for instance, if they're out of domain). The Root Name Servers tab contains a populated list of DNS Root Name Servers that are used when looking up Internet addresses; you can add servers to this list. The Exception tab allows you to enter resolution exception domains. In the Options tab (Figure 11-13) are check boxes to enable/disable several basic server functions, including round-robin DNS and incremental transfer. The last tab, Advanced, helps you manipulate parameters such as DNS cache TTL and size, as well as letting you change the TCP/UDP ports used by the server. Despite these available options, keep in mind that these are all parameters that you shouldn't change without very good reason.

NCR's DHCP Server

Network Registrar's DHCP server supports full integration with DDNS and is just as simple to administer. The DHCP configuration parameters are accessed via the CNR

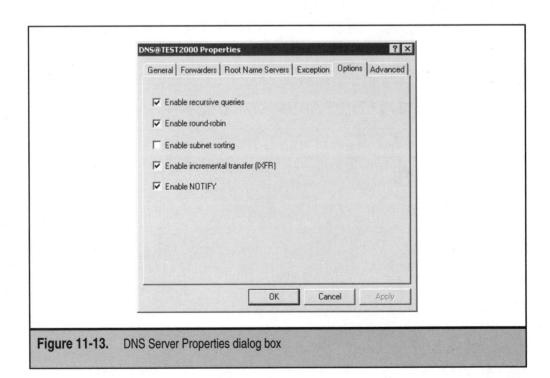

Figure 11-13.   DNS Server Properties dialog box

Server Manager interface. Select Server | DHCP@hostname | Properties to see the dialog box shown in Figure 11-14.

The tabs in this dialog include General, where you can change the server name; this dialog also displays the cluster name and CNR version. Additionally, the DHCP server can be configured to discover the LAN interfaces in the server machine, or they may be explicitly defined under the General tab. Under Policies, you can customize the information being passed back to the client during DHCP registration. These options include predefining the name servers, time servers, DHCP lease time, router default gateway, and a host of other options to fit your specific requirements.

The Advanced DNS tab includes parameters that allow you to tune how the DHCP server is communicating with the DNS server. The Scope Selection tab allows you to enable client class processing and to define and enable scope selection tags—very handy indeed. The Client Class tab allows you to create defined classes of clients grouped by host name, domain name, and policy name. The Clients tab lists the active clients, their MAC addresses and client class, and other information. The final tab, Advanced (Figure 11-14), helps you make changes that alter the underlying operations of the DHCP (in the rare event that they need to be changed).

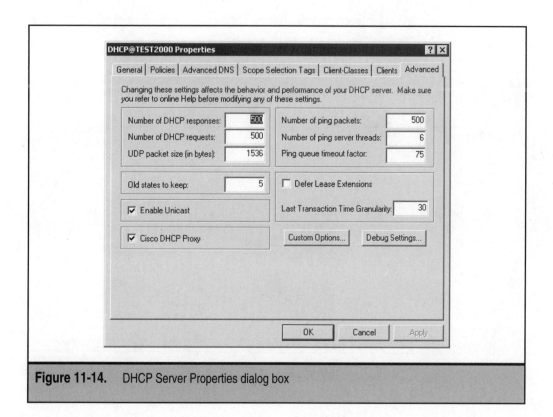

Figure 11-14. DHCP Server Properties dialog box

NOTE: You should decide on whether or not you will be using Cisco's or Microsoft's DNS and DHCP servers in your environment, and plan to stand by your choice. Although each vendor's DNS and DHCP servers are highly interoperable, attempting to incorporate both into a single network environment would be challenging and would unnecessarily complicate administration.

SUMMARY

In this chapter, we reviewed the basic components of key naming services, including DNS and DDNS, NetBIOS NBT name services, WINS, and DHCP. We also took a look at how each of these services works independently, as well as with each other, to provide a "seamless" set of naming services. We covered workgroup name resolution and how it differs from large-scale name services. We learned how to forward broadcasts on a Cisco network so that workgroups can see each other in the absence of WINS or DDNS. In addition, we studied the methods of each service for delivering information to the client, and how the services communicate. We also discussed several basic design options for the naming services and how the newest Windows 2000 and Cisco CNR DNS/DHCP tools are configured in their brand-new interfaces.

Next up is the last chapter in this section. Chapter 12 deals with designing Windows 2000 domains to fit your business needs. It also focuses on special issues in migrating from NT 4.0 to Windows 2000.

CHAPTER 12

Designing Windows 2000 Domains

One thing you can always count on in networking is that change is rapid and inevitable. Sometimes the change is small, such as moving from Windows 95 to Windows 98. But sometimes a change has impact on the entire network, all its users, and the organization as a whole. Windows 2000 will bring about this kind of wide-sweeping change for every organization that adopts its technologies.

All network engineers who design, implement, or support the network will want to be aware of the concepts and strategies outlined in this chapter. We will start by describing some of the high-level information you will need to make your Cisco/Windows network run efficiently and meet your business objectives. Then, we'll go through the technical steps required to build new networks or migrate existing networks to the new Windows 2000 domain model. These sections will touch on subjects such as client migration and namespace design, providing real-world examples of network designs appropriate for small-, medium-, and enterprise-sized organizations. Finally, we'll end by showing you some tools that you can use to avoid the "migration blues."

GATHERING INFORMATION

Before even a single cable is plugged in or a network diagram is created, a network designer must gather copious amounts of information that is, on the surface, somewhat nontechnical. For this reason, the information-gathering process is often difficult for technical people and is sometimes, unfortunately, skipped altogether. Omitting this part of the design process and jumping right into technical design issues will almost certainly result in a poor network design that fails to meet the goals of the business, goes over budget, and is quickly outdated.

Gathering information for network design involves three key stages: (1) determining business requirements; (2) identifying constraints; and (3) getting a grasp on the current network infrastructure by characterizing the network.

Determining Business Requirements

There is an axiom in business that permeates throughout an organization, even to its networking: All for-profit businesses are in business to make money. Such businesses use people to support this profit-making effort. To help their employees succeed, businesses provide technological tools such as applications, and these applications depend on the network to function properly. This simplistic view of a business is often overlooked by network designers, who may focus only on traffic and bits over the wires. At the early stages of network design, however, a successful network designer steps back and views the network as a tool to support the people who use the applications.

You'll probably learn how the business is served by the network through meeting with Management. At first, they will probably express their networking needs in terms of business needs. Because they don't understand how technology can fulfill these needs, they've called on an expert in the subject—that's you. You'll have to determine what technological solutions will allow the business to meet its needs. Some typical business objectives are

▼   Increase productivity of the workforce

■   Increase security of information

■   Provide better customer service

■   Decrease spending

▲   Reduce product-development time

All these business requirements are about bettering the bottom line, and many of them focus on doing this by improving conditions for employees. So, the first question you might ask is "How can a network improve the conditions for employees so that they will make the company more money?" The answer may be difficult to find, but it is paramount to the task of linking the network infrastructure to the needs of the business.

Let's use the first goal as an example. One way to begin is to ask Management for ideas about how they want to increase productivity of the sales staff. They might report that sales managers "don't have access to the right information half the time, and when they do get access, it takes a full minute to call it up." This sort of answer will at least get you started.

Eventually, you'll talk to the users of the network, trying to assess how you can make them more productive. To continue with our example, maybe you notice while interviewing several sales managers that they are frequently connecting to domains on the other side of the network to get information, and that sometimes they have trouble with permissions. Also, they complain about slow response times, especially around 9:00 A.M. This information is greatly useful because it puts you, the network designer, into the realm of people you're trying to help. In this case, you can now start thinking in terms familiar to you: domain permissions and bandwidth issues.

The next stage of information gathering will help you frame the solutions to issues you've identified.

Identifying Constraints

In the first stage of information gathering, you are charged with achieving a business goal. Now it's time to determine the constraints under which you must perform this feat. These constraints can come in many forms, including

▼   Time

■   Budget

■   Personal resources

■   Existing policies

▲   Technical feasibility

In addition to these more conspicuous constraints, you'll encounter many that are unspoken and potentially much more of an obstacle. These include the political boundaries, relationships, and history within an organization. For an outside consultant, these power struggles and turf wars can be very frustrating because you don't have any prior knowledge of the internal issues. You join the team, see what the business has to do, and are ready to get to work. Soon, however, you may find that your project has no chance of success without the buy-in from a certain VP. The best defense to the typical corporate political tangle is plenty of communication with everyone involved. Make sure each decision-maker clearly understands what you are going to do, and that you understand what it is they want in return. If there is a conflict or a lack of support on some level, get this out in the open early on.

Another constraint might come in the form of a service level agreement (SLA) or Quality of Service (QoS) requirement that is spelled out for you from the beginning. It might describe a condition that sales staff should wait no more than one second for a requested record to display on their monitor. Or that voiceover IP traffic shall have the same sound quality as the current phone systems. If such requirements are defined up front, you will certainly want to pay attention to them from the start.

Characterizing Existing Networks

At this point, you might feel that you have a pretty good understanding of what it is you are trying to accomplish for the organization. You feel that you have the right people behind you and have clearly defined what impact you will have on the business and the people who use the network. You might even have some ideas floating around in your head about how you're going to successfully design the network. But you can't know where you are going until you know where you are. You need to assess the existing network.

Determining the network infrastructure can be difficult because you have to rely on the organization for elements such as network diagrams, application profiles, and traffic patterns. Often, organizations have relatively little idea of how their network is running, so you may have to determine much of this information yourself. You can use network analyzers, probes, and network management tools as described in Chapters 8 and 10. Some items you will surely want to include in your analysis are

▼ Network topology

■ Windows design

■ Software versions of Cisco IOS

■ Network delay

■ Application response time

■ Security policies

■ Network traffic by protocol and application

- Current naming scheme
- Network addressing scheme (TCP/IP or IPX, for example)
- Inventory of hardware and operating systems in use
▲ Inventory of current and future software applications

Gathering and understanding this information will greatly increase your knowledge of the existing infrastructure and increase the likelihood that you will succeed with the current project.

BUILDING DOMAINS FROM THE GROUND UP

As you have just read, building a successful Cisco/Microsoft internetwork starts with a solid description of what the business requirements are, and the budgetary and physical constraints you must contend with. Once this is well understood, you can start planning the domain you will build.

You are limited to a specific set of elements when designing your Windows domain. Consider these the building blocks from which all domains will be constructed. There will certainly be unique properties for every internetwork, but all Windows 2000 networks will contain some of these fundamental pieces.

▼ **Domain controller**   A domain controller (DC) is at the head of any domain; it contains a copy of the Active Directory and allows users to use resources. The DC should always have at least one other peer DC to share the job of resource authentication.

- **Organizational unit**   Organizational units (OUs) are used to divide domains into security partitions. An administrator can create an OU and assign certain rights to users within the OU. This corrects the Windows 4.0 problem that users either have full control over a domain (domain administrators) or almost no control (domain users).

- **Active Directory**   The Active Directory (AD) is stored in the DCs and contains information about all objects within the domain. An *object* might be a printer, a user, or even a program. Details of any object are called *attributes*.

- **Schema**   The schema is a description of the objects and organization within the domain tree (defined in this list). The schema is not the data within an object (such as a user's name within the user object), but rather the structure of the objects as a group. For example, in your domain, you might add a user attribute called MobilePhoneNumber even though this is not a common attribute of the user object.

- **Site**   A site in Windows 2000 terms means a collection of devices that are connected via a high-speed connection (usually LAN speeds of 10 Mbps or higher).

■ **Global catalog** A Windows 2000 Server can be set up to host a global catalog (GC). This machine contains all of the objects of the Active Directory contained within the domain, but not all of the attributes. For example, all usernames are contained within a GC; but some attributes, such as home phone numbers, might be left out of the GC. This enables most queries to return results without having to copy the entire AD to all DCs within a domain tree.

■ **Trees** A *tree* in Windows 2000 parlance is a collection of domains that are structured hierarchically. That is, the root domain might be called company.com and have two children domains called finance.company.com and engineering.company.com. They share the same name structure, the same schema, and the same global catalog for the AD.

▲ **Forest** A *forest* is a collection of trees that have been joined via a trust relationship. They do not share the same naming hierarchy, but they do share the same global catalog and schema.

Planning a Migration to Windows 2000

The key to a successful migration to Windows 2000 lies in the preparedness of the network and the people that run it. That's why you should begin training now for the big event. An organization must have the support of all key groups that are part of the network management and design teams. These include desktop support, security policymakers, WAN groups, domain administrators, and server administrators. Since the organization of your future Windows 2000 network can be strongly influenced by the structure of the company, it's also useful to solicit input from Management. Getting all these people together and getting them to agree on a migration plan will take ample time, and that's why you start early.

One of the first decisions required is how to organize the new enterprise NT network. There are as many design possibilities as there are organizations. To begin thinking of your network as a Windows 2000 enterprise, you must be familiar with your current network domain structure, and the structure of the business that uses the network. You'll need to know the direction you want to take for the information infrastructure, as well. It's best to be intimately aware of how the business is organized—geographically, politically, and logically.

If your organization is very large and dispersed across the world, it might be prudent to design your enterprise based on geographical locations. Your root domain would be named something like company.com. The first-tier domains would be continent names (europe.company.com). Then you could break down the second-tier domains for each country or state. Finally, you'd have domains for departments, such as finance.ma.us.noamerica.company.com. If necessary, you could even subdivide this domain with OUs.

Beware, though—this model may lead to too many domains. For instance, you may have a lot of sites but not enough people at each site to warrant a domain. Instead, you can create domains based on business units or political boundaries. In this arrangement, your root domain could be company.com. A second-tier domain could be marketing.company.com, with child domains stemming from that domain, such as ma.marketing.company.com to indicate a domain that contains all of the marketing in Massachusetts. You'll need to do some vigorous pre-migration analysis before making decisions about domain arrangements. Table 12-1 offers a basic strategy for migrating from current NT 4.0 domain models to Windows 2000 models.

A major consideration in your design will be the amount of traffic traversing the WAN links as a result of the network design. For example, DCs update each other frequently, so placing a DC at each site may generate more WAN traffic than the users create in authenticating to a remote DC. Also, users will need access to the AD when searching for objects (such as a user's phone number). Instead of having all users cross the WAN to search a DC for objects, you can set up a Windows 2000 Server as a global catalog (GC)

NT 4.0 Domain Model	Windows 2000 Domain Strategy
Single domain	Use a single domain with multiple DCs for redundancy. Add OUs to parcel out administrative rights.
Complete trust	Because this model is totally decentralized, you create a separate Windows 2000 domain for each current NT 4.0 domain. Connect the domains to a tree or forest, depending on the namespace and type of trust relationships you want among the domains.
Master domain	Either create a single domain and use OUs for each of the previous domains, or create a tree using the parent and child domains.
Multiple master domain	If there must be equal control over all domains, create separate domains and connect them into a forest using explicit trust mechanisms. If there will be a single controlling group, make a tree using a parent domain and child domains. Divide the domains up using OUs for more granular administrative control.

Table 12-1.   Windows 2000 Conversion Strategies for NT 4.0 Domain Models

with partial records of the entire AD. Local queries first check with the GC before going across the WAN. If the GC doesn't contain the information the local user is requesting, the GC can point to the source across the WAN. Obviously, the GC must receive periodic updates from the DC, so the WAN traffic generated from this procedure may outweigh the benefit of having the local GC.

Namespace Design

Another primary consideration as you're designing your domain model is the naming scheme you will use. Getting this right from the start is crucial. Going back later and changing the naming convention can be costly and confusing for users. In addition, you will see that using a well-devised plan can actually increase network efficiency, and not just make things easier for managers and users.

Windows 2000 Domain Naming

Naming Windows domains and trees should be one of the first considerations in your design plans. Naming follows a strict hierarchical fashion. The name of the root domain is contained within all other domains within that tree. Figure 12-1 illustrates a Windows 2000 tree containing seven domains.

The root domain is called root.com and is located at the top of the graph. It is often wise to name child domains based on geographical location unless, of course, the domains are located in the same place. In that case, it might make more sense to name the domains after departments or other boundaries within your organization.

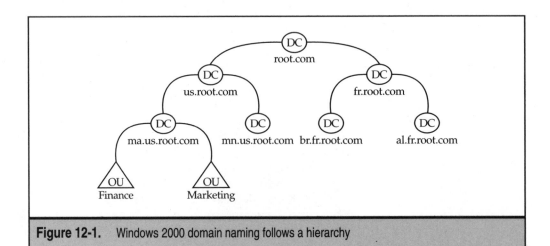

Figure 12-1. Windows 2000 domain naming follows a hierarchy

The child domains also contain the root domain and, in this example, are called us.root.com and fr.root.com. Second-level child domains are still named according to geographical location and contain the full domain name of their parent. Consider the example, ma.us.root.com. The name of the tree is the name of the root domain; so, in this example it would be root.com. You can see that the name of the domain is the DNS name of the tree, and all the child domains are considered to be using a contiguous namespace with the root domain.

Actual systems within a domain are just the name of the system concatenated with the domain name. For example, a server in the root domain might be called server1.root. com, and a server in a child domain might be xserver.mn.us.root.com. Users, on the other hand, are defined by username and the name of the tree. Thus, Joe User might be known as juser@root.com.

Within any given domain, you'll probably find it useful to name the OUs after functional groups of users rather than geographical locations. That is because OUs define administrative and user rights. However, you might want to stick to the convention you have been using, so that if you need to promote an OU to a domain controller, you won't be introducing an unfamiliar or incompatible domain name.

Following are some simple domain-naming guidelines:

▼   To maintain compatibility with DNS systems, don't use any characters other than letters, numbers, and the dash.

■   Follow the ISO 3166 convention for naming countries.

■   Use the two-letter postal codes for naming U.S. states.

▲   Keep the names short but descriptive.

Naming Cisco Devices

If you step one more layer into the design of a Windows/Cisco IP network, you'll be faced with the task of developing a naming convention for Cisco network devices and, ultimately, for providing IP addresses for every device in an IP network.

Nearly all Cisco devices can be managed by connecting to the device with a Telnet or HTTP session. Each device will have at least one IP address and one host name. Connecting to these devices thus involves entering its host name followed by the domain name, or typing in the IP address directly. Since people are better at remembering names than numbers, most of us use the device's name once the network grows beyond a few devices.

Naming Cisco devices should follow some orderly scheme but should not be easily guessed. You don't want a hacker guessing the names of some of the most crucial pieces of your network. So instead of using something like "wanrouter," which is easy to guess and not terribly descriptive, you might name your devices based on location. Many companies name their devices based on the closest airport code. For example, a Catalyst 5000 switch located in Boston might be named bossw09. When we apply the naming code, we then know that bossw09 is a device located in Boston, that it is a switch, and is the ninth device located there.

Designing an IP Naming Scheme

Today, few organizations use Internet-valid routable IP addresses, because of the diminishing number of valid Internet IP addresses and the prohibitive costs of obtaining them. Instead, corporations use a block of addresses that have been defined by the Internet Engineering Task Force (IETF) in RFC 1918, for use only on internal private networks. Table 12-2 lists those address blocks.

Your first reaction may be to grab the 10.0.0.0 (pronounced *ten dot oh*) block of addresses and start dishing them out—a range from 10.0.0.0 to 10.255.255.255 seems to offer an almost limitless supply of addresses. Take care, however, in assigning addresses to the subnets within your organization. Randomly assigning addresses to different subnets will result in very large route tables. If you dole them out properly, though, you can achieve maximum efficiency by allowing the routers to use *route summarization*.

Route summarization is illustrated in Figure 12-2. It's a pretty straightforward concept: When a group of routes can be grouped based on some characteristic of their address, then the group of routes can be described as a single route. The characteristic used for this summarization is the leftmost bit(s) in the addresses of the group. That is, if some leftmost portion of all their addresses is unique from all other addresses in the network, the group can be summarized as a single route. Then this information is used on more distant parts of the network to summarize the route to those addresses. For example, if there are three subnets with addresses 10.1.20.0, 10.1.30.0, and 10.1.40.0, and with the subnet mask 255.255.255.0, and there are no other 10.1 networks on the internetwork, then these three routes can be grouped together into a route to the 10.1 networks.

Class	Address Block
A	10.0.0.0 to 10.255.255.255
B	172.16.0.0 to 172.31.255.255
C	192.168.0.0 to 192.168.255.255

Table 12-2. IETF-Defined Private Network Address Blocks

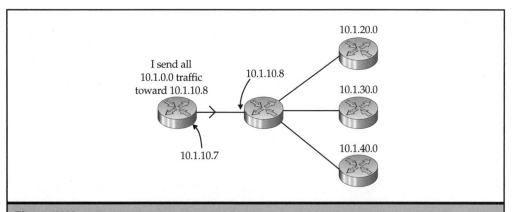

Figure 12-2.   Careful addressing in LANs can result in opportunities for route summarization

TIP: It can be useful to divide the network into areas, an area being a group of interconnected routers that are logically and physically grouped, that all use a contiguous block of subnets. First identify your backbone area, at the center of your network where all the remote sites connect. This is more easily illustrated in a hub and spoke topology where the hub is the backbone. Then group the remote sites that connect into the backbone area into their own area. An area may consist of a number of the spokes to remote sites; a site may consist of a router with a LAN and a WAN link homing back to the hub. One would keep the IP networks contiguous within each area; and all the subnets assigned to the LAN and WAN segments would be within one range of networks addresses, perhaps within a Class B network. One method is to have all the sites on one particular router be on one area, and sites homing into another area be grouped in another router. This would allow for the physical boundaries of the network to be consistent with the logical boundaries. Once you have grouped the sites into their respective areas, you can assign a full Class B address block to each area. For example, 172.16.0.0\16 for the Backbone Area sites; 172.17.0.0\16 for Area 1; and 172.18.0.0\16 for Area 2. And if you use Cisco's Enhanced IGRP, this arrangement allows you to take advantage of *auto-summarization* (one of EIGRP's best features). The routers will automatically summarize the routes to the single Class B network update, without having to manually configure the summarization.

Route summarization pays off for distant routers, as well as local devices. Instead of remembering three separate routes, the routers need only remember that all traffic destined for any 10.1 address (for example) goes toward those subnets.

EXAMPLE DOMAIN STRUCTURES

Although your internetworking requirements will certainly be unique, it is possible to take certain parts of other network designs and incorporate them into your own. This section offers four examples of Windows 2000 network designs, with the physical topology required to support each design.

Small Businesses

Smaller businesses (up to 1000 users) have many of the same requirements that larger organizations have (security, redundancy, and speed, for instance). However, the reduced number of users and resources in a small business allow for some simplification in the design. The small business is usually not spread out geographically and typically has only a single site.

The Windows Domain Model

The small business will almost always be well served by a single domain. Of course, there should be a peer DC for redundancy in the Active Directory. In this example, all machines will be known as *machinename*.company.com.

Figure 12-3 shows how a small business can use OUs to subdivide the domain into administrative segments. This allows an administrator to create certain users that can carry out administrative duties but only for certain parts of the network.

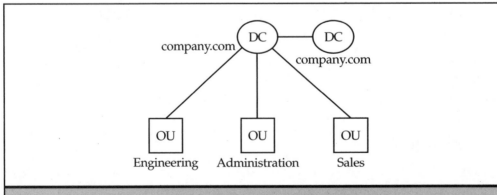

Figure 12-3. The Windows domain model (single domain) for a small business

The Logical Network Topology

At the center of this network (illustrated in Figure 12-4) is a Cisco 4000 Series router. It connects to switches and hubs for user access. It also connects to a Cisco PIX Firewall so that users on the inside can access resources on the Internet, but without allowing Internet users access inside the organization. The PIX also supports a separate LAN, where you can place Web servers or other servers that you might want available to Internet users but not totally exposed to the Internet. This LAN is called the *demilitarized zone (DMZ)*. Connecting to the Internet in this way is quite common and may be applied to any of the other domain examples here.

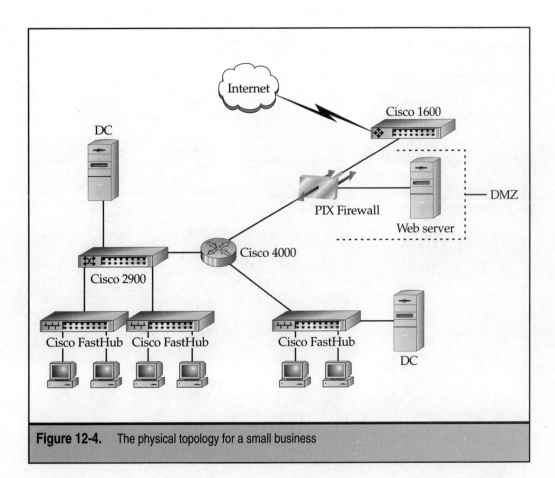

Figure 12-4. The physical topology for a small business

Users don't connect directly to routers. Rather, they typically connect to hubs (for normal users) and switches (for systems that require high throughput). In this example, a Cisco 2900XL switch is connected directly to the 4000. FastHubs, servers, domain controllers, and users that require high-speed access may be connected directly to the switches.

You may also connect a FastHub directly to the router. We have placed a second DC on this hub. This DC will service all local AD requests as well as provide backup in case the other DC goes down.

Medium-Sized Businesses (Centralized)

Some businesses grow into a larger version of the small business model. They add users, departments, and resources but do not spread geographically very much. In this example, a medium-sized business (1000–5000 users) has grown locally and has added a single remote location. This organization now comprises two sites (noted in Figure 12-5 by the dashed line separating sites).

The Windows Domain Model

Although a single domain could service this entire medium-sized organization, three domains are created to provide better security for the various departments. Adding more

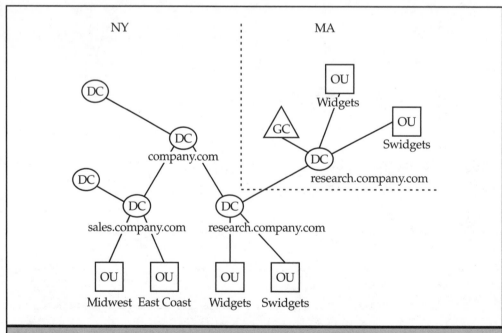

Figure 12-5.   The Windows domain model for a medium-sized business that is centralized

domains incurs the extra cost of DCs, but the two departments (Sales and Research) feel strongly about keeping control over their own departments. Each domain uses OUs to even better divide administrative functions. Central Administration is happy because they control the parent, root domain called company.com. Therefore, they have access throughout the domain tree.

This company has a Frame Relay connection to its remote site and has placed a DC there. This DC must contain the global catalog for the domain tree so that network traffic is reduced. The Frame Relay connection must support replication traffic the other DC will send in from the NY site. If this becomes too much, a separate domain could be created in MA, and it could be set up with a GC for the domain tree.

Future growth is quite simple. Domains can be added to any other domain, and OUs can be converted to their own domains at any time. Figure 12-5 illustrates this concept.

The Logical Network Topology

Figure 12-6 summarizes most of the major components that make up a centralized internetwork for a medium-sized company. In this case, the company has an FDDI backbone where the root DCs reside. Other heavily used servers are also part of this ring. Also connected to the FDDI ring is a small Cisco 2600 router that connects to the MA site using

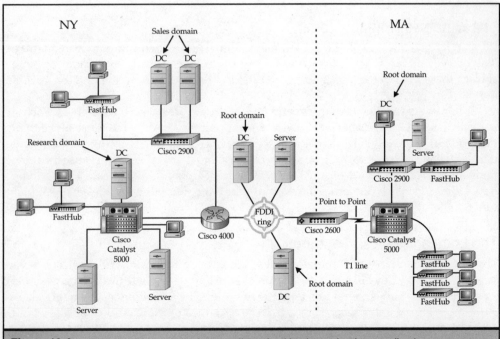

Figure 12-6. The physical topology for a medium-sized business that is centralized

Frame Relay. Since Frame Relay can accommodate more than one connection (PVC) for a single port on a router, this allows the company to grow easily without having to add much more equipment.

At the remote site, another Cisco 2600 connects the Frame Relay connection to a switch (maybe a Catalyst 4000). This switch then connects directly to servers, or to hubs. A DC for the research.company.com is also located here to serve local requests.

Back at headquarters in NY, a Cisco 4000 connects user switches and hubs to the FDDI backbone. Another router might be used in parallel here for redundancy. Either way, DCs, servers, and hubs will be connected to the switches depending on traffic patterns and speed requirements. The child domains (sales.company.com and research.company.com) should be located close (logically) to users, in order to minimize network traffic and provide the quickest service.

Medium-Sized Businesses (Decentralized)

Very often businesses grow by opening branch offices in other cities or by acquiring other businesses that are located remotely. This results in multiple sites (noted by dashed lines in Figure 12-7). Although each site might have its own domain, company headquarters may want to retain administrative control over the entire tree. The design shown in Figure 12-7 meets that objective while accounting for the remote location of most of the users.

The Windows Domain Model

We start by making the root domain at the headquarters (called company.com in this example). We might also include OUs to further subdivide users at this domain. In our example, these are called HR and Accounting. We also have another DC there for redundancy.

Each remote site has its own domain with two or more domain controllers. Each site may also use OUs to further partition users and administrative functions. Since the remote domains are all child domains of the root domain, administrators of the root domain will have administrative control over the remote domains. Also, because the remote domains are located across expensive WAN links, a global catalog for the entire domain tree is located in each domain. This should reduce the number of queries that need to be sent to other domains.

The Logical Network Topology

The physical layout for this domain model is illustrated in Figure 12-8. Each site is very straightforward. They all connect via Frame Relay to the main site (MPLS) using either a small Cisco 2600 Series router or a larger 3640 router. For redundancy, you might also include more Frame Relay links from site to site so that connections could survive a failure at the main site. Doing this will largely depend on budget and reliability requirements.

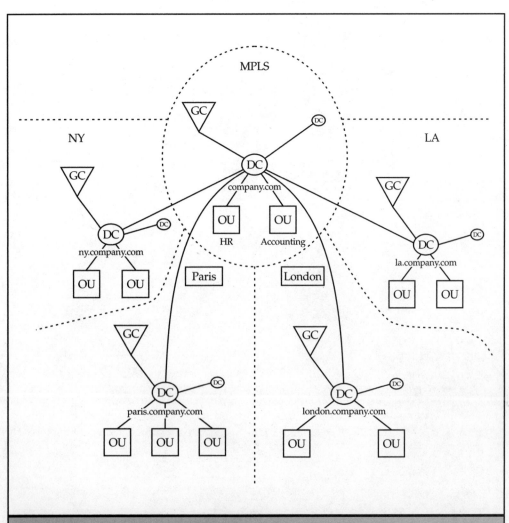

Figure 12-7.   The Windows domain model for a medium-sized business that is decentralized

Within each site, the router connected to the WAN also connects to other switches or hubs, so that servers (including the DCs) and users can attach to the network. Obviously, in this diagram, many users and servers have been omitted for clarity. As more sites are added, they can be incorporated as child domains sprouting from the current child domains or from the root domain directly. To attach to another tree, the two root domains would be connected via a trust relationship as illustrated in the enterprise example, next.

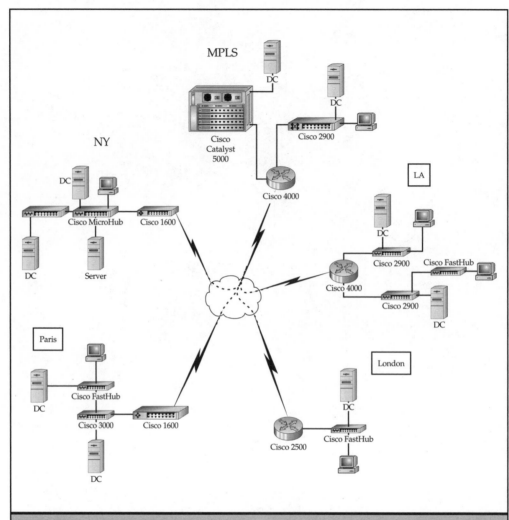

Figure 12-8. The physical topology for a medium-sized business that is decentralized

Enterprise Businesses

Large corporate or campus networks (from 5000 to more than 100,000 users) are large and diverse enough to have a personality of their own. Such networks must be hand-crafted and maintained by a large staff of network designers and engineers. In the example in Figure 12-9, only two of many sites are shown; the same model could be extended to as many sites as are needed.

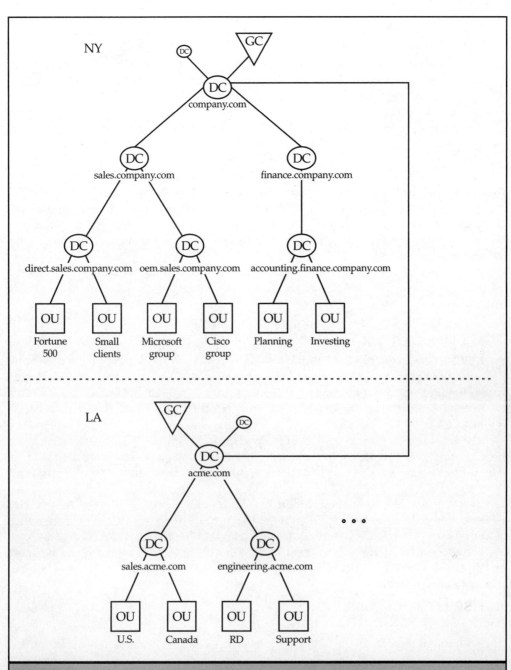

Figure 12-9. The Windows domain model for an enterprise

The Windows Domain Model

This enterprise example contains two trees, which may have been separate companies at one point but have now merged. Since we assume both trees share the same schema and GC but use different namespaces (company.com and acme.com), they are part of the same forest. Each tree keeps an updated copy of the GC for the forest. That way, we get fast searches for objects in other domains or trees, and consume the least amount of network bandwidth updating the AD.

In Figure 12-9, there are two sites (NY and LA) with a tree in each site. In the NY tree, the root domain (company.com) has two children domains (Finance and Sales). These two children also have children domains that further divide security boundaries. From there, we can use OUs to gain finer control of administrative power. Exactly how the domains and OUs are constructed depends largely on the organization of the company (political, geographical, and so forth); on the security requirements (more domains means more security issues); and on the financial constraints (more domains means more servers and administrators).

In LA, the root domain (acme.com) has two children domains that are split into OUs based on business function (R & D and Support) or geographical considerations (U.S. and Canada).

The Logical Network Topology

Figure 12-10 shows the physical design for the enterprise network example. In this example, we have connected the two sites using Frame Relay. We could provide a dedicated connection at D3 speeds (45 Mbps).

In the LA site, the Frame Relay connection goes through a Cisco 7206, which subsequently connects with a Catalyst 6000 that is fully loaded with a switch blade. These switch ports break out into more switches (2900s) and some hubs (Cisco FastHubs). From here, users, servers, and DCs are attached. This results in a very flat network for the LA site. Undoubtedly, VLANs would be incorporated to decrease the size of the broadcast domains.

In NY, the Frame Relay connection terminates at a Cisco 7206 Series router. This router connects to other devices, including other routers (Cisco 4000s) and a large switch (Catalyst 5509 or 8000). Users connect to hubs and switches that are hooked to these routers and the Catalyst. In a real enterprise network design, there would be many more switches, hubs, and users along with servers. This basic design could be repeated for additional network devices.

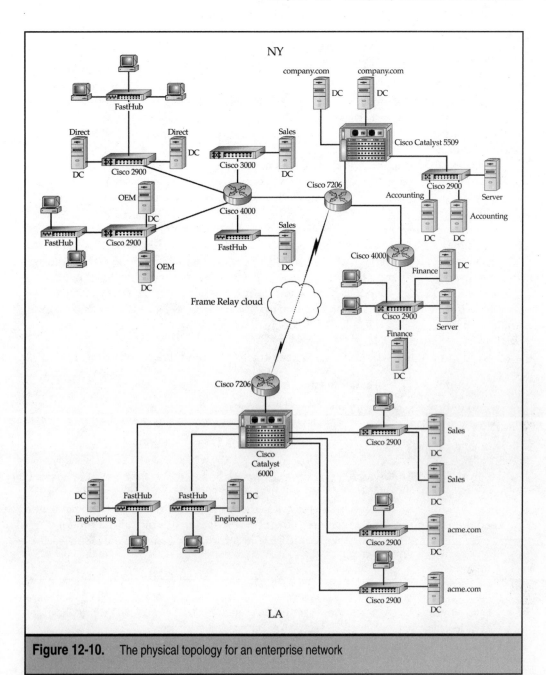

Figure 12-10. The physical topology for an enterprise network

WINDOWS 2000 MIGRATION

In all likelihood, you won't have the benefit of building a Windows 2000 domain structure from scratch. Probably you will have to migrate an existing Windows network. While this seems at first blush to be quite complicated, expensive, and disruptive, it doesn't have to be. In fact, Microsoft even proclaims that it can be done on the production network without any interruption of service. (Presumably, they don't count all those reboots as interruptions.)

This section describes the issues that occur when updating various Windows clients to Windows 2000. Then we'll move into a discussion of what you can do now to plan for your future migration. After that, we'll walk you through a sample migration of a domain.

At some stage of your Windows 2000 deployment, you will have to upgrade a multitude of client workstations. First of all, and let there be no confusion about this: Windows 2000 is, in fact, the next version of Windows NT. It was renamed from NT 5.0 to Windows 2000 for obvious marketing reasons. Microsoft pretends sometimes that Windows 2000 is a totally new OS built on NT technology, but this is misleading. Windows 2000 is NT; therefore, it should come as no surprise that upgrading from NT 4.0 is the easiest method, and administrators with NT skills will be more useful than those with only Windows 9*x* skills.

You can upgrade to Windows 2000 from the following operating systems:

▼ Windows NT Workstation 4.0

■ Windows NT Workstation 3.51

■ Windows 98

▲ Windows 95

Upgrading to Windows 2000 is accomplished in the same way for all Windows operating systems. You simply place the Windows 2000 CD into your computer when you are running Windows. A splash screen is displayed, and from there you click Upgrade and proceed. Before committing to the upgrade, you run a compatibility check on your system by typing **winnt32 /checkupgradeonly** at the command prompt in the i386 directory on the Windows 2000 CD-ROM.

NOTE: Windows 2000 Professional will continue to provide support for FAT16 and FAT32 file systems, provided that they are uncompressed before upgrading. You will, of course, be given the opportunity to upgrade the drive to NTFS version 5 at the time of the Windows 2000 upgrade.

Issues for Windows 9x Clients

For the first time, Windows 9x users will have the option of upgrading to a version of Windows NT without having to re-install all their settings and applications. This will bring about many more converts—especially considering there will be no more Windows 9x after Windows 98 has seen its last days. Nonetheless, converting from Windows 9x will prove difficult because of differences in applications, and in the Registry of Windows NT as compared with that of Windows 9x.

Many applications and devices will not run once you have upgraded to Windows 2000. In a standard desktop environment, you should first run the install on one of these machines and see what applications or devices give you trouble. If something fails to run, you'll have to figure out a way to allow Windows 2000 to work with the application or device. Microsoft offers a couple of solutions to this problem.

One answer is to uninstall the application before upgrading the OS, and then re-install it after Windows 2000 is loaded. This may not work for applications that were not designed to run on Windows NT.

The other solution is to write a *migration DLL file*, or obtain it from the original software vendor of an application. A migration DLL might be written to

▼ Replace Windows 9x files with files that are compatible with Windows NT.

■ Move Windows 9x application and user settings to the appropriate location in the Windows 2000 file system.

▲ Relocate Windows 9x Registry keys to the appropriate Windows 2000 locations.

Issues for NT Clients

As explained earlier, the best migration path to Windows 2000 is from Windows NT 4.0 systems. Versions 4.0 of Windows NT Server and Workstation have many things in common with Windows 2000, including

▼ Registry database and structure

■ NTFS file system

■ The same kernel architecture

▲ Similar security architecture

Although nearly all applications will continue to function after the upgrade, you might notice that some devices (such as NICs, cameras, and sound cards) do not function. You'll need to obtain an updated driver from the manufacturer to fix this problem.

Dual-Booting

You might be tempted to install Windows 2000 in a different directory so you can boot to either your NT system or the Windows 2000 system. This is called a *dual-boot* configuration. Although this is a good way to see whether you like the new OS, you should be aware of a few caveats beforehand.

The problems in dual-booting with Windows 2000 revolve around the new version of NTFS (v5). It offers many new features, including disk quotas, encrypted files, and release points. When you install Windows 2000, it will convert existing file systems to NTFS v5, rendering them unintelligible to NT systems. To fix this, you'll need to install NT 4.0 Service Pack 4 (or later) *before* you even insert the Windows 2000 disk into the computer. Service Pack 4 allows NT 4.0 systems to read NTFS v5 drives. With this in place, your NT system will be able to read its drive as well as any other NTFS volumes (versions 4 or 5). Unfortunately, however, your NT system will then not be able to take advantage of NTFS v5's powerful new features.

NOTE: When you use dual-booting, make sure each OS has its own unique name if they are being used in the same domain. Each machine must have a unique account in the domain for each OS it loads.

DOMAIN MIGRATION EXAMPLE

The standard practice for migrating domain controllers follows the top-down approach—that is, the primary domain controller (PDC) is the first system in the network to be converted to Windows 2000. Then other PDCs or backup domain controllers (BDCs) are converted, followed by normal servers and eventually user systems. In the following example, a Windows NT 4.0 PDC is converted to a Windows 2000 Server acting as a domain controller.

Easing the Migration Pains

In addition to planning the future network design, there are some things you can do now, before the actual migration, that will help it go smoothly. The first thing you can do is to standardize on TCP/IP throughout the network. The NetBIOS names that make up domain and computer names today can go away completely in a Windows 2000 environment. Moving to TCP/IP now will help you adjust to a NetBIOS free network—amen! Windows 2000 works best with TCP/IP, and you will ultimately have fewer headaches if you make this move now.

Also, get and install the components of Windows 2000 that are available now through Microsoft, and set them up in a test environment; this will allow you to work out the incompatibilities you might have with your current applications. You can download Dfs, the Zero Administration Kit, and the Microsoft Management Console (MMC) from Microsoft's Web site.

The last thing you can do before initiating a migration is to flatten your domains. If you have made multiple domains to circumvent the limitations of NT 4.0, you should consolidate them into a single domain before migrating to Windows 2000. Third-party applications can assist you (see the section on third-party migration tools later in this chapter). Doing this will allow you the most flexibility when you create your new domain. However, if you intend to keep all your domains separate after the migration, don't bother consolidating them first.

Converting Your First Domain

Once you have decided on an NT enterprise design and created an upgrade plan, at some point you will actually start converting your existing NT 4.0 domain over to the new Windows 2000 structure. Upgrading a domain can be broken down into four fundamental steps:

1. You will almost certainly upgrade a primary domain controller (PDC) to a new Windows 2000 domain controller (DC).

2. You can add OUs to better subdivide administrative rights.

3. You will create or upgrade other domain controllers to Windows 2000 DCs.

4. When all domain controllers are converted to Windows 2000, you will switch the domain into an "all Active Directory" mode to take advantage of all Windows 2000 technologies.

Step 1—Upgrading the PDC

Converting an NT 4.0 domain almost always starts at the top with the PDC. This is because the domain can then immediately join a tree if one exists, and administrators can use the administrative tools to create AD objects (such as OUs). Also, when other members of the domain are upgraded, they will have a domain to join.

Once the PDC is converted to a Windows 2000 DC, it will still be able to function with NT 4.0 BDCs, clients, and other NT Servers. Although the PDC migrates the Security Account Manager (SAM) database from the Registry to the directory store, it presents this information to down-level clients as a flat file. It can still authenticate users and maintains all the functionality it had before the conversion.

A safe approach is to take a copy of the PDC offline and upgrade that machine in a controlled environment. Run it through its paces there. If everything looks okay, then bring it up on the production network; prepare to turn on another copy of the PDC or promote an NT 4.0 BDC if anything goes wrong. Once you have a stable Windows 2000 DC online, you can proceed to the next step.

Step 2—Creating Organizational Units

By subdividing domains into separate OUs, you address a limitation in distribution of administrative rights in previous versions of NT. Basically, administrators had total control over the domain but were unable to dole out administrative rights to others. Regional administrators, therefore, couldn't manage their users and resources without having administrative rights in the entire domain. In step 2 of the migration, you can create separate OUs that subdivide your organization based on the design of the business or IT infrastructure.

Step 3—Creating More Domain Controllers

In this step, you will add more domain controllers so that you have redundancy at the level of the Active Directory. You should still maintain an NT 4.0 BDC just in case something goes wrong with the Windows 2000 DCs. It's best to keep this BDC turned off, so it has no interaction with Windows 2000. If something bad does happen, you can power up the NT 4.0 BDC and promote it to the PDC, and revert to the NT 4.0 domain.

The domain controller that used to be the PDC for the NT 4.0 domain is still regarded as such for the NT 4.0 system. It uses the old protocol for replication with BDCs, but also uses the newer protocol for replicating the AD with its Windows 2000 DC partners.

Step 4—Going Native

Once you have converted all the BDCs to Windows 2000 DCs and you are sure you'll never want to add another NT 4.0 domain controller, you can switch the domain from *mixed* mode over to *native* mode. Mixed mode operation is covered in more detail later in this chapter under "Finishing the Installation." Up to this point, you can have non-AD machines running alongside the Windows 2000 machines. When the network is in native mode, the multimaster replication for the AD is used. Also, clients can benefit from *transitive trusts*. This means they can see resources throughout the tree (see Chapter 1 for more information).

Making the Move

Migrating to Windows 2000 will be an arduous task for any enterprise, so is it worth it? That depends. If you are a small- or medium-sized company currently running NT 4.0, you might just want to stay put. Most of the advantages of Windows 2000 benefit larger networks. On the other hand, if you are an enterprise or a smaller company that needs some of the new benefits, start planning your move.

As any enterprise administrator can attest, many of the problems with previous versions of NT have stemmed from its inability to properly scale to the large enterprise environment. These limitations have been addressed in Windows 2000. The result is increased access for users, while decreasing the total cost of ownership by reducing management problems and centralizing domain information into the Active Directory. However, this conversion must be planned with great care. To ensure the minimal amount of downtime, Microsoft has built-in backward compatibility into Windows 2000. Thus you can at least migrate at your own pace rather than completely upgrading your enterprise all at once.

Single Domain Setup

In this example, we'll start with an NT 4.0 PDC and end with a Windows 2000 DC that is situated at the root of a new Windows 2000 tree and forest. Then we'll add OUs to subdivide the authority over resources.

A real migration is much more complicated than this, but this example will help you understand what is involved. Here are the steps of the basic process:

1. Upgrade NT 4.0 PDC to Windows 2000 DC.

2. Add the AD.

3. Configure the DNS service.

4. Add OUs.

Upgrading a Windows NT 4.0 PDC

To start the conversion, place the Windows 2000 CD-ROM into the PDC. This will bring up a splash screen and a prompt asking if you want to upgrade your NT systems to Windows 2000 or install a new copy (see Figure 12-11). If you're installing from the i386 directory, type **winnt32** at the command prompt from this directory.

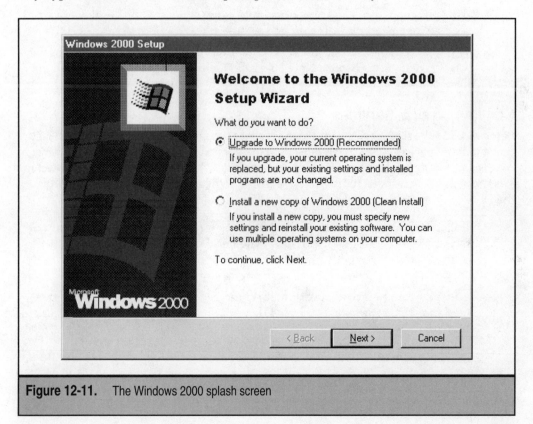

Figure 12-11. The Windows 2000 splash screen

TIP: Be aware that many of the flags used in NT 4.0 do not work in Windows 2000. Use the **winnt32 /?** command to get a listing of flags.

Before continuing with the installation, Windows 2000 will automatically check to see if any devices or settings are incompatible with Windows 2000. You will need about 700MB of free space to install Windows 2000 Server. After files are loaded locally, the system will reboot and enter the text phase, and then the graphics phase of setup. Unlike NT 4.0, users are prompted relatively infrequently for information. However, installation takes a good deal longer than with NT 4.0.

NOTE: Windows 2000 is heavily dependant on DNS as its nameserver and name locator. It's important to have your naming convention well defined before you start any migration.

Adding the Active Directory

The next step is to install Active Directory. After you reboot your newly upgraded system, a wizard pops up asking if you want to install AD. Here are the questions you must be prepared to answer:

▼ Are you going to create a new domain tree or a child domain? In this example, we want to make a new domain tree because this is our first Windows 2000 DC.

▲ Will this computer be part of an existing forest or will it be the first tree in the forest? We'll select Create a New Forest of Domain Trees in this example. If you have other Windows 2000 trees, you'll probably want to join an existing forest.

Configuring DNS Services

Before adding the DNS service, you should know the DNS name of the domain you are going to use—perhaps something like company.com. Since a child domain will incorporate its name as part of the top-level domain, it might be known as finance.company.com.

The next two questions in the Active Directory wizard are geared toward setting up the DNS services for the new DC:

▼ Because we are upgrading a PDC that isn't running DNS, we'll need to install DNS now. The next dialog box asks whether you want to install a DNS client or the DNS server on this machine. We choose to install DNS server because we don't have another DNS server running anywhere else.

▲ You are asked to provide the domain name. Since we are creating a new tree (and forest), this domain is the root domain, so its name would be something like company.com.

Now you have installed and configured DNS for your system. All future configuration will be through the DNS plug-in for the Microsoft Management Console called the DNS Manager. You will need to use the DNS Manager now to enable dynamic updates on the forward lookup zone. Open the DNS Manager by selecting Start | Programs | Administrative Tools | DNS Management.

Finishing the Installation

The Active Directory Wizard continues with questions about where to store log files, the AD database, and the system shared folders. You should carefully plan the location for the AD because it will require fast access and potentially plenty of space. You will be asked if NT 4.0 RAS users will be using the DC. If so, you'll need to temporarily weaken security settings to allow these users to connect. After this, you can review your selections and then proceed to building the Active Directory (see Figure 12-12).

When this configuration is finished, you should have a fully functional Windows 2000 DC that can service Windows 2000 systems as well as Windows NT 4.0 machines. The DC works for both Windows 2000 and down-level clients because it is acting in mixed mode. To take full advantage of all of Active Directory's features, you'll want to run in native mode, but this should only be done when all systems have been converted to Windows 2000.

NOTE: Unlike Windows NT, in Windows 2000 you can promote or demote a DC using a utility, rather than having to totally re-install the OS. The promotion/demotion process is started by simply typing **dcpromo** at the command prompt. This invokes the Domain Controller Promotion Wizard (DCPROMO.EXE).

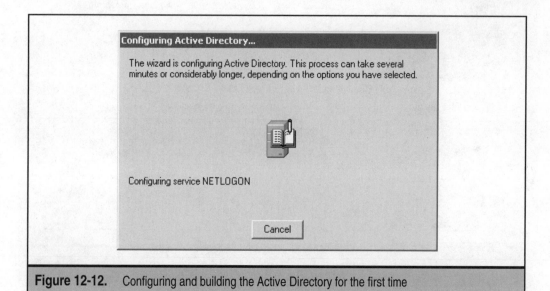

Figure 12-12.   Configuring and building the Active Directory for the first time

Adding an Organizational Unit

You will want to create several OUs to subdivide this domain for administrative reasons. This is accomplished using the Windows 2000 Configure Your Server application (shown in Figure 12-13). This application starts automatically when the Windows 2000 server starts. You can also get to it by selecting Programs | Administrative Tools | Configure Your Server.

In the left-hand frame, click Active Directory and then select Manage. This will open up the Microsoft Management Console. From here you can name the new OU. Right-click the domain name and select New | Organizational Unit, as shown in Figure 12-14. The new OU should appear under the domain name in the left pane of the Management Console. To set the OU's properties, including security, right-click the new OU and select Delegate Control from the menu. Next, you set the precise authority each group or user will have in the OU, using the Delegation of Control Wizard.

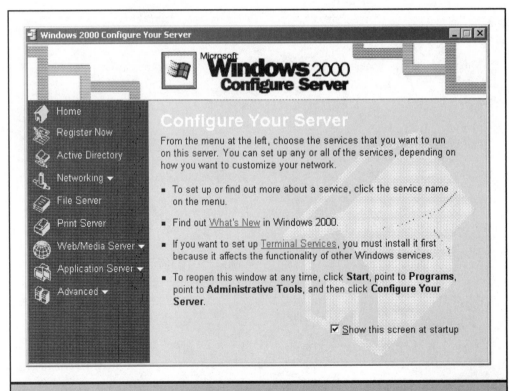

Figure 12-13.   Customize and manage your domain controller

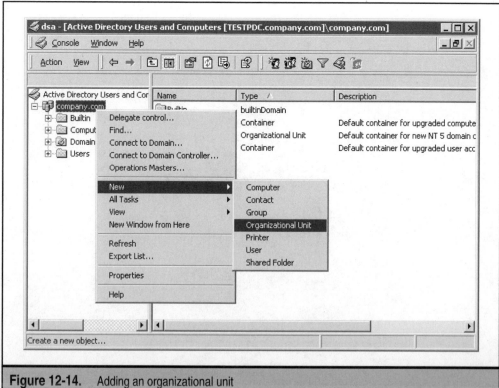

Figure 12-14.   Adding an organizational unit

Going Native

As mentioned previously, there are certain advantages to setting the network mode to native as opposed to mixed. They include the ability to use multimaster replication, and all members of a tree can browse resources throughout the tree.

WARNING: Only go native if you're sure you won't need to add more NT 4.0 DCs. You cannot reverse the change to native mode.

To make the switch to native mode, you must have administrative privileges. Go to the AD Management Console and right-click the topmost domain. This will bring up a window like that in Figure 12-15. Note the warning that this is an irreversible change. Simply click the Change Mode button to start the process.

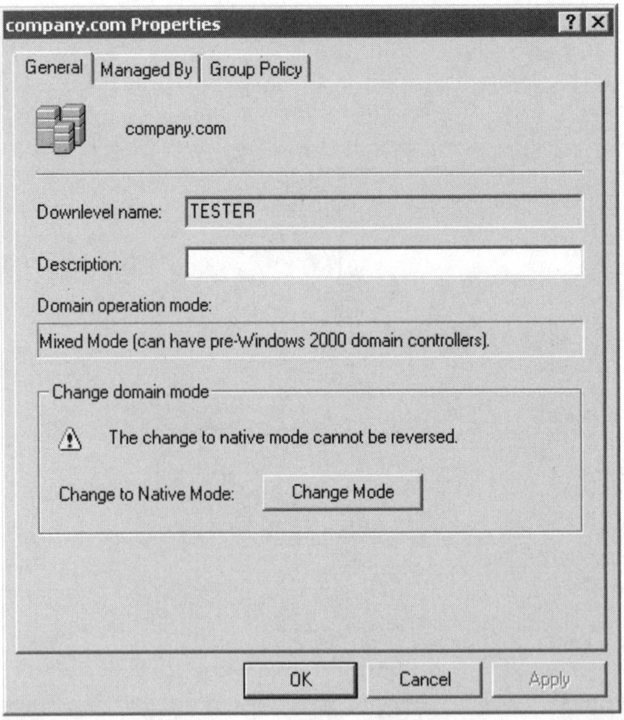

Figure 12-15.   Changing the mode over to native, which is irreversible

THIRD-PARTY MIGRATION TOOLS

Domain migration can get quite complicated, especially for multidomain networks. Fortunately, tools are already available to help you plan your migration as well as carry it out.

DirectManage

Active Directory; Windows 2000; migration . . . these are words you may be seeing or hearing every day, although you probably don't use these technologies in your daily tasks—yet. Entevo (www.entevo.com) has set out to change that, with their new Active Directory (AD) management product called DirectManage.

DirectManage is a valuable program that administrators can use to manage the AD. Moreover, it comes with a Migration tool—a wizard that helps you prepare your NT 4.0 or 3.51 domains for the conversion to Windows 2000 and AD.

Although Microsoft provides a snap-in for the Microsoft Management Console, the DirectManage program will help considerably in the tasks of AD management. DirectManage is actually two products in one: DirectAdmin and DirectScript. DirectAdmin is the primary management console. DirectScript extends the management capabilities by allowing scripts to automatically carry out custom administrative processes, such as searching for users that match a certain criteria and changing their properties.

Both DirectManage and DirectScript work with NT 3.51 and NT 4.0; and they are Active Directory Services Interface (ADSI) compliant, so they will work with Windows 2000 when it arrives in your enterprise. DirectManage, especially, can be used now to get control over your network, so you can easily move to Windows 2000 with one less thing to worry about.

DirectAdmin

DirectAdmin helps you manage the AD across multiple domains using an Explorer-like interface (shown in Figure 12-16). Objects of the AD are listed in the left pane, and the attributes of the objects are displayed in the right pane. The tools that allow you to manipulate the objects in the AD are located in the menus. You can drill far down into the AD to

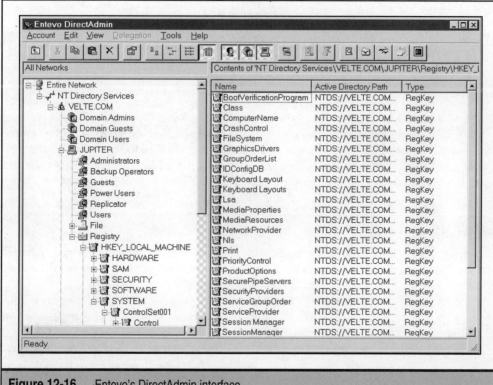

Figure 12-16. Entevo's DirectAdmin interface

view and change all sorts of minutia about the computers and users in your enterprise. For example, you can view the attributes of any file on any computer. Of course, you'll need administrator rights to successfully run DirectAdmin.

You can save some administrative time by delegating routine account/file management tasks to others, using the Delegation tool. (Although this does circumvent the problem with NT's all-or-none approach to user rights, Windows 2000 has addressed this issue anyway. Also, third-party applications already exist to do this same function—Enterprise Administrator by Mission Critical Software, for example.)

A valuable feature that sets DirectManage apart from other management applications is its Migration tool, which prepares your current enterprise organization (including user accounts) for Windows 2000 and the AD. You can easily move users from one domain to another or consolidate multiple domains. This will certainly alleviate some of the migration problems you are likely to face when moving to Windows 2000. The domain migration wizard also remaps file and Registry Key permissions so users will retain the access they had prior to the consolidation.

DirectAdmin also includes a set of canned reports that search the AD for objects that match your criteria. You can search on properties such as logon history or account attributes and then print out your reports, publish them to the Web, or use them to make changes to the accounts that matched your search criteria. This can be a valuable time-saver, especially when you are contending with hundreds or thousands of users.

DirectScript

For serious administration woes, DirectScript helps you write custom scripts that will automate your administrative tasks. You open DirectScript scripts from within DirectAdmin and run them there. The scripts can comprise VBScripts, Active Server Pages, or JavaScript. Since an object in the AD can be treated as a Component Object Model (COM), it can be used in a script. For example, a script could search for all users located within a particular site and then change their Registry settings to restrict their access to desktop settings. Administrators can make scripts as complex as needed. They can be used to examine a wide variety of information and make "intelligent" decisions. Learning how to write these scripts will require some time, but it'll save you administrative time in the long run.

Is DirectManage for You?

DirectManage is aimed squarely at enterprise networks and is priced at $19 per managed account. This means a 5000-user network would require a $95,000 license fee (however, Entevo has said it will give a discount for volume sales).

The only competition DirectManage has today is a few tools that overlap DirectManage in functionality (RoboMon and Enterprise Administrator, for example) and the administration tools within Windows 2000. If you can't wait for Windows 2000 to get cracking on Active Directory, or you want to ease the migration to Windows 2000, give DirectManage a look. Otherwise, it might be prudent to see if the built-in tools in Windows 2000 are adequate to do the job.

FastLane's Domain Management Suite

Certainly one of the most advanced sets of tools available today to help migrate to Windows 2000 is FastLane's Domain Management Suite (DM/Suite). The suite includes three separate applications: DM/Administrator, DM/Reporter, and DM/Manager. These applications assist in preparing for the move to Windows 2000, but also may be quite useful as stand-alone applications with only Windows NT.

DM/Suite Helps with Consolidation

One of the first things you can do before migrating your PDCs is to flatten your domain—converting multiple domains into a single larger domain. DM/Suite not only helps with your flattening tasks but lets you adopt some of AD's functions now.

▼   DM/Administrator will help you set up virtual domains and OUs in your existing Windows NT 4.0 environment, to better prepare for Windows 2000.

■   Before you move a single user, DM/Reporter tool will indicate if it expects any problems with the process, based on your domain and user rights. When you're ready, you can consolidate users, global groups, and local groups. During the process, you have the option of changing user rights as well as group rights. Subsequently, computer accounts are also transferred to the target domain.

▲   DM/Manager walks you through the flattening process in a careful, always reversible, manner.

DM/Administrator

One of the biggest drawbacks to the NT 4.0 security model is the "all-or-nothing" administrative model. In NT 4.0, an administrator either has total control over a domain or is just a normal user with no control. Windows 2000 will fix this problem by using OUs to delegate control of specified regions of the network to only certain users. You can take advantage of OUs now, without moving to Windows 2000, by using DM/Administrator.

This part of DM/Suite lets an administrator assign some administrative task to others without giving total control. In addition to creating virtual OUs, you can create virtual domains to further subdivide your existing domains. This arrangement will increase security today and help begin the migration to Windows 2000.

DM/Reporter

Getting a grip on data that transcend multiple domains can be challenging. DM/Reporter collects data from multiple DCs and multiple Exchange servers. Information about users, objects, and usage are consolidated and presented in a series of premade reports. You can also design custom reports to your specification.

One of the greatest benefits of DM/Reporter is that all this information is centrally stored even for the largest domain models. This way you can review summaries of vast amounts of data and look at historical data for comparisons. Figure 12-17 illustrates the results when DM/Reporter was asked to query all the computers in the network and display their general characteristics.

These reports can call on historical data for users, groups, and computers within your domain. They can be printed to the screen or a printer, or exported in a variety of useful formats.

DM/Manager

DM/Manager is a tool you use now to plan for, and later to help migrate to Windows 2000. This high-level tool allows you to consolidate domains and make them flat—a more suitable structure for Windows 2000 migration.

DM/Manager shows you your current domain structure in the upper pane and the proposed domain structure in the lower pane (see Figure 12-18). Making conversions is as simple as selecting a domain and indicating its position in the post-migration structure. Making these changes is as simple as clicking and dragging a domain to its future position. This very powerful tool also has an Undo Migration option that allows you to back out of erroneous changes.

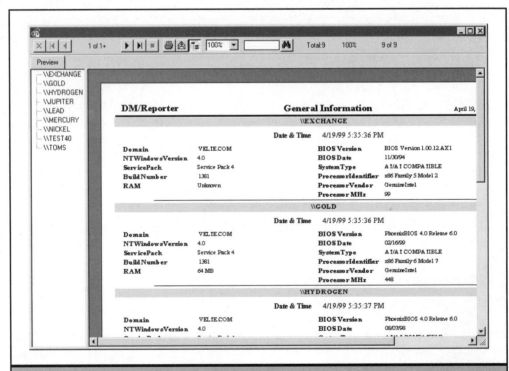

Figure 12-17. DM/Reporter, showing general properties for each computer in a domain

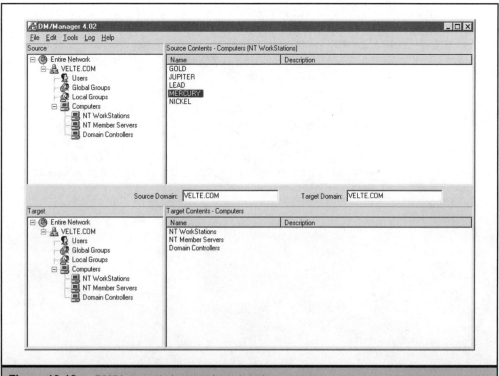

Figure 12-18.   DM/Manager helps transform domains

DM/Suite Pricing

More information about any of the DM/Suite applications can be found on FastLane's Web site at www.fastlanetech.com. They are individually priced on a per-managed-user basis. DM/Administrator goes for $7 per user; DM/Reporterm, $6 per user; and DM/Manager, $12 per user; or you can get all three for $25 per user. Of course, you can negotiate a site license for larger installations.

SUMMARY

Windows 2000 has much to offer an organization whose business needs can be better met by Windows 2000 technological advancements. Your organization will need an initial survey to determine if the benefits outweigh the effort that is required to implement Windows 2000.

Once the decision is made to upgrade, a certain amount of planning must be conducted before even a single system is upgraded. This planning applies to domain architecture, naming schemes, and administrative boundaries. Once the plan is in place, an upgrade strategy can be created and deployed—starting with the highest level systems in the network: the primary domain controllers.

Third-party tools can assist in the migration effort. You can even use them to start preparing today for a Windows 2000 environment, by implementing some of the Windows 2000 features into Windows NT systems. For example, you can begin now to build virtual domains and virtual organizational units.

This chapter concludes Part 3. Next, we are going to look at some strategies for building and managing network connections to the Internet, other corporations, and users.

PART IV

Intranet/Extranet Strategies

CHAPTER 13

Web Services

More and more companies today are relying on Web servers for the exchange of information in areas such as e-commerce, marketing, and advertising. Until now, the focus has been on the servers themselves. Organizations have implemented upgrades and redundant servers hoping to provide customers with better service and reliability. Cisco has taken a different approach—it has created external hardware and software solutions that assist in increasing efficient and reliable access to these servers.

This chapter discusses the Web-based services provided by Cisco's hardware and software solutions. The three tools described here are DistributedDirector and LocalDirector, which address load distribution and balancing of Web traffic, and the Cisco Web browser interface for hardware configuration.

CISCO'S DISTRIBUTEDDIRECTOR

In this section, you'll get to know Cisco's DistributedDirector product, which is designed to provide dynamic, transparent, scalable Internet traffic load distribution between geographically dispersed servers.

Today's innovative companies are using the Web to provide software distribution, customer service, and other business transactions. The resulting exponential growth of the global Internet is challenging these same companies with the following scalability issues:

▼ Sustaining high server availability

■ Maintaining server performance

▲ Reducing costs of server operations/administration

Solving the Problem of Scalability

The solutions that exist today for global WWW scalability are few and far between, and their downfalls are rapidly being discovered by system administrators. Let's take a look at the three solutions that administrators typically rely on to improve Web server availability and performance. Although popular, these actions are often not the best solution available.

UPGRADING SERVERS   For many administrators, the logical solution to WWW scalability is to upgrade their servers. Although larger and faster machines may temporarily relieve short-term pressures, continually upgrading servers is expensive and time-consuming. This is not the answer for meeting the requirements of long-term service growth.

MIRRORING SERVERS   Mirroring or duplicating servers is a way to improve the overall performance of the server arrangement. Administrators can build fault tolerance, which increases the reliability of access to their Web sites. They can use a round-robin load distribution that distributes the Web site traffic evenly across the duplicated servers. Although this method typically has good results, it, too, is expensive.

PLACING SERVERS IN MULTIPLE LOCATIONS   A company may decide to set up multiple mirrored servers in various locations in order to maintain an acceptable level of service to end users around the world. Round-robin Domain Name System (DNS) is typically used to distribute the load among these dispersed servers. Using round-robin DNS, users are connected to servers in a cyclical pattern. DNS does not know network topology or server availability, however. This means the connections may be too geographically distant or that the servers may be unavailable. The result is poor access performance and increased transmission costs. In addition, round-robin DNS treats all servers as equal. Thus, weaker servers may be oversubscribed while larger servers remain underutilized.

Cisco's Solution to WWW Scalability

Cisco's DistributedDirector is designed to address the issues of Internet service scalability by allowing you to

▼ Distribute network services transparently and cost-effectively across globally dispersed servers.

■ Maximize the ease and performance of access to distributed servers as seen by clients.

■ Reduce transmission costs associated with providing globally distributed network services.

■ Minimize time and cost associated with mirroring services.

▲ Redirect client traffic away from offline servers.

How Does DistributedDirector Work?

DistributedDirector resides on a dedicated box that looks similar to the PIX 520 Firewall. It is installed on the LAN and configured to share information with LAN and WAN routers, also referred to as Director Response Protocol (DRP) Server Agents. LAN routers acting as DRP Server Agents share internal routing information, as illustrated in Figure 13-1; and WAN routers acting as DRP Server Agents share external routing information, as illustrated in Figure 13-2.

The information shared between DistributedDirector and its DRP Server Agents relates directly to the end user (client) and the target Web server. Using the metrics provided by the DRP Server Agents, DistributedDirector determines the optimal server for the end user.

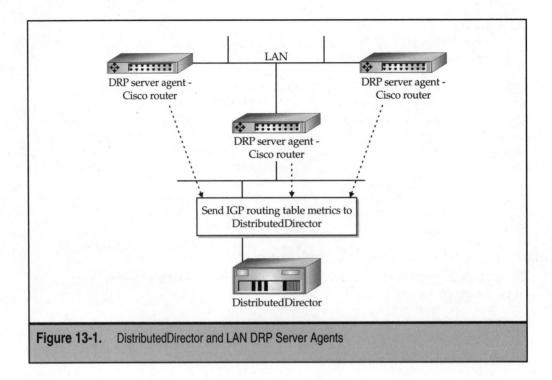

Figure 13-1. DistributedDirector and LAN DRP Server Agents

Director Response Protocol (DRP)

Director Response Protocol is a simple User Datagram Protocol (UDP) used by the DistributedDirector system to gather metrics. DistributedDirector sends two queries to the DRP Server Agents in the field, to acquire

▼ Border Gateway Protocol (BGP) and Interior Gateway Protocol (IGP) routing table metrics between the distributed servers and clients, to determine client-to-server distances. This allows the DistributedDirector to redirect clients to the topologically closest server and to localize traffic.

▲ Client-to-server link latency metrics using round-trip times. DistributedDirector can thus compare link latencies and maximize end-to-end server access performance by sending the user to the server with the lowest trip time.

Figure 13-3 illustrates the traffic generated by the DRP.

DistributedDirector Metrics

DistributedDirector selects the best server not only during the end user's initial access, but also for each additional request during the session. So, during a typical session, the end user's traffic may be redirected to one or several servers.

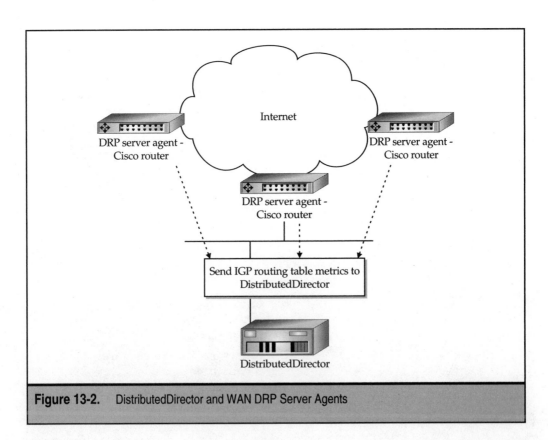

Figure 13-2.   DistributedDirector and WAN DRP Server Agents

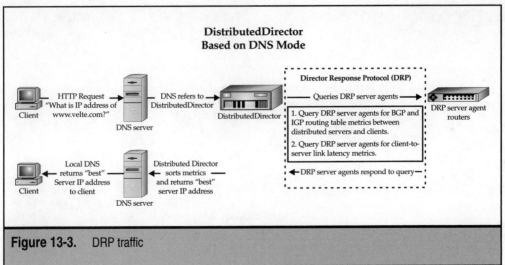

Figure 13-3.   DRP traffic

This section defines the various types of metrics that can be configured on the DistributedDirector (as summarized in Table 13-1). These metrics can all be collected, weighed, and/or ordered to define the "best" server for the client.

Metric Supported	Source of Metric Data	Description	Uses DRP or Routing Table Information?
DRP-External	BGP-AS (Autonomous Systems) hop counts	Measures distance from DRP routers to client	Yes
DRP-Internal	IGP	Measures distance from DRP routers to nearest BGP border router toward client	Yes
DRP-Server	IGP	Measures distance from DRP routers to associated distributed servers	Yes
DRP-Multi-Exit Discriminator (MED)	BGP-MED value, AS, IP address of AS exit point for each DRP Server Agent	Determines the distributed server with the lower BGP-MED value	Yes
DRP-Round Trip Times (RTT)	RTTs	Determines lowest RTT from server to client	Yes
Portion	Portion metric values	Assigns Portion metric values to each server; each server receives traffic corresponding to its Portion metric value	No
Random	Random numbers	Selects a random number for each distributed server; best server is the one with the smallest random number assignment	No
Administrative Cost	Statistical preference	Defines a server to have a statistical preference	No

Table 13-1.   DistributedDirector Metrics

DRP-External

The *DRP-External* metric defines the number of BGP autonomous system (AS) hops between the DRP server and the AS of the client requesting the Internet service. The DRP server having the least number of AS hops between it and the client is selected as the best server and provides the Internet service to the client. Figure 13-4 illustrates this metric.

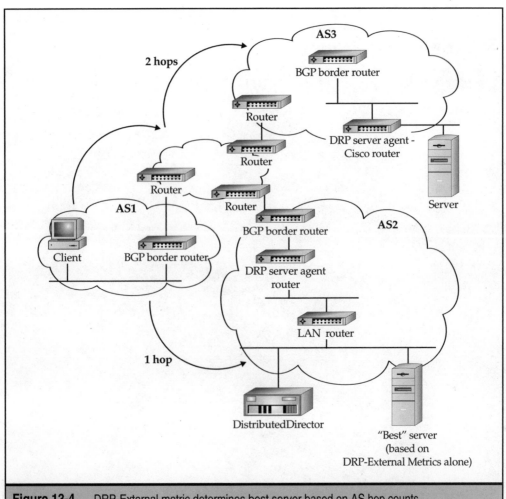

Figure 13-4.   DRP-External metric determines best server based on AS hop counts

DRP-Internal

The *DRP-Internal* metric can be used along with the DRP-External metric to get a finer distance calculation between the DRP Server Agents and the client requesting the Internet service. DRP-Internal uses the IGP route metric between the BGP border routers and the internal LAN routers. This metric helps determine the best server by discovering the hop count between BGP border routers and all internal LAN routers touched by the packets before they get to the DRP server. The best server is determined without consideration to DRP-External metrics. Figure 13-5 illustrates the DRP-Internal metric.

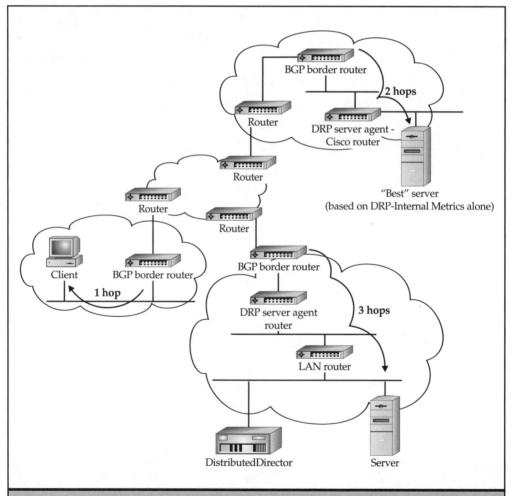

Figure 13-5.   DRP-Internal metric determines best server based on internal hop counts between BGP border routers and distributed servers

DRP-Server

The *DRP-Server metric* is used in combination with DRP-Internal to produce a finer internal distance calculation. Unlike DRP-Internal, which determines total hop count between BGP border routers and the LAN router connected to the distributed servers, DRP-Server determines total hop count between DRP Server Agents and the distributed server. Figure 13-6 illustrates the metric between DRP Server Agents and the distributed servers.

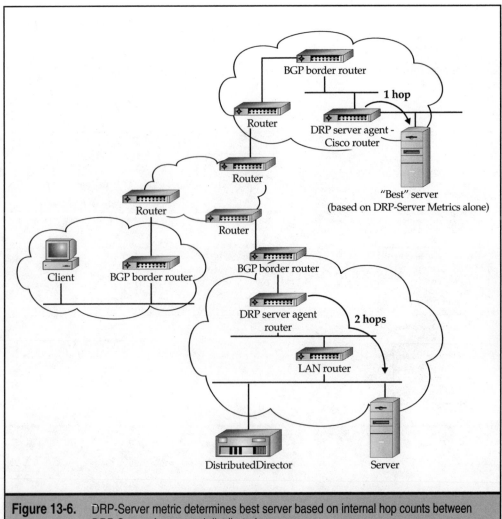

Figure 13-6.   DRP-Server metric determines best server based on internal hop counts between DRP Server Agents and distributed servers

DRP-Multi-Exit Discriminator (MED)

The *DRP-MED metric* is by far the most complicated. It is based on Multi-Exit Discriminator 5 attributes in traffic redirection decisions. DRP-MED is used to determine the best server when multiple DRP Server Agents exit one AS. DistributedDirector gathers the following information from the DRP Server Agents:

▼ BGP-MED value for a client's network prefix

■ Autonomous system (AS) number associated with each DRP Server Agent

▲ IP address of AS exit point for each DRP Server Agent

The AS number, and the IP address of the AS exit point, are used to verify that there are multiple DRP Server Agents located in the same AS that do *not* share the same exit IP address. The BGP-MED value is obtained from these DRP Server Agents, and the agent with the lower BGP-MED value selects its associated distributed server as the best server for the client. Figure 13-7 demonstrates the steps completed by DRP-MED to determine the best server.

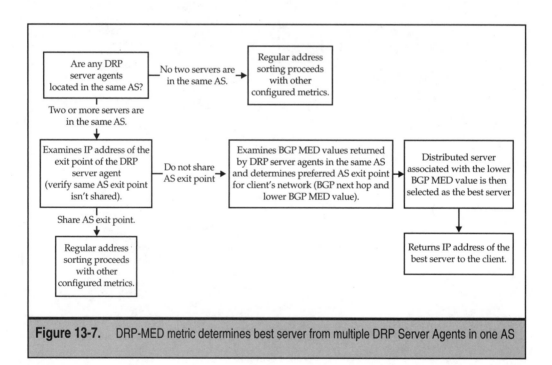

Figure 13-7. DRP-MED metric determines best server from multiple DRP Server Agents in one AS

DRP-Round Trip Times (RTTs)

The *DRP-RTT* metric determines the time it takes data to travel round trip from server to client. DRP-RTT helps you optimize server load distribution based on server-to-client link latency, resulting in maximized end-to-end server access performance. The DRP-RTT metric uses a TCP probe, not an ICMP echo, to determine round-trip times. DRP-RTT also has a tolerance parameter that defines the relative range of round-trip times (in a percentage) that should be considered as equal. For instance, consider the following DRP-RTT metrics for a specific client request:

▼ Server 1: 100 milliseconds

■ Server 2: 104 milliseconds

▲ Server 3: 140 milliseconds

Using the default DRP-RTT tolerance parameter of 10%, the DistributedDirector would determine that Server 1 and Server 2 are tied as being the best servers. Although Server 1 has the lowest DRP-RTT metric, the second-best metric (for Server 2) is less than 10% larger than Server 1's. Server 3 would be excluded from this decision because its DRP-RTT metric is greater than 10% as compared with Server 1.

Portion

Portion metric values are assigned to each distributed server. For example, one server is configured to receive 33% of the traffic, the second server is configured to receive 56% of the traffic, and a third server is configured to receive 11% of the traffic. The DistributedDirector uses these Portion metric values to determine what number of requests to give each server based on percentage of overall traffic. Figure 13-8 illustrates Portion metric.

Random

The Random metric simply assigns a random number to each distributed server, and the best server is the one with the smallest random number assignment. This metric allows random redirection of clients without the use of routing table information.

Administrative Cost

Administrative Cost metric is used to specify a statistical preference of one server over another. For instance, if you had a server that was being replaced with another server, you could give the new server a higher statistical preference. All traffic would then be directed to the new server, and you could remove the old server without any network downtime.

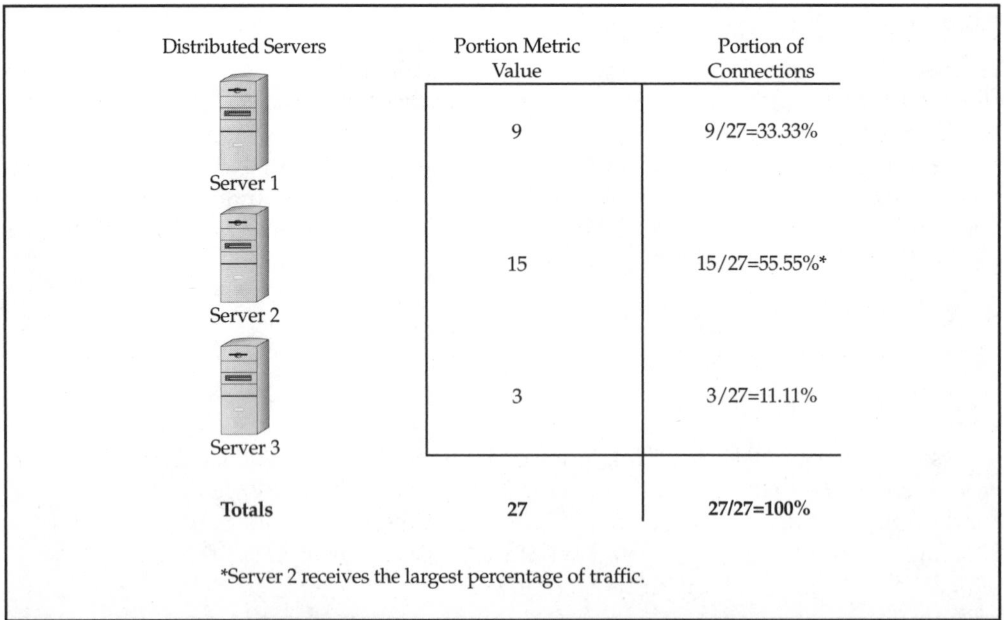

Distributed Servers	Portion Metric Value	Portion of Connections
Server 1	9	9/27=33.33%
Server 2	15	15/27=55.55%*
Server 3	3	3/27=11.11%
Totals	27	27/27=100%

*Server 2 receives the largest percentage of traffic.

Figure 13-8. Portion metric distributes traffic based on percentages

DistributedDirector Security

DistributedDirector supports access control lists (ACLs) and digital signature authentication for DRP queries and responses. (The digital signature is based on HMAC-MD5.) With ACLs you can limit DRP Server Agent access to devices having specific source IP addresses. DRP devices also support authentication for additional security. Hashing algorithm HMAC-MD5 is supported by DistributedDirector and used with digital signatures in order to authenticate the sources of DRP queries and responses. ACLs and digital signature authentication can be configured on all DRP Server Agents (assuming the agent is enabled on the DistributedDirector) and can be used to provide robust DRP-related security.

DistributedDirector Modes

DistributedDirector can be configured in either DNS Caching Nameserver mode or HTTP Session Redirector mode.

Initially, DistributedDirector was created to support the distribution of HTTP services. As the system was developed, the engineers realized DistributedDirector's solution had potential for application to other services, as well. For this reason, the DNS Caching Nameserver mode was made available.

DNS Caching Nameserver

In DNS Cashing Nameserver mode, DistributedDirector acts as the primary DNS caching nameserver for a specific subdomain. Using DRP, the DistributedDirector provides responses to DNS queries based on routing information contained in the network. Figure 13-3 (in the preceding section) shows the communication that takes place among the client, the DNS server, DistributedDirector, and DRP Server Agents when DistributedDirector is in DNS Caching Nameserver mode.

DNS Caching Nameserver works for all IP traffic and returns the single best IP address from a list of several possible servers. In addition, this mode enables load distribution of SMTP-based e-mail services through use of DNS Mail Exchange (MX) resource records. Not only can DistributedDirector issue the DNS address records that identify the best server, but it can also issue DNS MX records to identify the host name of the best mail server.

NOTE: DNS Caching Nameserver requires BIND version 4.9.3 or later on all DNS servers participating in any DistributedDirector traffic. This mode also requires that primary-domain nameservers provide iterative responses only. DNS recursion must occur as close as possible to the requesting client, in order to guarantee that the client's local DNS server issues the IP address request to the DistributedDirector.

DISTRIBUTEDDIRECTOR REPLY CACHING   DistributedDirector caches sorted replies from the DRP Server Agents on a per-client basis for a configurable default period of one minute. This functionality increases performance by reducing the traffic between the DistributedDirector and DRP Server Agents.

DISTRIBUTEDDIRECTOR REDUNDANCY IN DNS MODE   Two DistributedDirectors can be mirrored and be authoritative for the same virtual host names. This provides redundancy and failover in DNS mode. Both DistributedDirectors would be primary DNS servers. Besides the duplicated DistributedDirectors, you also need to configure multiple NS (name server) and A (address) DNS resource records (RRs) in the DNS server. Following this configuration, the client's local DNS server will initially attempt to contact the first DistributedDirector in the DNS list. If this DistributedDirector does not respond, the client's local DNS will automatically contact the second DistributedDirector in the DNS list.

You can also configure round-robin load distribution across multiple DistributedDirectors by setting ROUND_ROBIN to NS in the DNS server and adding a resource record for the distributed server's virtual host name.

Cisco Hot Standby Router Protocol (HSRP) can also be used to provide redundancy. Unfortunately, this feature requires that all redundant DistributedDirectors reside in the same subnet. We recommend using DNS to provide DistributedDirector redundancy. This eliminates the centralization requirement, and both device and network redundancy can be provided.

HTTP Session Redirector

This mode allows HTTP session redirection service. Unlike the DNS caching mode, this mode requires the DistributedDirector to be configured as the actual HTTP service host. This is accomplished by placing a DNS A-record in the primary domain name server, and binding a Web name (such as www.velte.com) to the IP address of the DistributedDirector device. Then, when a client sends an HTTP request to the Web name (www.velte.com), the DistributedDirector accepts the HTTP connection, issues DRP queries to the DRP Server Agents in the requested subdomain, sorts the DRP replies, and determines the best Web server for the client. Figure 13-9 illustrates these steps:

DistributedDirector is completely transparent to the client and DNS, so no changes in Web server software are required. While in HTTP session redirector mode, DistributedDirector

▼ Works only for HTTP traffic

■ Masquerades as the requested Web server

■ Redirects HTTP connections

▲ Works independent of BIND version

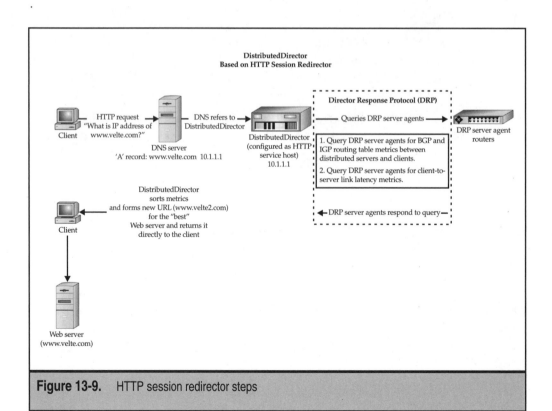

Figure 13-9. HTTP session redirector steps

Features of DistributedDirector

DistributedDirector has several features that provide additional functionality and configuration options.

Server Availability Parameter

When this function is enabled, DistributedDirector will try to establish a TCP connection to each of the distributed servers over a configurable interval (every 10 seconds, every 1 minute, every 10 minutes, etc.). Distributed servers yielding successful TCP connections are marked as being available. This function allows DistributedDirector to make sure the best server is an available server as well.

Multiservice Support

With multiservice support, DistributedDirector can enable load distribution of several services running on dispersed servers. Figure 13-10 illustrates the distribution of HTTP and FTP services across three servers.

SMTP-Based E-mail Load Distribution

In order to support transparent, global load distribution of SMTP-based e-mail services, DistributedDirector now supports DNS MX (Mail Exchange) Resource Records. This means DistributedDirector can be used to redirect client e-mail requests to the best SMTP server, through a single DNS MX Resource Record.

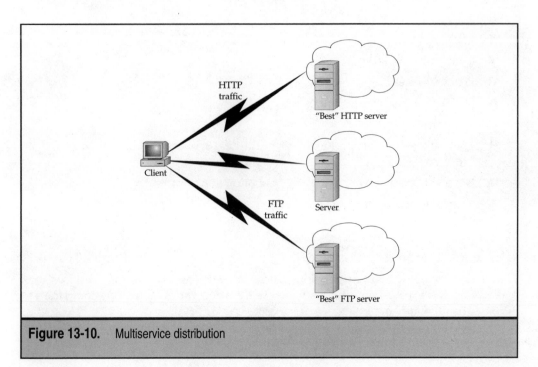

Figure 13-10. Multiservice distribution

> **NOTE:** This feature requires configuration of DistributedDirector in DNS Caching Nameserver mode.

Policy Redirection

Policy redirection uses access control lists (ACLs) to direct IP service requests to a single server or to distribute the service requests across a subset of servers based on client IP address and subnet mask. This feature is particularly useful when you want to redirect known clients to specific servers. Policy redirection can be used in both DNS Caching Nameserver and HTTP Redirect modes.

DistributedDirector Applications

As a rule of thumb, DistributedDirector can distribute any IP traffic across multiple servers provided that each server has a unique IP address. The distributed servers need not be on the same physical network. DNS Caching Nameserver mode allows distribution of all TCP and UDP traffic types. HTTP Redirect mode is only for the distribution of HTTP services.

The traffic types/applications that can be distributed by DistributedDirector include the following:

▼ Web (HTTP) services

■ FTP/TFTP services

■ Telnet services

■ E-mail posting servers

■ Proxy services

■ H.323 gateway services

■ Multimedia services

■ TN3270 session distribution access multiple Cisco Channel Interface Processors (CIPs)

■ Nearest home gateway discovery in conjunction with L2F or L2TP protocol

▲ Cisco LocalDirector traffic distribution

CISCO'S LOCALDIRECTOR

There is a growing demand for mission-critical TCP/IP-based application services such as e-commerce, video, e-mail, and many others. This demand is motivating companies to increase the reliability of networks and servers.

What Is LocalDirector?

Cisco's LocalDirector offers companies a network-based, server-and-application clustering solution. By using a hardware and software solution, LocalDirector balances the load of user traffic across multiple TCP/IP servers. All physical servers appear as one virtual server, requiring only one IP address and URL.

By tracking network sessions and server load conditions in real time, LocalDirector can direct each session to the most appropriate server. Tracking is based on the session distribution algorithm (SDA).

Session Distribution Algorithm (SDA)

The session distribution algorithm (SDA) is based on a passive approach that determines the most appropriate server based on the following criteria:

▼   Least connections

■   Weighted configured values

■   Fastest server

■   Linear random selection

▲   Source IP

SDA's many benefits include the following:

▼   Operating system independent

■   Hardware independent

■   Supports any TCP application

▲   Development of features instead of ports to operating system

Benefits of LocalDirector

LocalDirector ensures certain benefits to a distributed environment; these include continuous, high availability of content, and applications with proven techniques for actively managing servers and connections. By distributing user requests across a cluster of servers, LocalDirector optimizes responsiveness and system capacity, and dramatically reduces the cost of providing large-scale Internet, database, and application services. In addition, its integrated security device is capable of protecting servers from unauthorized access.

High Server Availability

The LocalDirector system uses a three-point system for detecting availability. This system

▼   Snoops TCP/IP handshake and data exchange between client and server to the port level, to analyze availability

■ Proactively probes Web servers with HTTP requests (This can be defined and customized by the user.)

▲ Uses a communication protocol to define server load and, if a server is down, to let LocalDirector know

Two LocalDirectors can be installed to provide a stateful failover mechanism that effectively eliminates all points of failure across the server farm. The second LocalDirector always maintains the states of current user connections. If the first LocalDirector fails, the second LocalDirector can take over immediately without dropping any sessions. In addition, configuration changes made to the first LocalDirector are automatically duplicated to the second LocalDirector. This reduces potential configuration problems and ensures a robust failover system.

Following are the primary high-availability features offered by LocalDirector:

▼ Stateful failover mechanism eliminates all points of failure and enables configuration of robust, high-availability server farms.

■ Automatic detection and removal of failed applications improves overall server-farm management and reliability.

■ Web-application probing technology monitors servers for application availability, application health, and database connectivity, effectively routing and directing traffic only to available applications.

■ "Auto-unfail" feature ensures a graceful shutdown that maintains existing connections without adding new connections to failed or removed servers.

■ "Hot standby" server allows servers and ports to back up other services and ports, increasing availability.

▲ "Hot standby" configuration is replicated, reducing administrative startup costs by automatically transferring the primary LocalDirector configuration to the secondary one.

High-Performance Load Balancing

LocalDirector provides a real-time, embedded operating system designed for load balancing and support of high traffic. The LocalDirector 430 model offers up to 240 Mbps actual load-balancing throughput, and 18,000 connections per second. The LocalDirector 416 model supports up to 80 Mbps of actual load-balancing throughput, and 7,000 connections per second.

LocalDirector has 16 interfaces for connecting to servers directly. Alternatively, an interface also can be connected to a switch, to support larger server farms and allow flexibility for a variety of network connections. Figure 13-11 illustrates this flexibility.

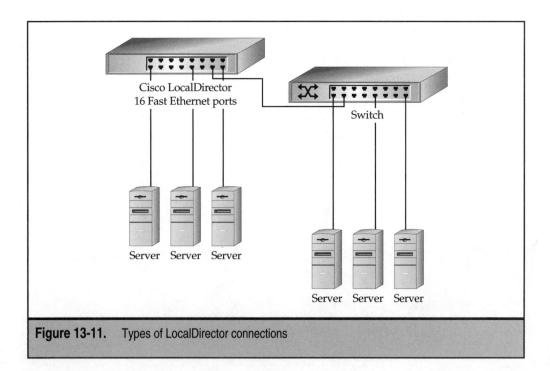

Figure 13-11. Types of LocalDirector connections

Server Connection Management

LocalDirector offers several types of connection management:

▼ Real or virtual servers provide mutual backup.

■ Maximum connection limits can be set for each server.

■ TCP traffic can be directed to different servers based on service, speed, source IP, or current quantity of connections.

■ Server resources can be added or relocated.

■ Servers can be gracefully shut down or automatically started.

■ Real and virtual IP addresses are allowed on different subnets. A user can enter a registered IP address and try to access Web traffic through traditional port 80. LocalDirector can map that registered (real) IP address to one or more virtual IP addresses, and to the same port 80 or to multiple virtual ports. Figure 13-12 illustrates the concept of virtual and real ports.

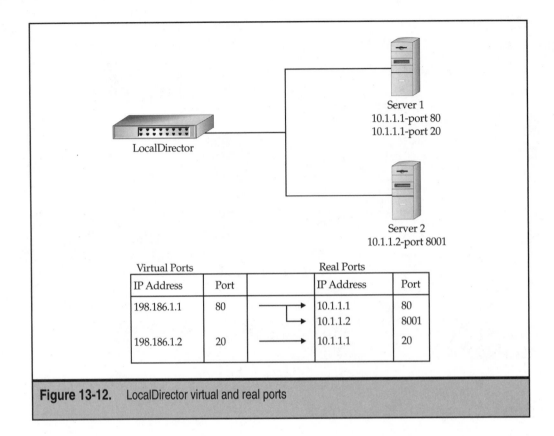

Figure 13-12.   LocalDirector virtual and real ports

- License counts or applications are not overwhelmed by setting a maximum connection.
- ▲ Packet coloring allows implementation of powerful quality-of-service networking.

Secure Access

Like DistributedDirector, LocalDirector allows the configuration of access control lists (ACLs) to control access by source IP address or service. The bridging capability of LocalDirector can be activated on a per-port basis to assist you in controlling direct access to individual servers via their registered IP addresses.

LocalDirector also supports Network Address Translation (NAT), which allows servers with unregistered IP addresses to access the public Internet—effectively preventing unauthorized external access to internal servers.

Applications Supported by LocalDirector

LocalDirector supports server farms in both Internet and intranet environments.

Internet Services

LocalDirector can manage servers that present Web content, electronic commerce applications, e-mail, host access via Telnet, and software distribution via FTP. All traffic is handled dynamically by LocalDirector. Typically, the LocalDirector 430 model would be used to support Internet services.

Intranet Services

Employees, customers, and suppliers can access internal servers for information. In addition to features for balancing the traffic load, LocalDirector provides firewall-type security features that protect these servers from unauthorized access via the Internet. These servers are protected by filtering based on source client IP address and service. Depending on traffic demands, the LocalDirector 416 model would be used to support intranet services.

DISTRIBUTEDDIRECTOR AND LOCALDIRECTOR CONFIGURATION EXAMPLES

DistributedDirector can be used to distribute traffic among several topologically dispersed LocalDirectors. Depending on the configured metric, DistributedDirector sends clients to the best LocalDirector. (Metrics are described earlier in this chapter.)

Use of the DistributedDirector's server availability parameter guarantees the existence of at least one responsive server within the cluster behind a LocalDirector. A failed server availability check would tell the DistributedDirector that any of the following conditions might exist:

▼ All servers in the cluster behind the LocalDirector are out of service.

■ The LocalDirector is out of service.

▲ The LocalDirector is not reachable from the DistributedDirector.

Based on the queries the DistributedDirector gathers from the DRP Server Agents, the DistributedDirector parcels out the traffic load to multiple LocalDirectors. These LocalDirectors then provide local, intelligent load balancing to ensure that connections are allocated to the best servers at each distributed server site.

The examples in this section are real configurations for a DistributedDirector and a LocalDirector. The comments within the configurations will assist you in understanding the functionality of certain commands. Figure 13-13 is a visual representation of the configurations.

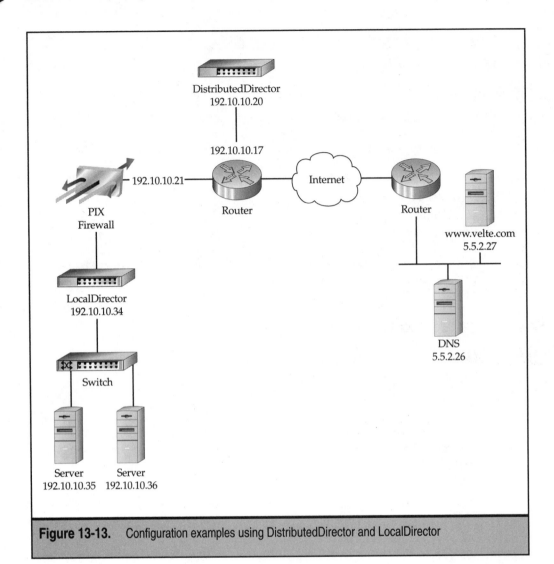

Figure 13-13. Configuration examples using DistributedDirector and LocalDirector

The DistributedDirector is typically located off the Internet router, in order to eliminate unnecessary traffic on the internal LAN. The LocalDirector sits in front of the switch (or hub) where your server farm connects, or the servers may plug directly into the LocalDirector. According to the configurations in the next two sections, a client requesting Web services from www.velte.com will be sent initially to the DistributedDirector. The DistributedDirector will determine whether the servers behind the LocalDirector can provide the best response, or whether the request should be sent to IP address 5.5.2.27. DistributedDirector uses Portion metric values assigned to both the LocalDirector and the IP address 5.5.2.27. If the traffic is directed to the LocalDirector, that system will select the best server based on the round-robin technique.

DistributedDirector Configuration Example

The DistributedDirector configuration file listed here, along with the LocalDirector configuration file that follows this section, are graphically illustrated in Figure 13-13. We have added comments within the DistributedDirector configuration file to help you understand the purpose of various commands.

```
!
version 11.1
service timestamps debug uptime
service timestamps log uptime
service udp-small-servers
service tcp-small-servers
!
hostname DistributedDirector
!
boot system flash c45dd_11.bin
enable password cisco
!
ip subnet-zero
!
interface Ethernet 0
  ip address 192.10.10.20 255.255.255.240
  no ip directed-director
  media-type 10BaseT
!
interface Ethernet 1
  no ip address
  no ip directed-broadcast
  shutdown
  media-type 10BaseT
!
interface TokenRing0
  no ip address
  no ip directed-broadcast
  shutdown
!
interface TokenRing1
  no ip address
  no ip directed-broadcast
  shutdown
!
/**next command binds http name www.velte.com to LocalDirector IP
/**address
```

```
ip host www.velte.com 192.10.10.34 5.5.2.27
/**next command specifies to the private DNS that Director should
/**send requests to
ip name-server 5.5.2.26
ip classless
/**next two commands configure static routes
ip route 0.0.0.0 0.0.0.0 192.10.10.17
ip dns primary www.velte.com soa distributeddirector.velte.com
hostmaster.velte.com 21600 900 7776000 86400
/**next command turns off the Director cache
no ip director cache
/**next four commands specify the simple preference of servers
ip director server 192.10.10.34 portion 1
ip director server 5.5.2.27 portion 1
ip director hosts www.velte.com priority por 1
ip director hosts www.velte.com connect 8
interval 10
logging buffered
!
line con 0
  transport input none
line aux 0
line vty 0 4
  password tryandgetin
  login
!
end
!
```

LocalDirector Configuration Example

The LocalDirector configuration file listed here, along with the DistributedDirector configuration file in the preceding section, are graphically illustrated in Figure 13-13. We have added comments within the LocalDirector configuration file to help you understand the purpose of various commands.

```
:saved
:LocalDirector 410 Version 2.2.1
syslog output 20.3
no syslog console
hostname localdirector
no shutdown ethernet 0
no shutdown ethernet 1
no shutdown ethernet 2
interface ethernet 0 auto
```

```
interface ethernet 1 auto
interface ethernet 2 auto
mtu 0 1500
mtu 1 1500
mtu 2 1500
multiring all
/**next three commands indicate that the external world
/**(i.e. Internet) can access the servers - no security is being applied
no secure 0
no secure 1
no secure 2
/**next three commands enable ping through each interface (0,1,&2)
ping-allow 0
ping-allow 1
ping-allow 2
ip address 192.10.10.37 255.255.255.240
/**next two commands show the LocalDirector has not been configured
/**for failover (other the IP address would be assigned and the
/**failover command would not be negated
failover ip address 0.0.0.0
no failover
telnet 192.10.10.1 255.255.255.0
no snmp-server contact
no snmp-server location
/**next command assigns the IP address as a "Virtual" IP address
/**that is 'is' (in-service vs. 'oos', out-of-service)
virtual 192.10.10.34:0:0 is
/**next command assigns the conditions traffic will be distributed
/**to applicable server. In this example the predictor is set to
/**roundrobin
predictor 192.10.10.34:0:0 roundrobin
/**next two commands assign the IP addresses as "Real" IP addresses
/**that are 'is' (in-service vs. 'oos', out-of-service)
real 192.10.10.35:0 is
real 192.10.10.36:0 is
name 192.10.10.36 Real2
name 192.10.10.35 Real1
name 192.10.10.34 Virtual
bind 192.10.10.34:0:0 192.10.10.36:
/** next three commands assign a name to an IP address so you don't
/**have to keep typing in the IP address
name 192.10.10.35 Real2
name 192.10.10.35 Real1
name 192.10.10.34 Virtual
/**next two commands bind the Real IP addresses to the Virtual
```

```
/**IP address
bind 192.10.10.34:0:0 192.10.10.36:0
bind 192.10.10.34:0:0 192.10.10.35:0
```

CISCO'S CACHE ENGINES

As stated often in this chapter, companies are depending on the Internet more and more for research, training, benchmarking, and other activities that help increase their bottom line. This growth of Internet traffic increases a company's WAN bandwidth congestion and fosters high transmission costs. Cisco Cache Engines can optimize the WAN bandwidth usage by localizing traffic patterns. WAN bandwidth costs go down, and the quality and availability of network service go up.

Cisco Network Caching Solution

The Cisco network caching solution is designed and optimized to work as a single caching system, in which are combined the following features:

▼ **Cache-aware internetworking equipment**   Cisco routers are capable today of allowing the network to optimize traffic flows based on type of content flowing through them. This is done by the Web Cache Communication Protocol (WCCP), a router/cache protocol that localizes network traffic and provides "network-intelligent" load distribution among single or multiple network caches for maximized download performances and content availability.

▲ **Network-integrated Cisco Cache Engines**   Cisco Cache Engines provide network management capabilities already available on Cisco networking gear, resulting in minimized management and operational costs. In addition, these engines are specifically designed as a caching network hardware solution. Therefore, they are generally a lot faster than other caching solutions. Cisco Cache Engines are transparent to end users. The end users do not have to change what gateway their computer systems point to. This means if the Cisco Cache Engine fails, the network knows this and sends the user's request directly out the Internet; the end users don't even know the Cisco Cache Engine failed.

The Cisco Cache Engine solution has several benefits. Some are highlighted here:

▼ Transparent network caching

■ Hierarchical deployment

■ Scalable clustering

■ Fault tolerance/fail safety

■ WCCP multihome router support

■ Overload bypass

- Dynamic client bypass
- Reverse proxy

How Do Cisco Cache Engines Work?

In order to localize Internet bound traffic, your network needs to now how to qualify certain traffic and send it out based on specified parameters. This capacity can be achieved by enabling *content routing technology.* Cisco IOS software's Web Cache Communication Protocol (WWCP) can be enabled on your network's routers to provide this content routing technology. Then, the next step after configuration of WCCP is the placement of the Cisco Cache Engine(s) at strategic points within your existing network. These two steps complete the traffic localization solution.

The network caches will now transparently cache (or store frequently accessed content) and then locally fulfill successive requests for the same content. This will reduce repetitive transmission of identical content over WAN links. Figure 13-14 shows how the two components work together to keep Web requests local when possible.

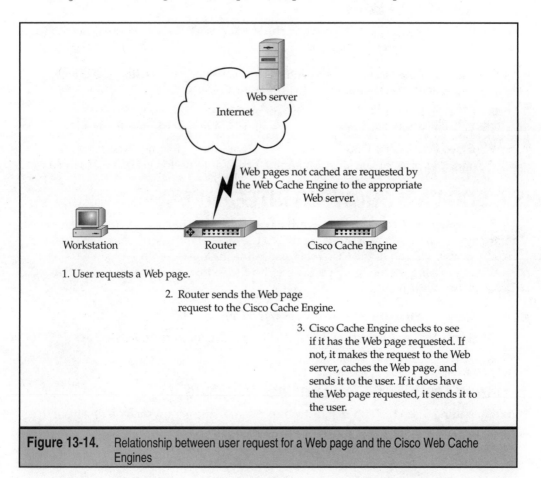

Figure 13-14.   Relationship between user request for a Web page and the Cisco Web Cache Engines

Other Alternatives to Cisco Cache Engines

The two most common types of caches on the market today are proxy servers and stand-alone caches. Proxy servers are software applications that run on servers and standard operating systems. The proxy server acts as a "gatekeeper." It receives all packets destined for the Internet and examines each packet to determine if it can fulfill the requests itself.

The downside to proxy servers is they are not a dedicated solution to provide Web caching, and so they fail under heavy network loads. In addition, since all clients need to be configured to point their workstations at the proxy server, the failure of the proxy server causes all users to lose network access. You would have to go to each workstation and change the gateway—a very tedious and time-consuming proposition.

Stand-alone cache systems are applications/appliances designed to improve performance by enhancing the caching software. Unfortunately, typical stand-alone cache systems are not network integrated, which means they have high ownership costs and are less desirable for wide-scale deployment.

Cisco Cache Engine Series

The Cisco Cache Engine is categorized in the 500 series, with each model designed for a different network environment:

▼ **Cisco Engine 505**   This is an entry-level cache engine for enterprise branch offices with WAN uplink bandwidth up to T1 rates.

■ **Cisco Engine 550**   This is a mid-range cache engine for Internet Service Providers (ISP) and enterprise sites with WAN uplink bandwidth up to 11 Mbps.

▲ **Cisco Engine 550-DS3**   This is the clustered Cache Engine 550 solution for ISPs and enterprise sites with WAN uplink bandwidth up to DS3 rates (45 Mbps).

THE CISCO WEB BROWSER INTERFACE

All Cisco routers and access servers loaded with Cisco IOS Release 11.0(6) or later have a home page. From this home page you can execute most of the Cisco IOS commands using a Web browser instead of the Cisco command-line interface.

Before jumping in, though, you have to do the following things in order to use the Cisco Web browser interface:

▼ Configure the Cisco Web browser interface.

■ Verify that you are using the correct browser hardware and software.

▲ Access the router's home page.

Configuring the Cisco Web Browser Interface

Prior to issuing Cisco IOS commands to your router using a browser, you first need to set up the Cisco Web browser interface as described in the following paragraphs. As stated earlier, the router must be running IOS release 11.0(6) or later software.

Enabling the Browser Interface

The first step in setting up the Cisco Web browser interface is actually enabling it on the router. Log into the router; enter enable mode, and then global configuration mode. Finally, enter the command to enable the Cisco Web browser:

```
Router>enable
Router#configuration terminal
Router(config)#ip http server
```

Changing the Browser Interface Port Number

The second step is to assign a port number to be used by the Cisco Web browser interface. By default, the browser interface uses port 80 on the router. Changing this is only necessary if you want to use a different port.

```
Router(config)#ip http port number
```

Controlling Access to the Browser Interface

To control client access to the HTTP server used by the Cisco Web browser interface, you need to assign an access list. The access list contains client IP addresses, allowing access by using a supported browser with the IP address and port number of the desired router. Here is the command:

```
Router(config)#ip http access-class access-list-number
```

Verifying the Browser Hardware and Software

Obviously, you need a browser to use the Cisco Web browser interface. The interface works with most browsers that can read and submit forms, including Netscape Navigator (version 4.06 or higher) and Microsoft Internet Explorer (version 4.01 SP1).

The computer running the Web browser must be connected to the same network as the router or access server.

Accessing the Router's Home Page

Once the router is enabled for IP HTTP server and your supported Web browser is properly set up, you're ready to connect to the router's home page.

1. Enter the name or address of the router or access server in the URL field of your browser and press ENTER.
2. Enter the user EXEC password of the router.

The browser will then display the home page for your router or access server. Figure 13-15 shows a home page for a Cisco 4500 router.

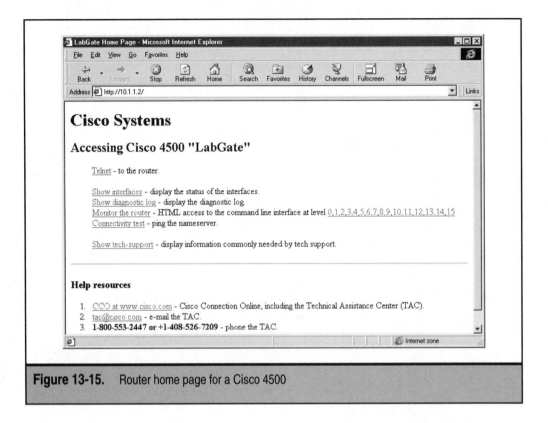

Figure 13-15.   Router home page for a Cisco 4500

Issuing Commands Using Cisco's Web Browser Interface

Once you have the home page displayed in your browser, you can click the link "Monitor the router" to display the Command Field Web page shown in Figure 13-16.

On the Command Field Web page you have three options for executing commands:

▼ **Enter Commands Using Hypertext Links**   To enter a command using hypertext links, scroll toward the bottom of the screen and click the desired command. If the command requires additional parameters, another list of command hypertext links is displayed. You then scroll through this second list and click the command you want. The **show** commands will display information in the Web browser window. Commands that require an argument will present a form on which the argument can be entered.

■ **Enter Commands Using the Command Field**   The Command Field is the white box at the top of the Command Field Web page. Here you can enter commands just like entering them at a terminal console. As in the Cisco IOS command-line interface, you can type a **?** to view the options for a particular command. The Command Field is also sensitive to the mode you are in and will only allow commands available in that mode to be executed. For instance, you can only apply access lists in the global configuration mode, so you'll have to enter that mode first by typing **config t** in the Command Field.

▲ **Enter Commands Using the URL Window**   You can also issue commands using the Web browser's URL window. For example, to execute a **show configuration** command on a router named **VelteRouter**, you enter **http://VelteRouter/exec/show/configuration** in the URL window. The Web browser then displays the configuration for the router.

Since the primary purpose in using a tool such as Cisco's Web browser interface is to simplify and reduce configuration time, your best bet is to use the hypertext links option for entering commands. The other two methods require that you know the exact command format, and you have to type in every command to be executed.

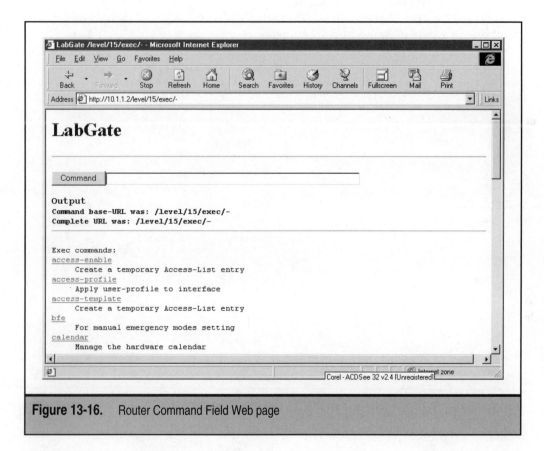

Figure 13-16.   Router Command Field Web page

SUMMARY

In line with advancing technology, today's companies have dispersed internally and have established multiple locations throughout the world. A single company may have a corporate headquarters office and multiple remote sites. Each location may support their own Web server or set of Web servers. Cisco's DistributedDirector simplifies access to multiple Web servers. The end user types in a single URL, and DistributedDirector then takes over to determine the lowest usage server and the fastest routes. DistributedDirector takes the best combination and sends the HTTP request to the best server.

LocalDirector operates similarly but at a local level. LocalDirector is placed in front of a server farm and balances the load among servers of the same functionality. Cisco Web Cache Engine helps you optimize WAN bandwidth, increase network scalability, and maximize network service quality and content availability. The Web Cache Engine works as a single caching system by combining Cisco IOS software's WCCP protocol and the network-integrated Cache Engine 500 series products, which are managed and designed like network products and will easily adapt to your network environment.

Cisco's Web browser interface is a utility supported by Cisco routers that allows the execution of the Cisco IOS commands through a Web browser. Although this simplifies keystrokes, you still need to know what each command does.

CHAPTER 14

Secure Connections

M ore and more data is shared over networks every day. As companies have focused on developing software and hardware to allow fast, stable, and reliable network connectivity among companies, business partners, and the Internet, the related security issues have been neglected. Risks resulting from this exchange of data were not initially considered, and mechanisms, therefore, were not available in the early hardware and software devices that allowed connectivity. Today the market for network security products is substantial and growing.

To get a grasp on today's security problems, and to proactively prevent security breaches, network administrators can choose from a variety of security tools from Cisco and Microsoft. This chapter discusses some of the most useful security hardware and software solutions.

CISCO ROUTER IOS SECURITY TECHNOLOGIES

First there was a single workstation that had no external connections other than maybe a printer or some other peripheral device. Then we gained the ability for two single nodes (such as workstations and servers) to communicate with each other. As more and more nodes sitting within a single building were connected, the concept of a local area network (LAN) evolved. The next major step in technology was communication among buildings within a company, and then the ultimate step (for now, at least): communication with other business partners and external resources of data. Routers were the initial network devices that connected these entities.

This technological evolution happened so fast that the security risks associated with connecting private networks to public networks were all but overlooked. Now Cisco and the majority of other vendors are continually modifying their operating systems to satisfy security requirements. Although the security capabilities of a router are obviously less than those found on firewalls, router security can still fulfill the needs of some companies with simple security requirements. This section describes the primary security features of Cisco routers.

Access Control Lists (ACLs)

Cisco IOS software can filter traffic based on network and transport layer information. Without a filter configured, the Cisco router is by default wide open and will allow all supported traffic through. A router's access control list (ACL) is its primary source of security, determining which traffic to block and which traffic to allow.

Filtering takes place by examining the IP or TCP/UDP and ICMP headers. Each of the fields within IP and TCP headers contains information that can include

▼   IP destination address

■   IP source address

■   IP protocol field

■   TCP source port

▲   TCP destination port

NOTE: Although this information is related specifically to IP traffic, packet filters do exist for other protocols such as IPX and AppleTalk. For simplicity's sake, this discussion primarily concerns IP ACLs.

Multiple filters are defined for various destinations, sources, protocols, and port numbers. Since each interface on a router can have ACLs applied, the filters are configured selectively based on the traffic that will traverse a certain interface. The combination of all the filters to be applied to an interface makes up a single ACL. Figure 14-1 demonstrates examples of router ACLs on one router.

NOTE: The example in Figure 14-1 does not depict Cisco ACL syntax, but rather general descriptions used in configuring an ACL.

Here are some things to keep in mind about ACLs:

▼ Each interface can have up to two ACLs for a given protocol: an ACL defining rules for inbound traffic, and an ACL defining rules for outbound traffic.

■ Almost always, if you have an ACL on an interface allowing outbound traffic, and an ACL on the same interface denying inbound traffic, you need to include a permission on the ACL denying inbound traffic to allow established traffic (responses to traffic initiated from inside).

■ If an interface does not have an ACL applied, then there are no filters applied and all traffic can flow freely.

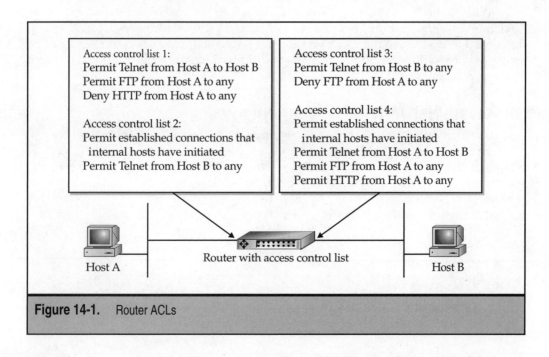

Figure 14-1. Router ACLs

- ■ If an interface has an ACL applied and there is only one entry in it, all other traffic is explicitly denied. (This makes it very important that, when an ACL is implemented, you make sure all authorized traffic has an entry.)
- ▲ Usually your ACL will reside on the last interface *before* the unprotected network—often an inbound filter on the outside address.

Network Address Translation (NAT)

Network Address Translation (NAT) is the process of converting one IP address into another IP address. Following is a summary of some of NAT's key features; this technology is discussed in greater detail later in this chapter.

- ▼ Network addresses can be translated statically or dynamically, depending on your requirements.
- ■ NAT is interface independent; it can be applied to any interface on the router that links inside-to-outside addressing schemes.
- ■ Typically, NAT operates on a border router between an inside private addressing scheme and an outside public addressing scheme.
- ▲ The configuration for NAT takes place both globally on the network device and on the interface to which NAT is being applied.

Port Address Translation (PAT) is a subset of NAT that allows you to map multiple IP addresses to a single IP address, and use PATs to decipher the various connections. PAT is beneficial in situations where limited registered IP addresses are available to use for NAT. Whereas PAT allows many inside addresses to be serviced by one outside address, NAT translates inside addresses to a pool of several outside addresses. Note that you don't need a one-for-one number of inside and outside addresses because NAT can be configured in overload mode, in which many inside addresses can be translated by just a few outside addresses.

Virtual Private Network (VPN) Technologies

A virtual private network (VPN) is a private tunnel between two devices, typically across an unprotected network. Although encryption is most often used to create this private tunnel, certain Internet service providers (ISPs) sell VPN solutions where the traffic is statically routed. Even though no encryption takes place, these ISPs consider this arrangement to be their own virtual private network.

VPN solutions can exist between several types of devices, including

- ▼ VPN routers
- ■ VPN firewalls
- ■ VPN servers
- ▲ VPN clients

Note that VPNs fill various roles. One VPN may be a single-user, remote access solution. Another may be a multiuser LAN-to-LAN connection across the Internet. These two interpretations of VPN have their own specific technical issues and may use different technologies.

Figure 14-2 illustrates a VPN across an unprotected network such as the Internet.

VPN solutions are sold by many vendors. As for any other technology, standardization among versions is needed to support interoperability. Internet Protocol Security (IPSec) is a collection of standards used to support an IP-layer VPN. By using encryption, security, and authentication protocols, IPSec ensures confidentiality, integrity, and authenticity.

Cisco offers IPSec across a wide range of platforms, including Cisco IOS software and Cisco PIX Firewall. IPSec is available in Cisco IOS software version 11.3(3)T. IPSec-supported platforms include

▼   Cisco 1600 Series

■   Cisco 1720 Series

■   Cisco 2500 Series

■   Cisco 2600 Series

■   Cisco 3600 Series

■   Cisco 4000 Series

■   Cisco 4500 Series

■   Cisco 5300 Series

■   Cisco 7100 Series

■   Cisco 7200 Series

▲   Cisco 7500 Series

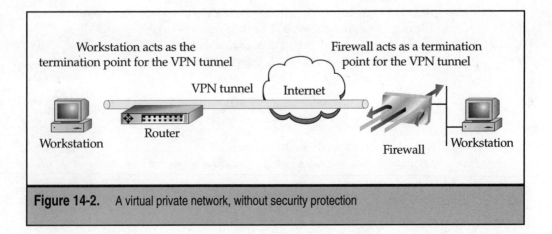

Figure 14-2.   A virtual private network, without security protection

If you don't currently have Cisco hardware in your network infrastructure (or you don't have the IPSec-supported platforms), enabling the Cisco VPN solution will require the purchase of extensive hardware and software. You'll need to obtain the components on each end to create the VPN tunnel—whether these components are IPSec-supported routers, firewalls, servers, or client software.

Microsoft offers a PPTP VPN client solution, included in their Routing and Remote Access Server (RRAS) Pack. By setting up a VPN server, any clients running the supported operating systems (Windows 9x, 2000, and NT) can be configured to establish a PPTP VPN connection for little to no hardware cost. (This assumes you have an NT server that could be configured as a VPN server and your users are currently using Windows NT, 9x, or 2000.) The configurations and requirements to set up Microsoft's PPTP VPN solution are defined later in this chapter.

Event Logging

Another security feature provided by Cisco IOS is the automatic logging of system output error messages to a console terminal or syslog server. This allows administrators to track and monitor abnormal activities and possible security breaches.

Identification and Authentication

Cisco IOS requires entry of two different passwords (user EXEC and privileged EXEC) in order to execute configuration commands. In previous IOS releases, access was pretty much all or nothing. Now the privileges offer 16 levels of access. User EXEC is level 1, fully privileged is level 15, and level 0 might be a guest who is only allowed to connect and disconnect.

The following commands show how to set up a user at level 5 and allow simple debugging, ping, and traceroutes. Remember that you must be in the highest level configuration mode (at privilege level 15) in order to perform these configurations.

```
Router(config)#enable password level 5 password
Router(config)#privilege exec level 5 debug frame-relay autoinstall
Router(config)#privilege exec level 5 debug frame-relay events
Router(config)#privilege exec level 5 debug frame-relay lmi
Router(config)#privilege exec level 5 ping
Router(config)#privilege exec level 5 trace
```

The following commands are two ways to configure the fully privileged (level 15) password:

```
Router(config)#enable password enablepassword
Router(config)#enable password level 15 enablepassword
```

Although the foregoing configuration options are useful, they may have certain limitations and can take time to accomplish for each potential user who needs access to network devices. Cisco offers, in addition, the following add-on tools that enable you to control authentication, authorization, and accounting:

▼ **TACACS+**   Terminal Access Controller Access Control System

▲ **RADIUS**   Remote Authentication Dial-in User Services

These tools are defined in detail in Chapter 16.

TIP: Always use a username for logging in, whether you are logging in locally or using an AAA server. Entering a username will provide an audit trail in the logs showing who has made changes.

Route Authentication

Route authentication is typically used in conjunction with Cisco router network data encryption. Route authentication enables peer encrypting routers to positively identify the source of incoming encrypted data. This authentication process occurs each time a new encrypted session is initiated, as discussed in the following section.

Cisco route authentication is also used to verify the authenticity of routing tables from other routers. Prior to the enabling of route authentication, routers trusted the sources sending them routing information. An intruder could develop faulty route information and send it to a router. The router would update its routing table accordingly, and might then start sending packets to the intruder packets. With Cisco IOS route authentication, routers can identify other routers and verify their legitimacy before accepting route updates.

Network-Level Encryption

With the development of networks came the flow of data from machine to machine. This data often passes through public or uncontrolled networks such as the Internet. Data that traverses these unsecured networks is subject to many types of attacks—the data can be read, altered, or forged by anybody who has access to the route your data takes. By configuring your network to apply *encryption* to the data before sending it out on a public network, you can significantly reduce the chances of your information being compromised.

What is encryption? Cryptography is the concept of keeping information, especially sensitive information, private; encryption is the process of modifying the appearance of data to make it private. Encryption is performed using an algorithm that takes plaintext data and converts it to *ciphertext*—encrypted data. A key applied to the algorithm determines the end result of the ciphertext. Different keys used on the same plaintext data will result in different ciphertext. The level or strength of encryption relies on the key and its length.

The most well-known encryption algorithm is the U.S. government-endorsed Data Encryption Standard (DES). This encryption is supported by Cisco's network encryption and is discussed further in a later section.

Cisco Network Data Encryption

Cisco provides network data encryption at the IP packet level. When the data is sent, the IP packet can be seen but the IP contents cannot be read. The IP header and upper-layer protocols, TCP or UDP, are not encrypted; but all the data within the packet is encrypted.

Encryption and decryption take place at *peer routers,* which must be specifically configured to perform the encryption and decryption of the data. No other routers take part in the encryption/decryption process. Your peer routers should be chosen based on the final destinations of the data. This means your peer routers typically would be perimeter routers placed in front of the public or unprotected network. Figure 14-3 illustrates encryption and decryption on the peer routers.

In conjunction with peer router–to–peer router encryption, router authentication also occurs. This is the process by which each peer router positively identifies incoming encrypted data to prohibit attackers from forging transmitted data or being able to identify data that has been tampered with. Router authentication occurs each time an encrypted session is established.

Cisco uses the Digital Signature Standard (DSS), the Diffie-Hellman (DH) public-key algorithm, and the Data Encryption Standard (DES) to implement network data encryption.

Digital Signature Standard (DSS)

Digital Signature Standard (DSS) is used by Cisco to authenticate that the data received is coming from the other peer router. Each router has both a public and private DSS key. The first step in setting up DSS is sharing and verifying the public key on each peer router. This step only occurs once. The public keys are shared by creating a public key on a router and propagating it to other peer routers. The verification of the public key on other peer routers is done verbally from network administrator to network administra-

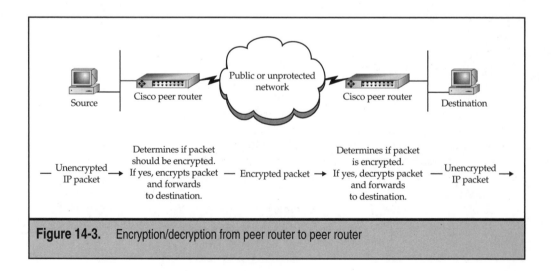

Figure 14-3.   Encryption/decryption from peer router to peer router

tor. Although the DSS public key is distributed to all peer routers, the DSS private key is not shared with any other devices. Figure 14-4 shows the sharing and verification of the DSS public keys.

In order for two peer routers to establish an encrypted session, they must first authenticate and generate a temporary Data Encryption Standard (DES) key. This key will be used to encrypt the data during the encryption session. Connection messages between peer routers provide authentication and the generation of the temporary DES key, as follows:

▼ **Authentication**   A router sending a connection message attaches its "signature"—a character string created by each router using the DSS private key. This signature is verified by the receiving router, using the DSS public key. Once this process is complete, the router is authenticated.

▲ **Key generation**   DES keys are generated by an exchange of Diffie-Hellman (DH) numbers during the connection messages. These DH numbers are then used to compute a common DES session key shared by both routers.

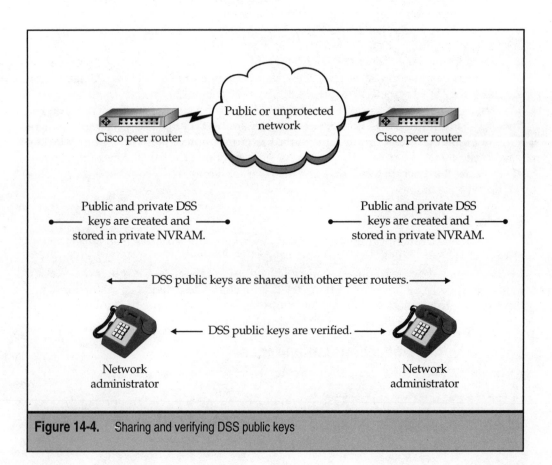

Figure 14-4.   Sharing and verifying DSS public keys

Data Encryption Standard (DES)

The Data Encryption Standard (DES) uses a key to encrypt and decrypt IP packets. The previous section described how the DES key is determined. When the encryption session terminates, the DH numbers and the DES key are discarded. New encryption sessions require another set of connection messages to establish new DH numbers and a new DES key.

There are several types of DES encryption algorithms. Cisco supports the following four types:

▼ Basic DES with 8-bit Cipher Feedback (CFB)

■ Basic DES with 64-bit CFB

■ 40-bit variation of DES with 8-bit CFB

▲ 40-bit variation of DES with 64-bit CFB

Basic DES uses a 56-bit key and an algorithm that scrambles data by running it through multiple iterations of its algorithm. Depending on the nature of your business, export laws may require you to use 40-bit DES. If you are running a nonexportable image, the DES default will be basic DES with 64-bit CFB.

DES is a *single-key (symmetrical)* cryptographic scheme. This means a single key is used to encrypt and decrypt the messages. As described for DSS, this key is generated by the exchange of DH numbers during the connection messages.

Certain network devices support *two-key (asymmetrical)* public-key cryptography. Two-key is an alternative to the private-key DES. In this scheme, everybody gets a set of keys—a public and a private key. The public key is distributed freely, and the private key is held secretly. To send an encrypted message, you obtain the public key being distributed and use it to encrypt the data. The data is sent, and only the destination's private key can decrypt the data.

Crypto Engine

Encryption and authentication are provided by a software service called *crypto engine*. The crypto engine resides on the router's Cisco IOS encryption feature-set software. All Cisco routers have at least one crypto engine, and some of the larger routers have more than one crypto. You have to configure the crypto engine to provide encryption and authentication. This includes enabling the crypto engine and assigning the router interfaces that will participate in the encryption and authentication.

Encryption/Authentication Configurations

Each router that is acting as a peer router must perform the following steps:

GENERATE DSS PUBLIC/PRIVATE KEYS   You must generate a public and private DSS key on each router—more specifically, on each crypto engine on a router, which means routers with more than one crypto engine will require each to be configured. The following commands are used to generate DSS public and private keys and save them to NVRAM:

```
Router(config)#crypto gen-signature-keys
Router(config)#privatekeyname
Router#copy running-config startup-config
```

EXCHANGE DSS PUBLIC KEYS   The DSS public keys must be exchanged between the peer routers. One router is the *active* router and the other router is *passive*. The passive router needs the following global configuration:

```
Router(config)#crypto key-exchange passive
```

and the active router needs the following global configuration:

```
Router(config)#crypto key-exchange ip-address key-name
```

The IP address in the active router's configuration command is the IP address of the passive peer router. These commands must be done simultaneously—typically with each network administrator on the phone. Once you have issued the preceding configuration commands, the following will occur:

1. The active router's DSS key serial number and fingerprint are displayed on the screen. (These are numeric values that should be identical on both peer routers.)

2. Identical numeric values means the passive router agrees to accept the active router's DSS key.

3. The passive router prompts the administrator to return a DSS public key. The administrator presses ENTER.

4. The passive router then prompts the administrator to confirm a public-key name. To accept, press ENTER.

5. The passive router DSS public key is now sent to the active router.

6. The passive DSS serial number and fingerprint are now displayed on both screens.

7. The two administrators verbally verify that the serial number and fingerprint are identical on both routers.

8. The active router administrator presses ENTER to accept the passive DSS public key.

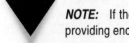

NOTE: If there are multiple peer routers, these steps must be completed for each peer router providing encrypted sessions.

Figure 14-5 illustrates the process for exchanging DSS keys.

ENABLE THE DES ENCRYPTION ALGORITHMS   The DES encryption algorithms must be enabled to provide encrypted sessions. This command needs to occur only once per router, even if you have a router with multiple crypto engines. One DES algorithm is enabled for your router by default. In a nonexportable image, the DES default algorithm will be basic ES with 64-bit CFB. In an exportable image, the DES default algorithm will be the 40-bit variation of DES with 64-bit CFB.

Use the following command to view the enabled DES algorithm on a router:

```
Router#show crypto algorithms
```

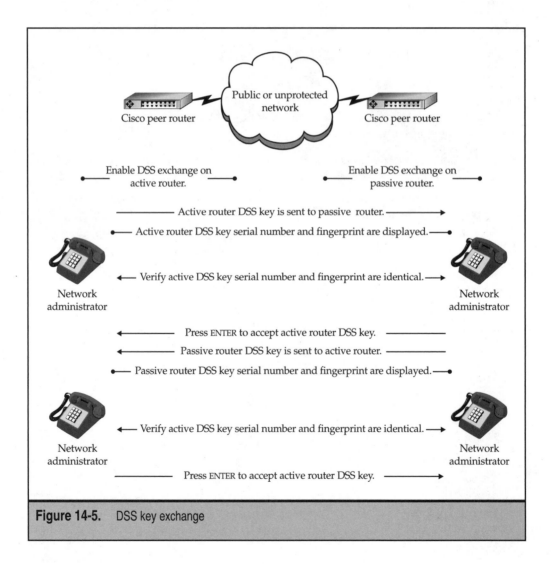

Figure 14-5.   DSS key exchange

To change the DES algorithm, type

```
Router#crypto algorithm
```

followed by one of the supported DES algorithm types:

```
des cfb-8
des cfb-64
40-bit-des cfb-8
40-bit-des cfb-64
```

NOTE: 8-bit CFB requires more CPU processing time than a 64-bit CFB.

DEFINE CRYPTO MAPS AND ASSIGN THEM TO INTERFACES   The preceding steps enabled the peer routers to have the capability to perform encryption and authentication. The next step is to tell the peer routers which traffic they need to encrypt and authenticate, and then apply this information to the appropriate interfaces. This is accomplished in three steps:

1. *Set up encryption ACLs.* These ACLs are similar to generic router ACLs. They define for the router what traffic is permitted and what traffic is denied, what permitted traffic is encrypted, and what denied traffic is not encrypted. Here is the command used to create an ACL entry:

    ```
    Router(config)#access-list access-list-number permit
    protocol source-ip-address source-mask destination-ip-address
    destination-ip-mask
    ```

2. *Define crypto maps.* A crypto map is used to specify which DES encryption algorithm will be applied to the ACL created. This is done by creating a crypto map, specifying the peer router and access list, and then setting the DES encryption algorithm. The configuration commands for this step are as follows:

    ```
    Router(config)#crypto map map-name
    Router(config)#set peer peer-router-name
    Router(config)#match access-list access-list-number
    Router(config)#set algorithm des-algorithm-type
    ```

3. *Apply crypto maps to interface.* The last step is to apply the crypto map you have just created to a router interface. You must apply one crypto map to each interface that will encrypt outbound data and decrypt inbound data. The following command is used to apply a crypto map to an interface. This command is performed on the interface to which the map should be applied:

    ```
    Router(config)#crypto map map-name
    ```

Denial of Service Detection and Prevention

The TCP protocol is a connection-orientated protocol used to carry the vast majority of Internet applications. As illustrated in Figure 14-6, TCP uses a *three-way handshake* to set up an end-to-end connection before data flows.

SYN-flooding attacks are a type of denial-of-service attack in which an intruder repeatedly sends synchronous packets with invalid source IP addresses. The acknowledge packets are therefore returned to illegitimate hosts, resulting in half-open connections. Too many half-open requests causes a server to exhaust its memory or waste processor cycles by trying to maintain state information on the bad connections. Many types of hosts will crash or perform a core dump when they are flooded with SYN packets.

Cisco IOS provides TCP Intercept, which prevents SYN-flooding attacks by tracking, optionally intercepting, and validating TCP connection requests. When used in intercept mode (the default setting), TCP Intercept will check for incoming TCP connection requests and validate the requests before sending them on to the server. Once a request has been validated between the client and the server, TCP Intercept stops intercepting the traffic and allows a single source/destination session. See Figure 14-7.

Recommended Security Configuration

By enabling a combination of the Cisco IOS security features described in this section, you'll make a good start toward designing a secure network environment. There are several other simple configurations that can be set to increase the level of system security.

▼ *Use **enable secret** rather than **enable password**.* It's important to set a password for controlling access to the privileged command mode. The use of **enable secret** instead of **enable password** will encrypt the password more securely.

■ *Put a password on the console port.* The console port should be considered as important a security risk as someone accessing the network device through any other interface. The **line console 0** command establishes a login password on the console port.

■ *Establish a username and password for administrator login to the router.* This feature provides limited authentication benefits. The command is

```
Router(config)#Username Bob password 7 mypassword
```

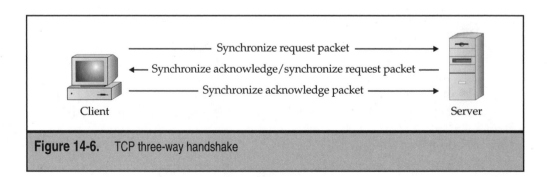

Figure 14-6.   TCP three-way handshake

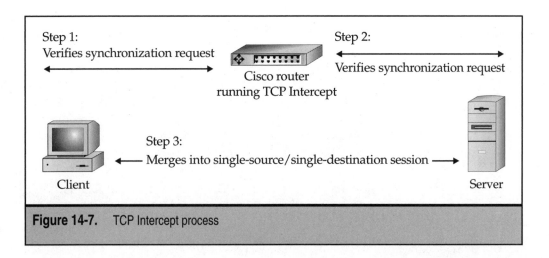

Figure 14-7.   TCP Intercept process

■ *Don't enable local services such as Telnet unless they're used.* If you support your network device 100% from the console port and don't require any other additional services to be provided by the router, then you should make sure these local services are not allowed. If you do need to access your router through a Telnet session, you can use the **line vty 0 4** command to establish a login password on incoming Telnet sessions for up to five sessions.

■ *Disable source routing.* IP source routing can sometimes be used to transport packets to parts of the network from which these packets should be blocked. Make it a habit to configure **no ip source-route** when you're setting up security-sensitive routers. Here is the command to disable source routing:

```
Router(config)#no ip source-route
```

■ *Disable minor services (TCP and UDP servers).* Unless they are disabled, the **small-servers** commands can be used to assist a variety of attacks. Use the following commands to disable the small servers:

```
Router(config)#no service udp-small-servers
Router(config)#no service tcp-small-servers
```

■ *Disable directed broadcasts.* Directed broadcasts can be used to assist intruders in denial-of-service attacks and therefore should be disabled on any interface where they are not actually needed. Here is the command to disable directed broadcasts:

```
Router(config)#no ip directed-broadcast
```

▲ *Turn off Cisco Discovery Protocol (CDP) on security-sensitive routers.* CDP provides information about the router and therefore should be disabled on security-sensitive routers. Here is the command to disable CDP:

```
Router(config)#no cdp enable
```

NETWORK ADDRESS TRANSLATION (NAT)

Cisco's Network Address Translation (NAT) process converts one IP address safely into another IP address. NAT is used primarily in the following roles:

▼ NAT allows you to hide your internal IP address scheme, for security purposes.

■ If you have an internal network configured with nonregistered IP addresses, NAT allows safe connectivity to a public network by translating these addresses to registered IP addresses before forwarding the traffic onto the public network. This saves you the time of redoing your internal IP address scheme.

▲ Internal machines that match up to static NAT IP addresses (mail servers, for instance) can be swapped without having to update records stored on the Internet.

Following are the advantages and disadvantages of NAT.

Advantages

▼ NAT conserves the number of legally registered IP addresses taken up for public network interaction.

■ Network design is simplified because of unlimited availability of addressing schemes (no more growth restrictions relating to lack of IP addresses).

■ When mergers occur, NAT allows for a seamless integration by maintaining previously implemented IP address schemes.

■ NAT eliminates the need to re-address a network that requires public network interaction.

▲ Security is increased by masking the internal IP address scheme.

Disadvantages

▼ There is a loss of end-to-end IP traceability.

▲ Switching path delays may occur when the IP addresses are translated (though this is typically imperceptible).

NAT hides end-to-end addresses, and so applications that use physical IP addresses instead of qualified domain names will not reach destinations that are translated across the NAT router. A possible solution to this problem may be to use static NAT rather than dynamic NAT.

Network Address Translation can be done *statically* or *dynamically* depending on your requirements. In static translation, an internal node initiating a connection to an external network receives the same NAT IP address every time. The NAT table has an entry for each static IP address, to map to the corresponding static NAT IP address.

A dynamic translation occurs when an internal node initiates an outbound connection and is assigned a random NAT IP address. In this case, there is a list of dynamic NAT IP addresses; every time the connection is initiated (by a permitted source) the next NAT IP address on the list is pulled and assigned as the new IP address for the internal node. Figure 14-8 demonstrates the difference between static and dynamic NAT.

NAT Availability

In Cisco IOS software releases 11.2 and 11.2P, full NAT functionality—including Port Address Translation (PAT), which is a subset of full NAT—is available only in Plus images.

In Cisco IOS software releases 11.3 and 11.3T, PAT is available in all base images on selected platforms. This means customers who only require PAT functionality do not need to purchase a Plus image.

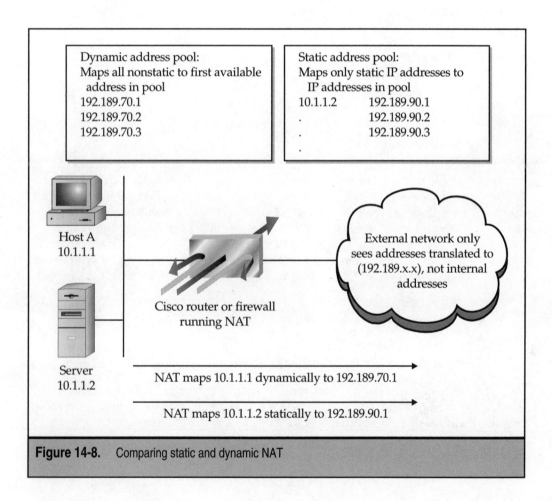

Figure 14-8. Comparing static and dynamic NAT

Beginning with Cisco IOS software release 12.0, complete Cisco IOS NAT functionality, including PAT, is available in all software images for platforms that support Cisco IOS NAT, at no extra charge. Although all Plus images will continue to deliver full NAT functionality, customers are not required to purchase Plus images in order to obtain full NAT functionality.

Beginning with Cisco IOS software releases 11.2(13)P, 11.3(3)T, 12.0(1), and 12.0(1)T, full NAT functionality is included in all 1600 and 2500 Cisco IOS Firewall images.

At the time of this writing, NAT is supported on the following platforms:

▼ Cisco 1000 Series

■ Cisco 1600 Series

■ Cisco 2500 Series

■ Cisco 3600 Series

■ Cisco 4000 Series

■ AS5200

■ RSP 7000 Series

■ Cisco 7200 Series

▲ Cisco 7500 Series

NAT Functionality Overview

NAT is interface independent, which means it can be applied to any interface on the router that links inside-to-outside addressing schemes. Typically, NAT operates on a border router between an inside private addressing scheme and an outside public addressing scheme. The configurations for NAT take place both globally on the network device and on the interface to which NAT is being applied. Specific configurations are discussed later in this section.

NAT can be done for both inbound and outbound connections and for both source and destination IP addresses. There are three basic circumstances for which NAT would be used:

▼ To translate an internal source IP address

■ To translate an external source IP address

▲ To translate an internal destination IP address

Although NAT can be applied to external IP addresses, typical NAT is used for internal IP address translations, to hide the internal IP address and/or translate nonregistered or private IP addresses to registered IP addresses that are routable on a public network infrastructure. As mentioned earlier, translating the internal IP address has several benefits. Let's take a closer look at these benefits.

Elimination of Re-addressing Overhead

Let's say you have a network that is composed of illegal, nonregistered IP addresses, and you want to connect your network to the Internet. In order for any packets to be routable across a public domain such as the Internet, the source and destination of these packets must be registered IP addresses. So, in order for any of your nodes to send or receive Internet traffic, you'll have to re-address your entire network—a conversion that would not only take substantial time and money to accomplish, but would also involve a good-sized investment for obtaining the required block of registered IP addresses.

NAT provides an alternative: By using NAT, all your internal IP addresses can continue to use nonregistered IP addresses. You obtain a small block of IP addresses from your Internet service provider (ISP), and a subset of these IP addresses are configured as the NAT IP address pool. With NAT addresses in place, any of your internal nodes initiating outbound connections will exchange their illegal source IP address for a legal NAT IP address. Any external nodes requesting a connection with an internal node will use the NAT IP address as the destination. NAT will then translate this NAT IP address to the actual internal destination IP address.

Port Address Translation (PAT)

Port Address Translation (PAT) is an additional address translation option. Typically considered a subset of NAT, PAT translates IP addresses to a single PAT IP address. PAT is only supported for UDP or TCP connections.

The PAT table contains a single registered IP address, and the source IP address of an internal node is mapped to this single PAT IP address. This part of PAT functionality is almost identical to NAT, except that only one IP address is being used. PAT earns its name because, in addition to swapping IP addresses, the port number associated with the connection is actually translated to a different port number. These translations are maintained in a table, which identifies the final location for the return connection.

PAT can be configured to use a specific IP address, or it can use the interface IP address on the interface on which PAT is configured. The following examples show configurations of PAT in these two situations. Pay close attention to the applicable privilege mode for both configurations. Both examples assume an access list 100 has been created.

Here's PAT configured using a specified IP address:

```
router(config-int)#ip nat outside
router(config)#ip nat pool NATAddresses 189.198.211.10
189.198.211.10 netmask 255.255.255.0
router(config)#ip nat inside source list 100 pool NATAddresses
overload
```

Here's PAT configured using the router's interface IP address:

```
router(config-int)#ip nat outside
router(config)#ip nat inside source list 100 interface Serial0
overload
```

When to Configure NAT, and When Not To

Although Network Address Translation has several compelling benefits, there are also situations when NAT should *not* be configured.

Cisco IOS NAT supports several types of applications or traffic. If you are planning to implement Cisco IOS NAT and already have traffic, you need to verify that Cisco IOS NAT does indeed support your requirements. A good rule of thumb is that Cisco IOS NAT will more than likely support TCP or UDP traffic that does not carry source and/or destination IP addresses in the application data stream. However, there are exceptions to this rule, including these applications and protocols:

▼ ICMP

■ FTP

■ NetBIOS over TCP/IP

■ RealAudio

■ CuSeeMe

■ StreamWorks

■ DNS's A and PTR queries

■ H.323 version12.0(1) and later

■ NetMeeting version 12.0(1) and later

■ VDOLive version 11.3(4) and later

▲ Vextreme version 11.3(4) and later

Table 14-1 lists the protocols and applications supported by Cisco IOS NAT at the time this book was written.

Supported by Cisco IOS NAT	Not Supported by Cisco IOS NAT
HTTP	IP Multicast
TFTP	Routing table updates
Telnet	DNS zone transfers
Archie	talk, ntalk
Finger	SNMP
NTP	NetShow
NFS	
Rlogin, rsh, rcp	

Table 14-1. Protocols and Applications Supported by NAT

NAT Configuration

There are three different parts to configuring Cisco IOS Network Address Translation: marking the interface; defining the pool of addresses; and enabling the address translation.

Part 1: Marking an interface to be inside or outside

In order for packets to be translated on an interface, that interface needs to be marked as to whether inside or outside packets are to be translated. Packets arriving on an unmarked interface will not be subject to translation. In the following example, an interface is designated as the one where the outbound (internal to external) packets are being translated:

```
router(config-int)#ip nat outside
```

Part 2: Defining the pool of NAT IP addresses

All IP addresses that are going to be translated will be pulled from the designated pool of NAT IP addresses. To allocate this pool of IP addresses, use the following command:

```
router(config)#ip nat pool NATAddresses 189.198.211.10
189.198.211.25 netmask 255.255.255.0
```

where **NATAddresses** is the name assigned to the pool.

Part 3: Enabling the translation of the IP addresses

The last part is to tell the router which addresses are going to be translated to the addresses in the global NAT IP address pool. There are three ways this can be defined, as shown in the following examples. The examples assume an access list of 100 and a pool named NATAddresses has been configured previously. (For more information on configuring access lists, refer to Chapter 5.)

Translating inside source addresses:

```
router(config)#ip nat inside source list 100 pool NATAddresses
```

Translating inside destination addresses:

```
router(config)#ip nat inside destination list 100 pool
NATAddresses
```

Translating outside source addresses:

```
router(config)#ip nat outside source list 100 pool NATAddresses
```

These three examples, using the form **list** *nn* **pool** *xx*, are used to enable dynamic NAT. In order to configure static NAT, use the following format:

```
Router(config)#ip nat outside source static global-ip-address
local-ip-address
```

VIRTUAL PRIVATE NETWORKS (VPNS)

A virtual private network (VPN) is a private connection between two different locations. This connection is typically encrypted, may employ a tunnel, and may have both. The Point-to-Point Protocol (PPP) remote access protocol is often used to establish a dial-up connection to an Internet service provider. Once a connection is established, a tunneling protocol creates the VPN channel.

Point-to-Point Tunneling Protocol (PPTP)

Point-to-Point Tunneling Protocol (PPTP) enables the secure transfer of data from a remote client to a private enterprise server. PPTP supports multiple network protocols, including IP, IPX, and NetBEUI. You can use PPTP to provide a secure virtual network using dial-up lines, over LANs, over WANs, or across the Internet and other TCP/IP-based networks. In order to establish a PPTP VPN, you must have a PPTP server and a PPTP client. Windows 2000 Client and Server software includes the necessary parameters to configure PPTP communication.

Planning for the PPTP Installation

The following is a list of key points that need to be recognized and understood before you implement PPTP.

▼ PPTP uses Microsoft's implementation of RAS and the Point-to-Point Protocol (PPP) to establish connections with remote computers by using dial-up lines. The mechanics of PPP are discussed in upcoming sections.

■ To use PPTP, you must install and configure RAS with Dial-Up Networking on the PPTP server as well as the clients.

■ For a dial-up solution, you must establish a PPP account with your ISP.

■ PPTP uses VPNs that are installed and configured in RAS as if they were physical devices.

■ PPTP is only installed on the client and on the server—not on any devices in between.

■ Consider placing the PPTP server on the external side of a firewall. The firewall can then check the traffic before allowing it onto the internal network.

■ PPTP clients must be authenticated.

▲ The IP address of the PPTP server must be a registered IP address when the tunnel goes through a public network. All other addresses encapsulated within the data packets are irrelevant to the PPTP connection.

In order for PPTP to be installed and supported, you'll need to verify that your network supports the appropriate hardware; your network must also meet the minimum server and client requirements. These stipulations are explained in the following sections.

Supported Network Protocols

TCP/IP is the protocol used on public networks such as the Internet. Conveniently, it is also the protocol required for you to use PPTP virtual private networking across these public channels. Even though TCP/IP is needed to transfer the data, it does not mean that only applications using TCP/IP can use PPTP VPN. Applications using protocols other than TCP/IP can also take advantage of PPTP VPN. The traffic of these protocols, including IPX and NetBEUI, is encapsulated first and then transferred across TCP/IP networks.

The PPTP packet needs to know the IP address of the PPTP server that, in return, will be visible on the public network. For this reason, the PPTP server must have a registered IP address. The destination addresses within the packet are not used until the packet arrives on the private network. At that time, the PPTP server disassembles the PPTP packet from the PPTP client and uses the address to forward the packet to the correct computer.

PPTP Server Minimum Requirements

Windows NT Server version 4.0 comes with the PPTP server software. To use VPNs, you must add the Routing and Remote Access Server (RRAS) add-on from Microsoft. Following are the hardware requirements for Windows NT Server version 4.0:

▼ Pentium or faster processor

■ 16MB memory (RAM); 32MB recommended

■ 110MB available hard disk space

■ CD-ROM drive or access to a CD-ROM over a computer network

■ VGA or higher-resolution display adapter

▲ Microsoft mouse or compatible pointing device

PPTP Client Minimum Requirements

The PPTP client software is included with Windows NT Workstation version 4.0 and Windows NT Server version 4.0. If the PPTP client is a remote user connecting via either dial-up lines or the Internet, then a telephone access device (such as a phone jack) and an analog modem or Internet connection device (such as an ISDN router) are required. The minimum hardware requirements for the Windows NT Workstation version 4.0 are similar to those for the Windows NT Server version 4.0 and are listed in the preceding section.

An Internet service provider (ISP) can also act as the PPTP client. The remote user would dial up to a network access server (NAS) at the ISP. The PPTP tunneling would then be from the NAS to the PPTP server, instead of between the actual remote user and the PPTP server. Although this presents some security vulnerability because a portion of the communication channel is not part of the tunnel, using an ISP also may reduce a bottleneck caused by the dial-up connection.

Figure 14-9 illustrates a VPN scenario using Microsoft's solution.

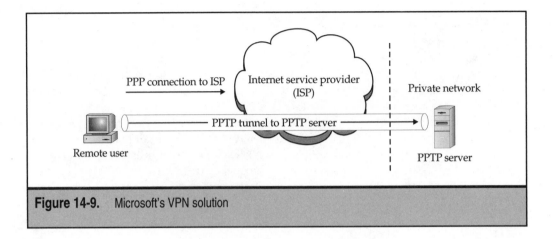

Figure 14-9. Microsoft's VPN solution

Installing and Configuring a PPTP Server

Prior to the actual installation and configuration of the PPTP Server, it is important for you to verify the following:

▼ Windows NT Server 4.0 is installed

■ One or more NICs are installed

■ TCP/IP is installed and bound to the network adapter connected to the private network, and the adapter is connected to the public network

■ The network protocol used on the private network is installed and bound to the network adapter connected to the private network

■ The Server is configured with a static IP address

■ RAS with Dial-Up Networking is installed and configured

▲ The number of PPTP simultaneous connections is identified

Once you have confirmed the above arrangement, you can begin the PPTP installation and configuration process. This process includes installing PPTP, adding the VPN devices, configuring encryption, and enabling LAN routing on the PPTP server. In addition, you can configure some other options to maximize the PPTP implementation. These options include configuring your PPTP server to accept only PPTP packets from the Internet. We'll take a closer look at these options later.

Installing PPTP on a PPTP Server

Following are the steps required to install PPTP on a Windows NT Server 4.0 computer.

1. Click Start | Settings | Control Panel.

2. Double-click Networks.

3. Click the Protocols tab.

4. Click Add, and the Select Network Protocol dialog box will appear.

5. Highlight Point-to-Point Tunneling Protocol and click OK.

6. In the Windows NT Setup dialog box, enter the drive and directory location of your Windows NT Server 4.0 installation files.

7. Click Continue. The PPTP files are copied from the installation directory.

8. Next you'll see the PPTP Configuration dialog box. Select the number of virtual private networks. This number represents the maximum simultaneous PPTP VPN connections.

9. Click OK.

10. Click OK in the Setup Messages dialog box.

11. In the Remote Access Setup Properties dialog box, click Add.

You're ready to move on to adding the VPN devices.

Adding VPN Devices

PPTP is now installed on the server. The next step is to add the VPN devices as RAS ports on the PPTP server. In the preceding steps, you configured the number of permitted VPNs. Each of these connections needs to have a VPN device assigned and acting as a RAS port.

Note that the following steps are for adding VPN devices on a computer running Windows NT Server 4.0. If you are coming directly from the preceding section you can skip steps 1–4.

1. Click Start | Settings | Control Panel.

2. Double-click Networks.

3. Click the Services tab.

4. Select Remote Access Service.

5. Click Properties to display the Remote Access Setup Properties dialog box.

6. Click Add. The Add RAS Device dialog box appears. All the VPN devices shown in the list box must be added and configured as a port and device in RAS.

7. Highlight one of the VPN devices and click OK.

8. Repeat steps 6 and 7 until all the VPNs are added to the Remote Access Setup Properties dialog box.

9. Now you'll do the configuration. Highlight a VPN port.

10. Click Configure. The Port Usage dialog box appears.

11. Select the Receive Calls Only option and click OK.

12. Repeat steps 9 through 11 for the remaining VPN devices.

13. Click Network. The Network Configuration dialog box is displayed.

14. Verify that only TCP/IP is checked in the Server Settings, and click OK.

15. In the Remote Access Setup Properties dialog box, click Continue.

16. Close the network configuration window; then shut down and restart the computer.

Configuring Encryption

Now you need to set up encryption for each VPN device that was added and configured. Point-to-Point Protocol (PPP) performs the encryption of data.

1. Click Start | Settings | Control Panel.

2. Double-click Networks.

3. Click the Services tab.

4. Select Remote Access Service.

5. Click Properties to display the Remote Access Setup Properties dialog box.

6. Highlight a VPN device on which you want to enable encryption.

7. Click Network. The Network Configuration dialog box appears.

8. Select Require Microsoft Encrypted Authentication and Require Data Encryption. With these settings, RAS and PPP will enforce Windows NT–based authentication of all remote clients connected to the PPTP Server.

9. Click OK.

10. In the Remote Access Setup Properties dialog box, click Continue.

11. Close the network configuration window; then shut down and restart the computer.

Enabling LAN Routing on the PPTP Server

Once the data packet has arrived at the PPTP server, that server needs to know how to route the packet to the appropriate destination. The following items are required in order for the PPTP Server to be able to deliver the data packet to the end destination.

1. The TCP/IP protocol of the PPTP Server must have IP forwarding enabled. This option is located in the Control Panel under Protocols. Select TCP/IP | Properties | Routing Properties. In the dialog box, turn on Enable IP Forwarding and click OK.

2. Windows NT Server and Workstation place a default route (0.0.0.0) on each network adapter. Then, when unknown IP addresses are routed, a route discovery is sent out each network adapter. You need to disable the automatic addition of a default route on all the PPTP network adapters. This can be done

by adding the Registry entry DontAddDefaultGateway with a value of REG_DWORD 0x1 in the following Registry key:

```
HKEY_LOCALMACHINE/SYSTEM/CurrentControlSet\Services\
<networkadapter>\Parameters\Tcpip\DontAddDefaultGateway
```

Now the default route will not be added to the network adapters when the server is rebooted. Static routes should be used instead.

3. Add a static route to allow the PPTP Server to know all subnets and computers on the private network. To add a static route, go to the command prompt. In the following example, we're adding a static route to the PPTP server type, by using the persistent (**-p**) option.

```
C:/>route add -p 10.0.0.0 netmask 255.255.255.255
gatewayIPaddress Metric 1
```

Accepting Only PPTP Packets

When PPTP filtering is enabled, all network packets are ignored except PPTP packets. This security mechanism is particularly beneficial in situations in which no other protection is being applied. For instance, if the PPTP server is intercepting all traffic between public and private networks without the help of devices such as a firewall or a router with firewall features, then it's probably a good idea to enable PPTP filtering.

NOTE: One downside of turning on PPTP filtering is that it prohibits the use of **ping** and **traceroute** commands in network troubleshooting.

Following are the steps for enabling PPTP packet filtering on your PPTP server.

1. Click Start | Settings | Control Panel.
2. Double-click Networks.
3. Click the Protocols tab.
4. Highlight the TCP/IP protocol.
5. Click Properties.
6. Click the IP Address tab.
7. Click Advanced.
8. Open the Adapter drop-down list and highlight the adapter connected to the public network.
9. Turn on Enable PPTP Filtering.
10. Click OK, and then click OK again.
11. Close the network configuration window; shut down and restart the computer.

Installing and Configuring a PPTP Client

Prior to installing and configuring the PPTP client, it's important to verify the following:

▼ Windows NT Workstation 4.0 or Windows NT Server 4.0 is installed.

■ TCP/IP is installed.

■ RAS with Dial-Up Networking is installed.

■ An analog modem, ISDN router, or another modem device is installed and configured in RAS (if you are establishing a dial-up PPTP connection).

▲ A PPP account has been set up with your ISP (if you are establishing a dial-up PPTP connection).

A PPTP client can connect to a PPTP server by using either a dial-up connection through the Internet, or a LAN connection (such as Ethernet).

NOTE: A PPTP connection can also be made using a network tap found in a mobile office work area, such as a conference room. Typically, however, a LAN connection is more desirable.

Regardless of what type of PPTP connection is being made, you'll need to install PPTP on a PPTP client and add a VPN device as a RAS port on the PPTP client.

Installing PPTP on a PPTP Client

Following are the steps required to install the PPTP protocol on a PPTP client running Windows NT Workstation or Server 4.0 or later.

1. Click Start | Settings | Control Panel.

2. Double-click Networks.

3. Click the Protocols tab.

4. Click Add, and the Select Network Protocol dialog box will appear.

5. Highlight Point-to-Point Tunneling Protocol and click OK.

6. In the Windows NT Setup dialog box, enter the drive and directory location of your Windows NT Server 4.0 installation files.

7. Click Continue. The PPTP files are copied from the installation directory.

8. Next you'll see the PPTP Configuration dialog box. Select the number of virtual private networks (one is usually fine). This number represents the maximum simultaneous PPTP VPN connections.

9. Click OK.

10. Click OK in the Setup Messages dialog box.

11. In the Remote Access Setup properties dialog box, click Add.

You're ready to move on to adding VPN devices as RAS ports on the PPTP client.

Adding VPN Devices as RAS Ports on the PPTP Client

PPTP is now installed on the client. The next step is to add the VPN devices as RAS ports on the PPTP server.

1. Click Start | Settings | Control Panel.
2. Double-click Networks.
3. Click the Services tab.
4. Select Remote Access Service.
5. Click Properties to display the Remote Access Setup Properties dialog box.
6. Click Add. The Add RAS Device dialog box appears.
7. Highlight a VPN device and click OK.

   All the VPN devices shown in the list box must be added and configured as a port and device in RAS. If you installed PPTP with more than one VPN device, repeat steps 6 and 7 until all the VPNs are added to the Remote Access Setup Properties dialog box.

8. Now you'll do the VPN configuration on the server. Right-click the Network icon and select Properties. The Network Configuration dialog box is displayed.
9. In the Dial Out Protocols section of the Network Configuration dialog box, verify that only TCP/IP is checked and click OK.
10. In the Remote Access Setup Properties dialog box, click Continue.
11. Close the Network configuration window; shut down and restart the computer.

PPTP Connections Across WANs: Dial-Up Networking

Remote users who dial in to the corporate network may check their mail, synchronize their laptops, upload or download sensitive information, and perform a variety of other functions that entail the transmission of proprietary information across a public infrastructure. A VPN solution can significantly reduce these vulnerabilities.

Point-to-Point Protocol (PPP) is a layer-2 protocol used to establish, maintain, and end the physical connection related to dial-up connectivity. Before you have the ability to transfer data, a PPP dial-up session goes through four distinct phases of negotiation.

PHASE 1: PPP LINK ESTABLISHMENT   The client and the remote access server select basic communication options, including the authentication protocol and network control protocols (NCPs). Even though the authentication protocol is selected at this time, it isn't actually implemented until Phase 4. The client and the server also negotiate whether or not to use compression and/or encryption. Like authentication, the types of compression and/or encryption are decided in Phase 4.

PHASE 2: USER AUTHENTICATION   The client sends authentication information to the remote access server. The remote access server compares the authentication information against its database (or a central authentication database such as TACACS+). Various types of authentication methods can be used, including

▼ **Password Authentication Protocol (PAP)**   PAP sends authentication information in cleartext. The remote access server requests the username and password, and then PAP sends them in cleartext. Obviously, this is not a very secure authentication process.

■ **Challenge Handshake Authentication Protocol (CHAP)**   CHAP encrypts authentication information before sending it to the remote access server. The remote access server sends the client a challenge, including a session ID and an arbitrary challenge string. The client uses an algorithm (MD5 one-way hashing algorithm) and the password together to encrypt the challenge, session ID, and password. The username is sent unhashed. Since the server already knows the password, it applies it to the algorithm and compares the result to the password sent. This is more secure than PAP because CHAP (1) encrypts the password; (2) sends arbitrary challenge strings for each authentication attempt; and (3) continues to send challenges throughout the duration of the connection.

▲ **Microsoft Challenge Handshake Authentication Protocol (MS-CHAP)** Microsoft's version of CHAP is very similar to plain-vanilla CHAP, with a little · more security added to the authentication process. MS-CHAP allows the remote access server to store hashed passwords instead of cleartext passwords. This version also supports password expiration and user permissions to change passwords. Under MS-CHAP, the client and server must independently generate an initial key for data encryption by MPPE (Microsoft Point-to-Point Encryption). Therefore, if MPPE encryption is being used, MS-CHAP authentication must also be used.

PHASE 3: PPP CALLBACK CONTROL   Microsoft's implementation of PPP uses Callback Control Protocol (CBCP). If CBCP is enabled, both the client and the remote access server disconnect after authentication. The remote access server then calls the client back at the specified number. This only works if you have a static number. Although it does provide an additional level of security, you have to decide if the security is worth the hassle.

PHASE 4: INVOKING NETWORK LAYER PROTOCOL(S)   The NCPs that were selected during Phase 1 are now enabled in Phase 4. NCPs can include protocols such as the IP Control Protocol (IPCP), which can assign a dynamic IP address to the dial-in user. Data compression and data encryption protocols (Phase 1) are also invoked. In Microsoft's PPP implementation, MMPC (Microsoft Point-to-Point Compression) for data compression and MPPE for data encryption are used.

Following the successful negotiation of these four phases, the data transfer process can begin. Each transmitted data packet is wrapped in a PPP header, which is then removed by the remote access server. Similarly, if encryption and compression were negotiated, each packet will be compressed and encrypted by the client and decompressed and decrypted by the server.

Layer-2 Protocol (L2TP)

PPTP is a Microsoft technology to establish a virtual connection across a public network. PPTP, together with encryption and authentication, provide a private and secure network. Cisco developed a protocol similar to PPTP, Layer-2 Forwarding (L2F), but it required Cisco hardware at both ends to support it. Cisco and Microsoft then merged the best features of PPTP and L2F and developed Layer-2 Protocol (L2TP). Similar to PPTP, L2TP provides a way for remote users to extend a PPP link across the Internet from the ISP to a corporate site.

CISCO FIREWALL IOS FEATURE SET

A risk assessment may uncover the need for a firewall in a network, but the risk level or return on investment may not justify the cost of a stand-alone firewall. Cisco has developed the Cisco Firewall IOS feature set as a cost-effective solution to a stand-alone firewall, for those companies requiring more security than Cisco's IOS can provide.

Cisco Firewall IOS is a Cisco IOS software image that can be deployed on supported Cisco routers. Security capabilities are enhanced when the Cisco Firewall IOS feature set is installed. The following router series support the Cisco Firewall IOS:

- ▼ 800 Series
- ■ UBR900 Series
- ■ 1600 Series
- ■ 1720 Series
- ■ 2500 Series
- ■ 2600 Series
- ■ 3600 Series
- ■ 7100 Series
- ▲ 7200 Series

As discussed just above, integrated security on Cisco's network devices is not a new concept. Existing Cisco IOS supports the following security technologies, as defined in the earlier section "Cisco Router IOS Security Technologies":

- ▼ Perimeter security
- ■ Identification and authentication
- ■ Denial of Service (DoS) protection
- ■ Data integrity and confidentiality
- ▲ Reporting

Cisco Firewall IOS Additional Security

Cisco has enhanced some of the security features of its IOS and included additional protection in order to offer Cisco Firewall IOS. These added features are defined in the following sections.

Context-Based Access Control (CBAC)

Access control lists (ACLs) can be applied to routers to permit or deny certain traffic. Context-Based Access Control (CBAC) is an extension of the ACL concept.

ACLs provide filtering on the following:

▼ IP destination address

■ IP source address

■ IP protocol field

■ TCP source port

▲ TCP destination port

They do not, however, keep track of these facts:

▼ How long ago the last packet in the session was transmitted

■ Whether the sequence/acknowledgment numbers are climbing as expected

■ Whether the session was initiated from the inside or outside

■ Whether the session is still open or has been closed

▲ What port or ports are being used by the return data channels

CBAC is a new packet-filtering mechanism introduced in the Cisco Firewall IOS feature set; it provides "stateful" packet filtering. CBAC bases decisions on the state of TCP sessions. Unlike ACLs, which only monitor the network and transport layers, CBAC also examines protocol information at the application layer in order to obtain the state of the session. This state information is collected and used to create temporary add-on filters. The result is an added layer of protection than what is provided by traditional access lists.

The CBAC process goes like this: Data is inspected as it comes in to or leaves the router. If the data passes inspection, it is forwarded and CBAC creates a state table. Return traffic is only permitted if the state table indicates the packet belongs to a valid session. When the session ends, the state table is deleted.

The CBAC packet inspection includes recognition of application-specific commands. Several applications are recognized by CBAC. You have the opportunity to specifically permit or deny these CBAC-recognized applications. Packet inspection also provides the detection and prevention of application-level attacks. CBAC recognizes the following:

▼ World Wide Web (WWW)

■ Telnet

■ Simple Network Management Protocol (SNMP)

■ Finger

■ File Transfer Protocol (FTP)

■ Trivial File Transfer Protocol (TFTP)

■ Simple Mail Transfer Protocol (SMTP)

■ Java blocking

■ BSD R-cmds

■ Oracle SQL*Net

■ Remote Procedure Call (RPC)

■ VDOnet's VDOLive

■ RealNetwork's RealAudio

■ Intel's Internet Video Phone

■ Microsoft's NetMeeting

■ Xing Technology's StreamWorks

▲ White Pine Software's CU-SeeMe

CBAC is configured on a per-interface basis. It can therefore be configured differently for each interface and deployed only on chosen interfaces.

Controlled Downloading of Java Applets

Cisco Firewall IOS feature set controls the downloading of Java applets. (Java is a programming language used to write Web applications and Java applets.)

Using Cisco Firewall IOS, HTTP connections can be configured to filter or completely deny access to Java applets that are not embedded in an archive or compressed file. These Java applets within HTTP traffic are blocked based on Web server IP address. All traffic from Web servers that contain Java applets can be explicitly permitted or denied via standard access lists.

Figure 14-10 illustrates Java blocking by the Cisco IOS Firewall feature set.

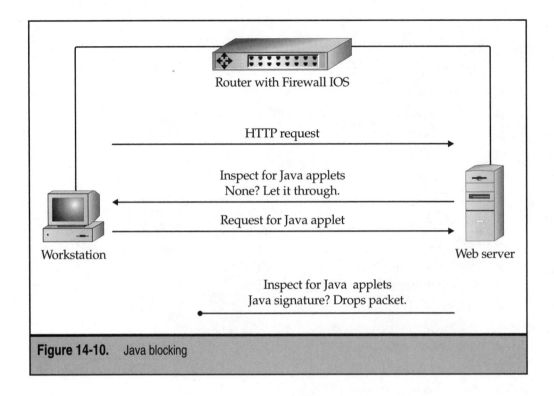

Figure 14-10.   Java blocking

Enhanced Denial-of-Service Detection and Prevention

Although Cisco IOS offers TCP Intercept to prevent SYN-flooding attacks, Cisco Firewall IOS takes it a step farther and provides the following attack detections:

▼ Compares the rate of requests for new connections, and the number of half-open connections, to a configurable threshold level. If the threshold is exceeded, an alert message is issued and other configured actions can be performed.

▲ Monitors TCP connections and packet sequence numbers. If the sequence numbers are not within an expected range, the suspicious packets are dropped.

In addition, Cisco Firewall IOS provides the following attack prevention:

▼ Drops old, half-open TCP connections if a configurable, maximum threshold is exceeded.

▲ Blocks all SYN packets from the host under attack, until expiration of the (configurable) automatic timeout period.

Real-Time Alerts

Cisco Firewall IOS can be configured to send syslog messages to a central management console upon detecting suspicious activity. This feature includes capability to

▼ Generate automatic alerts when attack prevention is enabled

■ Configure the types of alerts to be sent via the syslog management tool

▲ Send alerts for DoS attacks, SMTP command attacks, or denied Java applets

Cisco Firewall IOS Benefits

This section describes the benefits of Cisco Firewall IOS.

NOTE: It is important to determine your security requirements with care. Make sure that the Cisco Firewall IOS satisfies these requirements. If not, a dedicated firewall may be more appropriate.

Integrated Solution

Assuming you have a Cisco-based network and the supported platforms, Cisco Firewall IOS can be integrated into your system. Since it is a router-based firewall, there are fewer boxes to be managed. Existing knowledge of Cisco IOS can be leveraged, thus requiring a milder learning curve for a new platform.

No New Hardware Requirements

Cisco Firewall IOS feature set is available for a wide range of Cisco's router series. Any Cisco routers you currently have deployed will likely be capable of supporting Cisco Firewall IOS, so there's less chance you'll need to buy additional hardware.

Low Cost

Cisco Firewall IOS is extremely affordable, especially when comparing it to the cost of stand-alone firewalls. Again, assuming your network is based on Cisco technology, and you have compatible routers deployed and sufficient expertise on Cisco IOS, then the implementation, ownership, and management costs will be minimal in comparison.

Target Market and Pricing

The Cisco IOS Firewall feature set was developed as a cost-effective alternative to a stand-alone firewall. However, as a software-based solution on existing routers performing other functionality, it is limited by the platform capabilities. Therefore, it will be best deployed in the following environments:

▼ Small- to medium-sized businesses requiring Internet connectivity

■ Branch offices of large corporations using Cisco routers to access the Internet and the main office resources

- Internal perimeters within an enterprise network, to protect from casual access of vital assets such as financial databases and sensitive engineering projects
- Enterprises that are upgrading existing router-based infrastructure to enhance security
- Internet service providers offering managed solutions
- ▲ Companies wanting to enable secure communications with business partners

When deciding whether to implement the Cisco Firewall IOS or to invest in a dedicated stand-alone firewall solution, it's important to balance your company's business needs with its security requirements. Determine exactly what areas of security you would like to apply, and then define the firewall's access requirements. Table 14-2 defines several common requirements related to access and security.

Cost of Implementation

After your security requirements are defined, you need to weigh these requirements against the money you are willing to spend. The cost of implementing Cisco Firewall IOS varies according to the router series in place and the version of Cisco Firewall IOS you choose. Prices range from $700 for the lower end of the Firewall IOS series to more than $5,000 at the higher end of the series. Cisco Firewall IOS comes in these versions:

- ▼ IP/Firewall Feature Pack
- IP/IPX/AT/IBM Firewall Plus 56 Feature Pack
- IP/Firewall Plus 3DES Feature Pack
- IP/IPX/AT/IBM/Firewall Plus IPSec 56 Feature Pack
- IP/Firewall PLUS IPSec 56 Feature Pack
- IP/IPX/AT/DEC/Firewall Plus
- IP/IPX/AT/DEC/Firewall Plus Feature Pack
- Enterprise/Firewall Plus 56 Feature Pack
- ▲ Enterprise/Firewall Plus IPSec 56 Feature Pack

In order to determine the version most suitable for your environment, make sure you have considered the following:

- ▼ What protocols must be supported
- Whether Triple DES (3DES) must be supported
- Whether IPSec must be supported (in order to establish VPNs)
- ▲ What Cisco router series must support the Cisco Firewall IOS version you choose (not all series support all versions)

Business Needs	Security Requirements
Connectivity	Authentication
Performance	Authorization
Ease of use	Accounting
Manageability	Assurance
Availability	Confidentiality
	Data integrity

Table 14-2. Business Needs vs. Security Requirements

Configuration of Cisco Firewall IOS

Many of the configurations for Cisco Firewall IOS are similar or the same as for the Cisco IOS feature set. Following are the steps to set up Cisco Firewall IOS CBAC on a router. In addition to these tasks, a security-sensitive router should also include the recommended configurations under the router section.

1. **Configure Control-Based Access Control (CBAC) parameters.**

   CBAC parameters, more commonly known as inspection parameters, enable inspection for specific protocols and define session timeouts. Here are the commands:

   ```
   Router(config)#ip inspect name firewallrules tcp timeout 3600
   Router(config)#ip inspect name firewallrules udp timeout 15
   Router(config)#ip inspect name firewallrules ftp timeout 3600
   Router(config)#ip inspect name firewallrules http timeout 3600
   ```

2. **Apply inspection parameters to the appropriate interface.**

   Inspections are typically applied to the internal interface, so CBAC can be applied to packets initiating outbound connections. This means temporary access-list entries are created in response to initiated traffic from the internal network. Temporary access lists are configured on both interfaces (even though inspection is configured only on one interface). Typically, inspection parameters are configured (step 1) for only one interface, unless you have substantial traffic being initiated from the external network. Then inspection parameters could be created and applied to the external interface on the router for external initiated traffic to that interface.

   To apply inspection parameters to an interface, use the following command:

   ```
   Router(config)#ip inspect firewallrules in
   ```

3. **Define access lists.**

   Access is controlled by access lists, not by what's listed in the inspection parameters. The purpose of configuring inspection parameters is to set timeouts and define the protocols to which CBAC should pay attention. Access lists still need to be defined, just as they are for routers.

CISCO'S PIX FIREWALL

PIX Firewall is a hardware/software firewall that provides a wide range of security features without affecting network performance. During the writing of this book, the PIX Firewall was the leading product line in its segment of the firewall market. The following sections describe the features and functions of the PIX Firewall—some are common to other firewalls, and some are unique.

PIX Firewall Hardware

The PIX Firewall is an isolated design based on the interaction between hardware and software. Some competing firewalls on the market today are based on UNIX, Windows NT, or other operating systems that weren't developed specifically for a firewall solution. Knowing that a firewall is based on a familiar OS makes it easier for hackers to figure out a firewall's design and get to your data. Certainly we are not saying firewalls built on UNIX or NT have holes, but rather that their familiarity breeds opportunity to determine or generate holes.

Most firewalls operate by intercepting all traffic and validating its authenticity prior to sending it on. This process can generate excessive overhead and may possibly become a network bottleneck. The PIX Firewall design focuses not only on security but also on delivering outstanding performance. Other proxy-based firewalls run continuously at the application layer. In contrast, the PIX Firewall has software features that allow it to use the application layer level of security without having to run constantly at the application level. This reduces the firewall overhead and thus reduces possible network latencies.

Hardware and Software Scalability

By selecting appropriate options for licensing, NICs, and the Operating System that supports your requirements, you can design a PIX Firewall best suited for your network environment.

SOFTWARE LICENSING   A portion of the PIX Firewall price is based on your software licensing choice. Regardless of your licensing level, you enjoy the same level of PIX Firewall support. The only difference is that the PIX Firewall software is tweaked to satisfy only your licensing agreement, which is based on the number of simultaneous connections going through the PIX Firewall. There are three different levels:

▼   Entry Level (128 connections)

■   Midrange (1,024 connections)

▲   Unrestricted (up to 256,000 connections)

It's important not to equate every user with one connection—that is, if your network has 128 users who will be traversing the PIX Firewall, it doesn't mean the Entry Level is the right choice for your system. Certain traffic, such as Web and FTP traffic, uses multiple connections. A good rule of thumb for choosing a licensing level is to identify the number of employees who will be going through the PIX Firewall and multiply that number by five. The prices associated with each licensing level are outlined later in this chapter, in the section "Target Market and Cost of Ownership."

SUPPORTED TOPOLOGIES   The PIX Firewall supports multiple interfaces; you can set up an internal network, an external network, and multiple "demilitarized zones" (DMZs). DMZs, sometimes called *extranets*, are isolated networks separated by a firewall from the internal (protected) network and the external (unprotected) network. Web servers, FTP servers, and other servers accessed regularly by external users are examples of machines that would reside on the DMZ. You can thus permit access to these services without compromising your entire internal network.

Although not all networks require a DMZ, all deployments of the PIX Firewall will have at minimum an internal and external interface. Depending on the topology of the network on which the PIX Firewall is deployed, several types of NICs are supported:

▼ Single-port 10/100BaseT Ethernet (up to four NICs per PIX Firewall chassis)

■ 4 and 16 Mbps Token Ring (up to four NICs per PIX Firewall chassis)

■ Four-port 10/100BaseT Ethernet (may be combined with one or more single-port 10/100 Ethernet NICs)

▲ FDDI (up to two NICs per PIX Firewall chassis)

NOTE: Any Cisco PIX Firewall warranties are void if the NICs are not purchased from Cisco or its authorized resellers.

Virtual Private Networks (VPNs)

Like Cisco routers, the PIX Firewall offers an IPSec standard, virtual private network (VPN) solution. With IPSec encryption (described earlier in this chapter) running on a Cisco PIX Firewall (version 5.0 or greater), VPNs can be established between Windows PCs with the VPN client software, Cisco IOS routers, or other PIX Firewalls or encryption devices that are IPSec compliant. The PIX Firewall IPSec standard supports the Data Encryption Standard (DES).

Failover/Hot Standby

If you have two PIX Firewalls, you can use a failover cable to connect the two. Table 14-3 lists the pinouts for the failover cable.

After the two PIX Firewalls are connected, you then configure one firewall to be the primary unit and the other firewall to be the secondary unit. Both firewalls will receive network traffic; the primary firewall will also share information with the secondary

Pins for Primary PIX Firewall End	Pins for Secondary PIX Firewall End
1	10
9	14
2	3
10	1
3	2
4, 11, 12	6
5	5, 12
6	4, 11
14	9

Table 14-3.   Failover/Hot Standby Pinout Cables

firewall every 15 seconds. If the primary fails, the secondary takes over. The following conditions will result in a failover from the primary to the secondary PIX Firewall:

▼ The primary firewall stops receiving network packets, while the secondary firewall continues to receive packets for two consecutive 15-second intervals.

■ A cable error, such as a power failure.

▲ The primary firewall stops communicating with the secondary firewall.

Network traffic errors are detected within 30 seconds (two consecutive 15-second intervals). Power failure is detected within 15 seconds. Communication errors between the two firewalls are detected within 30 seconds.

By default, failover is active on the PIX Firewalls. Use the **show failover** command to verify the status of the connection and to determine which unit is active. Enter **no failover** in the configuration file if you will not be using failover; to reenable failover, enter **failover on**.

PIX Firewall Software

Several components of the PIX Firewall Software make it a step above the Cisco Firewall IOS and two steps above Cisco router access lists.

Adaptive Security Algorithm (ASA)

As discussed, Cisco takes pride in the high performance of the PIX Firewall in comparison to several others on the market. Since all traffic must traverse a firewall when traveling from the secure network to the unsecure network (or vice versa), high throughput is critical.

The heart of the Cisco PIX Firewall is the Adaptive Security Algorithm (ASA). ASA is a protection scheme that compares packets to entries in a table, similar to packet filtering in router access lists. However, ASA is more robust and dynamic than packet filtering.

As in the access-list operation, each packet is compared against a predefined set of rules. These rules can contain

▼   Source IP address

■   Destination IP address

■   Protocol

▲   TCP port numbers or application

Access is permitted only if an appropriate rule exists to validate that packet. Once the initial packet has been validated, ASA creates a dynamic entry in the list of rules. This entry can include

▼   Source IP address

■   Destination IP address

■   Randomized TCP sequence numbers

▲   Additional TCP flags

This dynamic rule now satisfies a stateful, connection-oriented session flow of traffic. As long as the session exists, the dynamic set of rules will continue to exist and be updated. After the last packet traverses the PIX Firewall, ASA removes the dynamic rule from its rules table.

Cut-Through Proxy

Cut-through proxy allows a user to be initially validated at the firewall, where they are permitted access to any TCP- or UDP-based application. A proxy server analyzes every data packet at the application layer of the OSI model. This takes time and processing cycles. In contrast, the Cisco PIX Firewall queries a TACACS+ or RADIUS database server for authentication, checks and validates the user, and then allows traffic flow directly between the two parties while the session state information is maintained. This cut-through proxy capability (see Figure 14-11) allows the Cisco PIX Firewall to perform dramatically faster than proxy servers.

URL Filtering

URLs (Universal Resource Locators) are the addresses of the various Web sites hit by every outbound Web connection. These addresses can be stored in log files on the PIX Firewall, which can then be used to monitor your users' Web hits. Although the PIX Firewall does provide this URL logging capability, it does not directly provide URL filtering.

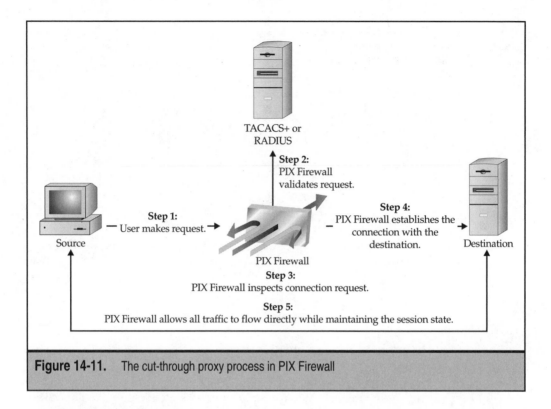

TACACS+ or
RADIUS

Step 2:
PIX Firewall
validates request.

Step 1:
User makes request.

Step 4:
PIX Firewall establishes the
connection with the
destination.

Source

Destination

PIX Firewall

Step 3:
PIX Firewall inspects connection request.

Step 5:
PIX Firewall allows all traffic to flow directly while maintaining the session state.

Figure 14-11.   The cut-through proxy process in PIX Firewall

For URL filtering, Cisco has established a relationship with NetPartner's WebSENSE server software. This software runs on a Windows NT or UNIX server located on your internal network. All Web traffic goes first to the WebSENSE server and then is routed to the PIX Firewall. In addition to URL filtering, WebSENSE provides statistics and reporting.

By handling URL filtering on a separate platform, you take this burden off the PIX Firewall. The disadvantages to this arrangement are that another hop is added to your users' destinations; another potential point of failure is added; and Web browsers must be configured to use the WebSENSE server as the gateway for Web traffic.

Supported Applications

PIX Firewall supports a wide range of applications (this section lists applications supported at the time of this writing). As more applications are developed and Cisco continues to collaborate with their vendors, the list of supported applications will grow.

IP-BASED PROTOCOLS AND APPLICATIONS

Internet Protocol (IP)
Transmission Control Protocol (TCP)
User Datagram Protocol (UDP)

Internet Control Message Protocol (ICMP)
Generic Route Encapsulation (GRE)
Address Resolution Protocol (ARP)
Domain Name System (DNS)
Simple Network Management Protocol (SNMP)
Boot Protocol (BOOTP)
HyperText Transport Protocol (HTTP)
File Transfer Protocol (FTP)
Trivial File Transfer Protocol (TFTP)
Archie
Gopher
Telnet
NetBIOS over IP (Microsoft Networking)
Point-to-Point Tunneling Protocol (PPTP)
SQLNet (Oracle client/server protocol)
Remote Procedure Call (RPC) services (Sun Microsystems)
Network File System (NFS)
Berkeley Standard Distribution (BSD) - Rcmds

MULTIMEDIA APPLICATIONS

NetShow (Microsoft)
CU-SeeMe (White Pine Software)
RealAudio and RealVideo (Real Networks)
StreamWorks (Xing Technology)
VDOLive (VDOnet)
WebTheater (Vxtreme)
Internet Phone (VocalTec)

VIDEOCONFERENCING APPLICATIONS

NetMeeting (Microsoft)
Internet Video Phone (Intel)
Meeting Point (White Pine Software)

Target Market and Cost of Ownership

The PIX Firewall offers a low cost of ownership for companies who require the additional security provided by a firewall—above and beyond access lists on a router or even Cisco's Firewall IOS. The PIX Firewall is scalable. The license you purchase can be upgraded from 128 sessions all the way to unlimited sessions (technically, 65,536 simultaneous connections), at a cost anywhere from $6,000–$13,000. Table 14-4 gives list prices for the various PIX Firewalls at the time of this writing.

PIX Firewall 520 Series with Two 10/100 NICs	List Price
128 sessions	$ 9,000
1,000 sessions	$16,000
Unlimited sessions	$22,000

Table 14-4.   PIX Firewall Prices

Installation and Setup

The PIX Firewall comes with an internal and external NIC. If you have any additional DMZ NICs, you'll have to install them yourself. Once you have all your hardware components installed, you're ready to begin the actual installation and setup of PIX Firewall. By default, the initial configuration

▼ Allows all outbound connections from the internal (private) network to external (public) networks.

▲ Denies all inbound connections from external networks to the internal network.

The initial PIX Firewall setup comprises the minimum level of settings required to allow connectivity through the firewall. In addition, each network will have its own specific requirements, and thus different configurations. These additional "advanced" settings should be done after the initial configuration is completed, and after connectivity is tested and verified at this initial state. Some of the advanced settings are listed later in this chapter.

The initial setup of the PIX Firewall is described next. There are two methods you can use to perform the initial installation: the PIX Firewall Setup Wizard, or a terminal emulator.

PIX Firewall Setup Wizard

The PIX Firewall Setup Wizard runs on Windows 9x or Windows NT, and offers the familiar Microsoft wizard-style graphical interface for stepping you through initial installation of the PIX Firewall. Although called a Wizard, it doesn't do a lot of magic. The GUI interface is confusing and not very user friendly. Since Cisco is in the process of releasing a new tool that will assist with PIX Firewalls, Cisco Firewall IOS, and Router ACLs, don't bother spending time learning how the PIX Firewall Setup Wizard works. Until Cisco releases their new tool to assist with security configurations, we recommend just configuring the PIX Firewall using the command-line interface through a Telnet session.

PIX Firewall Setup Using a Terminal Emulator

As with other terminal emulator–style connections to Cisco devices, you'll need to set some properties; Table 14-5 lists them.

When your terminal emulator software is ready to receive data from the PIX Firewall console, power it on. As in Cisco Router IOS, there are multiple levels of access. When you log into a PIX firewall, you'll be at the user mode, denoted by the > prompt. By typing **enable** (the enable password isn't initially required), you enter the configuration mode, denoted by the # prompt. Type **configure terminal**, and you enter the privileged configuration mode. Here is this series of commands:

```
pixfirewall>enable
Password: <Enter>
pixfirewall#configure terminal
pixfirewall(config)#
```

Now your actual configurations can begin.

Configuring the PIX Firewall

As mentioned, for your initial configuration it is recommended that you establish a basic firewall setup and verify connectivity before moving on to a more detailed configuration based on your network requirements. Following are the steps for basic firewall setup.

1. Specify the types of interfaces installed on your PIX Firewall.
The default configuration of the PIX Firewall uses the term *hardware_id* to describe the interface on which it resides. Replace the default label *hardware_id* with more descriptive labels for your interfaces. Typically, **ethernet0** or **tokenring0** is used to describe the external network, and **ethernet1** or **tokenring1** is used to describe the internal network. For Ethernet, use the **auto** keyword when you have 10/100 auto-sensing NICs, and use **10baseT** when you have strictly 10 Mbps cards. For Token Ring, use **4mbps** or **16mbps**.

Field	Value
Bits Per Second	9600
Data Bits	8
Parity	None
Stop Bits	1
Flow Control	Hardware

Table 14-5. Terminal Emulation Software Properties

Here are examples of the configuration commands for 10/100 auto-sensing Ethernet NICs:

```
pixfirewall#interface ethernet0 auto
pixfirewall#interface ethernet1 auto
```

2. Assign IP addresses to the network interface cards (NICs).

IP addresses for the internal and external interface must be on separate networks. The internal address can use nonregistered IP addresses since these can be hidden from the external world. If the external address exists on a public infrastructure, it must use a reg istered IP address. Following are examples of the configuration commands used to assign IP addresses to the interfaces. Notice the first two commands entered to get to interface configuration mode.

```
pixfirewall#configure terminal
pixfirewall(config)#interface ethernet0
pixfirewall(config-int)#ip address inside 10.1.1.1 255.255.255.0
pixfirewall(config-int)#exit
pixfirewall(config)#interface ethernet1
pixfirewall(config-int)#ip address outside 189.198.211.10
255.255.255.0
```

3. Allow all internal users (on the private network) to start outbound connections using Network Address Translation (NAT).

To enable users to initiate outbound connections using Cisco Network Address Translation (NAT), explained earlier in the chapter, you must configure a NAT statement. This NAT statement will take all the IP addresses specified (or all IP addresses if 0.0.0.0 is used) and translate them to the addresses in the global statement that follows the NAT statement (step 4.). The NAT statement and the global statement are linked together by the group number found in both of the commands, right before the IP addresses. Here is an example of a NAT statement allowing all IP addresses to initiate outbound connections using NAT:

```
pixfirewall(config)#nat (inside) 1 0.0.0.0
```

4. Create a pool of addresses that are used by internal users for connecting to external services.

This step goes hand in hand with the preceding NAT specification step. The NAT command states that address translation will take place for this group of users on this side of the PIX Firewall, and the global command states which IP addresses are going to be used.

Port Address Translation (PAT), discussed in a previous section, is also an option. It can be deployed in two ways:

▼   Enter only one IP address in the global command, and PAT will be used for every IP address that is defined in the preceding NAT command.

▲   Enter the range of NAT addresses to be used in the global command; then enter an additional global command with only one IP address. This configuration works when you would like to do NAT but have limited IP addresses. You set up NAT for as many IP addresses as you want to use, saving one for the global PAT command. As users are connected and their addresses are translated, they will use the IP addresses from the first global pool. Once those IP addresses are used up, any remaining connections will use PAT. For this arrangement, make sure the range of IP addresses is first in the configuration. Otherwise, PAT will be applied to all connections using the single IP address, and the range of IP addresses you designated won't be utilized.

Following is an example of a global command referring to group one of the previous NAT statements; here we use a range of IP addresses (NAT) versus one IP address (PAT). Instead of all outbound connections having the same source IP address (189.198.211.10), outbound connections will pull an available IP address from the pool (189.198.211.225-250). This global command allows all internal IP addresses from the step 3 NAT statement to initiate outbound connections by using an IP address from the range defined:

```
pixfirewall(config)#global (outside) 1 189.198.211.225-
189.198.211.250
```

5. Assign default routes to the inside and outside of network interfaces.

Assuming you are not running Routing Internet Protocol (RIP) and the routers aren't set up to share the routes with the PIX Firewall, you need to set up default routes for each interface. Here are the commands to do that:

```
pixfirewall(config)#route inside 10.1.1.3 255.255.255.0
pixfirewall(config)#route outside 189.198.211.11 255.255.255.0
```

The first command sets the default route for the internal interface to send everything to the internal default router. The second command sets the default route for the external interface to send everything to the external default router.

6. Write the current configuration to memory.

Of course, once you're done with any type of configuration, you write it to Flash memory to save it. This command is the same as for any other Cisco network device and is shown here:

```
pixfirewall#write memory
```

Testing and Verifying Initial Configuration

Whether you entered the initial setup for the PIX Firewall using the command line interface (CLI) or PIX Firewall Setup Wizard, your next step—prior to making any advanced settings—is to test and verify connectivity through the firewall.

NOTE: If you are not successful with any of the following steps, stop and determine the problem before you proceed. Use the debugging tools discussed in earlier chapters to diagnosis the problem.

The following testing and verification steps require access to the network devices' CLIs (including any related routers and the PIX Firewall); you also need access to at least one host on both the internal and external networks (routers will satisfy this requirement).

1. Enter a **clear arp** statement on all routers that intercept traffic to or from the PIX Firewall. This statement will flush any ARP caches that may have become incorrect once the firewall was installed.

2. Enter the **show ip address** command to verify that the IP addresses you wanted were correctly configured.

3. Enter the **show interface** command and look for the following in the output:

line protocol is up	The correct cable is used and it is connected properly.
interface is up	The interface is ready for use.
packets input	If this number is increasing, packets are being received.
packets output	If this number is increasing, packets are being transmitted.

4. Enter the **show arp** command and verify new entries in the ARP cache.

TIP: You can do a **clear arp** and then a **show arp** again to make it easier to determine new entries.

5. Enter the **ping** command to test the firewall's ability to reach a host on each network interface. Keep in mind that the PIX Firewall is not able to ping its own interfaces or any of its global addresses. Execute the following ping tests:

■ ping from the PIX Firewall to an internal host, and vice versa
■ ping from the PIX Firewall to an external host, and vice versa

Advanced Settings for the PIX Firewall

There are several advanced settings that are part of the PIX Firewall software capabilities. For explanations and help for the following list of options, refer to the documents located on Cisco Connection Online (CCO):

▼ Restricting outbound access

■ Providing inbound access to a mail server

■ Providing user authentication

■ Configuring failover

■ Configuring private links

■ Configuring SNMP

▲ Configuring FTP and URL logging

PIX Firewall Manager

The PIX Firewall Manager is a GUI developed to help network managers with PIX Firewall administration. The Manager consists of a management server and a management client. The server receives requests from the clients, sends them to the PIX Firewall, and then passes the firewall's responses back to the clients. The management client provides a GUI interface to the firewall, using supported network browsers. PIX Firewall has two access levels: user level with read-only access, and administrator level with read and write access.

PIX Firewall offers the following features:

▼ Management of up to ten PIX Firewall units.

■ GUI interface allows performance of most configuration tasks.

■ Encryption of all communication between the PIX Firewall and PIX Firewall Manager.

▲ Report generation.

Before Installing PIX Firewall Manager

Make sure the following have been completed and verified before you install PIX Firewall Manager:

1. You are running PIX Firewall version 4.2(3) or later.

2. To allow the Firewall Manager access to the PIX Firewall, enter a **telnet** configuration command on the PIX Firewall. In the following example, 192.189.10.1 represents the IP address of the Firewall Manager:

    ```
    pixfirewall(config)#telnet 192.189.10.1 255.255.255.255
    ```

3. The Firewall Manager must be installed on a Windows NT workstation or server running version 4.0 or later with Service Pack 3.

4. The Firewall Manager server must have a network browser that is Java 1.02 or 1.1 compliant. Any of the following browsers meets this requirement:

- Netscape Navigator 3.0 or 3.01
- Netscape Navigator Gold 3.0 or 3.01
- Netscape Communicator 4.0 or later
- Netscape Navigator (stand-alone) 4.0 or later
- Microsoft Internet Explorer 4.0 version 4.72.3110.8 (updated version: SP1)

PIX Firewall Manager Installation

The PIX Firewall Manager must be installed on the Windows NT system as Administrator (or any user who is a member of the Administrator group).

1. Put Install disk 1 in the disk drive and double-click **setup.exe**.
2. Continue to click Next to proceed with the installation without interruption.
3. Use the default port number (8080) for PIX Firewall's connection to the PIX Firewall Manager.
4. Click Finish, and the PIX Firewall Manager will start automatically when the server is running.

NOTE: To verify that the PIX Firewall Manager Server is running, select Start | Settings | Control Panel, and double-click the Services icon. "Started" should appear next to the PIX Firewall Management Server service name.

Setting Up Client Usernames and Passwords

The next step is to set up client usernames and passwords, as follows:

1. Select Start | Programs | Administrative Tools | User Manager.
2. Select User | New User.
3. From the Groups area, double-click PIX Admins for read and write privileges; and double-click PIX Users for read-only privileges.
4. Click Add.
5. From the Names fields, select the name of the user you want to add.
6. Click Add, and then click OK.

NOTE: Do not assign a user to both the PIX Admin and PIX Users groups.

Setting Up and Using the Management Client

Following are the steps to set up and use the PIX Firewall Manager management client:

1. Disable the proxies, as follows:

   ■ **For Netscape Navigator 3.**x   Choose Options | Network Preferences | Proxies tab. Then click No Proxies.

   ■ **For Netscape Communicator and Navigator 4.0 or later**   Choose Edit | Preferences | Advanced | Proxies. Then click Direct Connection to the Internet.

   ■ **For Microsoft Internet Explorer 4.0 version 4.72.3110.8 SP1**   Choose View | Internet Options | Connections tab | Proxies Server. Then disable the option to Access the Internet Using a Proxy Server.

2. Access the management client, as follows:

   ■ **In Netscape Navigator Version 3.**x   Choose File | Open Location and type

   ```
   http:// PIX_Firewall_IP_Address:8080
   ```

   ■ **In Netscape Communicator and Navigator 4.0 or later**   Choose File | Open Location and type

   ```
   http:// PIX_Firewall_IP_Address:8080
   ```

   ■ **Microsoft Internet Explorer 4.0 Version 4.72.3110.8 SP1**   Return to the main menu and type

   ```
   http:// PIX_Firewall_IP_Address:8080
   ```

Now you are ready to begin using the PIX Firewall management client. Unfortunately, understanding the management client may take as much effort as understanding the actual configuration file for a PIX Firewall! The management client does make it easier to enter the commands. (Instead of typing them at the CLI, you can click and drag.) But you still need to know about the relationships between global commands, NAT, conduit statements, and static route entries.

Although the PIX Firewall Manager may simplify things to some extent, in our opinion it's probably easier to use the command line interface and wait until Cisco tweaks the Manager up a bit.

CISCOSECURE INTRUSION DETECTION SYSTEM (IDS)

The CiscoSecure Intrusion Detection System (IDS), formerly named *NetRanger*, is a real-time intrusion detection system that discovers, responds to, and reports unauthorized activity, by using data derived directly from the network.

CiscoSecure IDS has two primary components. The Sensors act as sniffers, and the Director is the management console. In addition, a communication architect called the Post Office is responsible for communication between the Sensors and the Director.

Sensor

Sensors are network devices that reside on each network segment being monitored. They support the following topologies:

▼ Ethernet (10BaseT)

■ Fast Ethernet (100BaseT)

■ Token Ring (4 and 16 Mbps)

▲ Single and multimode Fiber Distributed Data Interface (FDDI)

Network Sensing

High-performance Sensors scan data and header portions of nearly every packet on a network segment. They look for attempts to access specific ports or hosts (*atomic* pattern) or sequences of operations across multiple hosts or time periods (*composite* pattern). They can also detect *named attacks,* single attacks that have specific names or common identities (such as Smurf, PHF, Land); *general category attacks,* attacks that keep appearing in new variations based on the same methodology (examples are Impossible IP Packet and IP fragmentation); and *extraordinary attacks,* extremely complicated attacks such as TCP hijacking and e-mail spam.

Custom Signatures

Custom signatures can be implemented to defend against specific security concerns. For instance, you might create the custom signature "proprietary" and the Sensor will detect all instances of the word "proprietary" on packets traveling onto an external network.

Attack Response

The Sensor can do several things after it determines an attack:

▼ Generate an alarm to the remote Director system.

■ Log the alarm event to a flat file on either the Sensor or the Director system.

■ Record the session to an IP session log, to gather evidence and trick the intruder by impersonating important documentation or information in order to obtain more information about the intruder.

■ Reset the TCP connection and kill the session generating an attack.

▲ Deny network access by reconfiguring the ACL of a Cisco router, using the Device Management feature, or configure it manually on the Director system.

Router Syslog Monitoring

CiscoSecure IDS monitors router ACL system logs. Any policy violations detected will generate alarms sent to the Director.

Director

The Director is a centralized software application that monitors and manages Sensors, collects and analyzes network security data, downloads new attack signatures, and facilitates user operation.

Although the Director does not offer reporting, it exports data to third-party reporting tools.

Network Security Database

The HTML-based network security database provides attack descriptions; possible countermeasures; and specific, customizable response procedures. The database interface is a map-based, color-icon GUI that displays visual forms of alarms.

Sensor Monitoring

The Sensors provide real-time security information to the Director. Using HP OpenView, this information is then presented via hierarchical icons on the network security maps. Each icon is used to access a particular layer, and the lowest layer contains Alarm and Error icons.

An icon can be a Machine, Application, or an Alarm. A state, represented by a color, is assigned to each icon. The state of an icon is propagated up to the highest layer of the network security maps, so at the highest level you can determine where the alarms are. Table 14-6 illustrates the relationship of icon colors to icon states.

Sensor Installation, Management, and Recovery

To install a SENSOR, you simply plug it into the desired network and assign it an IP address using a laptop and its console port. The Director can then detect the Sensor and provide the remaining configurations. The Director can also provide ongoing remote management and configuration changes for all Sensors on the related networks.

All existing and previous configuration files for the Sensors being monitored by the Director can also be stored by the Director. This means the Director can easily roll back to

Icon Color	Icon State
Green	Normal
Yellow	Marginal
Red	Critical

Table 14-6.   CiscoSecure IDS Icon States

a previous configuration or completely restore a configuration to a Sensor that has failed and needs to be recovered.

The following functions have parameters configurable by a user on the Director for the Sensor(s):

▼ Communications

■ Data management

■ Device management

■ Director forwarding

■ Event processing

■ Intrusion detection

■ System files

▲ Collection of Sensor data

Analysis of Sensor Data

Using third-party tools, the Director can analyze Sensor data and generate reports to show information such as number and levels of alarms, Web server activity, and a table of events, categorized by levels.

Post Office

Post Office is the communication tool between the Sensors and the Director. It is based on a unique three-part address with Organization, Host, and Application identifiers. The combination of these three identifiers distinguishes each node. This three-part addressing scheme can be layered on top of existing network protocols and allows for fault-tolerant connectivity across heterogeneous network architectures. It also addresses a much larger domain than the current 32-bit IP protocol.

Three-part addressing provides the following benefits:

▼ *Alternate routes are defined between hosts.* These allow automatic switching to the next route when the current route fails.

■ *Sensors send messages only to the Director; they are not broadcast onto multiple hosts.* The Director then propagates packets onto other affected platforms.

▲ *Multiple Directors can be used.* Local Directors can manage during core business hours, and Sensors know to send updates to the central Director during off-peak hours. By centralizing this operation, system management is simplified.

SUMMARY

In many companies, data is becoming the most important asset. This resource might describe how a company operates, and its future strategies with products, services, technologies, and so forth. Such information would be detrimental if placed in the wrong hands. Cisco's security options go far toward protecting a company's internal data from external hackers. Options include Cisco IOS access control lists (ACLs), Cisco Firewall IOS, and Cisco PIX Firewall. Each of these mechanisms offers a different level of security protection—from the basic protection of Cisco ACLs on up to Cisco PIX Firewall's high-level detection and prevention. The cost of these options increases in proportion to the measure of security provided.

Other methods, as well, can be used to secure a company's data in a Cisco environment. Cisco offers Network Address Translation (NAT) on the router IOS, on the router Firewall IOS, and on PIX Firewall. NAT is typically used to hide internal IP addressing schemes and/or reduce the expense of a registered IP address for each node on the network. Virtual private network (VPN) technology also exists. VPNs are encrypted tunnels that provide a means for traffic to traverse securely across a public network. VPNs are typically deployed for remote users accessing a company's internal data across a public network such as the Internet.

As with any network administration decision, the pros and cons must be weighed in order to determine the sacrifices the company will make in order to obtain the level of security desired.

CHAPTER 15

Ensuring Quality of Service

The Internet is a "best-effort" service. It's based on a first-come, first-served philosophy in which dropped packets and delivery delays are tolerated as inevitable by-products of fluctuating network traffic and available capacity. This isn't due to some fundamental design flaw—the Internet is that way on purpose. Its designers knew full well from the outset that things had to be kept simple in order to attain the stated goal of a "universal network." This is why IP provides little more than an elegant addressing scheme along with a message format, and TCP offers only a modest system for managing network connections. The Internet has no built-in infrastructure to handle such things as media access, security, foolproof error recovery, traffic management, and other advanced networking functions.

The designers had the foresight to push complexity out to the network's edge. In fact, they didn't have much choice in the matter. How else could the Internet accommodate so many different types of applications, and connections to virtually any make of computer? This commonality is made possible by keeping the network core fairly dumb. Consider the implementation of TCP/IP within the seven-layer OSI model, and you'll see that the Internet offloads as much as possible, assuming responsibility only up to layer 3, the network layer. The Internet's magic is that it pawns most complexity off onto LANs, end-host computers, and various kinds of edge network devices. Without this strategy, the Internet could not have grown to the stupendous size and capability we now take for granted.

But there's trouble looming in paradise. Best-effort delivery service is not sufficient to transport in a timely fashion all the traffic on the Internet and in corporate networks running TCP/IP. There is more traffic than ever, taxing the LAN and WAN links; moreover, a new breed of applications (including voice and video) can't tolerate delay. Organizations, ISPs, and the entire Internet community recognize the need to prioritize a network so that critical and time-sensitive data gets through as quickly as possible, and nonessential traffic is required to wait.

This chapter discusses the emerging technologies that promise to deliver prioritization of network traffic.

CONVERGENCE, MULTIMEDIA, AND RISING EXPECTATIONS

The Internet's future difficulties will probably all come in the form of new types of traffic. This expansion is driven by a whole new breed of network applications featuring real-time, two-way, time-sensitive characteristics. For these *convergence* applications, the 'Net is to become the unifying platform over which all mass communication takes place. Convergence has already started, represented by multimedia technologies such as WebTV, video-conferencing, Web radio, Microsoft's NetMeeting, distance learning, and others. Perhaps the most significant convergence medium is telephone service over the Internet.

These and other new-wave media are exposing IP's structural shortcomings, mostly because the applications require committed end-to-end service in order to work properly. As a result, IP's very strengths are increasingly becoming its weaknesses. This situation is similar to the emergence of the World Wide Web in the early 1990s. At that time, everybody was using some form of windows on their desktops, and the Internet's alphanumeric interface became unsatisfactory. This time around, the need for change is driven mostly by electronic commerce. For the Internet to indeed be the world's primary business venue, its infrastructure must be upgraded to include *all* important communications media, not just Web browsing, messaging, and file transfer. Therefore, IP must be somehow upgraded to handle the multimedia applications brought online by convergence.

Given the tremendous success of the Internet, however, only a fool would propose replacing IP (though a few actually have). What's needed instead is an IP-compatible technology that can give multimedia applications the end-to-end service levels they need. Even apart from the demands of multimedia, the Internet must be more reliable if it is to become a serious place of business.

The industry's response to these challenges is Quality of Service (QoS).

QoS Defined

If you're new to the subject, you may be tempted to dismiss QoS as the network variant of Total Quality Management or some other quality assurance methodology. That's not the case. QoS is an actual runtime technology, replete with data model architecture, protocols, message formats, algorithms, and commands. It is a not-so-distant cousin of routing protocols. In fact, QoS is growing into such a substantial technical discipline that it could emerge as an industry niche, much like network security and network management.

Dozens of QoS definitions are evolving, partly because the words *quality* and *service* themselves have been so abused over the years. Marry these two trendy words, and confusion really kicks in. But a more serious problem is that QoS is a nascent technology, with the Internet Engineering Task Force (IETF) still in the process of defining technical specifications for many important elements of QoS. In addition, there are competing commercial agendas for QoS, most notably the conflicting needs of ISPs versus corporate intranets.

But QoS is a real technology and it can be defined. A generalized explanation, that QoS is a collection of methods to differentiate traffic and services, is perhaps too broad. A more informative definition might be that QoS is a collection of runtime processes that actively manage bandwidth to provide committed levels of network service to applications and/or users. QoS implements a framework for service policy and action that extends end to end for serviced connections, even across autonomous systems. From there, a seemingly endless parade of variation ensues. We'll settle for this: QoS is a collection of mechanisms designed to favor some types of traffic over others.

Why Bandwidth Alone Is Not Enough

Until recently, increasing bandwidth has appeased most network users. When things slowed down, network managers simply put in a fatter "pipe." This is called *overprovisioning*. Until recently, overprovisioning has been the most common approach to QoS, especially in local networks, where installing media is much less expensive than upgrading WAN links.

But the amount of raw data that can be moved through a network is no longer the only issue. Now, timing and coordination are just as important. While it's true that most multimedia applications are bandwidth hogs, many also introduce operational requirements new to IP networks. For example, packet delay during a voice-over IP (VoIP) phone call can cause the speakers to talk out of sequence, making the conversation incomprehensible.

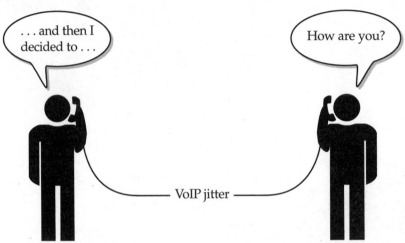

Packet delivery delay that causes a signal to lose its timing references is called *jitter*. For users, jitter in VoIP calls makes the calls unacceptable. The point here is that interactive, two-way network applications must maintain their sequential integrity above all, even when overall quality isn't especially high. We do this now with cell phone technology by tolerating occasional signal fade and persistent background noise. The cellular technology remains acceptable because it always maintains at least the sequential integrity of our phone conversations.

Traditional applications such as e-mail, Web browsing, and FTP aren't much affected by jitter or the other by-products of best-effort IP packet delivery. They're "elastic" in that they're not as sensitive to timing issues. Even when these transactions slow down, users still perceive the level of service to be sufficient—indeed they're usually unaware that a slowdown even took place. And when the overall service level slows too much, the network manager can simply install more bandwidth to maintain a desired level of service. By contrast, throwing bandwidth at a media application such as VoIP won't necessarily help. Even if overprovisioned with a high-bandwidth end-to-end pipe, sudden bursts of traffic would still manifest as jitter. Studies demonstrate that users are ten times more likely to remember an occasional service problem than the sustained level of good service surrounding it.

Network applications vary in their signal delivery requirements. The more an application's signal pattern is sensitive to delivery delay, the greater difficulty it has with IP's best-effort service approach. (By the way, *delay* is when a message is delivered intact but slowly; in contrast, *jitter* is when delay harms message integrity.)

In the following list, various traffic types are presented in order, from highest tolerance to jitter, to no tolerance:

Asynchronous	Fully elastic; delay causes no effect.
Synchronous	Delay can cause some effect, usually just slowness.
Interactive	Delay annoys and distracts users, but application is still functional.
Isochronous	Application is only partially functional.
Mission-critical	Application is functionally disabled.

Most traditional Internet applications are asynchronous and, therefore, very tolerant to jitter. For example, a user may not like waiting through the 30-second delay for a Web page to download, but the HTTP application still works fine from a functional standpoint. Convergence applications aren't so forgiving, although some are more tolerant to the vagaries of IP than others.

Let's cite some examples of traffic types:

▼ NetMeeting is a good example of interactive traffic, where delivery sequence is important but not critical.

■ VoIP is truly isochronous traffic because out-of-sequence speech causes information loss, and may even bug users enough to hang up.

■ Videocasting is another example of isochronous traffic, because each frame must be presented immediately after the other in perfect sequence and in quick succession.

▲ The classic example of mission-critical traffic is a process-control interrupt instruction to open a safety valve in a nuclear reactor's cooling system. Thankfully, mission-critical traffic does not exist on the Internet. (At least, we think not.)

VoIP (also called *IP telephony*) is hot because of its promise for huge cost savings. Also, it has the potential to weave spoken conversation into other applications, where text, graphics, and even financial transactions take place during a phone call. Major industry players are betting billions that VoIP will be the next "killer app" that binds all other mass communication onto a single transport platform: the Internet.

But for our purposes, VoIP is the best illustration of how bandwidth is no longer the only major factor in quality of service. An IP telephone conversation doesn't consume significant bandwidth (only about 9 Kbps each way), but the packets must be delivered quickly in order to maintain the conversational integrity. Even if you could afford to overconfigure bandwidth, traffic bursts would inevitably result in poor service, because round-trip delivery delays above half a second render VoIP unusable.

Overprovisioning bandwidth is an impossible dream because of burgeoning consumption. Millions of new users are coming online every day, and the level of activity per user is growing as Internet applications take on more and more routine tasks. These two factors alone have kept bandwidth consumption apace with advances in bandwidth technology. And now convergence is adding a raft of time-sensitive multimedia apps, most of which are bandwidth hogs (VoIP is an exception in this respect). Thus bandwidth is not a panacea for the technical challenges presented by convergence. To take the Internet to the next level, IP must be retrofitted to provide reliable network service levels, and the industry is convinced QoS is the answer.

QoS Is Nothing New

In truth, the industry has been using a QoS of sorts in WAN links for years. WAN links are more costly and have historically been the primary bottleneck in end-to-end connections. Very simply, it's expensive to pull a cable over long distances, across land belonging to others, under streets, and under oceans. The only way to cut WAN costs has been to install faster media, or to spread the cost among more users. While these measures have decreased WAN costs, long-haul links are still much more expensive than LAN bandwidth. The bottleneck problem persists, too. Even now, the routine configuration scenario for most companies is to have 100 Mbps Fast Ethernet in campus LANs connected to remote offices via 1.544 Mbps T1 links.

Both problems put intense pressure on the telecom industry to install various QoS mechanisms into their WAN transport technologies, which today are primarily Frame Relay and Asynchronous Transfer Mode (ATM). These mechanisms serve as a model for the architects of QoS solutions for the Internet.

Frame Relay QoS

Frame Relay is now the de facto standard technology for WANs. The technology is popular among remote users who cannot economically justify permanent point-to-point leased lines, but who need to connect to more than one site. From the technical standpoint, Frame Relay is a data-link layer protocol that uses a transport protocol based on

HDLC (the High-Level Data Link Control protocol). By using HDLC encapsulation, Frame Relay can form multiple virtual circuits within a network cloud—a fast and reliable arrangement that can be conveniently shared by otherwise unrelated enterprises.

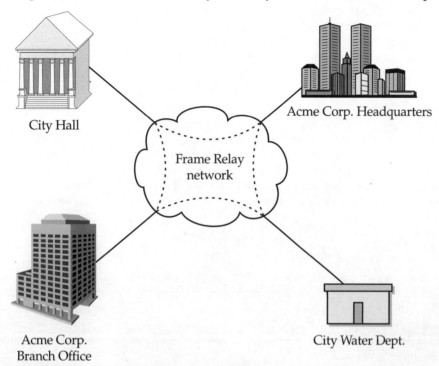

City Hall

Acme Corp. Headquarters

Frame Relay network

Acme Corp.
Branch Office

City Water Dept.

Frame Relay is especially popular for sites with intermittent data traffic. For example, a branch office that needs to talk to the headquarters mainframe in ten-minute spurts several times a day probably couldn't justify the cost of a dedicated link. The other option is long-distance dial-up, which tends to be slow, expensive, and unreliable. To use a Frame Relay service, the customer need only install a local loop line (either a 56/65 Kbps digital circuit or a T1 circuit) to the Frame Relay network's local access server. Everything beyond that point is transparent.

The challenge for the Frame Relay service provider is to balance the need for high-capacity utilization with the need to provide quality service to all customers. Frame Relay works by establishing a permanent virtual circuit (PVC) from end to end when a connection is made. To do this, Frame Relay defines a UNI (User-to-Network Interface) interface between the network and the client. The UNI maintains signaling between the endpoints by providing interim switches with information sufficient to maintaining proper PVC flow. The switches use the UNI signaling to identify the PVC to which a frame belongs, its direction, and its connection state.

The problem confronting Frame Relay is the "bursty" nature of the traffic it carries. A user dials into the network, goes through some setup, blasts a chunk of data through the pipe, and then logs off. Frame Relay handles bursty traffic with a service level called Committed Information Rate (CIR), in which the network operator commits to a customer that the PVC will operate at speeds no lower than a certain data rate. Like virtually all WAN operators, Frame Relay networks of course oversubscribe bandwidth on the assumption that seldom will all customers burst on simultaneously. In fact, Frame Relay network operators have to do this in order to compete and operate profitably.

Bandwidth congestion is inevitable under this arrangement, and Frame Relay has a safety valve to handle it. Frames have a Discard Eligible (DE) bit in the header. It's okay for a customer's transmission rate to burst above the CIR, as long as there's excess capacity in the network. But when the network is under pressure, the switches begin setting the DE bit in a customer's frames above the CIR, and this makes the frames eligible for discard.

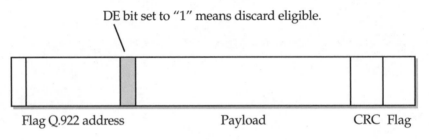

Frame Relay Frame Format

This practice is called *marking*. Frame Relay uses the DE bit as a place to mark excess frames, when necessary, to make good on CIR commitments to other users. Customers love Frame Relay because they get a bargain when traffic's slow, yet are assured service quality during peak times.

A CIR and other such commitments are called *service level agreements*, or SLAs. An SLA can consist of a single metric such as a CIR, but multiple metrics are more common. For example, an ISP and a customer might have an SLA that commits to guaranteed minimums for packet loss, average latency, and average available bandwidth.

When confronted with excess traffic, Frame Relay doesn't simply start dropping data frames. Another mechanism is used first, to ameliorate traffic congestion. When a switch in a Frame Relay network starts to become congested, the switch begins setting two particular bits in the frames passing through it: It sets the Backward Explicit Congestion Notification (BECN) bit to notify originating nodes of traffic queue build-up, so that the originating node can begin throttling back. The switch also sets the Forward Explicit Congestion Notification (FECN) bit to alert receiving nodes of potential future delays. If congestion continues to build beyond a second threshold, only then does the switch begin dropping DE-marked data frames. Frame Relay congestion control is quick because the FECN and BECN mechanisms are triggered at the actual moment and place of initial congestion, and the alerts are explicit notifications.

This ingenious Frame Relay arrangement reflects the essence of QoS: users can count on a certain level of service being consistently available. Yet, behind the scenes, the mechanisms also work to juggle user requirements, the goal being to yield more aggregate bandwidth than would otherwise be available from a finite resource (the Frame Relay network's bandwidth).

ATM QoS

During the 1980s, the telephone network infrastructure began to take on significant amounts of nonvoice traffic from corporate WANs and upstart Internet backbones. To help ensure service levels for everybody, the ATM protocol was introduced in the early 1990s. Since then, ATM links (with speeds up to 622 Mbps) have become the staple for high-speed WAN links, especially for ISP backbones. ATM transport is still relatively unknown to end users, remaining in the background because it rarely extends all the way to the desktop. Suffice it to say, though, that when you connect to a Web page or an FTP site, your download almost certainly passes through at least one ATM network along the way.

ATM has many QoS-enabling features built in, most notably the fixed-sized 53-byte cell it uses to transport information. This gives the hardware in ATM switches a substantial speed advantage over IP devices, which must process variable-sized packets. The variable-size packets force IP routers and switches to spend extra CPU cycles figuring out exactly where fields begin and end. The fixed cell size is what allowed ATM hardware to operate at speeds of 622 Mbps when Ethernet was still at 100 Mbps. Just as importantly, the fixed cell's inherent predictability lets ATM network managers meter out services with much greater precision than is possible with IP links.

Like Frame Relay, ATM is a switched-network technology that deploys UNI signaling to manage connections end to end within ATM networks. In contrast to Frame Relay, however, most ATM connections travel over *switched virtual circuits* (SVCs), on which connections are set up and torn down in response to UNI signaling. That is, an ATM SVC spans the entire network without the need to wire end-nodes into the network cloud via permanently connected physical phone loops. One of the principal attractions of ATM is its ability to deliver telephone network–like certainty without the need for PVCs, thereby offering both high performance and flexibility.

The ATM protocol spans layers 2 and 3 of the OSI model, so it's incompatible with IP at the native level. In other words, IP cannot operate over ATM as transparently as it does over Ethernet, Token Ring, and FDDI. IP can, however, interoperate with ATM, but only through emulation. Even so, the use of ATM for Internet backbone links is growing because of its inherently strong service quality. ATM is technically feasible for Internet backbone service because IP-to-ATM adapter technology is field proven, economically viable, and very fast.

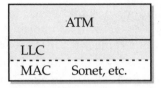

Because of its speed and manageability, ATM is considered by ISPs to be a desirable option despite its additional complexity and expense. Specifically, ATM switches have the capability to operate at these committed service levels:

▼ **Constant bit rate (CBR)** Service at a fixed data-transfer rate comparable to leased-line transfer, such as T1 or T3 (DS3). CBR is used for applications that require precise clocking to guarantee undistorted delivery.

■ **Variable bit rate (VBR)** Service at a variable bit rate to deliver a specified throughput capacity, but without sending the data evenly as in CBR. VBR is a popular choice for VoIP and videoconferencing applications.

■ **Available bit rate (ABR)** Service that guarantees a minimum capacity, but allows traffic to burst to higher levels when the bandwidth is available. ABR operation is similar to Frame Relay.

▲ **Unspecified bit rate (UBR)** Used to carry traffic that does not rely on time synchronization. UBR has no mechanism to dynamically adjust the amount of bandwidth available to a connection.

The important point here is that IP cannot specify any bit rate at all (at this juncture, at least). Because of its inherent QoS, ATM is especially capable for multimedia traffic, which must have CBR or real-time VBR to operate effectively. But ATM's QoS is also important for regular traffic, because it enables operators to tightly manage bandwidth in real time. Most Tier 1 ISPs use ATM to operate their Internet backbone trunks, because Tier 1's can cut a contract with a Tier 2 ISP or a big enterprise and use ATM QoS to deliver on their commitments, and also have detailed records documenting services rendered.

ATM switching works by combining multiple virtual circuits (VCs) into a virtual path (VP). Multiple VPs are in turn combined within a physical circuit, usually a fiber-optic cable operated by the Synchronous Optical Network (SONET) protocol at the physical level, as depicted in Figure 15-1.

Each ATM cell identifies itself with a VCI and a VPI (VC and VP identifiers) to tell ATM switches how the cell should be handled. As a cell hops between switches, its VCI and VPI values are rewritten to direct the cell to its next hop, thereby combining path integrity and adaptability.

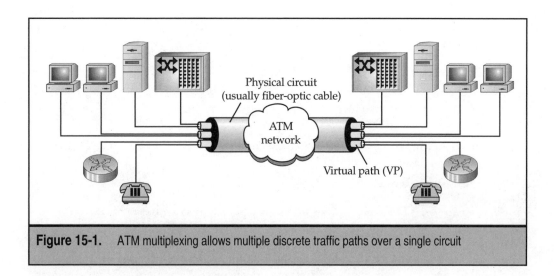

Figure 15-1.   ATM multiplexing allows multiple discrete traffic paths over a single circuit

A big part of ATM's ability is a second level of signaling through the Private Network-to-Network Interface (PNNI) protocol, which distributes topology information among switches in an ATM network. This is how ATM networks are able to calculate optimal end-to-end paths through ATM networks. PNNI maintains topology attribute information on individual ATM links to compute a cumulative score that ranks end-to-end ATM paths. PNNI is roughly similar to a link-state routing protocol in IP network, such as the Open Shortest Path First (OSPF) protocol.

What makes ATM so economically compelling is its proven ability to operate deterministic discrete paths (using SVCs) over a single cable. ATM's value is emphasized by the fact that fiber-optic bandwidth is more expensive over WAN links than on local networks.

ATM QoS Delivery Mechanisms

ATM uses a suite of traffic management mechanisms to deliver service levels. For example, there is a Cell Loss Priority (CLP) bit in the ATM cell format. When set to 1, the CLP bit marks ATM cells for selective discard during heavy traffic, in much the same manner as Frame Relay's DE bit marks frames for potential discard. ATM also uses a so-called "leaky bucket" mechanism to "shape" traffic flows as they enter the network. Other ATM mechanisms are used to separate traffic by service type, maximize bandwidth utilization, and so on.

ATM is probably the most complicated networking protocol there is; so, for brevity's sake, we won't go into detail on it here. For now, note that the reason ATM is able to offer granular service levels is that it implements a phalanx of sophisticated metrics. In order to form what is called a *traffic descriptor* for a connection, ATM uses four source traffic parameters:

▼ **Peak cell rate (PCR)**   A connection's maximum rate at which cells can be transported.

■ **Maximum burst size (MBS)**   A connection's maximum number of cells that may be transferred in a contiguous stream.

■ **Sustainable cell rate (SCR)**   A connection's allowable long-term cell transfer rate, on average.

▲ **Minimum cell rate (MCR)**   A connection's minimum allowable cell transfer rate.

As you can see, ATM characterizes traffic on a per-connection basis. These four traffic descriptors are enforced through the life of the connection. The tough part is calculating these rates in such a way that they balance the allocation of finite ATM bandwidth against the competing requirements of other simultaneous connections. Once the traffic descriptor is calculated, several additional QoS parameters are used to manage all flows over the ATM link. Combined with the PNNI protocol, these ATM QoS mechanisms serve to provide the best QoS solutions available in the industry today.

Yet the vast majority of ATM Internet backbone traffic still travels via unspecified bit rate (UBR) streams—ATM's least ambitious service category. This is the case for three reasons:

▼ Traditional traffic types are still prevalent. The majority of connections in the Internet today are asynchronous and therefore affected by delivery delay and jitter.

■ ATM is not end to end. Few end-stations are connected to ATM LANs. As a LAN technology, ATM proved to be too complicated to compete against Ethernet, so nearly all ATM networks are backbone links.

▲ No standards are set. Currently, there are no standards for mapping TCP/IP traffic types to ATM QoS mechanisms.

It's a cliché, but a chain is truly only as strong as its weakest link. The conundrum is that inelastic multimedia traffic such as IP telephony (VoIP) and videoconferencing won't flourish until end-to-end QoS is in place. End to end QoS, in turn, cannot be put into place until IP has at least some of ATM's QoS mechanisms. ATM QoS is a bit of a misnomer because no true QoS is possible unless it's end to end. This is why some experts are careful to call ATM's mechanisms "QoS enablers" instead of just plain QoS.

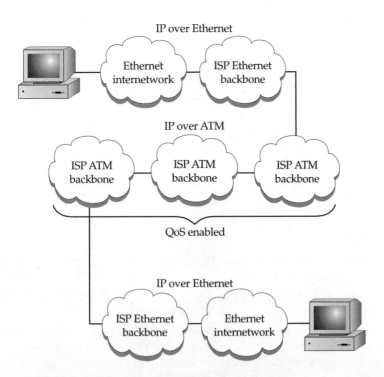

ATM is widespread in Internet backbones because, until the recent introduction of Gigabit Ethernet, ATM was the only network protocol technology capable of running over 1.544 Mbps OC-3 transport. But speed isn't ATM's only feature. ATM network operators are beginning to realize the economic value of ATM's inherent manageability, which can be used to offer customers better service packages.

No matter how good ATM becomes, however, it will remain at best a very important niche backbone technology. Therefore, QoS must be implemented in IP before the vision of Internet convergence can be realized.

NOTE: OC stands for *optical carrier* in the Synchronous Optical Network (SONET) specification. SONET is a physical-layer technology invented by BellCore to operate high-speed fiber-optic backbones. Now an ANSI standard, SONET is developing at a remarkable rate, having jumped from OC-3 to OC-12 (622 Mbps), then to OC-24 (1.244 Gbps), and now to OC-48 (2.488 Gbps). The next push is for an eye-popping 40 Gbps OC-768 in the 2001–2003 timeframe. A 100 Gbps OC level is already running in labs. These blinding speeds portend the ability to carry very large multimedia files, further intensifying the pressure for end-to-end QoS.

IP QoS

Convergence of the world onto IP for internetworking is a done deal, and the same goes for convergence onto Ethernet as the de facto LAN standard. But the convergence of virtually all communications media (telephone, television, and radio) onto IP is still somewhat problematic because, as discussed, IP by its very nature is antagonistic to the determinism of QoS.

The best-effort philosophy of IP is the fundamental result of the protocol's connectionless nature. When you send a packet, IP decides what route will be taken to the packet's destination. This contrasts sharply with transports such as Frame Relay and ATM, which operate by setting up virtual circuits to dedicate network resources to connections. Connectionless IP, of course, has no such capability.

In addition to its connectionless, best-effort architecture, there are other reasons why IP QoS is a tough engineering proposition:

▼ Network provisioning is a zero-sum game. Because bandwidth is a finite resource, every bps of capacity dedicated to one connection is consumed at the expense of all other simultaneous connections. QoS only finesses bandwidth; it doesn't create it.

■ Users will always take as much bandwidth as they can consume—as long as they don't have to pay extra for it. To be effective, QoS needs a way to authenticate users and a way to record utilization for billing. These authentication and accounting mechanisms must be unobtrusive and resource efficient.

▲ To remain universal, the Internet must be careful not to allocate so much bandwidth to inelastic applications that traditional (time-independent) applications such as HTTP and FTP are left wanting.

To succeed, IP QoS must build a suite of capabilities that systematically reduce complexity in identifying and allocating bandwidth resources. This isn't to say that QoS is an impossible dream. As a project, IP QoS is ultimately feasible because

▼ Most of the theoretical groundwork has been laid, and the IETF is well into the process of defining real-world technical specifications for missing QoS elements.

■ Frame Relay and ATM provide a real-world QoS experience base on which to build.

▲   In light of the immense profit potential at stake, full-blown QoS will eventually be realized. Money tends to have a coalescing effect on argumentative engineers and uncooperative vendors.

Given how well ATM and Frame Relay have done in WAN links, end-to-end QoS is now mostly a matter of implementing QoS within IP networks. The remainder of this chapter outlines the work done in this field to date. It's reasonable to assume that whatever is developed for IP QoS will be mapped back into ATM, Frame Relay, and other important non-IP networking protocols.

QoS FUNDAMENTALS

Certain IP QoS mechanisms have been in place for some time, but none powerful enough to handle end-to-end QoS on its own. Existing QoS mechanisms are manifested largely in the form of operating system commands. Cisco has led the way by implementing several QoS commands into its IOS operating system (we'll review them in action later). In addition, the IETF and other standards-setting bodies have busied themselves laying out broader QoS technologies. Until these superstructures are finally put into place, however, existent IP QoS commands will remain largely unused.

Before we go over these mechanisms, a review of QoS fundamentals will help put things in their proper context.

Two Kinds of QoS

There are two basic kinds of QoS, and they differ sharply:

▼   **Prioritization**   Individual packets are treated differently according to their assigned service class.

▲   **Resource reservation**   A connection is allocated a certain amount of bandwidth negotiated with routers and switches along its path.

Simple *prioritization QoS* is packet based. In other words, the treatment the packet deserves is in one way or another signified inside the packet itself. Although all QoS is priority driven, prioritization QoS is distinct because its implementation is constrained to a device inspecting packets. In other words, routers apply prioritization independent of other routers.

Reserved connections, in contrast, are far more complex. Reservation schemes must get all the routers along a connection's path to agree on a QoS regimen before transmission can begin. Moreover, the path itself must be defined before the reservations are made. In addition, it may be necessary for reserved-path bandwidth to make real-time adjustments to changing operating conditions, further adding to complexity.

That's not the case with packet-priority QoS, however. If operating conditions are changed when packets from another flow with the same or higher priority enter the same router, the original flow's packets are simply adjusted in its queue. As you'll see, some priority-based QoS mechanisms work by forming multiple output queues.

Reserving bandwidth, on the other hand, requires all devices in the path to converse and collectively arrive at a QoS service level commitment. Put another way, containing QoS in the packet itself does away with the need to establish and monitor connection flows across routers, across routing areas, and even across autonomous system boundaries. (Think of an *autonomous system* as a collection of routers under a single administrative authority using a common routing protocol.)

Flows and Connections

A *flow* is a stream of packets moving in a single direction between two end-host IP addresses identified by a TCP or UDP network application port number. When a packet stream travels back in the other direction between that same end-host pair, it constitutes a separate flow (because the "from-to" IP address pair is reversed). Frequently, there are multiple simultaneous flows running between a host pair. For example, a browser can run several flows at once. To keep them separate, multiple flows moving in one direction between a host pair are distinguished by port number.

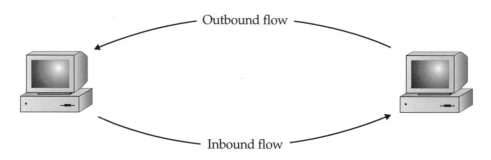

Flows are fundamental to QoS because, for every packet stream, they indicate the *where* (the path connecting the host pair), the *when* (the connection's sequence and direction), and the *why* (the application being run). Flows are identified using some or all of the following packet data elements:

▼ **Source host address**   The network address of the originating host (specific to a layer-3 protocol such as IP).

■ **Destination host address**   The network address of the receiving host (also specific to a layer-3 protocol such as IP).

■ **Protocol**   Network and transport protocols such as IP, TCP, and UDP.

■ **Source protocol port**   Network application protocol from the source host, such as HTTP and FTP.

■ **Destination protocol port**   Network application protocol dependent on the destination host network address.

▲ **Source device interface**   Network interface through which the traffic entered the device, usually a router.

Any combination of these flow-definition criteria is called a *tuple*. Those experienced with programming will recognize a tuple as a data object made up of two or more components. QoS functions use tuples to identify individual flows.

All flows between a host pair during an arbitrary time period constitute a *connection*. When flows are aggregated into connections, it simplifies the task of service level management by reducing the number of required flow-management instructions. Connections are also called *sessions*, the latter term being more often used in the context of the people using the connection. Flow identification is the most rudimentary QoS enabler because it tells network devices what connection a packet belongs to, and therefore what service level to apply (if any).

Stateless vs. Stateful QoS

QoS implemented on a per-device basis is by nature stateless. This kind of QoS (usually some variant of a prioritization scheme) works by holding a set of rules in router memory and matching packet headers to the rules. This takes some work to set up and some machine overhead to operate. Stateless, local QoS of this type doesn't scale well into large internetworks. It tends to fall apart due to inconsistencies in rules sets and because of the substantial administrative overhead usually required.

A second kind of stateless QoS modifies the simple priority-queuing approach. In this approach, which might be called *transitive stateless QoS*, routers change the content of a packet's header as it travels through the internetwork. Examples of message unit "marking" are Frame Relay's Discard Eligible (DE) bit and ATM's (CLP) bit, discussed earlier. But those mechanisms mark message units (frames and cells, respectively) only for selective treatment under stress load conditions.

IP can do what might be called "transitive stateless" packet marking to signify a preferential treatment value (as far as queuing priority) instead of a "discardability" value. As the packet travels into various layers of an internetwork—from the access layer into the distribution layer, and then into the core layer—the priority value can be changed according to a user-configured parameter. In this arrangement, the information needed to determine a queuing action is simply read from a field within the header. The router doesn't have to perform a painstaking match against a rules set. It's a faster and simpler procedure, as depicted in Figure 15-2.

Resource reservation is a *stateful* form of QoS. As illustrated in Figure 15-2, a flow state is defined within the sequence of routers along the path, and then the packets are marked as being part of a flow in the reserved path. This "connection path stateful" approach is more intelligent and presumably more reliable because it operates on a per-flow basis. There are many concerns, however, about the computational overhead needed to pull it off and potential latency the procedure might introduce to networks. This is because the flow's path must first be determined, and then QoS contracts for the flow must be successfully negotiated with every device along that path. If that can't be done, the same process must be attempted for an alternate path.

Why TCP Alone Cannot Support QoS

TCP is a flow-control protocol used to set up and manage connections over an IP network. It is sometimes said that TCP sets up "virtual circuits," but that's misleading. In the context of QoS, a *circuit* should be defined as a connection that arranges for specific de-

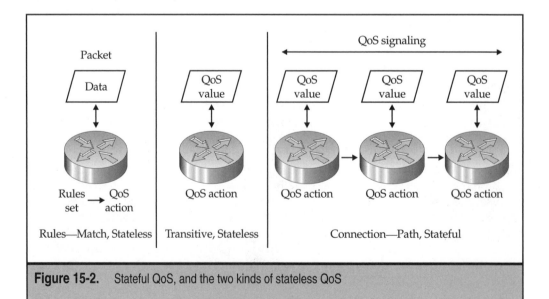

Figure 15-2.   Stateful QoS, and the two kinds of stateless QoS

vices (routers and switches) to be transited. TCP does not do this; the path is determined by the network devices.

Connection-oriented transports such as ATM and Frame Relay lend themselves better to QoS because having a virtual circuit (VC) gives more control over service quality. If a VC knows the routers handling a QoS connection, it reduces the number of variables necessary to help ensure priority, switching speed, average bandwidth, and other services along the connection's path. To take a specific example, Frame Relay uses the Explicit Congestion Notification (ECN) mechanisms to instantly alert both sender and receiver of incipient traffic problems. If the congestion persists, Frame Relay can then use the DE bit to selectively discard traffic to which it's not contractually committed. That's tight connection control in action.

Frame Relay Network

TCP's flow control relies on the acknowledgment (ACK) messages sent by receiver to sender after receipt of each packet stream. Unlike the explicit ECN of Frame Relay, TCP's ACK is implicit and therefore needs time to react to changing conditions.

In addition to acknowledging packet receipt for error control, the ACK informs the sending host of its current transmission window size. In TCP, a *window* is the number of bytes the host currently has available in buffer memory to handle packets being received in a connection. The more bytes available to the buffer, the larger the transmission window is. As the amount of buffer for the connection fluctuates, the value in the ACK window field is adjusted to notify the sending host of the change.

How TCP Manages Connections

Looking at the depiction of the process in Figure 15-3, you can imagine the "bounce time" involved for host pairs to adjust to changing network operating conditions.

TCP uses windowing to control the number of packets dropped for lack of host buffer memory. Constantly adjusting transmission window size also reduces overhead by greatly increasing the ratio of payload packets to ACK packets. TCP's transmission control method is fine for best-effort IP service; indeed, without this control the Internet wouldn't be what it is. But windowing is woefully insufficient for QoS, and for a number of reasons:

▼   **Limited scope**   TCP deals only with fluctuating host buffers. It has nothing to do with such in-network factors as available bandwidth, and router propagating errors.

- ■ **Speed of response**   Even for their limited mission, TCP hosts must iterate a number of ACK messages to settle on proper packet stream size, and that takes time.

- ▲ **Lack of control**   Inelastic applications such as IP telephony need service level assurances that TCP doesn't even attempt to provide, especially assured minimum latency.

QoS implies requirements that TCP/IP can't fulfill without significant enhancement. In a nutshell, then, it can be said that implementing QoS over IP networks is largely a matter of layering granular, real-time controls atop the TCP flow-control mechanism. But this must be done in a manner that doesn't impinge on TCP's time-tested ability to handle best-effort traffic.

The Need for a QoS Framework

To operate properly, QoS needs a separate framework of policies to layer atop IP networks. A service level agreement (SLA) is a policy, not unlike a network security policy.

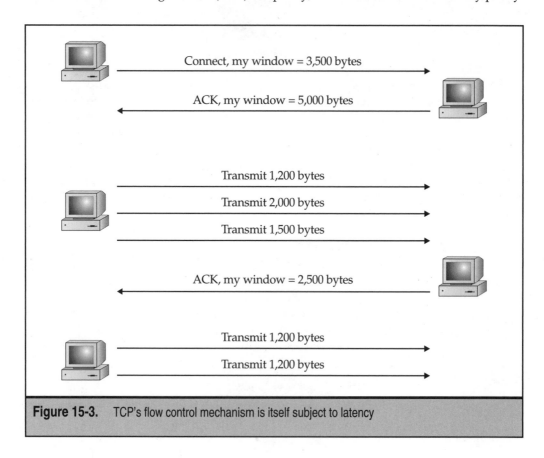

Figure 15-3.   TCP's flow control mechanism is itself subject to latency

But an SLA must be propagated to the devices that are to enforce it, and the policy must somehow be kept uniform across the topology. In other words, QoS needs a policy framework in much the same way that network access security measures are implemented within the framework of RADIUS or TACACS+.

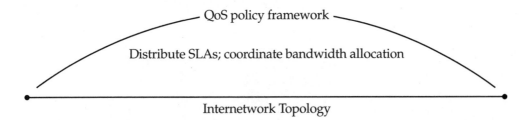

Coordinating QoS across large internetworks can get complicated. A communications infrastructure can serve as a framework for coordinating QoS policy across the topology. Those familiar with routing protocols or SNMP will understand that a cohesive suite of technical elements—a freestanding subsystem, in other words—must be in place for QoS to work.

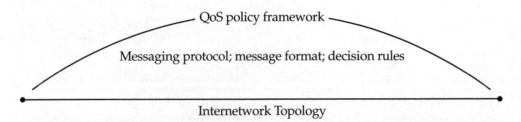

Without a framework, it would be necessary to separately maintain each QoS policy on a per-device basis. If administrators must "touch" each device (probably via a Telnet logon), QoS within an internetwork would be both labor intensive and mistake prone. Most couldn't imagine managing network devices or security in a large internetwork without the benefit of SNMP and RADIUS, and the same holds true for QoS. Indeed, QoS presents a much tougher implementation proposition than do system management and security because, for end-to-end service quality, the policy must be implemented across autonomous systems. Generally, this entails implementing QoS across ISPs, but extranets imply QoS between end-user enterprise internetworks also. Manual implementation of any meaningful QoS is virtually impossible.

In a typical internetwork, requests for service and changes in operating conditions take place several times a minute. It therefore follows that network teams will need to tweak fixed QoS policies with some frequency, probably at least weekly. This suggests the need for a layer of abstraction between the content of the policy and its application devices. For example, a router interface could have the role Priority Enforcer, but the actual rule of "give Gold packets 50% of available bandwidth" would be separately defined. So if the network manager decided to reduce Gold's priority to 40%, the change would be implemented only in the policy server, not in every device assigned the Priority Enforcer role.

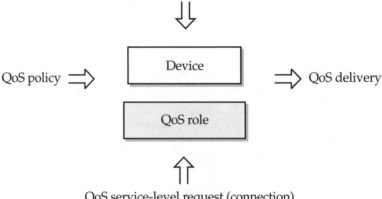

Binding rules to roles in real time would give a QoS system a lot more flexibility. QoS needs the ability to self-operate in the way routing protocols can. Routing protocols let routers update one another on topology changes, so each router can continually recalculate optimal routes to various destinations. The Internet was able to scale to its gigantic size because routing protocols imbue the Internet with a degree of self-awareness and self-operation—especially because of the Border Gateway Protocol (BGP) operating at the Internet peer routing level.

Specifically, QoS needs a way to continually account for finite bandwidth resources. Also needed are automated mechanisms to make decisions between competing QoS requests, and to set up and tear down QoS assignments as connections come and go. The mission of a QoS framework takes on high complexity as QoS services span autonomous systems.

Packet Manipulation and Overhead Costs

All networking subsystems work by manipulating packets in one way or another. Doing anything with a packet involves going through a CPU cycle. While it's true that smart engineering can pack more instructions into a cycle, the fact remains that every QoS action requires additional tasks that come at a cost. The trick is to get the most service-quality effect at the least processing-overhead cost.

Routers, switches, and other network devices don't need disks because their function is to forward traffic. Packets are only stored temporarily, where DRAM is used to set up and manage one or more packet queues while the CPU figures out how to forward them. Indeed, queuing is so important to router operations that most routers have separate DRAM called *packet memory* dedicated specifically to that purpose. One of the primary tools used by QoS to influence service levels is queue manipulation. Because virtually all routers use first-in/first-out (FIFO) ordering by default, queue manipulation mechanisms are often referred to as *non-FIFO queuing*.

The most common name for the practice, though, is *class-based queuing* (CBQ). CBQ works by somehow defining packets to a class by flow. If, for example, a router is instructed to favor one type of traffic over another, it must intervene and influence the queue's default FIFO order to bump the favored class of traffic toward the front. This process is shown in Figure 15-4, in which packet C is bumped to the front of the queue.

There's no avoiding the fact that queue intervention comes at a cost in processing overhead. The router must spend extra CPU cycles to inspect packets for class type and then to resequence the queue. As discussed, packets can be differentiated either by tuple or marking, but the favored CBQ method is marking because it costs less in processing and administrative overhead. It takes more CPU effort to match a four-tuple rule than to simply recognize the rule represented in a predetermined bit value.

No matter the recognition method used, however, overhead costs rise as queue manipulation schemes get more sophisticated. CBQ is the best example of how network administrators must weigh a cost-benefit analysis for each QoS policy. They need to balance improved network predictability against any unintended latency caused by packet inspection and queue manipulation.

QoS Topology Considerations

Network engineering literature describes a classical three-layer hierarchy design model. Illustrated in Figure 15-5, the three-layer model enforces segmentation in order to separate unrelated traffic. The access layer connects devices to the local network and contains such local traffic as database lookups and print jobs. The distribution layer is responsible for most

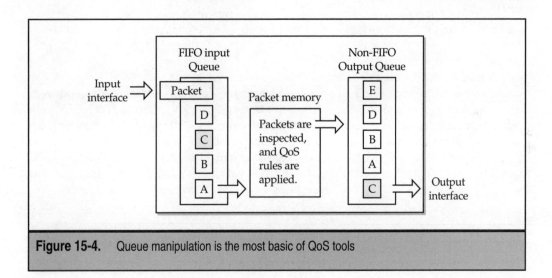

Figure 15-4.   Queue manipulation is the most basic of QoS tools

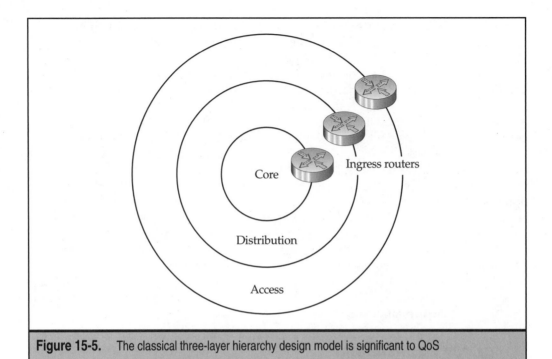

Figure 15-5. The classical three-layer hierarchy design model is significant to QoS

routing, security, and other intelligent functions—all of which require substantial packet manipulation. The core layer does minimal packet manipulation; it moves largely preconditioned flows at very high speeds, usually over switched Ethernet or ATM links.

Hierarchical topology is almost a requirement nowadays, and for reasons other than just traffic isolation. A second reason is that a rational topology layout facilitates route aggregation—a tactic aggressively pursued in large intranets using the OSPF routing protocol and on the open Internet using BGP—because it greatly reduces the size of routing tables and thereby increases overall network speed.

Hierarchical layering also helps QoS, which defines gateway routers between layers as *ingress points* (a natural place to differentiate service policy). Certainly, QoS ingress routers, too, are defined at gateways between autonomous systems, and even among declared multilayer QoS zones within an autonomous system. But it makes greatest sense to trigger QoS rules at ingress points between hierarchical layers. For example, an FTP packet might be accorded a Bronze CBQ service level entering the distribution layer, but be bumped up to Gold as it passes through the core layer's ingress router because the network manager has an SLA that favors long packet streams—due to the way the ISP has tuned its ATM QoS parameters, for example.

Putting QoS into the Access Layer

In order to help ensure performance levels, the application of QoS policy should be kept to a minimum in the core network. When QoS is applied closer to the network's edge, its application will have less impact on unrelated traffic. In other words, policy should be implemented at the lowest possible level in the internetwork hierarchy.

Congestion, too, must be managed along backbones also. An increasing volume of traffic is moving over the Internet's peer network, navigating across multiple ISP backbones to make remote connections. There used to be an "80/20 rule" in networking that said 80% of the traffic stayed in its local area, and only 20% percent went remote. With the rise of corporate intranets and consumer Internet use, experts now calculate that as much as 75% percent of 'Net traffic is remote. Traffic congestion mechanisms are therefore being developed to operate unobtrusively in high-speed backbone environments.

QoS and Autonomous Systems

Research has shown that most QoS implementations done to date are within private enterprise (non-ISP) internetworks. This is somewhat ironic given that ISPs invented the Service Level Agreement (SLA) as a way to do business, and the fact that ISPs operate most ATM networks. But it's understandable. Consider the following issues:

▼ When a packet passes through the ingress router to enter someone else's autonomous system, it becomes less of a priority. Why should they take on the added expense of the processing and administrative overhead needed to guarantee a QoS service level for the packet?

■ Even if another autonomous system wanted to help—say, an ISP that wants to win your business—how can your policies be distributed to, and implemented in, its routers?

▲ If your policy were implemented in another autonomous system, what would ensure that it was executed based on a common understanding of active conditions and resulting actions?

A lot of Internet gurus are asking these very questions nowadays, and it's a tough nut to crack. As you travel among autonomous systems, you pass through various policy domains that have their own operating styles. Not only will QoS implementation require a global policy framework holding uniform criteria, it will also need a global policy evaluation algorithm. Rules sets, tuples, bit precedents, policies, and other elements of QoS execution in each autonomous system (AS) must be kept uniform.

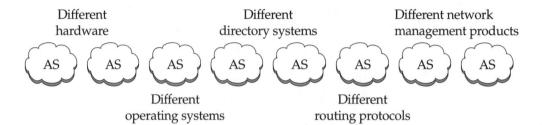

Compounding the problem of QoS among autonomous systems is the lack of uniform technical infrastructure. Any group of such systems is likely to be running a variety of routing protocols, network device hardware, computer platform operating systems, directory technologies, and network management systems. Their existence dictates that a truly interoperable QoS framework be in place in order for end-to-end QoS to work.

CISCO'S QOS DIRECTIVE

While it's true that end-to-end QoS is still in the future, that's not to say that the technology is "marketecture" hype from vendors. The idea of implementing "spot QoS" is catching on fast, with enterprise network managers and even ISPs putting QoS regimens into place in order to begin rationalizing services.

Doing QoS involves project risk and exacts a certain price in overhead, so look for early QoS adoption to take place when there exists the greatest discrepancy between classes of users. In this vein, it's not surprising that network managers at academic institutions are jumping on the QoS bandwagon. The idea of giving researchers and administrators precedence in campus networks over students playing Quake is just too tempting. And it's not the end of the world (or the ruination of the financial quarter) if the network goes out of whack for a day or two while the campus network team irons out QoS settings.

This is not to say that business isn't implementing QoS; it is. Let's take a look at the Cisco methods that can be used. Some of these QoS methods have been available for a while now. Others are just coming into existence, and others are still in the lab or exist only on the drawing board. Most or all of Cisco's methods are likely to be in play within the next two or three years, so they're important to all networking professionals today.

CiscoAssure

For some time, Cisco has identified end-to-end QoS as a goal the company wants to deploy in the enterprise. Even before the QoS technologies were ready for prime time, Cisco unveiled a QoS initiative called CiscoAssure. Like many of Cisco's terms that sound more like a program name, CiscoAssure isn't a discrete product. It's a total QoS solution that is implemented by using a family of products. Using all these products in their intended roles achieves all the benefits of QoS: prioritized traffic, central policy management, use of directory services, and so on.

The CiscoAssure architecture can be described in three components:

▼   **QoS-enabled network devices**   Routers, switches, and firewalls must be able to understand QoS policies and treat incoming traffic differently based on these policies. This feature must be supplied by the Cisco IOS. Most versions of IOS after 11.0 include a wide variety of QoS features that make the network devices running them QoS aware.

■   **Naming and directory services**   The CiscoAssure umbrella includes the services that provide IP addresses to end users (DHCP), as well as name-to-IP mapping services (DNS). It can be quite useful for QoS policies to be aware of users' IP addresses so that the policies can better prioritize traffic. Also, including communication to directory services (such as Active Directory) in the QoS decision will certainly enhance the ability to generate "intelligent" policy decisions. For example, you could build policies based on user attributes, such as the assigned user group.

Cisco does provide some of these services now through Network Registrar, as covered in Chapter 11. Also, as discussed in Chapter 2, the Directory-Enabled Network (DEN) initiative will bring network devices and directory services closer together.

▲   **Centralized policy management**   Creating QoS policies based on dynamic events (such as changing IP addresses) and directory information (such as user attributes) clearly will require a centralized control station and database. Also, sending policies out to many network devices will require some automation. Cisco is beginning to roll out this portion of CiscoAssure under the name of QoS Policy Manager.

The individual QoS technologies available today in Cisco IOS offer a vast array of methods to ensure traffic prioritization and control congestion. They can be used individually, but are most often combined in a customized solution that best fits a particular business and its QoS needs. These technologies are based on their method of delivering QoS:

▼   Packet classification

■   Congestion management

■   Congestion avoidance

■   Traffic shaping

▲   Flow signaling

The following sections describe Cisco's technologies in these categories and offer examples of their implementation on a Cisco router.

Packet Classification

In the broadest sense, packet classification involves tagging each packet with some descriptor that other downstream network devices can use to prioritize it. This *tag* might appear in the header of the packet or even within the payload, but most commonly the IP Precedence bits are used in IP networks.

In the header of an IP packet is a Type of Service (ToS) field reserved for tagging packets. Three of the bits can be used for IP Precedence. Of the eight possible combinations using three bits ($2^3 = 8$), six can be used to create six separate classes of service. Normally, these bits are untouched and ignored by network devices. If, however, these bits are set and the network device is instructed to look for them, the device can use them to make routing/queuing decisions.

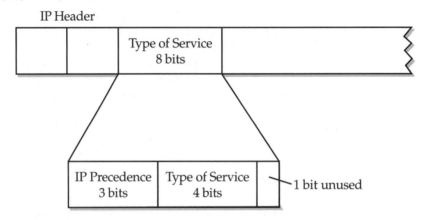

The intention is to set the IP Precedence bits on incoming data and then have the network devices handle traffic based on their reading of these bits. The first configuration issue, then, is how to set these bits for incoming traffic.

Setting the IP Precedence Bits

On Cisco devices, IP Precedence bits can be set using any of the following:

- ▼ **Policy-based routing (PBR)**   Allows setting the IP Precedence bits based on extended access lists; can even choose different routes based on these matches.

- ■ **QoS policy propagation via the Border Gateway Protocol (PB-BGP)**   For use on large internetworks, PB-BGP allows IP Precedence bits to be set based on BGP communities, BGP autonomous systems paths, and access lists.

- ▲ **Committed access rate (CAR)**   Can be used to classify as well as handle IP packets. Classification is based on matching traffic to extended access lists.

For our example, we'll use CAR to classify the IP Precedence bits, and then use it again to handle the packets.

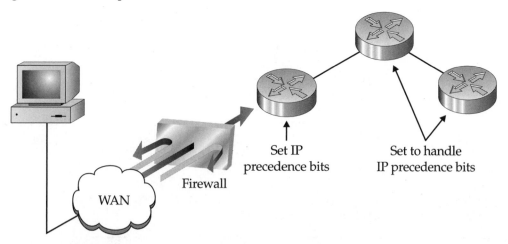

We first want to make an access list that will identify the traffic for which we want to set the IP Precedence bits. For example, to give a single user the IP Precedence bit value of 7 for Web traffic, we'd start by identifying this user based on IP address (10.1.1.10):

```
Router(config)#access-list 101 permit tcp 10.1.1.10 any eq www
```

The next step is to set the IP Precedence bits on all traffic that matches access group 101. First we set the interface to control, and then set up CAR to use the access group to set the IP Precedence bits.

```
Router(config)#interface ethernet 0
Router(config-if)#rate-limit output access-group 101 10000000 56000
56000 conform-action set-prec-transmit 7 exceed-action drop
```

Now when a user from 10.1.1.10 attempts to connect to port 80 (the Web) through this device, the user will be identified as matching access group 101. The **rate-limit** command tells the router to set the IP Precedence bit to 7 provided the user does not exceed the throughput of 10 Mbps (with an average and allowable burst rate set to 56 Kbps). If the traffic does exceed 10 Mbps, then the action is to drop the packet.

Controlling Traffic Based on IP Precedence Bits

For other network devices, we'll want them to see the IP Precedence bits that we set at the data ingress and handle them appropriately. We can use CAR to do this, as well. Since we don't want all the network devices to be setting the IP Precedence bits, we only need to match the access list to the bits already in the header and then proceed. First, we create an access list to identify each level of service.

```
Router(config)#access-list 101 permit tcp any any precedence 7
```

This identifies all TCP traffic carrying the IP Precedence bit of 7 as belonging to the access group 101.

Then we create a **rate-limit** statement to match this traffic and apply a policy to it, again on a specific interface.

```
Router(config-if)#rate-limit output access-group 101
5000000 56000 56000 conform-action transmit exceed-action drop
```

This policy states that traffic with IP Precedence of 7 gets transmitted as long as it doesn't consume more than 5 Mbps with an allowable burst of 56 Kbps. If the traffic doesn't conform, it will be dropped. Note that the first 56000 in this example identifies the normal burst; the second 56000 sets the maximum burst.

NOTE: Since there are many possible forms of the **rate-limit** command, and an almost limitless variation of applications, you should consult Cisco documentation before implementing any policies. (See www.cisco.com, then go to documentation | IOS commands | QoS.)

Differentiated Services (DiffServ)

A future classification model is called Differentiated Services, or DiffServ for short. Like the Resource Reservation Protocol (explained later in this chapter), DiffServ isn't a concept but rather a technology being developed under the auspices of an IETF working group. DiffServ, also called *soft QoS*, is meant to provide a relatively coarse but simple way to prioritize traffic.

DiffServ is a superset of the IP Precedence/CBQ mechanism, using a more sophisticated encoding scheme to mark packets. DiffServ does this by redefining the original IP ToS field bits into its own scheme, in which two of the eight ToS bits are used for congestion notification, and the remaining six bits for packet markings. This new scheme implements so-called *codepoints* within the six bits of marking space. Packets are marked for DiffServ class as they enter the DiffServ QoS network.

DiffServ attempts only to control so-called "per-hop" behaviors. In other words, policy is defined locally and DiffServ as a mechanism executes within a device to influence when the packet's next hop will occur and to where. Once policy is set across a toplogy, everything takes place within a device. DiffServ supports two service levels (traffic classes):

▼   **Expedited forwarding (EF)**   Minimizes delay and jitter. Packets are dropped if traffic exceeds maximum load threshold set by local policy.

▲   **Assured forwarding (AF)**   Provides for four subclasses and three drop-precedence codepoints within each subclass, for a total of twelve codepoints.

If traffic load exceeds local policy, excess AF packets are not delivered at the specified priority. Instead, they are demoted to a lower priority (but not dropped). This demotion procedure cascades through any configured drop-precedence codepoints.

Congestion Management

Congestion management attempts to alleviate some of the problems that occur when your link becomes saturated. Packet queues are created and used to store the packets until there is available bandwidth to send the transmission. There are several queuing methods, each offering different ways to control which packets get queued up and when they are transmitted.

FIRST-IN FIRST-OUT (FIFO)   This is the default method used on most routers. The first packet in is the first to go out. FIFO offers no prioritization and no QoS.

WEIGHTED FAIR QUEUING (WFQ)   Up to 256 individual queues are created, all with equal opportunity to transmit. Queues can be created based on source or destination address, protocol, source and destination ports, Frame Relay DLCI values, or even IP Precedence bits.

WFQ works by giving preferential treatment to low-volume flows, and then uses a congestion management algorithm to parcel out the remaining bandwidth to high-volume flows. Two output queues are set up, one each for low-volume and high-volume flows; the threshold separating them is a configurable parameter. WFQ is an automatic way to stop "bandwidth hogs" from starving off normal flows, allowing stabilization of network operations (and great reduction in the number of teed-off users). Most WFQ algorithms operate using the IP Precedence bits.

CUSTOM QUEUING (CQ)   In CQ, as in WFQ, individual queues (up to 16) can be created for outgoing traffic. However, in CQ each queue can be assigned a specific portion (in bytes) of the available bandwidth. This allows guarantee of some level of service to all users because even the lowest priority data gets its own queue.

PRIORITY QUEUING (PQ)   In PQ, up to four queues can be created for your data. You can set it up so that other queues do not get service unless a more important queue is empty. This allows absolute best service for some traffic but will snuff out lower-priority traffic altogether.

Configuring WFQ

Since weighted fair queuing is the simplest queuing method to set up, we'll use it for our example. If you do configure WFQ and then decide to switch to another queuing method, the new configuration will override WFQ.

Setting up congestion management is quite easy because it's already running by default on many interfaces. WFQ is automatically turned on for all serial links that run at or below 2 Mbps. Otherwise, you can turn it on by going first to the interface and then issuing this command:

```
Router(config-if)#fair-queue 64 128 16
```

The first argument (64) identifies the number of messages to hold in the queue; the second (128) sets the total number of dynamic queues to use; the last argument tells the router to create 16 queues for RSVP conversations.

Congestion Avoidance

Congestion is seemingly inevitable in IP networks, and it's a fact of life on the Internet. Traffic congestion leaves users disgruntled and can actually halt an internetwork altogether. With thousands of flows hitting a traffic aggregation point at once, it's possible for TCP itself to lock up. This phenomenon is called *global synchronization*, where all flows crossing the same node go into *TCP slow start* at roughly the same time. Slow start occurs when a TCP sender detects packet loss and retransmits, and keeps repeating the process until an ACK is finally received from the destination host. A network link that's sinking under the weight of exceeded load thresholds will be brought to its knees when hundreds or even thousands of TCP slow starts take place at the same time (synchronized). Once this relentless cycle is in motion, the link will crash altogether.

Random early detection (RED) and weighted random early detection (WRED) have been devised to avoid this fate.

Random Early Detection (RED)

The RED mechanism avoids congestion by randomly dropping packets after a user-configured traffic load threshold is exceeded. The packets to be dropped are selected arbitrarily from flows using the link, and RED continues dropping them until load has fallen back under the threshold. Load is sensed by monitoring queue depth. The dropped packets leverage the normal TCP connection control mechanism to signal senders to cut their transmission window sizes, thereby lowering the link's aggregate traffic load.

RED doesn't incur the overheads associated with the non-FIFO traffic-shaping mechanisms discussed earlier. FIFO queuing is left in place, but congestion avoidance is still provided. The drawback of RED is the amount of time this TCP-based adaptive signaling technique requires to work. The gurus anticipate that RED will prove insufficient in networks carrying bandwidth-heavy multimedia convergence application traffic.

Weighted Random Early Detection (WRED)

QoS is all about differentiation, and you can't differentiate with fairness. RED is "fair" in that it randomly selects the flows from which packets are dropped. WRED was devised to better marry congestion avoidance with QoS by introducing a measure of *un*fairness into the mechanism. WRED is a variant of standard RED that works by setting the threshold for packet discard according to the IP Precedence level of the packet. This "weighting" comes into play whenever RED is triggered at a higher threshold for packets belonging to higher IP Precedence classes. Non-IP traffic is treated as if its IP Precedence bit is set to zero. Therefore, non-IP traffic is more likely to get dropped when the link is congested.

NOTE: WRED is only useful when the majority of traffic is TCP/IP based. Other protocols do not indicate congestion in the same way, so WRED will be unable to detect congestion unless it learns about it from TCP/IP conversations.

Configuring Weighted Random Early Detection

To use WRED on a Cisco router, all you need to do is issue a single command at the interface where you want it to take effect. For example, the command

```
Router(config-if)#random-detect
```

will activate WRED on that particular interface. Although the IP Precedence bit determines how traffic is discarded, you can override the default by using the **random-detect** command with the **precedence** command.

Traffic Shaping

Currently, various mechanisms are used to control the characteristics of traffic being allowed into a network. Called *traffic shaping*, this process is primarily used at ingress routers. Network operators are starting to use traffic shaping to condition internal links for better service quality on their internal internetworks. Remember, network managers are faced with the reversal of the "80/20 rule" and transition to the current pattern in which as much as 75% of traffic in a private autonomous system is part of an external connection.

By definition, traffic shaping is the practice of controlling the volume of packets entering a network and controlling the rate of transmission in order to make traffic conform to a desired pattern. The name comes from the fact that a traffic flow is said to have been *shaped* when its pattern is changed. The two predominant ways to shape traffic are the *leaky bucket* and *token bucket* mechanisms.

The Leaky Bucket

A *leaky bucket* controls the rate at which packets enter a network, by manipulating inbound queues to smooth bursty traffic into less-variable flows. As mentioned, ATM invented the leaky bucket as a way to control the rate at which ATM cell traffic is transmitted over an ATM link. This mechanism has come into use more recently to condition IP packet datagram flows.

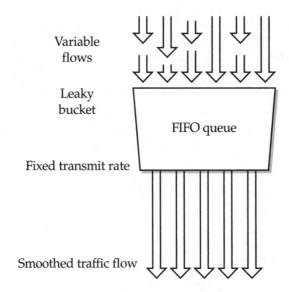

A leaky bucket is configured by setting two parameters: the maximum bucket depth (queue size limit), set as total bytes, and the maximum permitted transmission rate, set as bytes per second.

The primary benefit of leaky bucket traffic shaping is improved predictability of performance over a link. It's the most straightforward and easy-to-implement QoS mechanism there is, and it's especially popular for controlling flows when capacity is oversubscribed. The occasional dropped packet discourages congestion by triggering TCP to send reduced window sizes, or even negative acknowledgements (NACKs) back to the originating host.

Leaky bucket's downside is that the excess packets are discarded when traffic backs up beyond the bucket's depth. Also, because the "leak rate" is a fixed parameter that cannot adjust itself in real-time, bandwidth is wasted when traffic volume is less than the fixed leak rate.

The Token Bucket

The *token bucket* mechanism, though similar in name, is quite different from the leaky bucket. A token bucket is the practice of controlling the transmission rate based on the presence of so-called tokens in the bucket. In other words, a *token* is an abstract currency (measured in bytes) that must be available at any instant for the next FIFO packet to exit the network interface. There must be at least as many token bytes available as the number of bytes in the packet to be transmitted.

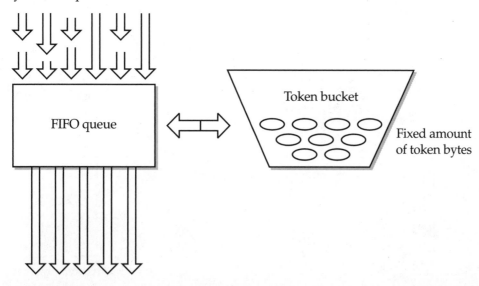

The number of tokens in the bucket is a configurable parameter. A burst-rate threshold parameter can also be configured to limit the number of tokens used by the packet stream of a single flow.

A token bucket is more flexible than a leaky bucket in that it will allow bursty traffic to transit the interface—as long as sufficient tokens are available. Although both the token bytes parameter and burst-rate threshold are fixed, a token bucket is more efficient than a leaky bucket because available bandwidth is more likely to be used when traffic is light.

Having one token bucket and one burst-rate threshold tends to negate the objectives of a Class of Service (CoS) prioritization scheme. For example, if there are gold, silver, and bronze traffic classes entering a router that's operating a single token bucket, token un-availability and peak rate threshold will weigh as heavily on gold as on bronze packets. A common practice, then, is to operate several token buckets, one for each class of service. Note that this requires implementing three separate output queues.

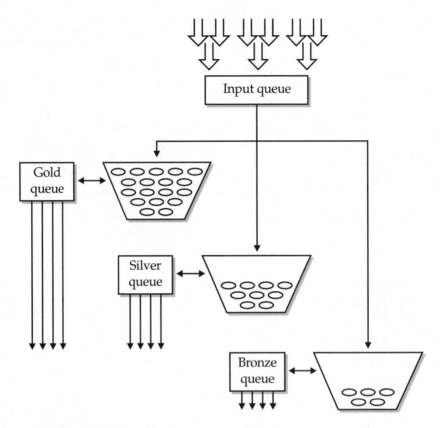

Gold-class packets would be afforded more tokens and a higher peak burst-rate threshold than would silver packets, with lower still parameters for bronze packets. Permitting classes to be shaped independently lets the administrator establish which types of traffic get the good (high peak burst rates) and which are most likely to experience the worst (packet loss for lack of available tokens). Properly configured, the token bucket mechanism doesn't incur the inherent bandwidth inefficiency of leaky buckets.

The Combined Traffic-Shaping Approach

A third form of traffic shaping is to combine leaky and token buckets within a single configuration. Combined shaping works by first conditioning incoming traffic through the leaky bucket queuing mechanism, and then sending it through a token bucket. The leaky bucket classifies traffic for its correspondent token bucket simply by assigning a packet stream to pass through that token bucket, as depicted in Figure 15-6.

Slower admission rates could be set for lower-priority traffic types (type B in this example) by directing such traffic from the input queue to the slower of the two leaky buckets. This combined approach gives more granular control over traffic by first freeing up

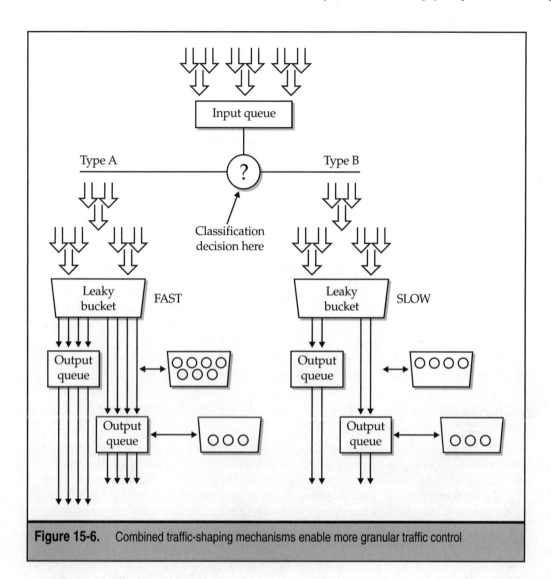

Figure 15-6. Combined traffic-shaping mechanisms enable more granular traffic control

bandwidth for the priority traffic, and also by allowing the assignment of aggregate throughput volumes and maximum burst rates for fast and slow traffic classes. One could configure as many combinations as desired—the limit being router overhead incurred for packet assignment and additional output queues.

Because it's only a network admission-control tool, traffic shaping alone can't deliver true QoS. Used in conjunction with other tools, however, traffic shapers help condition traffic for bandwidth priority and predictability.

Configuring Traffic Shaping

Let's take a look at how Cisco incorporated traffic shaping into its IOS. Cisco uses two types of traffic shaping:

▼ **Generic traffic shaping (GTS)**   GTS uses token bucket to shape the traffic output to match that of a particular interface or link. Once it leaves the token bucket(s) queue, the traffic must go through another queuing method if congestion still exists. GTS is configured on a per-interface basis, and the queuing method is WFQ.

▲ **Frame Relay traffic shaping (FRTS)**   FRTS is applied on a per-DLCI basis and doesn't support WFQ. Instead, CQ, PQ, or FIFO must be used as the queuing method.

The most basic implementation of GTS is when it is configured for all traffic leaving an interface. In the interface configuration mode, enter this command:

```
Router(config-if)#traffic-shape rate 5000000 56000 128000
```

Here, the bit rate is set to 5 Mbps with a burst size of 56 Kbps and a maximum burst size of 128 Kbps.

Configurations that are more complex can use access lists first to identify the traffic, and then selectively apply a specific shaping profile for that traffic.

Flow Signaling

Up to this point, we have described QoS methods that handle prioritized packets in a device-by-device fashion. Each network device acts independently and makes it own decision about the traffic passing through it. If any device along the path from client to server isn't using QoS, it creates the possibility that QoS won't be delivered. Another QoS method aims to remove this shortcoming and set up QoS parameters along the full length of the communication from one computer to the other.

The Resource Reservation Protocol (RSVP)

RSVP delivers QoS on a per-flow basis. As its name implies, RSVP "reserves" certain bandwidth resources along a path connecting source and destination devices in order to ensure a minimum level of QoS. Applications running on IP end systems will use RSVP to indicate the nature of the packet streams they want to receive, thereby "reserving" bandwidth that can support the required QoS. This is done by defining parameters for such characteristics as minimum bandwidth, maximum delay jitter, maximum burst, and the like.

RSVP is a nascent technology. Interest in RSVP has grown considerably in light of recently emerging convergence applications such as IP telephony and videoconferencing. The IETF and a number of vendors have devoted considerable resources to its development. An ambitious project, RSVP provides its own signaling to converse with devices for negotiating reserved QoS, and for monitoring flows once underway. This full-fledged protocol has a suite of messages, rules, and algorithms to integrate devices into a QoS service.

RSVP is complicated. It defines a *sender* and a *receiver* host for each flow. The sender sends a *PATH* message downstream to the receiver; the Path collects a roster of devices along the route. Once the Path message is received, the receiver sends a request called a *RESV* message back upstream along the same path to the RSVP sender. The RESV message specifies parameters for the desired bandwidth characteristics. Once all the interim devices are signed on to support the QoS levels, the session can begin. When the connection is terminated, an explicit teardown mechanism is used to free up resources on the reserved devices. The RSVP process is illustrated in Figure 15-7.

Route aggregation partially ameliorates RSVP complexity and overhead. For example, if thousands of RSVP receiver hosts were to receive a multicast (say, a Web TV videocast), the RESV messages would be rolled up and combined at aggregation points. Conversely, only one stream would be sent down from the videocaster, replicated at aggregation points to worm out to all endpoint destinations.

RSVP's large number of potential variables implies such complexity that it resembles ATM, but without the determinism. In light of this complexity, and the overhead likely in configuring and operating bandwidth reserved in this way, some experts openly question whether RSVP is even feasible. It seems likely that advances in hardware speed will solve the overhead problem. The complexity issue can be solved only through sustained R&D and standards-setting efforts. Those efforts are well underway and, if anything, intensifying under pressure from the demand for multimedia over IP applications.

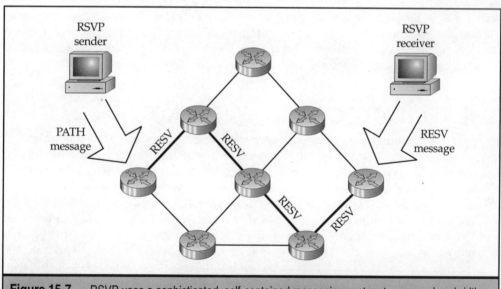

Figure 15-7.   RSVP uses a sophisticated, self-contained messaging system to reserve bandwidth

Configuring RSVP

There are three basic steps in setting up an RSVP session on Cisco routers.

First, RSVP must be enabled on the interfaces that will be used. This includes all interfaces on the path from the sender and receiver. We go to the interface configuration mode to set this up, with the following command:

```
Router(config-if)#ip rsvp bandwidth 10000 200
```

This command tells the router that the interface is a 10 Mbps connection and to use 200 Kbps as a single flow limit. In this arrangement, attempts to set up RSVP pipes of more than 200 Kbps will likely fail. Note that the **rsvp** command understands the bandwidth numbers to be in Kbps, whereas the QoS commands we've examined so far take numbers in bps.

Next, we tell the router about the sender so that the bandwidth can be reserved just for that individual. This is done with the **ip rsvp sender** command:

```
Router(config-if)#ip rsvp sender 2.2.2.2 10.10.1.10 tcp
5000 5001 10.10.11.1 eth1 100 16
```

This command tells the router that a session IP address of 2.2.2.2 is being set up by a user at 10.10.1.10, to use a TCP connection over the session port of 5000 and the sender's port of 5001, through the previous hop of 10.10.11.1 on the Ethernet interface 1. The last two arguments identify the reservation bandwidth (100 Kbps) and the burstable amount (16 Kbps).

The last step is to enter the receiver. The syntax for **ip rsvp receiver** is nearly identical to the **ip rsvp sender** command.

The RSVP command syntax is quite complicated, and configuring this manually on each device in the path for every communication is nearly impossible and very impractical. Fortunately, applications can do this automatically using RSVP PATH or RSVP RESV statements. Nonetheless, a centralized management application such as Cisco's Policy Manager must be used to prepare each interface on the network to use RSVP.

FUTURE TECHNOLOGY: TAG SWITCHING

Tag switching combines the intelligence of layer-3 routing with the speed and scalability of layer-2 switching. Essentially, tag switching works by inserting a tag into the packet, and this tag can be seen and quickly forwarded by a switch. Tag switching extends the IP routing model to work across a variety of data-link layer technologies, using the concept of *label swapping*. In label swapping, packets or cells are assigned short, fixed-length labels that are read by switching nodes to forward message units. Protocols such as Ethernet and PPP don't have swappable labels in their header formats, and this shortcoming is solved by inserting a *tag shim* header between the layer-2 header and the IP header.

Analogous to postal codes, tags are attached to a router's IP address table, which is then sequenced with tags in the tables of adjacent routers. Once a tag scheme is set up, *tag edge routers* assign a label to each packet (or cell) as it enters the tag-switched internetwork. This label assignment is made by matching IP routing protocol information with a tag to get things started. The tag label tells each device how to forward the packet. At each hop, the label is rewritten so that the output interface knows which device should get the packet next. (In this case, the tag label number is being used, not an IP address.) Tagged packets use the Tag Distribution Protocol (TDP) to obtain a tag binding from the adjacent node.

Figure 15-8 illustrates a tag-switched topology. Once the packet enters the tag-switched network, it is forwarded based on its tag label instead of a layer-3 IP address. The tag switches on the inside of the tag-switched network are logical peers, thus minimizing oper-

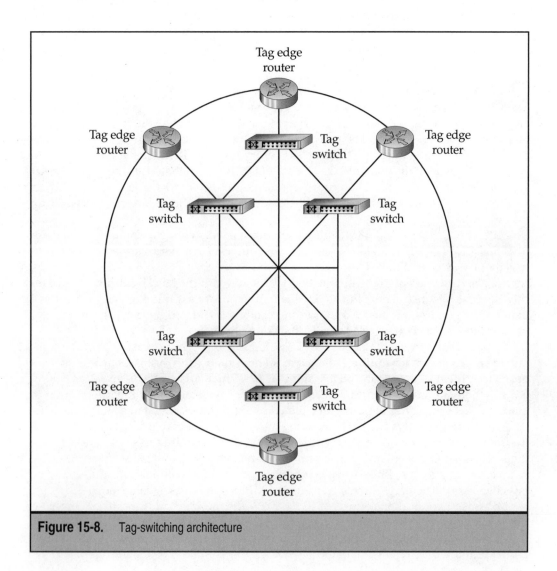

Figure 15-8. Tag-switching architecture

ating overhead and maximizing scalability because a minimum amount of signaling is required. When the packet exits the tag-switched network, the tag label is stripped off.

Tag switching is lightning fast and largely independent of network protocols. Tag routers can be implemented totally in software, avoiding the hassle and expense of a hardware upgrade. Therefore, an ATM switch in an Internet backbone topology can participate in tag switching by swapping a tag label for the virtual circuit identifier (VCI) in a cell. This results in an ATM switch that supports both conventional ATM and tag switching.

Tag switching enables QoS within a network by differentiating traffic by class. Packets carrying an inelastic application such as VoIP can be assigned tags in one range, packets that are part of an elastic application such as FTP are in another range, and so on. When congestion occurs, the network can be configured to drop elastic packets or cells first, and depend on TCP to handle error recovery on a best-effort basis.

Multiprotocol Label Switching (MPLS)

The IETF is developing Multiprotocol Label Switching (MPLS) as a protocol-independent packet-switching standard. In theory, at least, MPLS will be able to work with any media over which layer-3 packets can pass. MPLS supports fast label swapping similar to that in tag switching, applying the labels on entry into an MPLS-enabled network, and stripping them off at the point of exit. The use of labels means that MPLS need not dissect variable-length headers to obtain routing information—making the technology similar to ATM in that devices work with a predictable bit stream when processing forwarding information.

MPLS builds on early tag-switching technology by providing additional QoS attributes. Specifically, the MPLS label not only tells routers *where* to forward a packet, it also tells them *how* to send it. It does this by storing QoS service class information (priority, service class, and so on) in the forwarding tables to which the label binds in order to receive its next-hop instruction. But MPLS is actually more of a traffic engineering protocol than a QoS protocol, because MPLS routing establishes a fixed-bandwidth pipe analogous to the virtual circuits (VCs) of ATM or Frame Relay.

Perhaps the biggest advantage of MPLS is its scalability. The notion of operating committed service levels for multiple classes in an any-to-any network such as the Internet opens the threat of an uncontrollable number of virtual circuits being spawned, along with all their attendant overhead. MPLS curtails this by using IP routing information to map a packet's forwarding information ahead of time, and placing it in a table where the label can instruct routers and switches along the entire path. In other words, MPLS promises to deliver the benefits of VCs without the overhead required to set up and operate them. Thus MPLS potentially may combine the benefits of IP and ATM within a single service. For this reason, ISPs—always hungry to move high volumes of traffic as fast as possible—are particularly interested in seeing MPLS emerge as a viable technology.

MPLS isn't application controlled (it has no API); and it is "multi-protocol" in that it doesn't depend on any network protocol, not even IP. MPLS can work with IP, IPX, PPP, ATM, Frame Relay, and other protocols. It can do this because it exists only within routers, its primary mission only to determine which router should be the next hop.

MPLS uses a layer of abstraction to simplify the routing process. As shown in Figure 15-9, an MPLS-enabled router (called a label-switching router, or LSR) uses routing protocol intelligence to compute an MPLS label. The LSR attaches the label to the packet. The label contains a Forwarding Equivalence Class (FEC) value, a signifier that can be in-

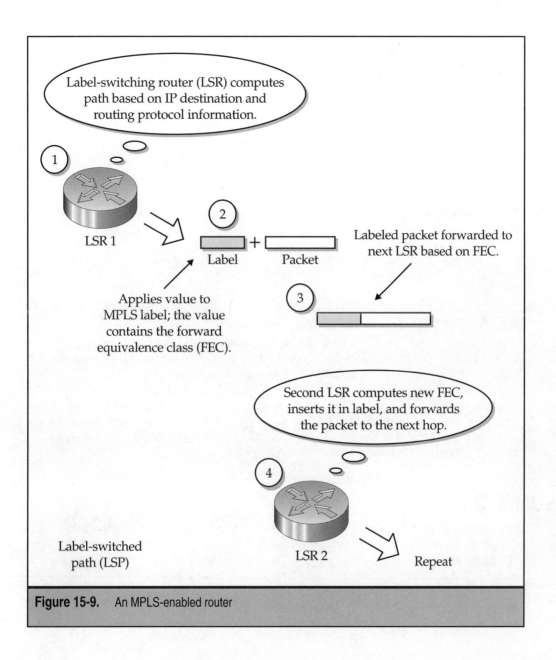

Figure 15-9.   An MPLS-enabled router

dexed to any other LSR's table to repeat the process. Rather than being forwarded based on a routing table, the packet is moved through the MPLS network by repeated application of the FEC in the MPLS label. In this sense, the packet is switched rather than routed, a faster and more resource-efficient process. The simplifying layer of abstraction is that MPLS just looks at the FEC to compute a next hop, instead of maintaining a routing table that accounts for the entire topology.

The packet is relabeled with a new FEC at each stop along the label-switched path (LSP). The big difference with MPLS is that routing and QoS policy are packaged within the label, or rather in the FEC value encoded into the label. The label's 32-bit format carries the FEC as its payload. The FEC's "class" never changes per se; it's only adjusted slightly at every stop to indicate the next hop.

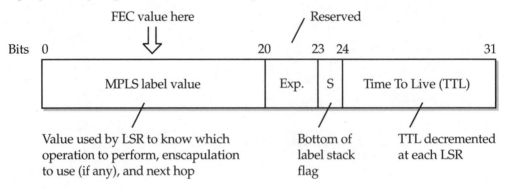

MPLS uses a TTL (time to live) in much the same way that an IP packet does. When an MPLS label's TTL is decremented to zero, however, the label isn't necessarily discarded as an IP packet would be. For a label, the action to take at TTL-zero depends on the FEC value, which (depending on the configuration of the MPLS network) may call for the packet to take a hop back to a predesignated router for redirection.

As you can see, the MPLS infrastructure is brutally simple, and savvy in the way it computes the initial FEC by using intelligence generated by routing protocols into routing tables. The complex part of MPLS involves the distribution and management of labels among MPLS routers. For these tasks, the Label Distribution Protocol (LDP) is being developed. Other protocols are being proposed, as well, including BGP and RSVP.

SUMMARY

As discussed in the first two chapters of this book, technologies are taking form that must be in place to enable QoS in the real world. The Lightweight Directory Access Protocol (LDAP) must be pervasively implemented to support the free exchange of information between directories within the Internet. This process is well underway, with Microsoft's implementation of LDAP in Active Directory with Windows 2000. This is also true of directory products from Novell, Netscape, and other makers of network software platforms. By letting the various directory technologies exchange information freely, LDAP effectively transforms widely distributed and otherwise incompatible directories into a central data store holding valuable information on virtually all network resources.

In addition to LDAP, QoS needs Directory-Enabled Networking (DEN). DEN itself is not a directory technology or an access protocol. Its role is to serve as a data model for designers to extend their directory repositories to finally also include information on network infrastructure—network hardware devices, links, media, network protocols, and the like. Integrating infrastructure data with extant directory repositories on applications and users will at long last support more-informed network operations. "Directory-enabled" portends the long-awaited dawn of the intelligent network.

CHAPTER 16

Authentication, Authorization, and Accounting

This book focuses on the technology and topologies for designing and implementing an efficient and effective network environment. Once you've done that, it's extremely important to protect your investment by allowing only valid users to have access to the network devices. One modification to a network device, intentional or unintentional, can result in hours of troubleshooting and network downtime.

This chapter discusses the precautions you can take as a network administrator to protect against unauthorized access, to control legitimate access, and to track detailed information about the who, what, where, and when of network access. We'll introduce some powerful tools you can use to simplify network access control configuration and management. Putting the information in this chapter to work will give you another measure of safety for your network equipment.

CISCO'S AUTHENTICATION, AUTHORIZATION, AND ACCOUNTING (AAA) SERVICES

Authentication, Authorization, and Accounting (AAA) are independent security services that, when implemented, will ensure that only appropriate administrators access the network hardware and execute appropriate commands. Cisco has grouped these three security functions together to help you configure AAA consistently and better protect your network architecture. AAA gives you the access controls you need for your network devices.

The benefits of using AAA include

▼ Increased flexibility and control

■ Scalability

■ Standardized authentication methods

▲ Multiple backup systems

AAA uses protocols such as RADIUS and TACACS+ to administer its security functions. These protocols can be applied to a server that functions as a RADIUS security server, TACACS+ security server, or simply "a security server." The AAA security functions use a router or access server acting as a network access server (NAS) to establish communication with the security server. The NAS does not have to communicate to a separate security server—it can use internal security-server functionality. Figure 16-1 is an example of a relationship between an NAS and a separate security server, configured to use AAA.

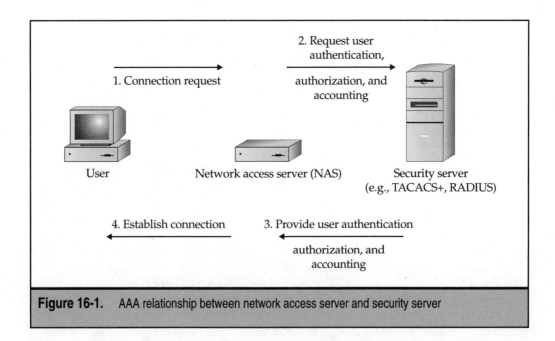

Figure 16-1. AAA relationship between network access server and security server

Configuring for AAA

Before you can use any of the services provided by AAA network security, you need to enable AAA on the NAS by executing the following command:

```
Router(config)#aaa new-model
```

If you decide to use a separate security server, you'll need to configure security protocol parameters such as RADIUS and TACACS+ as your chosen method. CiscoSecure is NT-supported software that can be used for access control with RADIUS or TACACS+. (There is also a version of CiscoSecure that runs on UNIX.) You'll find more information on CiscoSecure, TACACS+, and RADIUS later in this chapter.

After configuring security protocol parameters, the next step is defining the *method lists* for authentication and applying those method lists to the required interfaces or to the line of the NAS. A method list is simply a list of authentication methods to be used, in sequence, to authenticate a user. Designating more than one method ensures that you have a backup in case the initial method does not respond.

> **NOTE:** An authentication ERROR means the security server has failed to respond to an authentication query, and the next authentication method can be used. An authentication FAIL means the user has not met the criteria to be authenticated. The session is then terminated, and no additional authentication methods are permitted.

After configuring authentication, you then have the option to configure authorization and accounting.

AUTHENTICATION

Authentication is the process of verifying that you are who you say you are. Authentication requires administrators to identify themselves prior to obtaining access to a network device such as a router. The most common and simplest occurrence of authentication is entry and verification of the username and password. On a router, local authentication takes a username and password that are configured directly on the router or NAS. This data is used during the local (console port), line password (Telnet), and enable (EXEC privilege mode) authentications.

Cisco has developed both AAA authentication methods and non-AAA authentication methods (see Table 16-1). The AAA *authentication* methods were designed to be used in conjunction with AAA *authorization* methods and AAA *accounting* methods. All these methods are explained in the sections coming up.

AAA Authentication Methods	Non-AAA Authentication Methods
Login authentication using AAA	Line password protection
PPP (Point to Point Protocol) authentication using local password	Username authentication
ARA (Apple Remote Access Protocol) authentication using AAA	CHAP (Challenge Handshake Authentication Protocol) or PAP (Password Authentication Protocol) authentication
NASI (NetWare Asynchronous Services Interfaces) authentication using AAA	TACACS+ and Extended TACACS+ password protection
Password protection at the privileged level	
Authentication override	
Double authentication	

Table 16-1.   Types of AAA and Non-AAA Authentication Methods

AAA Authentication Methods

Within the several types of authentication methods are submethods. Figure 16-2 lists five AAA authentication methods and their submethods. A combination of submethods make up what is called a *method list* (you'd think it would be called a submethod list, but it's not).

Each authentication method list can have single or multiple authentication submethods (supported by each particular authentication method). When you define a *method_list* on the Cisco network hardware, you are defining the *login_authentication_methods* to be used and the sequential order in which to use them. This ensures a backup for authentication in case the initial method fails.

Figure 16-3 illustrates the configuration and authentication process for a *method_list* consisting of multiple authentication submethods, including TACACS+, a local username database, and enable password. For this arrangement, the administrator will be authenticated against TACACS+ first. If the TACACS+ server fails to respond, then the user will be authenticated against the local username database. If the local username database fails to respond, the user is then authenticated against the local enable password. These multiple opportunities for authentication will only occur, however, if the authenti-

Submethods that make up authentication method lists:	AAA authentication methods:				
	Login	PPP	ARA	NASI	Privilege-level password
* enable	✓			✓	✓
* if-needed		✓			
* krb5	✓	✓			
* local	✓	✓	✓	✓	
* none	✓	✓		✓	✓
* radius	✓	✓			
* tacacs+	✓	✓	✓	✓	✓
* line	✓		✓	✓	✓
* radius	✓				✓
* krb5-telnet	✓				
* guest			✓		
* auth-guest			✓		

Figure 16-2.   Authentication methods and submethods

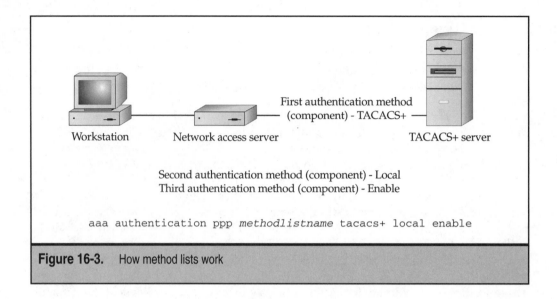

Figure 16-3.   How method lists work

cation service fails to respond. If the user generates an error, the authentication process stops and the session is terminated.

Authentication Method Components

In the following paragraphs we'll take a look at what makes up the authentication submethods. Here are definitions of the components:

- ▼ **enable**   Uses enable password for authentication
- ■ **krb5**   Uses Kerberos for authentication
- ■ **line**   Uses the line password for authentication
- ■ **local**   Uses the local username database for authentication
- ■ **radius**   Uses RADIUS authentication
- ■ **tacacs+**   Uses TACACS+ authentication
- ■ **krb5-telnet**   User Kerberos 5 Telnet authentication protocol when using Telnet to connect
- ■ **guest**   Allows guest logins
- ■ **auth-guest**   Allows guest logins only if the administrator has already logged in EXEC
- ■ **if-needed**   Does not authenticate if administrator has already been authenticated on a TTY line
- ▲ **none**   Uses no authentication

Login Authentication Using AAA

The Login Authentication allows you to create one or more lists of login authentication methods that are tried at login, including:

enable	Krb5	local	line	radius	tacacs+	if-needed	krb5-telnet	guest	auth-guest	none
✓	✓	✓	✓	✓	✓		✓			✓

To configure Login Authentication using AAA, you need to enable AAA globally, create a list of local authentication methods, enter the line configuration mode for the lines to which you want to apply the authentication list, and then apply the authentication list to a line or set of lines. Here are the commands to perform these tasks:

```
Router(config)#aaa new-model
Router(config)#aaa authentication login login_authentication_methods
Router(config)#line [aux|console|tty|vty] line-number [ending-line-number]
Router(config-line)#login authentication method_list_name
```

PPP Authentication Using AAA

When a user accesses a network access server (NAS) through a dialup or ISDN connection, the command line interface (CLI) is bypassed completely. A network protocol such as Point to Point Protocol (PPP) or Apple Remote Access Protocol (ARAP) is used as soon as the connection is established.

PPP Authentication provides a variety of authentication methods to be applied to serial interfaces that are running PPP, including the following:

enable	krb5	local	line	radius	tacacs+	if-needed	krb5-telnet	guest	auth-guest	none
	✓	✓		✓	✓	✓				✓

To configure PPP Authentication using AAA, you need to enable AAA globally, create a PPP authentication list, enter the interface configuration mode for the interface for which you want to apply the authentication list, and apply the authentication list to a line or set of lines. Here are the commands used to perform these tasks:

```
Router(config)#aaa new-model
Router(config)#aaa authentication ppp method_list_name
login_authentication_methods
Router(config)#interface interface_type interface_number
Router(config-if)#ppp authentication {chap|pap|chap pap |pap chap}
[if-needed] method_list_name
```

Password Authentication Protocol (PAP) and Challenge Handshake Authentication Protocol (CHAP) are standard protocols used to authenticate usernames and passwords. Either CHAP PAP or PAP CHAP is selected when Double Authentication is being configured (see upcoming section "Enable Double Authentication"). The main differences between PAP and CHAP are as follows:

▼ PAP sends passwords in the cleartext. CHAP sends a 64-bit signature instead of the password in the cleartext.

▲ CHAP requires that two username entries be configured, for both sides (assuming both sides are performing CHAP).

ARA Authentication Using AAA

These authentication methods are used when AppleTalk Remote Access (ARA) administrators attempt to log into a network device. Supported ARA authentication methods include the following:

enable	krb5	local	line	radius	tacacs+	if-needed	krb5-telnet	guest	auth-guest	none
		✓	✓		✓			✓	✓	

To configure ARA Authentication using AAA, you need to enable AAA globally and then enable authentication for ARA administrators. Here are the commands to perform these tasks:

```
Router(config)#aaa new-model
Router(config)#aaa authentication arap method_list_name
arap_authentication_methods
```

NASI Authentication Using AAA

NetWare Asynchronous Services Interfaces (NASI) authentication is used for NASI administrators who are attempting to log into the router. The following authentication methods are supported by NASI:

enable	krb5	local	line	radius	tacacs+	if-needed	krb5-telnet	guest	auth-guest	none
✓		✓	✓		✓					✓

To configure NASI Authentication using AAA, you need to enable AAA globally and then enable authentication for NASI administrators. Here are the necessary commands:

```
Router(config)#aaa new-model
Router(config)#aaa authentication nasi method_list_name
nasi_authentication_methods
```

Enable Password Protection at the Privileged Level

Enable Password Protection at the Privileged Level is used to authenticate an administrator prior to allowing access to the privileged EXEC command level. The following authentication methods are supported by the Enable Password Protection authentication:

enable	krb5	local	line	radius	tacacs+	if-needed	krb5-telnet	guest	auth-guest	none
✓				✓	✓	✓				✓

To configure Enable Password Authentication using AAA you need to enable AAA globally and then allow Enable Authentication for administrators. Here are the commands:

```
Router(config)#aaa new-model
Router(config)#aaa authentication enable enable_authentication_method
```

Enable Authentication Override

The Enable Authentication Override allows you to have the Cisco IOS software check the local user database for authentication before attempting another form of authentication. The command used to enable this authentication method is

```
Router (config)#aaa authentication local-override
```

Enable Double Authentication

Enable Double Authentication is used to provide two stages of authentication, PAP and CHAP, in order to validate a Point to Point (PPP) session. This is how it works:

1. The administrator logs in using the remote host name.

2. CHAP (or PAP) authenticates the remote host.

3. PPP negotiates with AAA to authorize the remote host (network access privileges are assigned to the administrator).

4. The remote administrator **telnet**s to the NAS to be authenticated.

5. The remote administrator logs in.

6. The administrator is authenticated with AAA login authentication.

7. The administrator enters the **access-profile** command to be reauthorized using AAA PAP (or CHAP).

Here are the steps to configure Double Authentication:

1. Enable AAA, configure your NAS to use login PPP authentication method lists, and apply those method lists to the appropriate lines or interfaces (see earlier section on PPP authentication).

2. Configure AAA network authorization at login (see the section "Authorization," later in the chapter.)

3. Configure a security protocol such as TACACS+ or RADIUS in the AAA server (see the later section on CiscoSecure).

Non-AAA Authentication Methods

Non-AAA authentication methods are used to require simple authentication prior to granting access to a network resource. There are four types of Non-AAA authentication configurations.

Configure Line Password Protection

This configuration is very important if you are planning to allow Telnet access to your network device. The following command assigns a password to the network device's vty lines (lines used to establish Telnet connectivity) and enables password checking:

```
Router(config-line)#password password
Router(config-line)#login
```

NOTE: The password you enter here is case sensitive, and spaces are allowed.

Establish Username Authentication

Cisco IOS also has the capability to create a database of usernames and passwords for use in validating an administrator trying to establish a connection. There are several options provided for these usernames and passwords. Although these options are more along the lines of authorization and accountability rather than authentication, we will discuss them briefly here in this section.

The usernames and passwords can be used for tracking configuration changes based on which administrator was logged in at the time of configuration. Privilege levels can also be assigned to the username to restrict administrator capabilities. By default, IOS has three privilege levels: 0, 1, and 15. Each level has a set of assigned commands. You can move these commands to other privilege levels by using the **privilege** IOS command. Here are some of the commands available to the three privilege levels:

Level 0	Level 1	Level 15
login logout exit help enable	All commands you can see when you issue a **?** at the > prompt	The rest of the commands, plus level 0 and 1 commands

Authentication can be applied to usernames in other ways, including the following:

▼ Usernames can be authenticated by access lists.

■ An **autocommand** can be configured to automatically execute when a particular administrator logs in.

■ A **noescape** login environment can be applied to the username to prevent administrators from using escape characters.

▲ A **nohangup** feature can be applied to prevent disconnect after using the **autocommand**.

Here's the command to create a username and password within the Cisco IOS:

```
Router(config)#username username password encryption_type password
```

NOTE: Passwords will be displayed in clear text in your configuration unless you enable the **service-password-encryption** command. This command encrypts the passwords in the configuration file.

Enable CHAP or PAP Authentication

As explained earlier, CHAP and PAP are two standard protocols used by ISPs to verify that only legitimate customers are dialing into the ISP access servers and establishing a PPP connection. To use CHAP or PAP, you must be running PPP encapsulation. The following command enables PPP on an interface:

```
Router(config-if)#encapsulation ppp
```

The next step is to enable CHAP or PAP on the interface. Here is the command to enable CHAP or PAP on an interface previously configured for PPP encapsulation:

```
Router(config-if)#ppp authentication {chap |chap pap |pap chap| pap}
```

where

▼ **#ppp authentication chap** will require CHAP authentication.

■ **#ppp authentication pap** will require PAP authentication.

■ **#ppp authentication chap pap** will try to authenticate with CHAP. If there is no response, then it will try to authenticate with PAP.

▲ **#ppp authentication pap chap** will try to authenticate with PAP. If there is no response, then it will try to authenticate with CHAP.

TIP: Here's a suggestion for CHAP and PAP: if you don't mark the box in MS DUN (Microsoft Dial-Up Networking) to encrypt the passwords, PAP will be used, and not CHAP.

PPP supports two-way authentication. Inbound authentication occurs when a remote device dials into an access server. Outbound authentication occurs when the remote device requires the access server to also verify its identity, or when the access server actually initiates the call to the remote device. Figure 16-4 illustrates this relationship.

Configuring TACACS+ and Extended TACACS+ Password Protection

TACACS can be configured to communicate with network devices to control login access to the router. First, you need to enable communication with a TACACS+ host on the network, and then set TACACS+ Password Protection at the Administrator level.

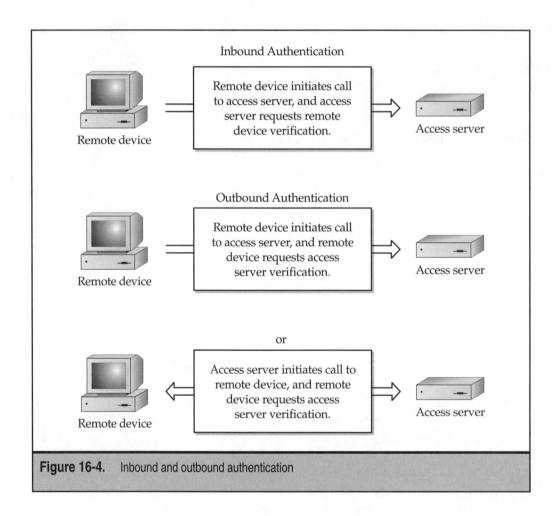

Figure 16-4. Inbound and outbound authentication

Most likely, it's critical that your routers are accessible at all times; and if the TACACS+ server is down you don't want to be locked out. Login failures can be prevented by

▼   Allowing an administrator to access privileged EXEC mode if that administrator enters the password set by the **enable** command

▲   Ensuring a successful login by allowing the administrator to access the privileged EXEC mode without further question

The commands to configure these options to eliminate login failure are as follows:

```
Router(config)#tacacs-server last-resort password
```

or

```
Router(config)#tacacs-server last-resort succeed
```

Additional specifics on the implementation of TACACS+ are included in the later section on the TACACS system.

AUTHORIZATION

The second *A* in Cisco's AAA services represents *authorization*, which determines whether or not a user has the rights to execute a given command. Authorization allows you to set administrators' limits for the privileges they have once they're authenticated on network devices. These limits are stored within an administrator's profile on either the network device's local administrator database, or on a security server (for example, CiscoSecure/TACACS+ or RADIUS).

Authorization is configured on an access server by defining the *authorization type* and *authorization method*. Authorization configuration is applied globally to the network device—unlike authentication, which can be applied uniquely to each interface. The following command is used to create an authorization method list for a particular authorization type and to enable authorization:

```
Router(config)#aaa authorization authorization_type
authorization_method
```

Authorization Types

Cisco IOS supports three types of authorization:

▼   **Network Authorization**   Enables network-related requests such as Point to Point (PPP), Serial Line Interface Protocol (SLIP), and Apple Remote Access Protocol (ARAP) connections.

- ■ **EXEC Authorization**   Enables the attributes associated with an administrator EXEC terminal session.

- ▲ **Commands Authorization**   Enables specific EXEC mode commands that are associated with a specific privilege level (0–15).

Authorization Methods

After you have defined the type of commands and/or connections that are going to be permitted, the next step is to define how the administrator will be authorized. There are six methods for authorization:

- ▼ **TACACS+**   The network access server (NAS) exchanges authorization with the TACACS+ security daemon. Each appropriate administrator has specific rights defined and stored on the TACACS+ server. These rights are communicated between the TACACS+ server and the network devices.

- ■ **If-Authenticated**   This authorization allows access to only the defined request function.

- ■ **None**   The NAS does not request authorization information since authorization is not performed over this line or interface.

- ■ **Local**   The router or access server consults its own local database to authorize specific rights for administrators. (This is defined by the **username** command.)

- ■ **RADIUS**   The NAS requests authorization information from the RADIUS security server, which then returns specific administrator attributes from the administrator information stored in the RADIUS database.

- ▲ **Kerberos instance map**   The NAS uses the instance defined by the **kerberos instance map** command.

Authorization Requirements

Before configuring authorization, you must perform the following tasks:

- ▼ Enable AAA on your network access server.

- ■ Configure AAA authentication (since authorization generally takes place after authentication and relies on authentication to work properly).

- ■ Configure your network access server to communicate with your RADIUS or TACACS+ server if possible.

- ■ If you are using local authorization, define the rights associated with specific administrators by using the **username** command.

- ▲ If you are using Kerberos, create the administrative instances of administrators in the Kerberos key distribution center by using the **kerberos instance map** command.

ACCOUNTING

The third *A* in AAA stands for *accounting*, which provides a method for tracking the commands executed by your administrators and/or the network resources they are consuming. Accounting information can be used for billing, auditing, and reporting functions. Tracked data may include information such as

- ▼ Administrator identity
- ■ Start and stop times
- ■ Commands executed
- ■ Number of packets
- ▲ Number of bytes

AAA accounting takes place when the NAS reports administrator activity to a security server such as TACACS+ or RADIUS. This activity (stored in the form of account records) can then be analyzed and used as needed. When accounting is enabled on a network device, all interfaces participate—the tracking is applied globally to the network device rather than to each interface.

Configuration

To configure AAA accounting, you need to enable AAA accounting for your desired accounting type (accounting types are defined in the next section). Then you define the characteristics of your security server. Some of these characteristics include

- ▼ **start-stop**   This provides additional accounting by instructing the specified security server to send a start-accounting notice at the beginning of the requested process, and a stop-accounting notice at the end of the requested process.
- ■ **wait-start**   This controls access even further by ensuring that the specified security server receives the start-accounting notice before granting the requested process.
- ▲ **stop-only**   This is used for minimal accounting only. It instructs the specified security server to send a stop-record-accounting notice at the end of the requested process.

Following is the command used to configure AAA accounting:

```
Router(config)#aaa accounting {system|network|connection|exec|command level}
{start-stop|wait-start|stop-only|} {tacacs|radius}
```

To view the active accounting sessions, use

```
Router#show accounting
```

Accounting Types

Cisco IOS 11.3 supports five types of accounting, defined in the paragraphs that follow.

Command Accounting

Command accounting tracks information (in the security server's command-accounting record) related to the commands executed in the EXEC level for each privilege level. In addition to listing the executed commands at each privilege level, command accounting also tracks information such as the date and time of execution, and the name and IP address of the administrator who executed the command.

NOTE: Cisco's implementation of RADIUS does not support command accounting.

Connection Accounting

Connection accounting tracks all the outbound connections made from the NAS and stores them in the security server's connection-accounting record. Types of outbound connections include

▼ Telnet

■ Local-area transport (LAT)

■ tn3270

■ Packet assembler-disassembler (PAD)

▲ rlogin

Here's an example of the information contained in a RADIUS connection-accounting record for an outbound Telnet connection:

```
Wed Jun 23 04:28:00 1999
NAS-IP-Address = "10.1.1.1"
NAS-Port = 2
User-Name = "jdoe"
Client-Port-DNIS = "4327528"
Caller-ID = "4082329477"
Acct-Status-Type = Start
Acct-Authentic = RADIUS
Service-Type = Login
Acct-Session-Id = "00000008"
Login-Service = Telnet
Login-IP-Host = "10.5.2.1"
Acct-Delay-Time = 0
```

```
User-Id = "jdoe"
NAS-Identifier = "10.1.1.1"
Wed Jun 23 04:28:39 1999
NAS-IP-Address = "10.1.1.1"
NAS-Port = 2
User-Name = "jdoe"
Client-Port-DNIS = "4327528"
Caller-ID = "4082329477"
Acct-Status-Type = Stop
Acct-Authentic = RADIUS
Service-Type = Login
Acct-Session-Id = "00000008"
Login-Service = Telnet
Login-IP-Host = "10.5.2.1"
Acct-Input-Octets = 10774
Acct-Output-Octets = 112
Acct-Input-Packets = 91
Acct-Output-Packets = 99
Acct-Session-Time = 39
Acct-Delay-Time = 0
User-Id = "jdoe"
NAS-Identifier = "10.1.1.1"
```

EXEC Accounting

EXEC accounting tracks information about user EXEC terminal sessions (user shells) on the NAS. The information is saved in an accounting record on a security server. This information includes

▼ Administrator name

■ Date of the session

■ Start and stop times

■ Access server IP address

▲ Telephone number where the call originated (for dial-in administrators)

The following example shows the information on a dial-in administrator, as contained in a TACACS+ EXEC accounting record:

```
Wed Jun 23 03:46:21 1999          10.1.1.1    jdoe    tty3
4082329430/4327528   start    task_id=2       service=shell
Wed Jun 23 04:08:55 1999          10.1.1.1    jdoe    tty3
4082329430/4327528   stop     task_id=2       service=shell
elapsed_time=1354
```

Network Accounting

Network accounting tracks information for all network sessions, including PPP, SLIP, and ARAP. The following example shows the information contained in a RADIUS network-accounting record for a PPP administrator who comes in through an EXEC session:

```
Wed Jun 23 04:44:45 1999
        NAS-IP-Address = "10.1.1.1"
        NAS-Port = 5
        User-Name = "jdoe"
        Client-Port-DNIS = "4327528"
        Caller-ID = "408"
        Acct-Status-Type = Start
        Acct-Authentic = RADIUS
        Service-Type = Exec-User
        Acct-Session-Id = "0000000D"
        Acct-Delay-Time = 0
        User-Id = "jdoe"
        NAS-Identifier = "10.5.2.1"
Wed Jun 25 04:45:00 1997
        NAS-IP-Address = "10.1.1.1"
        NAS-Port = 5
        User-Name = "jdoe"
        Client-Port-DNIS = "4327528"
        Caller-ID = "408"
        Acct-Status-Type = Start
        Acct-Authentic = RADIUS
        Service-Type = Framed
        Acct-Session-Id = "0000000E"
        Framed-IP-Address = "10.3.2.3"
        Framed-Protocol = PPP
        Acct-Delay-Time = 0
        User-Id = "jdoe"
        NAS-Identifier = "10.1.1.1"
Wed Jun 25 04:47:46 1997
        NAS-IP-Address = "10.1.1.1"
        NAS-Port = 5
        User-Name = "jdoe"
        Client-Port-DNIS = "4327528"
        Caller-ID = "408"
        Acct-Status-Type = Stop
        Acct-Authentic = RADIUS
        Service-Type = Framed
        Acct-Session-Id = "0000000E"
```

```
Framed-IP-Address = "10.3.2.3"
Framed-Protocol = PPP
Acct-Input-Octets = 3075
Acct-Output-Octets = 167
Acct-Input-Packets = 39
Acct-Output-Packets = 9
Acct-Session-Time = 171
Acct-Delay-Time = 0
User-Id = "jdoe"
NAS-Identifier = "10.1.1.1"
```

System Accounting

System accounting tracks all system-level events, such as system reboots and the enabling or disabling of accounting. The following accounting record is for a TACACS+ system, indicating that AAA accounting has been turned on:

```
Wed Jun 23 03:55:22 1999        10.1.1.1    unknown unknown unknown
stop    task_id=23    service=system    event=sys_acct
reason=reconfigure
```

NOTE: Cisco's implementation of RADIUS does not support system accounting.

Supplementing AAA

There's no denying the importance of implementing security for your network, including configuring Cisco's authentication, authorization, and accounting services on each network device. Doing so goes a long way toward protecting your network from attacks executed right at the command line.

However, there are additional security precautions you should take as well. These steps will supplement your security measures, helping to reduce your vulnerability to external attacks against your network devices. Hackers outside the network, if they find alternative means of accessing your equipment, can bring the hardware to its knees. For instance, they could set up a program to flood one of your devices with packets until its CPU can't handle any more and the device locks up entirely.

A *security vulnerability detection tool* tells you what types of vulnerabilities exist in your network. NetSonar, described later in the chapter, is Cisco's version of this tool that may or may not satisfy your requirements. Several other vendors, as well, offer this type of product.

REMOTE ACCESS DIAL-IN USER SERVICE (RADIUS)

Remote Access Dial-In User Service (RADIUS) is a protocol used for access control. Cisco has chosen to support this protocol in IOS Release 11.1 and later of IP Plus or above (not the IP basic feature set). RADIUS is also supported on the CiscoSecure Access Control Server (ACS).

RADIUS is based on a client/server model. The clients are network access servers, and the server is the RADIUS server. The client passes administrator information to the RADIUS server, the RADIUS server authenticates the administrator (if valid), and then returns all the configuration information necessary for the NAS to provide the administrator with the requested services. This communication between the NAS and RADIUS servers is based on the User Datagram Protocol (UDP), and is illustrated in Figure 16-5.

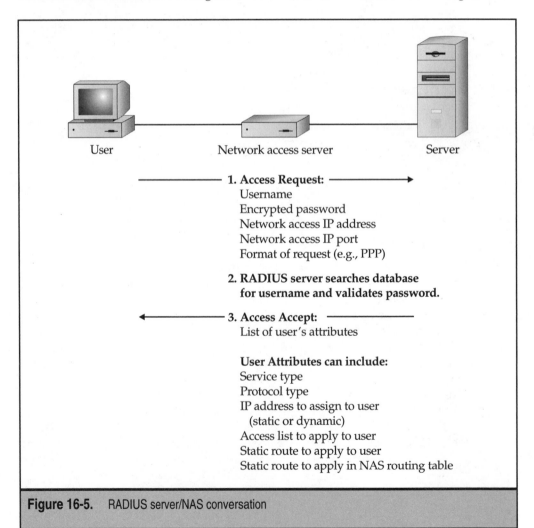

Figure 16-5. RADIUS server/NAS conversation

Unlike TACACS+, which uses the AAA architecture that separates authentication, authorization, and accounting, the RADIUS protocol combines the processes of authentication and authorization. The Access-Accept packets sent by the RADIUS server to the client contain all the authorization information. This simply means that, for example, if you were to use TACACS+ instead of RADIUS, you could use Kerberos for authentication and TACACS+ for authorization and accounting. RADIUS, on the other hand, mandates that you use RADIUS for both authentication and authorization.

Configuring for RADIUS

Before RADIUS can be implemented into your network, you need to

1. Configure a RADIUS security access server and populate it with valid user accounts.

2. Set up the network devices to use RADIUS.

Configuring RADIUS on the network devices has been described previously in this chapter. Configuring the RADIUS server is covered in the section on CiscoSecure, since we are focusing on the CiscoSecure ACS in this chapter.

TERMINAL ACCESS CONTROLLER ACCESS CONTROL SYSTEM (TACACS+)

Terminal Access Controller Access Control System (TACACS+) simplifies access management by providing the means to manage network security—authentication, authorization, and accounting (AAA)—from a server. The benefits of TACACS+ are

▼ Secure login to network devices

■ Multiple levels of user privileges

■ Centralized control over user accounts and privileges

■ Redundancy for TACACS+ servers and user database

▲ Accounting records

Unlike RADIUS, which uses UDP to exchange information between the network access server and the security server, TACACS+ uses TCP. Since TCP is a connection-oriented transport protocol, it provides immediate indication of an unavailable server.

The relationship between TACACS+ and the NAS is almost identical to that of RADIUS and the NAS. Here are the steps of the general process of logging into a network device, as illustrated in Figure 16-6:

1. A user initiates a Telnet session with a router acting as a network access server.

2. The NAS prompts the user for a username and password (cleartext).

3. The router encrypts the entire body of the packet and sends it to a TACACS+ server (RADIUS encrypts only the password).

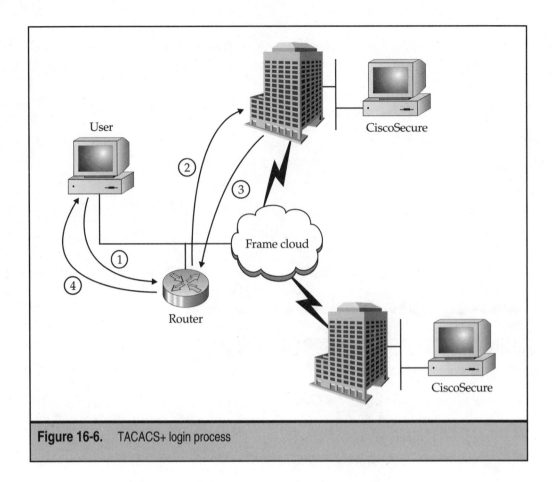

Figure 16-6. TACACS+ login process

4. The TACACS+ server checks its database to validate the user. If the user is valid, the TACACS+ server sends an OK to the router, as well as a privilege level for the user.

5. The router allows the user access and the Telnet session continues (cleartext).

Configuring for TACACS+

Before TACACS+ can be implemented on your network, you need to

1. Configure a TACACS+ server and populate it with valid user accounts.

2. Set up the network devices to use TACACS+.

Configuring TACACS+ on the network devices has been described previously in this chapter. Configuring the TACACS+ server is covered in the section on CiscoSecure, since we are focusing on the CiscoSecure ACS in this chapter.

CISCOSECURE ACCESS CONTROL SERVER

CiscoSecure Access Control Server (ACS) v2.1 is software installed on Windows NT to support the centralization of access control, and accounting for dial-up access servers and firewalls. This software, when configured properly, controls the authentication, authorization, and accounting (AAA) of administrators accessing thousands of network ports.

CiscoSecure ACS assists you in controlling users' login to the network, the privileges or authorizations of the administrator, and the accounting information to be recorded on the administrator. Key features and benefits include the following:

▼ Simultaneous TACACS+ and RADIUS support

■ HTML/JAVA GUI providing an administrator-friendly interface that simplifies and distributes configuration for administrator profiles, group profiles, and ACS configuration

■ Group assignments for administrators, to simplify changes in security policies

■ Domain stripping and authentication forwarding

■ Automatic replication

■ CHAP, PAP, and ARA password support

■ Time-of-day and day-of-week access restrictions

■ Administrator capability to configure permitted failed attempts before account is disabled

■ Administrator capability to view active sessions

▲ Windows NT performance-monitoring support for real-time statistic viewing

CiscoSecure for NT can reference the NT user database for the AAA request; therefore, user accounts need not be maintained in both the AAA and NT. In addition, CiscoSecure can access the Novell NDS database; this is actually done with a Microsoft utility that allows NT to access NDS. Plans for the next version of Cisco Secure include the capability to access information on the Windows 2000 LDAP directory, as well.

Following the system requirements for CiscoSecure ACS v2.1 for Windows NT.

Hardware	Memory/Disk Storage	Software
Intel-class Pentium 133MHz PC (or compatible)	32MB of RAM	Microsoft NT Server 4.0
CD-ROM drive	10MB of hard drive space	Microsoft Internet Explorer v3.02 or later; or Netscape Navigator v3.0 or later
Screen resolution of 800 × 600 or better		Cisco IOS 11.1 or later for TACACS+; v11.2 or later for RADIUS

Configuring CiscoSecure ACS

Once you've installed CiscoSecure ACS, you're ready to begin configuration. The complexity of the configuration depends on the level of detail you would like to apply to your security controls. The more granular you make your requirements, the more settings you'll have to make.

Using the CiscoSecure ACS Interface

The CiscoSecure ACS is managed using a browser-based interactive tool, shown in Figure 16-7. The icon buttons on the left side of the screen let you access the settings you need to administer the various functions of CiscoSecure ACS. We'll examine the purpose of each of these buttons as we work through this section.

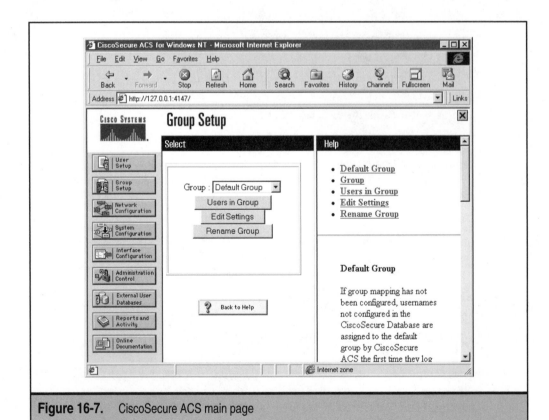

Figure 16-7. CiscoSecure ACS main page

LOGGING IN LOCALLY   You can log into the CiscoSecure ACS management interface locally via either a desktop icon or the Start menu. Simply log in using your administrator name and password.

> **NOTE:**   The initial CiscoSecure setup allows local login without username and password, but it is recommended that you change this to force local login. Click the Administration Control button to get to the settings for adding, deleting, and changing administrators.

LOGGING IN REMOTELY   Most often, login is done from a remote location. Remote login requires the use of a Web browser. You'll enter the address of the server in the browser Address field, as follows:

```
http://<IP-address of CiscoSecure ACS Server>:2002
```

where **2002** is the TCP port that the browser-based management interface initially uses.

Now let's work our way through the CiscoSecure ACS settings, using the icon buttons on the left side of the management interface main window.

User Setup

Click the User Setup icon to perform the following tasks:

▼   View a list of all users in the CiscoSecure database.

■   Find a particular user.

■   Add a user and assign the user to a group.

■   Edit a user's account information.

■   Change the user's authentication type.

■   Set the user's Network Access Restrictions (see the "Group Setup" section, coming up).

▲   Delete a user.

ADDING/EDITING USERS   Before CiscoSecure ACS can be of use, its databases must be populated with users. Here are the steps required to add a user:

1. Log in using the CiscoSecure ACS management interface.

2. Select User Setup.

3. Enter the new or changed username in the entry box.

4. Click Add/Edit.

5. Add any necessary Supplementary User Info. (The information requested here will depend on the settings in Interface Configuration Admin icon | User Data Configuration, described in a later section.)

6. Click Submit at the bottom of the page.

Each user's profile will have its own set of configuration parameters. As stated in step 5 just above, these settings are made using the Interface Configuration icon and selecting User Data Configuration. The user configuration parameters include the following:

Configuration Setting	Description
Password Authentication Method	This setting determines which database will be used for authentication:
	*CiscoSecure (simple username/password authentication using CiscoSecure's built-in database)
	*Windows NT (simple username/password authentication using Windows NT database)
	*CryptoCard (one-time password using Token Cards and a CryptoCard database; see "CryptoCard Admin," later in the chapter)
Password	This password is used along with the username for login to the NAS. If this user will be using a Token Card, no password is needed.
Group Assignment	User inherits the rights of his/her assigned group. Groups are defined using the Group Setup icon.
Advanced Settings	These can be used for limiting access to NASs based on features such as IP addresses, ports, etc.
Expiration Info	Used to disable username at a specific predefined date. Useful for contract employees.

The steps to delete a user are similar to the steps for adding/editing a user:

1. Log in using the CiscoSecure ACS management interface.
2. Select User Setup.
3. Enter the existing username in the entry box and click Add/Edit. Select List All Users, or click the first character of the user's name.
4. Click Delete User.
5. Click Submit.

Group Setup

Use the Group Setup icon to

▼   List all users in a group
■   Edit the settings for the group
▲   Rename the group

Group Setup helps ease the burden of rights assignments, by allowing many users with the same rights to be configured and edited together, rather than one at a time. CiscoSecure allows definition of up to 100 groups. Here are the steps for editing a group's settings:

1. Log in using the CiscoSecure ACS management interface.

2. Click Group Setup.

3. In the drop-down list, select the group to edit.

4. Click Edit Settings.

From here, the following group settings are available (some of these will appear only if defined in the Interface Configuration settings):

Group Setting	Description
Time of Day Restriction	Restricts group's access based on times of day.
Network Access Restriction	Restricts group's access based on parameters such as NAS, session origin, IP address, and port.
Token Card Settings	An advanced option for Token Caching. For use only with ISDN terminal adapters; should be fully understood before implementation.
TACACS+ Settings	A powerful section of the configuration process. From here, the administrator can specify and configure PPP (if enabled), privilege levels, services, access lists, and more. If you are using the Shell (exec) service, you can authorize particular commands with specific arguments.

The next step is to check the Command: box and enter the appropriate command in the text box. Arguments (the permitted or denied commands) can be subdefined (as in **show** *config*, **show** *running config*, **show** *version*, and so on). Here is the correct syntax for the Command/Argument:

```
Permit <Argument>
```

or

```
Deny    <Argument>
```

Although only one Command/Argument box is initially displayed, unlimited commands can be defined. Click Submit after each command entry, exit to any other screen, and return to the Group Setup | Edit Screen. Another Command/Argument box will be added.

NOTE: *Unlisted arguments* are anything not listed in the Arguments box. If the Arguments box is left empty, the Permit or Deny buttons apply to the command in general, including all arguments.

When you are satisfied with your settings, click Submit and Restart at the bottom of the page. This very briefly stops and restarts your ACS services. To make additional settings, just repeat the above steps.

Network Configuration

The Network Configuration settings are used to tie this CiscoSecure ACS in with the NAS. You'll need to enter information such as

▼ Host name

■ IP address

■ Key (secret value shared for authentication)

▲ Security protocol

Here are the steps to add an NAS:

1. Log into the CiscoSecure ACS management interface.

2. Click Network Configuration.

3. Below the Network Access Servers window, click Add Entry.

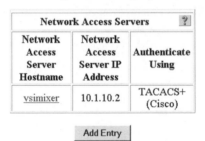

4. Populate the fields with the appropriate information. The following settings are available:

NAS Setting	Description
Key	Not the same as the Key used between CiscoSecure ACS servers. This is a case-sensitive encryption key of your choice, used to ensure that data between the NAS and the CiscoSecure ACS servers is properly encrypted. This key must also be entered into the NAS configuration as follows: **tacacs-server key** *<serverkey>*

NAS Setting	Description
Authenticate Using	In this drop-down box, select TACACS+ (Cisco) or Radius.
Single Connect	If you enable this feature, CiscoSecure will send a stop record in the TACACS+ accounting log for each user connected through the NAS.

5. To make your changes take effect, select Submit and Restart.

If modifications are necessary in the future, follow these same steps, but in step 3 you'll click the particular host name you want to change.

System Configuration

System Configuration options include

▼ Service controls to restart or stop services

■ Logging

▲ CiscoSecure ACS database replication

As with all other configuration changes, you must select the Submit button to make any changes take effect.

DATABASE REPLICATION *Database replication* is a feature that allows CiscoSecure databases to pass user, group, and other information between servers. With replicated databases in place, you ensure that in the event of a server failure, all other servers will have identical databases, thus allowing uninterrupted AAA services.

Replication Components	?	
Component	Send	Receive
User and Group Database	☐	☐
AAA & Network Access Server Tables	☐	☐
Distribution Table	☐	☐
Interface Configuration	☐	☐
Interface Security Settings	☐	☐

The parameters of database replication define whether the server is to send or receive the component information. It is generally a good idea to have one server send and the others receive, so that you are certain your databases will be identical. When using one server as the sender and all the others as receivers, all modifications to the database should be done from the sending server.

After configuring the components to be sent and received, and designating the sending and receiving servers, the next step is to identify the process and timeline in which this information is sent. This is known as *replication scheduling*. Following are the replication scheduling options:

Database Replication Setting	Description
Manual Replication	Replication will not be initiated unless the Replicate Now button at the bottom of the page is clicked; in other words, with this setting, the receiving server is configured by clicking this button.
Automatically Triggered Cascade	Used when there are more than two servers and you want the second-in-line server to automatically replicate to the third-in-line when the second-in-line receives the first server's information.
Each Backup Period (Minutes)	Allows you to specify replication time intervals.
At Specific Times	Allows you to specify what times and/or days replication is to occur. Useful when you want to replicate during off-peak hours, or on weekends.

Interface Configuration

Select the Interface Configuration button to configure the following settings:

Interface Setting	Description
User Data Configuration	Up to five fields can be defined to contain information you want to view for each user.
TACACS+ or RADIUS Protocol Configuration	Here's where you select the parameters you want to allow as configurable options in Group Setup. You can be very specific or implement a general overall policy.
Advanced Options	Includes settings for Maximum Sessions, Default Time-of-Day/Day-of-Week Specification, and Remote Logging.

Administration Configuration

The parameters for Administration Configuration are used to allow the CiscoSecure ACS to be remotely administered through a browser. In order for remote administration to occur, Java must be enabled.

External User Database

You can configure the following features for the External User Database:

▼ Actions to be taken if CiscoSecure ACS does not find a matching username

■ Whether CiscoSecure ACS can map an appropriate authentication/ authorization group profile to each external database

▲ Installation of support for communication with an external user

Reports and Activity

Click the Reports and Activity icon to bring up the navigation bar to view reports. The following types of reports can be viewed if configured:

▼ TACACS+ Accounting

■ TACACS+ Administration

■ RADIUS Accounting

■ RADIUS Administration

■ Failed Attempts

■ Logged-in Users

▲ Disabled Accounts

CISCOSECURE ACS LOG FILES   The log files for CiscoSecure ACS reports are generated daily and are enabled by default. They can either be viewed here in the management inter-face , or exported as .CSV files to other applications such as Microsoft Excel. About 40 dif-ferent items can be logged, ranging from username, to caller-ID (the IP address from which a user session is originating), to commands issued (such as **show running-config**), and more. These statistics can be a very powerful tool for troubleshooting and monitoring.

The data logged by CiscoSecure ACS can be as simple or complex as you designate it to be. This customization is performed by clicking the System Configuration button and selecting Logging, and then selecting the log to configure. If a checkmark appears below **use**, it means that the service is currently being logged; an X here means the service is not currently being logged. The next screen allows you to turn logging on or off, and to select the items you want included in the log files.

CryptoCard Admin

CryptoCard Admin is bundled with CiscoSecure ACS, allowing the use of *Token Cards* for authentication. Token Cards are used where the need for tightened security exists. In nor-mal Telnet sessions, a username and password sent in cleartext are used for authentica-tion. This username and password can be sniffed on the network and used by unauthorized personnel. Token Cards prevent this by using One-Time Passwords (OTP). In this arrangement, the username and password are still sent in cleartext, but the pass-word is only valid once, thus rendering it useless to any would-be sniffer. CryptoCards are small (about the size of a small, thin calculator) and simple to use.

Adding Administrators

As you'll see, you can arrange for administrators to be able to use Token Cards to log into the CryptoAdmin Client GUI. However, it is recommended that one default administrator is allowed username/password authentication in the unlikely event that one or more Admin Token Cards should fail. In case everyone gets locked out of the database, the default administrator can be used.

Here are the steps for adding an administrator:

1. Click the Admin Server Config icon and select option 2, Set Up Operator Information.
2. Enter the operator's (administrator's) name (maximum eight characters).
3. Enter the access mode (generally 0 for Unrestricted mode).
4. Enter the authentication method for authenticating the operator. A Token Card or a simple username/password can be used.

NOTE: If you choose Password for the authentication method, you'll be asked to enter the password (8–16 characters) for the operator. If you choose CryptoCard for the authentication method, the operator must have an established CryptoCard User Account before the Token Card can be used for authentication. (See the next section, "Adding CryptoCard Users.")

5. Type **yes** to set up another operator, if desired, and repeat steps 2 through 4.
6. Select 9 to exit.
7. Click the Client GUI Configuration icon.
8. Select Add and enter the name of the new operator.
9. Click the Plus (+) icon.
10. Enter the IP address of the host server (the default is local loopback).
11. Enter the port number (the default is 624).
12. Enter the packet encryption key (a 16-digit hex key).
13. Choose Operator Access Permissions on the right (Token, Policy, and Keys). These define what the operator can control.
14. Select Commit.

Adding CryptoCard Users

Users must be added to the CryptoCard database before the Token Cards can be used with CiscoSecure ACS for AAA. You add users via the Client GUI that is supplied by CryptoCard.

1. To start the client GUI, select Start menu | Programs | CryptoCard | CryptoAdmin.
2. Click the Client GUI icon.

3. Log in. Use the supplied Admin username and password. The server is the loopback address if you're operating locally, or the IP address of the remote server if you're operating remotely.

    If CryptoCard is used for login to the CryptoCard database, leave the password blank and select OK. You will then be prompted for Challenge/Response authentication.

4. Click the folder for the group to which the user will belong.

5. Select File | New | User.

6. Enter the new user's name and the serial number of the Card (RB-1 is the default).

7. Make any necessary changes to Token, Keys, and Policy.

8. Select Apply and Initialize.

9. Follow the instructions, entering information into the Card. (See the "User Profiles" bullet under "Other CryptoCard Settings," later in this chapter, for description of codes entered into the Card during initialization.)

10. Select Done.

The user is now ready to use the Token Card for authentication. The initial PIN depends on Card configuration. The user will be forced to change it during the Card's first use and may change it any time subsequently, using the CPIN key on the Card.

Resynchronizing Token Cards

In the event that a Token Card loses its synchronization with the server, a message will appear at login to NAS, to the effect of "Token out of Sync..." To fix this, attempt to log in again, and when issued a challenge, press the CH/MAC key on the Card and type **challenge** into the card. Type the Card's response into the terminal, and resynchronization is complete. If this doesn't work, there may be a problem with the card; see your administrator.

Other CryptoCard Settings

Following are the other CryptoCard settings available to you while running CryptoCard Admin.

▼ **User Profiles**   Step 7 in the procedure just above initializes the CryptoCard. This step-by-step initialization is based on user profiles previously configured. Settings for the user profile are converted to three-digit decimal codes for input into the Card during initialization. A default user profile is established with the most common settings (initial PIN, the number of failed login attempts before lockout, and so on). This default profile will be used for all Card initializations, but it can be modified on a per-user basis. If you wish to change this default setting, select File | Profile.

▲ **User Group Reassignment**   If at any point a user needs to be reassigned to another group, simply drag and drop the user from the old group to the new group. This has no effect on settings or authentication.

Network Access Server Configuration

In order for CiscoSecure ACS to function properly, the network access server (NAS) must be configured to acknowledge and use TACACS+. Many of these configuration commands have been discussed in the "Authentication," "Authorization," and "Accounting" sections; let's take another look at them here as a group. Following is a sample configuration for a Cisco 4500 router running IOS version 11.2 (15a). The configuration commands will vary, of course, with the hardware and IOS in use. The line numbers on the left are for reference and should not be entered into the NAS.

NOTE: The sample configuration shown here is for TACACS+ AAA security.

```
1. service password-encryption
2. aaa new-model
3. aaa authentication login default tacacs+ enable
4. aaa accounting exec stop-only tacacs+
5. aaa accounting commands 0 stop-only tacacs+
6. aaa accounting commands 1 stop-only tacacs+
7. aaa accounting commands 15 stop-only tacacs+
8. tacacs-server host <IP address of tacacsserver1>
9. tacacs-server host <IP address of tacacsserver2>
10.tacacs-server key <shared key>
11.aaa authentication login no_tacacs tacacs+ enable
12.line con 0
13.login authentication no_tacacs
14.aaa authorization exec tacacs+ none
15.aaa authorization commands 1 tacacs+ none
16.aaa authorization commands 15 tacacs+ none
```

Line 1 forces all passwords stored in the configuration file to be encrypted.

Line 2 creates a new TACACS+ model.

Line 3 defines the default login scenario. In this case, TACACS+ will be used for authentication; if no server can be reached, the enable password is used.

Lines 4–7 set up accounting for EXEC mode commands for privilege levels 0, 1, and 15.

Lines 8–10 specify the TACACS+ server host IP address and the shared key used for encryption between the NAS and the TACACS+ server. Whichever host is listed first will be the first server accessed for AAA.

Lines 11–13 define the console login. The parameter **no_tacacs** is a label; it does not mean "Do not use TACACS."

Lines 14–16 specify authorization checks to occur for all commands in the EXEC mode privilege levels 0, 1, and 15.

TIP: You should always ensure that the NAS configuration works, by trying to access the same NAS with another Telnet session before committing the configuration to memory. If it doesn't work, you can reload the old configuration by power-cycling the device.

NETSONAR

NetSonar (recently renamed CiscoSecure Scanner) is Cisco's vulnerability management tool for your network equipment. Using NetSonar, you can scan your network devices and obtain an electronic inventory of systems and services. Once these vulnerabilities have been determined, NetSonar compiles this data in the Network Security Database (NSDB), which is used to provide charts and reports visible through a browser-based interface. This comprehensive inventory helps you to determine where your system may be open external attack.

Following are the minimum system requirements for running NetSonar:

Hardware	Memory/Disk Storage	Software
A Pentium 266MHZ processor or faster CD-ROM drive	64MB RAM (96MB recommended) 2GB hard drive	Windows NT 4.0 Service Pack 3 or higher A TCP/IP network interface A Web browser (Netscape Navigator 2.0, or Microsoft Internet Explorer 3.0 or later)

Figure 16-8 illustrates the window displayed when you log into NetSonar. The Help menu contains standard help options. The File menu contains the following options:

▼   Preferences

■   NSDB Link (Network Security Database)

▲   Exit

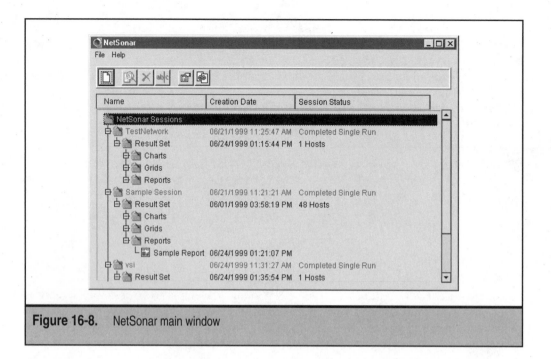

Figure 16-8. NetSonar main window

Setting Up NetSonar

The Preferences window contains fields that are to be configured when you first log into NetSonar.

NetSonar Parameters	Description
Names	This tab uses the information you entered when you installed NetSonar. This device name information is placed on the program's reports; you can change these names whenever necessary.
Session Browser	Sets the level of detail you want displayed on the main window of NetSonar's GUI. The default is full detail.
Grid Browser	Sets the level of detail you want displayed in the Grid Browser. Setting it to level 10 is usually sufficient, since there are seldom more than 10 levels of detail available.
HTML Browser	Sets the path to your Web browser, for the display of NetSonar reports and the Network Security Database.

NetSonar Parameters	Description
Misc Tab	Sets up what you want to appear on the main NetSonar window. By default both Toolbars and Session Status appear.

Network Security Database (NSDB)

The Network Security Database provides a unique insight into your system's security vulnerabilities. It contains descriptions of security problems and suggests options to improve or fix them. The database also provides severity ratings and online links for more extensive technical resources.

To view the NSDB, click the last icon in the toolbar of NetSonar's opening screen (Figure 16-8). This launches your browser and takes you to the database. Figure 16-9 is a snapshot of this view.

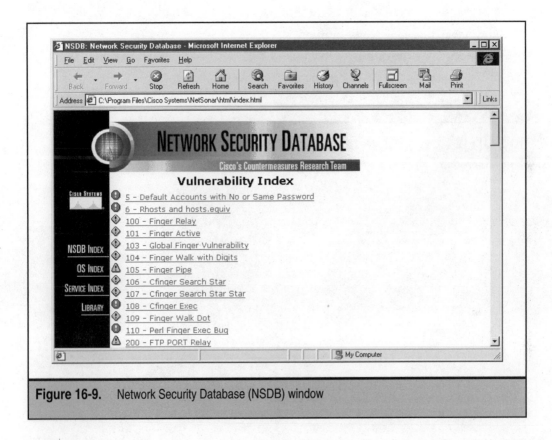

Figure 16-9.   Network Security Database (NSDB) window

Session Configuration

Before NetSonar can do its job, you need to define a session. A NetSonar session consists of either a *scan* or a *probe* (these network investigation operations are fully defined later, in "Working with NetSonar"). The results from the scan or probe are then used to create reports and even develop security policies.

To create a new session, click the first icon in the main NetSonar toolbar (Figure 16-8). The Session Configuration window is shown in Figure 16-10. This window has four configuration tabs, described in the following paragraphs. Once you're satisfied with your settings, you name your NetSonar session and press ENTER.

Network Addresses Tab

Figure 16-10 shows the Session Configuration window with the Network Addresses tab open. Here you define the following:

▼ Choose to scan the network or import previous scan data.

■ Enable/disable DNS resolution.

■ Specify IP address ranges to scan.

■ Specify IP addresses to eliminate from scan.

▲ Choose to export scan data, and designate the drive and file for storing it.

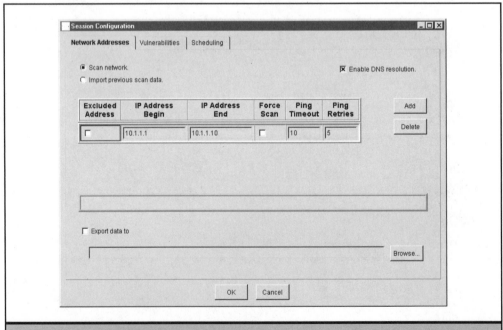

Figure 16-10. Session Configuration window

NetSonar uses **ping**s to discover live hosts and draw a map of the network. In Session Configuration you have the following additional options for the **ping**s:

▼ **Force Scan**   Conducts a port scan so you can discover the hosts behind routers or firewalls that block incoming **icmp** traffic (**ping**).

■ **Ping Timeout**   Maximum wait time for a response.

▲ **Ping Retries**   Number of retries before logging the address as dead.

Vulnerabilities Tab

The Vulnerabilities tab lets you define how specific or general you'd like the scan or probe to be. Depending on what you select as the level of scan or probe to execute, NetSonar will select or deselect vulnerabilities (from the Vulnerabilities confirmation window). You can also right-click on a specific vulnerability in the Vulnerabilities confirmation window to get a definition of the vulnerability. Your options for defining the intensity of the scan or probe are defined here:

▼ **TCP and UDP ports to be scanned**   Choose none, low-ports (1–1024), well-known ports, low plus well-known ports, or all ports.

■ **Active probe intensity**   Choose UNIX Heavy, Windows Heavy, All Heavy, UNIX Severe, All Lite, Windows Lite, UNIX Lite, Windows Severe, or All Severe. (You can focus on UNIX and/or Windows and then select a level.)

▲ **Vulnerabilities confirmation**   There are 13 categories of exploits, listed out on the NSDB page (Figure 16-9).

Scheduling Tab

Use this tab to define when and how often you would like this NetSonar session probe to occur. Your options include

▼ Time of day (run the probe immediately or at a specific time)

■ Recurrence pattern (Once, Daily, Weekly, and Monthly)

▲ Run the probe only once

Working with NetSonar

NetSonar has four main components: a GUI, a Network Mapping Tool, a Vulnerability Assessment Engine, and a Report Wizard. These components are used to perform scans and probes on a network at specific times or on a recurring basis.

▼ A scan is a passive analysis technique that identifies the open ports found on each network device and the associated port banner. This port banner is compared against a table of rules that assist in identifying the network device, its operating system, and all potential vulnerabilities.

▲   A probe is an active analysis technique that uses the information obtained during scanning to perform a more intense interrogation of network devices. The probe can confirm suspected vulnerabilities, as well as detect additional vulnerabilities that were not detected by the scan.

A scan and probe can target one node, a single network segment, or your entire network. You can also scan for specific vulnerabilities or for an entire spectrum of vulnerabilities. After the data is collected, NetSonar organizes it and provides reporting functionality.

NetSonar GUI

NetSonar's GUI is based on two components—the data management and scheduling organizer, and a grid browser.

THE DATA MANAGEMENT AND SCHEDULING ORGANIZER   Use this component to tell NetSonar

▼   What you want to be considered a vulnerability

■   How you want your data organized

▲   How you want your reports to look

THE GRID BROWSER   The Grid Browser is used to view the data based on the queries you defined. You select the fields of a particular network scan you are interested in, and use the Grid Browser to display this information. You decide the level of detail you want to see. The Grid Browser also will provide a "snapshot" of the views you like and include them in any reports you generate.

The Zoom feature lets you focus on more or less detail of your data. Scan data may include operating systems, services, and vulnerabilities running on various hosts. The drill-down feature reveals host-specific details such as

▼   All hosts running a particular service

■   All services running on one host

■   All vulnerabilities on one host

▲   All hosts with a particular vulnerability

By highlighting the data of interest, you are able to create graphics such as pie charts, area charts, and line charts.

Network Mapping Tool

Use NetSonar's Network Mapping Tool to perform a high-level passive analysis (scan) of your network. The Mapping Tool collects information such as active IP addresses, ports on each network device, and port banners. It then takes this collected information and compares it with the standard rules. This comparison is used to identify where potential vulnerabilities may exist and where additional probing is necessary. This analysis is performed by the Vulnerability Assessment Engine.

Vulnerability Assessment Engine

The Vulnerability Assessment Engine takes the results from the Network Mapping Tool and uses well-known exploitation techniques to perform an active analysis technique (probe). This probe confirms each suspected vulnerability and identifies other vulnerabilities not originally detected. The Vulnerability Assessment Engine also compares its findings with any additional set of rules you may have defined. This feature allows you to customize your probes to satisfy your network's particular requirements. There are two ways to customize NetSonar reports:

▼   Edit the HTML report after NetSonar generates it. This only applies to the current report. Assuming a standard installation, the report would be located in C:\Program Files\Cisco Systems\Netsonar\Udo*session name**session data**report name.*

▲   Edit the report template. This will apply to all subsequent reports. The report template is located in C:\Program Files\Cisco Systems\Netsonar\ ReportComponents.

Report Wizard

The Report Wizard does exactly what you'd expect—it generates the NetSonar reports after your network has been scanned and the data collected. These are HTML reports, which you can configure as desired, that can be viewed by any browser supporting HTML 2.0 or later.

To generate a report, right-click on the Result Set folder under the NetSonar session on which you want the report generated. Select Create New Report. The Report Wizard window will appear and step you through options such as these:

▼   **Type of Report**   Executive, Brief Technical, or Full.

■   **Report Components**   Cover Page, Executive Summary, Process Overview, and the selections under each of these components.

■   **Charts and Snapshots**   Created from data resulting from a network scan. (If you create this report prior to running Report Wizard, you can simply select and add the charts and snapshots to the Report.)

▲   **Report Name**   The name you wish to assign to this specific report, for this session.

NOTE: Multiple reports can be created for each session, allowing you to tailor each report for each recipient.

After all your options have been selected, you can view the report immediately if you wish. Report Wizard will launch the browser, showing the report with your selected components. Figure 16-11 illustrates an Executive Summary report including information such as vulnerability findings and recommendations. Figures 16-12 and 16-13 are views of later sections in the same report.

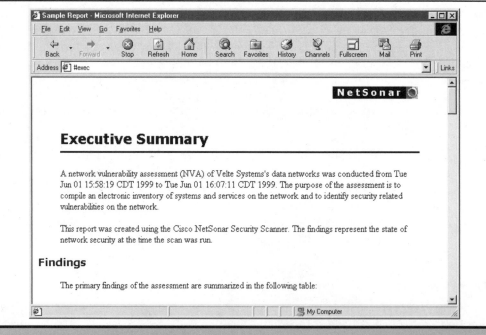

Figure 16-11. NetSonar Executive Summary Report

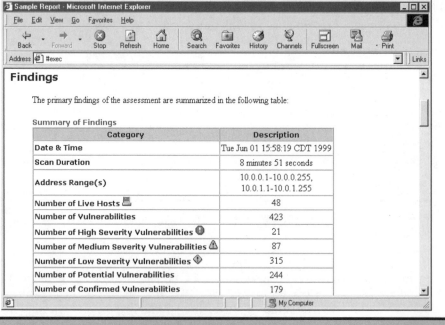

Figure 16-12. NetSonar Executive Summary Report—Findings

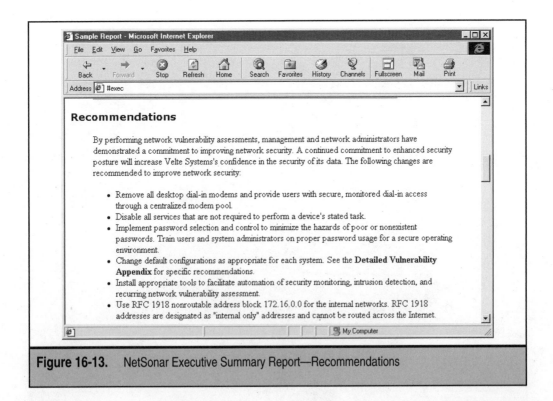

Figure 16-13. NetSonar Executive Summary Report—Recommendations

SUMMARY

This chapter introduced many important concepts and applications that aid you in ensuring that access to your network equipment is controlled and secure. Access control has several levels, depending on your security requirements. These levels range from simple non-AAA authentication methods, to a combination of AAA (Authentication, Authorization, and Accounting) safeguards. Cisco IOS on a Cisco network access server supports both non-AAA and full AAA.

For enhanced access control and a GUI interface that is easier to configure and manage, Cisco offers the CiscoSecure Access Control Server. The CiscoSecure ACS supports both TACACS+ and RADIUS, along with other security options including CryptoCards. NetSonar is a Cisco application used to determine security vulnerabilities within your network.

Although the concepts and applications discussed in this chapter do not offer a total security solution, they do provide the tools needed to control access to your network equipment.

PART V

Appendixes

APPENDIX A

Basic Cisco Router Configuration

C isco is the world leader in the production and sales of routers—from small routers with basic functions only, to large enterprise-level routers that can serve hundreds of virtual circuits supplying thousands of users with services designed to streamline network efficiency. In today's information systems, it is imperative that IT engineers understand at least the fundamentals of router functions, as well as the tasks involved in configuring these routers. At first glance, Cisco router configuration may seem a daunting task. With knowledge of a few good basic techniques, however, and a little time, it can be a fairly simple chore. This appendix explains the principal steps in a simple configuration of a Cisco router.

NOTE: Chapters 3, 4, and 5 address in detail much of the content in this appendix. Refer to these chapters for more information.

Routers function mainly at the network layer of the OSI model. Their role is to route data packets among networks while prohibiting broadcast data from being distributed. If these broadcast data packets were permitted to pass among networks, the volume of unwanted traffic on neighboring networks could result in *broadcast storms*. These broadcast storms can bring a network to its knees by swallowing up precious bandwidth. Routers not only save bandwidth, but also provide security to critical information systems.

START WITH A GOOD PLAN

Before beginning to configure any network device, including a router, have a plan for how you intend to use the device. Ask yourself, "Why am I adding this device?" and "What function will it serve in my network?" These questions may seem simple and the answers obvious, but you should consider them seriously or you may find yourself digging out of a deep hole later on. Take into account future growth, as well as possible technological advances. Make a list of all the possible scenarios affecting your router and plan accordingly.

Answer these questions:

▼ Which interfaces do you need to configure?

■ What addressing scheme do you have or plan to have?

▲ Which protocols will you use with these interfaces?

All the answers to these questions have direct impact on how you will configure your router.

THE ROUTER'S PHYSICAL INTERFACES

Start with the outside of the router. Pay close attention to the interfacing. Locate any 9-pin adapter interfaces (these are much like a PC's serial interface), 25-pin interfaces (like a printer port on a PC), or RJ-45 jacks (the most common Ethernet interface). These interfaces are the router's connections to the networks it will serve. See Chapter 4 for more information on router interfaces.

Before many of the features of the Cisco router can be used, these interfaces must have cables connected to them. Figure A-1 shows a view of the rear of a Cisco 4000 series router. Note the location of the *console port*; it's on the right, directly under the second Token Ring interface. The initial and possibly subsequent configurations will be done through the console port.

A connector cable from a *serial port interface* on a PC or laptop, when plugged into this console port, allows you to set up the router and define the interfaces. An RS-232 cable with the correct pinout will work for this connection. Cables designed specifically for Cisco routers are available, as well. These cables ship with new Cisco routers, or you can order them separately through Cisco. Chapter 4 offers more details on cable, connector, and interface specifications.

You can use any terminal emulation software for the console port connection. Windows operating systems come with the HyperTerminal application, which works just fine despite its limitations.

Cisco routers generally use the following settings for terminal connections:

▼ 9600 bits per second (bps)

■ 8 data bits

■ N(o) parity

▲ 1 stop bit

NOTE: Once the interfaces are in place, you'll be able to configure the router remotely via a simple Telnet session (provided you have configured the router to support IP traffic). We'll cover this shortly.

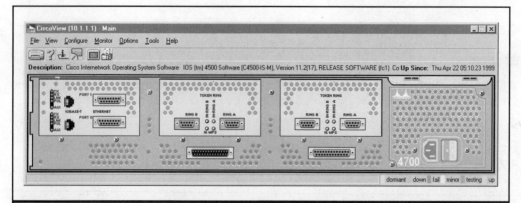

Figure A-1.   The back of a Cisco 4700 router

THE ROUTER'S OPERATING SYSTEM

Cisco routers use the Cisco Internetworking Operating System (Cisco IOS) to provide functionality to the user. Within the IOS is the Command Line Interface (CLI). There are other ways to configure a router, but for the configuration exercise in this appendix we'll enter the raw IOS commands through the CLI.

In addition to the CLI, the initial configuration dialog (Setup), which is initiated when a new router is powered up, can also assist you with the input of the initial configuration parameters. Another option is to use Cisco ConfigMaker to configure a device. The ConfigMaker application runs on Windows 95/98 or NT and is described in depth in Chapter 5.

NOTE: The Cisco IOS is the actual operating system of the router. The CLI is a function of the Cisco IOS that allows you to configure and use the IOS. The commands used in this appendix are a very small subset of the raw IOS commands commonly used in a basic configuration.

Within the Cisco IOS you will define and view interfaces over which data is routed among networks. When you power up the router, it goes through a series of self-tests and then loads the IOS:

▼ On a new router, or if the startup-configuration has been erased, you are led through the steps of an initial configuration setup.

▲ On a router with an existing configuration, or if you choose to cancel the initial configuration, the operating system is loaded. Then, unless you have set a password for the console port, the next message will ask you to press RETURN (in the Cisco router, it is referred to as Return) to get started.

You'll see the CLI prompt:

```
router>
```

where **router** is the host name of the router.

NOTE: You don't have to be connected to the router during its initial boot-up to make a console port connection. If the router is already powered up, you can connect to it, and simply press ENTER a time or two to get the **router** prompt. If you don't get the **router** prompt, check the cables and settings in your terminal application (9600, 8, N, 1).

Logging into the Router: User EXEC Mode

There are two modes in the IOS: user EXEC mode and privileged EXEC mode (also known as enable mode). The **router** prompt shown in the preceding section is the user EXEC mode prompt, from which you can execute limited router commands. These commands are actually a subset of the privileged EXEC mode commands.

At any time, you can enter **help** at the **router** prompt to display a list of available commands and command arguments. For example, the **show** command is used frequently in the management of the Cisco IOS. This command has many possible arguments, which you can list by typing one of these commands:

```
router>show help
```

or

```
router>show ?
```

Try this now; type

```
router>show privilege
```

In the response, you'll see that you have privilege level 1. Cisco routers can have up to 15 different privilege levels. The defaults are privilege 1 for user EXEC mode, and privilege 15 for enable mode (covered in the following section). Over time, with a little experience using the IOS, you'll know these common commands.

Using Privileged (Enable) Mode

Many more commands are available in privileged (enable) mode. This is where the router configuration changes are made. From here, you can enter the *global configuration mode* and set up the router and its interfaces. Privileged mode is usually password protected, and the encrypted **enable** password is stored internally by the router. See the section "Setting the Enable Password."

At the EXEC mode prompt, type

```
router>enable
```

(Remember, the **router** portion of the prompt you see will be the host name of your router.) Next you'll be prompted as follows:

```
password>
```

Enter your enable password after this prompt. If an enable password has not yet been set, the enable mode can only be accessed via the console port. If you are connected through the console port and no enable password has been set, simply press ENTER. The next prompt you see is

```
router#
```

The # in the prompt tells you that you are in privileged (enabled) mode. From this prompt you can set up interfaces, change passwords, and perform other router management operations.

Following are some of the more commonly used commands in the privileged mode:

▼ **show** Shows information about the running configuration.

■ **telnet** Initiates a Telnet session.

■ **disable** Returns you to the user EXEC mode.

▲ **configure** Enters global configuration mode.

To list these and other commands, type **?** at the enable prompt. Note that some of these commands can be executed in the user EXEC mode, as well.

Running Setup

As mentioned earlier, the Setup utility is run when you first boot up a new router. Executing the **setup** command on an already configured device will initiate a simple setup procedure that allows you to set passwords, establish interfaces with IP addresses, and more. This is an easy way to configure the router, but it is limited. If you want to dig in and get to the heart of the router configuration, use the CLI configuration mode.

Let's go back to the privileged mode prompt (the one with a # after the router name). After the prompt, type

```
router#>show running-config
```

The response to this command shows you the current *running* configuration of the router. The running configuration will be lost if you power down or reload the router.

If you use the

```
router#>show config
```

command, you will see what is written in *nonvolatile RAM (NVRAM)*. This configuration is not lost if the router is powered down or reloaded (with the **reload** command).

In order to ensure your configuration is safe, remember to use the

```
router#>write memory
```

command after you make changes to the running configuration. This takes the current running configuration and writes it to memory. Now it's safe to power down the router, and you won't lose your configuration.

NOTE: If you neglect to write your configuration to memory after changing the configuration, you won't see your changes when you use the **show configuration** command. Your changes will be in effect, but only in the running configuration, which you can view using the **show running-configuration** command.

Setting a Host Name

As you've seen, the prompt you see throughout your router navigation reflects the *host name* of that router. You can choose up to 80 alphanumeric, case-sensitive characters for the host name, but the name cannot begin with a space or a number.

To set the host name on your router, enter privileged EXEC mode using the enable password, and then enter the global configuration mode by typing

```
router#>configure terminal
```

The next prompt shows you're in **config** mode. Type

```
router(config#)hostname yourhostname
```

and notice that your prompt has now changed to reflect the new host name.

Use CTRL-Z, or type **end** at any time, to exit the global configuration mode.

WARNING: Nearly all changes you make in the configuration mode are instantaneous. When working in this mode, be careful not to shut down an interface you are using to communicate with the router, or you may lose your connection.

Setting the Enable Password

To set an enable password, use the following global configuration command:

```
router(config#)enable password yourenablepassword
```

By default, enable passwords are not encrypted when they are stored in the configuration file. To add encryption protection, use the following global configuration command:

```
router(config#)service password-encryption
```

This command encrypts all passwords in the configuration file.

WARNING: Don't forget these passwords! Passwords can be recovered, but only by an arduous process. So keep those passwords safe.

CONFIGURING A ROUTER'S INTERFACES

Interfaces are the lifelines of data passing through routers. In order for routers to work as designed, they need at least two interfaces. These can be serial interfaces that are connected directly to another router, or are connected via CSUs/DSUs to a WAN. These interfaces can also be Ethernet or Token Ring for LAN connection, or others. This section discusses the most frequently used interfaces today: serial, Ethernet, and Token Ring.

Serial Interface Configuration

For serial interfaces, the configuration varies with application. The following is a simple example of setting that up. First, we find out what interfaces we have. Take a look at the output from the following **show interfaces** command:

```
router#sh interfaces

Serial0 is administratively down, line protocol is down
 Hardware is HD64570
 MTU 1500 bytes, BW 1544 Kbit, DLY 20000 usec, rely 255/255, load 1/255
 Encapsulation HDLC, loopback not set, keepalive set (10 sec)
 Last input 6d02h, output 6d02h, output hang never
 Last clearing of "show interface" counters never
 Input queue: 0/75/0 (size/max/drops); Total output drops: 0
 Queueing strategy: weighted fair
 Output queue: 0/1000/64/0 (size/max total/threshold/drops)
   Conversations 0/3/256 (active/max active/max total)
   Reserved Conversations 0/0 (allocated/max allocated)
 5 minute input rate 0 bits/sec, 0 packets/sec
 5 minute output rate 0 bits/sec, 0 packets/sec
   257302 packets input, 22452373 bytes, 0 no buffer
   Received 72634 broadcasts, 0 runts, 0 giants, 0 throttles
   4577 input errors, 1 CRC, 0 frame, 0 overrun, 143 ignored, 1 abort
   423653 packets output, 123134542 bytes, 0 underruns
   0 output errors, 0 collisions, 48543 interface resets
   0 output buffer failures, 0 output buffers swapped out
   24 carrier transitions
   DCD=down DSR=down DTR=down RTS=down CTS=down
--More--
```

This output shows the first interface, serial 0. If there is output for additional interfaces, you can press the SPACEBAR to scroll an entire screen, ENTER to scroll line by line, and any other character to return to the prompt. As you configure interfaces for the router, check your changes by repeatedly using the **show interfaces** command. This will list the available interfaces on the router and give you some information about them, including their numerical identifier.

Let's assume you are configuring interface serial 0. From the enable prompt, type

```
router#configure terminal
```

This tells the router that you wish to configure the router using the terminal (or, in this case, the keyboard) for input.

The next prompt is the global configuration prompt:

```
router(config)#
```

At this prompt, type

```
router(config)#interface serial 0
```

to get the following prompt:

```
router(config-if)#
```

From here, all the configuration changes you make will affect serial port 0. You can add an IP address and subnet mask, as follows:

```
router(config-if)#ip address 203.146.202.86 255.255.255.0
```

This configuration command assigns an IP address 203.146.202.86 with the subnet mask of 255.255.255.0. In addition, a route for 203.146.202.0 is added to the routing tables.

You can designate encapsulation methods, for example,

```
router(config-if)#encapsulation ppp
```

This configuration command specifies the packet encapsulation method you wish to use for this interface. The default for synchronous serial interfaces is HDLC.

The last thing you need to do to activate an interface is to turn it on. This is done with the following command:

```
router(config-if)#no shutdown
```

Keep in mind that for almost every possible configuration command there is an opposite command. All you need to do is insert a **no** in front of the command, and the command is reversed. So if you wanted to disable serial interface 0, you would simply type its opposite command:

```
router(config-if)#shutdown
```

To see if the Ethernet interface 0 is administratively down, you type

```
router#>show interfaces
```

To bring the interface active again, from the interface configuration prompt type this command:

```
router(config-if)#no shutdown
```

or this shortened version:

```
router(config-if)#no shut
```

See the section "Testing and Troubleshooting," later in this appendix, for ways to test your interface configuration.

> **NOTE:** Many Cisco IOS commands can be executed with shortcuts or abbreviations. Some of the more common are **sh** for **show**, **conf** for **configure**, **int** for **interface**, **eth** for **ethernet**, and **ser** for **serial**. These abbreviations, which are usually just the first two or three letters of the command, help you speed up navigation and configuration of Cisco's IOS. Note, however, that for Cisco certification tests you will be expected to know and use the full version of the command.

Ethernet Interface Configuration

Ethernet interfaces are the easiest to configure. For the most part, they're used to connect separate networks in a LAN. These interfaces are generally RJ-45 female connectors. A 10BaseT (twisted pair) cable with an RJ-45 end plugs into the router, and then into another device such as a hub or switch. You must configure the Ethernet interfaces for them to function properly.

To configure an Ethernet interface, begin as you did with the serial interface configuration in the preceding section:

```
router#show interfaces
```

You can also type

```
router#show interfaces ethernet
```

This will show you only the Ethernet interfaces.

Assuming you have an Ethernet interface 0, type

```
router#configure terminal
```

and then

```
router(config)#interface ethernet 0
```

From here, you can configure your Ethernet interfaces any way you choose. You can assign IP addresses, specify encapsulation methods, choose media and connector types, and more. Assigning an IP address and subnet mask is as simple as typing the following command:

```
router(config-if)#ip address 10.1.13.1 255.255.255.0
```

where the IP address is 10.1.13.1 and the subnet mask is 255.255.255.0. This also adds 10.1.13.0 to the routing table of the router. The default encapsulation method for Ethernet interfaces is the standard ARPA version 2.0. There is no need to change this unless you have a conflicting application issue.

In some instances, you will have an interface on a router that has two possible media types, AUI and 10BaseT (twisted pair, RJ-45). In these cases, you must specify which you will use. For the sake of our example configuration later in this appendix, we will use 10BaseT. This is configured with the following interface configuration command:

```
router(config-if)#media-type 10BaseT
```

The configuration changes resulting from this command would set up Ethernet interface 0 with an IP address of 10.1.13.1. The subnet mask would be 255.255.255.0, and the encapsulation method would be the default ARPA version 2.0. The interface uses a 10BaseT cable.

Your next step should be to test and see if you have connectivity. Make sure that you have the Ethernet interface 0 physically connected to the network 10.1.13.0. See the section "Testing and Troubleshooting," later in this appendix, for ways to test your interface configuration.

Token Ring Interface Configuration

Although waning in popularity, Token Ring still has a considerable presence in the networking world. So it's essential to have a basic understanding of Token Ring interface configuration, which is similar to Ethernet.

First, enter the global configuration mode by typing

```
router#>configure terminal
```

or

```
router#>conf t
```

at the enable prompt. At the global configuration prompt, type

```
router(config)#interface tokenring 0
```

Set the IP address the same way you would for an Ethernet interface. Type

```
router(config-if)#ip address 10.1.14.2 255.255.255.0
```

The default encapsulation for Token Ring is SNAP. There is usually no need to change it.

Cisco Token Ring interfaces support *early token release*, in which the interface releases the token back onto the ring immediately after transmitting, rather than waiting for the frame to return. This can increase available bandwidth. To configure an interface for early token release, type

```
router(config-if)#early-token-release
```

in the interface configuration mode.

The default ring speed is 16Mbps, although you can change that with this command:

```
router(config-if)#ring-speed <4 or 16>
```

WARNING: Cisco warns that setting the incorrect ring speed will bring down the ring. Make sure the speed you set is correct for your ring.

Now you can test the Token Ring interface by pinging, the same way you would for an Ethernet interface. Again, if this fails, check your cabling and ring speed.

Configuring a Remote Router

After you have correctly configured at least one interface on the router and you can access its IP address, you'll be able to configure a router from a remote location. See the foregoing sections if you don't have an interface correctly configured. Windows operating systems come with a built-in Telnet application through which you can **telnet** to all Cisco devices that support the application.

Start Telnet from the command prompt:

```
C:\>telnet 10.1.13.1
```

This opens the Telnet application and attempts a connection with the 10.1.1.1 interface. In the Telnet window illustrated in Figure A-2, we have set a login password and an enable password. You'll notice that, for security reasons, the passwords do not appear as you type them.

From here you can explore the router's configuration, change configuration parameters, or just get a look at how the router is being used.

TIP: With Microsoft's Telnet application, you can add a scroll buffer on your Telnet session. Select Terminal | Preferences and increase the buffer size. (We recommend about 400 lines, so if text scrolls off the screen you can scroll back to look at it.)

Routing Protocols

Routing protocols assist routers with the task of path selection through a network. Some of the most popular routing protocols supported by Cisco routers are RIP (Routing Information Protocol) versions 1 and 2, the Cisco proprietary protocol IGRP (Internet Gateway Routing Protocol), EIGRP (Enhanced IGRP, also Cisco proprietary), and OSPF (Open Shortest Path First). See Chapter 3 for more information on routing protocols. Essentially, a routing protocol keeps a *routing table* that tells the router how to get a data packet from one network segment to another. Routers then share their routing tables with neighboring routers who are utilizing the same routing protocol. They do not, however, share tables with routers running dissimilar routing protocols (for instance, RIP shares only with RIP, IGRP shares with IGRP, and so on).

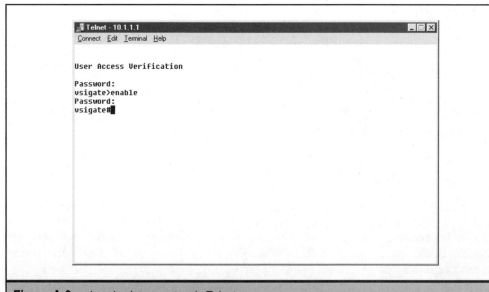

```
Telnet - 10.1.1.1                                         _ □ ×
Connect  Edit  Terminal  Help


User Access Verification

Password:
vsigate>enable
Password:
vsigate#█
```

Figure A-2. Logging into a router via Telnet

NOTE: You can define multiple routing protocols on a router. This increases overhead in the form of CPU and bandwidth utilization, but it allows you to keep routing tables for all possible routes in case you have devices that do not support a certain routing protocol.

In this way, the tables are propagated throughout the network, allowing the routers along the way to choose paths based on availability. If an interface or medium along the way is disabled for some reason, the routers around it will sense this and will detour data. Here we will look at RIP, one of the simplest and most common routing protocols.

RIP

RIP is a basic routing protocol that sends its entire routing table at regular intervals (30 seconds) to neighboring routers. This is an effective routing protocol except on larger networks, on which it has some limitations. For example, because the entire table is sent regardless of changes, you may see vital bandwidth being used to send unnecessary updates. RIP2 solves this by sending only when there is a change to the routing table. This saves a lot of bandwidth, especially over time. For a smaller network, however, RIP will suffice.

NOTE: Windows NT supports RIP and, therefore, can use the tables for its own routing decisions. This, of course, would be used on machines with more than one NIC, and is not generally recommended.

The use of routing protocols is a global configuration, meaning they are not interface specific. When you enable a routing protocol, you enable it on all the interfaces on that router. The configuration of RIP is simple:

```
router(config)#router rip
router(config)#network 10.0.0.0
```

The *network* command specifies that RIP should send its routing table updates to all networks in the 10.0.0.0 range.

EXAMPLE CONFIGURATION

Now let's see how all these configuration commands work together. Figure A-3 represents a simple network setup using a Cisco router. This router has two Ethernet interfaces and two Token Ring interfaces. One of each has been configured, while the others have been shut down. Additionally, we will set up OSPF as the routing protocol so that routes can be shared with other routers. See Chapter 5 for more information about OSPF.

Let's first examine the configuration that enables this network to function. You'll see the same commands we put to work earlier to set up the interfaces and get the router to function. We have used OSPF as our routing protocol, which requires you to set up the area number (Area 0 is the default area). Here is the command:

```
router(config)#router ospf 1
```

where **1** is simply a process identifier. There's only one additional configuration statement:

```
router(config)#network 10.0.0.0 0.255.255.255 area 0
```

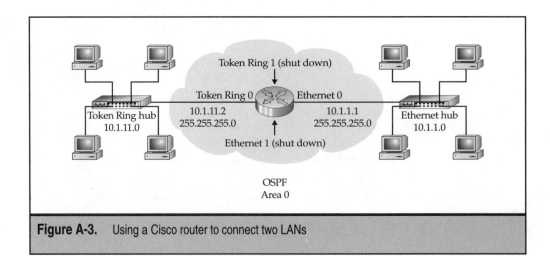

Figure A-3. Using a Cisco router to connect two LANs

OSPF uses *areas* to define the parts of a network its routing decisions should affect. All other devices "belonging to" area 0 would receive this router's table. You'll also notice the use of an *inverse mask.* The inverse mask does not delineate the network and host portion of the address, as in a *subnet* mask. Rather, it defines what part of the network address (10.0.0.0) should be considered part of the area. A zero means it must match to be included in the area. Therefore, in this example, any address starting with 10 will be considered part of area 0.

Note in the following example configuration that there are two interfaces not currently configured:

```
router#show configuration
Using 2634 out of 129016 bytes
!
version 11.2
service password-encryption
no service udp-small-servers
no service tcp-small-servers
!
hostname router
!
boot system flash
enable secret 5 $1$XtLe$qObJLGEyCmyqeBvsUEdQl/
enable password 7 094047071C45131D0C0B0D79
!
interface Ethernet0
  ip address 10.1.1.1 255.255.255.0
  media-type 10BaseT
!
interface Ethernet1
  no ip address
  shutdown
!
interface TokenRing0
  ip address 10.1.11.2 255.255.255.0
  ring-speed 16
!
interface TokenRing1
  no ip address
  shutdown
!
router ospf 1
  network 10.0.0.0 0.255.255.255 area 0
!
ip http server
```

```
snmp-server community public RO
snmp-server community private RW
snmp-server host 10.1.1.13 password
!
line con 0
  exec-timeout 0 0
line aux 0
  transport input all
line vty 0 4
  exec-timeout 0 0
  password 7 051D1506734E4B
  login
!
end

router#
```

TESTING AND TROUBLESHOOTING

Once configured, a Cisco router should be tested to ensure that connectivity and performance are acceptable. There are many tools in the Cisco IOS to aid in the testing and troubleshooting of a router's functionality.

The show Command

The **show** command is perhaps the most powerful tool in the Cisco IOS, though it doesn't change a thing in the configuration. All it does is report on the state of the router or certain elements of the router. The following is an abridged list of **show** commands available from the enable mode prompt. (Your list may vary depending on your Cisco IOS version and your hardware.)

```
router#sh ?
access-lists     List access lists
 accounting      Accounting data for active sessions
 arp             ARP table
 async           Information on terminal lines used as router
                    interfaces
 bootflash       Boot Flash information
 calendar        Display the hardware calendar
 cdp             CDP information
 clock           Display the system clock
 compress        Show compression statistics
 configuration   Contents of Non-Volatile memory
```

```
controllers        Interface controller status
dlsw               Data Link Switching information
flash              System Flash information
frame-relay        Frame-Relay information
history            Display the session command history
hosts              IP domain-name, lookup style, nameservers,
                      and host table
interfaces         Interface status and configuration
ip                 IP information
line               TTY line information
location           Display the system location
logging            Show the contents of logging buffers
memory             Memory statistics
netbios-cache      NetBIOS name cache contents
ppp                PPP parameters and statistics
privilege          Show current privilege level
protocols          Active network routing protocols
registry           Function registry information
reload             Scheduled reload information
rmon               rmon statistics
route-map          route-map information
running-config     Current operating configuration
sessions           Information about Telnet connections
```

As you can see, even an abbreviated list has many options. You'll probably not use many of these initially, but over time and in the course of router and network management, you will likely use most if not all of them.

Ping

Ping testing is one good way to test connectivity. A ping is merely an echo—much like yelling across a canyon, but instead of sending sound waves through air and bouncing them off a distant solid object, pings are ICMP echo packets that are sent to a destination. When they arrive, they are returned to their origin along data lines. If the echo packets are successful, you can be sure of connectivity.

```
router#ping 10.1.14.2

Type escape sequence to abort.
Sending 5, 100-byte ICMP Echos to 10.1.14.2, timeout is 2 seconds:
!!!!!
Success rate is 100 percent (5/5),
   round-trip min/avg/max = 36/37/40 ms
router#
```

If, on the other hand, the pings do not come back, that signals a connectivity problem that should be further investigated. You might try pinging other local devices and the local interface to see where the connectivity issue is occurring.

```
router#ping 10.1.14.2

Type escape sequence to abort.
Sending 5, 100-byte ICMP Echos to 10.1.14.2, timeout is 2 seconds:
.....
Success rate is 0 percent (0/5)
router#
```

The show cdp neighbor Command

Cisco's discovery protocol is a valuable aid for determining which devices are adjacent. You use the following **show cdp neighbor** command:

```
router#sh cdp nei

Capability Codes: R - Router, T - Trans Bridge, B - Source
 Route Bridge  S - Switch, H - Host, I - IGMP, r - Repeater

Device ID  LocalIntrfce Holdtme Capability Platform    Port ID
vsitest4   Tok 0        136     R     4500        Tok 1
Switch1    Eth 1        155     S     WS-C2924M Fas   0/8
vsitest7   Tok 1        174     R     RSP2        Tok 6/0
router#
```

This example shows sample output from a **show cdp neighbor** command. It tells you that there are three adjacent devices advertising using **cdp**. It gives information about the port in the local router, and the port to which each interface is connected on the other end. Such information may be helpful in determining how an interface modification might affect the immediate neighboring devices in your network.

HTTP Server

Your router can be monitored or configured from a Web browser interface. Use the **ip http server** command to turn the router into a Web server of sorts. From virtually any Web browser, you can view some basic parameters as well as configure the device.

```
router(config)#ip http server
```

This command turns on the http server on the router. To view the router in a browser, enter the IP address or host name of this router in the URL line of the browser. You'll see something similar to Figure A-4.

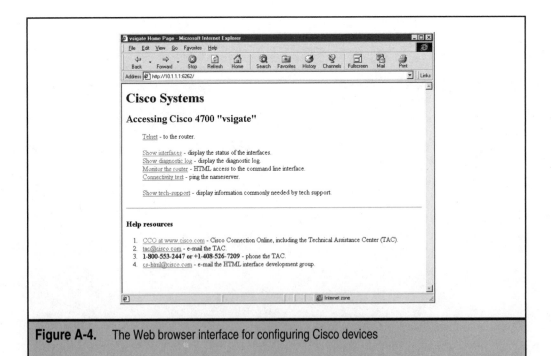

Figure A-4.   The Web browser interface for configuring Cisco devices

The http server interface allows you to interact with the router using a menu-driven interface. You can also use command-line functions and even Telnet from this interface. To disable the Web service, use the **no** form of the **http server** command:

```
router(config)#no ip http server
```

APPENDIX B

Map of the TCP/IP Protocol Suite

Transmission Control Protocol/Internet Protocol (TCP/IP) is a suite of protocols developed by the Department of Defense (DOD) to allow the connection of networks designed by different vendors. TCP/IP provides a common set of communication rules that support the delivery of basic services, including file transfer, e-mail, and remote login. TCP/IP can be used on a single LAN, or you can connect multiple LANs to form a network called an *internet* or *intranet*. In fact, TCP/IP is the protocol used to communicate on the World Wide Web (WWW).

This appendix provides a basic explanation of the evolution of the TCP/IP suite, and the position and role of popular protocols within the TCP/IP suite. The functions and properties of these protocols are illustrated in a condensed tutorial on how communication between two separate nodes is possible.

TCP/IP PROTOCOL SUITE

First, a little history: In the 1970s, it was becoming increasingly important to connect military computer systems that were using different hardware, operating systems, and network technologies. The Defense Advanced Research Projects Agency (DARPA), an agency of the United States Department of Defense, funded the research to determine a mechanism to resolve this connectivity problem.

A packet-switched network that provided communication among government agencies and military facilities was developed, called ARPANET. TCP/IP was implemented in the ARPANET and proved to be so successful that in 1983 the Office of the Secretary of Defense designated TCP/IP a network standard.

The TCP/IP protocol suite is the foundation that allows all connected hosts to communicate across a virtual network (internet) as if the hosts were part of a local network. The TCP/IP protocol suite is composed of several network protocols or rules that must be followed in order for data to be exchanged. TCP and IP are only two of the protocols within this suite, but they are the most important.

TCP/IP protocols are not only used on the Internet, but also widely employed to build private internets, which may or may not be connected to the global Internet. An internet used exclusively by one company is sometimes called an intranet.

Figure B-1 shows the layered architecture of the TCP/IP protocol suite.

TCP/IP's Documented Standards

TCP/IP protocols are defined by documents called Request for Comments (RFC). RFCs can be composed and submitted by anyone for approval. The RFC approval process is managed by the Internet Engineering Steering Group (IESG) based on recommendations from the Internet Engineering Task Force (IETF).

Not all RFCs specify TCP/IP standards. Some RFCs contain background information, hints for managing an internet, or descriptions of weaknesses in previous TCP/IP standards.

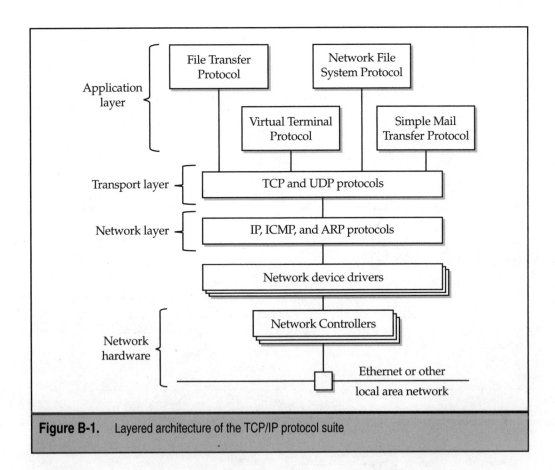

Figure B-1.   Layered architecture of the TCP/IP protocol suite

In the remainder of this appendix, RFCs for each of the protocols discussed are noted in the appropriate sections. The official RFC repository is the anonymous FTP archive maintained by the Information Sciences Institute of the University of California at ftp:// ftp.isi.edu/in-notes. The archive is reachable via the Web at http://www.rfc-editor.org.

OSI LAYERS AND PROTOCOLS

The most common model for describing data communications is the Open System Interconnection (OSI) model. This model was defined to provide a framework for examining the roles of each protocol within the TCP/IP suite. Each protocol of the TCP/IP suite belongs to a layer of the OSI model.

The OSI Model

The OSI model is based on a seven-layer architecture, each layer having a specific responsibility. Communication support services are provided from layers 1 through 4, and application support services from layers 5 through 7. Typically, layers 5 through 7 are only implemented in software closest to the end user. Figure B-2 illustrates the generic function of each layer and some questions that each layer might answer.

Each layer of the OSI model operates within the capabilities and limitations of the layers below it and provides services for the layers above it. As a Protocol Data Unit (PDU) is transferred through the network, it passes through all seven layers. Each layer adds a header to the PDU as it goes down the sending stack, and each layer removes a header as the PCU goes up the receiving stack. The OSI model has become the reference by which most protocols are compared.

TCP/IP in the OSI Model

The TCP/IP protocol suite specifically utilizes three layers of the OSI model: the network, transport, and application layers. Each of these layers provides services for the next layer and relies on services provided by the layers before it. The physical and data-link layers provide services for the network layer protocols, including TCP/IP. The TCP/IP layers are defined in Figure B-3.

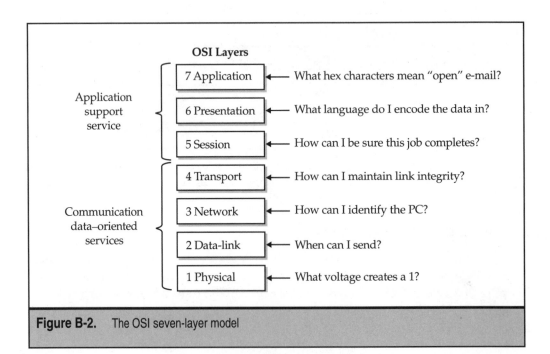

Figure B-2.   The OSI seven-layer model

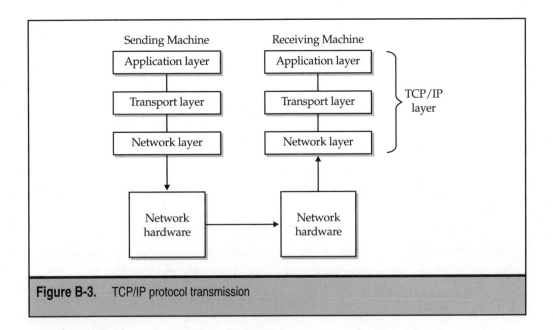

Figure B-3.   TCP/IP protocol transmission

Network Layer

One of the primary services supported by the network layer is the implementation of routable addresses. The network layer consists of two primary elements: the network, which provides routing information; and the host, which identifies the node within the network.

The network layer provides the following services for the transport layer:

▼   **Routing**   Geographical identification of destination

■   **Quality of Service**   Preferential treatment of specific traffic

■   **Segmenting**   Fragmentation of message to allow for transmission on various link services

▲   **Security**   Restriction of traffic to specific networks.

In TCP/IP, the Internet Protocol (IP) carries out the role of the network protocol. IP is discussed in more detail later in this appendix.

Transport Layer

The transport layer controls the quality and reliability of the data transmission. Packets are sequenced and acknowledged at this layer. The transport layer establishes a communication path with the destination node and can be responsible for end-to-end data integrity. This integrity is maintained by the ACK (acknowledge) and NAK (negative acknowledge) service. ACK is a message sent to respond to the preceding message arriving at its destination without error. NAK is a response to show receipt of a corrupted packet of information.

The sending transport node is primarily responsible for recovery from data loss. A timer is set for each message sent, and failure to respond within the set time results in re-transmission of the data.

User Datagram Protocol and Transmission Control Protocol are transport layer pro-tocols. These protocols are discussed in further detail later in this appendix.

Application Layer

This layer is the highest level in the protocol-layering model. The application layer is *not* the application itself that is doing the communication. The application layer provides the following services:

▼ Verification of other party's identification and availability

■ If appropriate, authentication of either the message sender or receiver, or both

■ Verification that resources necessary for communication exist

■ Negotiation of agreement at both ends regarding error recovery procedures, data integrity, and privacy

▲ Protocol and data syntax rules at the application level

Several protocols make up the application layer. Following are some of the more common ones:

Protocol	Function
Telnet	Provides remote login over the network
File Transfer Protocol (FTP)	Used to transfer files
Simple Mail Transfer Protocol (SMTP)	Used to deliver electronic mail
Domain Name System (DNS)	Maps host names to IP addresses
Routing Information Protocol (RIP)	Advertises routes to different subnets
Network File System (NFS)	Allows directories to be shared
Hypertext Transfer Protocol (HTTP)	The mechanism for WWW (World Wide Web)

Internet Protocol

Internet Protocol (IP), RFC 791, is the network layer protocol responsible for moving the packet of data from one machine to another. All other protocols in the suite rely on IP to provide the fundamental function of moving packets across an internet or the Internet.

IP is a very simple protocol that does not guarantee data delivery. It uses a "send and forget" theory; that is, after the data is sent, the protocol forgets it and doesn't look for any type of acknowledgment that it has been received.

IP *does*, however, care about the maximum size of a frame that can be carried on the medium. IP breaks large data packets down into a group of smaller data packets before transferring them. This activity is called *fragmentation,* and the packets are called *fragments*. The fragments are reassembled at the final destination.

Each packet includes an IP source and destination address, control information, and any actual data passed. When IP receives a packet, it compares the destination address with the routing table on a router. Packets are forwarded to the next destination (hop) based on the routing table. IP delivers packets with local addresses directly (local addresses being addresses on the same subnet). As the packet passes through the IP layer, an IP header is attached. A description of an IP header is shown in a following section.

Although IP is the most important protocol used for the Internet, there are also other protocols that are based on IP and supported on the Internet. These protocols include Internet Control Message Protocol, Address Resolution Protocol, and Reverse Address Resolution Protocol.

Internet Control Message Protocol (ICMP)

The Internet Control Message Protocol, RFC 792, provides the means for network devices to generate error messages, test packets, and informational messages related to IP. ICMP is basically IP's internal network management protocol and not intended for use by applications, but two well-known exceptions are the **ping** and **traceroute** diagnostic utilities:

▼   **Ping**   Sends and receives ICMP ECHO packets. The response packet can be taken as evidence that the target host is at least minimally active on the network.

▲   **Traceroute**   Sends UDP packets and tells you the route taken to the target host. (UDP is defined in an upcoming section.)

Address Resolution Protocol (ARP)

Address Resolution Protocol, RFC 826, translates a host's software address to the host's hardware address (data-link layer MAC address). When supported, broadcast frames are sent to obtain this information dynamically.

Reverse Address Resolution Protocol (RARP)

Reverse Address Resolution Protocol, RFC 903, translates a host's hardware address (data-link layer MAC address) to the host's software address. RARP is typically used to let a piece of diskless equipment discover its own IP address as part of its boot procedure. However, RARP is rarely used by modern equipment and has been replaced with BOOTP (a UDP protocol, defined shortly).

Transmission Control Protocol

The Transmission Control Protocol (TCP), RFC 793, is a transport layer protocol that provides a reliable service between two endpoints on an intranet or internet, depending on IP to move the packets. Since IP is inherently unreliable, TCP protects against data loss, data corruption, packet reordering, and data duplication. TCP is a *connection-oriented* protocol—data will not be transferred until the destination host accepts the connection request.

TCP also supports *windowing*. Unlike traditional connection-oriented services that use ACK and NAK services, windowing allows the sender to send multiple TCP segments one at a time before receiving an acknowledgment. Windowing helps to reduce traffic by reducing the number of acknowledgment packets.

TCP uses port numbers to identify applications running in the sending and receiving machines. Each TCP-defined protocol has an associated port or port numbers assigned to it. A list of common TCP and UDP protocols and their port numbers can be found at the following Web site: http://www.isi.edu/in-notes/iana/assignments/port-numbers.

The following sections describe application layer protocols that use TCP for reliable data transport.

Hypertext Transfer Protocol (HTTP)

The HTTP protocol, RFC 2068, is the network protocol used to deliver HTML files, image files, query results, and virtually any other file on the World Wide Web (WWW). HTTP also transmits resources or information identified by a Universal Resource Locator (URL)—for example, www.velte.com.

A browser such as Netscape Navigator or Microsoft Windows Explorer is an HTTP client because it sends requests to an HTTP server (Web server), which then sends responses back to the client. The default port for HTTP servers to listen on is port 80, although other ports can be used.

File Transfer Protocol (FTP)

The FTP protocol, RFC 1415, allows a user to log into a remote host and perform file operations such as listing directories and copying, renaming, or deleting files.

FTP requires two separate connections between a client and a server. The first connection is established when the client establishes an initial connection with the server and the server requests a username and password. The second connection is opened when the client requests operations from the server.

FTP supports most popular file formats, including ASCII and binary. Port numbers 20 and 21 are used by the FTP protocol.

Telnet

Telnet, RFC 818, provides a virtual terminal protocol to allow users on one host to access another host; users work as terminal users of that remote host. The Telnet server accepts data from the Telnet client and forwards it to the operating system. Responses generated by the server operating system are passed back to the Telnet client for display. Telnet uses port 23.

User Datagram Protocol (UDP)

The User Datagram Protocol (UDP), RFC 768, is a *connectionless* protocol that transports data to or from the application layer (again relying on IP to move the packets). UDP requires minimal overhead due to its lack of protection against datagram loss or duplication. UDP does not guarantee that the datagram will be delivered, that it will be delivered in the same order it was sent, or that the datagram will not be duplicated. For this reason, UDP should not be used in applications that require orderly and reliable data transport. As with TCP, UDP also uses port numbers to identify applications running in the sending and receiving machines. The following sections describe application layer protocols that use UDP.

Simple Network Management Protocol (SNMP)

Simple Network Management Protocol (SNMP), RFC 1441, provides a means of monitoring and managing systems over a network. SNMP defines a method of sending queries (GETs) and commands (SETs) from a management station client to an agent server running on the target system, and collecting responses and event notifications. SNMP can monitor various statistics or usage counters, collectively called the Management Information Base (MIB). SNMP uses port 161.

Bootstrap Protocol

The Bootstrap Protocol (BOOTP), RFC 1395, is implemented with both client and server software, which is used to request IP configuration information. BOOTP was designed for manual preconfiguration of the host information in a server database, while DHCP (described just below) allows for dynamic allocation of network addresses and configurations to newly attached hosts. BOOTP uses ports 67 and 68.

Dynamic Host Configuration Protocol (DHCP)

The Dynamic Host Configuration Protocol (DHCP), RFCs 2131 and 2132, is the standard method to automatically assign IP addresses. This automated process simplifies IP address management.

Like BOOTP, DHCP runs over UDP and uses ports 67 and 68. DHCP requires both client and server software compatibility in order to assign IP configuration information. The client issues a broadcast on startup of the IP protocol stack. The DHCP server examines the source MAC address of the workstation (contained in the broadcast). An IP address is then pulled from the DHCP server's pool of IP addresses and assigned to that MAC address. A DHCP server can assign addresses as follows:

▼ **Automatically**   Permanently assigns an IP address to a single workstation

■ **Dynamically**   Assigns an IP address to a workstation only for a predetermined time frame and then releases the IP address back to the pool

▲ **Manually**   Uses DHCP only to allow administrators to manually assign IP addresses (rarely used)

Trivial File Transfer Protocol (TFTP)

Trivial File Transfer Protocol (TFTP), RFC 1350, is a simple file-transfer protocol used for downloading boot code to diskless workstations. It is similar to FTP, except it is based on UDP and uses a limited set of commands. TFTP uses port 69. Most Cisco devices can use TFTP to download configuration files.

INSIDE THE INTERNET PROTOCOL PACKET

An IP packet is a logical grouping of information at the network layer that includes headers from the previous layers; the headers contain control information and user data. A *frame* is a series of bytes of data encapsulated with a header at the data-link layer. Each protocol type (Ethernet, Frame Relay, and so on) has a slightly different frame and thus a different packet structure. For simplicity here, we will define the Ethernet TCP/IP frame.

Structure of an Ethernet TCP/IP Frame

An Ethernet TCP/IP frame consists of the elements illustrated and defined as follows:

Preamble	Destination Address	Source Address	Type	IP	TCP	Data	FCS
8	6	6	2				4

Frame Element	Purpose
Preamble field	An 8-octet field that is used to allow the physical layer circuitry to reach its steady state synchronization within the received frame timing.
Address fields	Contains the Source and Destination addresses. These addresses can be individual addresses, group addresses, or broadcast addresses.
Length field	A 2-octet field whose value indicates the number of LLC (Logical Link Control) data octets in the data field.
IP	See the following section, "IP Header."
TCP	See the upcoming section "TCP Header."
Data	Contains the data being transferred.
Frame check sequence (FCS)	Provides error checking on received frames.

IP Header

When an IP packet passes through the network layer, a header is attached. The fields in an IP header are illustrated and defined as follows:

Ver	IHL	Type of Service	Total Length	
Identifer			Flags	Fragment Offset
Time to Live		Protocol	Header Checksum	
Source Address				
Destination Address				
Options + Padding				

IP Header
(minimum length = 20 octets)

Header Field	Field Contents
Ver	Version number
IHL	Internet header length
Type of Service	Specifies any precedence, delay, throughput, and/or reliability parameters
Total Length	Total length of the IP datagram
Identifier	Unique number to identify this datagram
Flags	Indicates if fragmentation is permitted/used
Fragment Offset	Indicates where each fragmented piece fits
Time to Live	Time to live in gateway (hops or seconds)
Protocol	Identifies the protocol that follows IP (TCP or UDP)
Header Checksum	Validation number that each gateway may or may not compute
Source Address	IP address of source
Destination Address	IP address of destination
Options+ and Padding	Ensures header is correct bit size

TCP Header

Once the IP packet passes through the network layer, it then goes through the transport layer. The transport layer, too, attaches a header to the IP packet. The fields in a TCP header are illustrated and defined as follows:

Source Port	Destination Port	
Sequence Number		
Acknowledgement Number		
Offset	Reserved	U A P R S F	Window	
Checksum	Urgent Pointer	
Options + Padding		

TCP header

TCP Header
(minimum length = 20 octets)

Header Field	Field Contents
Source Port	Port number of the source
Destination Port	Port number of the destination port
Sequence Number	Number to ensure the correct order
Acknowledgement Number	Attached to the acknowledgment data
Data Offset	Number of 32-bit words in the TCP header
Reserved	Set to zero
Flags	Control functions, such as the setup and termination of a session, expedited or urgent data flow, reset of a connection, or indication of the end of the data
Window	Number of octets (beginning with 1 in the acknowledgment field) the sender is willing to accept
Checksum	Points to the first octet that follows the urgent data and allows the receiver to determine how much urgent data is coming
Options and Padding	Ensures header is correct bit size

APPENDIX C

The Road to Certification

The idea of using certification as a way to validate an individual's proficiency level is not a new one. Your driver's license proves you have been tested and pronounced able to drive a car on the public roads. A teacher must be certified in a particular state in order to teach there. The IT industry may someday settle on—indeed, is striving to create—a set of standards. But for now, we must rely on vendor-specific certification standards.

There are various reasons to become certified, but for most of us it's a way to distinguish ourselves among peers and affirm to employers that we are knowledgeable in our field and proficient in our skills. In turn, we expect better positions and increased pay. The shortage of skilled IT professionals in the marketplace has created an immense vacuum in the IT workforce. Employers who can normally pick and choose from among the most qualified candidates available are increasingly looking for evidence of qualification outside of formal education and even without substantial accompanying experience. Certification enables many candidates to qualify and obtain the positions available in this growing field.

Microsoft and Cisco Systems, in need of a wider labor force to support their increasingly complex systems, have designed certification models to assist IT managers in hiring qualified personnel. In turn, waves of professionals are entering the workforce with expertise in Microsoft and Cisco products and services. There is quite a difference in the way these two corporate giants present and promote their respective certification processes. First, we'll take a look at the simpler of the two systems: Microsoft's. Then we'll examine Cisco's wide range of certification possibilities.

MICROSOFT CERTIFICATIONS

Windows NT and 9x hold a large share of the corporate desktop OS market, and the company shows no signs of retreating from its position. Microsoft's Certified Professional (MCP) program, particularly the Microsoft Certified Systems Engineer (MCSE) certification, has become a benchmark in the IT job-seeking world. All of the Microsoft certifications are designed to show proficiency in Microsoft operating systems and applications.

The program offers several varieties of professional endorsement, from the single-test MCP to the nine-test Microsoft Certified Systems Engineer + Internet endorsement. Microsoft Certified Professionals are required to pass any one of the Microsoft certification exams current as of October 1, 1998 (a "current" exam is one that has not been retired). *The exception is Exam 70-058: Networking Essentials, which does not apply toward MCP certification.* If you really want some clout in the IT world, however, set your sights on the MCSE or the advanced MCSE+I.

NOTE: If you plan to work through one of the Microsoft certification processes, you'll want to pay frequent visits to Microsoft's Web site at http://www.microsoft.com/mcp/. Here you'll find plenty of information to help plan your course of action. It's important to verify that a test you plan to take is not only valid, but will earn you credit toward your certification of choice. The Web site will help you answer these questions. Many other Internet sources are available, as well, to help you along the way. Try www.cramsession.com and www.braindumps.com if you're looking for a place where you can share study ideas and exam experiences with other examinees.

Testing Options

Sylvan Prometric, a company that specializes in testing, administers Microsoft certification exams (as well as Cisco's written exams). As of December, 1999, the tests cost $100 (U.S.) each. Call Sylvan Prometric at (800) 755-3926 when you feel you're ready to take an exam. The company will direct you to the nearest testing location and help you schedule your certification exam. Online registration is also available, at www.prometric.com.

Microsoft has traditionally opted for standard testing processes, using a 40-to-100-question multiple-choice format. Recently, however, *adaptive* testing has grown in popularity. In a nutshell, adaptive testing takes advantage of a "smart" testing process that can determine from the answers to 15–25 questions how an examinee would perform in the full 40–100 question format. The examinee is given a series of questions, each more difficult than the preceding one. As the test progresses, the test engine can extrapolate by degrees of difficulty how an examinee would fare if answering the full allotment of 40–100 questions. If you have the option, take advantage of the adaptive format; these exams are shorter, and many people report that they are easier to pass.

You need not take the exams in any particular order. Some of the tests, however, assume knowledge in another testing area; for example, the exam for Implementing and Supporting NT Server 4.0 in the Enterprise assumes knowledge of Implementing and Supporting NT Server 4.0. It can be beneficial to schedule your tests in some order, perhaps even taking related tests on the same day. Start with the ones you're most comfortable with, and work your way toward the more difficult ones. You may even want to take Networking Essentials first, to ensure you have a grasp of the technologies that you'll encounter in many of the other tests. (If your goal is simply to earn MCP status, you may elect to skip Networking Essentials, which doesn't count toward MCP certification.)

Certification Requirements

The requirements for each of the Microsoft certifications are different, although there is some overlap. On the way to one certification, you are allowed to obtain a lesser certification. For instance, you will earn your MCP on the road to your MCSE. This section describes the basic requirements for several Microsoft certifications.

▼ **MCP** Microsoft Certified Professionals are required to pass any one Microsoft certification exam current as of October 1, 1998, except for Exam 70-058: Networking Essentials.

■ **MCP +I** This requires 70-059 (Internetworking with Microsoft TCP/IP on Windows NT 4.0), 70-067 (Implementing and Supporting NT Server 4.0), and *either* 70-077 (Internet Information Server 3.0) or 70-087 (Internet Information Server 4.0).

▲ **MCSE** The MCSE certification exams are divided into two sections: Core and Elective. Microsoft has two tracks, NT 3.51 and NT 4.0. However, because the NT 3.51 track contains many tests that have been retired, and is no longer being pursued, we will concentrate only on the NT 4.0 track.

MCSE Exams

The MCSE NT 4.0 track has four mandatory core tests and two electives, for a total of six tests.

MCSE CORE EXAMS These consist of NT 4.0 Server, Server in the Enterprise, Networking Essentials, and your choice of client operating systems. Choose four of the following:

▼ **Exam 70-067:** Implementing and Supporting Microsoft Windows NT Server 4.0

■ **Exam 70-068:** Implementing and Supporting Microsoft Windows NT Server 4.0 in the Enterprise

■ **Exam 70-030:** Microsoft Windows 3.1 (retired)
or
Exam 70-048: Microsoft Windows for Workgroups 3.11 (retired)
or
Exam 70-064: Implementing and Supporting Microsoft Windows 95 (An acceptable alternative to this exam is certification in retired Exam 70-063: Implementing and Supporting Microsoft Windows 95.)
or
Exam 70-073: Microsoft Windows NT Workstation 4.0
or
Exam 70-098: Implementing and Supporting Microsoft Windows 98

▲ **Exam 70-058:** Networking Essentials (An acceptable alternative to this exam is certification in retired Exam 70-046: Networking with Microsoft Windows for Workgroups 3.11, or retired Exam 70-047: Networking with Microsoft Windows 3.1.)

Notice that you can choose among three different operating systems. The fourth option, Windows for Workgroups 3.11, has been retired. If an exam has been retired, you cannot take that test as part of your certification process. If, however, you've already taken and passed these retired tests, it's possible that, for now, you may not be required to take another, current exam to stay certified. This varies from test to test and is at the discretion of Microsoft. Current details on retired exams can be found at the Microsoft MCP Web site.

Microsoft generally gives fair notice of their plans to retire a particular test so that you can select a more contemporary topic.

MCSE ELECTIVE EXAMS   The MCSE certification also requires two elective exams from the following options.

NOTE: Some qualifying exams in this list have more than one alternative. Even if you complete more than one of these alternatives, only one will qualify as an MCSE elective. You must take two elective exams, each from a different subject.

- ▼ **Exam 70-013:** Implementing and Supporting Microsoft SNA Server 3.0
   or
   Exam 70-085: Implementing and Supporting Microsoft SNA Server 4.0

- ■ **Exam 70-018:** Implementing and Supporting Microsoft Systems Management Server 1.2
   or
   Exam 70-086: Implementing and Supporting Microsoft Systems Management Server 2.0

- ■ **Exam 70-019:** Designing and Implementing Data Warehouses with Microsoft SQL Server 7.0

- ■ **Exam 70-021:** Microsoft SQL Server 4.2 Database Implementation (Scheduled to be retired.)
   or
   Exam 70-027: Implementing a Database Design on Microsoft SQL Server 6.5
   or
   Exam 70-029: Designing and Implementing Databases with Microsoft SQL Server 7.0

- ■ **Exam 70-022:** Microsoft SQL Server 4.2 Database Administration for Microsoft Windows NT (Scheduled to be retired.)
   or
   Exam 70-026: System Administration for Microsoft SQL Server 6.5
   or
   Exam 70-028: Administering Microsoft SQL Server 7.0

- ■ **Exam 70-037:** Microsoft Mail for PC Networks 3.2-Enterprise (retired)

- ■ **Exam 70-053:** Internetworking Microsoft TCP/IP on Microsoft Windows NT (3.5–3.51)

or

Exam 70-059: Internetworking with Microsoft TCP/IP on Microsoft Windows NT 4.0

■ **Exam 70-056:** Implementing and Supporting Web Sites Using Microsoft Site Server 3.0

■ **Exam 70-075:** Implementing and Supporting Microsoft Exchange Server 4.0 (retired)

or

Exam 70-076: Implementing and Supporting Microsoft Exchange Server 5

or

Exam 70-081: Implementing and Supporting Microsoft Exchange Server 5.5

■ **Exam 70-077:** Implementing and Supporting Microsoft Internet Information Server 3.0 and Microsoft Index Server 1.1

or

Exam 70-087: Implementing and Supporting Microsoft Internet Information Server 4.0

■ **Exam 70-078:** Implementing and Supporting Microsoft Proxy Server 1.0

or

Exam 70-088: Implementing and Supporting Microsoft Proxy Server 2.0

▲ **Exam 70-079:** Implementing and Supporting Microsoft Internet Explorer 4.0 by using the Internet Explorer Administration Kit

MCSE+I

The MCSE+I certification, Microsoft's pinnacle of certification, is similar to the MCSE except that it comprises seven core tests and two electives.

NOTE: Some of the MCSE subjects also qualify as core exams for the MCSE+I, so careful planning may save you some steps. The following MCSE elective exams are also core exams for MCSE+I: Internetworking with Microsoft TCP/IP (#70-059), Internet Information Server 3.0 or 4.0 (#70-077 and #70-087), or Implementing and Supporting Microsoft Explorer 4.0 (#70-079).

MCSE+INTERNET CORE EXAMS   The MCSE+I core exams consist of the same four subjects listed as core exams for the MCSE, plus exams on Internet Information Server, Internet Explorer, and TCP/IP. Choose seven from the following options.

▼ **Exam 70-058:** Networking Essentials

■ **Exam 70-059:** Internetworking with Microsoft TCP/IP on Microsoft Windows NT 4.0

■ **Exam 70-064:** Implementing and Supporting Microsoft Windows 95
or
Exam 70-073: Implementing and Supporting Microsoft Windows NT
Workstation 4.0
or
Exam 70-098: Implementing and Supporting Microsoft Windows 98

■ **Exam 70-067:** Implementing and Supporting Microsoft Windows NT Server 4.0

■ **Exam 70-068:** Implementing and Supporting Microsoft Windows NT Server 4.0
in the Enterprise

■ **Exam 70-077:** Implementing and Supporting Microsoft Internet Information
Server 3.0 and Microsoft Index Server 1.1
or
Exam 70-087: Implementing and Supporting Microsoft Internet Information
Server 4.0

▲ **Exam 70-079:** Implementing and Supporting Microsoft Internet Explorer 4.0 by
using the Internet Explorer Administration Kit

MCSE+INTERNET ELECTIVE EXAMS   The MCSE+Internet certification also requires two
electives from the options that follow. As is the case with all Microsoft certification exams, more than one application version may be offered (see Administering Microsoft
SQL Server 6.5 and 7.0 in the following list); however, if both were passed, only one
would count toward certification. As a rule, take the most recent version of the exam.

▼ **Exam 70-026:** Administering Microsoft SQL Server 6.5
or
Exam 70-028: Administering Microsoft SQL Server 7.0

■ **Exam 70-027:** Implementing a Database Design on Microsoft SQL Server 6.5
or
Exam 70-029: Designing and Implementing Databases with Microsoft SQL
Server 7.0

■ **Exam 70-056:** Implementing and Supporting Web Sites Using Microsoft Site
Server 3.0

■ **Exam 70-076:** Implementing and Supporting Microsoft Exchange Server 5
or
Exam 70-081: Implementing and Supporting Microsoft Exchange Server 5.5

■ **Exam 70-078:** Implementing and Supporting Microsoft Proxy Server 1.0
or
Exam 70-088: Implementing and Supporting Microsoft Proxy Server 2.0

▲ **Exam 70-085:** Implementing and Supporting Microsoft SNA Server 4.0

Testing Strategies

There are many different ways to tackle the Microsoft certification testing process. With careful planning, you can minimize the amount of time and money spent. Here are some tips that may help:

▼ Make out your own certification schedule and stick with it. It helps to keep the material fresh in your mind!

■ The Networking Essentials test covers core networking concepts and terminology, so it really is "essential" to take this exam early (if not first) in your certification quest. Not only will it give you the basis for understanding key networking ideas, but it will make the rest of the exams much easier.

■ When scheduling exams, keep in mind the tests that contain similar objectives and material. Administering NT Server and Administering NT Server in the Enterprise cover many of the same configurations and concepts, so it may make sense for you to take both of these exams on the same day.

■ If you have decided to work toward the MCSE+Internet certification or are even thinking that you might, it's a good idea to choose two electives for the MCSE certification that also count as MCSE+I core exams. You'll save time and money.

■ Whenever possible, take the adaptive format of the exams. This shorter format has proven very accurate and will save you time. If you do opt for the adaptive format, however, be sure to focus on the questions one at a time; you won't be allowed to go back and change an answer to a previous question.

■ Take the exams when you feel comfortable. If you're not sure you're ready, you probably aren't. Also, try to schedule the exams at a time of the day when you feel most alert and energetic. If you're not a morning person, take your exams later in the day.

▲ Cramming until 3:00 A.M. for an 8:00 A.M. exam will probably only hurt your score. Get some rest.

CISCO CERTIFICATIONS

Cisco is the worldwide leader in network access products. Cisco routers, hubs, and switches connect more computers in today's LANs and WANs than any other manufacturer's hardware. The explosive growth of this company has spurred increased demand for talented engineers to design and configure network devices. Cisco has a certification program to address this demand.

Figure C-1 illustrates the two families of Cisco certification: *Network Support* and *Network Design*. Network Support certification focuses on technical support for the wide

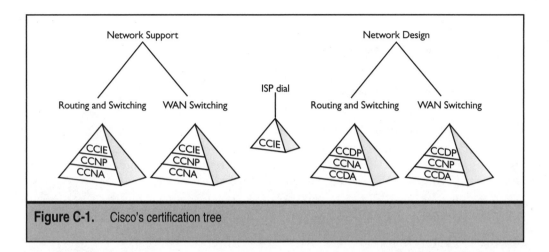

Figure C-1. Cisco's certification tree

range of Cisco devices and software running under traditional LAN and WAN technologies. Network Design certification, on the other hand, concentrates more on the design side of internetworking, emphasizing decision-making skills pertaining to designing networks using Cisco architecture.

Each of these two certification families is further divided into two sections: Routing and Switching, and WAN Switching. Let's take a look at the two families and their respective stepping-stone certifications.

Network Support: Routing and Switching

The Network Support/Routing and Switching certification track concentrates on an engineer's ability to design, configure, and support traditional Cisco-based networks that predominantly include LAN and WAN routers and LAN switches. This track has three levels of achievement: CCNA, CCNP, and CCIE.

Cisco Certified Network Associate (CCNA)

The CCNA is the first level of certification in the Routing and Switching track. To become a CCNA specializing in Routing and Switching, you take the Cisco written exam #640-407. You'll need to be proficient in Internetworking Technologies, Cisco Routing and Switching, and Router Configuration, as well as have significant hands-on experience. Cisco offers two options of recommended training for this certification. Both options are viable ways to train for CCNA certification; choose the option that suits you best.

Option 1

▼ Internetworking Technologies Multimedia (ITM)

▲ Cisco Routing and LAN Switching (CRLS)

Option 2

- ▼ Internetworking Technologies Multimedia (ITM)
- ■ Introduction to Cisco Router Configuration (ICRC)
- ▲ High-Performance Solutions for Desktop Connectivity (HPSDC)

Cisco Certified Network Professional (CCNP)

The CCNP certification is between the CCNA and the CCIE on the Routing and Switching track, and the CCNA certification is a prerequisite to CCNP. To earn CCNP certification, candidates are required to pass two to four exams.

Test Track 1

- ▼ Foundation R/S Exam #640-409
- ▲ CIT Exam #640-440

Test Track 2

- ▼ ACRC Exam #640-403
- ■ CLSC Exam #640-404
- ■ CMTD Exam #640-405
- ▲ CIT Exam #640-440

Upon completion of the CCNP certification, you may elect to study for a Cisco Career Specialization. These are a subset of the CCNP objectives and focus on specific skill sets for today's increasingly demanding networks. Five new specialties have been added, as listed in Table C-1.

Cisco Certified Internetwork Expert (CCIE)

The CCIE certification is the core of the Cisco certification program. A candidate for the CCIE must have a solid background in internetworking. For Routing and Switching CCIE certification, you must first pass the two-hour written CCIE-R/S Qualification Exam #350-001 administered by Sylvan Prometric. Then you must pass a two-day, hands-on lab exam that pits you against difficult build, break, and restore scenarios. You are only allowed a certain amount of time between passing the written exam and attempting the Lab exam, so plan carefully.

NOTE: To maintain an active CCIE status, CCIEs must complete a recertification requirement every two years.

Cisco offers and recommends training courses for the CCIE certification. Although these courses aren't required, don't pass them by without consideration. Both training

Specialization	Description
Security	Focuses on skills required in building and maintaining Cisco security solutions, including stand-alone firewalls and Cisco IOS software features.
Voice Access	Concentrates on the skills required to implement and support data/voice integration at the network access level. Some solutions include IP, ATM, and Frame Relay uplink access.
Network Management	Focuses on the skills needed to support network management solutions for routing and LAN-switching networks found in many enterprises.
LAN ATM	Builds skills designed for creating and maintaining campus ATM networks based on LAN emulation over ATM switches.
SNA Solutions	Focuses on the skills needed to install, configure, and troubleshoot Cisco routers in an SNA environment.

Table C-1.   Cisco Career Specializations

and study are highly recommended, but Cisco warns that experience is the number one factor when it comes to successfully completing the CCIE program.

Realizing that many candidates lack the resources to train effectively, Cisco sponsors practice labs. Unfortunately, there are only a limited number of these helpful labs available around the U.S., and the cost per day is a hefty $1,000 (U.S.). Also, in order to utilize the labs, you must have already passed the CCIE qualification written exam. Visit Cisco's Web site for a current listing of the labs.

Candidates are not required to earn Associate (CCNA) or Professional (CCNP) status before attempting to become a CCIE; however, these intermediate certificates are designed to act as stepping stones that confirm your relative expertise.

Network Support: WAN Switching

This career track concentrates on the skills required to manage WAN switched networks. Some of the skills needed are

▼ Frame Relay and ATM

■ Cisco-specific technologies such as WAN switch platforms, applications, architecture, and interfaces

▲ Service provider technologies, including packet encapsulations and network-to-network interconnections

The processes for the WAN Switching option are similar to that of the Routing and Switching track. Here are the differences.

Cisco Certified Network Associate (CCNA)

Cisco recommends the following training for the CCNA certification for WAN Switching:

▼ WAN Quick Start (WQS)

▲ Installation of Cisco WAN Switches (ICWS)

The exam for the WAN Switching CCNA is CCNA-WAN Sw Exam #640-410.

Cisco Certified Network Professional (CCNP)

CCNA certification is a prerequisite for the CCNP. Here are the training and testing options offered for the WAN Switching CCNP:

Training Option 1

▼ Multiband Switch and Service Configuration (MSSC)

■ BPX Switch and Service Configuration (BSSC)

■ MGX ATM Concentrator Configuration (MACC)

▲ Cisco StrataView Plus Installation and Operations (SVIO)

Testing Option 1

▼ MSSC Exam #640-419

■ BSSC Exam #640-425

■ MACC Exam #640-411

▲ SVIO Exam #640-451

Training Option 2

▼ WAN Switch and Services Configuration (WSSC)

■ MGX ATM Concentrator Configuration

▲ Cisco StrataView Plus Installation and Operations (SVIO)

Testing Option 2

▼ WSSC Exam #640-412

■ MACC Exam #640-411

▲ SVIO Exam #640-451

Cisco Certified Internetwork Expert (CCIE)

Although there is no certification prerequisite to the WAN Switching CCIE, Cisco strongly recommends that a candidate have earned the CCNP-WAN Switching certification. This, along with significant hands-on experience, will prepare you for CCIE-WAN Sw Qualification Exam #350-007. After you've passed this exam, a two-hour lab exam is required.

Network Design: Routing and Switching

The Routing and Switching certification track concentrates on an engineer's ability to design and configure traditional Cisco-based networks that predominantly include LAN and WAN routers and LAN switches.

Cisco Certified Design Associate (CCDA)

For training, Cisco recommends Designing Cisco Networks (DCN). The exam is DCN Exam #640-441.

Cisco Certified Network Associate (CCNA)

Training and testing is the same as the CCNA certification in the Network Support family.

Cisco Certified Design Professional (CCDP)

The CCNA and CCDA are prerequisites for the CCDP certification. Cisco offers the following training along with two testing tracks.

Training

▼ Advanced Cisco Routing and Configuration (ACRC)

■ Cisco LAN Switch Configuration (CLSC)

■ Configuring, Monitoring, Troubleshooting, and Dial-up Services (CMTD)

▲ Cisco Internetwork Design

Test Track 1

▼ Foundation R/S Exam #640-409

▲ CID Exam #640-025

Test Track 2

▼ ACRC Exam #640-403

■ CLSC Exam #640-404

■ CMTD Exam #640-405

▲ CID Exam #640-025

Network Design: WAN Switching

This career track concentrates on the skills required to design WAN switched networks.

Cisco Certified Network Associate (CCNA)

Training and testing for Network Design CCNA WAN Switching certification are the same as for Network Support CCNA WAN Switching.

Cisco Certified Network Professional (CCNP)

Training and testing for the Network Design CCNP WAN Switching certification are the same as for Network Support CCNP WAN Switching.

Cisco Certified Design Professional (CCDP)

The CCNA-WAN Switching and the CCNP-WAN Switching certifications are prerequisites for the CCDP-WAN Switching certification. Cisco offers DSWVS Exam #640-413 for certification. There is no lab exam required.

CCIE ISP-Dial

There is a CCIE certification for ISP-Dial. This CCIE certification has the following training and testing options:

Training

▼ Installing and Maintaining Cisco Routers (IMCR)

■ Cisco Internetwork Design (CID)

■ Managing Cisco Network Security (MCNS)

■ Cisco AS5200 Universal Access Server (AS5200)

▲ Significant experience

Testing

▼ CCIE-ISP Dial Qualification Exam #350-004

▲ CCIE-ISP Dial Certification Laboratory

Cisco Career Certifications Exams

Table C-2 summarizes all the Cisco certification exams.

Exam No.	Exam Name
640-403	ACRC 11.3, Advanced Cisco Router Configuration
640-425	BSSC 2.1, BPX Switch and Service Configuration
640-446	CATM 2.0, Campus ATM Solutions
640-410	CCNA WAN Switching
640-407	CCNA 1.0, Cisco Certified Network Associate
640-025	CID 3.0, Cisco Internetwork Design
640-440	CIT 4.0, Cisco Internetwork Troubleshooting
640-404	CLSC 1.0, Cisco LAN Switch Configuration
640-405	CMTD 8.0, Configuring, Monitoring, & Troubleshooting Dial-up Services
640-416	CSVIM 1.0, Cisco StrataView Plus Installation and Maintenance
640-417	CSVNO 1.0, Cisco StrataView Plus Network Operations
640-447	CVOICE 1.0 Cisco Voiceover Frame Relay ATM and IP
640-422	CSVP 1.0, Cisco StrataView Plus (retired 11/99)
640-441	DCN 1.0, Designing Cisco Networks
640-413	DSWVS 2.0, Designing Switched WAN Voice Solutions
640-409	FRS 1.0, Foundation Routing and Switching
640-411	MACC 4.0, MGX ATM Concentrator Configuration
640-443	MCRI 1.0, Managing Cisco Routed Internetworks
640-444	MCSI 3.0, Managing Cisco Switched Internetworks
640-419	MSSC 8.5, Multiband Switch and Service Configuration
640-445	SNAM, SNA Configuration for Multiprotocol Administrators

Table C-2.   Cisco's Written Exams

APPENDIX D

Getting Help: Cisco and Windows Resources

T he world of computers and networking can be very complicated. There will be times when you need help with your Cisco and Windows NT/2000 problems. This appendix lists some excellent resources.

In the case of NT/2000, solutions can be found through user groups and newsgroups, or through Internet or database searches. Cisco, on the other hand, provides a detailed level of assistance through their Web site, but external support such as user groups and newsgroups is hard to come by.

MICROSOFT ONLINE HELP

Microsoft Online Help helps eliminate paper clutter by providing access to your system's documentation with a few simple keystrokes. This documentation is installed on your Windows system and easily accessible through the Internet, as well. Online help is integrated into many Microsoft applications.

You can also find online help at the command prompt; in the locally installed HTML, .TXT, .PDF, .DOC, and other file types; and through the Windows NT/2000 help menus.

Help Books

When you're looking for help, go first to the *global help books* shown in Figure D-1 (click Help on the Start menu). These books contain highly detailed information on many subjects. You can search for a keyword using the Index tab, or ordinary words using the Search tab.

Command-Line Help

Sometimes you need help information in deeper detail, or maybe you don't want to traverse the help books' hierarchical organization to find your topic. You can get immediate information on specific Windows NT/2000 commands by using the **help** command at the command prompt. Simply type **help** followed by the command you want to look up; for example, here's how to get help about the **help** command itself:

```
C:\>help help
```

Not all commands are supported by the **help** command, however. To get a list of commands that are supported, type **help** without any arguments. When you need information about a command that's not on the supported list, type that command at the command line, followed by **/?**. In nearly all cases, this will give you a listing of how to use the command and its arguments.

Some commands (such as **ping**, **tracert**, and **telnet**) expect an address or other argument to follow the command, so they attempt to resolve the **/?** and report an error. For these commands, enter **-?** right after the command. For example, let's say we want help

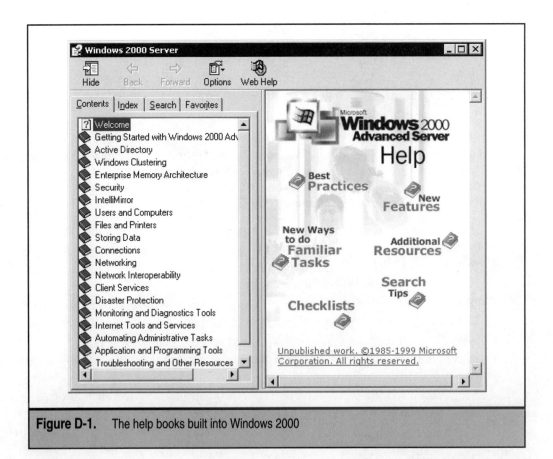

Figure D-1.   The help books built into Windows 2000

on the **tracert** command. Here is what happens when you type **help tracert**, then **tracert /?**, and finally **tracert -?**:

```
E:\>help tracert
This command is not supported by the help utility. Try "tracert /?".

E:\>tracert /?
Unable to resolve target system name /?.

E:\>tracert -?

Usage: tracert [-d] [-h maximum_hops] [-j host-list] [-w timeout]
    target_name

Options:
```

```
-d                    Do not resolve addresses to host names.
-h maximum_hops       Maximum number of hops to search for target.
-j host-list          Loose source route along host-list.
-w timeout            Wait timeout milliseconds for each reply.
```

Additional Documentation Files

Many applications include locally installed documentation ("help") files. These files may be installed automatically or selected for installation during the application's installation routine. Access is usually via an icon or menu selection in the application's program group. If you don't see an obvious path to these files, you can find them by searching the application's installation or working directories for filenames with the following extensions:

▼ **HTM, HTML**   HyperText Markup Language files, viewable using a Web browser.

■ **TXT, ASC**   ASCII-based text files, which typically include version-specific information and specific installation issues.

■ **DOC**   Microsoft Word-based files typically contain the same information as TXT and ASC doc files, and may also include full application documentation.

■ **WRI**   Microsoft Write–based files—another source of version-specific information and specific installation issues.

■ **PDF**   Sometimes these Adobe Acrobat files are used for version-specific information, specific installation issues, and full application documentation.

▲ **HLP**   Additional Windows application-specific information that may not be readily accessible through the application interface.

MICROSOFT TECHNET

Microsoft TechNet is a series of CD-ROMs that offer technical information, support information, support patches, drivers, and programs. This group of CD-ROMs is published every month. An annual subscription costs approximately $300 for single users and $700 for unlimited users. The TechNet CDs contain the following:

▼ Knowledge bases on many subjects

■ Supplemental drivers and patches

■ More than 150,000 pages of current technical information

■ Resource Kits (14 in all)

■ All recent service packs

■ CD-ROM seminars

■ The entire software library from Microsoft (current active library)

▲ Beta software

Figure D-2.   Search for recent technical notes on TechNet CD-ROMs

Microsoft TechNet gives serious engineers an opportunity to evaluate the most recent Windows software. Figure D-2 illustrates the search capabilities included with TechNet. For more information, explore www.microsoft.com/technet.

MICROSOFT ONLINE SUPPORT

In addition to support available through the OS application itself, Microsoft offers online Internet support. The Support Online site (www.microsoft.com/support) is one of the best places to go for support. You may have to fill out a registration questionnaire in order to get "premium content." Once registered, you can enter a question or a set of keywords to search through their databases. Your query goes through hundreds of megabytes of technical notes and knowledge bases in search of matches. Often a question or problem will be matched to a similar one, and you can see how that problem was resolved in another environment.

Figure D-3 illustrates the support query page at this site. You can search using either keywords (the default) or what Microsoft calls "natural language." Using natural language, you phrase your question in everyday sentence form, such as "How do I configure

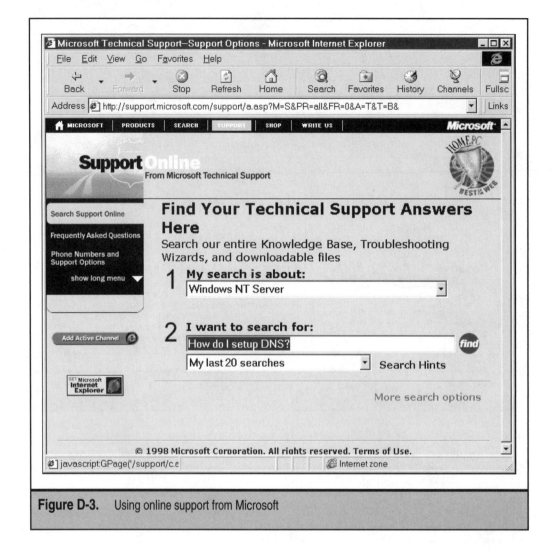

Figure D-3.   Using online support from Microsoft

a subnet mask?" To use natural language, click More Search Options in the site home page, and then select Natural Language.

For more comprehensive enterprise support, you might check out Microsoft's enterprise support options at www.microsoft.com/enterprise. Here you can read about phone-support packages and consulting services offered to large organizations.

MICROSOFT INTERNET SOURCES

In addition to Microsoft's supported Internet site, an abundance of other Internet locations exist to help you with information about Windows NT.

Unfortunately, since Windows NT is such a popular topic, general search tools many times return useless links. Table D-1 contains a few links that actually provide information of real value. The Resource Links in the table invariably lead to more links and focus on NT-related information. The Print Material links point you toward publishers of books and magazines. These publisher sites are also full of Windows-related information and instructions for obtaining the available publications. Most magazines publish much of their material on their Web sites.

Name	Type	Link
Resource Links		
Microsoft's FTP site	File repository	ftp.microsoft.com
Beverly Hills NT Resource Center	Resources, file repository	www.bhs.com
Jumbo NT Archive	File repository	www.jumbo.com
European MS WinNT Academic Centre	Resources, information, file repository	emwac.ed.ac.uk
Association of Windows NT System Professionals	Resources, user groups, information, file repository	www.ntpro.org
Print Material		
Osborne/McGraw-Hill	Beginning–Advanced	www.osborne.com
Microsoft Press	Beginning–Intermediate	mspress.microsoft.com
Wiley	Beginning–Advanced	www.wiley.com
Macmillan Computer Publishing	Beginning–Advanced	www.mcp.com
Windows NT Magazine	Advanced	www.winntmag.com
Back Office Magazine	Intermediate–Advanced	www.backoffice.com
Enterprise NT Magazine	Intermediate–Advanced	www.entmag.com
Windows NT Systems Magazine	Beginning–Intermediate	www.ntsystems.com
Windows Magazine	Beginner	www.winmag.com
Info World	Beginning–Intermediate	www.infoworld.com
Network World	Intermediate–Advanced	www.nwfusion.com

Table D-1.   Some Windows Resources on the Internet

MICROSOFT NEWSGROUPS

Newsgroups are discussion groups about a particular topic, with participants located throughout the world. Unlike chat rooms, newsgroup discussions do not happen in real time; you post a message, which other users can read and answer as desired.

Getting Started with a Newsgroup

There are thousands of newsgroup topics, so each group is narrowed down to a relatively specific subject. For example, one newsgroup on Windows NT is called comp.os.ms-windows.nt.misc.

It works like this: A user posts a message (an essay, a question, or any piece of text) to the newsgroup. The message gets distributed all over the world through *news servers*, which also keep copies of the messages and replies. Other users read the posted messages and post any reply using their own newsreader software. Responses are then posted to the news servers. A newsgroup may have many hundreds or thousands of associated users, and it can be challenging to keep up with the volume of information that passes through.

The first thing you'll need in order to participate is the newsreader software. Most Web browsers offer you a newsreader when you first install the browser. Otherwise, you can add the newsreader component at any time by going to the browser's add-on component site and selecting the newsreader. Many independent newsreader programs that work quite well are available free on the Internet.

Using Microsoft Newsgroups

Once your newsreader is functioning, point it to a news server so it can start retrieving posted messages. These servers are often inside corporations (for example, news.company.com) or located at your ISP on the Internet. Your server likely won't subscribe to all of the thousands of available groups, however. To get a complete list, check out www.liszt.com/news.

From the newsreader software, select the groups in which you're interested, and you'll be able to start reading and posting messages immediately, as shown in Figure D-4. This screen also shows some of the newsgroups related to Windows NT.

NOTE: A certain "decorum" is expected when posting to newsgroups. Newsgroup users are not particularly tolerant of novices and their mistakes, so it's best to read up on the proper etiquette for the group. Check out bell.ucs.indiana.edu/kb/menu/usenet for more introductory information.

People often use newsgroups to post a specific problem in hope that some guru will read it and know the answer. The disadvantage is that you may have to wait a long time before you receive a response, and you can't always trust the answer. But it *is* free, after all.

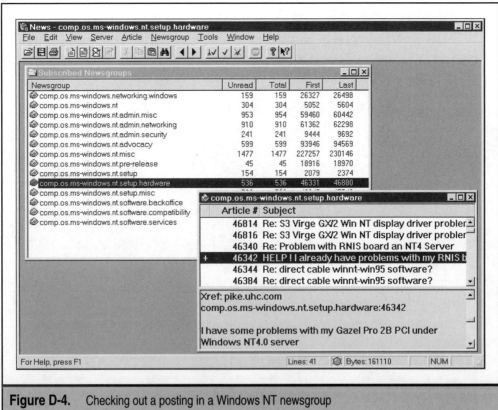

Figure D-4.   Checking out a posting in a Windows NT newsgroup

WINDOWS NT RESOURCE KITS

No review of Windows resources would be complete without a discussion of the Resource Kits. The Windows NT Resource Kit should be in every NT administrator's toolbox. Its wealth of utilities and technical information helps administrators, power users, and programmers alike to configure, troubleshoot, and tune their NT systems.

For Windows NT 4.0, the Resource Kit is offered as two separate products, one for NT Server and one for NT Workstation. Although both contain many of the same utilities and documentation on the CD-ROM, they each have specific enhancements for various needs. The NT Server Resource Kit is for network administrators who set up, administer, and support Windows NT Server–based networks. The NT Workstation Resource Kit is for power users, application developers, and administrators of smaller networks; this kit contains less information about networking NT systems.

The NT Server Resource Kit includes the following books:

▼ *Windows NT Server Resource Guide*

■ *Windows NT Server Networking Guide*

▲ *Windows NT Server Internet Guide*

Only one book comes with the NT Workstation Resource Kit: *Windows NT Workstation Resource Guide*. This guide is also included on the CD-ROM in the NT Server kit. The CD contains many utilities, including the following:

▼ **Batch Tools**   Perl 5 and Regina REXX

■ **Computer Administration and Configuration Tools**   C2-level security, automatic login, Command Scheduler, program to run an application as a service feature, time zone editor, and a uniprocessor-to-multiprocessor conversion utility

■ **Computer and Network Setup Tools**   Profile setup and Setup Manager

■ **Computer Diagnostic Tools**   Crystal Reports event viewer

■ **Desktop Tools**   Multiple desktops, animated cursor editor, image editor, and the *soft input panel*, a handwriting recognition software for pen users

■ **File Tools**   File and directory comparison, file compression and expansion, text file viewer

■ **Internet and TCP/IP Services and Tools**   SMTP and POP mail server, IP configuration tool, uuencoder and decoder

■ **Network Diagnostic Tools**   PerfMon MIB builder, Net Watch, Disk Probe for hard drives, Browser Monitor, Dependency Walker, Domain Monitor, Network Watch, Process Viewer, and SNMP Monitor

■ **Registry Tools**   Online Registry help

■ **Server Administration Tools**   DHCP Relay Agent, remote console, and Service Monitor application

■ **Tools for Developers**   Sixteen Posix tools, including **vi**, **ls**, and **mv**

▲ **User Account Administration Tools**   Tools to control floating profiles and copy user groups

Also included on the CD-ROM are a series of help books, including an online copy of the books included with the kit. In addition, you'll find the hardware compatibility list and an overview of all the tools included in the kit.

Microsoft updates the resource kits periodically with supplemental CD-ROMs. These provide the latest versions of helpful utilities and tools, as well as extensive valuable information taken from the TechNet CD series. For more information about the Resource Kits, look at mspress.microsoft.com/RESLINK/.

CISCO TELEPHONE SUPPORT

Microsoft is not known for accessible telephone support, but Cisco's is exceptional. Their Technical Assistance Centers (TACs) are available 24 hours a day, 7 days a week, from any touch-tone telephone.

Technical Assistance Center (TAC)

The quality of support offered by Cisco's Technical Assistance Centers can be attributed to the TAC team of engineers. This team is the largest, most highly trained and experienced team of engineers in the industry. Many of them have Cisco Certified Internetwork Engineer (CCIE) certification—the highest level of industry certification attainable. As a result, Cisco TAC engineers offer customers and Cisco Partners a superior level of networking experience.

There are four TACs, in San Jose, CA; Raleigh, NC; Brussels; and Sydney, Australia. These diverse sites collectively offer coverage to Cisco customers worldwide.

Who Are Cisco TACs' Clients?

Premier Cisco Value Added Resellers (VARs) and Service Providers have access to TAC in order to support their Cisco products in production, the products they are testing, and their products already deployed at customer sites. Cisco customers, too, may have access to TAC; they must first purchase a SMARTnet maintenance package for the Cisco product they want supported. Following are descriptions of the various SMARTnet maintenance packages.

SMARTNET ONSITE   This package includes 24x7x365 access to Cisco TAC telephone support, with critical problem escalation (this consists of telephone callback within one hour by the TAC for all hardware, configuration, and software problems from 9:00 A.M. to 5:00 P.M. local time, Monday through Friday, excluding Cisco-observed holidays). In addition, this package provides a field engineer to install advance replacement hardware parts for the customer. The customer defines (and purchases) response time in one of the following categories:

- ▼ 8x5xNext Business Day (request must be received by 3:00 P.M. for next business day service)
- ■ 8x5x4 (within four hours, Monday through Friday, 9:00 A.M. to 5 P.M.)
- ▲ 24x7x4 (within four hours, 7 days a week, 24 hours a day)

CISCO ADVANCE REPLACEMENT   This SMARTnet package allows an individual to receive expedited service when a part fails. It includes one telephone-based technical support incident from the TAC. In addition, it includes the following:

- ▼ One year cost-effective replacements for Cisco equipment

- Speedy hardware replacement
▲ Guest access to Cisco Connection Online (CCO) for one year

Accessing the TACs

Table D-2 lists contact information for qualified Cisco TAC users.

Qualified users can also obtain technical assistance through e-mail, as listed in Table D-3.

Region	Telephone Number
Asia-Pacific	61-2-8448-7107
Australia	1-800-805-227
China	Mandarin: 10810, then 800-501-2306 English: 10811, then 800-501-2306 In-country TAC support: 800-810-8886
Europe	32-2-778-4242
France	0800-90-75-94
Hong Kong	800-96-5910
India	000-117, then 888-861-6453
Indonesia	001-800-61-838
Japan	0066-33-800-926 In-country TAC Partners: 0120-086771
Korea	00798-611-0712: Seoul 00-911, then 888-861-5164
Malaysia	1-800-805-880
New Zealand	0800-44-6237
North America	800 553-2447 1-408-526-7209
Philippines	1-800-611-0056
Singapore	800-6161-356
Taiwan	0080-61-1206
Thailand	00-800-611-0754
U.K.	0800-960-547

Table D-2. Telephone Access to Cisco TAC

Language	E-mail Address
English/Spanish	Tac@cisco.com
Hanzi (Chinese)	Chines-tac@cisco.com
Kanji (Japanese)	Japan-tac@cisco.com
Hangul (Korean)	Korea-tac@cisco.com
Thai	Thai-tac@cisco.com

Table D-3.   E-mail Access to Cisco TAC

TAC Information Requirements

In order to obtain technical assistance from the TAC, be prepared to provide the following information:

▼ Cisco maintenance contract number for the site of the problem (required for Cisco maintenance customers)

■ Serial number of problem hardware/software

■ Purchase order number

■ Company name

■ Contact name

■ Physical location of equipment

■ Telephone number

■ E-mail address

■ Model number of unit experiencing the problem

▲ Accurate description and priority of problem priority

The TAC engineer will assign a case number to your call. Record this case number for any future references to the case. The report is then routed to the Customer Engineering Response Team for resolution. After the service has been delivered, the Customer Engineer will confirm with you that the problem is resolved and close the case.

The Online Cisco TAC is located at http://www.cisco.com/kobayashi/support/help.shtml. For more information on TAC, go to http://www.cisco.com/kobayashi/support/tac_wp.htm.

CISCO CONNECTION ONLINE (CCO)

Cisco Connection Online (CCO), the Cisco Internet Web site, enables customers and partners to access interactive Web-based applications that provide immediate, open access to Cisco information, resources, and systems. This support and information is available 24 hours a day, seven days a week. Figure D-5 shows the CCO interface. Features of CCO include the following:

▼ On-demand access to Cisco information, service and support resources, and systems

■ The latest downloadable upgrades, Cisco software registration

■ Assistance with design, implementation, and support of Cisco technologies through the comprehensive suite of Internet Technical Support Applications

▲ A variety of online commerce transactions, including purchase of Cisco networking products, services, merchandise, training kits and modules, brochures, and technical documents

Levels of CCO Access

There are two levels of access to CCO: contract and noncontract. Although each level is fundamentally similar, the contract level of access has several additional perks.

Noncontract Unregistered CCO Access

Noncontract, unregistered guest privilege to CCO is available to anyone browsing Cisco's Web site (www.cisco.com). This guest access link is for customers, prospects, the general public, and anyone else not yet a CCO Registered User. There is no charge for or restriction on using the guest option on CCO.

As stated just above, the guest-access features are only a subset of those available to the CCO Registered User. Some of these features are listed here:

▼ Cisco worldwide contacts and events calendar

■ *Packet* quarterly magazine

■ Press releases

■ Products, catalog, brochures, and announcements

■ Service and support information

■ Purchasing of promotional merchandise

▲ Complete library of technical documentation

NOTE: Cisco also provides 24-hour telephone support to guest users. This noncontract telephone support is billed at the prevailing Time and Materials rates. All noncontract calls are handled on a "first-come, first-server" basis, with response time depending on Cisco resource availability.

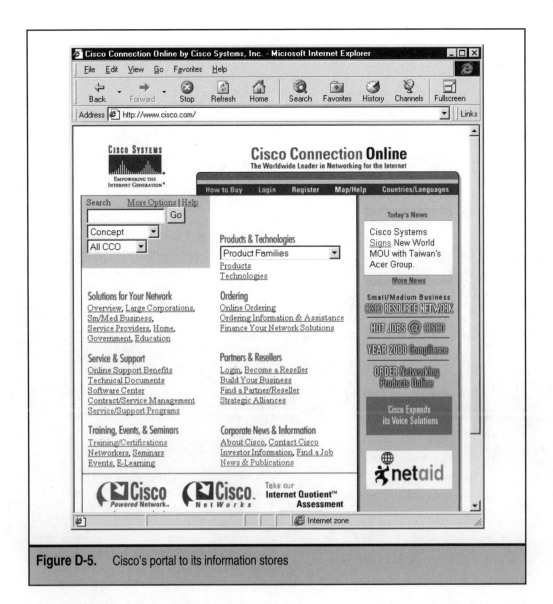

Figure D-5. Cisco's portal to its information stores

Contract Registered CCO Access

Four types of Contract Registered CCO users can access the extended support features of CCO. To have this privilege, you must register and have an assigned username and password for login.

▼ **Cisco Direct Customers** Cisco customers who have SMARTnet or comprehensive support contracts with Cisco

■ **Cisco Partner Initiated Customer Account (PICA) Customers**   Cisco customers who receive services from an authorized Cisco Partner

■ **Cisco Partner**   Cisco sales partners who have a reseller, distributor, or original equipment manufacturer (OEM) service agreement with Cisco

▲ **Cisco Premier Resellers**   Authorized resellers who have a reseller service agreement with Cisco

Table D-4 lists the level of CCO access for each of the above types of registered users.

	Cisco Direct Customers	Cisco PICA Customers	Cisco Partners	Cisco Premier Reseller
Ordering				
Internet Commerce Tools			✓	
RMA/Service Order tool			✓	
Lead Time tool		✓	✓	
Cisco MarketPlace	✓			
Configuration tool	✓	✓		
Pricing tool	✓	✓		
Order Status tool	✓			
Products and Technologies				
Product Approval Status	✓			
Service and Support				
Automatic Software Distribution			✓	
Stack Decoder			✓	
Software Center	✓	✓		
IOS Upgrade Planner	✓			
Technical Assistance Tools	✓			
Open Q&A Forum	✓	✓		✓
Technical tips				✓
Troubleshooting assistance	✓	✓		✓
Technical Assistance Center (TAC)	✓	✓		

Table D-4.   Cisco Partner and Customer CCO Access Level

	Cisco Direct Customers	Cisco PICA Customers	Cisco Partners	Cisco Premier Reseller
Open a TAC case	✓			
Query a TAC case	✓			
Update a TAC case	✓			
Software Bug Toolkit	✓	✓		✓
Field Notices tool				✓
Training, Seminars, and Events				
Cisco TV			✓	
EMEA training			✓	
Partners and Resellers				
Partner Initiated Customer Accounts (PICA) program			✓	
SMARTnet Partner notification			✓	
Cisco connection sales tools			✓	✓
CiscoLink			✓	
Cisco reseller news				✓

Table D-4.   Cisco Partner and Customer CCO Access Level *(continued)*

Users who qualify as one of the types listed in Table D-4 can register for CCO access at http://www.cisco.com/register/.

CCO Applications and Services

The following paragraphs describe existing CCO features that provide a wealth of information and support at your fingertips (and new applications and services are added frequently).

Ordering

Direct customers, Cisco Partners with Premier, Gold, or Silver Partner status, and Cisco distributors can obtain Direct Purchase agreements and use CCO ordering functionality. CCO eliminates some of the hassles of ordering by simplifying the process online. Following are descriptions of some of the tools associated with online ordering (they can be accessed from the site address http://www.cisco.com/kobayashi/ordering_info.shtml):

▼ **Product Catalog**   Online Cisco product overview with technical specifications and ordering information. The product catalog is also available on the Cisco Documentation CD-ROM Package and is discussed further in a later section of this chapter.

■ **Configuration Tools**   CCO configuration tools include a compilation of sample configurations, a calculator that can be used to simplify IP subnetting, and online tools that help you configure a subset of Cisco's products. The configuration tools help you search for configurable Cisco products and create a product configuration online, in addition to providing assistance with installation of new network products. Unfortunately, not all products are available for configuration, and certain products require separate Internet Commerce Tools registration. At the following Web site you'll find help in many aspects of Cisco product configuration: http://www.cisco.com/pcgi-bin/front.x/config_root.pl.

■ **Pricing Tool**   The Pricing Tool lets you access Cisco price lists and search for product prices based on a product family description or number.

■ **Order Status Tool**   The Order Status Tool produces quick status reports on your Cisco orders.

■ **RMA/Service Order Tool**   This tool lets you submit service orders, check status of RMAs and service orders, and view the Cisco parts catalog.

■ **Lead Time Tool**   This tool provides lead times from the point at which a valid purchase order is received by Cisco.

▲ **Cisco MarketPlace**   An Internet clearinghouse for ordering the tools described in this section. Cisco MarketPlace assists you in configuring, pricing, and submitting orders for Cisco products and promotional items. You must have Internet Commerce Tools registration in order to use the MarketPlace.

Products and Technologies

Cisco's success is founded on its quality products and its ability to market these products. The company Cisco offers a variety of resources to accomplish this task. CCO provides access to the following resources:

▼ **Product Approval Status**   Cisco Customers receive access to Product Approval Status reports, which review the approval status for Cisco products in countries worldwide.

■ **Product Catalog**   Cisco Systems Product Catalog describes all the internetworking products offered by Cisco, including potential configurations and part numbers for ordering. Available on Cisco Documentation CD-ROM Package and on CCO.

■ **Brochures**   Official Cisco brochures that highlight products, protocols, technologies, statements of direction, and customer profiles; photographs and figures are included.

■ **CCO Multimedia Gallery**   Video and high-quality color photographs of Cisco Systems products and presentations.

■ **Product Announcements**   Detailed descriptions of new Cisco products, with pictures, graphs, and figures.

▲ **Product Bulletins**   Important updates on Cisco products: enhancements, options, alerts, revisions and upgrade procedures.

Services and Support

In addition to marketing its products, Cisco also has to support them. Telephone support through the TACs is described in an earlier section. Here are the resources for Internet support.

AUTOMATIC SOFTWARE DISTRIBUTION   The Automatic Software Distribution (ASD) program can be used to retrieve master "translation images" to make EPROM software sets (SIMMs or Flash memory cards) for your Cisco devices. The ASD also contains links to the Cisco Software center.

STACK DECODER   Stack Decoder is an interactive tool that lets you analyze a stack trace on Cisco IOS router platforms. From this stack track you can show diagnostic results, including hardware failures and software defects. For information on Stack Decoder, go to http://www.cisco.com/stack/Stack_help.html.

SOFTWARE CENTER   At the CCO Software Center you can get upgrades and information. Learn more about Cisco's broad range of software products, including Cisco IOS for routers, switches, and gateway platforms; network management and security applications for workstation servers; and internetworking protocol suites for host systems. Although the Software Center has several features, one of its main functions is to upgrade planners and software for end-to-end network connectivity. Go to http://www.cisco.com/cgi-bin/ibld/all.pl?i=support&c=3&m=guest.

SOFTWARE APPLICATION SERVICES   Cisco excels in keeping up with and anticipating technological challenges. To ensure that you get the full benefit of your software investment, the company offers Software Application Support (SAS) and Software Application Support plus Upgrades (SASU). These support packages provide technical assistance and online support and maintenance updates, including the following:

▼ Quick resolution of problems, anytime, through access to Cisco expertise

■ Problem/workaround reports

■ Problem-resolution control through prioritization and escalation procedures that are put in the hands of the customer

▲ Maintenance updates and major software upgrades

The Software Application Support (SAS) package provides the following features:

▼   Minor release and bug fixes

■   Registered access to CCO

▲   24x7x365 telephone support

In addition to the SAS services, the Software Application Support plus Upgrades Features (SASU) package provides proactive shipment of all major and minor releases and bug fixes.

TECHNICAL ASSISTANCE TOOLS   CCO's industry-leading Technical Assistance Tools help save customers time by solving common technical problems online.

▼   **Open Q&A Forum**   A powerful search engine for the Cisco support database. You can tap the technical expertise of Cisco networking professionals by submitting a question or by searching through a database of questions and answers. You get help resolving common problems with hardware, configuration, and performance. Go to http://www.cisco.com/openf/openproj.shtml.

■   **Technical Tips**   Documentation that includes complete product manuals, technology overviews, and troubleshooting guides. Go to http://www.cisco.com/public/serv_tips.shtml.

■   **Troubleshooting Assistance**   Help with common problems involving hardware, configuration, and performance, using the "Step-by-Step Help." This help tool takes you through troubleshooting, one step at a time. Go to http://te.cisco.com/cgi-bin/webisapi.dll?New,KB=TE.

▲   **Technical Assistance Center (TAC)**   In addition to TAC support through touch-tone telephones, you can request TAC assistance through CCO. The online Cisco TAC is located at http://www.cisco.com/kobayashi/support/help.shtml.

For more information on TAC, go to http://www.cisco.com/kobayashi/support/tac_wp.htm.

SOFTWARE BUG TOOLKIT   Cisco offers a number of software bug-tracking tools, all of which are available through the online Bug Toolkit. This toolkit is an integrated set of applications that help you identify, evaluate, categorize, and track defects that affect network operations or planning. With the Bug Navigator you can search for known bugs based on software version, feature set, and keyword. With the Bug Watcher, you create named "bins" in which you can "watch" or monitor the status of any number of defects.

To obtain the Cisco Bug Toolkit, Bug Navigator, and Bug Watcher, go to http://www.cisco.com/support/bugtools/.

FIELD NOTICES TOOL   Field notices are designed to provide notification of any critical issues concerning Cisco products, including problem descriptions, safety or security issues, and hardware defects. Go to http://www.cisco.com/warp/public/770/.

Training, Seminars, and Events

Cisco clients have access to worldwide networking training on Cisco products and technologies. The company has developed certified proficiency for network design and support, and has established a Cisco Certified Internetwork Expert (CCIE) program to assist network engineers with a learning path. This training is offered through seminars, events, and *E-Learning*. Without traditional time and distance barriers, E-learning technologies offer virtual-classroom, remote-lab, and content-on-demand solutions for successful electronic learning programs. For example, Cisco TV provides a means to interact directly with experts as they discuss Cisco internetworking solutions.

Partners and Resellers

Many services are available to Partners and Resellers to assist with their customer relations.

- ▼ **Partner Initiated Customer Accounts (PICA) Program**   Allows Cisco Partners to provide their customers with contract numbers for use during CCO registrations.

- ■ **SMARTnet Partner Notification**   Allows Cisco Partners that sell SMARTnet contracts to request notification when their customers open and close cases, download software, request parts, and so on.

- ■ **Cisco Connection Sales Tools**   The online version of Cisco's CD-ROM for sales partners. It lists corporate and product information, sales presentations, product bulletins, the latest launches, and magazines and newsletters.

- ▲ **CiscoLink (a.k.a. Cisco Reseller News)**   Cisco's bimonthly Partner newsletter, with announcements, product details, regional information, and selling tips.

CISCO DOCUMENTATION CD-ROM PACKAGE

The Cisco Documentation CD-ROM Package is an interactive library of technical product information in HTML format. The CD-ROM Package includes the following:

- ▼ Cisco IOS release notes, configuration guides, command references, and command summaries

- ■ Debug command reference and system error messages

- ■ Cisco Management Information Base (MIB) User Quick Reference, and Access Services Quick Configuration Guide

- ■ Cisco product catalog

- ■ Router and hub installation and configuration guides

- Switch installation and configuration guides, switch command reference guides, and switch MIB reference guides

- Client/server software installation guides

▲ Configuration notes for memory upgrades, network interface cards, rack-mount kits, and other field upgrade products

You can purchase Cisco's subscription services to receive monthly Documentation CD-ROM updates throughout the year. To order the subscription services, call Cisco Systems Customer Service at 1-800-553-2447 or 408-526-7208. In addition, the latest versions of the documents can be assessed through CCO at the following URL: http://www.cisco.com/unvercd/home/home.htm.

Although the Documentation CD-ROM is produced monthly, the documents on CCO are updated constantly.

NOTE: Customers can request a free copy of the CD when ordering Cisco products.

CD-ROM Package Installation

To take full advantage of the features on the CD-ROM, you should install all of the following applications. The installation utility on the Cisco Documentation disc will install this software on your hard drive:

▼ Netscape Navigator 4.05

- Adobe Acrobat Reader 3.0

- Verity CD Web Publishers

▲ QuickTime (for Windows only)

The requirements for a Windows NT installation are a Pentium 300 MHz or faster with a minimum 16MB RAM and 39MB available disk space.

Here are the steps to install the CD-ROM Package:

1. Insert the Browser Software Installer disk (disk 1) into your CD-ROM drive.

2. Click the Install Software button and follow the installation instructions on your screen.

3. In the Cisco Documentation Installer window, click the Launch Documentation CD button. Netscape Navigator will launch, and additional instructions will be displayed.

4. Quit Navigator and remove the Browser Software Installer disk.

5. Insert the Cisco Documentation disk (disk 2).

6. Click the Launch Documentation CD button.

7. When you have finished, remove the CD.

In addition to Windows NT, the CD-ROM package is supported on Sun Microsystems, Macintosh, Hewlett-Packard, IBM, and other platforms.

Navigating the Documentation

After the documentation CD-ROM is up and running (see Figure D-6), you can look at the list of available documents and begin reading. Here's an overview of some of the features and functions supported within the Documentation CD-ROM Package:

▼ Hypertext links

■ Table of contents

■ Illustrations

■ Portable Document Format (PDF) files

■ Searching documents (single or multiple)

■ Bookmarks

▲ History window

Cisco Product Catalog

Included in the Documentation CD-ROM Package is the current Cisco product catalog. This catalog describes the internetworking hardware and software products offered by Cisco Systems for enterprise and service provider networks. Some of these products are available through two-tier distributors and their resellers. The product catalog includes the following:

▼ Product updates

■ Hardware

■ Software

■ Cables, transceivers, power supplies, and other peripherals

▲ Services and support

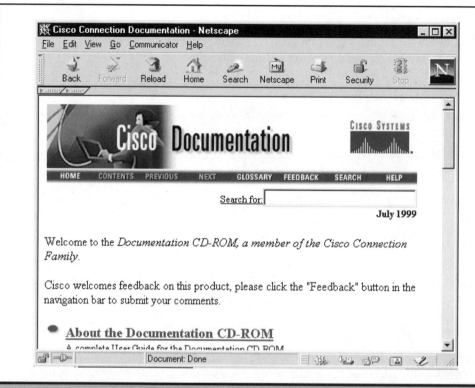

Figure D-6.   The Cisco Documentation CD-ROM main menu

Index

B

C

I

O

Q

R

X

Z